RUSSIA'S
Second Revolution

RUSSIA'S Second Revolution

The February 1917 Uprising in Petrograd

By

E. N. Burdzhalov

Translated and edited by

Donald J. Raleigh

Indiana University Press
Bloomington and Indianapolis

Originally published as E. N. Burdzhalov, *Vtoraia russkaia revoliutsiia: Vosstanie v Petrograde* (Moscow: Nauka, 1967).

This book was brought to publication with the assistance of a grant from the Andrew W. Mellon Foundation to the Russian and East European Institute, Indiana University, and the Center for Russian and East European Studies, University of Michigan.

Manufactured in the United States of America

Library of Congress Cataloging-in-Publication Data

Burdzhalov, E. N. (Eduard Nikolaevich), 1906–1985.
Russia's second revolution.

(Indiana-Michigan series in Russian and East European studies)
Translation of: Vtoraia russkaia revoliutsiia.
Bibliography: p.
Includes index.
1. Soviet Union—History—February Revolution, 1917.
I. Raleigh, Donald J. II. Title. III. Series.
DK265.19.B813 1987 947.084'1 86-45955
ISBN 0-253-35037-9
ISBN 0-253-20440-2 (pbk.)

1 2 3 4 5 91 90 89 88 87

This translation is dedicated to my grandmother,
Victoria K. Plaziak

Contents

Translator's Introduction

Eduard Nikolaevich Burdzhalov's *Vtoraia russkaia revoliutsiia: Vosstanie v Petrograde* (Moscow: Nauka, 1967) may well be the best book in any language on Russia's February Revolution of 1917 in Petrograd.[1] This essay is about this exceptional book and about the exceptional man who wrote it. Burdzhalov stood at the center of a major controversy in 1956–57, often called the "Burdzhalov Affair," when he published two sensational articles on the role of the Bolsheviks in the February Revolution and, as assistant editor of the historical profession's major journal, *Voprosy istorii* (Problems of History), facilitated publication of other articles and memoirs that challenged the status quo within Soviet historiography. His actions at that time contributed to the evolution of Soviet historical scholarship away from the rigid confines of Stalinism; his subsequent defense of his beliefs and behavior proved to be the driving force behind the researching and writing of his book. Its publication in 1967 marked a triumph for the author and a victory of sorts for the entire Soviet historical profession. There had been much more at stake during the "affair" than Burdzhalov's career alone.

A true representative of the romantic period of the Russian Revolution, Burdzhalov was born into a middle-class Armenian family in the colorful Volga city of Astrakhan in 1906. In 1912 the family moved to Baku. Fleeing the Turks, the Burdzhalovs returned to Astrakhan in 1918, where Eduard Nikolaevich enrolled in a local gymnasium. Civil war raging up and down the Volga interrupted his secondary education soon thereafter, and at age thirteen he went to work as a clerk in a military transit camp. That same year he joined the Komsomol and moved into a dormitory for young activists. His spirited commitment to the Communist youth movement, not understood by everyone in his family, earned him the nickname "Komsomol'skii Kirov" (S. M. Kirov was in Astrakhan at the time); his youth and compact size earned him the nickname "Komsomol'skii Baby." Thus, at this early age, Burdzhalov had already identified himself with the ideals of the revolution, especially with its internationalist appeals, which aroused a sympathetic response from the young Armenian. An important theme in his later writings appears to have taken shape at this time: the tsarist government had been a prisoner of nations.

After the establishment of Soviet power in Azerbaijan in 1920, Burdzhalov returned to Baku with his family and involved himself in the local Komsomol organization. His heroes, besides Lenin, were Shaumian and the twenty-six commissars of the Baku Soviet executed during the civil war. He was not to forget them when he took up his pen to write history. At age nineteen, young Burdzhalov joined the Communist party. The next year, in 1926, he enrolled in a *rabfak* (workers' faculty) at Moscow University (MGU). Upon completion of his secondary education in 1929, he matriculated at MGU, where he studied with E. A. Morokhovets, S. A. Piontkovskii, V. P. Volgin and S. V. Bakhrushin. While still a student, he began what would become a brilliant teaching career by offering courses at the university's *rabfak*, in the history department, and at the Kolkhoz Institute. Although Burdzhalov wished to further his education, the party packed him off to work in the Tula party organization's city committee in 1933 and to teach at the Tula Agricultural School. It was a grim assignment for someone who wished to carry out serious scholarly research. Nevertheless, this was a period of unparalleled social and political advancement for large numbers of young, newly trained Communists who were eager to serve the state; Burdzhalov's success in Tula led to rapid promotion within the party apparatus. Moreover, it was there that he met and married a young Jewish worker at the Tula Armament Factory, Gosia Borisovna Plotkina. It was love at first sight, Gosia Borisovna told me. Their only child, a son, Feliks, was born in 1936. Work and friends often took precedence over family in coming years, but Burdzhalov was a committed family man who enjoyed a happy, mutually sustaining conjugal relationship: he and his wife celebrated their fiftieth wedding anniversary the year Eduard Nikolaevich died.

Returning to Moscow in 1936, Burdzhalov assisted in the publication of *Istoriia grazhdanskoi voiny v SSSR* (History of the Civil War in the USSR). The titular editors of this project included Stalin himself, Maxim Gorky, V. M. Molotov, and other prominent political figures, while a large authors' collective of historians such as I. I. Mints and A. L. Sidorov were involved in the actual writing of the work. Burdzhalov's participation in this venture deepened his interest in the historical study of the revolution and forged some strong loyalties and enmities that were to play imprecise but nonetheless significant roles during the Burdzhalov Affair. He also wrote his candidate's dissertation at this time, "Proletarskaia revoliutsiia v Azerbaidzhane," which was published as *Dvadtsat'-shest' bakinskikh komissarov* (The Twenty-Six Baku Commissars). The book is written in a lively style, but it gives no indication that the author was capable of crafting the landmark study he published in 1967.

By the end of the 1930s—as the purges drew to a close—Burdzhalov's selfless service to the party was beginning to pay off. In 1939 he was appointed head of the Department of the History of the USSR at the Central Committee's Higher Party School. During the Second World War, Burdzhalov worked as a political lecturer in the Red Army, receiving numerous decorations for his service at the front and earning the rank of colonel by the end of the war. Following demobilization, he managed the lecturers' group of the Central Committee and served as assistant editor of the committee's tedious propaganda organ, *Kul'tura i zhizn'* (Culture and Life). He resumed teaching at the Higher Party School and taught in the Academy of Social Sciences. Many of his lectures, orthodox in every respect but written with flair and clarity, were published during 1940–53.[2] Not surprisingly, many foreign observers believed he was merely on a party assignment to challenge Stalinist historiography when he published his articles in 1956.

In fact, however, Stalin's last years were painful ones for Burdzhalov, for it was then that he fundamentally reassessed his own, Stalin's, and the party's past, while continuing to fulfill functions he found increasingly distasteful. He worked on *Kul'tura i zhizn'*, edited by the unsavory G. F. Aleksandrov. He published lectures presented at the Higher Party School, which contained historical distortions, simplistic formulations, gross omissions, and praise to Stalin's genius. To put Burdzhalov's moral tribulations in perspective, it should be noted that the political and academic climate during these years had taken a turn for the worse. The world of science and learning had become subject again to the party, creating a paranoid atmosphere of "anti-cosmopolitanism." The ugly campaign against foreign influence began taking into its sweep broader segments of the academic community. A controversy flared up over a reassessment of the historical legacy of Shamil, a north Caucasus hero who had battled against Russian expansionism. He was now called a reactionary. The crusade spread to the Central Committee's Academy of the Social Sciences and the pages of the historical journal *Voprosy istorii*, and it developed a strong anti-Semitic character. Serious writing in the Institute of History became gravely jeopardized. A. L. Sidorov, prorector and professor at Moscow University, stood at the helm in the attack against cosmopolitanism.[3] He assailed I. I. Mints and his students; he assailed N. L. Rubinshtein, and later E. N. Gorodetskii, Jews and friends of Burdzhalov. Some of the country's leading historians as well as vulgar careerists took part in the mud-slinging campaign.[4]

An intricate web of personal rivalries and loyalties, some dating from the 1930s, makes it exceedingly difficult to understand personal motivations during the campaign against cosmopolitanism and during the Burdzhalov Affair and afterward. Some people acted out of conviction, some out of self-aggrandizement, and some out of both. Loyalties changed, depending upon circumstances. And there were a few would-be free spirits like Burdzhalov who, once terror was no longer used as a direct control, would seek to make up for their past myopia. The bottom line, of course, was one of personal integrity, tempered with fear. Although it would be disingenuous to pretend to clarity about these personal links, several key relationships strongly suggest themselves. Burdzhalov's ties with Gorodetskii and, to a lesser extent, with Mints, both of whom fell under fire, may have contributed to his dissatisfaction with the state of things. A. M. Pankratova and N. M. Druzhinin come across well at this time; they, their students, and supporters appear to have lined up on Burdzhalov's side during the Burdzhalov Affair. More important yet was the conflict between

Burdzhalov and Sidorov, who had worked together since the 1930s. Sidorov was one of Burdzhalov's leading antagonists after 1956. The source of their animosity is unclear; that it was long-standing is certain.

During the campaign against cosmopolitanism, Burdzhalov decided to leave the Central Committee apparatus when the opportunity arose. In the summer of 1952 the journal *Voprosy istorii,* which had directed the assault against cosmopolitanism earlier, came under criticism. Academician I. M. Maiskii was arrested and the party group at the Institute of History had to denounce him. At the beginning of 1953 the Doctors' Plot was revealed, and the Presidium of the Academy of Sciences demanded the death sentence for those implicated in it. Then Stalin died. Beginning with the number 6 issue of *Voprosy istorii,* a new editorial board took over. A. M. Pankratova was now editor; Burdzhalov was her assistant.

De-Stalinization, beginning almost immediately after Stalin's death,[5] created the necessary conditions for Burdzhalov and others to stop being Stalinists. The isolation of the Stalin period ended. In September 1955 a Soviet team participated in the International Conference of Historical Sciences in Rome—the first international conference Soviet historians attended since 1933—and next joined a UNESCO project on the history of science and culture.[6] The second phase of the thaw was the public questioning of Soviet historical scholarship under Stalin. In January 1956 the editors of *Voprosy istorii* called a conference of its readers at which Pankratova impugned articles appearing the previous year for their dogmatism and shoddy scholarship, while Burdzhalov addressed those issues the editors felt needed greater attention in the future and called to task Soviet scholarship on many sensitive questions. Burdzhalov fired a broadside into A. L. Sidorov and the Institute of History "for not posing the principal questions." Other speakers ascribed some merit to M. N. Pokrovskii, the doyen of historical studies in the Soviet Union during the 1920s and later banned by Stalin, and to other Russian historians and those of the early Soviet period, and even suggested that Western historiography had its merits. In summing up the editorial board's position, Burdzhalov emphasized it was acting "according to party guidelines."[7] At the Twentieth Party Congress held the next month, Khrushchev denounced Stalin and passed judgment on a quarter-century of Soviet history: it was the most backward of the Soviet social sciences. Khrushchev lashed out against the official *Short Course of the History of the CPSU* and the *Brief Biography* of Stalin, which had served as prototypes for Soviet historical scholarship since the 1930s. Addressing the congress, the ever-cautious Pankratova appealed for more truthful historical evaluations and an examination of past mistakes. About the same time, state archives were opened to scholars.

Confusion reigned in the Soviet historical profession in the aftermath of the congress. For their part, the editors of *Voprosy istorii* felt they were in step with the new political climate when they put out the March issue of the journal in which virtually every article represented a sharp departure from previous norms. The editorial in this issue, devoted to the Twentieth Congress and written by Burdzhalov, called for a party history that would eliminate the "outright falsifications" of the past.[8] He reprehended the personality cult, Soviet writing on the nationalities problem in Russia, Stalin's overdrawn claims regarding his role in the siege of Tsaritsyn in 1918, and the whitewashing of Soviet defeats during 1941–42. He stressed that it was "necessary to illuminate correctly the situation within the party before Lenin's return to Russia. . . ." Speaking on behalf of the profession, *Voprosy istorii* intended to turn Soviet history into a real academic discipline, to expunge overtones of Russian patriotism from Soviet historical writing, and to somehow resolve the contradictions in regard to party history, especially those centered on the personality cult.[9]

If it was the journal *Voprosy istorii* that set the new tone for the historical profession, it was Burdzhalov and to a lesser extent Pankratova who set editorial policy for the journal. Subsequent articles continued the thrust of the reformers by attacking the Stalin cult, the state of historiography on the Communist Party of the Soviet Union (CPSU), and the practice of distorting memoirs of Old Bolsheviks. The real bombshell, however, fell when the journal ran two of Burdzhalov's own articles, "On Bolshevik Tactics in March–April 1917" and "More on Bolshevik Tactics in March–April 1917."[10] Supporting his conclusions with careful documentation, Burdzhalov demonstrated the extent to which the party had been ideologically disoriented before Lenin's return to Russia in April 1917. Petrograd Bolsheviks had failed to agree on such basic issues as the role of workers' demonstrations, the formation of the Soviet, and how to divide responsibility between the Central Committee Bureau and the lower-level Petrograd party organization. Neither one properly assessed the popular mood, and the resulting confusion was reflected in a manifesto the Central Committee Bureau put out on February 27. Outlining the party's minimum social program, the document appealed for creation of a "provisional revolutionary government," but failed to mention the Soviet. By the time the Central Committee Bureau decided to support the Soviet as the revolutionary government, the Petrograd Committee had already adopted the *postol'ku-poskol'ku* (only insofar as) formula of the other socialist parties, thereby agreeing to support the Provisional Government "only insofar as" it defended the gains of the revolution. Apart from addressing such taboo topics, Burdzhalov argued that the February Revolution was essentially a spontaneous affair in which the Bolsheviks, like the Mensheviks and SRs with whom they cooperated, swam with the tide of events. There was no communication to speak of between the party center abroad or the leadership within Russia. Further, when Kamenev and Stalin returned to Petrograd from exile, local party activists resisted their usurpation of *Pravda*. As Nancy Heer concluded, "it would not be far from the truth to say that the whole discussion of 1917 during all the years since is in reference to Burdzhalov's 1956 articles. . . ."[11]

It is not my purpose here to attempt to clarify why the party leadership decided to change course. By midyear, and in part owing to domestic ferment in Eastern Europe, the party leadership saw a need to retreat. E. I. Bugaev, assistant editor of the party journal *Partiinaia zhizn'* (Party Life), attacked Burdzhalov in an article appearing in that journal. An unsigned article in *Voprosy istorii* defended Burdzhalov against Bugaev's charges, and Burdzhalov's own essay "More on Bolshevik Tactics" did a convincing job of demolishing them.[12] Criticism against Burdzhalov did not stop here. Shortly after the Soviet invasion of Hungary, another readers' conference of *Voprosy istorii* was held, at which Sidorov censured Pankratova and Burdzhalov, demanding they admit that they had abused their power as editors and had violated party norms. Moscow University Professor V. Smirnov reprobated Burdzhalov on the pages of *Pravda* (November 20, 1956) and shortly afterward the Presidium of the Academy of Sciences called for the editors of *Voprosy istorii* to recant. On March 9, 1957, the Central Committee issued a decree "On the Journal *Voprosy istorii*," accusing the journal's editors of a variety of transgressions. *Voprosy istorii* itself failed to appear for two months and, when it did, its editorial board had been purged. Pankratova, who conceded her "mistakes" and was spared, died shortly thereafter; Burdzhalov and most of the others were removed for "intentionally bypassing official policy." When called before the appropriate Central Committee sector to absolve himself, Burdzhalov refused to admit any wrongdoing.[13]

Soviet scholars willing to discuss the Burdzhalov Affair bristle at the suggestion that Burdzhalov had not acted out of personal conviction. Penetrating the smokescreen covering the event is admittedly no easy matter, but an examination of the published record, of Burdzhalov's subsequent behavior, and of less tangible evidence uncovers a palimpsest upon which not all of the layers of writing have been erased. What emerges is an image of Burdzhalov the embattled historian who, once conditions had changed, rejected his earlier career and launched another. He was a passionate defender of his ideas. He was prone to stubbornness. He was optimistic. And he never regretted the course he took. As he began to see it, party history was wrought with shortcomings and failures, but all of these could be and should be explained historically, not falsified. What was at stake here, he believed, was the very future of the ideals of the revolution. He approached his own personal history the same way. Such were the qualities that saw him through the events of 1956–57 and through the subsequent struggle he had to endure. His emphasis on Stalin, however, was both correct and a little too convenient: it was easy to blame Stalin for everything; it was more difficult to blame oneself for having helped to fabricate the personality cult.

Removed from the editorial board of *Voprosy istorii*, Burdzhalov was sent to the Institute of History. There, the secretary of the party bureau, P. N. Sobolev, tried to have Burdzhalov's party membership revoked for his refusal to accept the Central Committee's decree. The Stalinists were outvoted on this matter, and instead of dismissal from the party, Burdzhalov received a severe reprimand. If the vote had gone the other way, Burdzhalov's career as a historian, maverick or otherwise, would have abruptly ended and he would not have been able to research and write his opus on the February Revolution. Shortly after he survived this ordeal, the institute's research council forced Burdzhalov in 1959 to submit to a reexamination of his credentials. On the grounds that he had not published enough academic literature to merit the title "senior researcher," and by a very close vote, he was removed from the institute. Unwilling to agree to the offer made to him by the editorial office of the trade union publishing house, Burdzhalov went without work for six months before securing a position at the Moscow Pedagogical Institute, where he taught until his retirement in 1976.

The events of 1956–57 had changed Soviet historical scholarship for the better. Once Stalinist practices were denied, the regime had to find new ways to shape its policies. History remained a highly politicized discipline, to be sure, but it was now viewed as being dependent upon a more sophisticated scholarship. Even the Stalinists had to make accommodations to the new climate and, in attacking the scholarly credibility of the revisionists such as Burdzhalov, had to speak to their level of academic discourse. Stalin was de-emphasized. Academic books now were better documented, more detailed, and were issued with a scholarly apparatus. Archives were opened, documents were published, new historical journals were founded, and multivolume works devoted to important issues began to appear. By 1960, more than twice the number of books and brochures on historical themes were published as in 1956.[14] In 1957–58 alone, on the fortieth anniversary of the revolution, 128 volumes of document collections on the history of 1917 were put out.[15] Institutions of higher education now offered required courses on party history.[16]

During this period, Stalin himself was subjected to historical reexamination, while Pokrovskii, who had fallen victim to the personality cult, was partially rehabilitated. In 1959, an authors' collective headed by B. N. Ponomarev came out with a replacement for Stalin's disgraced *Short Course,* in which Stalin was viewed positively until the Seventeenth Party Congress in 1934, after which he was reproached for having made serious mistakes. Further, he was reduced to an insignificant figure in 1917.[17] The practice of citing Lenin to buttress any argument now took hold. Meanwhile, S. M. Dubrovskii took the initiative in rehabilitating Pokrovskii. Graduates of the Communist Academy and former Pokrovskii students, such as I. I. Mints and M. V. Nechkina, supported the attempt.[18] Would-be reformers, however, continued to receive mixed signals. A lead article in *Voprosy istorii* on the eve of the Twenty-Second Party Congress in 1961, written by the conservative M. E. Naidenov, referred to the theoretical and methodological mistakes the journal had made back in 1956. Without alluding to Burdzhalov, Naidenov condemned some of the articles in the journal that had "incorrectly illuminated several principal questions in the history of the CPSU."[19]

The Twenty-Second Party Congress in 1961, however, went even further than the Twentieth Party Congress in discrediting Stalinism and gave impetus to the study of yet new themes formerly considered forbidden. In this climate, an All-Union Conference of Historians was held on December 18–21, 1962. Central Committee Secretary B. N. Ponomarev, editor of the one-volume history that had replaced the *Short Course*, and P. N. Pospelov, an old Stalinist who had tried to block publication of N. K. Krupskaia's memoirs because they underscored the insignificance of Stalin's role in 1917, addressed the gathering on behalf of the party. It is an important date in Burdzhalov's career, for it was here that he resumed the attack against Stalinist historiography and historians, and let it be known outside the Soviet Union that his career had not ended in 1957. The protocols of the conference document the sharp confrontation between the revisionist historians and the party apparatus that colored the conference proceedings,[20] and for this reason the protocols were published only after a long delay and only after some of the more vituperative exchanges had been struck out. Despite the warning that the Central Committee's decree of March 9, 1957, had resolved the matter of Stalin's role in the spring of 1917, Burdzhalov and others fired another salvo. They denounced the personality cult and the chauvinistic glorification of Russian history, and sought to restore Pokrovskii's reputation. They challenged those who still served the personality cult and who claimed to have known nothing of Stalin's crimes. Party veterans from the revolutionary period this time allied with the maverick historians. The anti-Stalinist mood had deepened, and many who now attacked Stalin had praised him on earlier occasions and had even been involved in the campaign against cosmopolitanism. In turn, the rebels were accused by their detractors, often justly, of having been official spokesmen under Stalin. The regime made an effort to present its case against the rebel historians, but the entire event ended on an ambivalent note.[21]

The conference merely emboldened Burdzhalov, who in 1964 published his first scholarly work since his 1956 articles, an essay entitled "Beginning of the Second Russian Revolution." This boldly argued piece traces the origins of the revolution to the spontaneous strikes and disturbances that began in Petrograd on February 18. Burdzhalov limned many ideas he was to develop further in his future book.[22]

The years before 1967 were full of contradictory trends for Soviet historians.[23] When Khrushchev was ousted in 1964, the new leadership reiterated the correctness of the party congresses under him. Stalin was not mentioned at the Twenty-Third Party Congress in 1966, however, perhaps because the months preceding it were rife with rumor that he would be rehabilitated. Revisionist historians may well have had the upper hand, but the neo-Stalinists had the edge by the time of the invasion of Czechoslovakia in 1968. This is important to note simply because Burdzhalov's manuscript was accepted for publication in 1966 (he had two sympathetic readers and he refused, at his editor's suggestion, to make any revisions) and published in 1967. It is doubtful that it would have been printed, at least without changes, had he tried to have it published a year later. At the time he submitted his work, Aleksandr Nekrich, Iurii Trifonov,

Ivan Maiskii, and others published books that took up the theme of the Stalin cult.[24] An article appearing on the fortieth anniversary of *Voprosy istorii* in 1966 criticized the cult, arguing that it had caused "great harm to historical science" by creating dogmatism, schematism, and falsifications. The editorial viewed the changes that had taken place since the Twentieth Congress positively. But true to the inconsistent signals given out by Soviet officialdom at this time, the article also pointed out that "some historians" had permitted methodological mistakes even on the pages of *Voprosy istorii*.[25] In early 1966 *Pravda* advocated dropping usage of the phrase "the personality cult." Within the Institute of History a heated battle raged between the Stalinists and more progressive historians, and historians such as Nekrich came under fire, he for publishing *June 22, 1941*,[26] which criticized Stalin's role at the beginning of the Nazi invasion. In February 1966 the Siniavsky-Daniel trial got underway, while in March the Chinese stated in a letter to the Central Committee that the Sino-Soviet split had been caused "by the dismantling of Stalin's heritage."[27]

It was in this mixed climate, then, that Burdzhalov's book appeared on the eve of the fiftieth anniversary of the February Revolution. As William G. Rosenberg said at the time, "ten years' silence have changed neither Burdzhalov's basic viewpoints nor his penchant for strong arguments."[28] Burdzhalov dealt directly with divisions and confusion within the Bolshevik leadership over tactics, chronicling the lack of coordination among Bolshevik organizations in Petrograd. He discussed the roles of the other socialist parties who, like the Bolsheviks, did not control or lead the movement, but joined it to add an element of leadership. He analyzed the key role of the Petrograd masses, that of the proletariat and soldiers. He examined the contribution of the Duma leadership, whom he viewed as a diverse lot with no common attitude on how to deal with the revolution.

Citing a rich array of archival material, émigré memoirs, and family archives, Burdzhalov showed the extent to which the Petrograd uprising took the revolutionaries by surprise. When the Bolsheviks played an important role, they did so in concert with Mensheviks, SRs, and Interdistrictites. Burdzhalov outlined the differences between the radically disposed Vyborg District Committee and the more cautious Russian Bureau of the Central Committee. Elaborating on his 1956 articles, he described the Bolsheviks' confusion and indecision in the clumsy efforts of the Central Committee Bureau in putting out a manifesto on February 27, which was more restrained than the mood in the streets, for it merely reiterated the party's minimum program and, not mentioning the Soviet at all, called for creation of a provisional revolutionary government. (In discussing the manifesto, incidentally, Burdzhalov settled an old score with Bugaev.) The Central Committee Bureau eventually came to recognize the Soviet as Russia's sole revolutionary government, but by that time the Petrograd Committee had already accepted the *postol'ku-poskol'ku* formula of the moderate socialists, which called for supporting the new government "only insofar as" it fought to protect the gains of the revolution. He even assessed Martov and

Trotsky more fairly than any other Soviet author, gave credit to the other revolutionary parties, and did not exaggerate the Bolsheviks' role in forming the Petrograd Soviet. Ignoring the criticism to which he had been subjected since 1956, Burdzhalov depicted the revolution as an essentially spontaneous affair in which the workers themselves occupied the forefront, assisted by the garrison. "The Petrograd proletariat played," he wrote, "the major role in the victory of the February Revolution."

It would be impossible here to touch upon all of the important contributions or historiographical issues dealt with in Burdzhalov's masterful study. He provided a wealth of new information on the strike movement in 1917, on worker and soldier demonstrations, and on the ferment in the barracks. He raised such issues as whether or not the Russian government seriously considered a separate peace with Germany, and the extent to which the Duma opposition had prepared for a palace coup. He offered a convincing explanation of the origins of Order No. 1 and, as an antidote to what is often assumed, pointed out that the February Revolution, in which two thousand people were killed in Petrograd alone, was far from a bloodless revolution. Finally, in focusing on the uprising, Burdzhalov relegates the Stalin question to the background, and this, in turn, further undermines history according to the *Short Course*.

Burdzhalov's history will not please everyone. Readers may well wish that the author had stated more clearly the underlying causes of the revolution and the relative importance of each of them. His panoramic background chapter, while fluently written and packed with information, often raises more questions than it resolves. After tracing the development of a new revolutionary upsurge in Russia circa 1912, Burdzhalov states that revolution was knocking on the door when World War I broke out and that the war actually delayed it. This thesis, also elaborated by Leopold Haimson, is not developed convincingly. Even his Soviet reviewers criticized him on this point, arguing that without the war there would have been no revolutionary garrison in Petrograd, and it was the garrison, after all, that swung the tide of events in favor of the people.[29] Startsev and Znamenskii also consider his discussion of the "second revolutionary wave" (see chapter 4) unconvincing and based on a priori arguments. (The Study Group on the Russian Revolution, in a discussion of the merits of Hasegawa's monograph, however, found Burdzhalov's ideas on this matter of considerable value.) Although I do not find it altogether convincing, recent scholarship suggests, ironically enough, that Burdzhalov may have underestimated the role of middle-level Bolshevik activists during the revolution.[30] Like most Soviet scholarly books from the period, Burdzhalov's lacks a bibliography and an index.

Nonetheless, when put into the context of either Soviet or Western historiography on the February Revolution, Burdzhalov's study remains a classic. From the 1930s until the end of the 1950s, Soviet scholarship did not produce a single valuable work on the February Revolution.[31] Between publication of Burdzhalov's articles in 1956 and his book in 1967, capable Soviet historians who examined this topic, such as E. D. Chermenskii, P. V. Volobuev, and I. P. Leiberov, tended to concentrate on the leadership crisis within the government (*krizis verkhov*), or to tap the newly opened archives to provide fresh evaluations of the labor movement.[32] Other historians ignored February and focused their attention on the party's role in the August–October period. Most authors stressed Bolshevik leadership of the revolutionary movement, but admitted Bolshevik collaboration with SRs and Mensheviks. Burdzhalov remained the only Soviet historian to have tackled the thorny question of factions within the party and the implications of this issue. The second volume of a six-volume history of the CPSU published in 1966 and edited by Burdzhalov's nemesis, E. I. Bugaev, for instance, emphasized the tight organization and singular influence of the Bolsheviks during the February Revolution, and thereby continued to falsify party history and skirt sensitive issues, even if on a higher "scholarly" level.

There were some other good works published on the fiftieth anniversary of 1917 that complement Burdzhalov's, but they either continued earlier trends of dealing with the crisis within the government[33] or hedged on the controversial topics with which Burdzhalov dealt.[34] The same year Burdzhalov's book was released, Soviet historians held two important conferences, one on the overthrow of the autocracy and the other on the Russian proletariat. Among other things, the conferences sought to address the problem of the role of spontaneity in the revolutionary process. When the conference papers were published with delays three years later, both were subjected to severe criticism and this represented a temporary setback for the profession.[35] It is probably correct to link this flood of criticism with the Twenty-Fourth Party Congress held in 1971, at a time when the leadership was still smarting after having snuffed out the liberalization drive in Czechoslovakia. As John Keep has observed, resolutions passed at the congress "made it clear that the present Soviet leaders intended to continue the hard line towards intellectuals which they embarked upon when they decided to crush the 'Prague spring' of 1968."[36] The collection of essays on the overthrow of the autocracy included an article by Burdzhalov, in which he again indicted Soviet historiography during the barren Stalin years and the many works published after 1956 for avoiding touchy topics and for often indiscriminately equating the role of the Mensheviks and Socialist Revolutionaries with that of the bourgeoisie.[37]

Since the early 1970s, Soviet scholarship has produced no book that challenges the leading position occupied by Burdzhalov's study. In 1971 the second volume of his work appeared, which examines the February Revolution in Moscow, in the provinces, and at the front.[38] Although the author may have restrained some of his arguments, he once again demonstrated mastery of the subject and sources. Perhaps because his standards were so high and his discussion of controversial topics so direct, no Soviet historian has attempted such thorough examination of the February Revolution itself, apart from joint-authored publications. Instead, historians have further illuminated the February Revolution in the provinces or specific aspects of the uprising in Petrograd.[39] The more serious authors acknowledge their intellectual debt to Burdzhalov, even if they criticize him for underestimating the role played by the "unified" Bolshevik center in Petrograd and the presence of a plan for the preparation and implementation of a general strike. Even though Burdzhalov never regained the personal stature he had once enjoyed, most of his views became incorporated over time into accepted treatments of the February events,[40] and have likewise made their way into mass-edition texts and popular accounts of the revolution.[41]

Overshadowed by the October Revolution that brought the Bolsheviks to power, the February Revolution until recently has not received comprehensive study by historians outside the Soviet Union. Works of a more general nature, such as those by M. T. Florinsky, Bernard Pares, and W. H. Chamberlin, have all described the February days, but the revolution itself was not their main concern. Although not without value, these studies are seriously dated.[42] Until publication of Hasegawa's impressive study in 1981, only two books dealt specifically with February, those of émigré historians George Katkov and S. P. Mel'gunov.[43] Concerned with high politics, both writers ignored the mass movement and as a result presented the actions of the liberals and high command as intrigues against the legitimate monarchy. Hasegawa's book and articles represent the most authoritative account in English; the author admits his intellectual debt to Burdzhalov. Recent Western studies of a general nature on the Russian Revolution have deepened our knowledge of 1917, while more narrowly focused monographs have offered fresh evaluations of key groups during the revolutionary process. In the latter case in particular the authors draw heavily from Burdzhalov and acknowledge his accomplishments.[44] When all is said and done, *Russia's February Revolution* has not outlived its usefulness and will continue to inspire historians for generations to come.

Eduard Nikolaevich Burdzhalov died in Moscow on December 31, 1985, after a ten-year-battle against Parkinson's disease. He was survived by his widow, Gosia Borisovna, their son, Feliks Eduardovich, and his family. Shortly after Burdzhalov's death, eighteen specialists on the Russian Revolution from Japan, Great Britain, Canada, and the United States sent a joint letter of sympathy to his widow. "All of us were meticulous readers of his brilliant book . . . ," the letter reads. "We respect its serious examination of the sources and its bold analysis." "I know," responded Gosia Borisovna, "that if his books continue to live, if historians continue to turn to them, then he has not lived in vain. Such thoughts give me strength in my never-ending grief."

E. N. Burdzhalov wrote in a lively, dramatic style. In translating his book, I have eschewed a literal rendering into English and have tried, instead, to capture the tone of his work. Rather than peppering the text with Russian words that do not lend themselves well to translation, I have attempted to find English equivalents as much as possible. I have kept my explanatory notes to a minimum, and have geared them to readers who lack a solid background in Russian history. Based on the author's footnotes, I have compiled a bibliography of sources used by Burdzhalov. For consistency and to avoid confusion, the original footnotes have been renumbered. I also have taken the liberty of tinkering with the title to make it more immediately comprehensible to English readers, and I have added several photographs and maps to the text. Readers must bear in mind that this is a work by a Marxist historian, and therefore they must learn to cope with what might be an unfamiliar terminology as well as with classifications, terms, and labels that are not always neutral.

All dates in this book are given according to the Julian calendar, which was thirteen days behind the Gregorian calendar of the West. Transliteration from Russian is based on the Library of Congress system. For stylistic considerations, however, I have deleted the soft signs from place names and proper nouns (e.g., Vasilevskii Island, rather than Vasil'evskii). In some surnames "ii" is rendered "y" to conform with common usage.

I am indebted to the National Endowment for the Humanities, whose generous financial support enabled me to devote the 1983–84 academic year to this project. Hugh F. Graham read the first draft of my translation and convinced me that it had to be redone. His experience and exacting standards showed me how to proceed in refining my work. Without his counsel at such an early stage in the project, I may well have been satisfied with a literal and flat translation that would have been a disservice to Burdzhalov. My colleague, Louise McReynolds, generously agreed to comment on a later version of my translation. Her good sense of style improved the final product. I am particularly grateful to my former graduate student G. Nelson Armitage III who, during the summer of 1985, provided valuable clerical help. Debra P. Heien, now with the Department of State, compiled the index. George M. Enteen of Pennsylvania State University read the draft of my introduction. Everett A. Wingert of the University of Hawaii and his assistant, Jodi Bailey, prepared the maps. The Museum of the Hungarian Labor Movement in Budapest provided me with some of the photographs published in this book. My thanks also go to the staffs of the University of Illinois Library, University of California at Berkeley Library, the Hoover Institution, and the University of Hawaii's Hamilton Library. I should mention Edward R. Kasinec, then head of the Slavic collection at Berkeley, who obtained most of Burdzhalov's earlier published works for me, and Patricia A. Polansky, Russian bibliographer at Hamilton Library, who assisted in a variety of ways. While expressing my appreciation for the efforts of these people, I wish to absolve them from responsibility for any remaining errors.

I am grateful to M. E. Sharpe, Inc., Publisher, for permission to include here, in altered form, excerpts of this work that were published in the Summer 1979 volume of *Soviet Studies in History* in a translation by William Mandel, edited by me.

Finally, I wish to record my indebtedness to Alexander Rabinowitch who, back in 1972, suggested I translate Burdzhalov's book. Alex has backed the project ever since. The author, E. N. Burdzhalov, gave me his blessing to undertake this translation and kindly discussed his book with me over the years. I am a richer person for having known him, and regret that I was unable to publish my translation before he died. After his death, his widow and son expressed their confidence in my ability to bring this project to fruition. As always, my wife, Karen, with good humor and patience, let Bolsheviks, Mensheviks, and the insurgent population of Petrograd invade her own life.

RUSSIA'S
Second Revolution

E. N. Burdzhalov, 1906–1985

Preface

In 1913 the reigning Romanov dynasty celebrated its tricentenary. Festive gatherings and public prayers were held; speeches and sermons were delivered; books and articles were written. . . . But within four years a mighty whirlwind of revolution wiped the Romanov dynasty and the entire autocratic system from the face of the earth. The revolution destroyed the tsarist regime and surged on toward a new, socialist stage of history.

At first, when it did not seem likely that the Russian Revolution would develop further, bourgeois newspapers called it a fantastic dream, "the second coming," a glorious holiday. They noted the establishment of freedom in Russia was "like the creation of the world." A miracle! wrote the Russian press. A miracle! resounded the echo from abroad. But there was nothing supernatural about the Russian Revolution; its victory was entirely the result of natural causes.

Could these causes have been eliminated? Was it possible to have prevented tsarism's downfall? These questions have been and still remain fundamental in bourgeois memoir and historical literature on the revolution. Pondering their fate at leisure, leaders of the Russian bourgeois-landowner camp accused each other of fostering the revolution. Devout reactionaries maintained that the State Duma[a] had undermined the foundations of the autocracy: if only it had been more accommodating, the revolution could have been avoided. Bourgeois liberals, on the other hand, believed the tsarist government itself was entirely at fault: if it had only been more flexible and granted concessions to the Duma, everything would have evolved peacefully, without revolution. Some declared that P. N. Miliukov[b] and M. V. Rodzianko[c] were guilty; some blamed Rasputin

[a] Russia's parliament or representative assembly established during the Revolution of 1905. The government dissolved the first two dumas, which convened in 1906 and 1907 respectively, because the opposition deputies held approximately two-thirds of the total seats. In June 1907 the government promulgated a new electoral law to guarantee a compliant legislature. Convening in November 1907, the Third Duma was the only one to serve its full five-year term; the Fourth Duma, elected in 1912, succumbed to the revolutionary changes in 1917.

[b] P. N. Miliukov (1859–1943), historian and leader of the Constitutional Democratic (Kadet) party, Russia's leading liberal party. His opponents have accused him of contributing to the collapse of the autocracy owing to his outspoken criticism of the tsarist government's prosecution of the war. See the abridged English-language edition of Miliukov's memoirs, *Political Memoirs: 1905–1917*, ed. Arthur P. Mendel and trans. Carl Golberg (Ann Arbor, 1967). See also Thomas Riha, *A Russian European: Paul Miliukov in Russian Politics* (Notre Dame, 1969).

[c] M. V. Rodzianko (1859–1924) was a leader of the Octobrist party (the Union of October 1917)

and the tsarina. Still others placed responsibility for the collapse of the autocracy on A. D. Protopopov.[d] "This revolution," said A. I. Guchkov[e] at a meeting of war industries committees[f] on March 8, 1917, "was not prepared by those who made it but by those at whom it was aimed. We, Russian society and the Russian people, were not the conspirators; the conspirators were representatives of the authorities themselves. . . . We might elect Protopopov an honorary member of our revolution!"[1]

The allegation that the tsarist dynasty destroyed itself, that the revolution was caused by the myopic policies of the autocracy or the criminal activities of its representatives, found its way from émigré literature into works and memoirs by foreign bourgeois historians, politicians, and publicists. "The conspirators who overthrew Czardom," wrote D. Lloyd George, "were the Czarina and Rasputin, with the help of incompetent Ministers they promoted and favoured. The unconscious head of the conspiracy was the Czar himself . . . there was only a crown without a head."[2] Edmund A. Walsh argued that if it had not been for the tsarevich's illness, the empress's mysticism, and Rasputin's pernicious influence, "Russia might have been spared the scourges that came upon her."

---

and president of the Third and Fourth dumas. By virtue of this post, he headed the Provisional Committee of the State Duma which played an important role in forming the Provisional Government. Rodzianko emigrated to Yugoslavia after the Civil War, where he remained in comparative isolation. Monarchists attacked him for betraying the tsar, while the liberals criticized his reluctance to set up a new government during the February Revolution. His inaccurate memoirs were published in English in 1927 (and reprinted in 1973), *The Reign of Rasputin: An Empire's Collapse*, trans. Catherine Zvegintzoff (London, 1927). See also Eleanor M. Eddy, "The Last President of the Duma: A Political Biography of M. V. Rodzianko," doctoral dissertation, University of Kansas, 1975.

[d] A. D. Protopopov (1866–1918) was the last minister of the interior and vice-president of the Fourth State Duma. Protopopov was elected to the Third and Fourth dumas as a member of the Octobrist party. During World War I his critics unfairly suspected him of promoting a separate peace with Germany. The fact that Aleksandra Fedorovna and Rasputin supported Protopopov's appointment to the cabinet in late 1916, about the time his progressive dementia worsened, contributed to his unpopularity. As M. T. Florinsky put it, "It was the last drop which filled to overflowing the cup of discredit of the Imperial Government." The Bolsheviks executed Protopopov in September 1918, following an attempt on Lenin's life. There are few sources on Protopopov available in English. For his role in the fall of the government, see Bernard Pares, *The Fall of the Russian Monarchy* (New York, 1939). Also of interest are Protopopov's "Iz dnevnika," *Krasnyi arkhiv*, vol. 20, no. 3 (1925), and his incoherent testimony in "Predsmertnaia zapiska," *Golos minuvshego na chuzhoi storone*," no. 2/XV (Berlin, 1926), and Vremennoe pravitel'stvo, Chrezvychainaia sledstvennaia komissiia, *Padenie tsarskogo rezhima* (7 vols: Leningrad and Moscow, 1924–27), esp. vol. 2, pp. 273–319; vol. 4, pp. 3–115; vol. 5, pp. 238–44.

[e] A. I. Guchkov (1862–1936). Born into a family of wealthy Moscow merchants, Guchkov became a founder and leader of the Octobrist party. He supported Prime Minister Stolypin's efforts to snuff out the revolutionary movement after 1907, and was elected president of the Third State Duma in 1910. He resigned, however, the following year and became a severe critic of the autocracy, lashing out against the government's bungling of the war and opposing Rasputin's growing influence. His memoirs appeared in *Poslednie novosti* on September 13, 1936.

[f] The Central War Industries Committee (WIC) was one of several voluntary organizations formed during World War I to mobilize the country's resources behind the war effort. Prominent members of industry and commerce founded the Central WIC in May 1915, in the wake of disastrous military defeats, to supply the Russian army more efficiently. By spring 1916, some 239 local committees existed throughout the country. See Lewis H. Siegelbaum, *The Politics of Industrial Mobilization in Russia, 1914–1917: A Study of the War-Industries Committees* (New York, 1983).

The history of the downfall of the Russian monarchy, he asserted, is "the story of the triumph of folly in Russia and the penalty she paid for that historic madness." Sir George Mavor maintained that if the despot had been stronger, perhaps tsarism would not have fallen. Bernard Pares reasoned that if it had not been for incompetent ministers, Nicholas II's weak character, etc., "everything might have been avoided."[3]

The policies of individuals and, even more, the activities of social groups and entire classes naturally exert considerable influence on the historical process, at times slowing it down, at times speeding it up. Given the nature of the autocratic system, the personality of the monarch was bound to affect the fate of the monarchy. Nicholas II met the same unhappy destiny as the English King Charles I and the French King Louis XVI. Like them, the last Russian tsar was a severe and remote man, obstinate and dull-witted, passive and weak-willed. He was surrounded by hopeless reactionaries and, during the last years of the empire, he entrusted its fate to his hysterical wife, the rogue Rasputin, and the demented Protopopov. The tsarist government's actions and the court camarilla's policies contributed to the isolation of the autocracy and hastened its downfall, but no other actions or policies could have saved tsarism. A dictatorship of the landowners, tsarism could not remain in power. Neither individuals nor groups nor even entire classes could have prevented its overthrow—the whole course of historical events had led up to it.

This does not imply that the autocracy was fatally doomed and collapsed by itself. Bourgeois historians and publicists frequently write about the monarchy's fall, collapse, and suicide. In his memoirs, P. N. Miliukov wrote "of the self liquidation of the old order." R. P. Browder and A. F. Kerensky note in the forward to their collection of documents, *The Russian Provisional Government*, that the Russian Revolution resulted more from the complete bankruptcy of tsarism than from radical ideology or a popular uprising.[4] Tsarism was indeed totally bankrupt, but it did not fall by itself, it did not quietly and peacefully pass away because it was senile and decrepit. It was overthrown by the people who rose against it. The Russian workers, actively supported by peasants in soldiers' greatcoats, were the ones who destroyed it once and for all.

Russian tsarism had earlier experienced severe vicissitudes: massive peasant rebellions had broken out in Russia; the Decembrists and populists *(narodniki)* from the educated commoners *(raznochintsy)*[g] had challenged the autocracy. Russian tsarism had tottered and cracked, but it had managed to survive.

[g]The Decembrist revolt took place in 1825 at the accession of Nicholas I. The Decembrists, who belonged to liberal revolutionary societies, hoped to place Nicholas's brother Constantine on the throne and to secure a constitution for Russia. The government crushed the revolt which often is viewed as the first major revolutionary challenge to the autocracy. The populists *(narodniki)* were groups of revolutionary-minded members of the intelligentsia, lacking a unified body of political or social doctrine other than their infatuation with the people *(narod)*, who went into the villages in the 1870s to radicalize the peasantry. The term *raznochintsy* literally means "persons of various ranks" (classes). The term refers to members of the intelligentsia of lower- and middle-class origin in the second half of the nineteenth century.

Tsarism was not faced with a truly mortal threat until the proletariat, the most progressive class in modern society, appeared on the scene. The militant Marxist party of the working class, the Bolshevik party guided by Lenin, led the proletariat and all working people of Russia into an assault on the autocracy. Once they had resolved this urgent task, they could undertake the realization of their goal—the building of socialism.

At the beginning of the twentieth century Russia endured the shocks and blows of three revolutions. Workers and peasants first battled against tsarism in 1905. At the time the autocracy barely managed to survive, but received a short-lived respite. A second onslaught followed in February 1917, when a new revolution broke out. Workers and soldiers overthrew tsarism and paved the way for a socialist revolution.

It is unfortunate that this great historical event has attracted little attention in our literature. Although Soviet historians in the 1920s published a number of serious studies on the history of the February Revolution, in later years scarcely any new scholarly work on this topic has appeared. The February Revolution of 1917 has occupied an insignificant place in general works on the history of the USSR. The struggle the working class and Bolshevik party waged against tsarism during the days of February–March 1917, the actions of the different classes and parties during the revolution, the complex and contradictory character of developments at that time—these and many other questions of the history of the "second" Russian Revolution have not received extensive or thorough treatment. Interest in further analyzing the history of this revolution has grown only recently.[5]

Historical literature commissioned by the party since the publication of the *History of the Communist Party of the Soviet Union (Bolsheviks): Short Course*[h] has underrated the significance of the February Revolution. Events of those days have been considered merely a phase of the imperialist war under a single rubric, e.g., "The Bolshevik Party during the Imperialist War: The Second Russian Revolution."[6] Textbooks on the history of the USSR used in institutions of higher education devote a chapter to the February Revolution, but immediately follow it with "Russian Culture and the Culture of the Peoples of Russia during the Age of Imperialism." Events surrounding the victory of the February Revolution are not discussed until the next volume. Such a limited exposition of what occurred makes it difficult to understand properly the process of how the bourgeois-democratic revolution became a socialist revolution. February 1917 was precisely the time when this process began.

The Revolution of 1905 preceded the February Revolution; October 1917 superseded it. The Second Russian Revolution continued the first on a much broader basis and prepared for the most important revolution in the history of Russia and of all mankind. V. I. Lenin called the cataclysm the "Third Russian

[h] The author is referring to the so-called *Short Course* first published in 1938 under Stalin's personal approval. Burdzhalov is making an oblique criticism here of Soviet historiography during the Stalin period. See my introduction to the text.

Revolution," and on the day it was victorious, October 25, 1917, he voiced confidence that this revolution would ultimately lead to the victory of socialism.

The fact that the three Russian revolutions are thus connected provides an opportunity to show more clearly and comprehensively the glorious march of the working people of Russia toward socialism, to shed more light on their historical experience, and to reveal the international significance of their victory. This book focuses on the February Revolution, when the same forces as in 1905 entered the political arena, but important changes had taken place in the alignment of these forces. The victory over tsarism enabled the revolution eventually to enter its socialist phase in Russia, and actually began the movement toward this phase. In chronological terms, my work deals with events that took place approximately until the middle of March 1917, when the autocratic structure was overthrown and dual power was established throughout the country. This was the first stage of the unified revolutionary process that led to the triumph of the Great October Revolution. I examine the harbingers of the revolution and the events during February and March 1917 in Petrograd. I discuss what was happening simultaneously in Moscow, in the provinces, and at the front in another volume readied for publication.[i] In it I consider the role of the February Revolution in the history of our country and of the entire world, and include a historiographical survey of the topic, which I have appended to the very end of the narrative of events set forth in this study, where it is best placed.

All revolutions are the result of a deep crisis, involving all aspects of life in a society, which inevitably causes the old order to fall. Before beginning an account of the course of the revolution we must answer a question at least summarily: how did the revolutionary crisis that led to the overthrow of the tsarist monarchy develop and mature?

[i] *Vtoraia russkaia revoliutsiia: Moskva, front, periferiia* (Moscow, 1971).

ONE

The Revolutionary Crisis

> Revolution is impossible without a national crisis (that affects the exploited and the exploiters).
>
> —V. I. Lenin

From the First to the Second Revolution

After suppressing the First Russian Revolution of 1905, tsarism sought to prevent a second. The autocracy hoped that brutal police terror and the support of the Russian and international bourgeoisie would smash the revolutionary forces. It determined to use Stolypin's agrarian reforms[a] to encourage bourgeois economic relations and relieve revolutionary pressures in the countryside.

Capitalism developed further in the years following the first revolution. Stratification among the peasantry, expanded trade, agricultural innovation, the growth of cities, vigorous railroad construction, and finally an arms race promoted Russian industry. In 1909–13, it experienced a new spurt during which coal mining, iron smelting, and steel production increased. This has led many bourgeois authors to maintain that Russia accomplished a great leap forward in its economic development during these years, that rapid growth occurred in Russian industry, and that peasants became petty proprietors. They write that Russia was reviving in the prewar period and the progress it achieved at the time had obviated the need for a new Russian revolution.[b]

Such claims do not correspond to reality. As in the past, gentry landownership and other remnants of serfdom not eliminated by the Stolypin

[a] Providing a legal and administrative framework for social transformation, the Stolypin agrarian reforms consisted of two 1906 laws facilitating the release of peasants from the confines of the commune and an edict of June 14, 1910, decreeing that members of communes who had not carried out a repartitioning of land recently became outright proprietors of their holdings. "A wager on the strong and sober," the reforms were conceived as a means to save the monarchical system by propagating private ownership in place of communally held land and by expanding the stratum of peasant landowners.

[b] Although fairly accurate at the time he wrote this book, Burdzhalov's assessment of Western scholarship has since become dated. During the past two decades a growing number of Western historians have taken a grim view of Russia's progress and the success of the government's reforms on the eve of the Great War.

reforms fettered the Russian economy. Industrial expansion did not rid Russia of her technical and economic backwardness. The advancement was insignificant. Even now Russia had four times fewer instruments of production than England, five times fewer than Germany, and ten times fewer than America.[1] The country continued to depend on more advanced capitalist countries technically and economically. Heavy industry was poorly developed, and Russia remained primarily agricultural.

The socioeconomic contradictions that caused the First Russian Revolution continued to exist as capitalism expanded further, and in fact they manifested themselves even more forcefully. Advanced industry and backward agriculture, a capitalist base and semifeudal superstructure, the supremacy of a small group of exploiters and an oppressed people—only a popular revolution could resolve these and numerous other contradictions, not partial government reforms and half-hearted concessions. In protecting the semifeudal order, tsarism continued as the major obstacle to the country's progressive development. After the reforms of the 1860s[c] it tried again to turn into a bourgeois monarchy, but it simply did not become one. Remaining a dictatorship of landowners, the autocracy strengthened the police regime in the country even more, cruelly suppressing every attempt at freedom and progress.

The immediate tasks of the Russian Revolution were to overthrow tsarism, eradicate the vestiges of serfdom, and democratize the political order. This revolution had a bourgeois democratic character but, in contrast with bourgeois-democratic revolutions in Western Europe, it took place later in the evolution of capitalism, after it had entered its imperialist stage.[d] Monopoly capitalism had developed in Russia as it had in other European countries, and in the years following the First Russian Revolution the process of concentrating production and capital intensified. The number of joint-stock companies and their capital increased several times. Syndicates occupied a leading place in ferrous and nonferrous metallurgy, in the fuel, machine-building, and other branches of heavy industry, and in several branches of light industry. Banks grew more involved in production and made industrial enterprises even more dependent on them.

Because Russia's backward technical and economic base prevented imperialism from achieving the same development that it had attained in Western Europe, the basic characteristics of modern imperialism were less manifest in Russia. Although Russian workers were more concentrated in large enterprises

[c] Here Burdzhalov is referring to the edict of 1861 that emancipated the serfs, an 1864 law that established *zemstvos* (local organs of self-government), and another 1864 law that reorganized the judiciary and introduced trial by jury and elected justices of the peace. Further reforms in the 1870s granted a measure of self-government to the towns and reorganized the army, making all social groups liable to military service.

[d] See Lenin's "Imperialism, the Highest Stage of Capitalism," first published in 1916. Tapping Marxist and non-Marxist writings, Lenin tried to demonstrate that the First World War was an imperialist war in order to justify his antiwar stand and to defend revolutionary defeatism. Lenin advocated Russia's defeat, arguing that it would hasten world revolution.

than in other capitalist countries, the technological level of these enterprises was lower than in the advanced countries. The formation of industrial trusts did not spread as widely in Russia, and the export of domestic capital to colonies was insubstantial. In fact, Russia itself was the object of the export of English, French, German, Belgian, and other foreign capital, which played important roles in Russian heavy industry and banking. Russian imperialism lagged behind the classical imperialism that existed in the USA, England, and Germany, and was dependent on it. Nevertheless, capitalist contradictions also became very acute in Russia. Even though a bourgeois-democratic revolution had not come about, the preconditions for the elimination of capitalism and for transformation to a socialist order already had been created in the country. Russia was not a major capitalist state and was economically less mature than such countries. Lenin referred to Russia as a country with an average-to-weak economic system. It was precisely in Russia, however, that a revolution took place that not only overthrew tsarism but actually advanced to liquidate the bourgeois order. This came about through the propitious combination of many objective and subjective circumstances. As Lenin put it: "Owing to a number of historical causes—the greater backwardness of Russia, the unusual hardships brought upon her by the war, the utter rottenness of tsarism, and the extreme tenacity of the traditions of 1905—the revolution broke out in Russia earlier than in other countries."[2]

The proletariat became the decisive driving force and leader of the Russian Revolution. At the beginning of the twentieth century there were three million factory, mill, mine, and railroad workers in Russia. This number was insignificant in comparison with the overall size of the population [128 million in 1897—D.J.R.], but the proletariat's share in the political life of the country was immeasurably larger than its size. The concentration of workers in large enterprises helped them to act cohesively and in an organized manner, and this had a powerful impact on the country's political life. Hired piece-rate workers in home and handicraft industries, workers in agriculture, mine workers, construction workers, workers in communications and retail trade, domestic servants, and others joined the proletariat of the factories and railroads.

The Russian proletariat had formed as a class later than the proletariat of Western Europe, at a time when the teachings of Karl Marx and Friedrich Engels already had been disseminated widely. The influence of petit bourgeois theories on the Russian working class was short-lived and the Russian workers' movement from the outset fell under Marxist sway.[e] The proletariat created a party of its own before any other class in Russia. Under its leadership, Russian workers undertook the struggle to overthrow tsarism as a precondition to social emancipation.

[e] Burdzhalov, like other Soviet historians, uses the term "petit bourgeois theories" as a pejorative referring to various neopopulist, populist, and reformist (rather than revolutionary) Marxist groups, and when convenient, to the other socialist parties.

Bent on overthrowing the domination of the landowners, the peasantry was the other driving force in the Russian Revolution, not as separate strata, but as an entire estate *(soslovie)* within a feudal society.[f] The spontaneous peasant uprisings that had repeatedly taken place in the past and invariably ended in defeat assumed a different character and led to different results after the proletariat entered the political arena, for only the latter's leadership made it possible to overthrow tsarism and destroy the vestiges of serfdom. The peasantry became the proletariat's ally. The union of the proletariat and peasantry was essential for the victory of the Russian Revolution.[g]

In contrast with the bourgeoisie of France, England, and some other countries, the Russian bourgeoisie was not the driving force behind the bourgeois-democratic revolution. It was dependent on foreign capital and tsarism, and its weak economic position made it politically lethargic and immature. Although interested in liquidating the vestiges of serfdom and establishing its own political supremacy, it was too closely connected to the autocracy. Needing the autocracy's support, the bourgeoisie could not decisively break with it. The Russian bourgeoisie entered the arena of active political struggle only after the proletariat had emerged as an independent political force. Fear of the working class constrained the bourgeoisie's actions. Apprehensive that a popular uprising against tsarism would turn against it, the bourgeoisie tried to secure reforms in order to avoid revolution. The bourgeoisie thus fought for a constitutional monarchy, hoping such a government would help it come to power and prevent the people from doing so.

Tsarism and the bourgeoisie both expected that a long period of peaceful development would ensue after the suppression of the First Russian Revolution. The Stolypin reaction had weakened the revolutionary movement. Mass arrests had debilitated its ranks and the number of strikes decreased and peasant uprisings declined. Many members of the intelligentsia and petite bourgeoisie withdrew from active political life. Yet the flames of revolution did not flicker out during this difficult time: the period of the Stolypin reaction was merely a lull between the two revolutions. The revolutionary forces did not

[f] A *soslovie* (estate) was a social class with a special legal status. Although it resembled that of the *ancien régime* in Western Europe, the legal estate structure of Russian society was established by the government itself in the eighteenth century. The reforms of the second half of the nineteenth century led to a disintegration of the estate structure, but the terms and formal division of the population into estates survived until the revolution. Circa 1900 approximately seventy-seven percent of the population belonged to the peasant estate.

[g] Burdzhalov's use of the expression "union of the proletariat and peasantry" is ambiguous, and perhaps purposefully so. At the time he wrote, Soviet historians were not in agreement as to which strata of the rural population represented the true allies of the proletariat. Burdzhalov gives credit to both the poorest elements of the peasantry and elsewhere to the entire peasant estate. From the early 1970s, an "orthodox" view has gained ascendancy in Soviet historiography, according to which only the poor peasants were the natural ally of the proletariat in this revolutionary union. P. V. Volobuev and other historians were chastized for arguing that the entire peasantry and not just its poorest elements had allied with the working class during 1917. See, for example, *Soviet Studies in History*, vol. 22, no. 3 (Winter 1983–84), ed. Donald J. Raleigh.

cease their struggle against tsarism. Returning to the underground, they passed to the defensive in order best to prepare themselves for a future offense.

New battles with tsarism were not far off. They were maturing because of the same socioeconomic contradictions and approximately the same alignment of class forces as in the battles of the First Russian Revolution. But there was an important difference: The growth of capitalism after the Revolution of 1905–1907 exacerbated previous contradictions, creating conditions that brought social revolution in Russia nearer. The revolutionary proletariat led by the Bolsheviks was now significantly more united than it had been during the First Russian Revolution. It relied on the vast political experience accumulated by this time and took into account the lessons of past revolutionary battles.

The workers of Russia recovered from the blows of the reaction slowly but steadily. The torpor and weariness caused by the defeat of the revolution gradually passed. A push was needed to speed up the development of and afford an outlet to the accumulated energy. In April–May 1912 a protest movement against the shooting of workers at the Lena Goldfields exploded into a new revolutionary upsurge. The peasantry rose behind the working class; revolutionary ferment infected the army and navy. All in all, tsarism's policies failed. The basic aim of Stolypin's System of the Third of June[h] was not achieved; a new revolutionary rising was bound to come. The sleeping Russian giant once again began to stir.

The revolutionary wave reached its greatest height during the summer of 1914. The proletariat in other cities of the country rose up in support of the workers of Baku who had gone on strike. A strike of Petersburg workers involving three hundred thousand people heated up. Armed police and Cossacks raided workers' meetings and broke up demonstrations. The Bolshevik newspaper *Trudovaia pravda* (Labor Truth) was shut down. Mass arrests began. Barricades were thrown up in response to police actions. Gripped by feelings of class solidarity and hatred of tsarism, the Petrograd proletariat yearned to strike back at the autocracy. Workers from Moscow, Warsaw, Kharkov, and other cities supported their Petersburg brothers, but the proletariat in the country as a whole lagged behind the proletariat of the capital and was not ready for decisive action. The peasantry and army had not yet been drawn into the nascent struggle.

The Petersburg workers ended their strike in order to prepare better for the approaching revolution. The Bolsheviks strengthened their forces, conducted propaganda, and agitated in the provinces among peasants and soldiers as much as possible in order to organize the country at large for the coming battle with tsarism. The specter of a new 1905 hovered over the country; revolution was

[h] In the aftermath of the Revolution of 1905 and establishment of the Duma, Prime Minister Stolypin embarked upon a sweeping campaign to crush the revolutionary movement. When opposition parties won majorities in the First and Second dumas, Stolypin dismissed the institution and promulgated a new electoral law on June 3, 1907, which guaranteed a progovernment legislature and introduced what Soviet historians call "the System of the Third of June."

imminent and was already making its presence felt. But developments outside the country now interrupted further revolutionary activities. While savage class struggles were taking place in the streets of the capital, clashes of a different sort were quietly being readied in government offices. Military conflagration had flared up in Europe. The international proletariat was unable to block the way to imperialist war, unleashed during the very days the workers of Petersburg returned to work after their strike had ended. The streets of the capital had barely been cleaned of workers' blood when torrents of workers' and peasants' blood began to flow at the front in the imperialist war.

Russia at War

The uneven way in which the imperialist powers had developed and the exacerbation of contradictions within the imperialist camp caused the First World War. In this war the imperialists fought over colonies, markets for their products, sources of raw materials, and ways to supplement capital. At the same time they expected to use the war to poison the working people's consciousness with the bane of nationalism, divert them from the class struggle, and weaken their offensive against the ruling order.

Tsarist Russia was one of the chief instigators of the war. Russian landowners and capitalists, like capitalists in other countries, sought to conquer new lands and thereby mollify internal contradictions. They wanted to annex Galicia and Turkish Armenia, the Straits, and Constantinople. The struggle over these aims led Russian imperialists to clash with those of Germany and Austria-Hungary. The bourgeoisie and landlords of Russia, together with the bourgeoisie of England and France, formed the nucleus of the Entente and embarked upon a fierce conflict with the Central Powers of Europe.

In announcing the beginning of the war, the tsar appealed to his "faithful subjects" to forget their internal quarrels and rally for a successful struggle against the foreign enemy. In newspapers, at meetings and rallies, from church pulpits and university lecterns, a hypocritical propaganda called upon working people "to defend the honor and dignity of Russia" and to help "their consanguineous fellow Slavs." The unbridled chauvinistic agitation for military victory clouded the consciousness of many. Crowds of people, including officials, office workers, and ordinary citizens, marched in processions through city streets, carrying portraits of the tsar and singing the imperial anthem. They forced those they passed to bare their heads and kneel before the portraits of the tsar.

The government's terror and chauvinistic propaganda caused marked confusion in the ranks of the proletariat and temporarily deflated its revolutionary activity. In all of Petersburg, only twenty-one enterprises with a total of some twenty-seven thousand workers took part in a strike protesting the war. In various parts of the country recruits occasionally looted state liquor warehouses, attacked induction centers, and demanded that the government provide for their families. Even at induction centers in Petrograd, however, cries of "down with the war" rarely resounded.

The landlords and capitalists wholeheartedly supported Russia's entry into the war. The outbreak of war caused a special session of the State Duma of the Third of June to be convoked on July 26, 1914, at which deputies sympathetically listened to addresses by tsarist ministers, greeted ambassadors of the Allied powers, and sang "God Save the Tsar." From the Duma tribune, speakers from the bourgeois-landowner parties declared they were ready to forget domestic disagreements and support the tsar and the war. The Constitutional Democratic (Kadet) party[i] read an appeal to the Duma which stated that "no matter what our relationship was to the domestic policies of the government, our main duty is to preserve the country one and indivisible . . . put aside internal disputes and not give the enemy even the slightest cause to hope he can divide us through our differences."[3] The capitalists expected territorial acquisitions from the war in the future and large profits in the present. Kadets and Octobrists[j] were thrown together with the tsar and Black Hundreds [extremely nationalistic, reactionary, monarchist forces—D. J. R.] for the purpose of conducting the war jointly.

The petite bourgeoisie's attitude toward the war was more complex and contradictory. Whereas the better-off peasants and part of the urban petite bourgeoisie were interested in territorial aggrandizement and planned to make a fortune out of the war, such aims were foreign to the toiling peasantry and poorer urban elements. It is not surprising that signs of duplicity and vacillation manifested themselves even in the Trudoviks'[k] declaration, read at the meeting of the State Duma on July 26. This declaration noted that "the responsibility of the governments of all of the European states, which in the interests of the

[i] Russia's most important liberal party to the end of the civil war. Although delegates to the second congress of the party in 1906 had changed the name to the Party of People's Freedom, party publications used both appelations. Party members called themselves Kadets, which is an acronym formed by joining the first two letters of the Russian spelling of Constitutional Democrats. See William G. Rosenberg, *Liberals in the Russian Revolution: The Constitutional Democratic Party, 1917–1921* (Princeton, 1974).

[j] A liberal party that stood to the right of the Kadets and drew its support from enlightened landowners and members of the bureaucracy. The party was founded in 1905 as the "Union of October 17," and was named after the government manifesto establishing a State Duma. Led by Guchkov, the party wanted little more than the fulfillment of promises made by the government in the October 17 manifesto. Although they were proponents of a constitutional monarchy, the Octobrists favored a strong executive responsible to the monarch rather than one responsible to the Duma. See Louis Menashe, "Alexander Guchkov and the Origins of the Octobrist Party: The Russian Bourgeoisie in Politics, 1905," doctoral dissertation, New York University, 1966; J. F. Hutchinson, "The Octobrists in Russian Politics, 1905–1917," doctoral dissertation, University of London, 1966; and Ben-Cion Pinchuk, *The Octobrists in the Third Duma* (Seattle, 1974).

[k] The Trudoviks (*Trudovaia gruppa* or Labor Group) was a major faction in the first two dumas, which strove to satisfy the peasants' land hunger by implementing the program of the Socialist Revolutionary and Popular Socialist parties. After the change in the electoral law resulting in the System of the Third of June, the number of Trudovik deputies dropped precipitously.

ruling classes have pushed their nations into the fratricidal slaughter, is unatonable."[4] Despite this theoretically sound position, the Trudoviks held that the war was defensive and that peasants and workers had a duty to defend the country from the attacking enemy. The Trudoviks charged tsarism with failing to rally all forces in the country while the war was being fought, and with failing to declare political amnesty and to mitigate the condition of the toiling people, saddling them instead with the main burden of wartime expenditures.

The Bolshevik faction of the State Duma vigorously condemned the war. Even before the convocation of the Duma a member of the faction, A. E. Badaev, responding to an inquiry made by journalists about attitudes toward the war, said: "The working class is going to struggle with all its might against the war. The war is not in the workers' interests. War against war—that is our slogan." Together with the Menshevik representatives, the Bolshevik deputies drew up a declaration regarding their position toward the imperialist war, and in the name of both Social Democratic factions a Menshevik, V. I. Khaustov, read it in the State Duma on July 26, 1914.

The Social Democratic declaration mirrored the workers' protest against the imperialist war and the covenant between tsarism and the bourgeoisie. It stated that "the present war, engendered by the policy of usurpation and violence practiced by all capitalist states, is a war for which the ruling circles in all the belligerent countries bear responsibility." The declaration emphasized that there can be no solidarity with forces that have enslaved the people. It expressed confidence that international proletarian solidarity would stop the war, and that a peace treaty would be dictated by the people themselves taking their fate into their own hands, and not by diplomats of the predatory governments. The joint declaration of the Social Democratic factions in the Duma did not reveal the character of the war in its entirety, and did not indicate the revolutionary paths of struggle against it. Nevertheless, the promulgation of this declaration in the Duma and the refusal of the Social Democratic factions and Trudoviks to vote for war credits played a distinctively positive role. The Social Democrats' declaration sounded a discordant note within the Duma chambers and showed that the call to join tsarism in fighting against Germany did not meet with the general support about which the bourgeois press wrote.[5]

Led by N. S. Chkheidze, the Menshevik Duma faction did not long adhere to the position set forth in the July 26 declaration. Answering the appeal of the chairman of the Second International, Emile Vandervelde, a member of the bourgeois government of Belgium, to create "a coalition of all vital forces of Europe" to struggle against the German danger, the group declared it "would not oppose the war." The policy of the Menshevik faction in the Duma was not remarkably consistent in the future either but instead reflected the hesitations and disagreements that the Mensheviks experienced during the war. Condemning defensism, L. O. Martov, L. D. Trotsky, and their supporters recognized the imperialist nature of the war, but they did not propose a revolutionary program of struggle against it. They were content with appeals for peace and did not make a decisive break with social chauvinism.[l] Such a position sowed the illusion that it was possible to obtain a just democratic peace under capitalism.

G. V. Plekhanov [the so-called father of Russian Marxism—D.J.R.] openly adopted a chauvinist position during the war. Together with a group of Socialist Revolutionaries (SRs),[m] he called for carrying out the war until Germany was completely routed and, forgetting previous disagreements, uniting harmoniously all vital forces of the country to fight against Austro-Hungarian imperialism. In a letter to A. Burianov, a member of the Menshevik faction of the State Duma, Plekhanov wrote: "Voice your reservations, they're necessary, but vote for credits."[6] The position of A. N. Potresov, S. L. Maslov, N. Cherevanin [F. A. Lipkin—D.J.R.], and other Russian Mensheviks grouped around the journal *Nashe delo* (Our Cause) was similar. Declaring that German imperialism was the main instigator of the war, this group summoned the population "to defend the country from the devastation threatening it." The Menshevik O. A. Ermanskii admitted that after promoting the slogan to defend one's country, these Mensheviks "were in glaring contradiction with the class position promoting the international solidarity of workers, since in essence 'the theory' of having each nation defend its 'fatherland' was tantamount to the slogan 'Workers of the world, seize each other by the throat.' "[7]

The Bolsheviks pursued a policy of proletarian internationalism. While Mensheviks and SRs broke up into several groups during the war, the Bolsheviks remained a united force. Only a few individual literary figures formerly connected to the party succumbed to the general epidemic and deserted to the defensist camp or else withdrew from active political life.[n] The Bolsheviks fought for the demands of the party program, and for the slogans of the First Russian Revolution; their proclamations invariably ended with the calls: "Down with the war!" "Long live international proletarian solidarity!" "Long live the Russian Revolution!"

Devising a specific program for the revolutionary proletariat and also their practical activities was complicated, however, by the weakness of local Bolshe-

[l] In 1907 the Second International had defined its position on the world war that threatened to flare up. If war should break out, socialists should take advantage of the resulting crisis "to hasten the downfall of capitalist class rule." However, in 1914 most socialist parties supported their own country's war efforts. Social chauvinists, then, were members of the Second International who adopted a "chauvinistic" position during the war. Lenin, who argued that the proletariat's task was "to transform the world war into a civil war" against the imperialists, was a striking exception.

[m] Russia's most important populist party claiming to represent the interests of the peasantry and all toiling people. See Oliver H. Radkey, *The Agrarian Foes of Bolshevism: Promise and Default of the Russian Socialist Revolutionaries, February to October 1917* (New York, 1958); Maureen Perrie, *The Agrarian Policy of the Russian Socialist-Revolutionary Party from its Origins through the Revolutions of 1905–1907* (Cambridge, 1976); Manfred Hildemeier, *Die Sozialrevolutionaere Partei Russlands: Agrarsozialismus und Modernisierung im Zarenreich* (Cologne and Vienna, 1978).

[n] Burdzhalov, referring here to N. D. Sokolov and Maxim Gorky, grossly exaggerates Bolshevik unity. The war introduced tremendous confusion into Bolshevik ranks.

vik organizations and the disruption of ties with the party center abroad. At first no news from this center reached Russia through the military fronts, but Bolshevik organizations definitely became more active when, by the end of 1914, material from Lenin was received in Russia. Lenin set forth his position on the war in his theses "The Tasks of Revolutionary Social Democracy in the European War," the manifesto of the Central Committee of the RSDRP entitled "The War and Russian Social Democracy," and articles in the central organ of the party, the newspaper *Sotsial-Demokrat* (The Social Democrat). A Marxist analysis of the nature of the war gave the Bolsheviks the opportunity to adopt a correct tactical stance. Unlike all other parties, the Bolsheviks based their actions on the goal of socialist revolution. They denounced not only the appeal "defend the fatherland" but also the abstract slogan of peace, for it did not summon the proletariat to struggle for a revolutionary overthrow of the existing order. During the war the Bolsheviks advanced their slogan—convert the imperialist war into a civil war. From this basic, definite formulation flowed the rest of their slogans: disenfranchise the bourgeois government, fraternize at the front, break with social chauvinism, and create a new, genuinely revolutionary International.

From the very first days of the war the Bolsheviks urged the working people of Russia to turn their weapons against the autocracy. A leaflet of the Petersburg Committee of the RSDRP issued in July 1914 concerning the war, predicted tsarism's approaching downfall. "Comrades," it read, "the government and bourgeoisie have sown the wind; they will reap the whirlwind! . . . The government of Nicholas the Bloody, the last autocratic government, and Nicholas the Bloody himself, this last swaddling child of the Romanovs, will be the last Russian tsar. . . . Revolution is coming. Let's do all we can to make it victorious."[8]

This prediction came true, but not immediately. Almost three years of war passed before the victorious revolution turned Nicholas II into Nicholas the Last. Many bourgeois historians and publicists maintain that without war there would not have been revolution. They write that tsarism failed because it could not cope with the difficulties of war, did not heed the advice "of true patriots," and rejected the helping hand extended to it.[9] In fact, a new revolution in Russia was brewing before the military conflict, and the country was in the throes of a serious revolutionary crisis in June 1914. The war did not speed up the revolution. It postponed it.

Like other countries at war, tsarist Russia subordinated the country's entire domestic life to the war effort. Instituting stern discipline at the front and a repressive regime at the rear, the autocracy fiercely repressed the revolutionary forces that opposed the war. Worker activists were arrested, exiled to Siberia, or sent to the front. The Bolshevik party was decimated. Party organizations were either completely routed or weakened by repressions and military mobilization. Trade unions and workers' educational societies were shut down, and the workers' press was silenced. Of all the legal workers' organizations at the factories, only the medical funds[o] survived, but the tsarist authorities attacked them too.

Chauvinist agitation, mobilization into the army, and repression at the rear told heavily on the revolutionary workers' movement. The leading strata of the proletariat led by the Bolsheviks remained faithful to the banner of proletarian internationalism and came out emphatically against the war; however, part of the workers succumbed to chauvinist propaganda. The number of strikes sharply decreased with the start of the war. The proletariat's traditional days of struggle such as "Bloody Sunday"[p] and May 1 passed unobserved in 1915. In November 1914 the autocracy arrested members of the Bolshevik faction of the State Duma for their spirited antiwar activity and banished them to Siberia. This arbitrary police action aroused indignation among the masses of workers, but protest against the arrests and the legal proceedings against the worker deputies did not assume wide-scale dimensions.

It appeared that the autocracy's calculations were vindicated and that war had snuffed out revolution. But it seemed this way only at first glance: the war could not stifle the revolution. In 1912–14, four-fifths of the politically conscious workers of Russia united around the Bolshevik newspaper *Pravda* (Truth). "Even if war, prison, Siberia, and hard labor should destroy five or even ten times as many," wrote Lenin, "this section of the workers *cannot* be annihilated. It is alive, it is imbued with the revolutionary spirit, is anti-chauvinist. It *alone* stands in the midst of the masses, with deep roots in the latter, as the champion of the internationalism of the toilers, the exploited, and the oppressed. It *alone* has held its ground in the general *debacle*. It alone is leading the semi-proletarian elements *away* from the social-chauvinism of the Cadets, the Trudoviks, Plekhanov and *Nazha zarya*,[q] and *towards* socialism."[10] In the difficult conditions of war the workers of Russia standing in the vanguard continued to carry on the revolutionary struggle, gathering and joining forces for a new, even more determined assault against tsarism.

The First World War interrupted the development of the revolutionary movement for only a brief period. A short time passed and this movement exploded once again with renewed vigor. The imperialist war shook the founda-

[o] Laws issued in June 1912, permitting the creation of workers' funds to aid victims of illness and accident, led to a proliferation of mutual aid societies and medical funds *(bol'nichnye kassy)*.

[p] The shooting of unarmed workers in St. Petersburg on January 9, 1905, usually considered the first violent episode of the Revolution of 1905.

[q] *Nasha zarya* (Our Dawn) was a monthly sociopolitical journal published (legally) in St. Petersburg between 1910 and 1914 by P. B. Axelrod, F. I. Dan, L. Martov, and others. Representing the Menshevik "liquidators," the organ called for the liquidation of underground Social Democratic activities and backed a united workers' party. When it took a defensist stand on the war, Lenin blasted it as "opportunist and chauvinist." See Lenin's "Socialism and War" which he penned in 1915 with the help of G. Zinoviev in preparation for a conference of antiwar socialist internationalists held at Zimmerwald, Switzerland.

tions of the existing order. Technically and economically backward, Russia proved to be less prepared for modern war than the other capitalist countries. The longer the war dragged on, the more obvious and palpable this became.

The Russian army was unable to resist the well-armed and organized German troops. At the beginning of the war the enemy destroyed two Russian armies in East Prussia. The Russian army routed Austro-Hungarian troops and occupied the Western Ukraine (Galicia), but this victory turned out to be temporary, and these lands were soon retaken by the enemy. The lack of guns, rifles, and ammunition during the first months of war caused Russian troops to endure heavy losses. Food, shoes, and clothing were in short supply at the front.

In preparing for war, the tsarist government thought that the conflict would be of short duration and that the reserves built up during peacetime would suffice. Soon, however, these reserves were exhausted. At many points Russian battalions could not return enemy fire. The number of killed, wounded, and sick soon mounted. Fresh reinforcements, poorly armed and clothed, were hastily thrown together. Under such conditions the Russian army failed to repel the opponent's offensive launched in the spring of 1915. Its defense lines were broken, and Russian troops retreated along the entire front. Taking heavy casualties, they withdrew even further into the interior. The morale of the Russian army declined; Russia's military situation became even more precarious.

The defeat of the Russian forces was the result of the utter incompetence of the tsarist regime, miscalculations by the tsarist government, and the folly of the high command. In January 1915, Minister of War V. A. Sukhomlinov assured Duma representatives the army had everything it needed and there were no grounds for concern. The Russian forces' retreat demonstrated that these were empty words. Regarded as the main culprit for the defeat, Sukhomlinov was forced to retire. The new minister of war, A. A. Polivanov, candidly told his colleagues at secret meetings of the Council of Ministers in August 1915 what was taking place at the front. "It's hopeless at the theater of war. The retreat is not stopping. . . . The entire army is gradually moving inland, and the front line changes almost hourly. Demoralization, surrender, and desertion are rampant. . . . As before, the situation is bleak and there's nothing consoling to report. [There's nothing but] a relentless picture of crushing defeat and confusion. I am counting on the impenetrable expanse, deep mire, and intercession of Saint Nikolai Mirlikiiskii, the guardian of Holy Russia."[11]

Retreat at the front created terrible confusion at the rear. Disarray, disorder, too much authority or not enough were the order of the day. The military authorities on the various fronts forced large numbers of civilians—old people, women, and children—forcibly to relocate. The territories they abandoned were destroyed, and supplies, property, and dwellings were burned. Terrible misfortunes accompanied the disorderly expulsion of all these people; thousands of people died along the way from hunger, cold, and illness. The death rate for children assumed appalling proportions. Unburied corpses rotted by the roads.

The war shook the Russian economy. As the conflict continued, it grew clear that the belligerents had not foreseen the character, dimension, or duration of military operations. The mightiest capitalist powers, supported by modern industry, quickly restructured their economies to meet the demands of modern war, adapting them to satisfy the army's needs. Tsarist Russia did not possess a comparable independent technical and economic base. Ferrous and nonferrous metallurgy were underdeveloped, and machine building and chemical manufacturing were in their infancy. Because there were no automobile, aviation, or similar industries, Russia needed to import many items from abroad. War severed former foreign trade ties: importation of goods from Germany stopped entirely and from other countries declined sharply. All this diminished Russia's industrial potential. Lack of raw materials and machinery forced many enterprises to produce less or shut down production.

By the end of the first year of war the enemy had seized the country's western regions, which caused Russia to lose up to twenty percent of her industrial capacity. Without plans or organization, enterprises were hastily evacuated from the Baltic region and Poland to the east. Few such enterprises resumed work at their new locations, and almost no new factories were constructed. State-owned military factories making armaments, artillery, gunpowder, etc., showed only small increases in their output. Some private concerns reorganized production on their own initiative and began manufacturing military equipment, but the government did not encourage this.

Faced with shortages of the items essential for conducting war, tsarism preferred to turn to its allies for help. Although the governments of England and France made credits available to the tsarist government, they had needs of their own to satisfy, and therefore did not share their supplies of armaments and ammunition and fell far short of meeting Russian war orders. The tsarist government also placed large orders for arms in the United States; however, American industry was slow to turn to the production of war materiel, often failed to meet deadlines, and supplied products that were sometimes of inferior quality. During the war military orders brought Russia rifles, machine guns, cannons, shells, cartridges, and even armored trucks and passenger automobiles, motorcycles, and the like from abroad. Picks, axes, wire, saddles, helmets, shoes, and other items were likewise imported. Nonetheless, the delivery of war materiel to Russia was extremely difficult; some military cargo piled up in American and Russian ports. Vladivostok and Arkhangelsk became warehouses for military materiel because railroads were unable to move it inland.

During the entire first year of war the government concentrated on foreign orders and made little use of domestic productive capacities of private industry. "It's too bad that we don't have a Krupp of our own," grieved the chief of staff,

General N. N. Ianushkevich. But in fact, Russia did have its own Krupps on a lesser scale who tried to keep up with the military orders, just as their counterparts in other countries did. At the very start of the war, city dumas and zemstvos [local organs of government—D.J.R.] established national organizations to serve the needs of the front—the Union of Towns and the Union of Zemstvos. They created a far-flung organizational network at both the front and rear, which occupied itself with medical and sanitation problems and organized aid for refugees and prisoners of war. The zemstvos and towns set up some enterprises of their own that worked at meeting war needs. At first the tsarist authorities were suspicious of these organizations, but then they resigned themselves to their existence and finally put large credits at their disposal, placing orders for military items and equipment such as uniforms, shoes, vehicles, shovels, etc.

During the summer of 1915 the bourgeoisie, offering to direct the country's entire efforts to repel the enemy, sounded the alarm as Russian forces withdrew and shortages of weapons and ammunition appeared. A congress of representatives of trade and industry resolved to mobilize Russian industry to meet the demands of the army in the field and to create war industries committees. Central and local war industries committees were organized, comprised of representatives of trade and industrial organizations, the Union of Zemstvos, the Union of Towns, and scientific-technical forces. The Central War Industries Committee was headed by the Octobrist A. I. Guchkov; the textile manufacturer A. I. Konovalov became deputy director. P. P. Riabushinskii, M. I. Tereshchenko, S. N. Tret'iakov, N. F. von Ditmar, and other large factory owners also entered the war industries committees. Thus a new organization of the bourgeoisie was formed, which wrapped its tentacles around all of the country's major centers.

At the same time the question arose whether the state should regulate the country's wartime economy. In the most developed capitalist countries, especially in Germany, such regulation had assumed massive dimensions. There, state organs of control had merged with large-scale monopolies. Utilizing the state apparatus, monopolies received profitable orders and influenced the economic and political life of the various countries. Monopoly capitalism became state-monopoly capitalism. The same process took place in Russia during the war. Here production grew more concentrated, banks expanded, and monopolies became stronger. The pursuit of wartime profits aroused feverish entrepreneurial activity and in particular facilitated the growth of joint-stock companies. Russian monopoly capital converged with the state apparatus of the autocracy, but an organic fusion between them did not occur and could not take place, because Russian monopoly capital was weaker than that of Western Europe and state power in Russia was in the hands of landowners, not the bourgeoisie.

In the autumn of 1915 the tsarist government created a "Special Council to Discuss and Unify Activities Related to the Defense of the Country" as well as special councils for various branches of the economy, such as transportation, fuel, and food supplies. Members of the State Duma and war industries committees and activists in the zemstvos and city dumas joined the so-called Special Defense Council. To tsarist officials, not capitalists, fell the chief responsibility for regulating the economy. Ministers with broad powers headed the special commissions. The decisions of the Special Defense Council were approved by the minister of war, who was given the authority to force state-owned and private enterprises to fill orders, remove factory directors, close private factories or place them under state control, establish rates of pay, etc.

The bourgeoisie tried to take the regulation of the country's economic life into its own hands. It protected itself against the reduction of high monopoly prices for goods, and its representatives protested the construction of state enterprises and the introduction of state monopolies for the sale of coal, oil, and the like. This caused disagreements between representatives of the bourgeoisie and the tsarist authorities, but both sides strove to keep their differences within bounds. Theirs was a struggle on the basis of cooperation. The special councils often made sweeping decisions that were not binding on anyone in any way, and in state institutions routine, red tape, and bureaucratism thrived as in the past. As before, officials in the War Department took bribes to allocate orders, finance enterprises, and distribute raw materials.

The militarization of production caused the output of armaments and ammunitions to increase in 1916, making it easier to supply Russian troops with materiel. Still, in technical equipment the Russian army lagged behind the other warring powers as before: it did not have enough mortars, explosives, airplanes, or automobiles. Russia continued to import weapons and ammunition, and also such items as telephones, wire, and much else. Russia's technical and economic base was too underdeveloped for the expansion of wartime production, and this had a pernicious effect on industry and the entire economy.

The war drastically worsened Russia's financial situation. Military expenditures grew tremendously, increasing during 1915–16 about nine times to reach 14.5 billion rubles.[12] Each day of war in 1916 cost 40 million rubles. Russia's peacetime financial condition had been fragile and it collapsed under the blows of war. In order to cover the growing deficit, the tsarist government resorted to the printing press and issued paper money not backed by gold. Fewer goods were produced; the ruble depreciated and the cost of living rose. Tsarism floated domestic loans with disappointing results; the mass of people did not want to hand over their meager resources to the autocracy to conduct a war that was alien to them. Tsarism also had recourse to foreign loans. Russia's main creditor, England, made loans at high rates, which caused gold to flow out of Russia. The ruble fell in value as Russia's national debt shot up; its foreign trade balance worsened. Exports amounted to only slightly more than one-fifth of imports. In sum, Russia's position in the world economic system weakened significantly while its dependence on the most advanced countries increased.

The war played havoc with transportation, which proved unprepared to meet complex military demands. Railroads did not have enough network and rolling stock to cope with the evacuation of factories and people from the western regions of the country, delivery of fuel and metal to factories and food supplies to cities, and other important deliveries without which the military economy was unable to function normally. The rear was not in the position to render to the front the help it needed. Rail transport lacked locomotives, wagons, rails; trains were worn out and were going out of service while the production of new engines and cars declined. The parlous condition of the railroads had a drastic effect on Russia's entire economy.

The country did not have enough metal. Military production required especially large amounts of it, which industry could not satisfy. In the south the extraction of iron ore and coke dropped sharply; as a result of the disruption of transportation their delivery to plants declined. Production of cast iron fell. Instead of the 151 blast furnaces operating before the war, only 115 were working in 1916. They now smelted 231.9 million poods of cast iron instead of the 257.4 million poods produced in 1913 [a pood equals approximately 36 lbs. *avoirdupois*—D.J.R.].[13] The war generated demand for copper, tin, nickel, and other nonferrous metals, but their production within the country diminished. Help from abroad was needed in order to supply military plants with nonferrous metals and special steels.

The country did not have enough fuel. Russia was deprived of the Dombrovskii basin and stopped importing English coal. Coal mining in the Donets basin [Donbass] increased somewhat, but it could not make up for the losses Russia endured. As a consequence of the disruption of transport in the Donbass, large coal reserves piled up which railroads were unable to transfer. Interruptions in the coal supply led to work stoppages at factories and hampered filling military orders. Industry and transport began using other fuels such as oil, peat, and wood. Although oil production increased slightly during the war, the supply of oil and oil-based derivatives lagged behind industrial needs.

Industry needed manpower. Army mobilizations siphoned off as much as one-quarter of the industrial workers, many of whom were highly skilled. The government was compelled to grant draft deferments to a significant number of workers employed in munitions factories, and to release some specialists from the army. During the war many peasants, artisans, and town dwellers went to work in factories. Women and children began to be employed more widely. At enterprises under the supervision of the factory inspectorate, the number of women increased 38.3 percent from 1914 through 1917, and adolescents and children of both sexes, 41.4 percent.[14] The number of workers hired in Russia by 1917 rose to 15 million. Those in heavy industry (including railroad shops) totaled 3.4 million.[15] The rest consisted of workers in handicraft and artisan industries, construction and agriculture workers, workers and clerks in offices of railroad and water transport, trade and communications workers, domestics, etc. Changes in the composition of the working class, lower workers' qualifications, the deterioration of their material position, and other factors brought about by the war led to the decline of labor productivity. Merchants and rich peasants (kulaks) hoping to escape military service flooded the factories, and this denigrated the ranks of the working class, infecting it with a petit bourgeois ideology.

During the war, food supply problems became acute. Several economists had predicted that in the event of war Russia would break off the export of grain and easily be able to provide the army and civilian population with food, whereas the disruption of peacetime economic ties would cause the industrialized powers grave difficulties. But these predictions did not come true. Russia's backward, semifeudal agricultural system could not cope with the trials of war, during which huge numbers of able-bodied males were drafted into the army and the labor of prisoners of war could not make up for this loss. The technical base of agriculture weakened: importation of farm machinery and implements almost completely ceased and domestic production of such equipment sharply decreased. The army requisitioned almost two million horses and a large number of cattle. All this was harmful to agriculture.

Capitalist forms of agriculture using a more advanced technology could take advantage of the state of the market to acquire large profits during the war. The kulaks became stronger, but poor and middle peasants found themselves in difficult straits. An ever increasing number of them, deprived of equipment and draft animals, were reduced to penury and ruined. The sown area and gross grain yields diminished. Meanwhile, the expanding urban population and especially the army made great demands for food. The country began to experience a shortage of supplies, and food prices began to rise.

The incipient breakdown of transport further complicated the food supply situation. Large amounts of food accumulated in agricultural regions were not delivered to the industrial centers; movement of grain decreased. The lack and high cost of industrial items and the depreciation of the ruble fostered rising speculation. Landlords and kulaks stashed away grain and forced up prices, battening upon the people's need. Government agencies prohibited the export of food from certain regions, established fixed prices, and in certain instances even requisitioned foodstuffs. Procurement of food preoccupied town boards, zemstvos, and cooperative societies. Speculation continued nevertheless. Merchants avoided prohibitions and restrictions, products disappeared from stores only to appear under the counter at higher prices. Landowners and rich peasants pressured the government to increase fixed prices on grain, and this led to a general rise in the cost of living. The tsarist government could not bring itself to curb speculators and regulate trade, for this would affect the interests of landowners and capitalists.

Urban working people and above all the working class suffered severely from the shortage of food and the high cost of living. The growth in nominal wages lagged behind the rise in food prices, and as a result workers and their families were undernourished. Many factories introduced mandatory overtime, which lengthened an already protracted workday. Sanitation and hygiene at the work place worsened; accidents and illnesses increased. Women, adolescents, and children were exploited at factories with especial cruelty; their pay was considerably lower than that of male workers. Moreover, factories were run like armies. The constant threat of being sent to the front hung over men of draft age, and the tsarist authorities and capitalists used army mobilizations to punish revolutionary elements.

The Mass Movement and the Politics of the Bourgeoisie

Tsarist repression, the changing composition of the working class, and chauvinistic propaganda were the chief reasons why workers' activities lessened and the revolutionary movement declined during the first months of war. As the war continued, the effect of these factors became less and less perceptible. Tsarist repression merely stoked the fire, arousing the workers to a more determined struggle. New cadres of workers "got seasoned" in the workers' cauldron. When going to work in factories, they came directly under the influence of the industrial proletariat. Chauvinistic ecstasy began to wear thin with Russian defeats at the front, disorganization at the rear, and the Bolsheviks' antiwar propaganda. By aggravating the misery and need of the toiling masses, the imperialist war made them more revolutionary. Once a brake on the revolutionary movement, the war now became its accelerator. A new revolutionary crisis developed in Russia.

The first signs of it could be seen clearly by the middle of 1915, chiefly in the revival of workers' strikes. Initially, these were mainly of an economic nature. Workers demanded more pay because the cost of necessities had gone up, yet they also wanted shorter hours and better working conditions. These demands drew into active struggle the broadest masses of workers because they could immediately understand them. Economic strikes inevitably assumed a political character, turning their wrath against the war and tsarism.

In the summer of 1915 strikes broke out in the textile plants of Vladimir and Kostroma provinces, where working conditions were especially bad and the Bolsheviks enjoyed considerable influence. The Department of Police reported that the "disorders" in Ivanovo-Voznesensk were caused by "(1) the presence of a Social Democratic organization and its intensive activity, and (2) the excessive increases in the cost of necessities."[16] In May 1915, a general strike took place in Ivanovo-Voznesensk and in Shuia. In the beginning of June a strike began at the Large Linen Mill in Kostroma; police opened fire on Kostroma workers as they demonstrated. The weavers of Ivanovo-Voznesensk once again quit work on August 10, held a rally, and organized a political demonstration. Tsarist authorities fired upon the demonstration of the Ivanovo-Voznesensk workers, too.

The Tver group of the RSDRP (as one group of Moscow Bolsheviks was called) wrote in a leaflet after the shooting of workers in Kostroma and Ivanovo-Voznesensk: "The spilled blood of our comrades calls for revenge. . . . Let's silence the factory whistles; let's bring the entire working people into the streets, let Moscow behold a great demonstration of our forces; let the tsar's executioners tremble!"[17] The protest movement the Moscow Bolsheviks called for against the crimes of tsarism in Ivanovo-Voznesensk and Kostroma did not turn into a major demonstration. Strikes and protest meetings, however, did occur at several Moscow factories and in many other of the country's cities. More than thirty thousand people took part in a protest strike in Petrograd. The workers' response to events in Kostroma and Ivanovo-Voznesensk marked the beginning of a turning point in the workers' movement from depression to a new animation. The strike in Petrograd in the beginning of September 1915 was clear evidence of this. It broke out at the Putilov Plant when several workers were arrested and coincided with the dismissal of the State Duma. The Petrograd Committee of the RSDRP appealed to workers to support their Putilov comrades with a citywide political strike. The Petrograd strike lasted three days. Between September 3–5, 150,000 workers went on strike. Workers from Moscow, Nizhnii Novgorod, Kharkov, and other cities supported them.

During the September strike an all-city strike committee was set up to direct the labor movement and to coordinate revolutionary activity in Petrograd with that in other centers. The question arose whether to organize a soviet of workers' deputies according to the example of 1905, and preparatory work to this end was already underway. The Menshevik defensists chose precisely this time to make a fresh attempt to direct the workers' movement to support the imperialist war and cooperate with the bourgeoisie. They endorsed the bourgeoisie's appeal for workers to take part in the work of war industries committees and make a joint contribution to the war effort. The Bolsheviks emphatically came out against the war and having workers serve on war industries committees. They were preparing a general political strike in the capital and in the country, which at the appropriate moment would be turned into an armed uprising against tsarism.[18]

The Bolsheviks' plan for revolution was set forth in "The Mandate of the Petersburg Proletariat to the Vyborg Collective." It stated that a historic task faced the Russian proletariat—"to lead the democracy [all groups to the left of the Kadets—D.J.R.] to sweep away the old regime in Russia and create a democratic republic on its ruins"; the proletariat's slogan was "to transform the present war into a civil war."

> To accomplish these tasks the proletariat of Petersburg, Moscow, and all of Russia must take practical steps first: (1) to stop work simultaneously at all factories; (2) to organize an armed people's militia according to neighborhoods; (3) to seize by force police stations, plants, factories, government offices, railroads, commercial storehouses, large stores, etc.; (4) to confiscate food supplies and other necessities; (5) to take over supplying the population with necessities; (6) to organize

> municipal, town, and zemstvo elections along democratic principles and to introduce democratic town and zemstvo self-government; (7) to prepare for general elections of a provisional government and constituent assembly; (8) to appeal to all reservists, militiamen, soldiers, and officers under arms to join the people in this rising.[19]

The Bolsheviks proposed to elect representatives at factories, proclaim the assembly of such representatives a soviet of workers' deputies with a mandate "urging the above steps be taken to bring out the proletariat and democracy in mass against the autocratic system based on the above slogans and program of the RSDRP led by central and regional organizations of the Russian Social Democratic party."[20]

Besides this document, the Bolshevik mandate to authorized electors of the War Industries Committee, which defined the tasks and slogans of the moment, was discussed at workers' meetings. It revealed the true character of the war and the slogan "in the defense of the fatherland," showing that the slogan "was the main enemy of every people in their own country." "The proletariat's efforts must be directed at achieving power by means of a civil war. The proletariat must give meaning to the slogan 'Down with the war!' and must amplify it further with the call 'Long live the socialist revolution!' " The mandate stated: "In advanced capitalist countries objective preconditions for a socialist revolution have already matured. In Russia the proletariat has still to achieve democratization of the state structure, that is, it has still to achieve a democratic republic."[21] The mandate called upon worker representatives "to declare publicly their refusal to participate in any institutions that further the war."

A stubborn fight over the question of participation in the War Industries Committee flared up at workers' meetings and at the meetings of electors. On September 27, 1915, A. I. Ul'ianova-Elizarova [Lenin's sister—D.J.R.] informed Lenin: "Our side suffered a fiasco at many factories. The Mensheviks, among whom were more experienced, eloquent people, had already celebrated their victory. Their chairman ran the meeting of worker electors and on the 27th, their agenda was approved. . . . They were already clapping their hands with joy. But the Bolshevik decision not to take part in the War Industries Committee and not to send representatives to it unexpectedly passed with a majority—true, it was a majority of only ten votes."[22] Having refused to select representatives to the War Industries Committee, the authorized electors declared that a decisive battle would be conducted against any workers who might somehow turn up on the committee as traitors and opponents of the will of the Petrograd proletariat.

The Bolsheviks carried the day at the meeting of authorized workers (electors), but leaders of the War Industries Committee and Menshevik defensists secured a reconsideration of the decision taken at it. Within two months, at a new meeting of representatives, Menshevik defensists succeeded in carrying their resolution to create a workers' group of the War Industries Committee, headed by K. A. Gvozdev. Despite protests by progressive workers, workers' groups headed by Menshevik defensists were also created in local war industries committees.

Petrograd Bolsheviks had correctly defined the general tasks of the workers' movement on the assumption that a revolutionary crisis had matured in Russia, but they overestimated the extent to which the crisis had developed: armed uprising and the proposal to organize a soviet of workers' deputies were premature in September 1915. Revolutionary crisis was imminent in Russia, but this still did not signify the revolution was beginning. In "Several Theses"[r] defining Bolshevik tactics at the start of a revolutionary crisis, Lenin wrote that "it is revolutionary Social Democracy's most pressing task to develop the incipient strike movement, and to conduct it under the slogan of the three pillars. . . .[s] soviets of workers' deputies and similar institutions must be regarded as organs of insurrection, of revolutionary rule. It is only in connection with the development of a mass political strike and with an insurrection, and in the measure of the latter's preparedness, development and success that such institutions can be of lasting value."[23]

The mass political strike by the Petrograd workers in September 1915 did not assume a national character. At that time, workers in the country's other industrial centers did not participate in major political activities. And even in Petrograd itself conditions for a decisive battle against tsarism did not yet exist. Among part of the workers of the capital, apathy, passivity, and the influence of defensists had not been eliminated. The tsarist authorities threatened striking workers with hard labor, mass dismissals, and dispatch to the front. A significant number of workers eligible for the draft had already been sent to the field army. This disorganized the workers' ranks but could not break their will. The struggle continued.

In order to organize an assault against tsarism, the Bolsheviks strengthened their own ranks. The Petersburg organization recovered from the blows tsarism had inflicted and gathered new strength after the arrests in the spring of 1915. Local working-class cadres appeared on the scene; V. N. Zalezhskii, V. V. Shmidt, S. Ia. Bogdat'ev, K. N. Orlov, and I. U. Lutovinov returned from exile or other cities. Together with Leonid Stark, M. I. Kalinin, N. P. Komarov, Kopylov, and other comrades, they constituted the guiding nucleus of the Petrograd Bolshevik Organization. Five hundred members of the party were represented at the Petrograd Conference the RSDRP held in July 1915. By the fall of 1915, the growth of the organization itself and the arrival of Bolsheviks from the front caused its ranks to increase to twelve hundred individuals. Dedicating number 47 of the newspaper *Sotsial-Demokrat* (October 13, 1915)

[r] "Several Theses," appearing as "A Few Theses" in the official English-language edition of Lenin's work, was published in *Sotsial-Demokrat*, no. 47, October 13, 1915.

[s] That is, a democratic republic, an eight-hour day, and the confiscation of landowners' estates. Lenin actually used the expression "three whales," which is an allusion to a Russian saying that the earth rests on three whales.

to the activity of the Petrograd Organization of the RSDRP, the editorial staff noted: "The material published in this issue shows the tremendous scope of the work being done by the St. Petersburg Committee of our Party. To Russia, and indeed to the entire International, this is indeed a model of Social-Democratic work during a reactionary war and in most difficult conditions the workers of St. Petersburg and Russia will bend every effort to give support to that work and will continue it along the same road ever more energetically and extensively."[24]

As before the war, Petrograd Bolsheviks enjoyed considerable influence over local party organizations. In the summer and fall of 1915 party work intensified both in Petrograd and in several other centers of the country. In Moscow, the Tver group of the RSDRP mentioned earlier was actively functioning at the time and a citywide committee was organized, which united five neighborhood party organizations. A party conference of the Ivanovo-Voznesensk region took place during the summer of 1915, which determined to conduct agitation for an armed uprising against the autocracy. The conference of Ural-area Social Democratic organizations, which took place in September 1915, promoted establishing the dictatorship of the proletariat and peasantry as one of its most important tasks. The Southern Regional Conference of the RSDRP taking place at the same time urged workers of the country "to join with the protests of the Petersburg and Moscow comrades, who have united around a single strong organization in order to staunchly and bravely meet the coming day of the Second Russian Revolution."[25]

The weak ties among the party organizations and with the Bolshevik center abroad negatively influenced their work. The restoration of such ties was important in devising the correct line and for the party's practical activity. In September 1915, A. G. Shliapnikov was co-opted into the Central Committee of the RSDRP. An old Petersburg worker and Bolshevik party member since 1901, he had carried out responsible missions abroad for Lenin. He was now charged with improving ties with Russia. Shliapnikov was sent to Russia to visit two or three centers, establish relations with the underground, and then return abroad to cement the links. Shliapnikov was able to carry out significant work in the difficult conditions of the underground. Following Lenin's instructions, he created a Russian Bureau of the Central Committee of the RSDRP made up of a worker from the Bolshevik paper, *Pravda*, K. Eremeev; a member of the Workers' Group of the Insurance Society, G. Osipov; a former leader among the workers of Ivanovo-Voznesensk in 1905, E. Dunaev; and K. Shvedchikov. A. I. Elizarova (Ul'ianova) actively participated in the bureau's work. She and Shvedchikov carried on correspondence, arranged transportation, and established ties with local organizations. Soon after Shliapnikov's departure abroad, however, new arrests took place and the Central Committee Bureau collapsed.

The revolutionary movement in Russia did not develop uninterruptedly in a straight ascending line. Instead, the revolutionary wave ebbed and flowed, but with each new swell the movement acquired still more force and assumed an even grander scale. After the stormy events in the summer and beginning of the fall of 1915, a slump in the workers' strike movement set in and the number of striking workers decreased. The lull was temporary, though, and from the start of 1916 the strike movement picked up once again. As during the first year of war, two groups of workers participated in it—metalworkers and textile workers. Workers from other branches of industry and also from small businesses and workshops took little part in strike activity. The overall number of strikes during the war was less, and the territorial limits of the movement narrower than in 1905. In the period of the First Russian Revolution half of all strikes had broken out in industrially developed outlying regions like the Baltic, Poland, and Baku, whereas now the strike movement was concentrated primarily in the industrial heartland. Petrograd workers stood at the head of the revolutionary struggle. The composition of the Petrograd proletariat had changed significantly during the war, but the cadres of the old Petersburg proletariat were preserved: men who had passed through the fire and storms of the First Russian Revolution were now drawing new workers into the struggle.

During the difficult wartime conditions the proletariat of Russia revived the glorious tradition of celebrating the most important dates in the revolutionary past in order to mobilize its forces. In 1916 mass workers' activities commemorated the anniversary of January 9. Close to one hundred thousand workers participated in a political strike that broke out that day in Petrograd. In 1916 workers celebrated the Lena Goldfields massacre, the anniversary of the trial of the Bolshevik faction in the State Duma, International Women's Day, and May Day. A leaflet from the Petersburg Committee of the RSDRP concerning International Women's Day that year noted that the ruinous war had made the women workers suffer more than anyone else. Knowing that the present war was the inevitable consequence of the existing capitalist order and that only the popular masses could organize action against the entire contemporary order of force and slavery to put an end to it, women workers of all countries added a demand for peace to the other slogan of the revolutionary proletariat: "Long live civil war!"[26]

The Putilov workers' strike in February 1916 was of considerable political significance. Entering into an economic struggle with capitalists to raise pay and shorten the workday, workers in the Putilov Plant declared that they would champion the rights of the entire working class. Having advanced basic political demands such as a democratic republic, the eight-hour workday, and confiscation of landowners' estates, the Putilov workers passed a resolution at a factorywide rally that noted that "only intensification of the revolutionary struggle of the democracy in all countries against their governments will save mankind from a bloody nightmare. Therefore we subscribe to the resolution promulgated by the Petersburg Committee of the Russian Social Democratic Labor party to oppose mobilization of reactionary elements by mobilizing proletarian forces for the Second Russian Revolution."[27] Petrograd Bolsheviks urged the proletariat of the capital to support the Putilovites in their just struggle. As an appeal from the Petersburg Committee of the RSDRP noted, "the cause of the Putilov workers is the cause of the entire Petersburg proletariat. . . . The government considers the Putilov Plant very dangerous, knowing that it always has been the leader of the revolutionary Petersburg proletariat. And the government is right: that's how it always was and that's how it always will be."[28]

The Putilov Plant was on strike for two weeks. More than one hundred thousand workers in the capital took part in a strike to show solidarity with the Putilov workers. As money was collected for the Putilovites and their families, the government took emergency measures to break the strike. Numerous workers ended up behind bars, and two thousand Putilovites were sent to the army. The government requisitioned the factory and sealed it off, while the War Department took over its management, pledging to consider the workers' demands within one month. The Putilov workers were forced to return to work. When the strike ended the Narva District Bolshevik Committee asserted in an appeal: "Comrade Putilovites, we have started to work; we have again mobilized our forces; now we must solidly be one; organize around our Russian Social Democratic Labor party and support it in every way possible. Call meetings and conferences to explain our position on the current moment and delay the human slaughter that threatens the democracy with ruin."[29]

The same appeal declared that the day of the decisive encounter with tsarism was drawing near, and that the workers of Petersburg and all over Russia were testing their forces for this encounter. The strike movement at that time seized many regions of the country. A strike at the Naval Shipyards in Nikolaev lasted almost two months. The authorities arrested strikers, prosecuted the ringleaders of the strike, and sent the militarily eligible to the front, but the struggle continued. Unable to move the stubborn workers, the Naval Department shut the factory down. Fifty thousand miners took part in a strike in the Donbass. A strike committee elected by workers conducted daily meetings, organized to defend the mine, and collected money for the strikers. Again in the spring of 1916, workers in the Briansk, Sormovo, and other major factories went out on strike.

Strikes usually began with economic demands caused above all by the struggle against hunger and the high cost of living. But the food supply crisis was brought about not by problems in the state of the market, but by the imperialist war and the resulting economic collapse. The question of war and power would determine the outcome of this crisis. Beginning with economic demands to increase wages and provide bread, the strikes inevitably led the workers to struggle against the war and tsarism. "What are we demanding?" asked a worker at the Briansk Factory at a meeting of strikers. He answered, "We are demanding the minimum; we are demanding bread. . . . They tell us it's not permitted to strike—there's a war on, we have to make shells. They threaten us with being sent to the front. But after all, we've already sent our fathers, brothers, and sons to war. We've given everything to the war, but what have the capitalists sacrificed? Nothing. We don't need the war."[30]

The food supply crisis was the most understandable and basic cause of unrest among the masses. The Bolsheviks strove to forge the movement this situation was creating into an organized, conscious struggle against the war and tsarism. The Central Committee of the RSDRP issued a brochure, "The War and the High Cost of Living in Russia," which stated that the main cause of the people's suffering was the system, the structure of the Russian state that had driven the country into the predatory war. Revolution must be the answer to the war and the high cost of living—the overthrow of tsarism, convocation of a constituent assembly, and establishment of a democratic republic were the first steps in breaking the yoke of capitalism and building socialism. "Raise up the red banner of revolt against our executioners, murderers, and robbers. To the street! It's better to die as free men than to live as slaves." A leaflet from the Petersburg Committee of the RSDRP, "Strikes and the Tasks of the Moment" (June 1916), stated: "It's necessary to intensify revolution and to animate the struggle of the popular masses to such a pitch until the hour has come to overthrow the thieves and murderers of the Romanov breed."[31] During each strike and at each demonstration the Bolsheviks advanced the slogans "Down with the war!" "Down with the tsarist authorities!"

Partial engagements took place that prepared for the decisive battles against the autocracy. The proletariat, involving other strata of the toiling population of Russia in the battle against tsarism and the war, matured and was tempered in these engagements. Rejecting collaboration with the bourgeoisie, the proletariat also strove to draw the peasantry into the revolutionary movement. The war had removed the most active element from the village; almost half of the adult male population was mobilized into the army. Mostly elderly people, women, old men, and adolescents remained in the countryside. The villages had been bled white and squeezed dry by the terrible calamities of war. Such conditions precluded peasant disturbances from taking on the same massive and critical character as during peacetime. Nonetheless, the villages continued to struggle during the war years.

The peasants now clashed more unexpectedly and spontaneously with the tsarist authorities. Peasants evaded performing such state service as fulfilling demands for military transportation and trench work, paying taxes and assessments, and they resisted giving fodder, horses, and livestock requisitions. Armed with pitchforks and scythes, peasants often hindered the authorities from seizing property to pay off debts or from conducting searches. The peasants freed those arrested. Wives of peasants mobilized into the army became active in the villages.

The war intensified the semifeudal oppression and serflike exploitation the peasantry felt, caused by the continued existence of gentry latifundia. Seizing the landowners' estates remained the basic aim of peasant disturbances. Simultaneously, the middle peasantry and peasant poor battled the rich (kulaks). Middle and poor peasants had no wish to leave the commune; they beat up *khutoriane, otrubshchiki* [peasants who had taken advantage of Stolypin's legislation—D.J.R.], and land surveyors and destroyed boundary markers. Rural constables and military units were called in to pacify the peasants. They beat, arrested, punished, and fired at the unarmed peasants. The police and constables won these clashes, but occasionally a crowd of peasants with pitchforks and scythes put them to flight. During the war the government was forced to suspend land conversions based on the Stolypin land reforms.

The shortage of necessary implements and the general high cost of living painfully affected the population of the countryside. The high cost of living and speculation gave rise to massive peasant disturbances in the villages in 1916. Women, mainly the wives of soldiers, looted shops. In November 1916 a communication from Irkutsk stated: "The countryside is becoming impoverished and ruined. Its wealth is being destroyed: horses and livestock have been taken, there's no one to plow and nothing to plow with. . . . Perhaps the landowners are getting rich, merchants and various rogues are getting rich, but the people, the common people, are undoubtedly growing poor. They are making all the sacrifices and enduring the entire burden of this war."[32]

From other parts of the country similar situations of the village population came to light. A letter from Poltava said: "Living conditions are awful in the countryside." A report from Ekaterinoslav: "The mood in the countryside is troubled and it can't be otherwise, they keep on taking people, it's becoming difficult to live. . . . Police officers and the other powers that be are on guard, trying to find sedition, but there's so much of it everywhere, they cannot stamp it out. Everyone has become a revolutionary, for it's impossible to be otherwise."[33] In the words of a representative of the Zemstvo Union who returned from the Volga region, "revolutionary ferment such as that which took place in 1906–1907 is being observed in the villages, political questions are discussed everywhere, resolutions are made directed against the landowners and merchants, cells of various organizations are being set up. . . . As of yet, of course, there is no unifying center, but it must be recognized that the peasants are uniting through cooperatives, which are popping up across Russia by the hour. In this manner the peasantry undoubtedly will turn out to be quite an effective participant in a new and inevitable movement."[34]

The soldier masses strongly influenced the peasants' struggle. Though he might be a soldier, the peasant continued to think like a member of his village; as in the past, questions about land, the landowners, Stolypin allotments, etc., continued to disturb him. In letters from the front, soldiers showed concern about the needs of the countryside and advised their relatives how to act in particular situations. They wrote that the peasants were offended, that they didn't even have a strip of land per person, that "you've got to watch out for the landowners," and that it's better to hide everything the authorities requisition. Soldiers arriving in the village on furlough told fellow villagers that after the war all land would be transferred to the people and that is why it was forbidden to permit it to be alienated and converted into private property. The authorities complained that the soldiers were inciting the peasants to withhold taxes, to ignore local and district police officers, to graze their cattle on landowners' land, etc.

The rear's influence on the front was even stronger, and the autocracy moved to curb it. The command checked the political reliability of new recruits, forbade the distribution of political literature in the army, and instituted strict supervision over the attitude and behavior of soldiers. As in the past the army was composed of peasants. But mass mobilization and dispatching workers to the front for participating in strikes had strengthened proletarian elements in the army significantly. Bolshevik workers mobilized into the army carried on revolutionary propaganda among soldiers. Revolutionary-minded reinforcements and letters from the rear arrived at the front. News reached there about shortages of food supplies and the breakdown of transportation, about strikes and disturbances among workers. All of this furthered a rise in the soldier masses' political consciousness.

The oppressive conditions prevailing in the Russian army assumed an even more brutal character during the war. The command sternly punished soldiers for the slightest disobedience and applied the most stringent measures of the laws of wartime to repress those who spoke out against the war. Corporal punishment was restored in the army because officers wanted to turn soldiers into a mute herd of cannon fodder. Gripped by stern military discipline, deprived of all of their rights, the soldiers expressed muffled discontent. In letters from the front, soldiers wrote they felt like prisoners; for the slightest disobedience they were thrashed and had to run the gauntlet, beaten with birch switches just as the landowners used to beat peasants. "They keep and treat us like cattle, perhaps even worse. It's absolutely impossible to hear humane speech, to meet humane company . . . the thought of enslavement oppresses us more and more."[35]

As the army suffered defeats, the soldiers' dissatisfaction intensified. In letters from the front, soldiers complained about the shortage of weapons, poor uniforms, meager rations, etc. Such terrible conditions made them think how senseless it was for the people to sacrifice so much in a foreign war. An elemental craving for peace sprang up under the enemy's guns; dissatisfaction spread even among the officers. During the war regular staff officers were supplemented by petit bourgeois elements of the population, students, people from various social groups, and white-collar workers. Officers were trained not only in military schools but also in short-term courses and in ordinary schools. Younger commanding officers were promoted in the field. The officer corps was democratized, and this was reflected in its mood. Many officers started thinking about the causes of the Russian army's defeat. Rumors reached them about treason in high places, disorder on the home front, and the ruinous policies of the tsarist government. The opposition mood of the bourgeoisie had an effect on army officers. Many pinned their hopes on the State Duma and sympathized with the demands it advanced. Others remained aloof from politics and considered it impermissible to criticize government actions. Dissension and friction arose among the officers, and this weakened the tsarist army.

The proletariat of the capital greatly influenced the sailors of the Baltic fleet. Among Baltic sailors the revolutionary movement grew steadily during the war. Spontaneous disturbances flared up during the fall of 1915 on the battleship Gangut and the cruiser Riurik. The Bolsheviks tried to harness the spontaneous movement. Bolshevik organizations existed on the vessels and in offshore units at Kronstadt, Helsingfors, Abo, and other cities. A ruling center was created in the Kronstadt Military Organization that established ties with the Petersburg Committee of the RSDRP, an accomplishment of the worker Kirill Orlov (Ivan Egorov), a member of the RSDRP since 1903. Several years in the underground, participation in the mutiny on the battleship Potemkin,[t] arrest, and sojourns abroad were all part of his past experience. Arriving in Petrograd from Riga in 1915, K. N. Orlov went to work at the Aivaz Factory and on instructions from the Bolshevik committee made contact with sailors. Together with I. D. Sladkov, T. Ul'iantsev, Nikolai Khovrin, and other comrades, he carried on revolutionary activity.

Tsarist repression weakened the Bolshevik organization in the fleet, but could not destroy it. The "Main Collective" in the Kronstadt military organization of the RSDRP was operating in 1916. A proclamation, "When Will It End" (August 1916), urged soldiers and sailors to support the working class's struggle against the war. "We are of the same flesh and blood. Our place is in the ranks of the working class. Together with the workers we must prepare for a decisive clash with the gang of aggressors who are pillaging the country and pushing mankind into an abyss. . . . Down with the criminal war! Down with the monarchy! Long live the Second Russian Revolution!"[36]

Military operations made it especially difficult to spread systematic revolutionary propaganda among soldiers in the field. More favorable conditions existed for revolutionary work in reserve and supply units. Soldiers in these units quartered in cities associated with workers, absorbed their attitudes, and joined in their struggle. Bolshevik organizations had connections in the garrisons of both capitals and the large towns, and also in several of the country's smaller ones. Party groups existed in individual units, antiwar literature was disseminated, discussions were organized with workers both singly and in groups.

Latvian Social Democrats carried on important work in the army units. Concentrated in a reserve regiment from which reinforcements were sent to the front, they spread revolutionary propaganda among Latvian sharpshooters fight-

[t]One of the most dramatic episodes of the Revolution of 1905, immortalized by Sergei Eisenstein's epic film, "Battleship Potempkin," in 1925. The crew of the battleship Potempkin of the Black Sea fleet mutinied in June. Not supported by the crews of the other vessels in the fleet, the Potempkin sailed to Rumania in search of political asylum. Some crew members returned to Russia where they were tried and sentenced to death or penal servitude.

ing there. Revolutionary propaganda among Russian soldiers was also conducted in Latvia. At a meeting in December 1916 of commanders in chief from the fronts, General N. D. Ruzskii declared Riga and Dvinsk were a great danger on the northern front: "They are two propaganda nests." General A. A. Brusilov added that the "completely propagandized" Seventh Siberian Corps, whose soldiers refused to attack, had arrived at the southwestern front directly from the Riga district.[37]

Conscription of political prisoners into the army in 1916 also facilitated the spread of revolutionary ideas among the masses of soldiers. In January 1917 the head of the Tomsk province gendarmerie reported to the Department of the Police that there were many exiles from the Nerchinsk region in the Eighteenth Siberian Rifle Regiment who had formerly been activists in the Petrograd, Moscow, and other organizations of the RSDRP. They attracted small groups of soldiers and tried to instill the notion that the government and privileged classes alone needed the war, that it brought only calamity to workers and peasants, and that therefore it was necessary to strive with all of one's might for the soonest possible conclusion of peace. The report further stated that V. Kosarev, a soldier who had been in exile, explained to his comrades, "It's important to have as many members of the organization as possible enter the field army where propaganda already is being conducted on a large scale under the leadership of the members of the Petrograd, Moscow, and Odessa organizations located there, who will also instruct Social Democrats who have arrived from the provinces."[38]

In "A Letter from the Front," P. Shatrov (apparently a Bolshevik) wrote that the army at the rear and especially at the front was packed with revolutionary elements, capable of becoming an active force during an uprising. The task was to unify them and convert isolated disorders, risings, and revolts into one general uprising of the army, once a definite aim, fully developed strategy, and tactics and proper organizational forms had been devised.[39] Shatrov proposed slogans such as a national constituent assembly, land and freedom, the eight-hour day, equality for nationalities, and a democratic republic. The revolutionary army must constitute the most important force in an uprising. He proposed that its officers be chosen from the ranks and that it must be at the disposal of a provisional revolutionary government. Opposing those arguing vaguely over "the process of an uprising" who did not understand the real conditions (he probably had the Mensheviks in mind), the author of "A Letter from the Front" wrote: "Esteemed comrades, 'the process of an uprising' is engulfing the entire Russian army and is everywhere, on every side. But revolutionary energy is being wasted and revolutionary creativity is being suppressed precisely among those who want most to revolt because they know there is no unity, organization, or final aim to an uprising." Shatrov expressed confidence that "with the help of the disaffected army it will not be difficult for the people who are up in arms to sweep away completely the loathsome gang that at present reigns and rules over Russia."

After reading "A Letter from the Front," War Minister M. A. Beliaev noted that its contents as well as several other pieces of information attested to the fact that "revolutionary forces were beginning to take advantage of the government's actual situation to plan an organization in the army made up of all unreliable elements, which were, of course, bound to penetrate the ranks during massive call-ups of the entire male population of the country liable for service."[40] The war minister ordered revolutionary elements suppressed by all possible means, but revolutionary activity in the army continued despite this.

The mass of the soldiers and some of the officers were becoming more and more determined for peace. Reports from the front indicated many officers were not convinced the war could be won, and that their attitude toward the government was very negative. Never before in the presence of other officers, let alone of persons from the high command, did such frank conversations take place about the possibility the dynasty would fall. A representative of the Zemstvo Union, traveling to the Baltic region in the fall of 1916, noted that soldiers accused the military authorities of corruption, cowardice, drunkenness, and even treason. All indications "certainly present a picture of the disintegration of the army, and this portends the imminent end of the war."[41] Doctors returning from the front told the Zemstvo Union of growing dissatisfaction, general war weariness, and a longing for peace. Soldiers in the front lines *[frontoviki]* wrote to relatives: "We're so sick of this war, so repulsed by it, that life's not worth living." "Everyone is utterly tired of the war." "Persistent rumors have begun to circulate among soldiers that there soon will be peace. It had better be soon, for we're fed up with it." "We're beginning to speak more urgently about peace . . . how wonderful that would be." "Damn this war."

Soldier desertions became more frequent, and reinforcements arrived at the field army far from full strength because some of the soldiers had run away en route. When the revolution broke out, the number of deserters from the Russian army already had reached two million men. Whole droves of soldiers voluntarily surrendered. "Why have our men begun to surrender like this?" asked a soldier. The answer: "Because they thrashed us soundly, fools that we are. The Germans have taken up positions, but at the rear they punish any insignificant breach of conduct with corporal punishment and beat us with switches."[42]

The soldiers' yearning for peace found more active forms of expression. There were cases when individual units refused to move to the front. The soldiers declared that they would stay on the defensive but would not take the offensive because they did not want to spill blood. The front borrowed such techniques as the strike from the working-class struggle. Command dispatches and soldiers' letters reported that the men "have gone out on strike." Serious disturbances repressed by the tsarist authorities accompanied the refusal to obey orders. The command transferred such units to the rear, shot ringleaders, and cashiered officers.

In October 1916 serious disturbances broke out at distribution points in

Gomel and Kremenchug. In Gomel soldiers beat up sentinels, freed the arrested, seized weapons, and exchanged shots with the police. Cries of "Down with the war!" rang out. The movement was brutally suppressed; nine participants were shot, but the situation around Gomel long remained strained. The governor wrote that he must either immediately transfer the distribution center to another place or set it off altogether from contact with the civilian population.

Fraternization at the front began to spread. The officers forbade it, but Russian and Austro-Hungarian soldiers unfurled white flags, went into enemy trenches or met at barricades where they exchanged gifts, and treated each other to bread, tobacco, and cigarettes. Such fraternization had not yet assumed a mass character, but the form it took at that time had great significance for the struggle against the imperialist war. Fraternization shattered the discipline of the bourgeois-landowner army and promoted international unity among working people in the belligerent countries.

The working-class revolutionary movement exerted considerable influence on the masses of soldiers. Despite close censorship, news about the strike movement of the proletariat reached the front. As soldiers' letters put it: "There cannot be peace until soldiers make it, and there are strikes in Russia's factories." "Write what people are saying at home about riots; if there are any you must intensify them: only then will the war end." "I was never so happy as when I learned that our comrades and brothers solemnly commemorated January 9" [the anniversary of "Bloody Sunday"—D.J.R.]. "Everyone is ready for revolution. And it's probably more than likely that the revolution will take place." "Soldiers aren't the same as they were during the Japanese war; under the mask of servile submissiveness lies terrible anger. . . . Just strike a tiny little match and everything will go up in flames."[43]

Russian and foreign bourgeois literature widely asserts that on the eve of the revolution the tsarist army was stable and ready to wage a successful struggle against the enemy in the upcoming campaign of the spring of 1917. But many bourgeois leaders were compelled to admit otherwise. Miliukov wrote that "fairness demands me to note that a breakdown in the army was not an exclusive phenomenon of the postrevolutionary period. Unwillingness to fight, decline in discipline, suspicion of the officer corps, and desertion: all these phenomena were in evidence before the revolution."[44] Rodzianko also pointed out that symptoms of disintegration in the army had already been noticed and felt during the second year of the war. Defeat at the front and breakdown at the rear, brutal conditions in the units and longing for peace encouraged soldiers to cross over to the side of the people. The revolutionary movement deprived tsarism of its armed force. This was one of the most salient expressions of the growing revolutionary crisis.

The imperialist powers conducted the world war under the slogan of "free and independent nations." But in fact both groups of imperialists sought increasingly to oppress other nations. This is why the question of liberating people from the yoke of nationalism developed more intensely during the war than before it.

The nationality question held a special place in the public life of Russia because tsarism oppressed many nations in Europe and Asia. More than half of the population of the Russian empire was composed of non-Russian nationalities who had achieved different levels of economic and cultural development, but all in one form or another were wronged by Russian officials, landowners, and capitalists. While appealing to the peoples of Russia to defend the fatherland, tsarism strengthened rather than weakened its oppression. Throughout the empire the autocracy continued to carry out brutal terror, fan great-power chauvinism, and stir up dissent among the different peoples.

Tsarism oppressed Finland. This oppression increased during the war when the autocracy restricted the Finnish constitution, hampered freedom of the press and assembly, and arrested and exiled to Siberia deputies of the Finnish Parliament (Sejm), members of town councils, and other Finnish leaders. The tsarist authorities hoped such measures would suppress the separatist movement in Finland, but the results turned out just the opposite. Even the tsarist minister A. F. Trepov was forced to admit that "the population of Finland in origin, language, faith, customs, and outlook is completely alien to everything Russian; the Finnish population negatively relates to the Russian government and strives for complete independence."[45]

Tsarism oppressed Poland. During the first days at war the tsarist command announced that Russian troops were bringing the Polish nation good news of "reconciliation and unification." It wrote: "Let the borders that have sundered the Polish nation dissolve. Long live reunited Poland under the sceptre of the Russian tsar! Under this sceptre a Poland free in faith, language, and self-government will be resurrected." But these were empty words. War did not bring any reconciliation and unification to Poland; as before the autocracy suppressed its self-government, language, and religion. In July 1915, at the height of a German offensive on Polish territory, the tsarist government declared Poland would be granted autonomy; however, the matter never went any further than devising numerous projects for Polish autonomy. The tsar postponed proclaiming it until after the war. Nor did the Kadets do anything to solve the Polish question. The Moscow branch of the Central Committee of the Kadet party in November 1916 concluded that "for the party to issue a declaration of independence or devise general plans for structuring Poland is inopportune. . . . Polish independence means a significant weakening of the military might of Russia."[46]

During the war the autocracy assailed the Ukrainian people with new repressions. It shut down periodical publications issued in the Ukrainian language, removed Ukrainian books from libraries, prosecuted local educational societies, and as in the past forbade instruction in the Ukrainian language. When Russian troops occupied Galicia and the Bukovina, tsarist authorities deprived the

Ukrainian population of these regions of the rights they had enjoyed as part of Austria-Hungary. Ukrainian schools, newspapers, and cultural institutions that had existed in Galicia and in the Bukovina were closed, and many Ukrainian leaders were arrested and exiled to Russia. The Uniate Church was subjected to persecution.

During the war the question of the future of the Armenian people took on new importance. Turkish authorities had exterminated the population of Western Armenia. This national tragedy surpassed all the Armenian people had previously suffered. Seeking salvation from Russia, Armenians organized volunteer detachments to fight on Russia's side. The Armenian population aided Russia, hoping to achieve autonomy. But the hopes of the Armenian people were dashed. The Russian command had its own plans for the Armenian regions won back from Turkey. Intending to turn Western Armenia into an ordinary province of the Russian empire, tsarist authorities drew up a plan to colonize it with Russian Cossacks. After Russian troops occupied Turkish Armenia, tsarist authorities did not permit Armenian refugees to return home. Tsarism needed Armenian lands without Armenians.

The Jewish population found itself in difficult straits, especially in the western regions threatened by invading German troops. The tsarist authorities accused the entire population of sympathizing with the enemy, and even of espionage. They seized rabbis and rich Jews as hostages, warning that some would be hanged for each act of treason. The Jews were largely evicted from the front zone. Their eviction was accomplished with terrible humiliation, torment, and often pogroms. A declaration by the Workers' Group of the War Industries Committee stated that the tsarist government was hunting the Jewish population like wild animals: "On the pretext of espionage and of similar false calumnies, the government has driven them out of their homes by the thousands, from one end of Russia to another, forbidding them to settle. The government has broken up families, torn children from their mothers—and finally, officially, through the Department of the Police, has organized pogroms. . . . Each day an entire nation is crucified and removed far into the depths of the country; the rear of the Russian army is littered with unmarked Jewish graves."[47] All former restrictions on the Jewish population were maintained. They were to reside only in the pale,[u] state service was closed to them, there were quotas for academic institutions, they were restricted to the lower ranks of the service, etc.

The autocracy also circumscribed other non-Russian nationalities. The Muslims of Turkestan, for instance, were deprived of representation in the State Duma and forbidden to acquire new lands; the number of their councilors in city dumas could not exceed one-fifth of the total number of deputies; and access of non-Christians was restricted on juries, in memberships of school councils, etc. Moreover, tsarism had slowed down the economic and cultural

[u] The pale of settlement was a limited region of southern and western European Russia, instituted in 1791 during the reign of Catherine the Great, beyond which Jews were not permitted to dwell.

development of the outlying regions of the country. In a note to the tsar dated October 1916, Grand Prince Nikolai Nikolaevich was forced to admit that "in the decades that have passed since the annexation of the Caucasus to the Russian empire, extraordinarily little attention has been paid to this richest of outlying regions, and concern has been shown not so much for economic and cultural prosperity as for maintaining police order and tranquility within the region's borders."[48]

The outburst of great-power chauvinism and the government's oppressive policies evoked a corresponding wave of local nationalism. The exploiting ruling class of the oppressed nations strove to divert the toiling people from the social struggle, unite them under a common flag, and place them under its influence. The struggle of this ruling class for national rights did not go beyond the limits of the existing political structure. It amounted to no more than demands to create national schools and other cultural and educational institutions, extend zemstvo and jury courts of law to the outlying regions of the country, lift national and religious restrictions, etc. The national bourgeoisie did not enter the revolutionary struggle against the autocracy. It supported the military efforts of tsarism, fought the war to a victorious end, and counted on receiving national rights from the top, from the hands of the tsar. The Dashnaks,[v] expecting emancipation from the Turkish Armenians through the victory of Russian arms, headed a volunteer movement to aid the tsarist army. The Latvian bourgeoisie, aspiring to eliminate the German barons and opposing the seizure of the Baltic region by the Kaiser's troops, formed volunteer sharpshooter battalions that entered the Russian forces. Even leaders of the Azerbaijani party, "Musavat," which contained strong pro-Turkish elements, announced their readiness to further the victory of tsarism.

The emancipation of the peoples of Russia from nationalist oppression depended on overthrowing the monarchy. The Russian proletariat led the working people along this road. Bolsheviks regarded the liquidation of nationalist oppression as one of the most important tasks of the Russian Revolution. They favored regional autonomy, democratic local self-government, and demanded all nations be granted the right to self-determination, even if they seceded and formed independent states. However, the liberation struggle of the nations in Russia during the war was difficult. The Baltic region, Ukraine, Belorussia, and Transcaucasia were located either directly in the zone of military operations or at the front. A large number of troops was concentrated here and martial law was in effect. The laws of war were operative and the slightest display of dissatisfaction or protest was savagely put down.

The eastern regions of Russia were far from the theater of military operations, and the military regime touched them less than in the western territories. But

[v] Dashnaktsutiun (The Armenian Revolutionary Federation), founded in Tiflis in 1890 with the goal of promoting democratic liberties for the peoples of Turkish Armenia. By 1907 the Dashnaks had adopted a socialist program (whose agrarian ideas resembled those of the SRs) and a program for Transcaucasia that called for an independent republic but one that would be diplomatically linked to Russia.

even here the war placed a heavy burden on working people, contributed to the economy's collapse, and impoverished the people. Enormous supplies of raw materials were extracted from Central Asia and Kazakhstan, while manufactured goods were in short supply. Prices for necessities grew, taxes were increased, and most working people became poor and were ruined. During the first two years of war the tsarist government refused to entrust weapons to or enlist the local population into the rear guard. Tsarist officials wrote of the "unreliability" of this population, of its penchant for "a vagrant way of life," or its unadaptability to climatic and everyday conditions of the theater of war, etc. But the war dragged on, and human resources ran dry; the authorities dispatched to the front those employed at the rear. To replace them, it was decided to mobilize the indigenous populations of Central Asia and Kazakhstan.

In June 1916, the tsarist government declared it would conscript "the non-Russian male population" of Turkestan and the steppe region and several other districts of the country, between the ages of nineteen and forty-three, to construct defense installations for the field army. This edict tore the most able-bodied part of the peasantry away from peaceful labor at the height of field work and "requisitioned" them for hard labor under unfamiliar conditions because of a war foreign to their interests. The tsarist edict mobilizing the male population provoked an uprising against the autocracy in Central Asia and Kazakhstan. Masses of workers armed with sticks, stones, hoes, and sometimes with handguns, attacked representatives of the tsarist administration, police, Cossacks, and officials, and tried to settle accounts with them. Those involved in the uprising destroyed lists of draftees and announced that they were not going to send people to war.

The long, drawn-out, and stubborn 1916 uprising in Central Asia and Kazakhstan unified heterogeneous social forces. Feudal-clerical elements took part in it, who tried to infuse a religious character into the movement and to use it to restore medieval observances, while bourgeois-nationalist groups strove to take advantage of the struggle of the popular masses to establish their supremacy. Reactionary forces incited the rebels to violence against the peaceful Russian population and provoked a series of bloody clashes among the nationalities. But neither these forces nor these clashes determined the character of the 1916 uprising. Its driving force was the working masses, who were struggling against the national-colonial oppression of Russian tsarism. These masses were insufficiently organized and conscious, but tsarism cruelly suppressed their spontaneous movement. Punitive expeditions of tsarist troops shot thousands of peasants, torched settlements and villages, destroyed crops, and seized livestock. Military field courts sentenced participants in the uprising to death, hard labor, and imprisonment. Lands were confiscated from the local population.

The 1916 uprising was not directly linked to the revolutionary movement of the Russian working class; it was isolated and not strong enough to overthrow the colonial yoke and win independence. Nonetheless, the uprising weakened the autocracy's colonial regime. Tsarism was compelled to curtail the number called up into the army, postpone call-ups, and in several places substitute volunteers for draftees. The national liberation movement shook the foundations of the tsarist prison of nations, and thereby promoted the general task of the working people of Russia—the overthrow of the autocracy.

The revolutionary crisis found reflection in the policies of the bourgeoisie. In the beginning of the war the bourgeoisie were united with tsarism in the name of the struggle against the external enemy. But cooperation with tsarism did not bring the desired results for the bourgeoisie, and the longer the war lasted the more obvious this became. Defeats at the front and breakdowns at the rear cast doubt on the prospects for victory for which the bourgeoisie so longed, and furthered the growth of the revolutionary forces the bourgeoisie so feared. From unity with tsarism the bourgeoisie moved into the opposition. Aided by the State Duma and new organizations created during the war, such as the voluntary organizations and war industries committees, the bourgeoisie tried to change the policies of the government, to force it to stand aside and to give the bourgeoisie a place in the sun. It tried to extract concessions from the autocracy that would allow it to take a more active part in the country's administration. While the tsarist government sought to keep the Duma in recess as long as possible and then dissolve it altogether, the bourgeoisie demanded that the Duma convene more often and remain in session longer. It insisted on changes in the government and formation of a Council of Ministers that could soundly organize the home front, preserve internal peace in the country, and "cooperate with society."

At the new session of the State Duma, which opened in July 1915, exactly a year after the beginning of the war, appeals again rang out to unite all forces in the country around the tsar to conduct the war to victory. Toward this end the head of the government, I. L. Goremykin, and the tsarist ministers proposed to restore cooperation between the government and Duma. This time, however, the appeals of the tsarist ministers did not meet with such enthusiastic support as they had at previous Duma sessions. Many deputies blamed the government for not "meeting society halfway," violating legality, provoking internal quarrels, and sowing national dissension.

The growing revolutionary movement inclined a large number of the State Duma members on the initiative of the Kadets to unite in August 1915 into the so-called Progressive Bloc. The entire bourgeois-landlord faction of the Duma (except for the far right) entered this bloc: Kadets, Progressists, Octobrists, the center, and Progressive Nationalists. Some members of the State Council (a group of the center and of academics) also joined. The bloc planned moderate liberal reforms designed to stave off the approaching revolution. The bloc's program noted that only a strong, stable, and vigorous authority, enjoying the confidence of the country, could win the war. It explained the need to introduce legality, preserve internal peace, revive local administration, amnesty individuals convicted on political or religious grounds, deal with the question of Poland's autonomy, conduct a conciliatory policy in Finland, abolish restrictions on Jews, and restore "the little Russian [Ukrainian—D.J.R.] press." The bloc's program spoke of the need to authorize workers' trade unions, bring the rights of peasants up to the rights of other groups, introduce volost (district) zemstvos, establish zemstvos in the outlying regions of the country, etc.[49]

In fear of frightening rightist groups away from the bloc, the Kadets decided not to advance demands for a ministry responsible to the Duma, or for the introduction of bourgeois-democratic freedoms like freedom of speech, press, assembly, etc. The leader of the so-called Progressive Nationalists, V. V. Shul'gin, wrote that they entered the Progressive Bloc to hold the Kadets to "a minimal program," but the Kadets drew them into the struggle for power: "Of course they are pushing from behind and forcing us to move forward. But we are holding back. We have locked arms and are not permitting the crowd to force its way through."[50] Shul'gin called the Progressive Bloc "red, white, and blue," that is, a nationalistic bloc, and its participants—a fire brigade determined to extinguish revolution and fan the flames of war.

The bourgeoisie also sought to use zemstvo and city governments and the war industries committees to pressure the autocracy. A convocation of representatives of war industries committees of the Moscow region, which took place in August 1915, demanded that the government be reorganized and individuals "enjoying the confidence of the country" be immediately included in it. Congresses of the Union of Towns and Union of Zemstvos, convening in September 1915, maintained that the only way out of the present situation was to create a "ministry of confidence" and implement the Progressive Bloc's program. The bourgeoisie had no intention of overthrowing tsarism. It wanted tsarism to join the fight against revolution for a victorious prosecution of the imperialist war. A. I. Guchkov declared: "We appeal to the authorities to reach agreement with society, not for revolution but rather to strengthen authority itself, and defend the fatherland from revolution and anarchy. It is necessary for us to make a last attempt through our representatives to open the eyes of the supreme authority to what is happening in Russia, and the possible terrible consequences."[51]

Congresses of the Union of Towns and Union of Zemstvos commissioned a deputation to the tsar, and instructed it to inform Nicholas II of its views on the country's situation and of the necessity to bring individuals to power who enjoyed the country's confidence. But the tsar refused to discuss questions with the deputation that did not pertain to the direct tasks of the Union of Towns and Union of Zemstvos. The tsarist government made no concessions to the bourgeoisie and its Progressive Bloc. It was rebuffed. The bourgeoisie, uncertain which way to go, wavered. Although realizing tsarism was incapable of preventing revolution or of winning the war, the bourgeoisie nonetheless did not wage a decisive struggle against it.

"A Tragic Situation" was what Kadet V. A. Maklakov entitled his article, appearing in 1915 in the newspaper *Russkie vedomosti* (Russian Gazette). He made the following comparison: the driver of an automobile, bearing along a steep and narrow road, does not know how to drive and is leading us and himself to destruction, but he tenaciously clutches the steering wheel and does not want to give it up to those who know how to drive. What can be done? Force the driver to give up his place? But can this be done descending a mountain road? The chauffeur laughs at your alarm and impotence: "Don't dare touch me." He is right: you will not dare touch him. "You will restrain yourself, you will postpone reckoning with the driver until the danger has passed, when you once again will be on a flat road. You leave the steering wheel in the driver's hands."

By his analogy, Maklakov meant that power must remain in the hands of the tsarist government during a dangerous period. Nevertheless, doubts gripped the Kadet leader; Maklakov's article ended with a question: "But what will you feel while thinking that your restraint will prove meaningless, that even with your help the driver will not be able to manage! How would you feel if your mother asked you for help at a time of danger and, failing to understand your behavior, accuses you of indifference?"[52] There was no answer to the question. Maklakov's article graphically reflected the Janus-like position of the Russian bourgeoisie, its vacillation and wavering. Deciding not to break with the tsarist monarchy even after defeat at the front, it wanted to take advantage of these defeats and the threat of revolution to win concessions from it. In either event, the former unity of the bourgeoisie and tsarism had been destroyed.

A split appeared within the tsarist government itself. Defeats of Russian troops at the front and the growth of a revolutionary movement at the rear forced the government to replace several ministers. After Sukhomlinov, extreme reactionaries such as N. A. Maklakov, V. K. Sabler, and I. G. Shcheglovitov were removed from office. The newly appointed ministers belonged to the more moderate wing of the ruling group and wanted to restore cooperation with the State Duma. The tsarina was dissatisfied with the new ministers and wrote to the tsar. Aleksandra Fedorovna asked Nicholas II to postpone convening the State Duma as long as possible. "You have to dismiss them . . . Russia, thank God, is not a constitutional country. . . . Don't permit them to harass you. It's terrible. If you make concessions to them, they'll simply want more."[53]

The changes in the government's composition caused the advocates of the former policies led by I. L. Goremykin to be in the minority within the Council of Ministers. There was discord between the two groups of ministers. At secret meetings of the Council of Ministers in August 1915, V. N. Shakhovskoi, A. A. Polivanov, S. D. Sazonov, and others pointed out to their colleagues that the country's situation was steadily growing worse, everyone was up in arms, was in a state of ferment, was being driven to despair, and an explosion was possible at any minute. Minister of Internal Affairs N. B. Shcherbatov announced that the troops were unreliable and there was no guarantee they would fire on a crowd—and one could not pacify Russia with policemen. Goremykin calmly objected, maintaining that talk about a growing revolutionary movement was clearly exaggerated and the monarchy was not in serious danger.[54] Goremykin was not

Tsaritsa Aleksandra Fedorovna. Prince Serge Wolkonsky, *My Reminiscences,* vol. 2 (London, n.d.).

the inoffensive, weak-willed old man he is often depicted. He and his supporters tenaciously executed the will "of the shady irresponsible individuals" grouped around Rasputin. Some ministers looked for new ways to pacify the country, but others recommended continuing to use the former methods of crude force.

In August 1915, Rasputin's clique secured the dismissal of Nikolai Nikolaevich as commander in chief. The tsarina suggested to the tsar that the grand prince was edging him aside and wanted to take the country's administration into his own hands. She tried to convince Nicholas II personally to assume the supreme command, as the tsar himself had been anxious to do. The tsar's decision to remove Nikolai Nikolaevich greatly alarmed the ministers, who pointed out to the tsar the seriousness of this step. They declared that the grand prince's removal could be the spark that would ignite a powder keg, and earnestly asked him to reconsider his decision. In a letter to the tsar, Rodzianko wrote, "On my knees I sincerely implore you not to delay your decision, and preserve from approaching misfortune the person of the Russian tsar, sacred to us, and the reigning dynasty."[55]

Rodzianko's entreaties and those of the ministers did not produce the desired effect. Convening a meeting of the Council of Ministers, the tsar patiently listened to their speeches, but responded, "I shall see," "I shall think it over," and in conclusion said, "I have listened to your opinions and remain of the same mind." He assumed the supreme command himself, assigning Nikolai Nikolaevich to the post of vice-regent of the Caucasian front. Now M. V. Alekseev, who had concentrated the administration of the army in his hands, was appointed chief of staff. The tsar's role as commander in chief amounted to no more than listening to Alekseev's reports and countersigning his orders.

The growth of mass dissatisfaction and strengthening of the opposition of the bourgeoisie made tsarism turn even more to the right. The reins of government passed into the hands of Aleksandra Fedorovna, Rasputin, and their ilk. Nicholas II now spent most of his time at headquarters, while the tsarina in Tsarskoe Selo gave instructions and directions to ministers and other statesmen. The tsar and tsarina conducted lively correspondence in which the advice of the "divine spiritual adviser" occupied a central place. Rasputin was called "our friend" in the letters, which mentioned him in the third person, invariably with a capital "H": "He said," "His advice," and so on. Aleksandra Fedorovna convinced her husband that carrying out the holy man's advice was the only way to save the monarchy. Following this counsel, the tsar removed "mutinous" ministers—not all at once, but one by one. In the beginning of 1916 he even had to part with Goremykin.

B. V. Stürmer was appointed chairman of the Council of Ministers. Like Goremykin, he was a fervent reactionary bureaucrat, but more stable and cunning. Stürmer was considered an advocate of a separate peace with Germany. He was a protégé of the tsarina and Rasputin, and his appointment aroused indignation even among the bourgeois-landlord opposition. At first this indignation was veiled. Moreover, the appointment of Stürmer, which coincided with a temporary slump in the workers' movement, stabilization at the front, and the bourgeoisie's receipt of numerous war orders, raised hopes among several Duma leaders that they could reach an agreement with the tsarist government. After a conversation with Stürmer, Rodzianko announced that the tsarist government was ready to come to terms with the Progressive

Rasputin. Robert K. Massie, *Nicholas and Alexandra* (New York, 1967).

Bloc on the basis of mutual concessions, and therefore he suggested to the deputies of the Duma that they should cease presenting the government with "untimely and excessive" demands.

On February 9, 1916, the State Duma resumed its sessions. Stürmer wanted to establish rapport with the Duma majority. At his suggestion, Nicholas II visited the Tauride Palace and in a speech appealed to the Duma deputies. Declaring he was happy to be among the deputies, the tsar evoked "God's blessing" upon the work of the Duma. The Duma was moved by the tsar's lofty

Tsar Nicholas II. Wolkonsky, *My Reminiscenses.*

"greeting." "Such joy for us, such happiness—our Russian tsar is here among us!" enthused Rodzianko. The chairman of the Duma urged the government to effect close and intimate contact with the Duma and to call in trust upon public organizations to help. The new chairman of the Council of Ministers in turn assured the deputies that the government would struggle against German domination and go on to victory over Germany. He suggested that internal differences be abandoned for the sake of this aim.[56]

Not all Duma deputies believed Stürmer, and criticism of the government continued. A semblance of unity, though, was nevertheless achieved. Hearing the government's declaration, the Duma did not adopt any decision but merely passed to routine business. Bourgeois leaders wanted to implement the Progressive Bloc's program but did not know how to reach an agreement with Stürmer's government on that basis. Miliukov finished his speech in the Duma with the following words: "I know where the door is, but I don't know how to pass through it. We lack resources to resolve this problem, and we refuse any longer to seek the wisdom of the governmental authorities. I leave this rostrum without an answer and without hope of receiving one from the present cabinet."[57]

At the congress of the Kadet party in February 1916, delegates from Moscow and other towns declared that Miliukov's moderate line would not achieve its goal, and insisted that the Duma adopt a more uncompromising line toward the tsarist government and seek rapprochement with leftist elements. A. I. Shingarev suggested they should not react to Stürmer's crafty tactics or enter into negotiations with him, but demand his immediate dismissal: "The authorities got themselves into this predicament. Let them sink: we should not throw even a scrap of rope to them."[58] But nothing came of this. After listening to radical speeches, the congress of the Kadet party reaffirmed its conservative positions. It had spoken in favor of the need for a rapprochement with such leftist elements as the Mensheviks and Trudoviks, but it did not want to sever its alliance with the Octobrists. Rejecting the demand "for a responsible ministry," the congress came out in favor of a "ministry of confidence."

Shrill antigovernment speeches were also delivered at congresses of the Union of Towns and Union of Zemstvos, which took place shortly after the Kadet congress. One of the leaders of the Union of Towns, N. I. Astrov, said that "the government has fallen into the hands of fools, rogues, and traitors, and it is necessary to tell it but one thing—resign." The majority of delegates to the congresses refused to support such a categorical demand, but nonetheless the unions and tsarism did not trust one another. Dissatisfied with the speeches of the bourgeois leaders, the government restricted the activities of zemstvo, town, and other public organizations in every way possible. The Council of Ministers prohibited zemstvo, town, and similar congresses and gatherings without prior permission. The Union of Towns and Union of Zemstvos and the Central War Industries Committee were ordered not to overstep limits the tsarist authorities determined for discussing practical programs. Tsarism also wrecked the material basis of cooperation with the bourgeoisie. It had needed the bourgeoisie when it had been almost impossible to supply the Russian army, but as soon as the situation began to improve, government orders started to decline. Capitalists began to worry. They protested against the government's actions, accusing it of disrupting the supplying of the army. They wanted to take full advantage of the favorable conditions in wartime to enrich themselves.

The Russian bourgeoisie were likewise anxious about the direction of tsarist foreign policy. There were Germanophile tendencies in top government circles, and rumors circulated to the effect that Aleksandra Fedorovna, Rasputin, and their group were striving to conclude a separate peace with Germany. Clearly aware of this, the German government sensed an opportunity to break tsarist Russia away from her allies. The empress's maid of honor M. A. Vasil'chikova, writing from Austria to Nicholas II, alluded to discussions with "high-ranking people" including the German foreign minister, Gottlieb von Jagow, and tried to convince the tsar that Germany sincerely wanted to conclude a durable peace that would guarantee Russia possession of the Dardanelles and save her from revolution. Aleksandra Fedorovna received a letter from her brother, the Duke of Hesse, who urged trustworthy individuals be sent to Stockholm to prepare for negotiations with Germany. Later attempts to reach a separate peace with Russia came through the director of the German Bank, a participant in the German syndicate of industrialists, and again from M. Vasil'chikova, who had managed to arrive in Petrograd.

The tsarist government rejected these feelers, removed Vasil'chikova from the capital, and declared its resolve to continue the war until the enemy was completely routed. Minister of Foreign Affairs S. D. Sazonov denied rumors about peace talks with Germany and confirmed that Russia was bound not to conclude a separate peace. But the Russian bourgeoisie's distrust of the country's foreign policy and that of her allies remained. In order to stop the maneuvers of German diplomacy and tie Russia more firmly to the Entente, the governments of England and France agreed to fulfill Russian tsarism's age-long dream—to annex Constantinople and the Straits. The French government sent to Russia Minister of Justice Rene Viviani and the deputy minister of munitions, socialist Albert Thomas, to strengthen military cooperation between the two countries. The ministers of republican France and autocratic Russia discussed questions of future military strategy and increasing military supplies, and agreed to send Russian troops to France to bolster the western front. "God Save the Tsar" and "La Marseillaise" sounded together. The Entente, it seemed, was stronger than ever.

But storm clouds gathered on the horizon. In July 1916 the minister of foreign affairs, the Anglophile Sazonov, was retired. Stürmer, the chairman of the Council of Ministers, took this post himself. The English press expressed dissatisfaction. Deputy Minister of Foreign Affairs Harding, of Great Britain, voiced regret at such "a serious change." But was it? Former officials continued to direct the Ministry of Foreign Affairs—Stürmer was only "in attendance." He assured the allies that Russia's foreign policy would remain the same. Whatever Stürmer's personal sympathies, he was unable to alter this policy. It was strange that a Russianized German was named head of the Russian government and the Ministry of Foreign Affairs during a war with Germany. This was why, despite Stürmer's assurances, the Entente and the Russian bourgeoisie remained apprehensive. Was Russia planning to ally with Germany? But there was no direct evidence. G. Buchanan and M. Paleologue believed that although Stürmer remained a Germanophile at heart and acted in concert with the empress, there was no basis for charging him with striving to conclude peace with Germany. On October 5, 1917, Paleologue wrote in his diary: "Officially we cannot accuse him of anything; his words and actions are absolutely correct. He is always telling us: 'War to the end . . . no mercy for Germany. . . .' "[59]

In August 1916 the English king, George V, warned Nicholas II that German agents were trying to sow discontent between Russia and England and were spreading rumors that the English government, in violation of the previous agreement, was trying to block Russia's acquisition of Constantinople. "We are resolved," wrote the English king, "not to back down from the promises we have made as your allies."[60] In turn Nicholas II assured George V that the feelings of deep friendship toward England and France were becoming stronger in Russia and that he would try to deal with individuals who did not share this view.

The protracted and exhausting war continued as both sides dug in across from each other at the front to a distance of more than twelve hundred kilometers and carried on a war of attrition in the trenches. In 1916 active combat operations revived. Launching an offensive on the Caucasian front, Russian troops seized Erzerum and Trapezund from the Turks. At the end of May 1916, troops on the southwestern front attacked an Austro-Hungarian army, dealing the enemy a crippling blow and seizing large spoils of war. This was the famous Brusilovsk breakthrough. It foiled important plans of the German command but did not go further, and proved unable to alter the course of the war. The summer engagements of 1916 once again revealed the weakness and defects of the Russian command, the insufficient maneuverability of Russian troops, the breakdown of transportation and of the entire rear. Prospects for victory over Germany grew remote and became even more doubtful. The revolutionary movement directed against the war and tsarism gained ground in the country. This alarmed the bourgeoisie and intensified the opposition mood within it.

The bourgeoisie sought a way out of the developing situation. In a letter written in August 1916, Guchkov asked General Alekseev for help, hoping he might bring pressure on the tsar. Sharply criticizing the government, he complained to Alekseev:

> They do not inform us, they deceive us, they do not take us into consideration, they do not ask our advice. . . . We at the rear are powerless or almost powerless to struggle against this evil. Our means of fighting may rebound on us and under the rising temper of the mass of people, especially the working masses, they could serve as the first spark to ignite a fire, the dimensions of which no one can foresee or localize. I can no longer say what is awaiting us after the war—a deluge is approaching—but the pitiful weak-willed authorities are preparing to meet this cataclysm as though it were merely a good pelting rain: they put on galoshes and open an umbrella.[61]

But the bourgeoisie itself did not take any more decisive measures. Afraid lest it would strike "the first spark to ignite the fire," it did no more than pressure the government, admonish the tsar, appeal to certain military leaders and statesmen, and raise the alarm from the Duma tribune.

The Crisis Intensifies

The revolutionary crisis in Russia steadily developed and deepened because its cause—the irreconcilable socioeconomic contradictions aggravated by the imperialist war—continued to intensify. At first glance it looked as if history would repeat itself. Once again, as in 1904–1905, there was war, Russia's defeat at the front, the growth of a workers' movement, discontent in the villages and the army, and opposition among the bourgeoisie. And again, as then, revolution drew nearer, urging the overthrow of the autocracy and the abolition of the final vestiges of serfdom.

Yet there was an essential difference. The Russian Revolution now had a better chance than in 1905. The further development of capitalism and the imperialist war created the possibility that a bourgeois-democratic revolution might win a quicker and more decisive victory in Russia and grow into a socialist revolution. The Russian revolutionary movement likewise enjoyed a more favorable international situation than in 1905–1907. The revolutionary tempest back then swept over only Russia, whereas now all the leading capitalist countries were moving toward revolution. "The imperialist war," wrote Lenin,

> has *linked* the Russian revolutionary crisis, which stems from a bourgeois-democratic revolution, with the growing crisis of the proletarian socialist revolution in the West. This link is so direct that no individual solution of revolutionary [problems] is possible in any single country—the Russian bourgeois-democratic revolution is now not only a prologue to, but an indivisible and integral part of, the socialist revolution in the West.
>
> In 1905, it was the proletariat's task to consummate the bourgeois revolution in Russia so as to kindle the proletarian revolution in the West. In 1915, the second part of this task has acquired an urgency that puts it on a level with the first part.[62]

The revolutionary crisis in Russia was the decisive link in the world revolutionary crisis caused by the war. Although capitalism in Russia was less developed than in the United States, England, or Germany, and although the Russian proletariat was smaller than the American, English, and German proletariat, the revolutionary crisis in Russia grew at a faster tempo and became more intense. Especially sharp contradictions had appeared in Russia. War shook the tsarist monarchy to its foundations; the disorganization of the rear was colossal in Russia, and the poverty and need of the working people had reached an alarming level. The breakdown of industry and disruption of transport steadily grew, and prices for essential items continued to rise. The exorbitant burdens of war, increasing taxes, the high cost of living, and the general disorder at the rear evoked smoldering ferment among working people. These factors contributed to the continuing development of the strike movement of the working class that was not limited to narrow economic issues. The economic and food supply crisis stimulated a broad political movement against the war and tsarism.

The Bolsheviks explained that the battle against hunger was closely connected to the struggle to overthrow the autocracy in order to achieve a democratic republic and end the war as quickly as possible. A proclamation by the Petersburg Committee of the RSDRP, issued on October 12, 1916, said: "Only by waging a decisive struggle against the war, only by stopping the raging world conflagration, will mankind save itself from imminent hunger, destitution, and degeneration. . . . It's time for the popular masses to seize the initiative; there's been enough waiting around and sitting still. The Russian proletariat must immediately raise its voice and take the lead of all active democratic elements in the country."[63]

The Bolshevik appeal struck a responsive chord and received active support from workers. On October 13–15, mass meetings to struggle with the high cost of living and the war were held at factories in the Vyborg region. "We shall not hand over our comrades to the slaughterhouse," said speakers. Workers quit work and took to the streets, singing revolutionary songs. The mass meetings turned into strikes and strikes into demonstrations. The strike spread from the Vyborg side to other neighborhoods in the capital. The police reported that on October 19, sixty thousand workers took part in it. Workers did not present economic demands; the strike had a political character. It was a protest against the war and the high cost of living. Workers and the police clashed in the streets of Petrograd.

During these days soldiers manifested open sympathy for the workers' movement for the first time. Soldiers of the 181st Reserve Infantry Regiment defended the Vyborg workers when police attacked them. The soldiers' action against the police alarmed military authorities. Soldiers were locked up in their barracks; many were arrested. The 181st Regiment was removed from revolutionary Petrograd. Even though the actions of the soldiers of the 181st Regiment were isolated, and received no support from other units, the precedent for joint actions of workers and soldiers had been set.

The strike of October 17–20 showed what the Petrograd proletariat thought about the war and tsarism. But at the time it still lacked means to begin a decisive battle with the enemy: ferment at the front and in the provinces had not yet assumed broad dimensions, and the Petrograd garrison was still unwilling to support the workers. The Bolsheviks appealed to workers to end the strike, to strengthen and close ranks, and at the appropriate moment to once again leave their benches in order to conduct the final assault on the autocracy by means of a general strike in union with the army.

Although the strike of the Petrograd workers came to an orderly end, the excitement among workers did not subside. The fate of the soldiers from the 181st Reserve Infantry Regiment and leaders of the Bolshevik organization in the Baltic fleet concerned workers. On October 26 a military trial began for Orlov, Sladkov, Uliantsev, and their comrades. The authorities threatened them with the death penalty and this caused a second strike to begin five days after the end of the first October strike. It broke out on direct political grounds in response to an appeal from the Bolsheviks who led it. "Comrade sailors and soldiers!" read the appeal of the Petersburg Committee of the RSDRP. "We are raising our voices in indignation over the reprisals taken against you. To show the revolutionary people's solidarity with the revolutionary army, we are shutting down our plants and factories. The hangman's hand is raised above your heads, but it will shake when faced with the powerful protest of the people rising up from slavery."[64]

The strike of Petrograd workers lasted three days (October 26–28); on its last day about fifty factories with 120,000 workers (twice as many as in the first strike in October) took part. Workers from smaller shops, from printing works, and students from higher educational institutions joined in. The tsarist authorities and capitalists answered the strike with a lockout; thousands upon thousands of workers were thrown into the streets. This prompted yet another wave of protest. The possibility of a new general strike compelled the tsarist authorities and capitalists to cancel the lockout. The threat of the death penalty for the revolutionary soldiers was lifted; the courts sentenced four defendants to hard labor and acquitted the rest. Still, the workers' struggle against the war and tsarism continued.

The workers' revolutionary movement also drew the petit bourgeois strata of the population into the struggle. The growing revolutionary crisis and an intensification of the revolutionary mood of the masses forced the petit bourgeois parties and groups to move to the left. Menshevik defensists, trying to adapt to the new situation, began speaking of the need for peace. At a meeting of regional war industries committees held in December 1916, the workers' delegation declared that the task facing the proletariat was to end the war as soon as possible and "conclude a peace without forced annexations and indemnities, explicit or secret."[65] Workers' representatives in the war industries committees appealed to workers to struggle to get rid of the existing regime and to democratize the country completely. But they did not assign an independent political role to the working class. The Gvozdevites[w] assumed that the bour-

[w] Refers to the members of the workers' groups within the war industries committees. Chaired by K. Gvozdev, the Workers' Group was a special contingent within the committee representing the Russian workers. Despite the vocal opposition of the Bolsheviks (the Mensheviks supported the special contingents), workers' groups were created in seventy war industries committees. In January 1917 the imperial government arrested the Workers' Group of the Central WIC in Petrograd. During the February Revolution workers and soldiers released the imprisoned members who afterward played important roles in the new political order. Gvozdev became minister of labor in the Provisional Government. Although opposed to Bolshevik rule, he later held minor posts in the Soviet economic apparatus.

geoisie had embarked on a struggle against the tsarist regime and that all the proletariat should do was exert pressure on the government and demand the repudiation of indecisive and half-hearted policies in its relation to the authorities. They believed that the propertied State Duma of the Third of June could be turned into a bulwark for the democratization of the country.

The foreign secretariat of the so-called Organizational Committee of the RSDRP, the Petrograd Initiative Group, and other organizations of Menshevik centrists censured the Workers' Group in the War Industries Committee for not representing the interests of the working class, and demanded its recall. P. B. Axelrod, L. Martov, F. I. Dan, I. G. Tsereteli, and others disassociated themselves from the defensist publication "Self-Defense," which contained articles by A. N. Potresov and his supporters. The publication of this volume aroused the Menshevik O. A. Ermanskii to issue a book entitled *Marxists at the Crossroads*. But Marxists were not at the crossroads: it was the Mensheviks who had turned away from Marxism.

The Interdistrict Organization of United Social Democrats *(Mezhraiontsy)* headed by I. Iurenev [K. K. Iurenev—D.J.R.] occupied a special position. Bolsheviks and Mensheviks who favored bringing both organizations into a single party joined this group. During the war the Interdistrictites took a position close to that of the Bolsheviks on fundamental questions, advancing the slogan "war against war." But on the question of party organization they, as before, took a different position from that of the Bolsheviks. The Interdistrict Group supported summoning a united party conference and invariably ended all of their leaflets with the call "Long live a united RSDRP."

The Bolsheviks opposed merging with other Social Democratic groups, but wherever possible they cooperated with them against the common enemy. This had particularly been the case during the strikes in October 1916. A letter sent from Petrograd to Irkutsk to the Interdistrictite member L. M. Karakhan explained that Bolsheviks, Interdistrictites, and the Menshevik Initiative Group had participated in the struggle against the war and the high cost of living that had broken out in 1916; that the Petersburg Bolshevik Committee had worked out a resolution adopted at mass rallies, which proved the indissoluble link between the food crisis and the general question of the war; and that the protest strike against the trial for the Kronstadt sailors "had been substantial and achieved dimensions the likes of which we have not seen since the beginning of the war, even though it did not take place at the same time everywhere, and was a bit disunited." The author of the letter noted the complete unanimity of all Marxist groups in these disturbances: "at factories all actions are discussed and carried out jointly."[66] The letter also mentioned that Bolsheviks, Interdistrictites, and the Initiative Group had boycotted the Workers' Group of the War Industries Committee. "A dark spot on a light background—the Gvozdevites—are losing ground more and more."

However, the background was not very light, the Gvozdevites were not so isolated, and the unity among different groups was not as close as one might conclude from the letter to Karakhan. A Bolshevik leaflet, *Proletarskii golos* (Proletarian Voice) (number 4, December 1916), noted that the Mensheviks united around the Initiative Group were still confused in terms of political ideology and coexisted with elements outside the bounds of Russian Social Democracy, that they "hamper the Menshevik comrades whom revolutionary events had forced to arrive at correct tactical insights from returning to revolutionary Social Democracy." The leaflet explained that "the Initiative Group is unequal to the internationalist tasks of the present moment, and the Inter-districtites persist in calling for unity among the various fictional fractions." *Proletarskii golos* noted the activity of the Petrograd group of Socialist Revolutionaries, which had gone largely ignored. The Bolsheviks had one mission with respect to all of the groups: "to enter into an informational association with them at a particular, definite instance to coordinate activities at the moment of the uprising, for which these socialist groups are ready."[67]

The Bolsheviks strengthened and united their organizations. They were subjected to continual persecution from tsarism and harassment by the bourgeoisie, but they overcame great difficulties and continued to increase their revolutionary activity. In March 1916 the Petrograd Bolshevik Organization numbered more than two thousand members. The Petersburg Committee of Bolsheviks printed leaflets on its own press, and maintained regular ties with the Central Committee of the RSDRP, from which it received literature. In August 1916 the head of the Petrograd secret police (Okhranka) informed his department that the efforts of the members of the Petersburg Committee of the RSDRP had caused "the activity of the Bolsheviks to expand constantly, take on clearer shape, and increase the means and methods of its criminal propaganda; in short, the committee has now become quite a serious and dangerous threat to public tranquility and governmental order."[68] The head of the secret police informed the authorities that "all the most active and leading Bolsheviks in the capital" had been arrested. But two months had passed and the two October general strikes showed that the tsarist authorities had not succeeded in challenging the activities of the Bolsheviks in the capital.

In the fall of 1916 the directing body of the Petrograd Bolshevik Organization was augmented with new members. Kirill Shutko returned. A member of the party since 1902, he had worked in Petrograd and Moscow early in the war, then was exiled to Irkutsk province and, escaping from exile for Petrograd, he again plunged into revolutionary work. N. Tolmachev participated zealously in party work, too. Nineteen years old in 1914, and a student at the Polytechnic Institute, he entered the party and soon developed into an important party organizer and propagandist. Returning from the Urals in the fall of 1916, Tolmachev undertook extensive revolutionary work in the capital. The Bolshevik worker G. F. Fedorov also returned from the Urals to Petrograd at this time. He was only twenty-six years old but already had been in the party nine years and had a great deal of experience in legal and illegal work in Petrograd, Moscow, and the Ural region.

Despite the fact that the party cadres were young, that there were few members of the intelligentsia among them, and that arrests constantly decimated their ranks, the Bolshevik organization of the capital carried out extensive propaganda and organizational work among local workers. Here is what Tolmachev wrote on October 24, 1916. "On the whole the undertaking is well organized. The main thing is people. And, it's really and truly great to live and work in Petrograd." On November 5: "And somehow I'm growing more and more convinced that momentous events are in the offing and coming closer to us. Soon history will be made; 'living' history that you'll live through yourself and not read about in a textbook by Kareev."[x] On November 15: "It's quiet on the streets now, but not in people's minds. We're rapidly growing both qualitatively and quantitatively. The political activity surrounding the State Duma is now stirring many of those who are with us as well as those with whom we shall now struggle. In general, the movement is taking shape, or rather its various components are elucidating their positions."[69]

The Bolsheviks also strengthened their organizations in other cities. A party conference in November 1916 in Ekaterinoslav showed that more than one hundred workers had formed cells in local factories. The conference noted that the working masses were very tense, that dissatisfaction and irritation were extreme, and that party organizations must organize the spontaneous and scattered movement.

In the fall of 1916 the Russian Bureau of the Central Committee of the RSDRP was reestablished; almost all the former members of the bureau were in prison or exile. Returning again from abroad, A. G. Shliapnikov restored party ties. The Bureau of the Central Committee was formed consisting of Shliapnikov, V. M. Molotov, and P. A. Zalutskii, who had returned from exile. Shliapnikov took charge of organization and communications with the émigrés and the provinces; Molotov managed publications; Zalutskii entered the Petersburg Committee of the RSDRP. A. I. Ul'ianova (Elizarova) and Shvedchikov took part in the work of the bureau as before. A group led by V. A. Tikhomirnov traveled to Finland to pick up literature arriving from abroad, and saw that it was disseminated.

As the economic and political crisis intensified, tsarism continued with its reactionary policies. In September 1916 the tsar entrusted internal affairs to A. D. Protopopov, a landowner and industrialist with close ties to the banks. He was a member of the Octobrist party and deputy vice-president of the State Duma. Going to Stockholm as a member of the Russian parliamentary delegation, Protopopov met with a representative of the German embassy, the banker Fritz Warburg, and spoke with him about concluding a separate peace with Germany. Upon his return he was graciously received by the tsar and tsarina

[x]N. I. Kareev (1850–1931), a Russian historian and political figure. Kareev published several groundbreaking studies on the peasantry and peasant question during the French Revolution. Tolmachev is most likely referring to Kareev's *History of Western Europe in Modern Times*, seven volumes of which were published in St. Petersburg between 1892 and 1917.

and, to the amazement of everyone, was soon elevated to high office. This was done with the approval of Rasputin and the tsarina. Henceforward, one of the leaders of the Duma became Stürmer's assistant and a friend of Rasputin and the empress. Bourgeois statesmen broke off relations with Protopopov, feeling he had deserted into the camp of extreme reaction, and conducted an extensive campaign against him. Criticizing Stürmer and Protopopov, they estimated that the government's policies might lead to revolution and facilitate conclusion of a separate peace with Germany. Bourgeois activists were determined to prevent either possibility.

The opposition mood of the bourgeoisie reached its peak at a session of the State Duma that opened on November 1, 1916. No sooner had Rodzianko in his opening speech said that "a government, strong in the country's trust, must lead society" than voices rang out. "Let the government retire!" Next Miliukov mounted the rostrum. He scathingly denounced the government, which had undermined the successful prosecution of the war. Rumors that the government considered it essential to end the war and conclude a separate peace especially alarmed the bourgeoisie. Miliukov quoted from German, Austrian, and Russian newspapers and from memoranda from right-wing groups, and told of his discussions with foreign leaders. He charged that the government was undermining Russia's relations with her allies.

Miliukov accused the government of betraying the national interests of Russia and transparently hinted that the source of this betrayal originated with the empress Aleksandra Fedorovna and her circle. Reporting rumor rather than fact, after each accusation he bombastically inquired—Is this stupidity or is it treason? Miliukov himself subsequently wrote about this speech: "I spoke about rumors of 'treason' circulating everywhere in the country, about the government's activities that aroused public indignation; moreover, in each instance I asked the audience to decide whether it was 'stupidity' or 'treason.' The audience emphatically chose the second interpretation—even when I myself was not altogether sure."[70]

Bourgeois circles called this speech an appeal for revolution. But neither Miliukov nor representatives of the bourgeoisie went further than demanding the government's replacement. After their speeches in the Duma the tsarist government remained in power, but the position of the head of the government was shaken. Stürmer was forced into retirement and A. F. Trepov was appointed chairman of the Council of Ministers. This was merely a change in personnel, not government policy; the course remained the same. Some leaders of the Progressive Bloc argued that Trepov should be given the benefit of the doubt; he was neither a traitor nor Rasputin's protégé. Others argued the opposite: Trepov was the same as Stürmer, only "more agreeable"; his government was composed of one-third decent people, one-third stupid people, and one-third who were good for nothing. Miliukov later wrote that at first Stürmer's retirement was considered an important victory. "But . . . it only seemed that way. The selection of one new head of government showed that the authorities had no intention of leaving their trenches and continued to find its servants among the same old gang of officials."[71]

The leaders of the Progressive Bloc continued their campaign against the government, but conducted it within so-called legal limits so as not to give the government a pretext for dismissing the Duma. They repeated the slogan "the Duma must be preserved," popular since the time of the First Duma. Two weeks after his appointment as chairman of the Council of Ministers on November 19, 1916, Trepov appeared before the Duma. But no sooner had the president announced that the new chairman of the Council of Ministers had asked to be recognized, than the Menshevik and Trudovik fractions pounded desks and cried "get rid of him," "retire him," and "get lost." They were so hostile that Trepov was compelled to leave the rostrum before even beginning his speech. The Duma decided to disassociate itself from such tactics and expelled its perpetrators for eight meetings. After the "guilty" deputies were dismissed, Trepov was able to speak. The new chairman of the Council of Ministers assured the State Duma the war would be fought to victory, promised to act in concert with the Duma and public organizations, and called upon the deputies to forget their arguments and quarrels and devote themselves to constructive work. The State Duma received Trepov's declaration with reservation. The deputies responded that vague promises set their teeth on edge, that the new declaration of the government was surprisingly similar to earlier ones and also was insipid and empty. Even the extreme conservative deputy M. V. Purishkevich declared that the traditional norms of authority were bursting like soap bubbles, leaving no trace, and that the irresponsible forces led by Rasputin were exerting decisive influence over the country's political life.

The speeches delivered on the floor of the State Duma in November 1916 provoked considerable uproar and fed rumors far beyond the Tauride Palace. The authorities tried to suppress the Duma speeches; readers could not find them in newspapers, entire sections were censored from the speeches, papers appeared blank, with small "bald patches" or large "bald spots." Then the Duma speeches were reproduced on typewriters or written out by hand. By criticizing the tsarist authorities and revealing the dark irresponsible forces behind them, the Duma speakers had further exposed the autocratic system, although this was not their intention.

Moderate Duma resolutions followed caustic Duma speeches. A broadside passed by the Duma in response to Trepov's declaration noted that the changes in the composition of the Council of Ministers were no more than a substitution of individuals, not a change in the system, and was not enough to alter the State Duma's attitude toward the government. The Duma declared that the influence of the dark irresponsible forces must be eliminated; it would adopt all available legal means to form a cabinet responsible to the State Duma and willing to implement the program of its majority. The Duma, however, never went beyond making speeches and passing resolutions.

The Progressist M. A. Karaulov observed that the government was strong because the Duma was weak. "It is fully confident that you will do no more than assail it with words, that actually you will deny it nothing, all your indignation amounts to is hysterical cries, not the threatening order of an enraged master. You yourselves do not feel masters of the situation . . . you blindly trusted the government during the most critical moments in the state's history, gave it complete command of the state chariot, and crawled from the driver's seat into the back where you fell sound asleep, waking only when you were jolted by potholes."[72] Karaulov maintained that the country placed its hopes on the Duma and was waiting for action, not declarations.

In private correspondence Duma deputies candidly admitted they were weak and powerless. Here is what one deputy, Kadet G. V. Gutop, wrote on November 21, 1916: "We're stewing in our own juices here, venting our feelings in futile speeches, feeling we're standing before a blank wall, which no words can penetrate, and we have no heavy artillery at our disposal." On November 22, 1916: "I am one of the nonentities bending my jaws, providing material for newspaper stories and arousing the populace that fancies that the Duma can actually achieve something. It can't do a thing, and we are filling the air with our cries to no avail." On December 17, 1916: "People more and more are dangerously exaggerating the hopes they place in the State Duma and excessively estimating its strength and importance. To date the Duma has neither initiated nor led the movement that has become so tense . . . whatever the Duma could have done, without exceeding the limits of the law, it has already accomplished."[73]

The Duma had exhausted all its possibilities of bringing peaceful pressure to bear on the tsar and government. It would not overstep the limits set for it by the Stolypin legislation of the Third of June. Everything had already been said, all wishes and requests had been expressed, and matters had come to a standstill. On November 28, 1916, the Progressist A. I. Konovalov wrote: "The future is completely unclear. How dreadful it is that at this threatening moment in history there is such a vile pitiful government, that the people's representatives were elevated on the basis of the electoral law of the Third of June." The Octobrist Blazhkov formed similar impressions. "The mood here is disgusting; we all realize we can't escape from the dead end to which the dark forces have brought Russia. All the wishes of the State Duma and State Council and the Congress of the All-Russian Nobility are but voices crying in the wilderness."[74] He expressed the same thoughts in other correspondence from Petrograd. "Speeches, no matter how eloquent, are still speeches." "Everything has been said, nothing is left of our old strength. We continue riding in the train which, so far, apparently hasn't derailed."[75]

The bourgeoisie had one more device with which to fight the government—its public organizations. In December 1916 the congresses of the Union of Towns and Union of Zemstvos and the Conference of Representatives of Public Organizations Dealing with Food Supplies were supposed to begin work in Moscow. The tsarist authorities, however, did not permit these congresses to open. Delegates gathered nonetheless and passed a resolution on the country's political situation. The resolution adopted by representatives of the zemstvos noted that the weak and undistinguished government, utterly distrusted by everyone, had become an obstacle to victory over the enemy and that its policies had shaken the tsarist throne. To replace it, delegates proposed as soon as possible to create a government "strong in its responsibility before the nation and its popular representatives." The State Duma should assume responsibility for the fate of the country. "There is no time to be lost; history will allow us no further respites."[76] N. I. Astrov, an activist in the Union of Towns, noted that the December resolutions adopted by the delegations of the zemstvos and towns, "testify how deeply we recognize the situation is hopeless. These were already cries of despair. The old hulk has sunk. We must save ourselves."[77]

Not only bourgeois public organizations, but also institutions inseparably identified with the autocracy protested government policies. The State Council, which not long before had considered the most moderate projects undertaken by the State Duma dangerous, began to speak out. The State Council passed a resolution proposing to ban the dark irresponsible forces (Rasputin and his gang) from state affairs and to form an effective government, enjoying the confidence and sympathy of the country, capable of working with existing legislative institutions.[78] The "united nobility" on which the Stolypin reaction earlier had relied also spoke out. The Congress of United Nobility noted that the monarchy was rocking on its foundations, that it was essential to get rid of the dark forces once and for all in the affairs of state and create a government responsible to the monarch, while enjoying public confidence and capable of working with legislative institutions. "The bedrock is beginning to speak," contemporaries remarked when these two resolutions were passed.

The bourgeois-landowner opposition spoke out not so much against tsarism or even the government, as against "the dark irresponsible forces" behind it. Rasputin was the main target. Bourgeois oppositionists, several extreme rightist spokesmen, and members of the royal family came out against him. Even many reactionaries considered that Rasputin was discrediting the tsar and tsarina and was destroying the entire monarchy, that he was the cause of all the misfortunes and disasters, and that his removal would save tsarism from ruin. Rasputin's influence, however, was exaggerated and his role was inflated in order to direct attention from tsarism. Rasputin was called "chancellor of the Russian empire," the "uncrowned monarch," and the like.[79] Irate speeches from the tribune of the State Duma and State Council demanded Rasputin's removal in order to save the autocracy. The fervent Black Hundredite and one of the founders of the so-called Union of the Russian People, M. V. Purishkevich, appealed to the deputies of the Duma: "Step over to tsarist headquarters, throw yourself on your knees before His Majesty and ask the tsar to permit himself to open his eyes to the terrible reality, ask him to deliver Russia from Rasputin and his followers young and old."[80]

Not surprisingly, a conspiracy was soon hatched against Rasputin. The tsar's cousin, Grand Prince Dmitrii Pavlovich, Prince F. F. Iusupov, and Purishkevich were convinced the tsar would not deliver the country from Rasputin, and resolved to take the matter into their own hands. Rasputin was killed on the evening of December 17, 1916, in the palace of Prince Iusupov. Newspapers were prohibited from publishing anything about Rasputin's murder, but news of the death of the renowned Grisha quickly spread throughout the city and country, causing a sensation. From Petrograd it was reported that for several days people joyfully spoke about nothing save Rasputin's murder.

The tsar and tsarina, however, were deeply distressed by what had happened. Learning of Rasputin's murder, Nicholas II interrupted a meeting at Supreme Headquarters called to plan impending military operations, and immediately left for Petrograd in order to share his family's grief. The entry in Nicholas II's diary for December 21, 1916, reads: "At 9 o'clock I set off with my entire family past the building with photographs and turned to the right toward a field, where we were present at a sad scene: the coffin containing the body of the unforgettable Grigorii, killed on the night of Dec[ember] 17 by monsters in the home of F. Iusupov, had already been lowered into a grave. F[ather] Al[eksandr] Vasil'ev performed service after which we returned home. The weather was gloomy at twelve degrees below zero."[81]

Many in the bourgeois-landowner camp believed that Rasputin's murder would end the dark period in Russian history and a new, brighter period would dawn. In a letter from Moscow to Lenin someone named Sidorov wrote: "The events of the past few days, when so-called progressive society clearly showed how helpless it was, are reducing the great struggle of the people to a vulgar hunt for a single individual. . . . A newspaper [*Utro Rossii* (Russian Morning)—E.B.] has raised this drunken insignificant altercation to the level of historical events. In this society people long for heroes and individual fighters, needed in order to move the Russian cart from historical potholes."[82]

Bourgeois activists also had doubts that Rasputin's murder would do any good. Guchkov wrote to his brother Nikolai in Moscow: "We have taken a leap. We threw caution to the winds. But will these bloody events do any good? And where will it all end? . . . There is little hope the crisis will be resolved safely."[83] The Kadet V. A. Maklakov, who was directly involved in Rasputin's murder, later admitted that it did not achieve the desired results: "It caused new animosity in the heart of Aleksandra Fedorovna against everyone who condemned her, that is, against all of society. Her feelings were transmitted to His Majesty. The political move to the right became sharp and aggressive. Dead, Rasputin turned out to be even more powerful than when he was alive."

Rasputin's murder deepened the split inside the royal family. Members of the royal family petitioned the tsar to mitigate the lot of Grand Prince Dmitrii Pavlovich, who had been sent to a military unit stationed in Persia for his participation in Rasputin's murder. They saw the extent to which danger threatened the entire Romanov dynasty, and self-preservation prompted them to search for a way to save themselves. Grand princes Aleksandr and Nikolai

Mikhailovich and several other members of the tsarist dynasty wrote to Nicholas II and requested an audience in order to open his eyes and to secure the tsarina's removal from conducting affairs of state. They tried to convince Nicholas II to form an "intelligent government," maintaining that the present government with its prohibitions, constraints, and suspicions was driving people into the camp of the leftists and thereby paving the way for revolution. But the memoranda of the grand princes had no effect; the tsarist government continued its former policies. Rasputin had merely been the most despicable personification of the corrupt tsarist regime. His murder did not force tsarism to make concessions, nor did it destroy the influence of dark forces. On the contrary, they began to show even greater malice and intransigence.

Protopopov replaced Rasputin. Sophisticated in a European manner, the Simbirsk nobleman occupied the place of the unscrubbed Siberian spiritual adviser, but even so, events continued on the same course. Indignation against the new favorite of the tsar and tsarina grew and the Octobrists expelled him from their Duma fraction. The nobility of Simbirsk province felt guilty for having selected him as their marshal and demanded that he account for his actions. There were so many protests against Protopopov's behavior that on January 24, 1917, the Department of Police instructed the head of the Simbirsk gendarme administration "to take all measures to hold all telegrams and even letters from the nobility involving political agitation against the minister of internal affairs."[84]

Protopopov remained in power. It was Trepov who was forced into retirement. Trepov did not enjoy the tsarina's trust, and as soon as the dirty work of dismissing the Duma was over, he was removed. In January 1917, Prince N. D. Golitsyn was appointed chairman of the Council of Ministers. He was a politically unsophisticated nonentity so ill that he could barely drag his legs along. But he had assisted Aleksandra Fedorovna on charitable committees and was devoted to the empress. This alone was enough to enable him to become head of the tsarist government at a critical time for the autocracy. The tsarist camarilla, determined to maintain its position, took the offensive. The convocation of the State Duma was postponed one month. To put down opposition in the State Council, its membership was changed: many conservative figures were brought in and I. G. Shcheglovitov was appointed its president.

These measures seemed inadequate to the extreme conservative camp. The Black Hundreds were alarmed and confused. Sensing that the ground was shaky and that the monarchy was dying, taking its supporters along with it, the Black Hundreds saw revolution everywhere. They found it among workers and soldiers, in the *Zemgor* [Union of Towns and Union of Zemstvos—D.J.R.] and in the war industries committees, in the State Duma, and even in the Union of the Nobility. The extreme conservatives urged the government to further strengthen its reactionary course and, in particular, demanded the State Duma's dissolution. They created the United Council of Monarchist Organizations, which was determined to prevent any reforms in the country and suppress any opposition. The ringleader of the Astrakhan Black Hundreds, Tikhanovich-Savitskii, offered "to surround His Majesty only with conservatives and draw closer to the tsarina." He also wrote Maklakov: "Tell me candidly, Nikolai Aleksandrovich, if an uprising occurred that was even more powerful than that of 1905, in which the troops participated, would you suppress it if you were minister of internal affairs once again? Do you have a plan for such an emergency? Can you find and show me several military leaders, popular with the men, very conservative, upon whom one can completely rely?"[85]

It is not known how Maklakov reacted to this appeal, but in December 1916 he sent a letter to the tsar in which he wrote that the time had come when the fate of the tsarist dynasty would be decided, that in the capital an assault on tsarist power had already begun and Russia "may be left without the monarchy, like a cupola without a cross." Maklakov thought it was still possible to avert the approaching calamity, but in order to do so it was necessary to work together as one, postpone convening the State Duma as long as possible, and limit activities of the public organizations. In the beginning of February 1917 the tsar instructed Maklakov to draw up a draft manifesto to dissolve the State Duma. Receiving this instruction, Maklakov advised the tsar to prepare, immediately, carefully, and without further delay, to meet as they should be met any difficulties that could arise if the State Duma were dissolved, and to concentrate his forces in the struggle with the domestic enemy "that has long been growing more dangerous, more embittered, and bolder than the foreign enemy."[86]

An extensive program to combat "the domestic enemy" and a possible popular uprising was set forth in two documents, a memorandum and a letter to the tsar, composed by an extreme right circle headed by a member of the State Council, A. A. Rimskii-Korsakov. The authors of the letter and memorandum offered to appoint people to the highest government posts who were capable of decisively suppressing "revolts and anarchy," to introduce immediately martial law (and if necessary declare a state of siege) in the capitals and large cities, to supply military units with machine guns and artillery, to close all organs of the leftist press and to strengthen rightist newspapers, to militarize all factories working for defense, to appoint government commissars to all public organizations, to dismiss the present State Duma, and to call elections for a new Duma, after undesirable and harmful elements were removed from it, at all costs guaranteeing a government majority.[87]

The long memoranda sent by the extreme conservative circles to the tsar were reinforced by the brief but unequivocal advice of the tsarina. In letters to Nicholas II in December 1916, Aleksandra Fedorovna urged the tsar to cease wavering and demonstrate firmness: "Be master." "For a long time, for many years people have been saying over and over again to me: 'Russia loves the knout.'" "Be Peter the Great, Ivan the Terrible, Emperor Paul—smash them all."[88]

The question how to continue to conduct the war also arose. Exhaustion of economic and human resources had awakened a desire in ruling circles of the belligerent countries to substitute imperialist peace for an imperialist war. In Russia, where the war had been especially ruinous, and in her ruling circles where a pro-German group had long existed, the urge to make a separate peace was particularly strong. The opinion was widespread in highest government circles and among the nobility that tsarism's alliance with the bourgeois democracies, England and France, was unnatural and the defeat of the German empire would lead to the collapse of Russian tsarism. Contradictions between the imperialists of Russia and Germany existed, but no less sharp were contradictions between the imperialists of Russia and England. During the war, combinations of forces might change and the imperialist powers might cross from one camp into another. Lenin noted that both tsarism and the Russian bourgeoisie wanted the same thing—to despoil Germany, Austria, and Turkey in Europe and to strike at England in Asia. "These 'dear friends' disagree only as to *when and how* to turn from a struggle against Germany to a struggle against England."[89]

But the time had not arrived to resolve this dispute, and there was scant possibility for Russia to reorient its foreign policy. Leaders of the bourgeois opposition accused the tsarist ministers of wanting to break with the Entente and conclude a separate peace with Germany. At both the rear and the front spy mania spread—all the failures and defeats the Russian army had sustained were explained away as machinations of German spies. It was said that treason had found a home in the highest government circles and the high command, and that the tsarina and her camarilla were preparing to make a separate peace with Germany. These were merely assumptions and conjectures. Bourgeois leaders took them up and spread them in order to inflame militant nationalism and discredit the tsarist ministers.

In the fall of 1916 the foreign press reported that Russia and Germany were conducting talks about a separate peace and that both powers had already reached agreement in principle. Were such negotiations going on at the time, or did Germany spread rumors about them in order to drive a wedge between Russia and England? No one can be sure. In any case, if negotiations were conducted they did not produce any results; the ruling elite of Russia would not forsake alliance with England and France to make a separate peace with Germany. Tsarist Russia was too dependent on the English and French imperialists and was burdened by obligations to them. It had gone too far in its battle against Germany and Austria to change sides during the war. Such a step meant the autocracy would have had to part company with the majority of the Russian imperialist bourgeoisie, which was disposed to alliance with the Entente powers, and would have placed its future in jeopardy. By making a separate peace, tsarism might have destroyed itself. Self-preservation dictated it restrain from such an about-face.[90]

Tsarism preserved the alliance with the Entente powers. In a declaration of November 19, 1916, Trepov assured the Duma the government would fight against Germany until victory was achieved. He announced in the Duma that a secret agreement had been concluded with the Allies to give Russia Constantinople and the Straits. They did this obviously to rally Russia's military efforts and to bind her even more tightly to their cause. Within ten days, again from the tribune of the Duma, the new minister of foreign affairs, N. N. Pokrovskii, said that the Entente powers were utterly determined to achieve the crushing defeat of Germany. At precisely this time the German government made peace overtures to the Entente. The German imperialists began talking about peace because of agitation among the popular masses weary of war. It was a device to calm the working masses and influence public opinion in the belligerent and neutral countries. In fact, though, neither they nor the imperialists of the Entente genuinely wanted to end the sanguinary war. Tsarism rejected the peace proposals: "The time for peace has not yet come" read an order of the tsar to the troops in response to the declaration of the German government.

In January 1917 Pokrovskii ordered Russian ambassadors to assure the governments of France and Italy that Russia's foreign policy "would remain unshakable both in its general principles and in particular in its close unity with our allies."[91] The Allied states remained somewhat skeptical of these declarations and were not entirely convinced that all elements in the population of Russia were imbued with warlike sentiment. On the contrary, facts showed that the Russian people were tired of war and were yearning for peace. This was the cause of the disturbances in Russia. The *chargé d'affaires* of the tsarist government in France, M. M. Sevastopulo, in a letter to Pokrovskii reported that rumors were circulating about disorders in Petrograd and there was concern that these disorders might unfavorably affect the war effort. *Chargé d'affaires* Nabokov communicated from London that "local parliamentary and financial circles are daily becoming more anxious over the internal situation in Russia." In January 1917 Russian Ambassador M. N. Giers wrote that Rome was completely convinced "that Russia's foreign policy will not change" but "fears we may weaken as a consequence of events which, as reflected in the foreign press, appear to constitute an internal upheaval."[92]

The disagreements between the tsarist government and the majority in the State Duma worried the Entente powers, and in their desire to conduct the imperialist war successfully they strove to achieve unity between them. At the end of 1916, Buchanan decided to act as mediator between the tsar and the Duma. He first spoke with Rodzianko, who told the English ambassador the State Duma would be satisfied if an individual were appointed chairman of the Council of Ministers who enjoyed the trust of the people and had the power to select other members of the government. After his conversation with Rodzianko, Buchanan approached the tsar. Buchanan recounts in his memoirs that he told the tsar an insurmountable barrier had risen between the tsar and the nation which must be eliminated, that in the event of revolution only a small stratum of soldiers could be relied on to defend the dynasty. Buchanan wrote that at the end of the conversation he allegedly exclaimed: "You have, Sir, come to the parting of the ways, and you have now to choose between two paths. The one will lead to victory and a glorious peace—the other to revolution and disaster. Let me implore your majesty to choose the former. . . . The Emperor was visibly moved by the warmth which I had put into this appeal, and, pressing my hand as he bade me good-bye, said, 'I thank you, Sir George.' "[93] But besides conversations and handshakes, no other results emerged from this meeting.

The imperialists of the Entente wanted to help regulate relations between the tsarist government and the State Duma in the interests of conducting the war more successfully. But did they want to liquidate the Russian autocratic system or at least replace the tsar? Buchanan has been accused of allegedly paving the way for the Russian Revolution, and of influencing the Duma leaders to break with tsarism. The French ambassador Paleologue wrote in his diary on December 28, 1916: "Several times already I have been questioned about Buchanan's dealings with the liberal parties and I have been asked very seriously whether or not he secretly is working on behalf of revolution. Each time I protest with all my might." The same accusations were flung at Buchanan upon his return to England, and he was forced to vindicate himself.[94] There can be no doubt that Buchanan and Paleologue had close ties with the Russian opposition leaders and both were filled with indignation at the behavior of Rasputin and Protopopov. They condemned Aleksandra Fedorovna, criticized the tsarist government, and so forth. But it is highly unlikely that they participated in preparing even a palace coup in Russia. Buchanan wrote in his memoirs: "I had been at one with the Duma leaders in holding that the course of the military operations must not be compromised by any grave internal crisis. . . . I was personally devoted to him [Nicholas II—D.J.R.], and it was the fear of the consequences of a possible palace revolution that made me warn him of the danger in which he stood of assassination."[95]

Whether Russia would continue to participate in the war especially worried the English bourgeoisie. Although admitting the tsar was weak, Buchanan did not doubt his loyalty to the allies and desire to continue the war. On February 5, 1917, the English ambassador telegraphed London: "Though attacks are occasionally made on us in the reactionary gutter press, the anti-British campaign has died out and Anglo-Russian relations were never better than at present. The emperor, most of his ministers and the bulk of the nation are all firm supporters of the Anglo-Russian alliance. The emperor, the supreme factor, is deplorably weak; but the one point on which we can count on his remaining firm is the war, more especially as the empress, who virtually governs Russia, is herself sound on this question."[96] In view of such confidence in the anti-German stand of the tsar and even the tsarina, it was hardly possible to risk a palace coup. Buchanan hoped tsarist Russia would remain in the war if the allies would render her the necessary help.

The plan for future military operations rendered the issue of stepping up military and economic aid to Russia acute in the beginning of 1917. Since peace sentiments were growing, the Allied powers decided to launch a broad offensive on the front as soon as possible in order to defeat Germany in 1917. To this end a conference of the Allied powers, England, France, Italy, and Russia, was held in January and February 1917 in Petrograd. The Petrograd Conference was designed to coordinate their political and military efforts and find ways to guarantee the Russian army with military materiel, which was still in short supply. Lloyd George afterward admitted that it was already too late to raise this issue. Why, he asked, hadn't those responsible for military policy ever met before February 1917 for joint discussions of strategic questions? Lloyd George wrote about the disastrous consequences of "Russian ineptitude and Western selfishness," which were so evident that military leaders in France and England insisted all efforts must be concentrated on the western front to the neglect of the difficulties of their Eastern ally.[97]

The Petrograd Conference decided to spare no efforts or energy in conducting the upcoming campaign so that the allies might achieve a decisive success in 1917. The offensive was planned to begin between April 1 and May 1. The allies promised to extend Russia credits to pay for orders placed abroad and for stimulating foreign loans. They admitted it was necessary to pool their military resources and divide them up as efficaciously as possible, thereby assuring each front a minimum of military supplies in proportion to the number of fighting units and to the extent and scale of upcoming operations. However, it at once became clear that it was impossible to do this. Delivery of cargoes to Russia was difficult because of the shortage of ships, German submarines, the limited capacity of Russian ports, and the poor condition and lack of rolling stock on Russian railroads, etc. Apart from this, "the arrogance of the Western powers" of which Lloyd George wrote also had its effect on the Petrograd Conference. It cut the requests of the Russian military departments in half.

The conference of the Allied powers was unable to influence the course of the war. In his memoirs Paleologue noted that the results of the conference, which was surrounded "simultaneously by so much mystery and sensation—were meagre." Lord Alfred Milner, head of the English delegation, informed the British war minister that the sessions seemed extremely empty and superficial and the entire conference was exceptionally poorly organized. The delegates from the Allied powers understood that tsarism's military efforts depended upon the country's internal situation. They explored the situation in discussions with Russian statesmen, heard conversations censuring the activities of the tsar and tsarina, and were aware of the conflict between the bourgeoisie and the tsar. But the delegates of the Allied powers did not see the people and therefore concluded that there would be no revolution in Russia before the end of the war. In response to the question of whether the Russians had the will to fight, only one delegate, Sir Walter Layton, answered: "No, they are much too busy thinking of the coming revolution."

Emphasizing this fact, Lloyd George wrote: "Having regard to the warnings which were blaring at them in every direction, it is incomprehensible that they should have been so deaf and blind. It is one more proof of the way the most intelligent human judgment has always been misled by the tapestries of an established order without paying sufficient regard to the condition of the walls they hide and on which they hang."[98] Buchanan had a different explanation why the British delegates, after returning to London, issued a reassuring statement about the internal situation in Russia. He wrote: "The session of the conference had synchronized with a temporary improvement in the internal situation, and there had been but few outward or visible signs of political unrest. It is hardly, therefore, to be wondered at that the Allied delegates, on returning to their respective countries, should have expressed themselves somewhat too optimistically with regard to the Russian outlook."[99] Not expecting anything serious to develop, Buchanan himself left Petrograd to vacation in Finland after the conference.

Russian bourgeois statesmen, particularly G. E. L'vov and M. L. Chelnokov, wanted the representatives of the Allied powers to help them apply pressure on the tsar and force him to collaborate with the State Duma and Zemgor in order to carry out essential reforms. Milner promised them that he would inform the tsar that the Union of Zemstvos and Union of Towns had made a favorable impression upon him, but he observed that the Allied delegation had not come to discuss the internal situation in Russia. In a letter of February 4, 1917, Milner assured the tsar that England was ready to do everything it could to support Russia: "She wishes to render her aid as an ally enjoying absolute trust."[100]

Buchanan and Paleologue were aware that the highest strata of Russian society were seriously considering the idea of a palace coup.[101] The conspiracy involved members of the State Duma. Rodzianko wrote: "The notion of forcing the tsar to abdicate was persistently advanced in Petrograd by the end of 1916 and the beginning of 1917. Representatives of the highest society repeatedly came to me from various quarters to say that the Duma and its president for the sake of the country must assume the responsibility of saving the army and Russia."[102] But the president of the State Duma did not take the responsibility, and the grand princes in opposition or the leaders of the bourgeoisie did not wish to do so. Everyone was waiting to see what the other would do. . . . V. A. Maklakov noted that none of the grand princes "dares display the slightest initiative; each wants to work exclusively for himself. They would like the Duma to explode the charge. . . . The result is that they wait for us while we wait for them."[103]

Several groups discussed a palace coup. They were not united, although they were planning similar courses of action. In October 1916, P. N. Miliukov, A. I. Shingarev, N. V. Nekrasov, A. I. Konovalov, Prince G. E. L'vov, M. I. Tereshchenko, S. I. Shidlovskii, and others, fifteen people in all, took part in a conversation. At the meeting the view was expressed that efforts to make the tsar listen to reason were futile, that the existing authorities were in no position to stave off the victory of the street, that the personality of Nicholas II was the source of dissatisfaction in the country, and that it was impossible to keep him on the throne. They took out the law code and started looking for articles that provided for the replacement of one monarch with another; they wanted to set up a regency and to choose a Regency Council; they spoke of who should compose the government. Then a ruling triumvirate of conspirators formed, including Guchkov, Nekrasov, and Tereshchenko.

Contemplating a plan for a palace coup, the organizers proposed to force Nicholas II to abdicate, after which Aleksei would be proclaimed tsar and Mikhail Aleksandrovich [the tsar's brother—D.J.R.] regent. To avoid a savage clash with the tsar's guards, they wanted to seize the royal train en route to Supreme Headquarters and make him abdicate there. Guchkov maintained the conspiracy was complete in all its detail, and they were so certain it would be implemented that they did not bother to consider what steps to take should His Majesty refuse to abdicate.[104] The young prince D. L. Viazemskii, who had joined the conspirators, began approaching guards officers below the rank of regiment commanders. The plotters hesitated to draw the army high command into the conspiracy for fear of provoking civil war, although they did mention several generals who were involved in the conspiracy. Yet this remained rumor and conjecture. One general was certainly implicated in the plot: the commander of the cavalry corps, A. I. Krymov. At the beginning of January 1917, Krymov had a conversation with several members of the Duma gathered at Rodzianko's apartment. The general argued it was impossible to hope for victory with the present government, as everything had been tried and the only alternative was a coup: "If you should decide to take this extreme measure, we shall support you," he declared. "It's obvious there are no other options." Many agreed with Krymov, but no one took any action.[105]

Tereshchenko noted: "The prophetic Duma sirens tried to convince us the hour had not yet struck and those closer to government affairs than we, who they considered hotheads, saw more clearly it was necessary to wait longer. January and the first half of February passed. Finally the sagacious words of experienced politicians ceased to convince us, and in language we had prearranged to communicate among ourselves, General Krymov was summoned to Petrograd from Rumania in early March. However, it turned out to be too late."[106] Talking to staff members of the Commission Investigating the Participants in the Events (the Society to Study the Revolution of 1917), Tereshchenko, relating the plans for a palace coup, noted the leaders of the Progressive Bloc, Miliukov and Shidlovskii, had argued that "serious politicians must not be involved in a coup, and should wait until everything has been settled and then take power. But this idea was impermissible and received no support. We argued that by then it would already be too late to take advantage of what others had accomplished; those who kill a bear will not allow others to skin it, and power could not be given to the common people. We were five in all. We decided a coup should take place immediately and discussed concrete measures to accomplish our task. Since His Majesty had left for headquarters, it was impossible to move directly. Therefore we chose the first days of March for the time of the coup."[107]

The leaders of the Progressive Bloc, Miliukov, Shingarev, and others, were not really very enthusiastic about a palace coup. Miliukov said they were not as interested in a palace coup as in what sort of government would be established after the overthrow and what role the State Duma would play. Wrote Miliukov: "The impending coup from above was not discussed seriously. Everyone expected it, but no one did anything about it. Some members of the Duma were only in agreement about how to act after the tsar was overthrown."[108] And some bourgeois activists were in principle opposed to a palace revolution. Prince P. D. Dolgorukov, a Kadet, wrote that a palace coup was undesirable, even fatal, since the house of Romanov had no one to replace the present tsar and to overthrow the ruler "would not bring conciliation" but, on the contrary, "would actually force us inveterate constitutional monarchists to support a republic." Dolgorukov saw a solution if the tsar would voluntarily form a responsible ministry.[109]

At the end of 1916 and the beginning of 1917 rumors of an impending palace revolution were widely circulated in both capitals and in the provinces. The conspirators probably talked boldly about a coup more than they actually prepared for one, because they wished to frighten the tsar and force concessions from him. Kadet Chelnikov, then mayor of Moscow, said no one was seriously contemplating a palace revolution, but people talked about what a good idea it would be if someone organized one. Kadet Iziumov afterward wrote in disappointment to S. P. Mel'gunov:[y] "A revolutionary mood existed and people talked about it, but no one showed himself to be resolute. The conspiratorial center was little more than salon gossip; people thought they were in the middle of things but the revolution passed them by."[110] On the very eve of the revolution, conditions for a coup were unfavorable, and the Russian bourgeoisie and the Anglo-French alliance were not really anxious to replace the tsar at the moment.

In the beginning of 1917, after the government and the tsar himself had explicitly declared they intended to fight until Germany was completely routed and the Allied states agreed at the Petrograd Conference to cooperate, pro-German sentiments diminished in Russian governmental circles. A palace revolution might arouse forces deleterious to the Russian and foreign imperialists. If the tsarist throne tottered under the circumstances, the result might be directly contrary to what the conspirators wanted. It might lead not to further prosecution of the war and prevent revolution, but to the conclusion of peace

[y] A historian and publicist active in the Popular Socialist party (1879–1956). Apart from writing on a wide variety of topics in Russian history, Mel'gunov collaborated in publishing the newspaper *Russkie vedomosti* (Russian News) and was one of the editors of the journal *Golos minuvshego* (Voice of the Past). Following his emigration in 1923 he authored several works on the Russian Revolution and civil war, which were highly critical of the Bolsheviks. See, for example, *The Bolshevik Seizure of Power* (Santa Barbara, CA, 1972).

and hastening of the revolution. Such apprehension apparently restrained the conspirators in bourgeois and military circles and caused them to waver and act indecisively.

Tereshchenko and Guchkov had designated the middle of March as the time when a coup was supposed to take place. This was not set down or discussed, however, until after the revolution, obviously with the intent to prove they, too, were against the tsar, and that the palace revolution they were planning was some two weeks late.

A. F. Kerensky subsequently argued that a well-timed palace coup in the winter of 1916–17 could have averted revolution, and he lamented that one had not taken place. V. A. Maklakov, on the other hand, believed even a palace revolution would have had trouble saving the dynasty. He wrote that there was no fitting successor to the tsar; those who strove for the throne had no real support.[111] The issue was not the absence of a successor to the tsar: the entire autocratic structure lay in ruins. No palace coup could have saved it.

On the Eve of Revolution

While the talks were underway about replacing the government and even the tsar himself, the Russian economy declined even further. There was not enough bread, fuel, iron, coal, coaches, or locomotives. In February 1917, Rodzianko presented a memorandum to the tsar: "The situation in Russia at present is catastrophic and also most tragic. . . . From all over Russia each piece of news is more cheerless than the next, and more bitter than the other."[112] Lack of fuel, metal, and electricity forced many industrial enterprises to shut down. Metal smelting in the south and Ural region steadily fell off. The disruption in transport left many million poods of coal in the Donbass. The railroads were short of at least eighty thousand cars and two thousand freight locomotives. Transportation plans and schedules to move transport collapsed, rolling stock wore out; broken-down trains were repaired most ineffectively, productivity in wagon-building and engine-building factories fell precipitately and orders remained unfilled. Rodzianko's memorandum spoke of "disorder in the labor market," the low productivity of labor, the total disruption of trade, the government's "senseless" financial policies, the lack of a general economic plan, etc.

The country's food supply continued to deteriorate. The army was supplied with provisions intermittently and in smaller amounts than before. The fronts informed the rear that there was not enough bread, meat, fat, or groats. Soldiers wrote: "We are all hungry." "We have nothing to eat, you could pound nails with the bread." "They feed us badly, it's a wonder we don't die." "They serve us food fit for fast days and rotten fish." "There's nothing to eat, they cook porridge dogs wouldn't even eat." "The food is terrible; we get fed only once a day." It was even more difficult to provide food to the civilian population. Because government agencies were unequal to the task, public organizations tried to take charge of food supplies. A Central Committee of Public Organizations to Deal with Food Supplies *(Tsentral'nyi komitet obshchestvennykh organizatsii po prodovol'stvennomu delu)* existed, which included representatives from zemstvos, war industries committees, and other public organizations. However, the tsarist authorities did not wish to surrender altogether to these organizations the task of supplying food. A proposal to entrust the supplying of food to the military authorities or the Ministry of Internal Affairs was rejected. It remained in the hands of the Ministry of Agriculture.

The tsarist authorities resorted to emergency measures to fulfill the state plan for food procurement. They instituted mandatory grain deliveries to the state at fixed prices and apportioned mandatory procurements by province. The allotment, proving excessive, was scaled back, but even so was not fulfilled. The tsarist authorities were compelled to ration sugar, bread, and other products in a number of cities. Yet even these measures did not improve the situation, as the transportation system could not cope with grain shipments. The food supplied in January 1917 to Petrograd was only half of what had been ordered. The shortages fanned speculation. Obtaining large profits, landowners, merchants, and dealers raised food prices while the mass of the working people starved. Long lines formed in front of bread shops and bakeries, and threatening signs appeared on the doors of many of them: "There is no bread today, nor will there be." The food situation in Petrograd and in the entire country deteriorated unabatedly. In Moscow they wrote that famine was imminent: "This probably will be the straw that breaks the camel's back." The food crisis also reached remote outlying districts. Khabarovsk, Chita, the Ural region, and other places reported lack of flour, sugar, meat, kerosene—"in a word, there was only hunger, cold, and despair."[113]

The worsening economic situation in the country, and above all else the exacerbation of the food supply crisis, intensified antigovernment feelings. Indignation at the policies of tsarism seized all strata of the population, assuming a national character. Practically every police report now mentioned the First Russian Revolution and compared it with the present situation. One report stressed that the developing situation was reminiscent of "the situation that preceded the revolutionary excesses of 1905." Others maintained that the mood of the population was even more strained and more revolutionary than then. The head of the Moscow secret police in October 1916 reported:

> Such phrases as acute irritation, extreme bitterness, indignation, etc., fail to reflect the reality. We are sure we have not had to cope with similar unrest and animosity. In comparison with the present mood, that of 1905–1906 without doubt was more favorable for the government. Back then, bitter hatred of the government was felt by a comparatively narrow circle, the working class, part of the peasantry, and part of the intelligentsia; now almost all of society is being united in irreconcilable condemnation of the government. . . . The masses' irritation and animosity is so great that they are no longer shy in expressing their feelings to the government and to the supreme authorities. . . . The entire

> responsibility now falls on the government, in the person of the Council of Ministers, and also on the tsar himself. Even extreme conclusions are being drawn.[114]

The summary report of the Department of Police in that same month noted that the greatest irritation and animosity were observed in the capitals. A comparison of the mood of the population of Petrograd and Moscow between the present and the 1905–1906 period showed that "now opposition feeling has reached such exceptional levels, far above what it was among the broad masses in the troubled period mentioned."[115] Police authorities reported that the population of the capital experienced growing animosity toward the government, the tsar, and the royal family, and everyone expected something exceptional to happen. No one was afraid any longer and people were openly criticizing the authorities on the streets, on streetcars, in theaters, and in shops.

Analogous sentiments not only infected the population in the capitals, but in varying degrees were typical of inhabitants of other regions of Russia. The head of the Kazan gendarmerie on January 8, 1917, wrote:

> The mood of society in Kazan is excitable. The overwhelming majority of society is aroused against the government; no one takes pains to hide it, they speak about it quite openly. They condemn the new course taken by the government, they say that it is a step back; what was possible earlier is now unacceptable.[116]

The Saratov Governor S. D. Tverskoi wrote in a private letter:

> What is happening? It is not yet eleven years since the year 1905. Yet once again, there's the same individuals, the same words on one side and the same paralysis of the authorities on the other. Once again, zemstvo activists from the nobility are taking up politics in the provinces. Once again, there are ringing resolutions about the hated government, etc. And what will come of all of this? In the future the unlettered muzhik once again will have the say and will have his way. The situation is utterly disgusting.

The Governor of Tula, A. Troinitskii, reported:

> Such terrible times have set in that I don't know how to cope. It's very bad with food supplies; nothing is being brought in, there are lines everywhere. . . . I am sitting on a powder keg.[117]

Appeals to struggle against the war and tsarism were heard not only in the center of the country. In the settlement of Shostka in Chernigov province printed leaflets were disseminated, the text of which read:

> Comrades, it's high time to end the war with the Germans and to begin to fight our real enemy—tsarism and the government. . . . We shall show the police we have not forgotten 1905. Send the police to the front; that's where they belong.

> Get ready, brothers, come to an agreement, advise each other, and when you have to, stand up and be counted. Rise up, raise yourself up, working people! Rise up and struggle, hungry people. Forward, forward![118]

Leaflets were posted throughout the town of Murom in Vladimir province that read:

> Free citizens of the town of Murom! Are you going to put up with the government's injustice much longer? The whims of the sovereign make the people and the fatherland endure disaster. Let us rise up in rebellion, brothers, against the sovereign and the government and hoist the red flag of people's freedom. Let's get to work immediately.[119]

The bourgeois-landowner opposition also contributed to the general dissatisfaction. Although not exceeding the limits of the existing system, its actions unmasked tsarism and furthered its isolation. The speeches of the bourgeoisie were made legally and provoked considerable attention, creating an impression that the clash between tsarism and the bourgeoisie was the most important phase in the developing struggle. The tsarist government itself did not clearly understand the source of the main danger. Tsarism exaggerated the opposition of the Russian bourgeoisie and the threat it presented: "There is no beast stronger than a cat." This phrase turned up specifically in police reports in the period immediately preceding the revolution. One can agree with Kadet N. I. Astrov that involvement of bourgeois public organizations in the country's political life was unusual for the tsarist authorities, and therefore the police and its political department kept a close eye on the Unions [Union of Towns and Union of Zemstvos—D.J.R.] and reported on them factually and fancifully. For example, the police accused the Union of Towns of trying to take advantage of the difficulties facing the tsarist government in order to overthrow the autocracy. But as a matter of fact what the Union of Towns wanted was to save tsarism, prevent possible catastrophe, and "influence as much as possible the developing spontaneous protest, prevent it if possible, and not let it develop into anarchy and a senseless, merciless brawl."[120]

The court camarilla considered the leaders of the Duma opposition their deadly enemies. In a letter to the tsar, Aleksandra Fedorovna wrote that "the loathsome Rodzianko and those other creatures" requested the convocation of the Duma, but the thing to do is dismiss them. They chatter too much. She demanded the tsar threaten the bourgeois leaders and put them in their place. Still, this was not enough for her. "Oh, if only it were possible to hang Guchkov!" dreamed the empress in September 1915. Aleksandra Fedorovna's suggestion became even more concrete at the end of 1916. "Dismiss the Duma this minute . . . ," she wrote Nicholas II on December 14 of that year. "Calmly and with a clear conscience before all Russia I would send L'vov to Siberia (as was done for far less serious misdemeanors), I would remove Samarin from office . . . Miliukov, Guchkov, and Polivanov[z]: off to Siberia with them, too."[121] Analogous demands were also heard from the camp of the extreme right.

The tsarist government, however, did not move in this direction. It did not employ the police to repress the bourgeois leaders as it did in its dealings with worker revolutionaries. The authorities did no more than dismiss the State Duma, town and zemstvo congresses, and other organizations. Both sides—tsarism and the bourgeois-landowner opposition—were opposed to each other, yet they could not bring themselves to break the bonds uniting them and embark upon a course of irreconcilable struggle.

This was not the main arena of struggle. The working class and the masses of working people marching behind it led the revolutionary war against tsarism. The revolutionary mole had burrowed underground and its activity was not always visible on the surface. Driven underground, the revolutionary movement dug its way to the surface in the form of massive workers' strikes. Bourgeois leaders often attributed workers' disturbances to the provocative activities of pro-German elements who strove to disorganize the rear and provoke internal disorder in Russia. Bourgeois circles were largely of the opinion that Protopopov wanted to provoke the workers to come out so that he could drown their disturbances in blood, consolidate his power, and, alleging the difficult internal situation in the country, make peace with Germany. In fact, Protopopov, like the entire tsarist government, was doing all he could to prevent workers from becoming active.

Many petit bourgeois activists who considered themselves close to the proletariat likewise failed to notice the growth of the revolutionary workers' movement. S. Postnikov, an SR who worked at this time in the Union of Towns, wrote:

> It was possible to observe how comparatively weak the workers' political movement was. It more often promoted economic demands during strikes, whereas other classes and strata of Russian society such as the prominent bourgeoisie, zemstvo and town activists, the high military command, and even people in court circles conducted a persistent and systematic struggle against the tsarist government. All these groups, the best organized and politically well informed, understood and realized the tsarist regime would not survive the war and would lead the country to ruin.[122]

It was actually the proletariat, not the bourgeoisie, that led the most sustained and systematic struggle against the tsarist government. The local organs of tsarism saw the main sources of danger to the autocracy. The head of the

[z] A. D. Samarin was procurator of the Holy Synod. In the summer of 1915 he and other members of the cabinet protested Nicholas II's decision to assume personal command of the army. He was dismissed in October. General A. A. Polivanov, who had replaced V. A. Sukhomlinov as minister of war in 1915, was dismissed in March 1916 for refusing to deal with Rasputin and for his willingness to enlist the Duma's support to revitalize the army.

Perm Provincial Gendarmerie wrote: "The most important centers in the province where workers' disturbances may be expected are the Lysvenskii Factory and the Motovilikh and Verkhne-Isetskii factories."[123] On January 29 Governor Kreiton of Vladimir province reported to the Council of Ministers: "Animosity in several regions, especially where there are factories, is palpable. The strike movement at the factories has assumed an unyielding character and has made factory owners unusually nervous. Manufacturers from Orekhov and Ivanovo are almost in a panic over their fate and that of their enterprises."[124]

The tsarist government readied forces to suppress possible popular disturbances. It relied above all on the police and therefore strengthened them. In the fall of 1916 measures were adopted to increase the number of secret police agents, substitute mounted constables for unmounted police, increase the strength of the police, and raise salaries. Governors were instructed to bring the guards up to full strength and station them appropriately. It was recommended that police officers should be formed into detachments and placed in the more important centers of the province, especially where workers were concentrated. The police, however, were inadequate to suppress large-scale popular disturbances. The tsarist authorities were intending to use the army for this purpose.

Meanwhile, the army had become a less reliable prop for the autocracy. The same sharp dissatisfaction with the war and tsarism had affected reserve units of recently mobilized, poorly trained and inadequately armed recruits, just as it had the mass of the civilian population. In February 1917 the head of the Perm Provincial Gendarmerie reported to the Department of the Police that a rather large number of reserve infantry regiments were stationed in the most important centers of the Ural region. But he added: "The number of reserve regiments does not indicate how many bayonets are available to suppress risings. Each of these regiments contains much raw, untrained material, unfit to put down disorders, and in addition, they have few rifles and cartridges."[125]

The revolutionary proletariat gathered and organized its forces in all the large centers in the country. The Bolsheviks of the Ural region, Donbass, Nizhnii Novgorod, Tula, Kharkov, Kiev, Ekaterinoslav, Baku, and other regions of Russia were conducting their revolutionary activity under difficult wartime conditions. Reestablishing an all-Russian organization, the Russian Bureau of the Central Committee of the RSDRP set up ties with the provinces. In January 1917 it began to publish "Informational Sheets" that provided information on the activities of local Bolshevik organizations.

The Moscow Bolsheviks carried on extensive revolutionary work. There were many provocations and failure followed failure; no sooner had the Moscow Committee of the RSDRP organized than its entire membership ended up behind bars. But party work continued in Moscow almost without interruption. Underground factory circles were set up, printed and lithographed leaflets and proclamations to workers and soldiers were issued, and literature was distributed. Students were drawn into the revolutionary struggle. In the cafeteria of the Commercial Institute, meetings, talks, reports, and discussions on political themes were organized in which workers and students took part. It was a center for conspiratorial activity and for disseminating illegal literature. In the fall of 1916 an Oblast Bureau of the Central Committee of the RSDRP was formed, which included such leading activists of the Bolshevik party as M. S. Ol'minskii, I. I. Skvortsov (Stepanov), V. P. Nogin, M. Savel'ev, V. P. Miliutin, and others. The legal journal *Golos pechatnogo truda* (Voice of the Printing Trade) began to appear in November of the same year under Ol'minskii's editorship. Close ties were established between the Bolsheviks of Petrograd and Moscow. An employee of the Petrograd secret police reported that representatives of the Moscow Bolshevik Organization had arrived in Petrograd to make contact: "They reported that the mood in Moscow was aroused to the extent that an armed uprising is conceivable. Strong ties have been forged with all industrial enterprises, and this makes a mass strike possible. Workers are only waiting for the signal to conduct a general uprising."[126]

The revolutionary crisis that gripped the entire country was most critical in Petrograd. It was here above all that the main forces of both warring camps were concentrated and where the decisive battle between them was unfolding. The eyes of the entire nation were focused on the Petrograd proletariat. Workers in other cities placed their hopes on them to move; they waited for them to give the signal for a general assault on tsarism. The tsarist secret police reported the Petrograd proletariat was ready to do battle with the autocracy and to use its well-tried methods of the strike in this engagement. "The idea of a general strike is gaining new adherents from day to day and is becoming popular as in the year 1905. . . . The masses of workers have again realized that a general strike is necessary and feasible and will result in revolution."[127]

The Bolsheviks led the revolutionary struggle of the Petrograd proletariat. Despite the difficulty of the wartime situation, frequent arrests, provocations, lack of technical equipment, etc., the Petersburg and almost all the neighborhood committees of the RSDRP continued their activity.

Representatives of other Social Democratic groups were drawn to the Bolshevik organization. On February 11, Shliapnikov wrote to members of the Central Committee of the RSDRP abroad: "Here and there in Petrograd and in the provinces Menshevik 'unifiers' and others who had broken away are again entering the party. We welcome such a mobilization of proletarian forces." "The centrist In[itiative] Gr[oup] and the 'Unit[ed]' Interdistrictites are negotiating to create a general organization. We are suggesting they enter our ranks."[128]

As the revolutionary crisis deepened the Socialist Revolutionaries also strove to intensify their activities. Their organizations in Russia had literally ceased to exist during the war. A leaflet of the SR Initiative Group "written in February 1917 noted 'there is no party. . . . It has collapsed and degenerated into small uncoordinated weak groups, cells, that are practically helpless, powerless, and lacking theoretical and moral authority.'" The appeal called upon activists young and old to reunify the party, help the illegal press, and prepare for an all-Russian party congress. "Don't you feel how all gigantic Russia is waking from its slumber as the storm approaches? Don't you hear the call to go forth?" The Initiative Group of Socialist Revolutionaries called for a rising against the imperialist war and for a struggle with the tsarist autocracy to make Russia a genuine democracy, socialize the land, and institute the eight-hour day. It greeted the "energetic and indefatigable activity, which our friendly competitors in the Marxist camp are displaying," and it proposed to revive the SR party and coordinate its activities with those of the Social Democrats.[129] In an appeal, also issued in February, the Moscow Organizational Group of Socialist Revolutionaries called for a declaration of war against the oppressors of the people: "Only a National Constituent Assembly," it wrote, "can deliver Russia from the blind alley down which the government has led it with the tacit agreement of the State Duma. . . . Set up revolutionary organizations and conduct revolutionary propaganda among the proletariat, peasantry, and soldiers."[130]

The strike that took place on the traditional date of January 9, 1917, was an important step along the road to revolution. The Petersburg Bolshevik Committee urged workers to commemorate that day with a political strike and mass meetings, which must explain the "aim of this political strike and must state the need to intensify the revolutionary struggle now." It proposed to conduct the January 9th strike under the slogans "Down with the tsarist monarchy!" and "Down with the war!" Preparations for January 9, 1917, were undertaken in all neighborhoods of Petrograd. A meeting of the Vyborg District Committee of the RSDRP on December 18, 1916, explained that economic conflicts were breaking out in the factories, that funds were being collected to aid the arrested comrades, and that many groups were getting ready to come out on January 9. "The general mood of indignation is growing."[131]

The tsarist authorities decided to spare no efforts to break the workers' strike on January 9. They engaged in their typical "diversionary tactics," arresting many active Bolsheviks, including the entire membership of the Petersburg Committee of the RSDRP at that time. Police seized the Bolshevik underground printing press, and Bolshevik attempts to use a legal press met with no success. Among the Petrograd Bolshevik organizations only the Vyborg District and Latvian committees succeeded in issuing proclamations for January 9. Despite this, preparations to come out on that day continued. Between January 5 and 7 political mass meetings and assemblies took place in factories in the Vyborg District, at the Putilov and Obukhov plants, and in the Moscow and Petrograd districts. Appeals to strike on "Bloody Sunday" rang out at these meetings.

Other Social Democratic organizations also shared in the preparations for January 9, 1917. The Interdistrict Committee of the RSDRP issued an appeal for January 9, in which it exposed the policies of tsarism and the bourgeoisie and their accomplices in the Workers' Group of the War Industries Committee. In calling all to support the imperialist war and cooperate with the bourgeoisie, the Gvozdevites, it said, were betraying the cause of the working class. The Interdistrictites urged workers: "Let us remember that our proletarian tasks are not yet resolved, and that the demands inscribed on our banners on January 9, 1905, are still unmet."[132] On the day set aside to review the forces of the organized proletariat, the Interdistrictites advanced slogans to struggle against the autocracy and the war, to achieve the victory of the revolution, to create a provisional government, and to establish a democratic republic.

A leaflet of the Initiative Group of Menshevik Social Democrats issued in honor of January 9 also urged workers to mark that day with a strike and mass meetings. It noted that the tsarist monarchy stood in the way of the peace the people desired; however, it had no answer to the question of how to overthrow the monarchy and how to deal with the bourgeoisie. The Menshevik leaflet avoided major problems in the struggle of the people that was developing.

The workers' movement assumed such a dimension that even the Workers' Group in the Central War Industries Committee could not stand aside. The Workers' Group earlier had opposed strikes, believing they undermined the country's military efforts, but now, pressured by the mass of workers, it supported the strike. The Workers' Group wanted to use January 9 not to strengthen the revolutionary struggle of the proletariat but to make it an adjunct of bourgeois liberalism: it took the view that the activity on this day would arouse the bourgeoisie and unify all progressive forces around the State Duma.[133]

But the actions of the workers of Petrograd were not at all directed toward that goal. January 9, 1917, constituted an important revolutionary event. The strike that broke out involved the majority of Petersburg workers, and its dimensions surpassed all the strikes that had occurred during the years of war, including the powerful strike of October 1916. An Information Sheet of the Bureau of the Central Committee of the RSDRP reported: "All party cells conducted agitation in favor of the strike, and the strike this year was distinguished for the large number of participants. The Putilov and Obukhov works went out on strike, and so did the St. Petersburg Arsenal, which had not known a strike since 1905. The strike reached the following levels by neighborhood: Vyborg—general; Nevskii—general; City—the majority; Vasilevskii Island—weak; Petersburg side—the majority. The strike involved 300,000 workers."[134]

The activities of January 9, 1917, were not limited to strikes. Mass meetings took place at factories on the Vyborg side where speakers called for the overthrow of tsarism and an end to the war. Workers left the mass meetings singing revolutionary songs and here and there displaying red flags. Workers in individual workshops of the Putilov Plant spent the day not in working but in organizing demonstrations with red flags. A speaker made a speech in the street; the demonstration was broken up by mounted police. A letter of the Executive Committee of the Petersburg Committee to the Bureau of the

Central Committee of the RSDRP noted that January 9, 1917, "was an index of how tremendous the revolutionary consciousness and activity of the Petrograd proletariat had grown during the past year."[135]

The Petrograd political police felt sure that the strike of January 9 had not justified the hopes of the Petrograd proletariat, that the Bolsheviks had intended that energetic and militant demonstrations should accompany the activities of January 9, and that the strike was peaceful and orderly. The Okhranka reported that revolutionary organizations had given the signal for the strike, but the arrest of the Petersburg Committee of the RSDRP and of many other party workers had deprived the strike "of a unifying ruling center" and resulted in a "peaceful" strike. Of course, the presence of a center that could unify and lead would have caused events to assume a more active, militant, and purposeful character, but the strike was not as peaceful as the police described. Clashes occurred. "Order was broken": workers went out on strike and did so carrying red banners and Bolshevik slogans.

The Okhranka was compelled to admit that the number of strikers compared with January 9, 1916, had increased, and that the growth resulted both from a rise of the total number of workers and because the masses had moved to the left. "Many things caused this. A scarcity and rise in the price of basic commodities, war-weariness, rumors that excited the population, etc., and the habit of the working people to take part in strikes on 'special' days."[136]

The Workers' Group of the War Industries Committee interpreted the events of January 9, 1917, in its own way. Recognizing that memories of January 9 had acquired special poignancy, it wrote that organized workers' circles strove to take advantage of the strikes and meetings that took place that day in order to support the bourgeois opposition and demand immediate convocation of the State Duma. But in fact, workers did not advance such demands. Few of them thought about the State Duma on January 9: the strike had taken place under revolutionary slogans and greatly furthered the struggle against the war and tsarism. A letter of the Executive Committee of the Petersburg Committee of the RSDRP pointed out that the January strike of 1917 had surpassed all strike activity during the war years and raised the spirit of the masses considerably: "The mood at the factories is very spirited and politically conscious and opens the way to broad revolutionary possibilities."[137]

Impressive action on the part of workers also took place in Moscow on January 9, 1917. After numerous failures, the Bolshevik organization in Moscow partially regrouped its forces and carried on preparations for January 9. At a gathering of district representatives, which occurred a week earlier, it became clear that the working masses were ready to take to the streets whenever the Bolsheviks summoned them. It was a time when, as participants in the events asserted, everything was in ferment and "there was discontent in abundance, the masses of people were deeply enraged, everyone was confident that we were witnessing the birth and growth of a revolution."[138]

A proclamation of the Moscow Committee of the RSDRP, dedicated to that date, began with the words: "The tsarist crime of January 9–10, 1905, lives on; workers have not forgotten it. . . . And now in the days of endless war it is even more important than before that the proletariat should demonstrate on January 9." The proclamation declared only revolutionary action by the working class would end the war and all violence. "It is necessary to wrest power from the tsarist government and transfer it to a government created by the revolution in order to conclude that peace and establish that political order workers need. Workers of all countries must struggle for a democratic republic and an end to the war. We call Moscow workers to a general strike on January 9. Comrades, stop your work all at once and take to the streets! Raise your heads. Defend those dying at the front! Defend yourselves! Show that the revolutionary force of the proletariat is alive and the red banner of the working class has not been rent."[139]

The workers of Moscow responded to this appeal. The Okhranka estimated the strike of January 9, 1917, involved forty-one enterprises and more than twenty-eight thousand workers.[140] Compared to the total number of Moscow workers this figure was insignificant. To compensate for this, the strikers acted vigorously. Many went out into the city streets, demonstrated with red flags, and sang revolutionary songs. The demonstration in the center of Moscow took place somewhat earlier than had been intended.

An Information Sheet of the Bureau of the Central Committee of the RSDRP reported:

> About one o'clock in the afternoon at the instance of the Moscow Committee 2,000 to 3,000 workers gathered on Tverskoi Boulevard, among whom were probably some three dozen students. The police who had assembled earlier made a demonstration impossible. Arrests began when the demonstrators attempted to break into song. Mounted police appeared. The comrades headed in small groups to Theater Square. By two o'clock a crowd of workers and a few students formed on Theater Square. They began singing "Let us renounce the old world" and, holding a red banner on which was written "Down with the war," "Long live the Russian Social Democratic party," they proceeded from Neglinnaia Street halfway up Okhotnyi Row and back again.[141]

At Neglinnaia Thoroughfare they clashed with police and armed gendarmes. Cossacks and gendarmes cordoned off Theater Square and beat and arrested the participants in the demonstration. This was the first time during the war that a red banner was raised on the streets of Moscow. The same day demonstrations occurred on Elokhovskaia and Nemetskaia streets, beyond Presnaia, on Lubianskaia Square, at the Red Gate, and in other parts of the city.

On January 9, 1917, Bolshevik organizations in many Russian towns called on working people to fight tsarism. Proclamations and leaflets issued by these organizations in honor of January 9 were permeated with staunch confidence that the Second Russian Revolution was at hand. A leaflet of the Tver Organization of the RSDRP stated: "Only revolution can end the war, only at the barricades shall we win our rights, overthrow the autocracy, and save ourselves from starvation. Organize yourselves, comrades! Get ready for civil war!" The Ekaterinoslav Committee of the RSDRP wrote in its proclamation: "Isn't it time to mention the year 1905 in the proper spirit? Who besides workers can stop the production of cannon and shells and end the carnage? Who else can raise high the glorious banner of the Russian Revolution? The final denouement is near, as is the final judgment on the perpetrators of the greatest crime in history against mankind. . . . There have been enough victims for the glory of Capital. Our common enemy is behind our backs."[142]

In late 1916 and early 1917 the revolutionary proletariat of Russia fought in the vanguard against the autocracy. The hour of the decisive engagement was now at hand. The revolutionary crisis enveloping the entire country and all elements in the population was now acute.

How was this crisis transformed into an uprising and revolution?

TWO

The Beginning of the Insurrection

> And the muscular arm of millions of working people shall raise itself, and the yoke of despotism, though protected by soldiers' bayonets, shall be smashed to pieces.
>
> From the speech of a weaver, Petr Alekseev, before a tsarist court in 1877.

From Strikes to Insurrection

The proletariat entered the Second Russian Revolution guided by the experience of the glorious year 1905. Tapping this experience, it realized it was first necessary to strengthen the militant revolutionary workers' party and, under its leadership, to organize and direct the growing revolutionary movement toward the desired goal. In spite of the difficult conditions during the war, the Bolsheviks' efforts scored genuine successes.

On February 11, 1917, A. G. Shliapnikov reported to the Central Committee of the RSDRP abroad:

> Our organizational affairs are adequate, but they could be far better if only we had more people. At the present we're successfully organizing the South and the Volga and Ural regions. A Moscow Regional Bureau has been set up. We are awaiting news from the Caucasus. They are demanding people and literature. To produce more [literature] inside Russia is the immediate task of the Central Committee Bureau. We have been able to pick up good, stable, capable cadres. Compared with the other parties our situation is fine. One can say we have the only national organization at the present.[1]

Nonetheless, the organization of the revolutionary movement lagged behind spontaneous developments. Local reports presented at a meeting of the Petersburg Committee of the RSDRP on January 15, 1917, made it clear that harsh repression had created difficulties for the Bolshevik organization in the capital. In explaining their causes, a representative of the Executive Commission of the Petersburg Committee announced that its work "was especially difficult and arrests were constant." The Petersburg Committee decided to appeal to factory and district Bolshevik organizations to intensify local work, particularly to acquire their own printing equipment.[2]

New members A. K. Skorokhodov and I. D. Chugurin were brought into the Petersburg Committee's Executive Committee. They were worker activists who had inseparably linked their fate to the party. Skorokhodov had become a Bolshevik in 1912. After enduring exile to Vologodsk and working at the Naval Factory in Nikolaevsk, he established himself at the small factory Deka on the Petrograd side, led party circles, chaired illegal gatherings, and forged ties with soldiers. Ivan Chugurin was originally a worker from Sormovo. The Bolshevik organization sent him abroad to the small town of Longjumeau in France where he studied at the party school headed by Lenin. The tsarist authorities arrested Chugurin at the border and exiled him to Naryma. He escaped, however, and in 1916 arrived in Petrograd where he worked in the Promet and Aivaz factories on the Vyborg side, actively participated in the party organization in this region, and represented it in the Petersburg Committee of the RSDRP.

The spontaneity of the developing movement posed the threat that the revolutionary forces might be dissipated and routed during premature skirmishes. A leaflet put out in January 1917 by the Vyborg District Committee of the RSDRP noted that each day the people's anger was growing stronger and might explode at any moment.

> But, reluctantly we must not get involved in individual actions since we must husband our forces. We are going to strengthen our old cells and create new ones. Comrade workers, form circles in your plants and factories, make close contact with your collectives of propagandists and factory and plant committees right up to the very center, and prepare for a general offensive. Time does not wait, events are unfolding at incredible speed and insistently demand our cooperation, pooling of forces, and common tactics.[3]

The leaflet urged workers to struggle for peace, bread, and freedom.

The Bolsheviks planned a mass political strike. At a meeting of workers of the metal workshop in the Kharkov plant Helferikh-Sade on January 25, 1917, a worker, Vakulenko, read aloud a letter from Petrograd, which mentioned that "now is not the time for economic strikes; these strikes will not give the working class anything. The thing to do is to organize a general political strike in order to achieve a better life. There are indications that such a strike may occur at the end of February of this year." On February 9 a mass meeting of workers from various enterprises assembled near the square by this very factory. Speakers at the meeting called for a general strike, demanded an end to the war, and declared the State Duma was deceiving the people. Shouts of approval from those assembled interrupted the speeches.[4]

The Revolution of 1905 had given workers extensive experience in utilizing diverse tactics. Preparing for a new revolution, the proletariat relied on this experience, yet new conditions also had to be taken into account. The proletariat could not organize a national railroad strike similar to the one of 1905. To halt rail communications during such a serious food supply crisis would doom the urban population and the army to hunger and disorganize the workers themselves. Massive political strikes in plants and factories in the city remained one of the proletariat's most important tactical means of struggle. The political strike was the chief means to draw the masses of the working class into the struggle, and it also awakened other elements in the working people and brought them to the critical phase of the revolution—armed insurrection. As before, the people's victory over tsarism would be impossible until they reached this stage. The imperialist world war caused the proletariat to do so by other routes than in 1905: a strike became an uprising during the Second Russian Revolution in an entirely different way. After January 9, 1905, the Bolshevik party had organized workers into armed guards, procured weapons for them, and trained them for military action. These workers' guards also provoked armed uprisings against tsarism in December 1905. Even then the proletariat had tried to win over tsarist troops to its side to make the revolution victorious, but armed detachments of workers were the main striking force of the revolutionary army.

Matters turned out otherwise on the eve of the February Revolution. The armed forces of tsarism were immeasurably stronger than in 1905. By the end of the Russo-Japanese War millions of Russian soldiers were concentrated in the Far East; during World War I, fifteen million men were mobilized. In 1905 the war was waged in a remote outlying area; now military operations unfolded close to the country's vital centers. Numerous garrisons were located in all the large cities, especially in Petrograd. Statistics of the Military Commission of the State Duma showed that during the revolution more than 170,000 soldiers were billeted in Petrograd, 152,000 in the environs as far as Luga and Novgorod, totaling 322,000 in the capital and the surrounding area, which was more than two and a half times greater than in peacetime.[5] There were fourteen reserve battalions whose guards regiments were at the front and other infantry, cavalry, and special units in which many workers from Petrograd itself served. Bolshevik organizations had ties with military units and exerted considerable influence over the soldiers.

The imperialist war prevented the proletariat from creating its own armed guards or detachments capable of resisting tsarist troops. To win over the soldier masses to the side of the people was therefore more urgent than it had been during the First Russian Revolution. Tsarism had mobilized millions of workers and peasants into the army. The revolutionary proletariat had to turn its weapons against tsarism itself. It was necessary to bring the troops over to the side of the workers, and then to act jointly to ensure the revolution's victory. Some party workers suggested obtaining arms and organizing armed workers' guards. Shliapnikov wrote that the Bureau of the Central Committee of the RSDRP had rejected these proposals. "And I deliberately voted down all requests to procure and acquire weapons, urging those who desperately wanted them to get them 'from acquaintances' in the barracks. We harbored no delusion that our arms could compete with military units, and combined our understandable longing for arms with the tactical need for ties between workers and the barracks. We encouraged extensive contacts with troops and fraternization with soldiers at street meetings, etc."[6]

Street demonstrations now became the most important of all the forms of the working class's struggle. Strikes almost never brought workers in contact with the armed forces of tsarism, but street demonstrations gave workers the opportunity to appeal to the troops and draw them into the revolution because tsarism used soldiers to suppress the disturbances. The mass of the workers could not be armed, and armed guards could not be organized, until after such street clashes turned into battles that would arouse soldiers to come over to the side of the revolution. In sum, a general strike and street demonstrations were essential preliminaries to an armed uprising.

The émigré party center that Lenin led saw that events were approaching this decisive stage. However, the news from Russia received in far-away Switzerland was meager. Regular contact had broken down and reports on the workers' movement and the activities of local organizations came irregularly. It was difficult to obtain any clear idea about what was taking place in Russia from the bourgeois press. Despite this, Lenin correctly assessed the situation in the country and was convinced revolution was at hand in Russia. In January 1917 Lenin delivered an address on the twelfth anniversary of the First Russian Revolution to a meeting of Swiss working-class youth. He said that the new revolution in Russia would be the prologue to the coming European revolution. "Ilich did not doubt for a moment," observed N. K. Krupskaia, "that such prospects existed. Of course, though, he had no way of knowing how soon the approaching revolution would arrive. 'We older men perhaps will not live to see the decisive battles in this coming revolution,' he said with resigned sadness in a concluding remark, but Ilich thought only about the coming revolution and worked for it."[7] Exactly at this time, January 31, 1917, number 58 of *Sotsial-Demokrat* appeared, in which Lenin wrote that it was impossible to predict exactly when the revolution would break out and how great its chances were for success. "The revolutionary situation in Europe is a fact. The extreme discontent, the unrest and anger of the masses are facts. It is on strengthening *this* torrent that revolutionary Social-Democrats must concentrate all their efforts."[8]

The conscious proletariat of Russia directed all its thoughts and actions to utilizing the developing revolutionary situation to overthrow the existing order. Lenin heard that the revolutionary struggle of the working people of Russia was expanding unabatedly. On February 6 (19), 1917, he wrote Inessa Armand:[a]

[a] Inessa Armand (1874–1920), an active member of the Bolshevik party and of the international communist movement. Armand was born in Paris, but after her father died she was raised in Moscow in the home of the manufacturers Armand. She participated in the Revolution of 1905, was arrested and exiled (often), and collaborated with Lenin at his party school in Longjumeau. Lenin's letters to Armand, published in his *Collected Works* (5th edition, vols. 48–49), have spawned speculation as to the true nature of his relationship to her.

"The other day we had a gratifying letter from Moscow. . . . They write that the mood of the masses is a good one, that chauvinism is clearly declining and that probably our day will come. The organization, they say, is suffering from the fact that the adults are at the front, while in the factories there are young people and women. But the fighting spirit, they say, is not any the less."[9]

That day Krupskaia wrote to S. Kasparov:[b]

> You'll have to get to Russia right away or else you won't get in on "the beginning." In all seriousness, the letters from Russia are filled with good news. Just yesterday one came from an old friend, a highly experienced person, who wrote: "The difficult period apparently is passing, a turn for the better can be seen in the mood of the workers and educated young people. Organization is poor because all the adults are either at the front or subject to call-up. The influx of women and adolescents into the work force is lowering organizational capacity but not the mood. Even so the organizations are growing. Despite arrests, they are functioning quite well in the Volga region and southern Russia. As regards Petrograd, of course, as you know, the influence of the chauvinists is quickly weakening. I wish you good cheer. Our day is coming soon. . . ." They also sent a leaflet from the Bureau of the Central Committee; it's fine.[10]

Leading the workers toward revolution, the Bolsheviks resolutely struggled against attempts by Menshevik defensists to have the proletariat compromise with the bourgeoisie. At the end of February 1917, during the growing revolutionary crisis, the Workers' Group of the War Industries Committee launched a campaign "for the democratization of the country." Workers in several enterprises in the capital passed a resolution this group had devised. It made two demands: 1) the immediate and decisive transformation of the existing order, and the organization "of a government to save the country" supported by the people, the Duma, and all existing workers' and democratic organizations; 2) the immediate declaration of general and complete amnesty, especially the release of the exiled Social Democrat deputies of the Second and Fourth state dumas and restoration of their rights. The Menshevik defensists believed that it was the bourgeoisie that must lead the struggle to democratize the country's political system. As before, they conceived that the working class's task was to put pressure on the bourgeoisie and arouse it to take the initiative.

Even after the workers' strikes in October 1916 and January 1917, the Menshevik defensists continued to maintain that the "conflict between the propertied classes and the government" was the decisive factor in the country's political life. The Workers' Group of the War Industries Committee called upon the proletariat to become involved in this conflict and to force bourgeois activists to struggle against the tsarist authorities. It declared that the proper-

[b] S. Kasparov probably is V. M. Kasparov (pseudonym of M. Kaspar'iants) (1884–1917), a Bolshevik active in the Baku, St. Petersburg, and Rostov committees of the RSDRP before 1912, and in emigration in Switzerland afterward. During the war years he corresponded with Lenin and, on behalf of the Central Committee, with clandestine party groups in Russia.

tied elements alone could not lead the country out of the fatal impasse; it was necessary for the proletariat to throw its organized weight on the scales. The Gvozdevites invited the workers to send delegations with demands to the president of the Duma and the chairman of the Duma faction.

The Menshevik Gvozdevites decided to use a massive workers' demonstration to put pressure on the forthcoming session of the State Duma. When the revolutionary movement, the leading force of which was the proletariat, was at its height, the Gvozdevites called upon workers to enter the political arena to force the bourgeoisie to struggle aggressively. In a letter to the workers of Petrograd signed by "organized SD workers," the Gvozdevites proposed to demand the Duma eliminate the autocracy and create a provisional government supported by the people and, on the day the Duma convened, to march together to the Tauride Palace "in complete order, not disturbing the peace of the inhabitants, not antagonizing anyone, not offending anyone, and not inciting the police to violence."[11]

The Bolsheviks took a firm stand against the Gvozdevites' conciliatory policies. A number of workers' meetings carried a resolution introduced by the Bolsheviks. It stated that under the influence of the bourgeoisie the chauvinistic groups of workers *(Gvozdevtsy)* calling for the creation of a "government of salvation for the country" were actually weakening the proletarian revolutionary movement. "The ruling classes want to save the country from the external danger only so that they can mercilessly crush the popular masses within the country aspiring to freedom. . . . Only transfer of power to the hands of workers and poor peasants in a provisional revolutionary government after the tsarist government is overthrown will ensure—through the convocation of a constituent assembly—the realization of political freedoms, and an end to the war."[12]

The Gvozdevites' appeals did not meet with sympathy among workers. The proletariat was directing its revolutionary struggle to overthrow tsarism and the bourgeoisie, not in support of it. An ideologist in the Workers' Group, the Menshevik Evgenii Maevskii, admitted that the proposal to send workers' delegations to the president of the State Duma or to chairmen of the factions had little success "because it encountered inveterate Bolshevik boycottist[c] prejudices in workers' circles."[13] The Gvozdevites' appeal, however, began to worry the tsarist authorities. They reckoned that the Workers' Group had abandoned its immediate tasks, and had become revolutionary in hopes of creating favorable conditions for a coup d'etat by seizing power and forming a provisional government. On the night of January 26–27 the majority of its members were arrested.

The leaders of the War Industries Committee, A. I. Guchkov, A. I. Konovalov, and others, defended the Workers' Group. The bureau of the committee passed a resolution assuring the tsarist authorities that the Workers'

[c] A reference to the fact that the Bolsheviks had encouraged workers to boycott elections of worker representatives to the war industries committees (and also to the State Duma).

Group did not employ methods of struggle utilized by the revolutionary parties, and that its members had supported one of the most moderate tendencies among Russian workers. Testifying to the loyalty of the Workers' Group, the Bureau of the Central War Industries Committee noted that the group had participated in the country's military efforts and had rendered "very active assistance in preventing a strike movement among workers in defense industries. Moreover, the group resolutely opposed the excesses toward which several elements sometimes pushed workers."[14]

The Bureau of the War Industries Committee held that arresting members of the Workers' Group would increase ferment among the proletariat, result in the isolation of workers "from so-called bourgeois elements," and that this would pose "a grave danger to the normal political development of the country and the maintenance of internal tranquility." It insisted upon a more flexible policy toward workers and upon bringing them into bourgeois organizations. Approving the activities of the Workers' Group, the bureau condemned its arrest.

Not all bourgeois leaders took such a stand. At a meeting of representatives of public organizations on January 29, Miliukov accused the Workers' Group of exceeding its authority. He declared that only the State Duma had the right to assign the duration of political activities and define their goals, that "besides the State Duma, no one, no class in the population, no social group, has the right to advance slogans and independently launch or conduct the designated struggle." The majority participating in this meeting, however, approved the stand of the Workers' Group and supported cooperation with workers' organizations. "We have already said everything that needs to have been said, done everything that needs to have been done. Our backs are to the wall," declared the Kadet M. S. Adzhemov. Professor D. S. Zernov noted that the time for paper resolutions that do no good had passed, and that the time for concerted actions of all social classes was at hand. N. S. Chkheidze warned that in opposing the workers, Miliukov might be left behind by events: "If things remain the same, the simple if obvious result will be that only workers will be left to head political activities."[15]

Despite the arrest of the majority of members of the Workers' Group of the Central War Industries Committee, the demonstration of workers at the State Duma was not canceled. Supporters of the Workers' Group continued to prepare for it. The Duma was scheduled to meet on February 14; the workers' demonstration was planned for that same day. The Bolsheviks, preparing for a revolution designed to liquidate both the State Duma of the Third of June and tsarism, emphatically condemned this move. The Bureau of the Central Committee of the RSDRP passed a resolution concerning the appeal of the Workers' Group, which stated: "The Bureau of the Central Committee favors resisting the call of the Gvozdevites to organize a procession to the State Duma on February 14 for the following reasons: 1) the movement organized by the Gvozdevites is intended to support the Duma and the counterrevolutionary leaders; 2) participation in the movement organized by the Gvozdevites obscures the present political stand of the revolutionary working class; 3) it is necessary to expose the traitorous antiworkers' policies of the Gvozdevites and how they are opposed to our own Social Democratic policies."

To counterbalance the demonstration planned by the Gvozdevites, the Central Committee Bureau favored another political demonstration by workers, unconnected to the opening of the Duma. It proposed to conduct a one-day strike to commemorate the anniversary of the trial of the workers' deputies of the State Duma on February 13 (the trial was held February 10–13, 1915). "At the right moment for broader action," stated the resolution of the Central Committee Bureau, "the organization should call for a demonstration under our slogans. If the movement lasts until February 14, expand and deepen it, universally opposing the Gvozdevite policy of support for the Duma and liberals. In this way the Gvozdevites will lose initiative for the movement."[16]

The Petersburg Bolshevik Committee discussed the Central Committee Bureau's proposal on February 2 with delegates from eleven organizations, representing some eight hundred participating party members. The committee flatly condemned the procession to the State Duma and supported the proposal to conduct a strike and demonstration as a sign of solidarity with the exiled workers' deputies in the Duma; the Petersburg Committee of the RSDRP assigned them not to February 13, however, as the Bureau of the Central Committee had recommended, but to February 10, to distance themselves even further from the demonstration planned by the Workers' Group.[17] On this occasion the Petersburg Committee exposed the hypocrisy of the liberal bourgeoisie and the Gvozdevites who supported it. It unmasked the reactionary nature of the slogans "continue the war to a victorious end," "create a provisional government," "strengthen the public significance of the Duma," etc.

A leaflet issued by the Petersburg Bolshevik Committee stated that processions to palaces of the tsars and the ruling classes would cost the gullible dearly. The Petersburg Committee proposed to struggle earnestly against the war and tsarism for a democratic republic, a provisional revolutionary government of workers and poor peasants, and international worker solidarity.

> On February 10 when a tsarist court laid its heavy hand on our deputies who had struggled bravely to advance our slogans, we send them our brotherly greetings, demand their immediate return, and commemorate that day with a one-day strike to show our readiness to lay down our lives in the struggle on behalf of the slogans our exiled deputies openly proclaimed. Down with the tsarist monarchy! Make war on war! Long live a provisional revolutionary government! Long live a national constituent assembly! Long live a democratic republic! Long live international socialism![18]

The Interdistrict Committee of the RSDRP and the Menshevik Initiative Group also condemned the procession to the State Duma, only both these groups approached the question from their own viewpoint. The resolution of the Interdistrict Committee noted that a demonstration by the broad masses of workers, to coincide with the opening of the State Duma, would play into the hands of the bourgeoisie, who had betrayed the workers' deputies and offered its own slogan, "war to victory." Appealing to the workers not to fall for the ruse and become servants of the bourgeoisie, the Interdistrictites pointed out that the final decisive rising by the proletariat must eliminate both the tsarist autocracy and the State Duma in one blow and raise "from the depths of the people in revolt a provisional revolutionary government that will convene a constituent assembly to replace the autocratic order with a democratic republic." The Interdistrictites feared, though, that the moment was premature. Cautioning against impulsive actions, they pleaded that the working class was not organized adequately, that the RSDRP was experiencing a difficult organizational crisis, that "the army was not united closely with workers' organizations and that at the present moment there was no basis for counting on its active support."[19]

A leaflet put out by the Initiative Group noted that the Duma of the Third of June could never be considered a true fighter for the people's interests. At the critical moment the Duma would more likely side with the government against the people rather than with the people against the government. Pointing out that the struggle of the working class would sweep away both the Duma and the government, the Initiative Group spoke in favor of convoking a constituent assembly and establishing a democratic republic, a speedy end to the war, confiscation of gentry land, and the eight-hour day. Unlike the Bolsheviks and Interdistrictites, however, the Initiative Group did not call for a provisional revolutionary government and took the view that bourgeois power must replace tsarism. It declared that the people must fight for a constituent assembly and a democratic republic "specifically to secure a parliamentary regime in Russia and bring the bourgeoisie to power."[20] After taking a negative stand on the appeals of the Workers' Group, the Interdistrictites and Initiative Group called upon workers to gather their forces, organize, and prepare themselves, as it was time to take direct action.

Threatened by the growing revolutionary movement, the autocracy mobilized all its forces to nip all possible "disorders" in the bud. On February 5 the tsarist authorities withdrew the Petrograd Military District from the jurisdiction of the northern front. In order to better use the district's units for the struggle against the "internal enemy," the district was isolated and formed into an independent unit. General S. S. Khabalov was appointed district commander. Civil authorities also prepared to suppress the revolution. Protopopov threatened to drown Petrograd in blood if disturbances broke out. Tsarism was relying chiefly on mounted and regular police and a gendarme division, numbering thirty-five hundred. Part of them were in police stations, part were held in the reserve. Because these forces were insufficient to suppress large-scale revolutionary actions, the tsarist authorities planned to recruit military units to help the police. These units, however, were not reliable defenders of tsarism.

The large garrison in the capital comprised mainly reserve units. They had been augmented by new recruits, drafted mostly from Petrograd and the provinces near the capital. The proportion of workers was significantly high in the reserve units. For example, workers, artisans, and unskilled laborers made up more than half the personnel in the First and Second companies of the 180th Reserve Infantry Regiment. The garrison units contained companies of so-called evacuated soldiers who had been at the front and had been taken out of action after having been wounded. The horrors of combat turned them against the war and tsarism all the more. The training detachments in the reserve battalions constituted the autocracy's most reliable support; they were assigned to an obedient and disciplined unit of the garrison.

The troops of the Petrograd garrison were poorly armed. More than half the soldiers in the reserve battalions for the Izmailovskii, Egerskii, Moscow, and other regiments had no rifles. The reserve battalions of the Pavlovskii Regiment had only 2,626 rifles for 6,573 soldiers; the Lithuanian Regiment, 2,743 rifles for 6,553 soldiers; the Petrograd Regiment, 2,206 rifles for 6,775 soldiers; and the Finland Regiment 2,313 rifles for 7,011 soldiers.[21]

The headquarters of the Petrograd Military District and the city of Petrograd devised a detailed plan of action, and police and troops were distributed "in case of disorders." This plan, prepared back in 1905, was revised in accordance with changing circumstances. It was proposed that regular station policemen, reserves, and the mounted gendarme division would act first. Then, as needed, cavalry units would reinforce the police, and as a last resort the infantry would be called out. If that happened, command of all units and the police would be transferred to the military authorities. Petrograd was divided up according to districts in which military units were assigned. A police chief headed each district. On his order troops would occupy buildings and installations and dispatch mounted and foot patrols.

The plan of action against possible disorders was presented to the tsar. According to the city governor,[d] General A. P. Balk, Protopopov had informed Nicholas II that he had only twelve thousand reliable troops to deal with the revolutionary movement in Petrograd, a sufficient number to "cope with disorders." He believed the remaining troops "would not mutiny." Despite Protopopov's reassurances, it was decided to reinforce the Petrograd garrison with reliable troops from the front. The Guards Cavalry was ordered to Petrograd, but in its place less trustworthy troops, including the Maritime Guards Unit, were sent to the capital. It was stationed at Tsarskoe Selo where the imperial family lived. The authorities strove to isolate the sailors from the outside world, forbidding them to visit Petrograd or read newspapers. The authorities in the capital hoped that with help from the combined guards regiment, the tsar's escort, the railroad battalion, and other units they could repel a possible attack on Tsarskoe Selo from revolutionary Petrograd.

The military relied heavily on Cossack regiments to struggle with possible

[d] City governor *(gradonachal'nik)* was the urban equivalent of a governor.

"disorders." Supplementary measures were taken to guard military factories "from attacks by workers," and military warehouses, which could "serve as a source of arms for the mob." The police, armed with machine guns they had been trained to use, prepared for street battles. Such was the situation in Petrograd and several other cities.[22] Rodzianko noted that members of the Special Defense Council asked the minister of war what right he had to place "a large number of arms needed at the front at the disposition of the Ministry of Internal Affairs" without the sanction of the Special Defense Council.[23] There was no answer.

On February 8, 1917, City Governor Balk conferred with the highest authorities and civilian officials concerning what measures to take to preserve order and tranquility in the capital. The head of the Petrograd secret police informed those assembled that "the socialists and workers' organizations may organize street disorders on several consecutive days between February 10 and 14." General Balk ordered the police to prevent and break up assemblages and street "disorders," "so that crowds will not be permitted to form anywhere. Any group of people who appear the least suspicious on the streets and sidewalks must be dispersed at once. If more sizable groups materialize, cavalry units must be called out immediately."[24]

Obeying the instructions of the city governor, the police reinforced controls on bridges, crossings, and routes over the Neva "to prevent striking workers from crossing over into the center of the city." The commander of the river police and other responsible officials received special assignments in connection with this. Night clerks and watchmen were more closely supervised and ordered not to allow revolutionary proclamations to be posted or distributed. One leaflet, however, was widely circulated throughout the city. It was the order of the commander of the Petrograd Military District, in which General Khabalov admonished workers not to leave work, declaring that strikers were traitors to the fatherland and threatening them with punishment. "I remind those who ignore my appeal," wrote Khabalov, "that Petrograd is under martial law and any attempt to resist or use force against the legal authorities will be stopped forthwith with the use of arms."[25]

The imminent demonstrations also alarmed several bourgeois leaders. Miliukov published a letter in the newspaper *Rech'* (Speech) in which he called upon workers "not to take part in the demonstration of February 14 and to remain calm on that day."[26] Miliukov labeled calls to demonstrate against the war and tsarism as dangerous advice that proceeded "from a most suspicious source," by which he meant German agents. Miliukov and his supporters sought to discredit the growing revolutionary movement by alleging it was provocative and would pique Protopopov. Miliukov stuck to his guns. He wrote in his memoirs: "Rumors about a march on the Duma on February 14 took concrete form, and behind them it was not difficult to divine police provocation. Protopopov was apparently ready to excite an artificial 'revolution' and then gun it down as he had done in Moscow in 1905."[27]

The Bolsheviks exposed the slanderous fabrication that workers were yielding to Protopopov's provocations. Information Leaflet No. 2 from the Bureau of the Central Committee of the RSDRP noted that his purely police point of view "does not at all take into account the fact that there are numerous reasons for the growing dissatisfaction of the popular masses in Russia enslaved by the tsarist government. Liberals are demagogically speaking out as though they were the thoughtful guardians of workers, and in doing so are receiving support from the tsarist government."[28]

The authorities were fully prepared to drown the workers' demonstration on February 10–14 in blood, but no decisive skirmish with tsarism took place during these days. The attempts to organize a mass strike and demonstration on February 10 to protest the treatment of the workers' deputies did not succeed. The day chosen for this purpose proved unfortunate: Lent had begun the night before, so some industrial enterprises were closed and other factories worked only until noon. Moreover, the contradictory appeals from party organizations confused many workers. The failure of the Central Committee Bureau to come to an agreement with the Petersburg Committee of the RSDRP over the date for the demonstration also hurt it. On February 10 mass rallies took place at several plants and factories, resolutions were adopted, literature was disseminated, but a mass movement failed to materialize.

The demonstrations on February 14 were much more significant. The police reported that ninety thousand workers went out on strike in Petrograd that day. Most workers left their factories and went home, although some took part in street demonstrations. The movement of February 14 did not develop into what the Menshevik defensists tried to make it become, and the response to the appeal of the Workers' Group of the War Industries Committee to go to the State Duma was feeble. On February 14 a small crowd gathered outside the Tauride Palace; however, most of the demonstrators went to the center of the city. Striking Putilov workers emerged on Peterhof Chaussee carrying banners inscribed with the words "Down with the war!" "Long live a democratic republic!" "Down with the government!" "Long live the Second Russian Revolution!" Workers from the New Lessner Factory quit work and marched through the city, singing revolutionary songs. As they crossed Bolshoi Sampsonievskii Prospekt to Liteinyi Bridge they shouted "Bread!" and "Down with the war!" At 3:00 P.M. crowds came out on Nevskii Prospekt and joined the demonstration. The police dispersed those who had gathered and made arrests.[29]

During these days the protest movement also engulfed the Moscow proletariat. Moscow Bolsheviks called upon workers to conduct a protest strike on February 13, the anniversary of the trial against the workers' Duma deputies. The Bolsheviks had been unable to prepare extensively for the strike because tsarist authorities had arrested many leaders of the Bolshevik organization on the eve of the event. They readied their armed forces for action in order to suppress possible revolutionary disturbances promptly. At 10:00 A.M. on Febru-

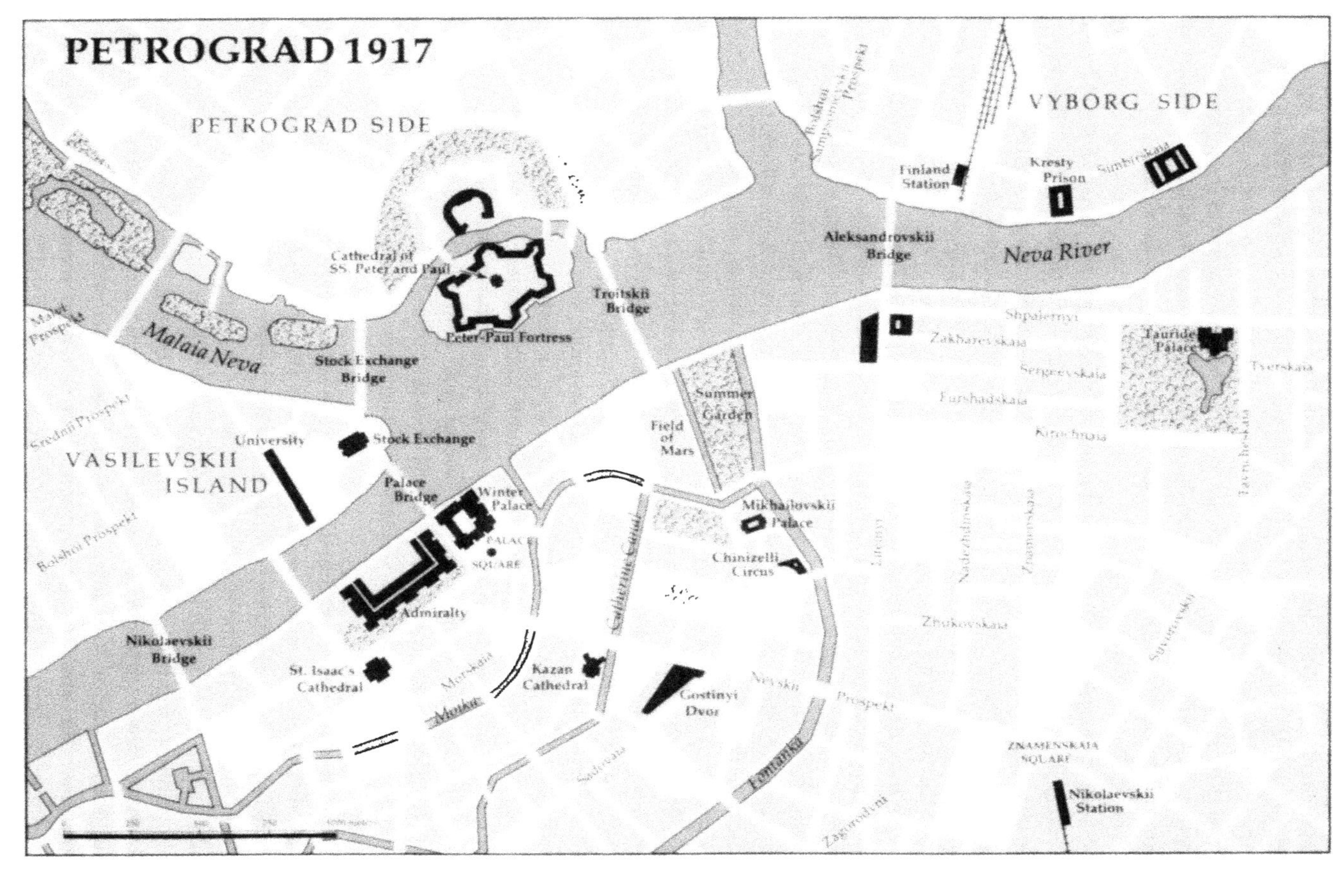
PETROGRAD 1917
PETROGRAD SIDE
VYBORG SIDE
VASILEVSKII ISLAND
Neva River
Malaia Neva
Cathedral of SS. Peter and Paul
Peter-Paul Fortress
Troitskii Bridge
Stock Exchange Bridge
Stock Exchange
University
Palace Bridge
Winter Palace
PALACE SQUARE
Admiralty
Nikolaevskii Bridge
St. Isaac's Cathedral
Kazan Cathedral
Gostinyi Dvor
Field of Mars
Summer Garden
Mikhailovskii Palace
Chinizelli Circus
Aleksandrovskii Bridge
Finland Station
Kresty Prison
Simbirskaia
Bolshoi Sampsonievskii Prospekt
Shpalernyi
Zakharevskaia
Sergeevskaia
Furshadskaia
Kirochnaia
Tauride Palace
Tverskaia
Tavricheskaia
Liteinyi
Nadezhdinskaia
Znamenskaia
Zhukovskaia
Suvorovskii
Nevskii Prospekt
ZNAMENSKAIA SQUARE
Nikolaevskii Station
Catherine Canal
Moika
Morskaia
Sadovaia
Fontanka
Zagorodnyi
Srednii Prospekt
Bolshoi Prospekt
Malyi Prospekt

ary 13 workers from the Dinamo Factory struck; an emergency meeting took place on the factory grounds. Two hundred workers descended upon the Tsindel Factory, unfurled a red flag, and marched with cries of "Down with the war!" and "Bread!" Police dispersed this workers' demonstration and arrested some of its participants. On February 13–14 Moscow workers from the Bromlei Factory, the Sokolnicheskii Tramshops, the Mikhelson Mechanical Plant, the Dobrov Factory, and several other enterprises went out on strike.

The strike of February 13–14 in Moscow remained limited in scope; however, the toiling people were in a revolutionary mood and the head of the Moscow secret police concluded his report on the strike with these words: "The excitable condition of the masses of workers and of the public is aggravated in Moscow by bread shortages, and has been used by revolutionaries at the first sign of strikes and demonstrations. The masses' mood can be expected to become even more threatening to state order and public tranquility."[30]

The mounting revolutionary crisis roused Petrograd's students, and they took part in the demonstration on February 14. Student assemblies at the university, the Psychological Institute, the Higher Courses for Women, and other academic institutions resolved that students should abandon their studies and join the demonstrators. Students at an assembly in the Polytechnic Institute passed a Bolshevik resolution protesting the trial of the workers' deputies of the Duma and calling upon students to strike. Military officers could also be found among the demonstrators on February 14. Police agents reported that on Nevskii Prospekt ensigns and students enthusiastically sang "La Marseillaise." They cried out to the police: "You shouldn't be fighting here. They ought to send all of you fatsoes to the front." The Social Democratic factions likewise called for a strike that took place at institutions of higher learning in Kharkov on February 13–14. Students protested the punishment of the workers' deputies of the State Duma and demanded a provisional revolutionary government and an end to the war. The student organization at Kazan University put out a journal, *Klich* (Call), which stated: "Revolution, Revolution, Revolution. That is our main slogan. Down with the war! Down with the government! Long live the revolution!"[31]

The dissolution of the Duma, postponement of its new session, and prohibition of public organizations from meeting in December evoked numerous protests. Liberal capitalists and landowners believed that by hamstringing the State Duma and public organizations tsarism had brought revolution and Russia's defeat in the war closer. Town dumas and zemstvos favored replacing the government, regulating food supplies, and instituting measures to permit public organizations to solve economic questions. The tsarist government approved the resolutions of the city dumas and zemstvos when they supported its positions. Yet now the government "happened to remember" that political questions lay beyond the competency of local administrative organs. The Ministry of Internal Affairs ordered local authorities to repeal decrees by zemstvo assemblies and city dumas regarding these questions and to do their best to suspend discussion of them. It proved impossible, however, to divorce zemstvo and city activists from politics. The situation was strained, the revolutionary crisis was becoming more acute, zemstvo and town institutions continued to criticize the government and, insisting upon its replacement, to support the State Duma. Even organizations of the nobility came out in favor of summoning the State Duma and State Council. A resolution by the Nobility of Novgorod stated that if these institutions were not convened and people who intrigued against them prevailed, "the gloom of unbridled passions and irrepressible malice will set in. And then the throne, Russia, and her hopes will be plunged into an abyss."[32]

Moscow remained the center of bourgeois opposition. Here were concentrated the main forces of Russian capital. The bourgeoisie of the Central Industrial Region[e] and representatives from public organizations from across the country gravitated here to attend national congresses. The Union of Towns and Union of Zemstvos, the Regional War Industries Committee, and the Stock Exchange Committee, headed by such powerful capitalists as P. P. Riabushinskii, A. I. Konovalov, S. N. Tret'iakov, and others, were located in Moscow. Furthermore, the strongest Kadet party organizations existed here and meetings of its central committee took place frequently.

At the beginning of 1917 the Moscow Stock Exchange Committee decided to create yet another bourgeois organization, the Trade-Industry Union. Stock-exchange committees in other towns, the Society of Factory Owners and Manufacturers, the Council of Congresses of Industry and Trade, and other entrepreneurial organizations supported this proposal. The government, however, distrusted the Moscow capitalists and, fearing the new organization would become antigovernment, it prohibited the trade-industry congress to convene. Preparations for the congress continued anyway.

During those days in Moscow, zemstvo leaders, the city's political activists, representatives of the nobility and trade and industrial circles, and the intelligentsia met in private apartments. Guests from Petrograd also often showed up. Police documents containing numerous reports about these gatherings and meetings are contradictory, and it is difficult to extract from them a clear notion of what exactly the participants discussed. In any case, bourgeois activists in early 1917 did not simply repeat what they had said before; they had some new ideas. Earlier they had spoken about revolution in the distant future. Now they thought it might happen during the war and voiced the opinion that it could come about in the near future. As in the past bourgeois leaders did everything they could to prevent revolution, but they saw that their efforts were not achieving the desired results, that hope for a peaceful outcome was constantly fading and revolution was drawing near.

A new question arose: what would the Kadets do if revolution actually broke

[e] The Central Industrial Region comprises those provinces surrounding Moscow in which textile production predominated.

out? At meetings of bourgeois leaders in January 1917, the left Kadet N. V. Nekrasov maintained that the government was pushing the country toward imminent revolution, that the only reliable support the government had was the Kadets, but they would not enter into an agreement with tsarism and would take advantage of the revolution. "In the trials Russia will face," said Nekrasov, "we will not appear in the role of suppressors of the revolution. The government has destroyed itself. Our task will be entirely constructive; in the storm and chaos we will have to create a new government that will be able to calm the country immediately and get down to vast creative work."[33] Nekrasov stood for establishing a new government, but Miliukov believed it was necessary to preserve the old one. "Revolution," he declared, "must not take us by surprise. We are the only restraining and organized force, the only force that could save the government and reconcile it with the rough raging sea of people."[34]

The Kadet historian A. A. Kizevetter took refuge in history. At a meeting of the Central Committee of the Kadet party in Moscow early in February 1917, he noted that events in Russia were developing as systematically as European events had unfolded in the eighteenth and nineteenth centuries. "The government has gradually lost support and now hangs by a thread. And it is pulling on this thread with all of its might. History has already once seen how this game ends; one fine day a majestic throne becomes a simple, broken chair."[35] Kizevetter suggested discarding Aesopian language and facing the question directly: "One ought to save oneself and not the suicide victim." Still, the Kadets continued to deal with the tsar—"the suicide." Moreover, bourgeois opposition had peaked in November–December 1916, and now was declining. Although revolution was approaching, the bourgeoisie was not actively opposing the autocracy.

Bourgeois leaders called for resisting provocation and utilizing parliamentary means in the final struggle. They proposed to use the impending Duma session to vent their anger on the more hated tsarist ministers, but not on tsarism itself. At a meeting of the Kadet party Central Committee Miliukov said: "November 1 was Stürmer's day, and we will arrange Protopopov's during the first days of the new session."[36]

Three days before the opening of the Duma, a new attempt was made to wring a concession from the tsar, to change the government's composition and policies. Rodzianko brought a written report to what turned out to be his final audience with Nicholas II on February 10, 1917. In the report, the president of the State Duma complained that the government did not trust the Duma or public forces and used old bureaucratic methods to impede their work in all sorts of ways. He complained that the government was undermining the rear and that its policies were permanently dissipating its authority and losing supporters each day. Rodzianko urged the tsar to replace the government and change the style of administering the country. Seeing the Duma as the main bulwark against revolution, Rodzianko considered it impermissible to serve the present government, for this would undermine the country's trust in it, and "then the country itself would rise to defend its legal rights. This," wrote Rodzianko, "cannot be allowed to happen. This must be avoided at all costs. Here is our fundamental task."

Rodzianko noticed the tsar conversed with him in an unusually cold manner, was distracted, and finally, interrupted him, saying curtly: "Hurry up. Grand Prince Mikhail Aleksandrovich is waiting to have tea with me!" In answer to Rodzianko's statement about the threatening mood in the country and the possibility of revolution, the tsar declared: "My information is altogether different, and if the Duma permits such acrimonious debates as last time, it will be dismissed."[37]

Rodzianko told the leaders of the Duma opposition about the tsar's warnings, and they gave him an account of their activity. The Duma session that opened on February 14, 1917, was less fractious than and more of a pale copy of the November 1916 meeting. Breaking with tradition, the chairman of the Council of Ministers, Golitsyn, did not deliver a speech from the throne as his predecessors had done. Golitsyn remained silent. Minister of Agriculture A. A. Rittikh grew loquacious. In a long speech he defended the grain requisition he had established and called upon the Duma to give up politics and join the government in solving the food supply problem. Rittikh tried to justify the course he had taken of abolishing fixed prices and returning to free grain trade, and on this question he met support within the Progressive Bloc itself. Representing the large landowners, the Octobrists approved his policies. In contrast, the Kadets favored keeping grain prices fixed. The Progressive Bloc split. Of course, the Octobrists and Kadets claimed they were in complete agreement on all fundamental political questions, but their quarrel over the government's economic policies could hardly strengthen this unity.

In the political realm the Progressive Bloc continued to defend its former program. Its leaders declared the government could not supply the army and population with essential items unless the executive power was reorganized, and as before, they considered as the main evil the fact that the people who ran the ministries did not enjoy the country's trust, were not up to the tasks facing them, and were incapable of working in harmony with the legislative institutions. The Progressive Bloc once again did no more than request that "a ministry of trust" be created, referred to the tsar's rescript and insisted the government change its attitude toward and cooperate with the State Duma.

The bourgeoisie boasted several legal organizations. The opposition it offered met with sympathy in the army high command, among the United Nobility, and even among the grand princes. Yet it continued to mark time. Addressing the Duma, Miliukov mentioned that people wanted it to act, not talk. They say everything has been said, every conceivable speech has been made, now act boldly. "These appeals, these hopes," recalled Miliukov, "deeply touch us, but I must say that they also slightly embarrass us. Words are our currency. Words and votes remain our only weapon."[38] Many deputies admitted that the Duma was full of idle chatterers, did not live up to its obligations, and did not justify the hopes placed on it. The deputies said the first day of the session was uninteresting and boring and offered no fresh alternatives. Speeches in the Duma had lost their cutting edge, deputies listened to them indifferently, and the Duma lacked a quorum. "Returning from the Duma," wrote Deputy Ern, "I felt ashamed. The entire country was waiting and hoping for something . . . the day had not become 'important' but turned out to be quite dull."[39] Even though the time for talk had passed, the Duma was incapable of action.

While bourgeois leaders were busy with verbal disputes in the Tauride Palace and conversations were held in fashionable hotels over the necessity of a palace coup, the working class continued along the road to revolution. A leaflet issued by the Petersburg Committee of the RSDRP after the events of February 14, 1917, declared it was impossible to achieve freedom by leaving the stones of the palaces unturned. The State Duma, with its "lordly" nature, could not arouse the workers' hopes by demanding continuation of the war and protracting the grief and calamity that were the lot of the popular masses. Only the people could help themselves. "It is impossible to wait and remain silent any longer. The working class and peasants, dressed in soldiers' greatcoats and dark blue smocks, must extend a hand to each other and must conduct a struggle with the entire tsarist clique in order to end the shameful oppression of Russia once and for all."[40] The Petersburg Committee of the RSDRP wrote in a leaflet: "The time has come for an open struggle!" The committee called upon workers to overthrow the autocracy, form a provisional revolutionary government that would establish a democratic republic, introduce an eight-hour workday, and transfer all gentry lands to the peasants.

When encouraging the working class to enter into an open battle against the autocracy, the Bolsheviks did not fix a specific date for beginning the decisive engagement. Afterward, in 1918, Lenin said:

> Recall December 1916. How could we guarantee that two months later the tsarist monarchy would be overthrown in the course of a few days? We in this country, which has experienced two revolutions, know and realize that the progress of the revolution cannot be foretold, and that revolution cannot be called forth. We can only work for the revolution if you work consistently, if you work devotedly, if this work is linked up with the interests of the oppressed masses, who make up the majority, revolution will come; but where, how, at what moment, from what immediate cause, cannot be foretold.[41]

The leaflet of the Petersburg Committee of the RSDRP quoted above said: "Let each day in the history of the workers' movement become a call to demonstrate. The trial of the workers' deputies, the Lena massacre, the first of May, the July shootings, the October days, January 9, and the like serve as a summons to mass action."

The Russian Bureau of the Central Committee of the RSDRP, although promoting the idea of a street engagement, did not have a day for the decisive skirmish in mind. Shliapnikov wrote: "When will it come? We did not guess which event or day would spark it, we didn't even pose such a question, but carried out our work persistently and consistently. The triumph of our slogans turned out to be not far off."[42]

The situation in the country and particularly in Petrograd became ever more strained. Economic strikes took place at many enterprises in the capital. Some of them had already broken out before February 14 and continued afterward. On February 9 workers in the Petrograd suburb of Kolpino struck at the Izhora Factory, which filled war orders. The Izhora workers rose up to struggle against and protest lower wages. Factory assemblies discussed the workers' economic situation, and even raised political questions. Workers declared it was necessary to bring the Bolshevik deputies back from exile, end the war, and establish a democratic republic. Leaflets put out by the Petersburg Committee of the RSDRP circulated at the factory, and the Bolshevik workers Panov, Mareev, Zimin, and others appealed to workers not to pin their hopes on the State Duma but to work to convoke a constituent assembly and create a democratic republic themselves. A meeting of Izhora workers proposed coordinating activities in Kolpino with those in Petrograd. A representative of the Petersburg Committee of the RSDRP came to the factory.

The head of the district gendarmerie reported what took place at the factory on February 15:

> Around 9:00 A.M. a rally began at the chapel in the factory yard. They shut down the ammunition workshop. Panov was the first to speak. . . . A police officer wanted to arrest him, but the crowd protected him and wouldn't let the officer make the arrest. Then the police and officers withdrew and returned before long with Cossacks. During the interim Mareev spoke on economic themes and called to continue the strike. He could not finish his speech, however, because Cossacks appeared and began to herd the workers together with their horses. A Cossack officer approached Mareev, turned to him and said: "Russia is in danger and you are calling for a strike. What are you doing? Don't you know you can't do this!" At that moment a speaker from the Petersburg Committee got up on the railing and cried to the officer: "Shame on you, Mr. Officer. It is you who are destroying Russia. People are demanding bread." The noise intensified, the spokesman from the Petersburg Committee hid, and someone cried: "To the rolling mill!" From all directions the entire mass poured into the narrow passageways of the rolling mill where the Cossacks were unable to follow. This last circumstance enabled an extensive political rally to take place in the workshop at which the speaker from the Petersburg Committee turned up and made a fiery speech reflecting the spirit of the Petersburg Committee's leaflet. . . . The speaker from the Petersburg Committee went over to the armor-casting workshop, where a similar rally was also under way.[43]

After exhausting all other means to pressure the workers, the administration of the Izhora Factory resorted to a lockout. The head of the factory reported: "At 6:00 A.M. on February 16, I ordered the whole factory to shut down and discharged all factory hands who did not show up for work. Two infantry companies were brought in and the disturbance came to an end."[44] Yet in fact, "the disturbance" continued; the lockout did not break the determination of the Izhora Factory workers to continue the struggle.

In Petrograd itself the ferment at the large Putilov Plant was almost uninterrupted. On January 9, 1917, 20,000 workers struck. In January and early February workers in the boiler factory, cannon, and other workshops walked out. On February 18 workers in the gun-carriage punching workshop struck. They demanded a pay hike and the return to the factory of their comrades who the administration had unjustly sacked. Announcing he would close the plant if the workers did not return to their machines immediately, the factory director rejected the workers' demands. The threat produced no effect. Although no more than 486 people out of 26,700 total workers at the plant worked in the gun-carriage shop, other groups of workers supported them. Workers in the machine, shrapnel, and assembly workshops struck. Mass rallies took place in the factory at which workers discussed wage rates, the high cost of living, the bread shortage, the exhausting war, and the autocracy, without whose overthrow it was impossible to escape poverty and misfortune. The strike, which had broken out in individual workshops, threatened to become general.[45]

The factory management let it be known that those guilty "of unauthorized work disturbances" would be held accountable and, without waiting for a factorywide strike to be declared, announced a lockout. On February 22, 1917, the factory gates were closed and an announcement was posted: "I announce that recent systematic disruption of the normal flow of work and order at the factory by workers has made the continuation of normal production impossible and therefore, beginning on the morning of February 22, the factory will be closed until further notice. [Signed] Factory Director Major-General Dublitskii."[46] The worker A. Grigelevich recalled: "They didn't let us into the plant. The entrances were closed. We held a meeting. Some favored breaking down the doors to get into the factory. Others favored starting for town. We marched along Peterhof Chaussee toward the Narva Gate, joining workers of the Tentelev Chemical Factory and the Paper Factory along the way."[47] The Putilov workers elected a strike committee and decided to appeal for support to other Petrograd workers.

A strike beginning on February 20 also occurred at the Putilov Shipyard, site of four thousand workers. Demands for increased wages resounded at a workers' rally. Men spoke about the war and tsarism. On February 21 the entire shipyard shut down. Although workers showed up in the workshops, they stood at their machines and did not work. The administration complained that workers were acting provocatively, demanding satisfaction of all their demands and intending to wheel their hated bosses out in wheelbarrows.[f]

[f]It was not uncommon for Russian workers to toss their bosses in wheelbarrows and cart them out of the factory in protest. As S. A. Smith put it, it "was a symbolic affirmation by workers of their

The Putilov workers' struggle strongly influenced subsequent events. The Petersburg Committee of the RSDRP called upon the proletariat of the capital to render all possible support to the workers of the Putilov Plant. With strong ties to the workers of Petrograd and the entire country, the thirty thousand Putilov workers had always been in the front ranks of those struggling for revolution. It is understandable why their struggle elicited deep sympathy among the proletariat of the capital. The Socialist Revolutionary V. M. Zenzinov related that on February 22 a group of workers from the Putilov Plant went to Kerensky and informed him of the situation that had arisen at the factory because of the lockout. They declared that recent events could have serious consequences and might mean the beginning of a major political movement. Zenzinov wrote: "The warning turned out to be fateful in the full sense of the word, and later I often remembered it and was surprised how well the Putilov workers understood the crisis at the time . . . they were the real harbingers of the coming revolution. Their intuition probably can be attributed to the fact that they were at the very heart of the movement and sensed how strained the atmosphere had already become in workers' circles in Petrograd."[48]

The Putilov strike was the forerunner of the revolutionary storm, but it was not the storm itself. A campaign to defend the Putilov workers never truly got underway; instead Petrograd became the scene of new events that involved all elements of the population. The campaign of solidarity with the Putilovites joined and became a component part of this powerful movement.[49]

The Petrograd workers' revolutionary battle took place during the ever growing food crisis. For the whole of February 1917 the inhabitants of Petrograd, especially in the workers' regions, were short of bread. Long lines stretched in front of shops and bakeries. A winter unprecedented in severity had set in, filling the streets with ice and piling snowdrifts on the roofs of homes, sidewalks, and bridges of the city. Shivering from the cold, poorly dressed young people, women, and old men waited hours for bread and often went home empty-handed. Food shortages provoked an even greater ferment among the masses. In line they discussed why there was no bread and why prices were still rising; they wondered who was responsible for the people's misery and who needed the war. The Petrograd Okhranka observed that on days of severe crisis the queues had the same force as revolutionary meetings and tens of thousands of revolutionary leaflets. The street had become a political club.

All segments of the population, especially working people, were resentful and flooded the city and its environs like a powerful wave. Crowds of hungry people, mostly women and young people, sacked bakeries and bread shops when they received no bread. Stones and pieces of wood pounded the doors and store windows. The sound of shattered glass rang out; broken shop signs

---

dignity as human beings and a ritual humiliation of those who had deprived them of this dignity . . . and had the same significance in the factory as did tearing off an army-officer's badges of rank." S. A. Smith, *Red Petrograd: Revolution in the Factories, 1917–1918* (Cambridge, England, 1983), p. 57.

clattered. In the streets of Petrograd the people's demand "Bread!" could be heard louder and louder. Notices appeared in the newspapers that coupons for bread and other items would soon be distributed in the city. The matter of transferring food distribution to the city administration was discussed. As before, though, there was not enough bread and the agitation among the population swelled.

On February 22 it assumed an especially ominous character. That day a police officer in the second section of the Vyborg police district reported: "The working masses inhabiting the district entrusted to me are in strong ferment because there is a shortage of bread. . . . [I must] listen each day to complaints that they have had no bread for two or three days. This is all the more reason why we can readily expect disorders."[50] Strikes and disturbances occurred on February 22 in a number of enterprises. Demanding bread, nine hundred textile workers in the joint-stock company of Voronin, Liutch and Chesher stopped work and stood idly at their machines until the end of the workday. Workers in the Lebedev Jute Factory, Factory Number Two of the Society of United Mechanized Factories, the Baranovskii Pipe Factory, and other enterprises presented the same demands. Emergency meetings were held at many factories and plants to take up the bread shortages.[51]

The disturbances caused by bread shortages charged the air—all that was needed was a spark to ignite the flames of revolution. The food supply affected the vital interests of the widest numbers of the toiling masses and the difficulties with it drew them into the battle. The proletariat, led by the Bolsheviks,[g] made the battle of the toiling masses an uprising against tsarism.

How did this uprising begin?

The First Day

The Second Russian Revolution began with strikes, political meetings, and demonstrations that took place in Petrograd on International Women's Day, February 23, 1917 (March 8 New Style).[h] The war and the high cost of living had seriously affected the situation of working women. Many of them had husbands at the front. They had to hold down jobs and take care of their children, as well as cope with shortages of bread and other foodstuffs.

The Bolsheviks agitated among the working women. The Petersburg Committee of the RSDRP had created an all-city women's circle whose task was to conduct "organization and propaganda among the female factory proletariat." As the Bolshevik A. Shalaginova (Fedorova) wrote, the members of this circle and the women's circle of the Interdistrict Committee (represented by Anna

[g] Needless to say, Burdzhalov is stretching the point here.

[h] The Julian calendar (Old Style), which was thirteen days behind the Gregorian calendar of the West, was in use in Russia until 1918.

Itkina) decided to commemorate International Women's Day with an antiwar demonstration.[52] Supporting this proposal, the Bureau of the Central Committee and the Petersburg Committee of Bolsheviks scheduled rallies and meetings at factories that day in order to explain why the position of working women was difficult, and to urge male and female workers to undertake a decisive battle against the imperialist war and tsarism. "The war, the high cost of living, and the situation of women" were the agenda on that day.

The Bolshevik organization sent speakers to workers' meetings and mass rallies. A. Kostina, a participant in the events, recounted that demands for agitators were relayed by special individuals to the apartment of Tolmacheva, a student at Bestuzhev Women's College. From there another individual went to a different apartment where many of the comrades who were prepared to speak at the workers' meetings had gathered. The Bolsheviks had intended to publish a leaflet for Women's Day, but the loss of their press prevented them from doing so.

The Interdistrict Committee of the RSDRP, however, succeeded in issuing an appeal for Women's Day. It addressed the oppressive exploitation of workers, tsarist repression, and the terrible calamities brought on by the war.

> Dear women comrades, are we going to put up with this in silence much longer, now and then venting our smoldering rage on small shop owners? After all, they're not to blame for the people's suffering, they are being ruined themselves. The government is to blame! It started the war and cannot end it. The government is ruining the country and causing us to go hungry. The capitalists are to blame! The war brings them profits. It's high time to cry out to them: "Enough!" Down with the criminal government and its whole gang of robbers and murderers! Long live peace![53]

The movement on February 23 was particularly widespread in Petersburg's Vyborg quarter, one of the most important industrial districts in the capital. Here there were no towering buildings of giant enterprises like the Putilov Plant, but it did contain many large and medium-size metalworking enterprises like the Old Lessner, New Lessner, Aivaz, Erikson, Rosenkrantz, Renault, Phoenix, Promet, and other works. The textile enterprises located on the Vyborg side of town employed mostly women. The Vyborg District had a glorious revolutionary tradition and a strong Bolshevik organization enjoying great prestige among the masses of workers.

When rousing the masses of working men and women to struggle, the Bolsheviks did not believe that the moment for the final clash with tsarism had yet come. On Women's Day in 1917 they intended to conduct meetings and rallies. I. D. Chugurin related that in preparing the decisive struggle against the war and tsarism, the Bolsheviks had proposed a general strike for the traditional day—May 1. "Previous directives," said Chugurin, "told us to stir the workers to the boiling point by the first of May."[54] V. N. Kaiurov, a leader in the Vyborg District Committee of the RSDRP wrote:

> We could feel the storm coming, but no one could determine how it would be manifested. The highly charged mood of the masses forced the district committee to decide to stop agitating, cease direct appeals for strikes and the like, and focus attention primarily on the maintenance of discipline and restraint during the upcoming demonstrations. On the eve of 'Women's Day,' that is, the night of February 22, I was sent to a women's meeting in the Lesnoi District. While describing the significance of 'Women's Day' and the women's movement in general, I had to call attention to the current situation, chiefly to urge people to refrain from abortive deeds and act exclusively in accordance with the instructions of the party committee.[55]

The meetings and rallies at the factories on the Vyborg side on February 23 were stormy. The working women said that they had run out of patience. Their husbands were at the front, their young children stood in line for bread and had to leave without any. At many plants and factories rallies and meetings ended with the proclamation of strikes. Some working men and women stopped work, dispersed, and went home. For example, police records show this is what happened at the Aivaz Works. A police official in the Lesnoi precinct reported that over three thousand workers from that factory, returning from lunch, assembled in the automation section for a rally to celebrate Women's Day. "The workers decided not to work today and began to talk about the bread crisis." The women asked the men to join them in a strike, and together they "peacefully dispersed" at 4:00 P.M. Apparently, however, this kind of "peaceful" end to a meeting was the exception. Mass meetings and strikes that day snowballed into demonstrations.

Deserting their departments and workshops, the working men and women took to the streets in a vociferous crowd demanding "Bread!" In front of stores and bakery shops stood long lines of frustrated people. At first glance, the disturbances occurring on February 23 over the bread shortage were no different from those of preceding days. But in actuality the difference was profound. Earlier outbursts of popular discontent over the bread shortage had not been linked to the organized struggle of the working class; by the end of the day they would die down as rapidly as they had flared up. Now the street demonstrations of the city's toilers demanding bread merged with those of the striking workers. Led by the workers, the movement was directed against tsarism, the principal culprit responsible for all the misery.

It was the women who initiated action in most cases, primarily working women from the textile mills. Regarding the events of February 23, Information Sheet No. 2 published by the Bureau of the Central Committee of the RSDRP stated: "In connection with Women's Day, and at the insistence of the organized women, a number of rallies were held on the Vyborg side that culminated in a strike and in calling workers from other districts off the job. The appeal of the Putilov workers for support and the lack of bread created a militant mood among the masses that turned into demonstrations, rallies, and clashes with the police."[56]

Stopping work, men and women abandoned plants and factories and headed for neighboring enterprises to bring them into the strike and demonstrations. Working women at the Neva Thread Mills heard a noise in the street, which at first was unclear but then resolved into impassioned cries and demands to stop work.

> "Into the street! Stop! We've had it!" And the entire first floor of the thread mill opened its windows in a flush, or rather they were knocked out with sticks, stones, and pieces of wood. The women thread-spinners surged noisily into the passageway. . . . All the doors were thrown open. And crowds of thread-makers pushed out into freedom.[57]

The women textile workers then went to the metalworkers. I. Gordienko, a Bolshevik worker in the Ludwig Nobel Machinery Works, tells how on

> the morning of February 23, women's voices were heard in the alley onto which the windows of our department opened, shouting "Down with the war! Down with the high cost of living! Down with hunger! Bread for the workers!" Myself and a few other comrades immediately went to the windows. . . . The gates of Bolshoi Sampsonievskii Mill No. 1 were wide open. Throngs of militant women workers filled the alley. Those who spotted us began waving their arms and yelling "Come out! Stop work!" Snowballs pelted the windows. We decided to join the demonstration. . . . A brief rally was held near the main office, at the gate, and we took to the street. . . . They linked arms with comrades up front and with yells of "Hurrah!" set off to Bolshoi Sampsonievskii Prospekt.[58]

In the light of unfolding events, such considerations as "the time was not yet ripe" for a general strike or for street demonstrations lost their meaning. The question arose: how should the revolutionaries evaluate the new situation and react to events? Bolshevik workers in each enterprise had to settle that question quickly and, furthermore, on their own, for no directives had come from the party centers by the morning of February 23. Five Bolsheviks from the Erikson Plant held an emergency meeting in a hallway. Kaiurov recalled that at the gathering Nikifor Ilin reported on strikes at several textile mills, and women delegated by their factories had come with requests for support. The meeting continued with Socialist Revolutionaries and Mensheviks participating. They adopted a resolution

> to support the striking women workers, and accepted my proposal that, once we decided to protest, we should immediately direct all workers without exception into the streets, and lead the strike and demonstration ourselves. Comrade Ivan Zhukov without hesitation brought our resolution to the attention of the district party committee. And remarkably, neither the district committee nor the workers' representatives from the various departments were surprised at such a resolution. The idea of an uprising had long been growing among the workers, but at that moment no one foresaw how it would end. . . . No one thought the revolution could be so very close.[59]

With no contacts among themselves, Bolshevik workers at the various enterprises nevertheless reached the same conclusion: they had to take the lead in the workers' strike and demonstrations and direct them into a struggle against the war and tsarism. This unanimity is explained by the fact that the Bolshevik workers, drawing on the experience of the First Russian Revolution, had long been ready for a decisive encounter with the autocracy. Knowing the moods of the workers, they saw that the time for this clash was coming. It was time! The conditions for decisive action had been prepared, and the workers were only waiting for a signal to go into action.

SRs and Mensheviks as well as Bolsheviks could be counted among the workers. In the decisive days of the struggle against tsarism, a mighty outburst of revolutionary enthusiasm seized the entire mass of workers and welded them into one. I. Mil'chik, an SR worker from the same Erikson Plant, wrote that on February 23 the workers were especially tense. Every minute they would leave their machines and approach activists to ask "what shall we do?" No longer inert, the masses were urging the most advanced workers to lead.

> We quickly assembled at the office of the workers' medical fund—ten or twelve of us, the leading core of the plant. We raised the question: should we strike? If we strike, should we take to the streets to demonstrate and call out other plants? We queried each other about the moods at other factories, and whether a decision had been made anywhere to strike and take to the streets. . . . Despite the absence of assurance that other factories would go out, the decision to strike, and take to the streets and utter the slogans "Down with the autocracy!" "Down with the war!" "Give us bread!" was unusually quick and unanimous. Young boys were the first to hear of the decision to go out. Shouting joyfully, they ran through the workshops: "Stop work! To the meeting!"

Climbing on piles of scrap metal and discarded machines, workers made speeches to the crowd.

> The speakers were our own people; they were known by everyone, yet they somehow seemed transformed by the moment, imbued with revolutionary spirit. There was no need to raise spirits, no need to agitate. The speeches gave instructions how to conduct ourselves in the streets. . . . Tomorrow we should show up at work at the usual hour, but were not to begin work. The masses perceived the seriousness of the moment, were on the alert, and disciplined. Even noisy and mischievous young boys quieted down, and listened to familiar and knowledgeable leaders as they never had before.[60]

I. Markov, an SR worker from the Arsenal Plant, recounted that on February 23, after lunch break, there came loud knocks at the gate and windows of Arsenal. Workers of other plants, who had marched to Arsenal, shouted: "Quit work, come out!" The Arsenal workers stopped working, dressed quickly, went to the exit, and despite threats and exhortations by management, joined the crowd. In a large column they went to enterprises along the Poliustrov

Embankment of the Neva River, and then emerged at the corner of Bezborodkin Prospekt and Simbirsk Street. Cossacks and mounted police herded the demonstrators toward the Finland Station, where they were jammed up against lines of streetcars. Worker speakers addressed the crowd from the cars, station stairs, and curbstones. "The moment has arrived," they shouted, "the time has come. We must carry through our cause." Speakers urged people to go to Nevskii Prospekt and call out workers in other districts.[61]

The Bolshevik A. Taimi described a political meeting held on February 23 at a precision machine factory. At first people spoke about International Women's Day. Then Taimi, taking the floor, dwelled on the questions of bread, the war, and the tasks of the revolutionary struggle. "And of course, as soon as I began to speak about these questions that were uppermost in everyone's mind, the crowd was transformed; it came alive, moved and buzzed. . . . When I proposed we join other factories on strike and take to the streets, hundreds of hands were raised. In a few minutes we came out of the factory and headed for Nevskii Prospekt."[62]

After the metalworkers joined the strike and demonstration, the workers' actions became more purposeful and better organized. While some of the striking workers went to their homes, others went from factory to factory to shut down those still at work. Factory administrators and police vainly sought to prevent the strike from spreading. When the mass of workers approached the Metalworks they found its gate locked tight. Undaunted, the workers started singing "Dubinushka,"[i] and pressing against the gate. They tore it off its hinges and entered the factory yard. The place was shut down. Then the workers headed for the machine factory belonging to the Russian Company for Aerial Navigation, and the police were unable to stop them. A police supervisor drew his revolver and began threatening the crowd. Workers knocked the revolver from the hands of this zealous official and, after beating him up, stormed into the plant.[63] Another large detachment of workers had joined the strikers' ranks.

The strike spread to other parts of the capital. The Bolshevik N. Ignatov related how workers in the Lorenz Works on the Petrograd side rose up in struggle. A worker named Ziablikov ran onto the floor and informed them that the women workers were on strike and had taken to the streets. Somebody yelled "Stop work!" In a few minutes the workers of the Lorenz Works had poured out onto Kamennoostrovskii Prospekt, turned over a streetcar, headed for the Langenzippen Works, broke into the shops, and pulled workers off the job. A large demonstration headed for Troitskaia Square.[64]

There were exceptions to the rule. Some workers with large families to support feared losing their jobs. Others, subject to military call-up, were afraid of being sent to the front. At first they could not make up their minds to join the ranks of the strikers and waited to see how events would develop. Thus, on

[i] "Dubinushka," ("La Marseillaise," "Varshavianka," "Comrades, Boldly in Step," and others) were revolutionary songs that became popular among workers at the turn of the century.

February 23, three thousand workers in the Franco-Russian Factory gathered in the machine shop for a political meeting. "The speakers mainly spoke about the lack of bread, and there were speeches both for and against the war. Some spoke in favor of supporting their comrades from Vyborg. The majority spoke against the disorders. . . . It was decided to meet again the next morning to settle the question of what to do next."[65]

Spontaneous demonstrations with the demand "Bread!" took place in various parts of the city that day. Police reports and dispatches from February 23 note that crowds of women and young people demanding "Bread!" and singing revolutionary songs marched along Srednii Prospekt, Sadovaia, Mikhailovskaia, and other streets.[66] The striking workers, pouring out beyond the walls of factory buildings and flowing in an increasingly powerful wave through the wide streets, played the principal role. The strike became a revolutionary demonstration as masses of people filled the sidewalks and bridges of the capital. The people had become masters of the city. In many neighborhoods transportation was interrupted. Workers stopped rapidly moving streetcars, forced motormen to halt, took away their operating wrenches, made passengers get out, turned the streetcars over, and with shouts of "Hurrah!" moved on. Some streetcars were returned to the barns, others lay overturned on the rails or stayed motionless. The interruption of streetcar traffic paralyzed life in the city and disorganized the tsarist camp.

Workers marched through the city's streets in a militant and joyous mood, singing "La Marseillaise," "Varshavianka," "Comrades, Boldly in Step," and other revolutionary songs. As they moved, the demonstrations became living speakers' tribunes. Calling for struggle against the war and the monarchy, speakers were carried on the demonstrators' shoulders. Red flags waved here and there above the moving crowds. The revolution had begun.

Workers on the Vyborg side headed for Bolshoi Sampsonievskii and Bezborodkinskii prospekts and for Simbirsk and Nizhegorodskaia streets. Bolshoi Sampsonievskii Prospekt linked the different parts of the Vyborg District and led to the Liteinyi Bridge, which was the way to the center of the city. Bezborodkinskii Prospekt also led to the Liteinyi Bridge, but from the other end of the district. Having occupied this vital route, the workers of the Vyborg quarter established contact with other parts of the city and opened a path to the center of town.

"To Nevskii!" became the slogan shouted in the workers' districts of Petrograd on the very first day of the revolution. Why there? Because it was the traditional site of political demonstrations in Petrograd, beginning with the very first demonstration at Kazan Cathedral in 1876,[j] where the central institutions of the government, residences of the tsar's ministers, the General Staff, the Admiralty,

[j]The demonstration at the Kazan Cathedral in 1876 was an attempt by the revolutionary intelligentsia to forge an alliance with the people. A populist organization, Land and Liberty, sponsored the demonstration in which Plekhanov took part.

and other bastions of tsarism were located. To come out on Nevskii Prospekt meant that the movement was becoming citywide. The proletariat was taking a stand as an independent political force against the autocracy. In those decisive days, it did not parade to the Tauride Palace to bow before the liberal bourgeoisie; nor did it enter into an agreement with the liberal bourgeoisie and its stronghold, the State Duma.

The slogan "To Nevskii!" struck a responsive chord among the demonstrating workers and alarmed the camp of the defenders of the autocracy. The tsarist authorities, acting on the basis of their experience in the First Russian Revolution, sought above all to separate the various segments of the Petrograd proletariat, isolate workers' neighborhoods from each other, and break off their contact with the center. The troops and police received an order to hold the bridges at all costs and not to permit demonstrators to cross them.

Although the gendarmes and police threatened reprisals and attempted to bar the workers' way, the threats did not work. Overturning the barricades set up by the police along the approaches to Liteinyi Bridge, the demonstrators encountered new police forces on the bridge itself. A squadron of cavalry stopped the flow of demonstrators, and only scattered groups of workers filtered through to Liteinyi Prospekt. At another time of the year seizing the bridges by police and troops, and thereby isolating the neighborhoods of the city, would have had a devastating effect on the mass demonstration of workers of the capital. The winter had been a severe one, however, and thick ice covered the Neva. The workers began to cross the ice to the other bank. There they joined their comrades and moved together along Liteinyi Prospekt to Nevskii. Another group of workers from the Vyborg quarter crossed Sampsonievskii Bridge to the Petrograd side and broke through police blockades to Troitskaia Square. A group of Vyborg District workers also reached the center via Upper Lebiazhii Bridge.

Workers from the Putilov Plant, men and women from the Ekaterinhof Mills, from the sawmills, chemical factories, and other enterprises assembled during the day on February 23 at the Narva Gate. A political meeting began. Unlike previous years, speakers did not hide their faces, pull their caps down over their eyes, or fear attacks from the police. Revolutionary slogans were openly proclaimed for the first time in a long while. "A cry suddenly rang out from the crowd: 'To Nevskii! March in ranks!' The crowd roared: 'To Nevskii! Demand bread! Peace! . . . Down with the war!' Bolshevik slogans against the war and the autocracy were heard once again. Revolutionary songs rang out in various places; red banners appeared from somewhere. They were grasped by the women: 'It's our holiday. We'll carry the banners! Putilov workers, let's go!' was heard at the Narva Gate."[67] Police detachments stopped the Putilov workers at the Kalinkin Bridge. The Putilov workers met them by dividing into small groups and continued by various roundabout routes along the Fontanka, the Obvodnyi Canal, and intermediate bridges to force their way to the center.

The workers moved to Nevskii Prospekt from various directions. Reports arrived from police stations: "At 4:40 P.M. a crowd approached Kazan Bridge along Nevskii Prospekt from Mikhailovskaia Street, singing songs and crying 'Give us bread!'" "Between 4:00 and 5:00 P.M., a crowd of about 150 workers, primarily young people, came from Sadovaia Street onto Nevskii Prospekt singing the workers' 'La Marseillaise.'" "On Liteinyi Prospekt workers formed a crowd some 1,000-strong and headed for Nevskii Prospekt from Znamenskaia Square." "At about 6:00 P.M. a crowd moved along Suvorov Prospekt to Nevskii. . . ." "At about 7:00 P.M., during the disorders on Nevskii Prospekt, a crowd of demonstrators appeared from Znamenskaia Square. . . ."[68]

Emerging onto Nevskii Prospekt in the afternoon of February 23, the workers did not disperse until late in the evening. Upon arriving at Nevskii, workers from the Lorenz Factory found large crowds there. "The police were powerless to disperse them. They would gather in bunches and then break up again. Pieces of red fabric knotted to staffs began appearing. The police tried to break through to them, but workers pushed the police onto the pavement, and in some places chased them away."[69]

On February 23 worker demonstrators moved along Nevskii Prospekt in separate groups as they had not yet formed a single mass. Their principal demand was "Bread!" This led tsarist authorities and casual bourgeois observers to characterize the movement that had begun as "food disorders" and a "hunger riot." "Bread!" was indeed the most popular slogan on the first day of the revolution. It touched the most vital interests of the people and made the masses understand the real cause of their sufferings, thereby facilitating the involvement of all toilers, including the most backward, in the revolutionary movement. The movement "based on the bread shortage" was transformed into a political struggle and a revolution against the war and tsarism.

Even on February 23 the demand "Bread!" had been supplemented with other, more ominous demands. Captain Chikolini reported that on February 23, as he made the rounds of the striking factories in the Vyborg quarter as garrison duty officer, he encountered a peaceful procession of workers demanding bread. "At that moment a rather hostile crowd started approaching them with cries of 'Down with the war!'"[70] These and other slogans merged. The Petrograd proletariat was on the way to revolution by demanding bread, peace, and liberty.

We have already noted that even before the revolution began the Bolsheviks had demonstrated the connection among these three slogans. A brochure, "The War and the High Cost of Living in Russia," published abroad in 1915 by the Central Committee of the RSDRP, in part was dedicated to the battle against hunger, the war, and tsarism. An associate of the procurator of the Petrograd District Court, I. Gromov, subsequently testified that he was struck by the fact that the workers who took to the street on February 23 did so in a rather organized manner, with identical slogans that corresponded with the words in the Bolshevik brochure mentioned above, which declared: "They drove our sons, brothers, and husbands away to war, and deprived us of bread." At the end of the brochure was found a call to take to the street with the red banner of insurrection.[71]

As the workers' demonstrations on Nevskii Prospekt broke off late in the evening, tsarist authorities began to assess the day's events. The head of the Petrograd secret police reported:

> In the morning of the aforesaid day skilled craftsmen *(masterovye)* from the Vyborg District present in the factories gradually began to stop work and to go out into the streets in crowds, openly expressing protest and dissatisfaction over the shortage of bread. The mass movement for the most part took on such a provocative character that it was necessary to reinforce police details everywhere. News of the strike that had broken out spread to enterprises throughout all of Petrograd, and their skilled craftsmen began to join the strikers.[72]

The tsarist secret police noted the extraordinary drive and determination of the workers. "The majority of workers who left the factories spent almost all of the time on the streets, where they would organize demonstrations and disorders at the first convenient opportunity. . . . Strikers, who were dispersed in one place, would soon assemble in another, displaying dogged determination in all of this."[73] The Okhranka report gave statistics on the enterprises on strike—forty-three (with 78,444 workers). A different figure is adduced in a police memorandum on the events—fifty enterprises involving 87,534 workers. According to the compilation of I. P. Leiberov, based on police and Okhranka data, and on information from the factory inspectorate and the administrations of enterprises, more than 128,000 workers participated in the strike of February 23.[74]

The authorities were particularly anxious to prevent street demonstrations. On February 23 they were not yet employing firearms, but they did make extensive use of mounted and foot police, gendarmes, and cavalry units to break up demonstrations. Detachments of policemen, Cossacks, and cavalry would cut into the crowd of unarmed demonstrators. Participants in the demonstrations fell under the hooves of the policemen's horses and felt police whips on their backs. City Governor Balk claimed the police were acting most innocently. "During the day," he said, "the police merely dispersed crowds; no one was detained, weapons were not used, and there were no victims."[75] Nevertheless, even official records admitted that twenty-one workers were arrested on February 23. The protocol concerning the detention on February 23 of a worker from the Putilov Plant reads that he was arrested "for instigating street disorders conducive to the breaking of public order." The worker's entire guilt consisted of "disobeying an order to return and luring others to follow him." "Weapons were not used," Balk assured. But it depends upon what one means by weapons—sabers, pikes, and whips were widely used already on February 23. "There were no victims." But aren't men beaten with whips and sabers and mutilated under the hooves of police horses victims?

The entire point is that the police and Cossack onslaughts did not achieve their aim and evoked still greater hatred and determination to fight among workers. "Be damned, you bloodsuckers!" they cried out to the police and gendarmes. Even though the police operated most zealously against the workers, they failed to disperse the demonstrators for long. The workers assembled again; they were not afraid of a new clash with the minions of tsarism and, if they got the chance, even to attack them. Demonstrators injured an auxiliary policeman at the corner of Finskii Lane and Nizhegorodskaia Street after he had tried to arrest a worker who had stopped a tram. Demonstrators beat up another policeman near the Finland Station.

A worker, A. Kuznetsov from the Metalworks, told about the clash between workers and mounted police at the Moscow Gate. The workers had gone to the center, after occupying a bridge and sidewalks.

> The gray, sullen faces looked stern and determined. . . . Suddenly the din subsided. A small piece of red cloth appeared on the bridge above people. . . . Kovalev's loud voice was heard: "Comrades! For the third year rivers of the blood of working people of all countries have been flowing. The rich have used the proletariat to protect their capital. . . .' 'The Pharaohs are coming!'[k] the crowd suddenly began to cry. Everyone shuddered. The speech abruptly stopped. A detachment of mounted police rushed to confront the workers. The demonstrators pressed together closely but continued their advance, for the threat of reprisal roused their will to fight. Stones began flying at the approaching police. People shouted, groaned, sang out, and cursed. Sabers clanged; whips whistled. The square was filled with moans. The police in a frenzy went to work with their whips and sabers. . . . The people were cruelly beaten and forced to retreat . . . only a small group of brave souls savagely defended themselves with stones, pressed together on all sides.

Still, the workers' movement did not end. The demonstrators gathered in small groups and forced their way downtown.[76]

On February 23 the proletariat, the principal force spearheading the revolution, rose to the struggle. In order to triumph, however, it had to bring the mass of the soldiery over to its side. On February 23, vacillation and indecisiveness were already evident among part of the troops fighting the revolutionary movement. While the police were furiously attacking unarmed workers, many soldiers and Cossacks carried out the orders of their superiors with much less zeal than the regulations demanded. Acting passively and flaccidly, they sometimes directly refused to carry out their officers' orders.

A Bolshevik working woman from the Promet Factory, A. I. Kruglova, described an encounter between workers of this enterprise and soldiers of the Novocherkassk Regiment and Cossacks.

> A detachment of Cossacks bore down on us quickly. But we did not waver; we stood in a solid wall as though turned to stone. An officer of the Cossacks yelled:

[k] People colloquially referred to the police as pharaohs.

> "Who are you following? You are being led by an old crone!" I said: "No old crone; but a sister and wife of soldiers at the front." What happened next was totally unexpected. The soldiers of the Novocherkassk Regiment lowered their rifles. . . . Someone at the rear yelled: "Cossacks, you are our brothers, you can't shoot us. . . ." And the Cossacks turned their horses around.[77]

Although instances of this kind were still isolated, they excited in workers the hope that when the decisive conflict came, the soldiers and Cossacks would not shoot the people. The Cossacks, loyal servants of tsarism during the First Russian Revolution, had ceased to play the role of executioner.

Like the tsarist authorities, the bourgeoisie saw the action of Petrograd's workers on February 23 as merely a hunger riot by an unorganized mob. Maintaining that the disturbances in Petrograd were occurring "because of the bread shortage," it feared that if the food question were not settled and the policies of the government remained unchanged, the consequences both for tsarism and for itself would be most lamentable. Some bourgeois figures kept asserting it was the government itself that was provoking the workers in order to find an excuse to suppress the movement and make a separate peace with Germany. The writer Zinaida Gippius,[1] who was close to these individuals, wrote in her diary on February 23: "Today disorders. . . . Again the Kadet fable that it is a provocation, that everything has been brought about 'provocatively,' that bread, if you please, has allegedly been deliberately concealed so that rebellions caused by hunger would justify a separate peace desired by the government. What stupid and blind distortions."[78]

After a short interval, the Fifth Session of the Fourth State Duma, where the main activities of the bourgeois parties were concentrated, returned to session on February 23. The Duma was out of touch with the turbulent events that had unfolded that day on the streets of Petrograd. Not a single demonstrator had paid any attention to it, and it, in turn, had not tried to establish contact with the demonstrators. Yet the threatening revolutionary din had penetrated even the thick walls of the Tauride Palace. This din forced the State Duma to discuss the food supply question. At the meeting on February 23, Duma deputies talked about fixed grain prices, the grain tax, and how to supply the army and cities with food. They criticized the government. Minister of Agriculture Rittikh and the conservative deputies told the State Duma to stay out of politics and concentrate all its attention on practical work to improve the food supply. The members of the Progressive Bloc ignored this appeal. They maintained that the street disturbances had been provoked by the government's policies that had to be decisively changed. Declaring policy to be indispensable, A. I. Shingarev suggested they must distinguish between short-sighted and dangerous policies that were leading the state to destruction, and judicious and

[1]Zinaida Nikolaevna Gippius (Hippius) (1867–1945) was a Russian symbolist poet and writer married to D. S. Merezhkovskii. Gippius presided over an important literary salon in St. Petersburg before the revolution; in 1919 she emigrated to Paris where she lived until her death.

constructive policies that would further strengthen it. Shingarev, assuring that the Kadets had helped and would continue to help the tsarist government resolve the food supply and other problems, called upon the tsarist authorities to embark upon a judicious and constructive path and "not quarrel with legislative institutions." He said the Duma should demand the government "either learn how to come to grips with its affairs or simply step aside."[79]

Representatives of the petit bourgeois parties made especially critical speeches at the Duma meeting on February 23. The Menshevik Skobelev said that the country was reaping the whirlwind. The measures the tsarist authorities were taking amounted to stoking the fire. By closing factories, the military administration was protracting workers' strikes. By condemning the population to hunger, the government was furthering the destruction of the existing order. Women and adolescents, driven to despair, had taken to the streets of the capital, demanding bread. Skobelev warned against possible consequences. "We know of cases in history when the authorities demoralized the country once and for all, and reduced the population to hunger. The indignant population cruelly punished those who had starved them."[80]

Mensheviks and Trudoviks complained that a proposal to organize the food supply and change the government had not been passed in good time, and a situation had been created that was now difficult to correct. Kerensky showed contempt for the people when he said: "After all, the masses are primitive. Hunger is turning into the only thing goading them. Their wits are dulled. All they want is to gnaw a crust of black bread. They have no sense. They just savagely hate everything stopping them from filling their bellies. You can't reason with these primitive masses any more, they just won't listen to words of conviction any longer."[81] Kerensky called on the Duma deputies "to struggle to prevent the insane authorities from destroying the state that is equally dear to us all." He proposed to demand the government's resignation and to reorganize the food supply by entrusting it to public committees that would include workers' representatives.

The State Duma simply refused to demand the government resign and confined itself to yet another statement to the tsarist authorities on the food supply question. The Duma believed the government must take immediate measures to guarantee food for the population of the capital and other cities, particularly workers in defense industries, and have town governments and other public forces involved in distributing the food. The Duma asked the government why it had closed the Izhora and Putilov plants. It asked the chairman of the Council of Ministers and the military and naval ministers what they intended to do "to restore normal production in the factories and take care of the tens of thousands of workers thrown into the street." The Duma wanted all the discharged workers of the Putilov and Izhora plants returned to work and to have these factories quickly back into operation. However, these measures, even if taken, could no longer remove the causes of the events of February 23.

The movement that broke out that day was immeasurably broader and more significant than it seemed to the bourgeoisie and landowners in the Duma.

Petit bourgeois leaders similarly failed to grasp what had occurred. The SR Zenzinov wrote that the strike movement of the Petrograd workers "was not considered abnormal. No one thought that movement presaged imminent revolution."[82] A Menshevik, O. A. Ermanskii, related that he was astounded by the demonstrations and street clashes on February 23, and to interpret them "as an overture to mighty events was something that really didn't enter my head at the time."[83] The Menshevik N. N. Sukhanov recalled that on February 22 and 23 "the city was full of rumors and a feeling of 'disorders.' Contemporaries had seen disorders of such dimensions dozens of times before; . . . that's all they were—there had not yet been any revolution."[84] The SR S. Postnikov wrote that everyone he had chanced to run into considered the events of February 23 no more than minor demonstrations owing to a shortage of bread. Only a female acquaintance, E. Evreinova, who had connections with the medical funds and workers' cooperatives, told him that "in peaceable working-class circles a most unusual mood and inclination to overt action exists, and there is no special agitation and propaganda."[85] Assuming the events were hunger rebellions and disorders, the leaders of the Mensheviks and Socialist Revolutionaries remained inactive on February 23, refraining from involvement in what was happening in the streets.

The authorities claimed they had not expected the workers to demonstrate. "The events of February 23 broke out suddenly. I did not anticipate the movement among the troops or the powerful swell among the workers," Protopopov said. General Balk maintained the same: "Prior to February 23 the units were not ordered to strengthen details in the streets and elsewhere. Early on February 23 a strike involved half of the factories and plants. I had no idea this would happen. This movement took us by surprise. No police units were on the streets. I called the units always available, mounted police, gendarmes, and cavalry detachments."[86]

The police authorities saw that revolutionary ferment was growing. They knew they might expect a revolution very shortly, and therefore they mobilized all their forces to crush it. The worker demonstrations on January 9 and February 10–14, 1917, were known in advance; the authorities had been informed about them and prepared to suppress them beforehand. But February 23 was different. As they had done before, the tsarist authorities had made available police, the gendarmerie, and large military units, and, on command, they could swing into action in accordance with an established plan, similar to how it had been done on the eve of the events of February 10–14. However, the limited extent of the revolutionary movement during those days had dulled the tsarist authorities' vigilance. They did not know the workers would come out again precisely on February 23, and when the movement actually began they did not comprehend how truly dangerous it was to tsarism. The revolution caught the tsarist government by surprise and sowed confusion in its midst. Its suddenness helped the revolution to succeed in its early stages.

At a meeting in the city governor's office on the evening of February 23, Balk reproached the police for not informing him in good time of what was taking place. If the disturbances should resume he ordered all the police ranks to go into the streets, continue to use former methods to disperse the crowd, prevent more than five or six individuals from gathering, yet not to resort to shooting.

At the same time the tsarist authorities tried to convince the population there was no food crisis. Why, then, did lines form in front of shops and tens of thousands of people remain without bread? The commander of the Petrograd Military District, General Khabalov, provided an answer in an address to the population. He said: "During the last few days flour has been distributed to bakers and as much bread has been baked in Petrograd as before. There should not be any shortage of bread for sale. If bread was short in a few shops it was because many, fearing shortages, bought up reserves to make into biscuits. There was sufficient rye flour in Petrograd. The delivery of this type of flour has been uninterrupted."[87] A declaration of that sort could not dispel hunger, however, and as before there was simply not enough bread.

Summarizing the events of the day, Protopopov noted in his diary that "the day of the 23d was not all that bad; several policemen were injured; but there was no shooting." The Department of the Police reassured itself and its command that the movement could not have serious consequences and hopefully several factories would resume work on the twenty-fourth. It was openly assumed that the movement that had broken out was not political and was possibly limited to the strikes and demonstrations that had taken place on the twenty-third. Employees of the Petrograd secret police were less optimistic in their appraisal of developments. A memorandum by one of its agents dated February 23 read that "the shortage of bread is driving the working masses into the streets, and the idea that an uprising is the only means to escape from the food crisis is becoming more and more popular among the masses. Now everyone on the street in lines for bread and other essentials is saying an uprising is imminent and inevitable; soldiers, sailors, and intellectual circles are talking about it."[88] The Petrograd Okhranka observed that some soldiers of the Semenovskii Regiment were readily saying they would "shoot into the air" should an uprising begin.

The tsarist authorities believed the movement that had flared up on February 23 could be suppressed without special difficulty because it was spontaneous. It was precisely the fact that the revolution possessed an uncontrollable spontaneous force, however, that testified to its deep roots and vitality. Lenin observed that "the spontaneity of the movement is proof that it is deeply rooted in the masses, that its roots are firm and that it is inevitable."[89] Revolutions in which the masses would rise up immediately and in an organized manner did not occur. "Spontaneous outbreaks become inevitable as the revolution matures," Lenin said. "There has never been a revolution in which this has not been the case, nor can there be such a revolution."[90]

Spontaneity manifests itself with even greater force in bourgeois-democratic revolutions that attract wider strata of the unorganized masses of the people than in socialist revolutions. The higher the degree of organization in bourgeois-democratic revolutions, the more active is the working class's participation in them. The experience of many countries and of Russia in particular testifies to this. The actions of workers on February 23, 1917, were not foreseen, they did not unfold according to a definite plan, and they were not directed from a single center. They consisted of a great number of skirmishes and clashes, largely independent of one another.

Nonetheless, the Russian bourgeois-democratic revolution, led by the proletariat, was immeasurably more organized than the bourgeois-democratic revolutions, led by the bourgeoisie, that had occurred in Western Europe in the earliest days of capitalist development. The workers who came out into the streets of Petrograd on February 23 had a well-defined aim and previous revolutionary experience. They acted with a certain consistency. They quit work, assembled for political meetings, went out into the streets, "removed" workers from other enterprises, and after fusing with them in a general demonstration, went to the center of town. Although they came out alone, the workers drew other elements of the toiling people, soldiers above all, into the struggle.

The workers' movement took place under the influence of Bolshevik ideas. Although it had been prepared by the party's entire previous activity, it immediately assumed such vast dimensions and aroused so many of the masses to struggle that it was impossible to direct it into a tightly organized channel. The insignificant size of the underground party organizations rendered it impossible for them to guide the movement that had broken out; however, they tried to influence it as much as possible, to strengthen its organization, and to lead it in a more reliable manner toward the designated goal.[91]

On the evening of February 23 the Bolsheviks discussed the results of the first day of the revolution and outlined the tasks of the future struggle. The Bureau of the Central Committee of the RSDRP had a secret rendezvous in the very center of the Vyborg side, in the Pavlovs' apartment on 35 Serdobolsk Street. A great deal of information was brought together here about events at factories and in the streets of the capital. Members of the Petersburg and Vyborg district party committees came here to share their impressions of the events and coordinate their activities. Reports from the field noted that the next day all the factories on the Vyborg side and a number of enterprises in other regions of Petrograd would also go out on strike. At the time the tsarist authorities and bourgeois figures saw the actions of February 23 only as "hunger riots," the Bolsheviks evaluated them as having great political significance with a definite revolutionary character. Would these events become the decisive skirmish with tsarism? Shliapnikov wrote:

> We did not regard the movement that started on February 23 as the beginning of a resolute assault on the tsarist throne. But we took objective conditions into account. The workers' economic position had sharply worsened, people were dissatisfied with the war, the bourgeoisie was displeased with the failure to win the war, and also the entire economic ruin was intensifying and the reaction was fierce, and thus we admitted a revolutionary hurricane might arise even from an insignificant wind. Therefore we watched the movement of February 23 with extreme care and attentiveness, and all organizations were directed to develop the movement, not to limit it to a fixed period as was common in those times.[92]

To fix dates when the movement should end, to declare a one- or three-day protest strike would mean to place foreordained limits on the movement and slow it down. That is why the Bureau of the Central Committee of the Petersburg Committee of the RSDRP, as Shliapnikov stated, proposed to expand the movement "to its extreme limits." The skirmishes armed workers and soldiers fought with the police and troops loyal to the tsar suggested such limits.

Late in the evening of February 23 Bolsheviks met in the Vyborg District to discuss the situation created by the workers' actions. The meeting was held in the room of a worker, I. Aleksandrov, on Golovinskii Lane. In attendance was a representative of the Bureau of the Central Committee, Zalutskii, members of the Petersburg and Vyborg committees, and workers from other parts of the capital—A. K. Skorokhodov, I. D. Chugurin, K. I. Shutko, N. F. Sveshnikov, I. Ivanov, P. Alekseev, S. Lobov, V. Narchuk, A. Efimov, N. Agadzhanova, and others. This meeting, Sveshnikov related, "dragged on until late evening and adopted a series of important decisions, such as strengthening agitation and forming ties among soldiers, acquiring weapons, continuing the strike, and organizing a demonstration on Nevskii on February 25. It was recommended that all the comrades go to the factories in the morning, not take up work, and after a brief meeting lead as many workers as possible in an antiwar demonstration to Kazan Cathedral."[93] All participants at the gathering spoke in favor of advancing the slogan of overthrowing the autocracy, believing that its entire prior historical experience had prepared the masses for it. "Our agitation," wrote Sveshnikov in his memoirs, "was facilitated wonderfully by the objective course of things. To overthrow the autocracy was, in everyone's mind, a perfectly comprehensible act. Although our relationship to the slogan 'Down with the war' was more complex, many still went to the demonstration."

Few imagined the events of February 23 meant the Second Russian Revolution had started, but within several days this became quite clear. Just as January 9, 1905, marked the beginning of the First Russian Revolution, and October 24, 1917, the beginning of the Great October Socialist Revolution, February 23 marked the first day of the Second Russian Revolution.[94]

The first Bolshevik chronicle of the revolution, which M. I. Ul'ianova and A. I. Ul'ianova-Elizarova compiled, stated:

> On Women's Day, February 23, a strike was declared at the majority of factories and plants. The women were in a very militant mood—not only the women workers, but the masses of women standing in line for bread and kerosene. They held political meetings, they predominated in the streets, they moved to the City Duma with a demand for bread, they stopped streetcars. "Comrades, come out!" enthusiastic voices shouted. They appeared at factories and plants and called workers off the job. All in all, Women's Day went brilliantly and the revolutionary mood began to rise from that day on.[95]

A leaflet, "A Great Day," issued on March 2, 1917, by the Bureau of the Central Committee of the RSDRP, noted that women were the first to take to the streets of Petrograd and that Women's Day was the first day of the revolution.

> In the bleak war years, women assumed unprecedented burdens: heartfelt pain for their dear ones swallowed up by the war alternated with pain for their hungry children. Yet women did not yield to desperation. They raised the banner of revolution. . . . February 23—Women's Day—was the day of the Russian Revolution, the first day of the Third International. . . . Hail to women! Hail to the International! Hail to the Great Russian Revolution![96]

The beginning of the Second Russian Revolution differed radically from the start of the first. On January 9, 1905, masses of Petersburg workers had marched on the Winter Palace with a petition, believing the "little father" tsar would grant concessions to the people. Tsarism shot away their faith and taught the proletariat an object lesson in civil war. The procession of workers to the tsar became the start of a popular revolution against tsarism. However, almost a full year of embittered encounters had to pass. The stormy October and November strikes were needed before that revolution reached its highest stage on the barricades of Moscow and other cities of Russia in December 1905. The Second Russian Revolution did not go through these stages. It picked up where the first one had stopped. The proletariat of Russia was not the same as it had been in 1905. It had outlived its tsarist illusions long ago, acquired experience in revolutionary struggle, and received a baptism by fire in its battle against the autocracy.

The strikes and demonstrations of the Petrograd workers on February 23 marked the beginning of the uprising. The workers took to the streets of the capital that day not to protest particular measures of the tsarist authorities or to win partial concessions from it. They rose up to overthrow tsarism, which had brought the people nothing but hunger. Not all demonstrators fully understood this goal at the time, and the slogan "Down with tsarism" was drowned out by the demand "Bread!" Still, the objective meaning of the actions on February 23 was precisely that.

Strikers and demonstrators on the first day of revolution became insurgents, even though they had embarked on a revolution against tsarism without weapons or organized fighting detachments like those the Moscow workers had formed during the December battles of 1905. Nevertheless, this was an unarmed uprising and remained such. It could not gain a victory, but as the struggle developed such an uprising could acquire armed force. By drawing tsarist troops to the side of the people, which meant arming the uprising as it went along, the workers created the basic condition to overthrow tsarism. How did the struggle unfold on succeeding days?

The Revolution Broadens and Deepens

On the second day of the revolution, Friday, February 24, Petrograd workers assembled at their places of employment at the usual morning hour, but many of them went to political meetings and not to their machines. Appeals rang out: Don't go to work, continue the strike, demonstrate as you did yesterday. The workers responded to these calls good naturedly. The strike acquired a new powerful impetus; it involved a significantly larger number of enterprises and workers than the day before. About two hundred thousand people were on strike. From participation in strikes workers now got involved in revolutionary actions. They took part in street fighting and during the struggle were transformed into soldiers of the revolutionary army that overthrew the tsarist autocracy.

As on the previous day, Petrograd was the site of numerous demonstrations. Clashes with police took place, and crowds of people stopped streetcars and interfered with traffic. Waiting in line for bread, women and teenagers looted shops and bakeries. This was no replay of what had already occurred; demonstrations became larger and larger, and clashes with the police sharper. The army of the revolution was still unarmed, but it had boldly begun the decisive battle against the enemy. The strikes and demonstrations begun on February 23 turned into insurrection and were now proceeding on a greatly enlarged scale and taking on more distinct forms. The workers, forcing their way to the streets, squares, and boulevards of Petrograd, had learned from the first day of struggle. They had won their first positions for the decisive assault on tsarism. The task was now to fortify and broaden it.

The Vyborg District was, as before, in the vanguard of the movement. On February 25 the overwhelming majority of workers in the district continued the strike and took to the streets. A demonstration began as early as 8:00 A.M. in the Vyborg quarter. Workers moved along a route already "familiar": along Sampsonievskii Prospekt to Liteinyi Bridge, to penetrate the center of the city. Detachments of police, Cossacks, and soldiers tried to stop the procession. A mass of workers, as many as forty thousand in number, moved across the entire width of the Liteinyi Bridge, pressing against the mounted police guard. At the end of the bridge, it broke through the line of cavalry: one part of the demonstrators surged onto Liteinyi Prospekt; another was driven back to the Vyborg side. As on the first day of the revolution, many workers began crossing to the other bank of the river over the frozen Neva.

Workers from other districts of the city joined those from Vyborg. On February 24 Vasilevskii Police Headquarters reported that workers in the Laferme Tobacco Factory, the Siemens and Halske Works, and other enterprises had struck, and crowds of workers singing "La Marseillaise" were demonstrating on Bolshoi and Srednii prospekts, the Nikolaevskii Embankment, and on Fifth, Eighth, and other avenues of Vasilevskii Island. On the Petrograd side, workers of the Mechanical Plant struck and took to the streets, while on Kamennoostrovskii Prospekt and elsewhere, workers' demonstrations and clashes with civilian police and Cossacks occurred. Workers in the Military Horseshoes Factory in the harbor district stopped work. At the Shchetinin Works, a meeting took place where speakers called for support of the workers in the Vyborg quarter and for following their example with a strike. They shouted slogans: "Down with the tsarist government!" "Down with the monarchy!" "Down with the war!" The police agent reported that "after these speeches, all hands left the plant and headed for the Slesarenko Factory."[97] Near the Moscow Gate, workers of the Westinghouse Plant struck on February 24, and those of the New Cotton Spinning Mill joined them. United, they headed for Nikolaevskii Station.

Young people played an active role in the events of the second day of the revolution, as they had the day before. Before the revolution, progressive young workers had engaged in underground work, occupied themselves in study circles, distributed leaflets, and participated in strikes. Now both they and the entire mass of working-class youth had joined the street fighting. They marched in the front ranks of the demonstrators, attended rallies, and clashed with the police. Working-class adolescents were the point men of the revolution. They were the first to inform the workers that troops and police were approaching, tell them where demonstrators were to assemble, what rallies were scheduled, and so forth. Young workers organized pickets to prevent resumption of work. The police reported on February 24 that crowds consisting chiefly of young people and adolescents were stopping streetcars, singing revolutionary songs, and throwing chunks of ice, bolts, and other objects at the police. Workers from sixteen to twenty years old figured in the list of those arrested that day.

Detachments of police, Cossacks, and soldiers tried to disperse workers' demonstrations and restore "order" on the streets of the capital. This was the first time the overwhelming majority of the demonstrators had had to endure the onslaught of police and troops, but participation in the demonstration had fused the disparate parts into a whole. More experienced comrades advised the ranks of the workers: "Lock arms. It will be harder for cavalry to break the chain." And, in fact, it was becoming harder and harder to disperse the crowds of workers. Working men and women sought to win the tsarist troops to their side or at least to neutralize them. As on the first day of the revolution, the defenders of the autocracy overtly vacillated. On February 24 considerably more Cossacks appeared on Bolshoi Sampsonievskii Prospekt than the day before. A Bolshevik worker, I. Gordienko, related that the situation grew tense and a clash appeared inevitable.

> The working women took the initiative. They surrounded the Cossacks in a solid wall. "We have husbands, fathers, and brothers at the front!" they cried. "Here there is hunger, intolerable toil, insult, outrages against us, and humiliation. You too have mothers, wives, sisters, children: we are demanding bread and an end to the war!" The officers, fearing the influence of this agitation upon the Cossacks, gave their command. The Cossacks put their horses into a gallop. People dashed out of the way, each with a rock or wrench at the ready, but the Cossacks passed us by, didn't touch us, turned, and rode back to their former position. They were welcomed with cries of "Hurrah!"[98]

V. N. Kaiurov recalled in his memoirs a similar case when peaceful relations were established between the Cossacks and worker demonstrators in the vicinity of Bolshoi Sampsonievskii Prospekt.

> The Cossacks drew themselves up about sixty or seventy feet in front of the demonstration. . . . The officer's command rang out, and the Cossacks, sabers bared, drove down on our totally defenseless unarmed column. . . . Forcing their way through with their horses, their eyes bloodshot, the officers were the first to break into the crowd, and the Cossacks galloped behind, across the full width of the boulevard. . . . But such joy! The Cossacks rode single file into the aperture the officers had just opened. Some of them smiled, and one actually winked at the workers. There was no end to our delight. Yells of "Hurrah" for the Cossacks rose from thousands of chests.[99]

On February 24 there were as yet few such instances. The armed forces of tsarism were still defending the existing order. They ringed bridges and occupied main street crossings to prevent the workers from reaching the center of town. Workers had to clash with squads of Cossacks in order to break through to the center of the city. On February 23 individual groups of workers managed to get there by midday, but on the twenty-fourth the entire mass of striking workers was stubbornly determined to achieve this goal in the morning. To which district in the center did the workers head? Not long before, the Workers' Group of the War Industries Committee had called upon the workers to march to the State Duma, but all was quiet and empty around the Tauride Palace. The State Duma was remote from events and the workers paid no attention to it. As on the previous day, they went to Nevskii Prospekt. Crowds of workers streamed toward it from all parts of town.

The authorities reported that at about 1:00 P.M. a large crowd of workers had assembled between Kazan and Police bridges. "This crowd sang 'La Marseillaise,' 'Arise, Raise Yourselves Up, Working Folk!' and with such cries as 'Give us bread!' they uttered revolutionary slogans like 'Down with the tsar!'

and 'Down with the government!' and unfurled red flags." At 4:20 a crowd of workers singing revolutionary songs again approached Kazan Bridge. "Efforts to disperse the crowd were made for an hour and a half, but the people in the crowd, when driven from one place, would immediately regroup in another."[100]

Large masses of workers headed for Kazan Cathedral where rallies took place in the square in front of the building. Speakers urged demonstrators to make a decisive assault on the war and tsarism. Still larger rallies took place on Znamenskaia Square. The first groups of worker demonstrators broke through to there at about 3:00 P.M. on February 24. Mounted police tried in vain to disperse the workers who had arrived at the square. They were met with a hail of stones and chunks of wood, and the frightened horses carried their riders away. Cossacks were also present, but they did not attack the demonstrators. The crowd greeted the Cossacks with cries of "Hurrah," and the Cossacks responded by bowing low to the crowd. Worker demonstrators converged from various directions upon the granite pedestal above which towered the cast-iron, heavy-set body of Alexander III seated on an enormous horse. A virtually nonstop political rally went on at this monument, at which speakers shouted, "Down with the war!" "Down with tsarism!" "Long live a democratic republic!" A daring individual in an unbuttoned coat and hatless crawled from the shoulders of others onto the tsar's pedestal. This bold spirit rose to his full height and raised his right hand: "Comrades! Russia's blood continues to flow from beneath this brainless cast-iron blob. The senseless military slaughter undertaken by the camarilla has already led the entire nation to ruin!"[101]

The armed forces of tsarism sought to fragment the mass of workers and to prevent separate groups from forming a united revolutionary demonstration. Squads of police, Cossacks, and soldiers fell upon the demonstrators who had broken through to Nevskii Prospekt. Kaiurov reported that on February 24 Cossacks were incessantly attacking demonstrating workers on Nevskii, and later dragoons made their appearance. The revolutionary mass held firm. The workers continued to gather at one and then at another part of Nevskii to resume the demonstration. "The dragoons and Cossacks again and again attacked the demonstrators until nightfall, preventing the demonstration from moving ahead and breaking it up into parts."[102]

By the evening of February 24 the struggle on the streets and squares of Petrograd had quieted down, and the worker demonstrators dispersed to their neighborhoods. What would the next day bring? A report of the police authorities on February 24 stated: "A crowd of about 3,000 workers moving along Nevskii Prospekt paused at house no. 80 and listened to a speaker who called for the overthrow of the existing system and proposed they assemble tomorrow, the 25th of February, at noon in front of Kazan Cathedral."[103]

Nevskii Prospekt was quiet only for the night. The revolutionary movement in the capital resumed with new force on the third day of revolution on the morning of February 25, reaching a new height. The number of strikers that day increased by another one hundred thousand to total over three hundred thou-

Unidentified orator addressing demonstration in Mariinskaia Square. From a photograph in the Museum of the Hungarian Labor Movement, Budapest.

sand.[104] The strike became general. Large and medium-sized factories and mills had stopped work, and now printshops, small enterprises, workshops, and commercial establishments did too. . . . Streetcar traffic came to a complete standstill, and newspapers ceased publishing.

As on the previous day, the workers of the Vyborg side began February 25 with rallies at their factories. A Bolshevik, A. Kondrat'ev, described a rally at the New Parvianinen Factory. The workers sat in front of half-finished products, on ceiling trusses, practically under the roof, and every word the comrades spoke elicited a storm of approval. "The speakers were Bolsheviks, Mensheviks, and Socialist Revolutionaries. The slogan was to march to Nevskii. . . . One speaker ended with the revolutionary verse: 'Out of the way, obsolete world, rotten from top to bottom. Young Russia is on the march!' The atmosphere was tense. . . . There was comradely enthusiasm. We would live or die together in the struggle."[105] The mass of workers from that factory poured into the street and, joining with workers from other enterprises on the Vyborg side, moved in a united demonstration along Bolshoi Sampsonievskii Prospekt.

Workers from other quarters of the capital also demonstrated with determination on February 25. Workers in the largest enterprise on Vasilevskii Island, the Pipe Plant, went out on strike that day. The enterprise belonged to the state, and its manager decided to resort to arms to force resumption of work. When soldiers in a reserve battalion of the Finland Regiment were summoned, the workers approached them and tried to persuade them not to shoot. The soldiers hesitated. Then an officer shot one of those who had approached, a young worker named Dmitriev, and killed him on the spot. Dmitriev's murder provoked the masses of workers of Vasilevskii Island to an explosion of outrage. Downing tools, they took to the streets. The marching demonstrators took Srednii Prospekt as their main route.

Workers of the Geisler, Vulcan, and other enterprises formed a common demonstration on Bolshoi Prospekt on the Petrograd side, determined to bring out the remaining factories of their district. They marched while singing, organizing political rallies along the way and stopping streetcars. Overcoming police blockades, the demonstration grew and added new elements. The workers headed for Troitskii Bridge to break through to Nevskii.

The workers of the Obukhov Factory joined the movement. At 9:00 A.M. on February 25, fourteen thousand striking workers from the Obukhov Factory, revolutionary songs on their lips, headed for the center of the city. Their red banners were clearly inscribed: "Down with the autocracy! Long live a democratic republic!" The revolutionary movement now encompassed every district of Petrograd. Workers from Petrograd's outlying districts—Okhta, Novaia Derevnia, Kolpino—rose in struggle as well. There were street demonstrations on Galernyi Island and in the harbor district. The general strike spawned a general demonstration. As before, striking workers headed for the center of the city, to Nevskii Prospekt. No force could bar their way. On the morning of February 25, mounted police and Cossacks attempted to prevent demonstrating workers of the Vyborg side from marching to Liteinyi Bridge. Police Chief Shalfeev rode up to the crowd and told the workers to disperse, but they pulled this high police official off his horse and beat him up. Heavy objects were thrown at the police. Overpowering police resistance, the workers crossed the bridge and emerged on Liteinyi and Nevskii prospekts. Demonstrators from other parts of Petrograd also marched to the center of the city.

"The workers are coming!" resounded along Nevskii, and soon the capital's major avenue and adjacent streets were filled with workers. The entire appearance of this part of the city changed rapidly. Stores, restaurants, and cafes soon closed, streetcars stopped running, and cabmen disappeared. There was virtually nothing left of the usual strolling public. Crowding the sidewalks, local residents watched the unusual spectacle. Meanwhile the working people paraded down the road in motley, irregular ranks, but even so they instilled fear in the masters of the city. Well-fed, dandified aristocrats and the bourgeoisie disappeared from Nevskii Prospekt, replaced by people with lean emaciated countenances from the workers' suburbs. Beaver hats and fur coats were no longer to be seen on Nevskii. Instead there were stiff visored caps, neckerchiefs, head scarves, well-worn cloth coats, and double-breasted jackets. Nevskii had been won by the worker masses. It had beheld no such mass of workers since the First Russian Revolution.

Mounted police, Cossacks, and soldiers sought to break up the rallies and demonstrations on Nevskii. The crowd retreated under their onslaught but did not leave the field of battle. The workers moved from one place to another, scattered and assembled anew. The police and military pressed the workers into side streets, yet the workers kept striving to reach Nevskii, clashing again and again with the defenders of tsarism. An enormous mass of demonstrators was concentrated on the corner of Liteinyi and Nevskii prospekts. Scattered by mounted units, they quickly assembled again and moved toward Kazan Cathedral. Another column of demonstrators emerged onto Nevskii Prospekt from the Spasskaia area. Shouts of "Down with the tsar!" "Down with the government!" and "Give us bread!" were heard constantly.

The demonstrators carried red flags along Nevskii and sang militant revolutionary songs—"La Marseillaise," "Varshavianka," and "Comrades, Boldly in Step." For the first time in many years free speech was heard in the Russian capital. Unknown speakers uttered impassioned words to the crowds: "Comrades! The time has come to put an end to the bloody war and the tsarist autocracy. Long live the revolution!" And in response there would come a mighty "Hurrah" and the confident words of the militant song:

> With a mighty hand we shall sweep away
> Fatal oppression forever.

On the capital's main avenue, near the royal palaces and ministries, the rebellious proletariat loudly enunciated its demand in a mighty chorus: "Bread!" "Peace!" "Liberty!" The three slogans became one. Threatening demands of "Down with tsarism!" "Long live a democratic republic!" were now added. These appeals and slogans expressed the aspirations of the entire people, not merely the working class, and rallied all the toiling population around the workers. The proletariat was the first to rise up against tsarism and initially fought it single-handedly. As that battle developed the social base of the revolution began to broaden and the movement assumed the widest possible popular nature.

The proletariat's selflessness and persistence roused wide masses of people to struggle against tsarism. The urban petite bourgeoisie—including artisans, office workers, professionals, university, institute, and upper-level secondary-school students, and others—began to join the workers. These elements demonstrated more passively than the proletariat. Crowds of inhabitants of the capital supported the workers' demonstrations and were outraged by police actions. Some joined the ranks of the demonstrators and became participants rather than mere spectators. The nonproletarian city dwellers, diffused in the general mass of insurrectionists, could not exercise a decisive influence on the revolution. Events were determined as before by the working class. Nonetheless, the participation of these elements of the population afforded the revolution new scope and furthered its success. An atmosphere of mutual empathy was created, which raised the morale of the insurrectionists and reinforced their determination to continue the struggle.

Students demonstrated great activity during these days. They gathered at numerous assemblies to discuss current events and the question of joining the workers. On February 25 students at Petrograd University declared a strike and students in other higher educational institutions in Petrograd resolved to join them. A memorandum of the Police Department stated: "Complete sympathy with the movement is to be observed among the students of higher educational institutions. Speakers are holding assemblies within their walls. High school students are taking part in the street disorders."[106]

Classes were suspended at the institutes of higher education. Of course, not all students joined the ranks of those fighting for the revolution; some went home. Student demonstrations on Vasilevskii Island took place. Crowds of students, primarily from the Psychoneurological Institute, demonstrated near Znamenskaia Square. Students did not usually march in groups of their own but in the general ranks. Student caps flashed here and there among the enormous mass of workers proceeding through the streets of Petrograd. These were student youth who had left the classroom and taken to the street in support of the workers.

The major centers for demonstrations and meetings were, as previously, Kazan Cathedral Square and Znamenskaia Square. Groups of demonstrators started assembling at the cathedral at noon on February 25. A member of the Interdistrict Committee of the RSDRP, a woman student, R. Kovnator, recounted that when two red banners bearing the inscriptions "Down with the autocracy" and "Long live the revolution" appeared over the crowd at the cathedral, joyous cries arose, "for it was exactly such banners of hope and struggle that served to unite the mood of the enormous crowd of many thousands." A rally took place at Kazan Cathedral. I. Iurenev [an Interdistrictite—D.J.R.] "moved from one group to another. As I recall, he spoke of the struggle of the working class, appealed to the tradition of great revolutionaries of the past, and called upon the crowd of workers to swear that this time it would not disperse until it had gained its objective. . . . Suddenly the police flung themselves upon the crowd and several persons were arrested. The crowd rushed to release them. The arrested were rescued from the police."[107] Then the demonstrators moved to Znamenskaia Square, where a new rally took place at the monument to Alexander III, accompanied by a fierce clash with Cossacks and police. The police and Cossacks threw themselves upon the demonstrators with whips. Those who fell were trampled by horses; one heard the whistle of the whips and screams of pain blending with yells of outrage.

The rallies at Znamenskaia Square were particularly broad in scope. At midday on February 25 the precinct police captain Krylov tried to disperse the rally at the Alexander III monument and wrest the red flag from the workers, but Krylov was cut down by a saber on the square. Who did this? The secret police reported that it was a Cossack. A number of other sources indicate that the Cossacks drove the mounted police away and prevented their attempts to disperse the crowd. The demonstrators gave an ovation to the Cossacks; the rally on the square continued.

In other places as well, monuments to the tsars were used as sites for revolutionary rallies. A Bolshevik workingman, Gavrilov, wrote: "The monuments to the Russian emperors became the tribunals of the revolution. A young worker grasping the sword of Peter the Great called on those assembled on Sampsonievskii Prospekt to rise in armed struggle."[108] A thunderous call directed against tsarism arose around the monuments to the tsars. The demand for bread receded. The workers' struggle grew with slogans to overthrow the autocracy and to end the imperialist war. Bolshevik workers from the Erikson Plant and other enterprises turned out red banners with the slogans "Down with the war" and "Down with the autocracy." On February 25 demonstrations took place under those banners on Nevskii Prospekt and Znamenskaia Square.

The clashes between the two camps of revolution and tsarism grew steadily fiercer. The workers defended themselves against police and troops, also taking the offensive when they could. They carried bolts, nuts, and scraps of iron with them from the factories to use against the enemy. They utilized such "materials at hand" as lumps of frozen snow, pieces of ice, stones, chunks of wood, etc., for they had no rifles or revolvers. Avoiding clashes with the soldiers, the workers fell upon isolated policemen and gendarmes, taking their weapons from them. During these days hatred for the gendarmerie and police, universal among the people, was rampant.

For many years the people had endured their arbitrary behavior, brutality, oppression, and humiliation. During the imperialist war, while millions of soldiers lay dying on the fronts, the police sat it out at the rear, taunting the population and suppressing all attempts to win liberty. In the early days of the revolution the gendarmes and police were the most zealous defenders of tsarism. "Disperse! Fall back!" mounted police would holler, cut into the crowd on their horses, and strike the demonstrators with pikes, sabers, and knouts. The people referred to the city police as "hides for sale" and "pharaohs" and reserved their greatest wrath for them. The demonstrators initially defended themselves against the attacks of the police, but later began to take the initiative themselves, and settled accounts with the police at every opportunity.

On Bolshoi Sampsonievskii Prospekt workers pulled several police off their horses and gave them thorough beatings. Suffering losses, city police were beaten and disarmed at the Anichkov Bridge, Suvorov Prospekt, and many other points in the capital. On the embankment of Catherine Canal, empty bottles were thrown at mounted police and Cossacks, and a few shots were fired as well. At the corner of Nevskii and Vladimirskii prospekts the crowd surrounded and disarmed three police inspectors. By the close of February 25, disarming and beating of the police had become so widespread that they were afraid to be alone. For security some of them donned military overcoats or even changed to civilian clothing.

The workers took a different attitude toward the soldiers and Cossacks, whom they wanted to win over. Workers went to barracks to fraternize with soldiers. Groups of working men and women would gather around guards and patrols and hold conversations with the soldiers. One participant in the revolution recalled: "Soldiers and Cossacks are welcomed and greeted; no trace of the former bitterness toward them remains. . . . A worker comes up to a barracks and says to a soldier: You tell your guys to support us, not to attack their own kind. This time we're out for the real thing, no fooling. The soldier would nod."[109]

On February 25 cavalry units and Cossacks continued to be used extensively against worker demonstrators. They helped the police to scatter crowds of workers and beat demonstrators. Shots were fired at the people for the first time. In clashes with the police and troops on February 25, workers' blood was spilled on the streets of Petrograd, and the people made their first sacrifice. At the City Duma building on Nevskii Prospekt, soldiers of the Ninth Reserve Cavalry Regiment opened fire on the crowd, killing nine persons and wounding nine others.

In many cases, however, the soldiers and Cossacks were passive and left it to the police alone to move against the people who neutralized the tsarist army. Male and female workers seized rifles pointed at them and pleaded with the soldiers to support the people. The workers' actions confused the soldiers and Cossacks and disorganized their ranks. Guns aimed at the people stopped firing. In some instances, soldiers and Cossacks indirectly aided the worker demonstrators, and individual soldiers actually joined them. It was hard to capture such soldiers, for the crowd helped hide them.

A worker, Ershov, described a clash with Cossacks on Nevskii Prospekt:

> An order rang out. The demonstrators slowed their pace. "La Marseillaise" died down. . . . It looked as though the demonstrators would stop and the Cossacks would hurl themselves on them and beat them with their short, heavy, braided leather whips. First isolated voices and then a general cry rose from the crowd: "Bread!" "Peace!" The ranks of horses parted, and trickles of demonstrators would flow through the gaps that appeared, which soon became a living current of workers. They yelled greetings at the Cossacks. "Long live the army!" "Down with the war!" "Bread and peace!" "La Marseillaise" rang out again. The Cossacks formed a column and rode off.[110]

The worker Taimi reported on a demonstration on Nevskii Prospekt:

> In front they carried a flag on which was written: "We demand bread! Down with the tsar!" When we approached Anichkov Bridge, we saw a Cossack unit in front of us on the far side of the bridge. They rode slowly toward us in ranks of four. An officer rode in front. The distance narrowed minute by minute. Now our columns

> set foot on the bridge. We sang "La Marseillaise." . . . And suddenly a voice rang out from the crowd: "Long live the comrade Cossacks!" . . . The crowd picked it up. The Cossacks did not answer. Some smiled. That's how we got across Anichkov Bridge.[111]

Police supervisors and agents reported on February 25 that some of the military units failed to struggle against the people. Here are several excerpts: "While speeches were made the military units stood idly by." "A platoon of Cossacks of the First Don Cossack Regiment that had arrived took no steps whatsoever to restore order." "Some military units called out to suppress the disorders are cooperating with the demonstrators, and some units take a protective attitude toward them and encourage the crowd with promises: 'Put the heat on higher.' "[112]

Colonel Khodnev, head of the training command of the Finland Reserve Regiment, complained bitterly about the Cossacks. "The Don Cossacks," he wrote,

> were extremely slack in the capital and indecisive. They subsequently refused categorically to take action against the rebels, and even turned their arms against the defenders of legitimate rule and order. The inaction of the Cossacks was particularly apparent when they formed an individual patrol, mounted patrol, or platoon without senior officers, under the command of sergeants or young junior lieutenants. More than once I heard them threatening: "This isn't 1905. We won't carry whips . . . we won't move against our own kind, against the people."

Khodnev commanded a detachment composed of soldiers, Cossacks of the Fourth Don Cossack Regiment, and police. He ordered the Cossacks to deny passage over the Nikolaevskii Bridge to a crowd of workers who had marched from the Sixth Avenue on Vasilevskii Island. Khodnev wrote:

> A junior lieutenant slowly led his platoon from a yard and had them mount. Only when I pressed them they moved forward. The crowd had already reached the embankment and one could now hear yells, noise, and a kind of dull rumble. Imagine my amazement and rage when the Cossacks calmly let the crowd pass, which waved flags, shawls, and hats at them, and shouted words of greeting. The demonstrators, after getting by the Cossacks, again quickly closed ranks and ran for the bridge.[113]

The conduct of the soldiers and Cossacks showed that this time the army would be with the people. Joyous and sometimes exaggerated stories that soldiers had promised not to shoot, that Cossacks had chased away police, and so forth, circulated broadly. This augmented the forces of the revolution and strengthened the masses' determination to struggle until tsarism was totally routed. The enemies of the revolution also noted the significance of this fact. A police agent reported:

> Since military units did not block the crowd and in some cases even took measures to paralyze the police, the masses grew confident they would not be punished. Now, after two days of parading the streets unhindered, with revolutionary elements raising the slogans "Down with the war!" and "Down with the government!" the people are encouraged to think that a revolution has begun, that success is on the masses' side, that the authorities are powerless to suppress the movement because the military refused to support them. They believe final victory is near because military units will, tomorrow if not today, openly side with the revolutionary forces and the incipient movement will not subside and will grow uninterruptedly until final victory and the government is overthrown.[114]

Assessing events of February 25, the Department of Police observed that that day had to be considered an extremely difficult one for the police of the capital in their effort to end street disorders. The department stressed that the police were helpless and some soldiers and Cossacks sympathized with the people's movement.[115]

By the evening of February 25, as on the previous day, Petrograd grew quiet. Street lamps burned dimly, isolated shots rang out, muffled cries from the thinning crowd were heard. The city seemed to stand still. But lights burned brightly that evening at the Aleksandr Theater where the premier of Lermontov's *Masquerade* was being performed, memorable for its elaborate decorations, magnificent costumes, rich staging, and the fabulously expensive tickets, while not far from the theater crowds of people were demanding bread. In the last scene of *Masquerade* they sang a requiem to Nina, poisoned by Arbenin. To all intents and purposes the imperial theater and tsarist Russia also came to an end with the passing of the white figure of Death sung in the dirge. "The disaster of Khodynka[m] at the beginning of the tsar's reign and the grimaces of the splendid masquerade at the end. A bloody christening and a magnificent theatrical funeral!"[116]

On February 25 the funeral of the autocracy was still just symbolic; the authorities were still guarding the tsarist regime and taking measures to suppress the revolution. Police arrested demonstrators. It is clear from the protocols that have been preserved that those arrested were accused of violating police instructions and established order. Workers from the Arsenal, A. Zaitsev and A. Shevchuk, were arrested for refusing to obey the order of a gendarme officer, and the student Volkov for "failing to execute the orders of the city

[m] Refers to the tragedy that occurred on May 18, 1896, as part of the ceremonies planned to celebrate Nicholas II's coronation (which had been postponed owing to the period of mourning following his father's death). Perhaps as many as a half million people had gathered in Khodynka Field outside of Moscow in expectation of refreshments and coronation souvenirs. A stampede somehow began which resulted in the death and injury of several thousand people. Nicholas showed poor judgment in accepting the counsel of his uncles and court officials who urged him to attend an elaborate ball given by the French ambassador that evening. This left him open to the charges of critics of the regime.

governor himself." The workers Erokhin and Stanislavenkov, the tram driver A. Trubach, and others were arrested "for instigating strikes and street disorders." Police officials stiffly fined them all.[117]

The police could still make arrests; however, to guard those who had been apprehended and convey them to police stations was becoming steadily more difficult, for the crowd often freed the arrested. The police herded demonstrators they detained into courtyards, in hopes of restoring "order" in the main streets. But order was not restored and the popular masses set the arrested free. As an example, demonstrators found out that some sixty arrested workers had been confined in the courtyard of number 46 Nevskii Prospekt, and they started demanding their immediate release. When a police officer refused, workers stormed into the courtyard and released the arrested themselves.[118] A group of workers went along Kazan Street to house number 3 where twenty-five arrested demonstrators were held in the courtyard. The workers demanded their comrades' release. The worker V. Shepelev related:

> Here Cossacks with whips rode up and tried to convince the workers to disperse. What happened shows that the workers' revolutionary spirit somehow influenced the Cossacks. They became hesitant. Sensing a change in their mood, a worker cried out: "Comrade Cossacks, join us! Help us to free our comrades!" It was a tense moment. All eyes were fixed on the Cossacks. They formed a circle and began whispering to each other. Then, without saying a word, whooping and whistling, they charged into the courtyard where the arrested workers were. . . . Since the guard had not expected such a frenzied charge it was taken aback and within several minutes surrendered and gave up the arrested whom we met with the warmest welcome.[119]

The release of arrested demonstrators was characteristic of the third day of revolution. The workers grew more resolute. Toward evening on February 25 the demonstrators returned to the workers' neighborhoods, determined to continue the revolutionary fighting the next day. "Till tomorrow," they said to each other as they left Nevskii. Three days of strikes and street fighting had united and tempered the Petrograd workers and set new goals for them. The streets of Petrograd were the scene of the final and decisive battle with the tsarist autocracy.

The revolutionary forces had not yet launched an armed uprising, but events were leading up to one.[120] Now the question of who was to lead the revolution that had unfolded with the force of an impetuous, irrepressible whirlwind grew especially acute. On the evening of February 24 the best organized Bolshevik district committee, the one of the Vyborg side, met. P. Sveshnikov wrote: "All members of the district committee were present, and new ones also showed up—Comrades Moiseev and N. I. Medvedev—who were included in the district executive committee. The mood was animated, yet a lack of overall leadership and information from other districts was felt; precise revolutionary directives from the Central Committee were persistently demanded."[121] The same mood held sway at the meeting of party workers that took place on February 24 in the Pavlovs' apartment. "Everyone knew," Shliapnikov wrote, "that the revolution had begun, that Russia 'was on the move.' The revolutionary movement had affected so many that no one could doubt the decisive battle was underway."[122] This raised the issue of the need to increase fraternization with the soldiers and win the armed forces over from tsarism or at least to neutralize them. To this end it was decided to strengthen work among the soldiers, infiltrate their barracks, establish strong ties there, and secure arms.

Zalutskii related that several members of the Petersburg Committee at first were apprehensive how the struggle would develop now that tsarism had brought troops and Cossacks into the picture. Yet everyone soon agreed it was necessary to strengthen and deepen the ongoing movement and draw the soldiers into it. Only Ozol (Chernomor), who was subsequently unmasked as a provocateur, continued to object to actively involving soldiers in the movement. "The Executive Commission of the Petersburg Committee, however, was entirely against him and was on our side."[123]

On February 25 the Petersburg Bolshevik Committee drew up a far-reaching plan to develop and deepen the revolution. Unfortunately, only a police account of it has been preserved. A memorandum found in the Police Archive which, judging from its contents relates to February 25, says:

> The Petrograd organization of the RSDRP at the end of two days of disturbances that have taken place in Petrograd, decided to use the movement that had broken out to advance the aims of the party, take over the leadership of the masses participating in it, and give it a clearly revolutionary direction. Toward this end the said organization has proposed: (1) to publish a leaflet today, February 25 (draft appended); (2) to convene the committee tomorrow morning, February 26, to resolve the question as to what is the best and most expedient way to control the masses of striking workers already aroused but as yet insufficiently organized. Moreover, it was proposed to start erecting barricades on Monday, February 27, disconnect all electrical equipment, and shut off the water supply and telephones should the government take measures to suppress disorders.

This document stated that the Petrograd Bolshevik Organization had decided to form factory (obviously party) committees at enterprises right away to select representatives among their members to serve on the so-called Informational Bureau to Direct Factory Committees and transmit them directives from the Petersburg Committee of the RSDRP. It was further proposed to reorganize the Informational Bureau into a soviet of workers' deputies "like the one that had functioned in 1905."[124] The police memorandum also noted the Bureau of the Central Committee of the RSDRP had sent delegates to Moscow and Nizhnii-Novgorod on party business.

The extant sources do not say how the draft plan was fulfilled. The arrest of members of the committee prevented the meeting of the Petersburg Committee of the RSDRP called for the morning of February 26 from taking place.

Judging by Shliapnikov's memoirs, however, this police document correctly conveys the Petersburg Bolsheviks' intentions.

On February 25 the Petersburg Committee of the RSDRP issued a leaflet, the text of which, as Shliapnikov wrote, was composed by members of the Central Committee Bureau. The leaflet began: "It's become impossible to live. There's nothing to eat. There's nothing to wear. There's no fuel for stoves. At the front there's nothing but blood, mutilation, and death. The country has been devastated. There's no bread. Hunger has set in." Who is responsible? the leaflet asked, and answered plainly: the tsarist authorities and the bourgeoisie are guilty. It is they who rob the people and for the sake of profits and acquisition of new territories drag on the war without end and drive the people into a slaughterhouse. "Liberals and Black Hundreds, ministers and the State Duma, the nobility and the zemstvo—all have during the war formed one brutal gang." Flinging these awesome charges at tsarism and the bourgeoisie, the Bolsheviks urged workers to take to the streets, to fight for their interests, their children, and their brothers.

The leaflet by the Petersburg Committee of the RSDRP called on workers and soldiers to organize for the struggle against the oppressors and toward this end to establish first "committees of the Russian Social Democratic Labor party" in workshops, factories, neighborhoods, towns, regions—in barracks and throughout Russia.

> They will be committees of struggle, committees of liberty. Explain to peasants, city folk, and soldiers that their salvation depends on the victory of the Social Democrats. The time for an open struggle is nigh. Strikes, mass meetings, and demonstrations will strengthen, not weaken this organization. Take advantage of every opportunity, each suitable day. As much as possible be with the masses, delivering your revolutionary slogans. Let the lackies of capital call our activities strike provocations and a bunch of hot air—our salvation lies in immediate universal struggle; do not postpone it to a later date. . . . One simple action must grow into a national revolution that could foster revolution in other countries. We have a struggle in front of us, but victory awaits us. Everyone must be under the red banners of revolution! Down with the tsarist monarchy! Long live a democratic republic! Long live the eight-hour day! All landowners' estates to the people! Down with the war! Long live the brotherhood of workers of the entire world! Long live the Socialist International![125]

At a meeting of the Bureau of the Central Committee of the RSDRP on the evening of February 25, Zalutskii reported on the situation in various districts of Petrograd. Things were clearly going very well; underground Bolshevik organizations were striving to take control of the movement and to continue revolutionary demonstrations and fraternization with soldiers. The strike had become general and the workers' mood was becoming stronger and more militant. The workers had decided to keep on striking until they had won total victory over tsarism and had won over the soldiers to the revolution to help achieve this goal.

> The Petersburg Committee's ties with the barracks and in the districts have been mended. The Vyborg District is taking the lead. Several reserve regiments and detachments of bicyclists are stationed there, our comrades have begun to conduct heated agitation among them. . . . Thousands of workers are keeping an eye on the mode of life and the activities of soldiers in the barracks. The unrest reigning in the barracks has not gone unnoticed by them, and the slightest signs of insubordination on the part of the soldiers invigorates them and inspires hopes for victory.[126]

"To the barracks! To the soldiers!" This was the most important task of the day. The Petersburg Committee of the RSDRP addressed soldiers with an appeal to join the people. "Brother soldiers!" read a leaflet from the Petersburg Committee. "For the third day we, workers of Petrograd, are openly demanding the destruction of the autocracy, which has caused the people to shed blood, made our country hungry, and condemned our wives, children, mothers, and brothers to ruin. Remember, comrade soldiers, only the brotherly union of the working class and revolutionary army will emancipate the enslaved people and end the fratricidal senseless war. Down with the tsarist monarchy! Long live the brotherly union of the revolutionary army and the people."[127]

At this time the Interdistrictites also issued an appeal to further struggle. On February 24 the Interdistrict Committee of the RSDRP addressed a leaflet to workers and soldiers. The leaflet to workers said: "Hunger will not be eliminated by sacking shops or marching on the Duma. Revolution alone will lead us out of the blind alley of war and destruction. Get ready, comrades! Our enemy is awake. It's been two days already since 30,000 Putilovites were thrown into the street, demanding their discharged comrades be reinstated. Organize, comrades! The day of reckoning with your inveterate enemy is at hand."[128] The Interdistrictites proposed a three-day strike to protest the dismissal of the thirty thousand Putilovites, "the slaughter of people, autocratic arbitrariness, the prevalent hunger," and to take up collections on behalf of the Putilov workers and the illegal workers' press. They urged workers and soldiers to unite, to involve soldiers in the struggle, and to fight together for a democratic republic, socialism, the establishment of a provisional revolutionary government, and convocation of a constituent assembly.

The Interdistrict Committee's leaflet was a day late. Revolution had already begun and the battle cry of the day could no longer be a three-day protest strike; now the battle had to go on to total victory over tsarism, and this victory had to be won in street battles. I. Iurenev admitted the leaflets of the Interdistrictites expressed "uncertainty over whether the present battle is decisive, and the appeal to soldiers was distinctly half-hearted. We did not call for the soldiers to stage an immediate uprising."[129] Nevertheless, the emphatic protest found in the leaflet of the Interdistrictites against the imperialist war and the policies of tsarism proved to be of value.

On the streets of Petrograd, Mensheviks, SRs, and nonparty people fought alongside Bolshevik workers. During this struggle a unity of purpose was forged and unity of action began. The minimum Social Democratic program—which was the "three whales" of a democratic republic, an eight-hour workday, and the confiscation of landowners' estates—penetrated the vanguard of the working class and won genuine support among the masses of toiling people. Men and women, industrial workers and white-collar workers, students and pupils marched through the streets of the capital under the slogan "Down with tsarism!"

Although the movement was uncoordinated and lacked a single leadership, the insurgents adhered to a common tactic. They left factories and plants for the street, united into powerful demonstrations, and worked to draw the armed force of the autocracy to their side. As the revolution developed, the struggle to win the troops became the main goal for the insurgents because the outcome of the incipient struggle depended on achieving it. The Bolsheviks urged the working masses to strive toward this end. The workers had learned from the lessons of the long preceding struggle that this task was essential. They knew that it was the most reliable way to accomplish their desired goal.

In their common actions the workers were not directed, however, by comparable party centers. Unlike Bolshevik organizations, the other parties fumbled during these days. The SRs had no united center at all at this time. Zenzinov noted that on the eve of the revolution in Petrograd "the SR party organization was in shambles—here and there isolated party members carried on work on the outskirts and distributed homemade proclamations without any coordination."[130] During the revolution only a small group of Left SRs (P. A. Aleksandrovich, S. Maslovksii, and others) functioned, cooperating with the Interdistrictites. The two leading Menshevik organs, the Organization Committee and the Initiative Group, were isolated from events during the first days of the revolution. A member of the Initiative Group, Ermanskii wrote: "Events broke out very quickly. The strike became general. . . . If I had been asked at that time what would come of this movement, I would not have been able to answer concretely. . . . The leadership of the movement and of the actions of the masses was not visible. I don't know what other party organizations were doing at this time. Our admittedly weak Initiative Workers' Group didn't meet at all during these days; it existed only as the sum of its parts, not as a whole."[131]

Leading SRs and Mensheviks came out against the autocratic-landlord system, believing it must be replaced by bourgeois rule. They considered it the task of the proletariat to further the establishment of bourgeois power. This is why Menshevik and SR leaders during the decisive days of the revolution were moved to meet with Duma leaders to discuss creation of a bourgeois government. The SRs and Mensheviks included workers in their organizations, but they championed the interests of the petite bourgeoisie who suffered from lack of rights, police repression, the constraint of censorship, and who wanted the sort of parliamentary order that existed in Western Europe to replace tsarism. They feared the revolutionary struggle unfolding on the streets of Petrograd would go beyond permissible limits and frighten the bourgeoisie. Deputies belonging to the Social Democratic and Trudovik factions in the State Duma, publicists, literary men, and leaders of the cooperatives assembled during these days in private apartments to exchange opinions and discuss events. A conversation would typically begin with a discussion of the food question, and end with current political events. Appeals for militant street actions were few and far between at these meetings. The majority argued it was necessary to act moderately, not to push ahead, and to keep in step with the State Duma.

The meetings of petit bourgeois activists often took place in the apartment of the lawyer N. D. Sokolov. The master of the apartment, recently a Bolshevik, had taken up a defensist position during the war and enjoyed extensive ties with various political groups. Representatives of different political persuasions came here, including populists, such as Kerensky, N. Rusanov, Zenzinov, Chernolusski, and others. A participant in these conversations, Sukhanov, related that those who assembled discussed the problem of the war and of political power; they believed that the movement that had broken out would be victorious only if the bourgeoisie joined it, and they feared the antiwar slogans advanced by the Bolsheviks would scare the bourgeoisie away. Yet the petit bourgeois leaders at the time were unable to exercise any real influence on the movement. Sukhanov admitted: "I feel totally removed from the center of the revolution and completely helpless. I did not count on having even the slightest influence on the ruling centers of the movement. During the conversation with Sokolov I could think of nothing besides the consciousness of my helplessness to influence events somehow."[132]

Sukhanov actively contributed to the journal *Letopis'* (Chronicle), edited by Maksim Gorky. Representatives of the democratic intelligentsia had grouped themselves around this journal. During the revolution many people came to Gorky to share impressions, ask questions, get information, and seek advice. Also present were Bolsheviks who were attached to Gorky by long-standing tradition. Arguments broke out, during which the gulf between the two camps of the petite bourgeoisie and the proletariat revealed itself clearly. Mensheviks and SRs argued it was necessary to establish bourgeois power and called, as Sukhanov put it, "for work on Miliukov." The Bolsheviks insisted it was necessary to establish a dictatorship of the proletariat and peasantry. Sukhanov observed that the Bolsheviks represented a different milieu, unlike that of the men of letters from among the intelligentsia. They came "straight from workers' cauldrons and party committees. During these days these people were up to their necks in work of an altogether different nature, coming with the details of the movement, forcing a decisive skirmish with tsarism, organizing agitation and an illegal press."[133]

Now political questions were discussed at mass meetings as well as in small groups in private apartments. On February 25 the Petrograd Union of Consumer Society Workers, in cooperation with the Social Democratic faction in the State Duma, called a meeting of workers' representatives from various districts in the capital. Some thirty to thirty-five people were present. Besides workers, Chkheidze, Cherevanin, Kopelinskii, and other Mensheviks involved in the legal workers' movement were present. The gathering heard local reports and resolved to create a soviet of workers' deputies on the 1905 model in order to organize the workers' movement better.

That evening Ia. Anasovskii and Ia. S. Ostapenko, members of the Workers' Group of the War Industries Committee who had avoided arrest, summoned representatives of workers and cooperative employees to discuss the food supply. The meeting met openly, according to an agenda distributed earlier. Police quickly appeared at the building of the War Industries Committee and shut the meeting down, detaining its participants on the committee's premises. M. I. Tereshchenko, who had been summoned as a result of this, found police and a detachment of soldiers from the reserve battalion of the Volynskii Regiment. Tereshchenko failed to convince the police officer that the meeting that had been convened was legal; the police officer and the commander of the regiment were intractable. Twenty-eight workers were escorted to the police station, where they were interrogated; some were arrested and others released. Tereshchenko recalled how one of the detained workers cheerfully addressed the others: "'Just one more attempt—and we'll have won. Just don't give in!' It seemed strange to me that such a mood could exist in these circumstances, that under these conditions one could speak of success."[134] Although the tsarist authorities arrested the workers, they remained unwilling to take the same measures against bourgeois activists.

That day, February 25, the Petrograd Duma discussed the food supply. It was an unusual meeting for the Duma dominated by merchants and property owners. Deputies and representatives from public organizations and workers came to the large white Duma hall on Nevskii Prospekt. Such a mix of participants, plus a powerful demonstration taking place near the Duma on Nevskii, strongly influenced the meeting. Speakers declared the government was responsible for the serious supply crisis because it had spurned society's help. The gathering was told the tsarist authorities were delaying liquidation of the crisis by refusing to allow workers to be elected to food supply committees. In answer to this many proposed "to ignore what they think in the highest circles" and elect workers in a revolutionary manner.

During the meetings the food supply question was placed on the back burner; the situation of the workers and the countermeasures taken by the tsarist government in the capital were discussed. Indignation was unbounded when it was learned that demonstrators had been shot on Nevskii and the wounded were carried into the Duma building during the meeting. "Something must be done no later than tomorrow morning," a speaker declared after the shooting of the workers. Someone in the hall cried out: "We have to do something to stop them from shooting people." The Kadet Kogan maintained, "We must not discuss the food supply, but realize that a revolution has begun and we must do everything to prevent 'irresponsible elements' from leading it."

He insisted the Kadets and other "progressive" forces (the bourgeois parties) immediately assume leadership of the revolution.[135]

News soon arrived that the police had arrested the workers on their way to the City Duma to express their view on the food supply. The meeting charged Mayor P. I. Lelianov and Deputy A. I. Shingarev to negotiate with the government and secure the immediate release of the arrested. The two Duma representatives soon returned and told those present that Chairman of the Council of Ministers Golitsyn knew nothing of what had taken place, but promised to find out why the workers had been detained. In this situation the question of supplies became a question of power. A representative of the workers' cooperatives, I. G. Volkov, argued that the food supply problem could only be solved when the political structure was democratized and said: "The workers don't need any guarantee from the government, since they don't believe at all in the government's promises." A worker, Saval'ev, maintained the same: "We don't believe 'the highest authorities,' for they are conducting a fratricidal war and have driven us to hunger." The deputy Shitikov declared the present government to be so utterly incompetent that it should resign to make way for a coalition cabinet. Skobelev proposed to take advantage of the authorities' confusion and force the resignation of a government that was spilling the blood of innocent people and "coping with the food supply crisis by shooting people who eat."[136]

The City Duma meeting of February 25 did not reach a decision on power, and merely carried a resolution on the food supply question, declaring the city administration would organize the food supply if the government would guarantee delivery of sufficient products and invite representatives of all the population to participate. Although the Duma did no more than adopt a resolution on the food supply question, its meeting showed the deep changes the workers' movement had brought about among the petite bourgeoisie. Petit bourgeois elements swung to the left and began talking about a change in power. The tsarist political police dubbed the assembly "a mass revolutionary meeting," which served as a reminder of the meetings of 1905. It was exasperated because the chairman of the gathering did not interrupt speakers.

The deputies of the State Duma could not escape the turbulent events unfolding in the streets of the capital. The spirit of revolution in the streets was more insistently reaching the Tauride Palace. On February 24, the second day of revolution, the State Duma had resumed discussion of the food supply. Again speakers in the Duma offered figures and made estimates and computations, mentioning the work of government entities and city governments, the breakdown of railroad transportation, fixed prices and allocations for individual provinces and the entire country. Soon examination of the food supply focused on the capital. The Duma had addressed an inquiry to the chairman of the Council of Ministers—what measures was the government taking to regulate the food supply in Petrograd?

The State Duma deputies were extremely alarmed by the turbulent events in Petrograd. They believed that a dangerous moment had arrived, that "the street" had flared up and that it was necessary to put out the fire. A Duma deputy, the priest S. Krylov, began his speech with the words: "I have mounted this platform filled with a fresh impression of what I have just seen on the streets of Petrograd. . . . I have just seen a huge mass of people filling, literally filling all of Znamenskaia Square, Nevskii Prospekt, and all the adjacent streets." Krylov urged the deputies to give bread to the population, introduce order, "and not force hungry people to stand from early morning until night in freezing cold, trying to obtain a miserable little chunk of bread."[137] The Duma members thought the only solution to the existing situation was to transfer distribution of food supplies to the city administration, which would involve inhabitants of the towns and their regular civilian committees in the matter. Many deputies expressed hope that the government finally would hear their voice and hand over the resolution of the supply question to the whole population.

Just as the day before, however, several speakers expressed doubts: were the present authorities capable of dealing with the situation? The Kadet F. I. Rodichev said that the authorities were leading the state to ruin, and that the country was standing over an abyss. There still was time to stop and not crash down into it, but the government would have to be replaced. "We demand it co-opt people whom all Russia can trust; we demand above all the expulsion of people whom all Russia despises."[138] The Kadets' talk about co-opting some and expelling other ministers meant that, faced with a rising revolutionary tide, the liberal bourgeoisie wanted to replace individuals, not the regime. The Kadets did not intend to destroy but to repair and renovate the dilapidated tsarist monarchy.

The Menshevik and Trudovik Duma factions tried to drive the bourgeois leaders to the left. They appealed to the Duma deputies to refuse to make an agreement with tsarism. Chkheidze spoke of the opposing interests of the nation and tsarism, and said there should be no compromises with the tsarist government. He urged the Duma to lead the burgeoning movement and use it to get rid of the tsarist authorities. "The street has begun to speak," Chkheidze intoned, "the only thing we can do now, the only remedy, is to find the street a course it can follow as it organizes. If so, it may find the government it needs."[139]

The Mensheviks and SRs strove to harness the energy and activity of the workers participating in cooperatives, local citizens' committees, and other public organizations. They tried to win freedom of action for these organizations so as to afford workers and the entire urban population an opportunity to take part in regulating the food supply. At the Duma meeting of February 24, Kerensky said that the nascent movement was propelling the country to anarchy when "reason is stifled, and naked hunger and hatred master it." He called for the immediate creation of self-regulating public workers' democratic organizations, which would throw up a bulwark against "unbridled passion" and spontaneity, and could organize public opinion in a democracy and gird the masses for action.[140]

Almost all day on February 24 the State Duma discussed the food supply question, yet took no decisions. Meanwhile, events in Petrograd continued to escalate. Rodzianko told the deputies that the strained situation required prompt, urgent measures to calm the population. He communicated with the government, and that evening on February 24 an extraordinary session chaired by Prince Golitsyn was convened in the Mariinskii Palace to deal with the food supply. Tsarist ministers, members of the State Duma and State Council, the city mayor, and the chairman of the provincial zemstvo administration participated in it. For a long time the tsarist government had stubbornly refused to transfer jurisdiction over food supplies to the city government, but now, as the powerful movement was developing on the streets of the capital, for which the lack of food was responsible, tsarist ministers became more accommodating. At the meeting in the Mariinskii Palace they finally agreed to allow the City Duma to handle the food supply.

The next day, February 25, Rittikh informed the State Duma that the government was prepared immediately, today or tomorrow, to transfer control of the food supply to the city government. Rittikh tried to assure Duma deputies that Petrograd had sufficient reserves of flour, and that the enormous lines in front of bread shops were caused by some misunderstanding or panic. The Duma approved the transfer of the food supplies to the city government and charged its own committees to devise an appropriate bill. Better late than never, the deputies said. Still, many had their doubts: wasn't it already too late? In any case, the Duma declared the city administration might assume responsibility for the food supply only on condition that the government would not impede the work of public committees and would guarantee the delivery of bread.

The Duma had no intention of exceeding the "limits of the law." It did not pass a resolution to remove the present government, create a new government subordinate to popular control, guarantee freedom of speech, assembly, organization, and person. Even so, its days were numbered. The meeting on February 25 turned out to be its last. It had already been decided to prorogue the Duma. The next meeting, scheduled for February 28, did not take place.

At this decisive moment for the country the bourgeoisie was confused. It did not know how to handle the movement unfolding in the streets of the capital. It feared the people and could not support their struggle against tsarism, but neither could it bring itself to support the authorities. As the Kadet S. Gessen explained, the festivities on February 24 to celebrate the regular anniversary of the newspaper *Rech'* were more like a requiem: "Champagne could not dissipate the sullen mood or loosen tongues, there was nothing to talk about or argue over and it was awkward to look at each other and ask the meaning of the shots that we heard in the streets which were trying to scatter the people."[141] The Duma leaders saw storm clouds threatening the tsarist monarchy and desired to save it. Some believed that if the food supply were transferred to the city administration, and Golitsyn's government resigned, tsarism could stay in power. "I am convinced," Rodzianko subsequently said, "that if this had happened, and if on the 25th a responsible ministry had superseded them and Aleksandra Fedorovna had gone off to live permanently in Livadiia,[n] it would have been possible to contain the movement and defeat the revolution. This was our salvation."[142] Rodzianko was deluded. There were no longer any lifelines to save tsarism.

The tsarist government itself at first did not attach any importance to the events. Protopopov announced to his ministers that nothing alarming was happening. At a meeting of the Council of Ministers on February 24, he maintained that "hooligans had incited a riot," with which the police could easily cope. The next day, February 25, at a meeting of the Council of Ministers, however, Golitsyn reported that despite the assurances of Protopopov, the popular disturbances were assuming a threatening character and they must discuss what to do. In vain Protopopov again tried to assure the ministers their apprehensions were unfounded: the police were on the alert, armed to the teeth, and Khabalov had promised to send thirty thousand soldiers, artillery, and armored cars to suppress the uprising. No one believed him any longer. N. N. Pokrovskii and several other ministers declared that the suppression of disturbances with armed force would be useless; the time had come to make serious concessions and form a new cabinet composed of individuals popular with the Duma. As possible candidates for new ministers he named Count P. N. Ignat'iev, A. A. Polivanov, General M. V. Alekseev, and others.

The Council of Ministers sought a peaceful way out of the existing situation. It decided to negotiate with State Duma leaders and leaders of the Duma factions to explore whether they could achieve agreement with them.[143] The government commissioned Pokrovskii and Rittikh to conduct discussions with Duma activists.

These ministers conversed with Duma deputies N. V. Savich, V. A. Maklakov, P. Balashov, and I. Dmitriukov. Savich declared the only solution would be to form a ministry responsible to the Duma, and he proposed to begin forming a new cabinet right away and to suspend the Duma in the meanwhile. Dmitriukov also supported immediate creation of a responsible ministry, but considered it inexpedient to disband the Duma even for a short time. The tsarist ministers, however, rejected the proposal to set up a responsible ministry and nothing came of these discussions with Duma personnel.

At approximately the same time the president of the State Duma met with the chairman of the Council of Ministers. Rodzianko tried to convince Golitsyn to retire voluntarily, but Golitsyn refused to follow this advice. "It turned out," reported Rodzianko, "that eloquence did not touch his heart; he did not heed

[n] Livadiia is a resort on the shore of the Black Sea some three kilometers southwest of Yalta. It was the site of the neo-Renaissance Great Livadiia Palace built in 1910–11 and a residence of the imperial family.

my admonishments, and did just the opposite. 'You want me to retire, but do you know what I have in my folder?'" Golitsyn handed Rodzianko a folder containing a tsarist decree to dismiss the State Duma. The edict to dismiss the Duma had been signed by the tsar on February 13, just before the Duma session opened, in case it should be needed. Like his predecessors, Golitsyn did not need the tsar's sanction to dissolve the Duma. That had been left to his discretion; the prime minister himself could designate a date to dismiss and even decide which day to publish the edict the tsar had already signed.

Golitsyn threatened Rodzianko with dismissal of the Duma, knowing Duma leaders feared this. During that conversation Golitsyn also offered Rodzianko a peaceful settlement. "I am keeping this for emergencies," he said, nodding at the folder containing the tsarist decree. Meanwhile, the prime minister requested the chairman of the State Duma to summon leading Duma members for a friendly talk with him. "Let's get together and chat. It's no good to live at daggers drawn all the time," Golitsyn urged. In turn Rodzianko also called for conciliation, proposing to Golitsyn "to slip the daggers back into their sheaths." Golitsyn promised to telephone Rodzianko to arrange a time and place for the upcoming meeting with Duma members. The meeting never materialized.

The Council of Ministers decided to dismiss the Duma and postpone any changes in the government's composition. The tsarist ministers wanted to reach agreement with Duma leaders without granting concessions. The government's obstinacy isolated and weakened the Duma's authority. A police agent reported on February 26:

> The situation is aggravated because bourgeois groups are also demanding the government be replaced, and this means the government has no support from anyone. At the moment, however, there is something positive as well—the bourgeois groups only demand the government be replaced. They still believe the war must be pursued to victory while workers are advancing the slogans "Bread," "Down with the government," and "Down with the war!" This last point causes friction between the proletariat and the bourgeoisie and prevents them from supporting each other. This difference of opinion is the one good thing as far as the government is concerned. It saps the strength and diffuses the undertakings of individual groups.[144]

Nevertheless, events had developed so quickly and decisively and the revolution had gone so far that the government's ability to take advantage of the differences between the bourgeoisie and proletariat became even less likely.

Among all persons in the autocracy, the tsar himself was almost the last to learn about the revolution in Petrograd. Nicholas II was at Tsarskoe Selo for more than two months before departing for Supreme Headquarters on February 22, just before the revolution began. There was no apparent warning of the coming storm. We have already noted that the authorities considered it impossible that serious events might occur inside the country in the days immediately ahead; otherwise the tsar would not have left for headquarters. In his railroad car Nicholas read a letter from his wife. She wrote how terrible times were, how she would like to hear "the consoling and approving" voice of Rasputin, and how the tsar must be firm. "Things will probably straighten out. But be firm, my dear, show a mighty hand. . . . Now they have started to 'feel' you and Kalinin (the name the empress called Protopopov—E. B.), they have begun to calm down. . . . But no matter where you are, they have to be kept trembling all the same."[145] Aleksandra Fedorovna thought that Nicholas was needed much more in the capital than at headquarters and asked him to return home in ten days. Nicholas actually did return within ten days, though no longer as tsar.

At headquarters the tsar and his entourage followed an already established routine. Nicholas would invariably arrive at 9:30 A.M. to hear a report from General Alekseev; then he breakfasted, went for a walk, took tea, read mail, and had dinner. Nothing unusual was anticipated and no changes were planned. General D. N. Dubenskii, who had ceased to be a specialist in horse breeding and a Black Hundred publisher and was now the royal historiographer, as headquarters had commissioned him to describe the tsar's travels, wrote in his diary on February 24: "A quiet, luckless life; everything will be as before. Nothing can be expected of 'Him' (the word Dubenskii used to refer to the tsar—E.B.) unless chance external causes bring about a change."

Nicholas also kept a daily diary as he had regularly done for a long time. However, one would search the pages of the diary of the ruler of the Russian empire in vain for any reference to the momentous political events of the time. The diary simply listed mundane facts of everyday life. It vividly shows how empty were the interests, how limited the outlook, and how insignificant the last Russian autocrat was. For February 23–26, 1917, Nicholas wrote in his diary: "Spent all my free time reading a Fren[ch] book on Caesar's conquest of Gaul . . . dined with all the foreigners and our people . . . stopped in at the monastery to kiss the icon of the Mother of God. Took a trip along the highway to Orsha. At 6:00 P.M. went to vespers. . . . Wrote to Aliks [his nickname for the tsarina—D.J.R.] and drove along Bobr[uisk] Highway to the bell tower, where I took a stroll. The weather was clear and cold. After tea I read and received Senator Tregubov before dinner. Played dominoes in the evening."[146] While the tsar was going to vespers and playing dominoes, the struggle to overthrow tsarism was underway in the streets of Petrograd.

Although the empress was closer to events, the information about what was happening that reached her at Tsarskoe Selo was quite vague. Protopopov phoned soothing information to Tsarskoe Selo pertaining to the situation in the capital, and assured the empress everything would soon be calm and return to normal. After receiving such information, Aleksandra Fedorovna, in her letters to the tsar, referred to events in Petrograd as trifling disturbances caused by the food problem. On February 24 she wrote: "Yesterday there were disorders on V[asilevskii] Island and Nevskii, because the poor stormed bakeries."[147] On February 25 the empress told the tsar: "This is a hooligan movement; boys and girls run about shouting they have no bread merely to create excitement, as do workers, who prevent others from working. If the weather were very cold, they would probably all be at home. But this would all go away and die down if the Duma would only behave itself."

Not waiting for everything to "go away and die down," Aleksandra Fedorovna proposed in her letter to take immediate steps to restore order, issue ration cards, and militarize factories. "Strikers have to be told flatly not to strike or they will be sent to the front or severely punished. No need for shooting; all you have to do is maintain order and not let them cross bridges the way they are doing."[148] During the afternoon of February 26, while worker demonstrators were being shot down in the streets of Petrograd, Aleksandra Fedorovna visited Rasputin's grave to seek solace after the last turbulent few days. "It seems to me everything will be alright," she wrote her husband. "The sun is shining so brightly, and I felt such calm and peace at His dear grave! He died to save us."

Rumors about the disturbances in Petrograd reached headquarters from people who had chanced to arrive from Petrograd; the government and the Petrograd military authorities took a long time to make up their minds to "alarm" the tsar, hoping everything would turn out alright. Only on the third day of the revolution did news reach the tsar. At 5:00 P.M. on February 25, Khabalov sent his first telegram to Supreme Headquarters: "I report that on February 23 and 24 strikes broke out at many factories owing to the shortage of bread; on February 24 some 200,000 workers were on strike and they forced those who continued to work off the job. Workers have halted streetcars. About noon on February 23 and 24 some workers forced their way onto Nevskii, but they were driven off. . . . Today, February 25, attempts by workers to enter Nevskii have been successfully stopped. The Cossacks are dispersing those who have broken through."[149]

One might assume Khabalov's message meant that nothing unusual had happened and order was being maintained in the capital. The conclusion of the message, however, contradicted its otherwise soothing tone. Khabalov wrote: "The Petrograd garrison, five squadrons of the Ninth Reserve Cavalry Regiment brought from Krasnoe Selo, and a bodyguard unit of the Cossack regiment from Pavlovsk are helping to suppress the disorders. Moreover, five squadrons of the Guards Reserve Cavalry Regiment have been ordered to Petrograd."[150] This showed the "disorders" had taken a serious turn; the Petrograd garrison had proved inadequate to suppress them and it was necessary to use military forces stationed outside the capital.

When he learned what was happening in Petrograd, the tsar sent a stern order to the city authorities. On the evening of February 25 he signed a telegram to Khabalov which read: "I command the disorders in the capital end tomorrow. They are impermissible in the difficult time of war with Germany and Austria. Nicholas." The following day the tsar wrote to his wife: "I hope Khabalov will be able to stop these street disorders quickly. Protopopov must give him clear and definite instructions. If only old Golitsyn doesn't lose his head."[151] Exactly the opposite happened. Khabalov did not know how to stop the "street disturbances," Protopopov was unable to give him any instructions, and old Golitsyn lost his head. Khabalov declared he was thunderstruck by the tsar's command to stop the disorders: "How could they be stopped by the next day? . . . When people said 'Give us bread,' we gave them bread and that was the end of it. But when inscriptions on banners read 'Down with the autocracy,' what kind of bread could calm them?"[152] The city military authorities decided they could only carry out the tsar's order by resorting to armed force, if necessary, by shooting the demonstrators. Khabalov said: "The tsar has issued a command: we've got to shoot."

Each evening Khabalov conferred with the chiefs of the military defense sectors. They would report to the commander of the forces of the military district on events that had occurred during the day and receive instructions how to act the next day. An hour after receiving the tsar's telegram on the evening of February 25, the regular conference of the chiefs of the military defense sectors assembled. After reading the telegram from Nicholas, Khabalov declared: "The sovereign has ordered the disorders be stopped by tomorrow. We have a last resort, and we must use it. . . . You have been assigned a cavalry detachment to each sector: if the crowd is small and not aggressive, carrying no banners, use cavalry to disperse the crowd, but if the crowd is aggressive and carrying banners, act according to regulations. I mean, warn them three times, and after the third warning, open fire."[153]

The tsarist authorities carefully informed the population of the capital about these measures. On February 25 Khabalov signed a proclamation: "In recent days disorders have occurred in Petrograd, accompanied by violence and assaults on military and police personnel. I forbid all street gatherings. I announce to the population of Petrograd in advance that I endorsed the use of arms by the troops and that they are to stop at nothing to bring order to the capital."[154]

Khabalov said in a telegram to General Alekseev: "I report that during the afternoon of February 25, crowds of workers assembled on Znamenskaia Square and near Kazan Cathedral were repeatedly dispersed by police and the military. At about 5:00 P.M. demonstrators near Gostinyi Dvor[o] sang revolutionary songs and unfurled red flags bearing the inscription 'Down with the war!' On February 25, 240,000 workers were on strike. I have issued a proclamation forbidding crowds to gather on the streets and informing the population in advance that any display of disorder will be suppressed by force of arms."[155]

In carrying out the tsar's command, the Petrograd authorities were preparing an assault on the revolution. They decided it was most important to behead the forces of the revolution by seizing the leaders and, if street "disorders" resumed, to use firearms against the workers. On the night of February 25–26, the Council of Ministers discussed measures the military authorities and police should take to crush the revolution. Khabalov and Protopopov reported that, in

[o]A shopping bazaar built in the mid-eighteenth century, located on Nevskii Prospekt.

order to fulfill the tsar's command to suppress all disorders immediately, troops and police had been authorized to fire on street crowds. The ministers approved the military's measures, declaring armed force was needed to put down the "disorders."

On arriving at city hall, Protopopov called upon the defenders of the autocracy bravely to suppress the "disorders." Protopopov expressed the hope that "the Lord God will not suffer our righteous cause to perish." "Pray and hope for victory," said the tsar's minister on the eve of tsarism's offensive against the revolution.

What did this offensive accomplish? How did it affect the next stage in the struggle to overthrow the autocracy?

THREE

The Decisive Clash

> The proletariat came forward with bare hands and naked chests—and found a brotherly response in the revolutionary army. . . . The army is with you, comrades, and this guarantees the victory of the Second Russian Revolution.
>
> —From an RSDRP leaflet, February 27, 1917

Bloody Sunday

Tsarism attacked on the evening of February 25–26. That night the authorities made mass arrests. The Department of Police reported it had taken into custody some 100 members of revolutionary organizations. Protopopov, in a telegram sent to the palace commandant, gave a different figure: 136. These were the last repressive acts of the last tsarist government of Russia. The authorities hastily locked up those they had arrested in station houses, but apparently never had a chance to interrogate them.[1]

A worker, M. Efimov-Vinogradov, related that early on the morning of the twenty-sixth, a sharp knock on the door brought him to his feet. A sergeant and two policemen conducted a search, arrested him, and took him to the station house, where he was lodged in the duty officer's room. He then was taken to the captain.[2] A. Sudakov, a Bolshevik seized that night, spent the whole day in a Lesnoi precinct detention cell packed with workers and students. Late that evening, a group of arrestees in two wagons accompanied by a sizable police convoy was sent to the other end of the city to the Spassk headquarters. "Demonstrations in the city had virtually died down," Sudakov recalled, "except that on the Field of Mars[a] a small group of workers tried to free us. Nevskii was completely empty and brightly lit by a powerful searchlight from the Admiralty. . . . In Spassk headquarters we were frisked and locked up in separate cells."[3]

The morning of February 26 the tsarist authorities arrested the basic core of

[a] A large parade ground and war memorial field located at the approach to Troitskii Bridge, across from the Peter-Paul Fortress. The Pavlovskii Regiment was billeted next to it.

the Petrograd Committee of the RSDRP in A. Kuklin's apartment on Bolshoi Sampsonievskii Prospekt: Secretary A. K. Skorokhodov and Petrograd Committee members A. Kuklin, P. Gan'shin, E. Eizenshmidt, and A. A. Vinokurov. This major operation involved about fifty infantry and mounted police. Arresting the members of the Petrograd Committee of the RSDRP at the height of the revolution significantly harmed it, but did not interrupt it.

February 26 was special in the history of the Second Russian Revolution. It was Sunday. Factories and offices were shut down. The heart of Petrograd was quiet and empty. Stores were closed, streetcars did not run, restaurants and cafes were not functioning, and above all, the large numbers of worker demonstrators who had filled the streets and squares of the city center the previous day were not to be seen. Instead, troops were picketed and posted everywhere, mounted patrols and cavalry rode back and forth, and field telephones had been set up. They were deployed to occupy major buildings and key points in the capital and the approaches to the bridges. The center of Petrograd had become an armed camp. It was as though an enemy armed to the teeth was attacking and the Petrograd garrison had been brought to full alert to avert it.

On the morning of February 26 disorders no longer occurred in the center of the city and the troops stood idle. It seemed the reprisals against demonstrators on the previous days and Khabalov's threats to shoot had intimidated people and depressed the revolutionary movement. Khabalov had already reported to Supreme Headquarters: "Today, February 26, there has been quiet in the city since morning." Yet that was the calm before the storm. While order reigned in the center of town, unusual bustle and enthusiasm seized the workers' suburbs. The workers poured into the streets and squares. The people had undertaken a showdown battle with the monarchy, and no threats by the authorities could hold them back any longer. Khabalov's proclamations were torn down from the walls of buildings.

Initially in neighborhood groups, masses of workers from midday on again headed for Nevskii. Reinforced details of police and troops sought to bar them from the center of the city, defending the bridges with particular tenacity. But the lines of police and tsarist troops were not solid enough and, as before, the demonstrators found passages through them. They crossed the Neva on the ice or broke through the hostile detachments. At first everything went as it had on previous days; however, as people moved to the center of the city, the picture began to change. Considerably larger numbers of troops, resorting to firearms, now met the workers. Police and soldiers had shot at people during the first days of the struggle, but only rarely. Although many thought this would be the case again, on February 26 shooting unarmed demonstrators became widespread. Bugles—the signal to fire—were heard at the City Duma building, on Liteinyi and Suvorov prospekts, on Znamenskaia Square, and other places. Sometimes after this signal soldiers first fired into the air or used blanks; sometimes real shots were fired from the outset. Bullets struck crowds of demonstrators or hit building walls and windows. Cries of terror filled the streets. Dead and wounded collapsed on the sidewalk.

The struggle on Nevskii Prospekt became particularly savage as workers' blood stained Petrograd's main thoroughfare. On February 26, dozens of freedom fighters fell. Hospitals were filled with wounded, and morgues with corpses. This was the Bloody Sunday of the Second Russian Revolution.

Here are some individual instances of attacks on demonstrators. An enormous mass of workers was moving down Nevskii Prospekt. The front ranks were singing revolutionary songs. Near the Moika Canal, a detachment of soldiers from the reserve battalion of the Pavlovskii Regiment barred the way.

> When the masses of people approached the soldiers of the Pavlovskii Regiment, the soldiers were ordered to sink to one knee and brace their rifle butts against their shoulders. Although the crowd stopped, the rear ranks pressed forward. The situation, uncertain for a short while, was soon resolved when the soldiers fired twice. The demonstration collapsed: the majority fled, some fell, a number of them dead. People often had to step in puddles of blood of the dead and wounded sprawled along the road and sidewalks. They were immediately picked up and taken away, most to the City Duma building. People's faces reflected bitterness and anger.[4]

The same thing happened to workers from the Vyborg quarter approaching Nevskii Prospekt on February 26:

> Suddenly, scattered shooting broke out. Then we heard the chatter of machine guns, and saw people running toward us, their faces distorted with terror. An appalling scene awaited us on Nevskii. A few people were hugging the pavement. From Sadovaia to the Kazan Cathedral and from Kazanskaia to the Znamenskaia police and other armed forces were shooting in all directions. It could only mean the uprising was being routed. The unarmed demonstrators could not retaliate against the government that had resorted to decisive measures. Ambulances raced along Nevskii, carrying off the dead and wounded. People did not disperse but pressed closer to buildings, while youths taunted the police from around corners.[5]

Since the authorities had resorted to massive use of firearms they now brought out infantry instead of cavalry, primarily training detachments from the reserve battalions of the guards regiments, to put down the insurrection. The soldiers in these units were the best disciplined among the reserve battalions, and the military district command intended to rely on them to contain the rebellious populace. The principal training unit in the reserve battalion of the Volynskii Guards Regiment was ordered to prevent assemblies on Znamenskaia Square. It was difficult to carry out this order. Crowds of people surrounded the patrols and struck up conversations with their members, telling them not to fire at the people. The soldiers showed no great enthusiasm for carrying out their officers' orders. Captain Lashkevich, commander of the training detachment, arrested Corporal Il'in for failing to act, and sent new, reinforced patrols to the square to break up the demonstrators. They also failed. Then the signal to fire was given, and the soldiers raised their guns. The crowd still formed a solid wall, unable to believe the soldiers would fire at them. Volleys rang out. When some soldiers shot into the air, enraged officers tore the rifles out of their hands and fired at the people themselves. After several volleys the crowd thinned out and people scattered, leaving their dead and wounded on the square.

On February 26, after the tsar ordered them to shoot, the troops did not behave as they had earlier. Their actions were reminiscent of 1905. Stringent discipline, blind obedience to superiors, and the ignorance and cowed nature of most soldiers had their effect. Many refused to let workers approach them. Responding with ugly curses and threats to appeals for fraternization, they fired into the people at their officers' orders. The troops' actions on February 26 satisfied the authorities. Protopopov reported that on that day large crowds gathered on Ligovskaia Street, Znamenskaia Square, as well as at the intersection of Nevskii and Vladimir prospekts and on Sadovaia Street, "at all these points the crowds conducted themselves provocatively, throwing stones and chunks of ice. When shooting into the air failed to disperse the crowds and brought about ridicule of the troops, the latter were compelled to put an end to this by firing live cartridges into the crowd, resulting in dead and wounded." The Department of Police noted that demonstrators "hid in interior courtyards of the nearest buildings and came back into the streets when the shooting stopped."[6]

On the day tsarism attacked the revolution, the police started using machine guns. Subsequently, former police chiefs and some so-called witnesses, anxious to absolve the authorities from the responsibility for gunning down the unarmed inhabitants of the capital, declared that desperate defenders of the autocracy, knowing their cause was lost and acting spontaneously and individually, adopted this last hopeless form of resistance, and that machine-gun fire was not employed until the evening of February 28, after the tsar's main armed forces had capitulated. However, such reasoning leaves a question unanswered: how did machine guns get into the hands of these madmen? The truth is that the authorities had already decided to use machine guns to quell popular disturbances. They put their plans into practice on February 26 when the autocracy launched its counteroffensive against the revolution.

The police set up machine guns to fire at demonstrators on roofs, in church bell towers, and in fire lookout towers. Machine guns fired that day from the fire tower of the Aleksandr Nevskii Monastery, the tower of the Nikolaevskii Railroad Station, the roof of Gostinyi Dvor,[b] and other places. Here is a description of one of the numerous instances when machine guns fired on workers and students on February 26: "A group of demonstrators carrying a red flag and singing 'La Marseillaise' moved from the left along the Catherine Canal. These were young students, both male and female. We welcomed them and merged

[b] Aleksandr Nevskii Monastery, founded in 1710, Nikolaevskii Railroad Station (now the Moscow Station), and Gostinyi Dvor, were all strategically located on Nevskii Prospekt.

into a single group . . . when suddenly there was a deafening rattle, tra-ta-ta-ta! Machine-gun fire! . . . An officer yelled: 'Anyone who wants to live had better lie down!' . . . Two corpses and many wounded lay on the bridge. . . . Hangmen, damned bloodsuckers!"[7]

The events of February 26 alarmed prominent Duma members, who understood that the tsarist troops' shooting of worker demonstrators would make it difficult to achieve a peaceful solution to the existing crisis. They held that another way must be found to "resolve the conflict." For this reason a group of State Duma members addressed a statement to Rodzianko on February 26, protesting Khabalov's threats and the policy of shooting demonstrators. They asked the chairman of the State Duma "to use his influence with the military authorities to prevent spilling the blood of peaceful demonstrators and, incidentally, of ordinary citizens going about their business, among whom were many women and children."[8]

Rodzianko proposed another way to disperse the demonstrators. He advised the military authorities to have men scatter them with fire hoses. Beliaev and Khabalov told the Duma chairman that it was forbidden to use fire companies to combat disorders, and furthermore that "some say drenching with water produces the opposite effect; it stimulates."[9] Thus ended any attempt by Duma members to influence Petrograd's military authorities. That same day, Rodzianko attempted to intervene in "high politics." Realizing tsarism was in mortal danger and convinced that tsarist authorities were acting irrationally and that it was hopeless to appeal to them again, he telegraphed General N. V. Alekseev at headquarters, asking him to win concessions from the tsar needed to save the monarchy. He wrote:

> The spontaneous disturbances that have begun in Petrograd are assuming threatening dimensions. Their cause is the shortage of bread and the inadequate supply of flour that inspires panic. But our main concern is total lack of confidence in the authorities, who are incapable of saving the country from this crisis. This means that events will undoubtedly take place that can be temporarily subdued only if peaceful citizens suffer. Such occurrences cannot be controlled if repeated. If it spreads to the railroads, the movement will paralyze the country at a very dangerous time. Defense industries in Petrograd will have to shut down owing to lack of fuel and raw materials, workers will be idled, and a hungry, unemployed mob will resort to elemental, unrestrainable anarchy.

Rodzianko's telegram said that the danger was unprecedented and fraught with horrifying consequences; order had broken down and the government was completely paralyzed and totally powerless to reinstitute it.[c] To avert a possible catastrophe, Rodzianko proposed to form a "ministry of confidence." "I believe

[c] Hasegawa argues that Rodzianko's telegrams purposefully distorted the situation in the capital to serve his own goal—the formation of a ministry of confidence.

that the necessary and only way out of the existing situation is to entrust someone enjoying the confidence of the country with the formation of a new government. . . . There must be no delay. Procrastination is tantamount to death. Your Excellency, the fate of glorious and victorious Russia is in your hands."[10] Rodzianko's telegram was referred to the tsar, but he gave no answer.

The authorities believed they had won the bloody encounter of February 26 and the revolution had been checked. Balk, the city governor of Petrograd, later declared the troops had produced "brilliant results" on February 26, by "twilight the streets were quite normal again. If decisive measures had been taken earlier it would have been possible to have stopped the disorders entirely. But resolve was lacking."[11] Balk asserted that the military authorities, led by "weak individuals who had lost their nerve," had been unable to take advantage of the situation, which had taken a favorable turn for tsarism as a result of the massacre of February 26. In reality, the resulting situation had improved not for tsarism, but for the revolution. Tsarism enjoyed only fleeting success on February 26.

Shooting demonstrators agitated the people and failed to destroy the workers' resolve to continue the struggle. Demonstrators dispersed when they were shot at, fled to building entrances and interior courtyards, but when these were later locked by order of the authorities, people headed for side streets and alleys and, as soon as the firing died down, assembled once again on Nevskii. Here enormous crowds gathered around the soldiers who had been shooting a moment before; revolutionary songs were sung, and speakers addressed the crowd. The people had been baptized by fire. Revolutionary enthusiasm and determination to take the struggle that had begun to complete victory over hated tsarism had triumphed over the fear of death. Risking their lives, workers had fearlessly clashed with soldiers and Cossacks, defended themselves, and sometimes even attacked. Crowds were shot at but they fired back, primarily at the police. Individuals armed with revolvers fired, and each bullet that struck its target inspired the masses. The news that a policeman had been killed somewhere in town spread rapidly through the city. A call went out to disarm the police and seize their weapons.

The entry in the logbook of the Petrograd secret police for February 26 noted:

> During the disorders the rioting throngs generally behaved in an extremely challenging way toward the military detachments. In response to orders to disperse, they threw stones, snowballs, and ice from the streets at our men. When troops fired warning volleys into the air, the crowds refused to disperse and greeted them with laughter. Only live ammunition fired into the thick of the crowd could scatter the mobs, but most of their members hid in the courtyards of the nearest buildings and came back into the streets again after the firing ceased. . . . Once crowds were dispersed on Znamenskaia Square, mobs began gathering on Nevskii Prospekt, along the stretch known as Old Nevskii (from Znamenskaia Square to the Aleksandr Nevskii Monastery), and Goncharnaia Street. They hid behind corner buildings, firing revolvers at military patrols.[12]

Shooting unarmed demonstrators outraged the population of the capital, which supported the insurrectionists. Students were particularly active in backing the workers. The victims shot by the authorities needed medical aid, which the students provided. The logbook of the Petrograd secret police on February 26 recorded:

> During today's disorders at various points in the capital, groups of secondary school students wearing broad Red Cross armbands and white aprons beneath their uniforms volunteered to go to Nevskii Prospekt to take away the wounded and provide first aid. Students in the women's higher educational institutions went to where the wounded had been brought for that same purpose, and acted brazenly toward the police who sought to remove them.[13]

Although the tsarist commanders used some military units to snuff out the revolution, they wanted to isolate the bulk of soldiers of the Petrograd garrison. Most soldiers were confined to barracks and knew little of what was happening outside. Nevertheless, news of events in the city reached them. Worker agitators and ordinary citizens told soldiers huddled behind barrack walls, fences, and gates of what had occurred. Soldiers called out to put down the disorders also described the bloody clashes in the streets of the city to their comrades. News that worker demonstrators had been shot provoked mute discontent among part of the soldiers.

That very day, February 26, the discontent first made itself felt. It involved the reserve battalion of the Pavlovskii Guards Regiment. The training unit of the battalion had helped shoot demonstrators on Nevskii. The rest of the soldiers in the battalion heard of this from workers, who approached the Pavlovskii barracks. They told the soldiers about the bloody slaughter on Nevskii in which members of the Pavlovskii Regiment had taken part.

"Pavlovskiis are firing at the people!" This news flashed through the barracks like lightning. Soldiers in the Fourth Company of the Reserve Battalion grew agitated and demanded that pickets composed of soldiers from the Pavlovskii Regiment be withdrawn from the streets. "No more shooting at the people!" they cried. A shout was heard, "To the streets!" A few soldiers hurled themselves against the company storeroom, broke the heavy bolts on its doors, burst in and seized rifles. There were only thirty for the fifteen hundred men. They thus took to the streets virtually unarmed, marching along the Catherine Canal toward Nevskii Prospekt. On the side of the canal mounted police rode from Mikhailovskaia Square to stop the Pavlovskiis. Riding to the very railing along the canal, the police fired a volley at the soldiers, who hit the ground and returned fire. Several horses reared and some policemen fell; the others turned their horses and galloped back. Then soldiers of the Preobrazhenskii Regiment came out to face the Pavlovskiis and barred the street with rifles at the ready. Two detachments, one armed, the other virtually unarmed, advanced upon each other. A signal to shoot was given. "Don't shoot, brothers!" the Pavlovskiis yelled. The Preobrazhenskiis, returning their rifles to their shoulders, fell back.

What would happen next? It was growing dark and there were no more cartridges. The Pavlovskiis had not won over other soldiers and had not joined the workers. The military authorities feared most of all that soldiers and workers would unite. Khabalov later said he had ordered the battalion commander and the chaplain to persuade the Pavlovskiis to go back to their barracks. According to the soldiers, however, that was not quite the way it had been. The company returned there on its own accord because it was alone, received no support from other units, and did not know what to do next.

Officers tried to soothe the soldiers who had gone back to their barracks. The officers announced that an order had been issued to withdraw patrols of Pavlovskiis from all streets and thereafter the Pavlovskii Battalion would not stain its hands with the people's blood. But by nightfall, the Fourth Company was in danger of suffering reprisals. The company was isolated and locked in the barracks, all its rifles were removed, armed bands of soldiers surrounded it in an iron ring and cut it off from the outside world. Although the authorities had planned to arrest the entire company and court-martial it, all they did was take into custody the ringleader of the disturbance. Nineteen soldiers of the Fourth Company were escorted to the Peter-Paul Fortress under unusually heavy guard for the sole reason that they had protested shooting at people. They were assigned cells in Trubetskoi Ravelin,[d] where those who had first risen against the autocracy had been immured long ago. Sixteen soldiers from the Fourth Company were also sent to the battalion guardhouse.

On the morning of February 27, Khabalov personally appeared at the Fourth Company barracks. He questioned platoon commanders and individual officers and soldiers, and threatened dire punishment for the previous day's mutiny. Only, the situation in the capital had changed. After they returned to the barracks following the unsuccessful sally the day before, the Pavlovskiis might have expected to face firing squads or exile to hard labor. By February 27 it was now the authorities who had to fear arrest and execution. The Fourth Company of the Reserve Battalion in the Pavlovskii Guards Regiment did not directly influence the subsequent course of events. What they had done was still an isolated action. News of the Pavlovskiis' behavior had not yet reached other units of the Petrograd garrison or the workers of the capital. Nevertheless, their actions showed that soldiers would go over to the people.

After the revolution's triumph the Soviet of Workers' and Soldiers' Deputies published an appeal to the soldiers written by a lawyer, S. Bogoiavlenskii, and approved by Private Savel'ev, secretary of the battalion committee. It said:

> On Sunday, February 26, while servants of the tsarist government were perfidiously shooting people on Nevskii Prospekt and elsewhere in Petrograd and the

[d]The Peter-Paul Fortress was founded in 1703. Later, stone bastions were added to the structure and were named after Peter the Great and five of his generals. One of them, the Trubetskoi Bastion or Ravelin, was especially notorious owing to the large number of political prisoners it had held over the years.

> power of that government not only seemed but actually was a threatening force of splendidly armed gendarmes and police, you were the first soldiers to raise the glorious banner of the Great Russian Revolution in a noble outpouring of wrath, and with a selfless bravery unheard of in history. Virtually unarmed, since you had no more than 30 rifles for the entire company and not more than 100 cartridges, you took to the streets from your company headquarters around 5:00 P.M., after taking an oath to each other to triumph or perish. Comrade soldiers! To your great feat of valor! You will be greeted enthusiastically. Millions of Russian people will send you brotherly thanks and bow to the ground when they learn who were the first to fight for the people's freedom.[14]

By evening on February 26 shooting in the streets of Petrograd had ceased. As on the previous day, demonstrators left the center of the city for the outlying factory districts. Yet not everything was the same as the day before. Tsarist troops firmly occupied the center of the city, guard posts stood at every crossing along Nevskii Prospekt and some other streets, and mounted men patrolled the bridges. A powerful searchlight illuminating Nevskii was mounted on the Admiralty building. Emboldened by their success on February 26, the authorities intended to continue their offensive against the revolution the next day. They readied military units in the capital itself and called for reinforcements from the suburbs. To intensify the struggle against the insurrection, they called in two companies of the First Reserve Machine-Gun Regiment from Oranienbaum.[e]

The people's struggle against tsarism was entering a decisive stage. The workers knew they could not triumph at this point unless an armed insurrection of the entire people occurred. On the streets, in factories, and in teahouses the workers said:

> We'll see what'll happen tomorrow! They routed us today? You're joking. They didn't. Maybe they killed a couple of hundred, but there are thousands of us! Many thousands! They've closed the bridges? We don't need them! We'll cross on the ice! And workers will come from Sestroretsk[f]—Didn't you hear, they're already on strike. And workers will flock to Petrograd from all over Russia. . . . They're strong and we are too! Tomorrow won't be like today. Tomorrow we'll be armed. You'll see what tomorrow will bring!

A speaker at a rally showed the same spirit.

> Comrades, we went out armed only with songs and banners. They came out with volleys of shots and machine guns. But who won? Are we dispersed, disunited, defeated? Aren't we stronger? Haven't we acquired strength and gotten angrier under their bullets? Comrades! Tomorrow is the day of reckoning. No more naiveté! Let's go with arms in hand! We'll storm their fortresses. We'll find

[e] Now Lomonosov, located on the Gulf of Finland, opposite the naval base at Kronstadt.

[f] A railroad center and seaside resort on the Gulf of Finland. Important metalworking factories were located there, including a major armaments plant.

> revolvers, rifles, and bullets in the arsenal and gun shops. We'll head for Kresty,[g] the Peter-Paul Fortress, all the jails where our brothers fighting for liberty languish. Comrades! It's now or never.[15]

The fighting on February 26 was bound to alarm some workers over the outcome of the struggle underway. It was reasonable to assume that the following day the authorities might use arms on an even wider scale and tsarism's offensive would spread from the center of the capital to the outlying workers' districts. In view of this, Mensheviks and SRs discussed the need to curtail the movement in order to avoid the possibility of total rout. Kerensky and V. M. Zenzinov subsequently tried to say the Bolsheviks were the ones who favored winding down the movement. To support this contention, Zenzinov wrote that I. Iurenev was alleged to have said at a meeting in Kerensky's apartment that "no revolution is taking place, the movement among the soldiers is going nowhere, and we must prepare for a long period of reaction." Iurenev proposed "to wait and see."[16] However, Iurenev was no Bolshevik, he was an Interdistrictite. Moreover, even they, despite all their vacillation and doubts, had no wish to curtail the movement and fought beside the Bolsheviks against tsarism. At the Sixth Congress of the RSDRP [July 1917—D.J.R.] Iurenev said: "On February 27, when the revolution's success was still in doubt, our organization decided it must stand with the masses; together with the Bolsheviks and anarchists we seized the printshop of the newspaper *Russkaia volia* (Russian Liberty) and issued a leaflet appealing to the workers and soldiers to organize soviets."[17]

After the bloody slaughter on February 26, the revolutionary forces continued the struggle they had launched and prepared for the decisive battle with tsarism. A report by a police agent from February 26 spoke of a joint meeting held by Bolsheviks and Interdistrictite-Unifiers[h] on Vasilevskii Island. "In the Vasilevskii Island District, SDs are agitating fiercely to continue the strikes and street demonstrations. . . . Today Bolsheviks and Unifiers, some twenty-eight persons, met at Grismanov's, a worker residing in Apartment no. 1, 95 Fourteenth Line, Vasilevskii Island." They gave appeals to those present to distribute among soldiers and adopted a resolution to continue strikes and demonstrations "and carry them to the ultimate extreme," which meant to collect arms to form fighting squads and to make surprise attacks to disarm police.[18]

Again on February 26 worker activists met at the Edinenie Cooperative in Novaia Derevnia (in the Vyborg District). A police agent reported that as many as fifty people attended, who decided

[g]"The Crosses," officially the Petrograd Solitary Prison and the Women's Prison. A large Petersburg prison built in 1892 whose two structures are joined together in the shape of a cross. After the Revolution of 1905 mostly political prisoners were incarcerated there.

[h]Once again, at this time few tactical issues separated the Interdistrictites, who promoted unification of the different Social Democratic factions into one party, from the Bolsheviks.

> tomorrow (February 27), to notify everybody in all factories not to work and assemble at 10:00 A.M. at a stated place on Nevskii from which they would go to funeral services at the Pipe Plant where the body of a fallen comrade, sacrificed to the struggle for freedom, was lying. Danilov, a speaker from the Shchetinin Factory, cried: "Comrades, let us march boldly together. No hiding behind corners. Down with the tsar! Down with the government! Long live a provisional government and the Russian Social Democratic Labor party!" With this the meeting ended and all left one by one, out the back.[19]

As on previous days, members of the Bureau of the Central Committee of the RSDRP and party workers associated with them, Chugurin, Kaiurov, Lebedev, A. Bubnov, and others, met in the Pavlovs' apartment to discuss plans for further action. The first question was: who should replace arrested members of the Petrograd Committee? It was impossible to organize a new committee, for fighting was at its height. It was proposed instead that the Vyborg Committee, the strongest and best organized, assume the duties of the Petrograd Committee and cooperate with the Bureau of the Central Committee of the RSDRP in leading the movement. All present took note of how powerful the movement had become and the popularity of Bolshevik slogans. How was the movement to be brought to a triumphant conclusion? Many proposed to obtain arms, to organize fighting squads, and to use them to rout autocracy's defenders. But the majority felt workers' squads could not resist the armed forces of tsarism. Only if some of the tsar's soldiers came over to the people could the workers be armed and the success of the revolution be guaranteed. Those attending the meeting agreed to continue the struggle and try to win military units to the revolution, and decided the Bolshevik organizations should strive to this end.[20]

The principal driving force of the revolution was always the working class, which had transferred its activities to the streets and squares of Petrograd. Still, even now factories and mills remained the bulwarks and bastions of the revolution. There workers' rallies and meetings took place, from there the working masses went forth to battle in the streets. This is why voices in the camp of tsarism urged keeping the striking workers from the enterprises, and temporarily locking up the factories. On February 26 a police agent wrote:

> It should be borne in mind that tomorrow the workers will appear at the factories, but only to assemble, agree what to do, and again move into the streets in an organized and planned fashion in hopes of achieving complete success. At present the factories are serving as vast clubhouses. Therefore, temporarily closing the factories, even for two or three days, would deprive the masses of information centers where experienced speakers electrify crowds, regulate actions in individual factories, and coordinate and organize the demonstrations.[21]

During the first days of the revolution, cooperative actions by the proletariat determined the outcome of the struggle against tsarism. Now the destiny of the revolution depended upon the troops. Soldiers could no longer remain aloof.

On December [*sic*—February—D.J.R.] 26 they had shot at the people. Who would they shoot at tomorrow? V. D. Bonch-Bruevich recalled that after the shooting on February 26, discussions took place in workers' neighborhoods, apartments of party members, public places, and clubrooms. Participants did not yet know the mood of the troops, and "only late at night did rumors, wishes, and hopes begin that next morning the soldiers would contest the government's onslaught."[22]

A police agent observed in a memorandum: "Now everything depends upon the military units. If they do not go over to the proletariat the movement will quickly die down, but if the troops stand against the government nothing will save the country from revolution."

Returning to their neighborhoods, workers discussed tomorrow's strategy. Mutual communication dispelled fresh doubts and reinforced the workers' determination to triumph or perish in the struggle against autocracy. The shooting of February 26 had not dissipated the militant mood of the first three days of the uprising. Workers parted expecting to meet one another and the soldiers again tomorrow. The insurrection against tsarism entered its final stage. The time for the decisive battle had come.

How did this battle unfold?

February Twenty-Seventh

The morning of the fifth day of the revolution came. The authorities ordered workers to return to work on Monday, February 27, but to no avail. Work was not resumed. Only a few enterprises blew lonely whistle blasts calling workers to their machines. Working-class Petrograd continued on strike. The Petrograd workers again went out into the streets, and the factory districts remained in their hands. This time workers did not hasten to the center and Nevskii Prospekt, the site of the previous bloody clash. A danger existed that tsarist troops would attack the outskirts of town, which would lead to further slaughter and prolong the people's struggle against the autocracy. The workers were determined to prevent tsarism from an offensive against the outskirts, to involve the soldiers in the revolution, and to overthrow tsarism by their joint forces.

Early in the morning of February 27, the Vyborg Bolshevik Committee met with factory representatives in V. N. Kaiurov's apartment. Some forty people were present. K. I. Shutko represented the Petrograd Committee of the RSDRP. A majority of those present voted to continue the struggle. After making that decision, the participants departed for their workplaces.[23]

Again on the morning of February 27, I. D. Chugurin informed the Bureau of the Central Committee of the RSDRP that workers were assembling in factories and deciding to continue the strike. A short leaflet appealing for further struggle was needed. Such a leaflet was written right there in Pavlov's apartment and given to Chugurin for distribution. It read:

> Working people no longer will endure violence, discontent, and ruin. To the demands of the workers and other citizens of Petrograd, as evinced by demonstrations throughout the city, the henchmen of the tsar-autocrat replied with bullets. Soldier executioners fired into an unarmed crowd. May the curses of the people, and of the hundreds killed, and their wives and children, haunt their drunken consciences the rest of their lives. Tsarist authority cannot satisfy the needs of the workers, of the people. . . . May the soldiers, our brothers and children, march in our ranks with their rifles in their hands. Then the final hour of the Romanov monarchy will have struck! Down with the tsarist monarchy! Long live the People's Republic! All landlords' estates to the people! The eight-hour workday for working people! Long live the Russian Social Democratic party! Long live a provisional revolutionary government! Down with butchery![24]

The workers, fully determined to continue the struggle to final victory over tsarism, did not think of going back to work. Enormous masses of workers gathered in squares and at intersections and held rallies. Workers who had previously vacillated now joined the ranks to fight for the revolution. Fear of losing a job no longer influenced men subject to the draft or those who had large families to support. A mass rally took place that morning at the Treugolnik Factory. K. Zaitseva, a woman worker in the factory remembered: "The armed Putilov workers were greeted with tremendous rejoicing. People shouted: 'We are with you! Everyone in the streets!' We left the shop, a noisy, joyous crowd, and went through the gates to a place where many workers had already assembled . . . all moved to the Narva Gate."[25] At that moment, the workers in the Treugolnik Factory, sixteen thousand strong, began a new life. Working women in the rubber industry took to the streets, went to neighboring enterprises, participated in demonstrations and rallies, listened to speakers, and sometimes ventured to speak at such gatherings themselves. Well-attended meetings now occurred in the yards, cafeteria, shops, and departments of the Treugolnik Factory itself.

The workers believed they had to draw the soldiers over to the side of the people. They marched to the barracks, organized rallies nearby, sent notes into the barracks, struck up conversations with soldiers standing at the barracks gates—in short, they tried to end the troops' isolation from the people and deprive tsarism of its armed support. Attempts to fraternize with soldiers were not always successful. Sometimes gunfire dispersed rallies, but individual failures did not stop the attempts to achieve the goal. Appeals to soldiers to join the people started striking a responsive chord. Influenced by the events of the previous days, the soldiers' mood began to change. Doubts and vacillation made them ask themselves whether they had done right to obey orders to shoot at demonstrating workers. They heard the military authorities intended to continue the bloody reprisal against the people and had already issued an order to many units to be ready to undertake new actions against the workers on February 27. Life posed the question point-blank: either remain loyal to their oath and discipline and fire at the people or break their oath and discipline and join forces with them.

Military discipline weighed heavily upon the masses of soldiers. The workers' movement had evolved from strikes and demonstrations to insurrection. A military insurrection, on the other hand, could not have an intermediate stage and would immediately assume the extreme form of an armed mutiny. The officers treated expressions of dissatisfaction or protest on the part of a soldier as a violation of the oath and as a breach of discipline, subject to the harshest punishment: execution, hard labor, or consignment to a punishment battalion at the front. These considerations tormented the soldiers. Workers penetrated the barracks of some units, explained the meaning of events that had occurred and called on the soldiers to join the people. A decision had to be taken.

A training unit in the reserve battalion of the Volynskii Guards Regiment acted first.[26] Soldiers in the regiment had initially participated in the struggle against workers on the streets of Petrograd, but they refused to serve as executioners any longer. Platoon leaders and some officers of the Volynskii training unit conferred in the barracks on the eve of February 27 and decided not to take part in putting down the people but to join forces with the insurrectionists. They rejected a proposal to attack battalion headquarters and kill hated high-ranking officers. They agreed to harm no one but to arouse the main training unit an hour earlier than usual in the morning, win over the rest of the soldiers in the battalion, and then all would go over to the people.

At 6:00 A.M. on February 27, the four hundred soldiers in the main training unit of the Volynskii Battalion were ready to go. They approved the decision taken the night before and promised not to obey orders, and only to carry out the instructions of their platoon leaders and certain officers. Cartridges were issued and the training unit, in full battle array, lined up in parade formation. Officers began arriving, the soldiers greeted them as always, responding to the officers' salutations in accordance with regulations. Yet, as agreed, when greeting the chief of the unit, Captain Lashkevich, the soldiers unanimously responded with a yell, "Hurrah!" Lashkevich asked noncommissioned officers T. Kirpichnikov and M. Markov what this meant, but they did not answer. The soldiers again shouted, "Hurrah!" Lashkevich issued the order "at ease," took out a paper, declared it contained an order of the tsar, and was about to read it. He didn't get a chance. A rousing "Hurrah" again rang through the ranks, and cries were heard everywhere. "We won't kill any more. Enough blood!" "Gentlemen officers," said Kirpichnikov, "I request you all to leave," and the entire unit banged rifle butts against the floor. At this threatening sound the officers fled. Someone shouted: "Cut them down!" A few excited soldiers lunged at the officers. Crossing the yard, the officers drew level with the barracks window; shots rang out from the ventilation window. Captain Lashkevich fell dead.

The main training unit of the Volynskii Battalion marched out into the yard. Several men headed for other battalion units to win them to the side of the

Soldier demonstrators who joined the revolution. From a photograph in the Museum of the Hungarian Labor Movement, Budapest.

insurrection. Soon the Fourth Company came out, followed by the First and Second companies, the preparatory training units. Soldiers opened the battalion storerooms and distributed rifles and cartridges to those who did not have them. Armed soldiers filled the entire courtyard of the barracks. Buglers sounded the tocsin. A few shots were fired in the air and a hearty "Hurrah" rang out. Thus began the rising of the Volynskii Battalion.

From the beginning, the Volynians' rising was more serious than that of the Pavlovskiis. The Volynians did not go to companies of their own battalion located far away. The enormous barracks of the Preobrazhenskii and Lithuanian regiments were immediately adjacent to the barracks of the Volynskii Regiment. The insurrectionists rushed there to rouse soldiers in those regiments to fight for the common cause. Drill instruction on the parade ground at the Preobrazhenskii barracks halted. The Volynians appeared and called on their neighbors to join them. Here too they were ready for revolution and only a push was needed. The Preobrazhenskii troops joined the Volynian contingent.

Soldiers in the reserve battalion of the Lithuanian Regiment temporarily vacillated. Officers told them to stay out of it. But the mighty revolutionary wave overwhelmed the opposition. "Get dressed!" resounded through the barracks, and the men of the Lithuanian Regiment began to emerge. Soon the barracks yard was transformed: buglers sounded their calls, the regimental bell rang, and shots were fired. The soldiers, overcome with joy, shook hands all around. The traditional camaraderie among soldiers, which sprang from the uniformly degrading status in which the lower ranks of the tsarist army were held, now was reborn in a revolutionary setting, strengthened because the soldiers understood the community of interest and were conscious of their unity with the people.

The soldiers strove to leave the hated barracks and get out into the streets as quickly as possible to join other military units and the people. One column moved along Kirochnaia Street to the gray barracks of the Sixth Engineer Reserve Battalion. O. Sipol', a soldier in that battalion, remembered that on the morning of February 27, when the battalion was preparing for training as usual, they heard a loud volley of rifle fire. Shouts of "Hurrah" reached them from the street as did the cries of soldiers approaching their battalion: "Come out, comrades!" The engineers hadn't long to wait before the barracks gates opened. "Those who had come up ran into the barracks shouting: 'Hurrah, comrades, get your rifles!' . . . Voices cried: 'Cartridges too!' The locked doors of the storerooms were broken down, a shot rang out, and the quartermaster lay 'where he belonged.' "[27] Posting guards in the barracks, the engineers joined the insurrection. They took to the street with their band, and the horde of soldiers marched to music along Liteinyi Prospekt.

Mikhail Slonimskii,[i] the writer, then serving in the Sixth Engineer Battalion, told how a lad from the Volynskii Regiment striding alongside him down Liteinyi Prospekt yelled, flapping his arms like wings: " 'We're going forward into the unknown!' . . . He uttered these words enthusiastically with pathos and with great hope. . . . We indeed were marching forward into the unknown. The school for engineer ensigns, where I was destined to receive my first rank as an officer, now succumbed. A gendarme at the entrance to the school office fired a shot, but the rifle was instantly torn from his hands and he, pale and encircled by angry soldiers, begged: 'Don't kill me! I didn't know you were having a revolution.' "[28]

Soldiers from different units intermingled. Some marched alone, others in groups. No one was in command, and scarcely any officers were to be seen. When an officer appeared to take charge, the soldiers drew themselves up and marched with greater confidence, since they had grown accustomed to military organization and discipline. They willingly obeyed an unknown ensign riding about on a horse who sought to bring order into the ranks. They responded approvingly to the voice of Second Lieutenant Georgii Astakhov: "Brothers, I'm with you!" This cry encouraged the soldiers. "Forward! The lieutenant is with us!" the men exclaimed. Again there were cries of "Hurrah," and shouts of

[i] Mikhail Leonidovich Slonimskii (1897–1972), Russian writer and member of the Serapion Brotherhood literary group founded in 1921. Slonimskii published a collection of grotesque stories about the war and revolution *(Shestoi strelkovyi)*.

"Long live freedom!" Few detachments were organized. Most soldiers walked in no order. Some hung their heads, not knowing what awaited them. But many were confident they knew what to do.

Journalist N. Iordanskii[j] remembered conversing on the street on February 27 with soldiers of the Preobrazhenskii Regiment. The soldiers, calm and businesslike, understood fully what was happening. They said they had to carry through to the end or else they would be executed. Iordanskii noted that his advice to the soldiers was superfluous, that they knew what to do. This made Iordanskii think the insurrection of February 27 had been organized by a secret military group composed of liberal generals totally independent of the revolutionary organizations.[29] There is absolutely no evidence to support this hypothesis. "Liberal" generals had no military organization to prepare an insurrection. Soldiers rose inspired by the self-sacrificing struggle of the workers in response to the appeals of the latter's revolutionary organizations.

The first joyous encounter between the rebelling workers and soldiers took place at the barracks of the Volynskii and Preobrazhenskii regiments. There were brief speeches and happy greetings. " 'That's it!' a resident of the capital in a ragged cap said to a cook holding her basket. 'Look at all the soldiers with their guns! No pharaoh will stand up to them!' People on the sidewalks shouted and dashed to the ranks of soldiers, and fused with them. They cried loudly and excitedly. Someone said the tsar might dispatch troops from the front. A member of the Preobrazhenskii Regiment answered: 'They're just like us . . . now no one can resist the people.' "[30]

Soldiers merged with workers. This was the revolution's turning point. "The inevitable happened," wrote Kaiurov. "The soldiers came with us. The revolutionary masses had triumphed."[31] "Indefatigable Comrade Chugurin, rifle in hand and a cartridge bandolier over his shoulder, terribly dirty but beaming triumphantly," came to the Pavlovs' apartment. " 'We've won!' He was the first to tell us that soldiers with weapons in hand were joining us by units. Here and there workers had managed to join the soldiers, infiltrate the barracks, and secure arms."[32]

The revolutionary soldiers mostly headed for the principal center of insurrection, the Vyborg District. As before, on February 27 people filled Vyborg streets. After the previous day's slaughter in the center of the capital, the Vyborg workers expected government troops to attack their district and kept close watch on Bolshoi Sampsonievskii Prospekt toward Liteinyi Bridge, where troops might appear. They did, but they were no longer defending tsarism. "At about 1:00 P.M.," I. Mil'chik remembered,

[j] N. Iordanskii (1863–1941), a well-known educator and political activist who played an important role in the Russian Sunday School Movement and in the advancement of education for women. Iordanskii was one of the organizers of the All-Russian Teachers' Congress of 1913–14. Although he was not a Bolshevik, Iordanskii served in various capacities in the Commissariat of Education after the revolution.

> a powerful force stirred that dark mass of workers into action. A truck packed with soldiers, rifles in hand, parted the crowd as it roared down Sampsonievskii. Red flags waved from the bayonets of the rifles, something never before seen or heard of. The soldiers turned to the crowd, waved their arms at the Villier Clinic, and shouted out loud. The noise of the truck and the murmuring of many thousands drowned out their words. Yet no words were needed. Red flags on bayonets and excited and gleaming faces, instead of the wooden dullness of the past, foretold victory. . . . The news the truck brought—that troops had mutinied—spread like wildfire.[33]

Soldiers appeared on the corner of Nizhegorodskaia and Lesnaia as a dense crowd rather than in formation. Workers greeted them with immense joy. Although many soldiers were distraught and lacked confidence, the workers merged into the mass of them, bringing cheer and determination to fight to the end. Workers and soldiers united to form columns. Soldiers' gray coats blended with workers' black garb. Civilian caps appeared on soldiers' heads and soldiers' caps on workers. Many workers now were armed; they had received weapons from the soldiers, a rifle, a saber, or a revolver.

Workers in the Vyborg District and soldiers of the rebel units made for the barracks of the reserve battalion of the Moscow Guards Regiment located in that district in order to draw its soldiers into the revolution. A large crowd of workers and soldiers concentrated at the regiment barracks. "Comrade soldiers!" the crowd shouted. "Come out: join the people. Down with the war!" The Moscow training unit drew itself up in ranks at the gate on Lesnoi Prospekt, barring entry into the barracks and refusing to allow soldiers on the street. An officer threatened to shoot in an attempt to persuade the workers to disperse, but they exhorted the soldiers not to listen to their officers. "Brother soldiers, join us! All the regiments have risen up in the city and march with the people. Don't be traitors!"

For a while both sides were confined to arguments or threats. Then something happened:

> Suddenly the low weak fence started to shake. It gave in at several points, and streams of people poured in from the avenue to the yard. Now the gate too swung open. The workers and soldiers came together. The training unit handed over its rifles, and the workers seized them from their hands. The commander of the training unit shouted: "Fire in bursts!" and fired his own revolver, but he was so agitated that he shot into the air. He was felled on the spot and someone killed him. Soldiers loaded their rifles and began shooting at the building where the officers met and at the barracks where soldiers who were hesitating were lurking. "Out of the barracks! Everybody out! In formation. . . ." Crowds of workers and some soldiers besieged the arms cache of the Moscow Regiment and broke the locks. Soon all the rifles and cartridges were in workers' hands.[34]

Two tasks were thus accomplished simultaneously: the soldiers of the reserve battalion of the Moscow Regiment joined the revolution and the workers of the Vyborg quarter acquired arms.

This success inspired the insurrectionists. Until then the workers had learned how to "bring out" factories and make them go out on strike. Now they learned how to "bring out" military units and involve them in the revolution. "Comrades! Bring out the regiments!" the crowd strongly urged. The mass of people divided into groups and set off in various directions to make that slogan a reality.

A bicycle battalion was stationed in a wooden barracks on Sampsonievskii Prospekt in the Vyborg District. The battalion differed from most units, as it accepted only people who could ride bicycles. Usually they were the sons of prosperous parents, a fact that was bound to affect the battalion's attitude toward the revolution. The first attempt to draw them into the insurrection failed. A new group of workers and soldiers, approaching the barracks of the bicycle battalion, met a firm defense prepared in advance. The battalion had dug trenches and erected barricades in the yard; it had placed machine guns on the ready in the barracks windows. Workers appealed to the bicycle troops to come out and join the people. Speakers climbed up the barracks fence and made brief speeches, but they were answered by machine guns and an exchange of fire ensued. Most of the soldiers were locked into the barracks. Only a small group of bicycle troops ran from the barracks without their weapons to join the people. The siege of the bicyclists' barracks continued until evening without results.

Prisons were among the most important targets of the rebellious workers and soldiers. Petrograd jails and police stations were overflowing when the revolution broke out. Designed to hold 4,000, they contained 7,600 prisoners, of whom 2,400 were held in solitary confinement in the Kresty Prison, 958 in the house of preliminary detention, and 1,436 in the prison for those assigned to hard labor.[35] The prisoners included a considerable number of progressive workers, activists of the Petrograd Bolshevik Organization and trade unions, and members of other political parties who had been sentenced for revolutionary activity. A few members of the Petrograd Committee of the RSDRP also languished behind bars.

Several groups of insurrectionists simultaneously decided to free political prisoners, especially leaders in the workers' movement, as quickly as possible. M. I. Kalinin[k] recalled how, on February 27, he and a crowd of workers approached the Finland Station when some military unit appeared.

> Even though the station guard was immediately disarmed, the crowd still hesitated. What was to be done next? Soldiers yelled: "Where are our leaders? Lead us." I myself hesitated. I still didn't know where our force could go and what might be done here and now on the spot. One thing, however, was absolutely clear: we had right then, without a moment's delay, to incite them to battle, for everybody felt the same way and wanted action. I climbed to a station platform

[k] M. I. Kalinin (1875–1946), an old Bolshevik party leader elected a candidate member of the party's Central Committee in 1912. After the death of Ia. M. Sverdlov in 1919, Kalinin was appointed chairman of the All-Russian Soviet Executive Committee, a position that corresponded to that of head of state.

> and hollered: "If it's leaders you want, Kresty Prison is right here, but first you have to free your leaders." My idea was picked up and expanded upon instantly. Somebody yelled: "Let's free those in the military prison first. . . ." Detachments were formed and leaders appeared. Thought turned to action: some made for the military prison, others for Kresty.[36]

Workers and soldiers attacked Kresty on two sides, the Neva embankment and Simbirskaia Street. A crowd of workers and soldiers in front of the prison greeted the prisoners, waving caps and shawls and shouting. Prisoners began breaking windows to hear what the crowd was saying. People discussed how best to get into the prison: climb over the fence or breach the wall. They finally decided to storm it. Rifle butts smashed away and the iron gates gave in. The crowd rushed into the building, disarmed guards and administrators, opened cells, and freed the prisoners. Prison records and papers were burned in the courtyard.

Among the political prisoners, active workers in the Bolshevik party[1] were freed from Kresty: they included Ivan Emel'ianov of the Phoenix Factory, Nikolai Bystrov of the Rosenkrantz Works, Kazenkov of the Putilov Plant, Sergei Gessen, secretary of the Putilov workers' medical fund, Georgii Pylaev, Semen Roshal', and many others. Bolshevik workers N. Antipov and Fedor Lemeshev were confined in the same cell. "The window of our cell," Lemeshev recounted,

> looked out on Bolshaia Neva. Every day Antipov and I watched through the window to see if smoke was coming from the factory. If there was no smoke, the workers were on strike. On the morning of February 27 there was none. . . . Suddenly, at 1:00 P.M., we heard rifle fire and noise near the prison. Workers and soldiers had come to free us. . . . The political prisoners, though grown men, cried like babies and embraced one another. An emergency meeting was held outside the jail. The freed political prisoners joined the soldiers and workers and set out to agitate among the remaining regiments to have them join the revolution.[37]

V. Shmidt, a member of the Petersburg Bolshevik Committee, was freed from Kresty. He described what he saw upon his release:

> What greeted my eyes made me extraordinarily happy. Thousands of armed soldiers were standing on the embankment along the entire prison wall handing out arms to workers of the Vyborg quarter. Dozens of trucks containing weapons and cartridges were unloaded almost instantaneously. I hastily grabbed the first gun that came to hand and set off for the State Duma building along with everybody else.[38]

The prisoners in the hard-labor transfer prison beyond Nevskii Gate were freed the following day. Having learned what was happening in the city, the

[1]As well as Menshevik and SR leaders.

hard-labor prisoners rebelled. Two thousand of them, housed in fifty-two cells, began smashing windows and breaking down doors in the hated prison. Throwing down their keys, the keepers fled. Led by Bolshevik workers and sailors—K. Orlov, V. Naumov, Peterson, I. Sladkov, T. Ul'iantsev, and others—they rushed into the yard, tore down the gate, and poured into the street. A rally took place. Some prisoners headed for the barracks of a nearby Cossack regiment, opened the storeroom, seized arms, and swept the Cossacks along with them. Orlov recalled: "We were on our way to the city. Clanking chains and handcuffs were heard amid the roaring, noisy crowd. . . . In the Cossack Regiment smithy we unshackled each other. . . . Armed to the teeth, we drove the whole Cossack regiment into the yard, posted guards in the barracks, organized another rally, and led the Cossacks to the Tauride Palace."[39]

February 27 was the decisive day of the Second Russian Revolution: that day the people finally won the upper hand. They deprived tsarism of one support after another and forced the police to capitulate. Backed by the troops that had come over to the revolution, the people mercilessly settled accounts with the detested police and wiped out their strongholds. Although the authorities called in remaining patrols and concentrated the police in the stations, it was already too late. The sacking of the stations had begun. When the commander of the Third Precinct in the Petrograd quarter asked his superiors what to do, they replied: "Do your best." He told his men to change into civilian clothes and disperse. The police ceased to exist as an organized, armed defender of the tsarist regime, although determined individual policemen continued to resist for another few days.

On February 27 the soldier masses began shifting to the side of the insurrection. During the first days of the revolution, the troops had vacillated. Some had participated in suppressing the revolution, while others remained passive or benignly neutral. The revolutionary proletariat intensified its struggle to win over the troops and achieved remarkable success on February 27, although the number of soldiers who openly joined the revolution was still relatively small. Here are the figures:

February 26, evening	600
February 27, morning	10,200
February 27, noon	25,700
February 27, evening	66,700[40]

Moreover, units in the garrison not yet identified with the people no longer represented a dependable support for the monarchy. Revolutionary ferment had penetrated all the military units in Petrograd. During the early days the police and some soldiers had fought the unarmed people. Now the people had seized the military arsenal, storerooms, and warehouses and had procured weapons. Many civilians appeared in the streets with rifles slung on their shoulders and sabers and revolvers in their belts. Together with soldiers, they stopped officers, took away their sidearms, and armed the people. Henceforward, the insurrection against tsarism would be armed. Although the revolutionary forces lacked proper organization and command and traditional military organization, and an experienced officer corps still held together the forces of tsarism, the advantage lay with the revolution. Generals and officers feared having no soldiers left.

Petrograd kept sending encouraging reports to Supreme Headquarters. At 1:15 P.M., February 27, Beliaev telegraphed: "Companies and battalions faithful to their duty are with resolve and vigor suppressing disturbances that began in the morning. The mutiny has not yet been put down, but I am fully confident that order soon will be restored. Relentless measures are being taken. The authorities are calm."[41] In reality, dismay and disarray reigned at the headquarters of tsarism's defenders. Senior army and police personnel, assembled in city hall, could not decide upon a course of action. Constant telephone messages reported that more units were rebelling, and even the most zealous defenders of the old order began to feel it was useless to resist. Commands and directives were issued, yet almost no one knew to whom or why they were issued. Police Chief Galle was called to the military district headquarters to acquaint the highest officers with the city plan. Galle related that upon appearing at city hall, he found it in a state of confusion. Nobody ever asked him about the plan. Khabalov and a few colonels, the commanders of reserve battalions, wandered aimlessly from room to room. Chief of Staff Telezhnikov paced up and down. Colonel Kutepov found the same scene in the city government building: "All of them (the higher military ranks—E.B.) were greatly distraught and confused. I noticed that General Khabalov's jaw trembled while we talked."[42]

Many supporters of the monarchy later blamed the Petrograd military authorities for the monarchy's fall. In their opinion, the authorities had acted indecisively during the revolution. They had failed because Khabalov, a mediocre man of weak character, had lacked energy and will. General Sheifon wrote that the highest administrative officials held long conferences each day in military district headquarters. "The 'rulers of the capital,' weak and distraught, lost precious time. Deciding nothing at the morning meeting, they scheduled another for the evening. At each conference everyone understood that it was necessary to use force against the rebellions on the street. They tried, but so feebly that the uncultured mobs invariably won."[43]

The street prevailed not because force was used "feebly" nor because Khabalov was confused and indecisive. The authorities were active: they feverishly tried to save the dying regime, but no commander, no matter how bold and decisive, could have saved the moribund autocracy.

Learning of the rising by the reserve battalion of the Volynskii Regiment, Khabalov instructed its commander to do everything possible to end the disturbance, bring the soldiers back to the barracks, and disarm them. The battalion commander, of course, could not comply. Khabalov then enjoined a reserve squadron of armored cars to combat with the insurrectionists. The crews of the squadron turned out to be unreliable, and the armored cars, as the squadron commander said, could not function effectively against the crowd. At the front they fought the enemy facing them, but now their rear was unprotected. Khabalov ordered the cars be rendered inoperable and threatened to execute the squadron commandant if even a single vehicle fell to the rebels. What Khabalov feared happened: all the armored cars passed into the insurgents' hands. The writer V. Shklovskii,[m] who was serving in the armored-car squadron, related that parts were removed from the cars on the orders of the command, and the disassembled vehicles were hauled to the Mikhailovskii garage. But at the decisive moment of the revolution the armored cars were restored to fighting readiness and moved to Nevskii Prospekt to support the insurrection.[44] The letters "RSDRP" were etched into the gray steel of one, and a red pennant waved from it.

Fighting on the side of the revolution, the armored cars helped attack the telephone building. One operated on Morskaia Street, another on Kirpichnyi Lane. The police set up an ambush and fired a machine gun but they were crushed. The policemen, wearing soldiers' coats, laid down their arms, thus opening the road to the telephone exchange. Workers and students ran in, swiftly climbed the stairs, bid the operators to disconnect government wires, searched the building, and posted sentries. From this point on, telephones would serve the revolution. The military automobile school, in which V. V. Maiakovskii was serving,[n] joined the revolution. The poet and the entire school went to the State Duma, and later he commanded the school for several days.

From the morning of February 27 when revolution took hold of the capital, constant requests for reinforcements flooded military district headquarters. The command could not satisfy them. Most unit commanders responded that they had no one to send to headquarters. The authorities were particularly alarmed when they learned at 11:00 A.M. on February 27 that rebel troops were moving along Kirochnaia Street and Liteinyi Prospekt. A punitive shock detachment was quickly put together and placed under the command of Colonel A. P. Kutepov of the Preobrazhenskii Regiment, on leave in Petrograd.[o] General Sheifon expressed indignation that Khabalov had called upon the decisive Kutepov too late, when every opportunity had been missed and the "senile authorities had for all practical purposes already abandoned the city to the raging mob." Nothing would have changed, however, even if they had acted earlier.

[m] V. B. Shklovskii (1893–1984), a Russian essayist, novelist, and literary scholar. See his *A Sentimental Journey: Memoirs, 1917–1922*, trans. Richard Sheldon (Ithaca: Cornell University Press, 1970).

[n] V. V. Maiakovskii (1893–1930). One of the great poets of the twentieth century, Maiakovskii joined the Bolshevik party before the revolution and afterward devoted himself to popularizing its ideals. A tragic love affair and probable growing disillusionment with the regime drove him to suicide.

[o] A. P. Kutepov had arrived in Petrograd only a week before and admitted he was still unfamiliar with the situation in the capital at the time of his appointment.

Kutepov's detachment was supposed to move along Liteinyi and Suvorov prospekts and thus surround the rebels. This meant he would have had to enclose an enormous area, from Liteinyi Bridge to Nikolaevskii Station. Kutepov declared he would not hesitate to shoot the insurrectionists but he needed at least a brigade to encircle such a huge area. Khabalov irritably replied, "We're giving you all we've got." He assigned two Preobrazhenskii companies to Kutepov: one reserve battalion of the Keksholm Regiment, a machine-gun company from Oranienbaum, and a Ninth Reserve Cavalry Regiment squadron. Khabalov also promised Kutepov he would dispatch chasseurs and anything else he could. No punitive detachment could have saved tsarism, however, even if an entire brigade had been available. One new chink after another appeared in the defenses of the tsarist troops. Kutepov had barely set out for the intersection of Liteinyi and Nevskii prospekts when he was ordered to retreat, for the insurrectionists were moving on the Winter Palace. Kutepov obeyed the new order and intended to enter the Field of Mars, but a perilous situation developed where the First Artillery Brigade was located and he had to remain to reinforce the situation there.

Kutepov's punitive detachment launched its military operations. It shot at crowds on Liteinyi Prospekt, on Sergeevskaia Street, near the Artillery Factory, and other places, and fired upon trucks filled with workers, killing some. This tsarist punitive force raged unchecked for a few hours, "restoring order" along Liteinyi Prospekt. But in vain! Workers packed the entire district. Dissatisfaction showed even in Kutepov's detachment, and more and more of his soldiers crossed over to the people. Kutepov tried to phone Khabalov, but no one answered because headquarters' communications were out. By evening there was almost nothing left of Kutepov's force. "When I went into the street," he recalled, "it was already dark and all Liteinyi was filled with crowds pouring in from the side streets. . . . A large part of my force mixed with the crowd and I understood that my detachment could put up no further resistance. I went home and ordered the door closed."[45]

Other attempts the tsarist authorities made to rout the revolutionary forces ended in the same manner. By midday on February 27 the tsar's position had become critical. The insurrectionists held the Vyborg quarter, parts of the Petrograd side, and much of Liteinyi Prospekt. In view of this position, the military district staff decided to unite its forces, forge battle-ready detachments, and send them to suppress the principal centers of the insurrection. The staff managed to assemble loyal units in front of the Winter Palace: a company in the reserve battalion of the Preobrazhenskii Regiment, units of reserve battalions in the Chasseur (Egerskii) and Petrograd regiments, some Pavlovskii men, and a batch of sailors from a guards unit. A band was playing on Palace Square, shouts of "Hurrah" went up, but no one moved. Some units had no cartridges. The insurrectionists had seized the weapons' depository in the Vyborg quarter. If cartridges had been sent from other units they would almost inevitably have fallen into the rebels' hands. Above all, the soldiers in the square became steadily infused with revolutionary zeal, and it was risky to send them to fight the insurrectionists.

Some officers decided they should negotiate with the State Duma to find a peaceful solution. Captain Skripitsyn of the Preobrazhenskii Regiment proposed this to Khabalov. The commander rejected it, preferring to use force against the mutinous soldiers. But how and where he would act remained unclear. The soldiers were stamping their feet in Palace Square and huddling against the cold. Khabalov reported the situation to the Council of Ministers yet could not offer any plan of action. Prime Minister Golitsyn subsequently said that Khabalov had "impressed him as a slow-witted person, hopelessly lacking in energy, and poorly informed. He was totally confused, it was impossible to form an impression from his report of what the situation actually was, what was to be expected, or what measures he proposed to take."[46] Beliaev also observed that "Khabalov made a very negative impression on the members of the Council of Ministers. His hands were shaking, and he obviously had lost the capacity to manage things at so serious a moment."[47] Interestingly enough, the same description was made of Beliaev himself, Balk, and the other tsarist generals in Petrograd. And no wonder. They all had reason to be distraught—the Petrograd garrison had slipped out of the authorities' control.

When it became clear that Khabalov could do nothing, the Council of Ministers made Beliaev responsible for subduing the insurrection. Khabalov, however, remained at his post until the tsar could issue an order. Beliaev was present at Khabalov's headquarters, as he himself mentioned, only "to support him with energy and boldness of spirit or advise him if necessary."[48] On February 27, Beliaev proposed that Colonel Zankevich, chief of the General Staff, should take command of the troops. After this it was altogether unclear who was subordinate to whom and who was in command. Zankevich, Beliaev, and Khabalov were all issuing orders, although Khabalov held that the war minister had no right to interfere in the affairs of a military district directly subordinate to the commander in chief. Zankevich donned the uniform of the Pavlovskii Regiment, which he had once commanded, and appeared at Palace Square to explain how the force standing there could be used to curb the revolution. Zankevich's conclusion was discouraging: the soldiers could not be relied on. At nightfall, the troops who had been passively waiting there gradually dispersed to their barracks. Palace Square emptied. The defenders of the monarchy had lost another detachment.

General Balk later criticized the tsarist authorities' behavior during the revolution. He wrote that Beliaev and Khabalov, unequal to the task, had failed to take firm measures to put down the insurrection, and had been utterly surprised by the rising of the reserve battalion of the Volynskii Regiment.[49] Late in the evening on February 27 the former commander of the guards corps, General Bezobrazov, advised Khabalov to send a detachment to the Tauride Palace to destroy the "principal nucleus of the rebels" that had formed there. Yet Khabalov took no action. Balk further upbraided him for not using the military schools in the struggle against the revolution; however, by the evening of February 27 Khabalov could not rely on them either. The infantry, artillery, engineering, and other military schools were in ferment.

The military authorities had no forces available in Petrograd to strike at the revolution. All they could hope for was salvation from the front. Expecting such help, they went over to the defensive. Withdrawing forces from some districts, they were reconciled to the temporary loss of much of Petrograd. Troops loyal to tsarism held the area from the Neva embankment and Mariinskii Palace to Zimnaia Kanavka. The authorities elected the Admiralty as the focus of their defense. Why did they choose the Admiralty? From there, streets radiated to the capital's three railroad stations, Nikolaevskii, Tsarskoe Selo, and Warsaw stations, from which the arrival of troops from the front was awaited. Moreover, these forces could advance into the city supported by artillery and machine-gun fire from the Admiralty. At approximately 7:00 P.M. the military district headquarters moved there. Responding to a call from headquarters, a reserve battalion of the Izmailovskii Regiment, a squadron of the Ninth Reserve Cavalry Regiment, and two batteries of a guards artillery squadron came to the Admiralty. All told, five infantry companies totaling six hundred men, with twelve artillery pieces and forty machine guns, assembled. The command decided not to defend the Admiralty outside but to entrench themselves inside the building. They closed all entrances and exits, blocked all gates with piles of wood, and posted guards, turning the Admiralty into a fortress in a raging revolutionary sea. The troops in the Admiralty were told to hold out until the evening of February 28. The assistant commander of the Izmailovskii Battalion, B. Fomin, related that the military authorities of the capital had assured the Izmailovskii Regiment that troops from the front would reach Petrograd by then, and "would immediately restore order in the capital and shoot the mutinous reserve battalions and the crowds of demonstrators."[50]

Despite these assurances from the officers, members of the detachment in the Admiralty felt doomed. Neither strong walls nor iron gates nor barricades of timber and firewood could guarantee their safety. The officers could not vouch for those they commanded. The Admiralty had nothing to feed hungry soldiers. To wait with empty stomachs undermined morale. The troops loyal to the autocracy had been called to defend the tsarist government until units arrived from the front. But did a government still exist? It continued to meet in Golitsyn's apartment or in the Mariinskii Palace. At 2:00 P.M. on February 27, Beliaev told the ministers about the disturbances among the soldiers. The ministers severely criticized Protopopov for misleading the government with reassuring declarations. Protopopov defended himself, saying the disturbances were spontaneous and could not have been anticipated. The imminent danger to the autocracy thoroughly alarmed the tsar's ministers. Their council, always apathetic and passive, suddenly began to show signs of life. Except it was already too late.

The Council of Ministers put Petrograd under martial law and authority in the city passed into the hands of the military command. Some tsarist generals later claimed they had objected to this because only the tsar could proclaim martial law. Beliaev replied: "You can assume that an imperial command to proclaim martial law has been issued." Yet what significance could the measure have when real power in the capital was increasingly concentrated in the hands of the revolutionary people?

On the eve of the monarchy's downfall, the government decided to augment the powers of the chairman of the Council of Ministers, who previously had had but limited influence on the ministers. At its February 27 meeting, the council gave the chairman the right to direct all governmental affairs. There was now nothing to direct, however, for by February 27 few remained loyal to the tsarist government. At last, the Council of Ministers sacrificed one of its members. It removed Protopopov, whose actions more than others had aroused the popular wrath, as minister of internal affairs. By law, only the tsar could replace ministers, but they found a way out by suggesting Protopopov should say he was ill and retire. He did so, to Prince Golitsyn's relief. What significance, though, did Protopopov's retirement on February 27 have when the people had in effect retired the entire tsarist cabinet Golitsyn led?

The government no longer had either the strength or resources to implement its own decisions, and it could not even inform the population about them. After Beliaev proposed the government's decree on martial law be printed in the government print shop, it proved impossible because the people had captured it and the tsar's mandate was no longer valid there. When the Naval Ministry finally printed the decrees of the Council of Ministers, there was no way to post them. "I reported," Balk recalled, "I couldn't do it because I had neither glue nor brushes, but General Khabalov said that some way must be found to hang and post them by the Admiralty. The way General Khabalov spoke I got the impression that he ascribed no significance to the declaration."[51]

After adopting these meaningless and already outdated resolutions, the government had come to the end of the road. The final meeting of Russia's last tsarist government took place on the evening of February 27. Golitsyn remembered: "We sat in the Mariinskii Palace from 7:00 P.M. to 11:30. . . . No decisions were made. We walked about in distraction. We saw that the situation was deteriorating and anticipated we would be arrested."[52] They learned that people were advancing on the Mariinskii Palace to arrest the tsarist ministers. Fear of the people's retribution seized the high-placed royal officials. Extraordinary turmoil and panic now set in. The palace lights went out and, as one member of the government said, when they came on again he was amazed to find himself beneath a table.[53] The ministers, so recently all-powerful, now sneaked out of the palace by the back way. Two hid in a dark room reserved for couriers to avoid the people, and waited for a good opportunity to slip out of the palace. Tsarist authority had ceased to exist in the capital.

The messages from Petrograd on February 27 reaching the headquarters of the commander in chief differed fundamentally from those of the preceding days, and alarm grew by the hour. The military district command urgently requested headquarters to send help immediately from the front. At noon Khabalov telegraphed the tsar: "I'm doing all I can to put down the revolt. I consider it essential to send reliable troops from the front at once."[54] Wires from Petrograd officials in the evening had lost the reassuring tone of previous messages. Beliaev too now requested help from the front. At 7:00 P.M. on February 27 he telegraphed Alekseev: "The situation in Petrograd is becoming very serious. The few units still loyal have had no success as yet in quelling the military mutiny. Worse than that, more and more units are steadily joining the rebels. Fires have broken out and we have no means to combat them. Genuinely dependable units must come at once, and in numbers large enough to act in concert in different parts of the city."[55]

An hour later, 8:00 P.M., February 27, Khabalov informed Alekseev and the tsar that all efforts to suppress the insurrection in Petrograd had failed and that the insurgents held most of the city. "I request His Imperial Majesty be informed," wrote Khabalov,

> that I have been unable to fulfill his command to restore order in the capital. One after another, most of the units have mutinied, refusing to fight the rebels. Others have been fraternizing with the rebels and turning their arms against troops loyal to His Majesty. Those still loyal have been fighting the rebels all day, suffering heavy losses. The insurrectionists now hold most of the capital. Only a handful of men from different regiments have remained loyal. They are concentrated at the Winter Palace under the command of Major General Zankevich. They and I will continue the struggle.[56]

Even later, at 12:35 A.M., February 28, the Naval Department sent a telegram from Petrograd. Count I. I. Kapnist reported to the Chief of the Naval Staff at Supreme Headquarters what parts of the city the rebels occupied. He mentioned a provisional committee had been formed in the State Duma to restore order but commented that "it is doubtful that the raging crowd can be calmed. The troops are willingly going over to the rebels. Officers are disarmed on the street. The mob is commandeering vehicles. . . . Although Beliaev has assumed command, in view of what is happening it is unlikely he will be able to control the situation."[57]

At this point no tsarist general could have taken charge of the situation to save the autocracy. Petrograd workers who had begun the insurrection all alone had won over the soldiers. Together they had overthrown the autocracy. "The St. Petersburg workers have vanquished the tsarist monarchy. Having started the uprising unarmed in face of machine guns, in their heroic struggle against the police and the tsar's armies, the workers won over the majority of the soldiers of the St. Petersburg garrison."[58]

After the soldiers joined the people, the composition of the revolutionary army changed both in quantity and quality. The movement expanded enormously and the struggle became general, assuring the revolution would triumph. The expansion of the movement was bound to have an impact on the level of consciousness and degree of organization of those who took part in it. The vast mass of the soldiers, chiefly unstable, vacillating, and petit bourgeois, had risen against tsarism. This influenced the following course of events. The State Duma, remote from the movement in the early days of the revolution, unexpectedly emerged as a leading force. A proposal put forth by Menshevik defensists just before the revolution to proceed to the State Duma found no support among workers. They did not go to the Tauride Palace during the first days of the revolution either—the Petrograd proletariat had placed no hopes on the Duma. At that time the struggle lay in the streets and squares of the capital. Now circumstances had changed and a move toward the Tauride Palace got underway. Some authors explain this by arguing that the barracks of the military units that joined the struggle against tsarism first (Volhynskii, Lithuanian, Preobrazhenskii, and others) were located on Kirochnaia, Tavricheskaia, Zakharevskaia, and Shpalernaia streets near the Tauride Palace. Understandably they would first head for the closest familiar center. Geography, however, was of secondary importance.

The pull toward the State Duma ushered in a fresh stage in the movement that began on February 27. New social groups, entering the revolutionary struggle for the first time, considered the Duma something akin to a popular organ and its leaders fighters against the tsarist regime. They thought the Duma was the device to help them painlessly break with the past. Soldiers who had violated their oath to the tsar and joined the people desired to win approval from what they regarded as a "legitimate institution." Officers who had thrown in their lot with the soldiers and the mass of urban people supporting the insurrection wanted Duma authority to sanction their actions. Thus the slogan "To the Tauride Palace! To the State Duma!" won strong support among the masses.

Another factor favoring the State Duma was that on February 27, rumors spread throughout the city that the tsar had dissolved the Duma, but it had ignored the royal edict and decided to organize a new government. *Izvestiia Komiteta petrogradskikh zhurnalistov* (News of the Committee of Petrograd Journalists, hereafter *Izvestiia zhurnalistov*) clearly stated that "in extraordinary session the Council of Elders, after studying the order of dissolution, has resolved that the State Duma shall not disperse and all deputies shall remain on duty." *Izvestiia zhurnalistov* also reported that Rodzianko had told a delegation of insurrectionary soldiers appearing at the Tauride Palace that the State Duma would proceed most vigorously to substitute a new government for the old one. The bourgeoisie had the opportunity to use the Duma to seize power and the workers had no legal entity available. It would have been difficult to forge one during fierce street fighting. The Bolsheviks, involved in direct clashes with tsarism, failed to pay sufficient attention to this question. "The Russian Bureau of the Central Committee," the *History of the Communist Party of the Soviet*

Union states, "devoted all its energies to the armed uprising and underestimated the issue of power."[59]

Correctly understanding that "actions from below" were decisive in overthrowing tsarism, the Bolsheviks were lax about combining them with "actions from above." The Bolsheviks of the Vyborg side tried unsuccessfully to create a revolutionary center in the Finland Station (more on that later). Many Bolshevik workers instead went with the masses to the Tauride Palace on February 27. S. Skalov subsequently justified this, alleging it would deprive the State Duma of independence.

> I thought I was correct in refusing to go to the Finland Station and form our own separate group, as some suggested. On our way to the Tauride Palace we saw a note at the corner of Shpalernyi and Liteinyi prospekts. I don't recall which organization posted it. It invited all workers to congregate at the Finland Station. Had we isolated ourselves in this way we would have immediately opposed our own weak organization to the State Duma and would thus have untied its hands and allowed it full freedom of political action and independence to lead. This might have led to grave consequences.

Skalov asserts:

> It was out of the question for us to oppose the Duma on February 27, 1917, nor could we have done so. Our organization was too weak. Our leaders were in prison or exile or emigration. Therefore we had to draw the Duma into the revolution. . . . We had to create revolutionary chaos, paralyze any initiative the Duma might direct against the revolution, and this could be done only from within the Duma, by flooding it with the objective reality of revolution."[60]

It is difficult to accept Skalov's contention. The proletariat unquestioningly had to prevent the Duma from acting independently, check its instability, and deny it an opportunity to conspire with tsarism. This could be done only by the revolutionary people acting on their own to form another genuinely revolutionary body as a counterweight to the Duma. To suck the Duma into the revolutionary whirlpool and to instill in it a revolutionary spirit was impossible. Petit bourgeois leaders thought they could make the bourgeois-landlord Duma a bulwark of the revolution. Asserting bourgeois rule alone could take the place of tsarism, they believed that the Duma must establish such rule. Some Duma leaders, particularly Kerensky and Chkheidze, were well known. Their Duma speeches attacking the tsarist government had enjoyed wide circulation. The petit bourgeois figures took advantage of their popularity to mediate between the bourgeoisie and the people. They urged the bourgeoisie to take power and used their influence with the people to have them accept it.

SR and Menshevik leaders called on workers and soldiers to make the Duma deputies stop wavering and break with the old ruling order. The appearance of workers and soldiers at the Tauride Palace did influence the State Duma leaders. "When the troops came to the Duma," Kerensky related, "all doubts vanished. . . . We knew we had to act decisively: either seek support to counteract this new elemental force or become reconciled to it."[61] Leaders of the Workers' Group freed from prison typically made for the Duma. V. N. Zalezhskii recalled meeting them on the street on February 27: "'Where are you going?' we asked in amazement, seeing they were heading for Liteinyi. 'To the Duma.' 'Well, we're on our way to workers' neighborhoods,' we shot back as we parted."[62]

Hastening to the workers' districts, Bolshevik activists paid little attention to the petit bourgeois leaders. Before the revolution they had sent their representatives to exchange information with them. Now this connection was broken. Shliapnikov wrote: "Visiting N. D. Sokolov's apartment, meeting with Chkheidze, Kerensky, and other members of the intelligentsia no longer mattered. . . . Street fighting and demonstrating under the red banner of revolution needed no agreements made in offices by the various political groups. We consciously avoided slogans calling for a nonparty body and instead put forward our battle-tested, disciplined, and centralized party collective to lead the semispontaneous movement."[63] It was impossible to ignore the fact, however, that the petit bourgeois leaders had influence with the masses. Their plans and intentions needed to be known in order to detach the masses from them and prevent them from concluding agreements with Duma leaders to establish bourgeois rule.

The first column of soldiers and workers arrived at the Tauride Palace at about 1:00 P.M. on February 27. It stopped at the entrance to the garden and the front door and sent representatives to discover the Duma's intentions. Kerensky, Chkheidze, and Skobelev addressed the assembly. On his way out Kerensky asked Miliukov: "What shall I propose to the people?" "The program is clear. It is the program of our Progressive Bloc," answered Miliukov. Kerensky waved him off: "What program of the bloc? Does it really have any validity now?" It did not, even though the revolution had not yet reached its culmination on February 27.

The principal issue that concerned the masses was the question of power. The crowd asked: "Where's the new authority? Where's the new government?" Skobelev replied: "The State Duma is now in session. Its members are still vacillating and have not made up their minds to take power. We are pressuring them." Emphasizing that to form a new government was not easy, Skobelev called upon the assembly to remain calm and orderly. "This may last a couple of days. Have patience. The first thing to do is establish revolutionary order."[64] Chkheidze felt the same: "Maintain order," he said. "Organize. That's what we need." In response came cries, "Give us leaders, we need leaders!"

The masses of soldiers who had come to the Tauride Palace on February 27 did not represent an organized military force. They were disorganized groups mixed with civilians. The first task was to organize and guide them, unite the

Soldiers carrying revolutionary banners to the Tauride Palace. From a photograph in the Museum of the Hungarian Labor Movement, Budapest.

workers and rebellious soldiers throughout the city, secure the defense, and again take the initiative in the successful but not yet triumphant revolution. An insurrectionary military and technical center could have done this, only none existed. Under these circumstances the initiative the participants in the revolution displayed assumed decisive significance. A soldier, Fedor Linde, a former student of mathematics and philosophy at Petrograd University, a loner associated with no party, climbed onto the Tauride Palace fence and commanded in a loud voice: "Soldiers, fall in. Civilians, move aside." The soldiers obeyed. "It was decided to form them into an armed detachment, which was drawn up in the courtyard behind the railing in front of the Tauride Palace. All had seen service at the front. At once they chose their leaders from among former platoon noncommissioned officers and people of generally greater experience. After soldiers and armed volunteers were grouped into detachments, their numbers turned out to be quite considerable. It was decided to move them to points in the city where an armed clash might be anticipated."[65] Detachments of armed workers and soldiers set out to occupy the enemy's fortified positions and guard important places. This was not done from above, or at the initiative of the masses themselves or of individuals acting independently. The revolutionaries needed no one's permission to accomplish these tasks.

On the morning of February 27 the movement in the direction of the Tauride Palace assumed massive proportions. A tsarist official, G. Rein, regretted that the order to dissolve the Fourth Duma had not been accompanied by one to seal off the Tauride Palace, as Stolypin had done when he dissolved the First and Second dumas to prevent its becoming a "place for the people to assemble." Duma member A. A. Oznobishin observed that if the gates had been closed and the Tauride Palace had been guarded by "gallant mounted police," the "rebels" would have been arrested and events would have followed a different course. No locked gates or "gallant policemen" could have stopped the popular movement. When it was learned that soldiers and workers were moving toward the Duma, Rodzianko was compelled to order the chief of the palace guard to offer no resistance and not to employ arms.

The people replaced the former palace guard with a new one. Preobrazhenskii Regiment soldiers who had come over to the people composed the first revolutionary guard. It occupied all entrances and exits of the palace, the telegraph office, etc., and stationed guards at all public telephones. The Tauride Palace became the principal focus of the revolution. The mighty avalanche of workers and soldiers no longer stopped at fences or the entrance to the building as they had done, but entered its numerous halls and rooms. A second and third followed.

The real masters of the capital and the entire country who had never before been inside the Tauride Palace had arrived. S. D. Mstislavskii recalled: "I remember how distraught doormen and janitors were as crowds of armed workers and peasants tramped through the halls and chambers: 'they'll make the floor so dirty we won't be able to clean it in a week.' Palace administrators held this 'doorman's point of view.' They plaintively requested admission to the building of the State Duma be orderly." Permission slips granting the right of entry to the palace were issued. But "as might have been expected, for each individual entering with a card three hundred pushed in without any."[66] Miliukov commented that by the evening of February 27, Duma members felt they were not the only ones in the palace, and were not fully its master. By that time a center had been established there to unite all revolutionary forces.

What was it?

The Emergence of the Soviet

As the Second Russian Revolution unfolded, the need to create an administrative body capable of bringing the national uprising to a conclusion and establishing revolutionary authority became more pressing. The First Russian Revolution had demonstrated that a soviet of workers' deputies was precisely such an organ. Revolutionary workers had elected soviets at the height of the disturbances in 1905; they were products of the people's spontaneous action. Arising from massive political strikes, these nonparty organizations of the broad working masses even then had become organs of national struggle and armed uprising, embryos of revolutionary authority.

The soviets declined when the revolution collapsed and now revived when it resumed. Remembering the experience of 1905, workers in Petrograd and other cities began to organize soviets as soon as the revolution broke out. As in 1905, the worker masses took the initiative in creating them. Lenin wrote: "The spontaneous formation of soviets of workers' deputies in the February Revolution was a repetition of the experience of 1905."[67] Talk of organizing soviets arose simultaneously at several different meetings of Petrograd workers and became a public issue. A participant in the revolution remembered: "On February 25 at the base of the huge monument of Alexander III on Znamenskaia Square the first call resounded: 'Let's elect a soviet of workers' deputies!' This call was born in the street and with it was born the revolution."[68] A youth, P. Slovatinskii, noted in his diary that the mass rally of some thirty thousand people that took place on Znamenskaia Square on February 25 shouted the slogan "Long live a soviet of workers' deputies," along with others.[69] A Bolshevik worker, I. M. Gordienko, recalled February 25 on Znamenskaia Square in his memoirs: "On a high teetering box by a lamp post, holding onto the gray pillars with one hand, stood a tall, broad-shouldered man with an animated face who looked like both a worker and a student. Gesticulating with one hand, he cried: 'Comrades, the long-awaited hour has finally come. The people have risen against their oppressors. Don't lose a minute, form neighborhood workers' soviets and draw soldier representatives into them.'"[70]

The working masses responded sympathetically to his appeal to create a soviet. Sukhanov noted that the idea "was immediately picked up by party organizations and, as is known, was successfully realized in the factories of the capital during those days. . . . On Friday evening (February 24—E.B.) people were saying that elections to a soviet of workers' deputies were being conducted in the city's factories."[71] As has been already mentioned, a police department document from February 25 reported that the Petersburg Bolshevik Committee proposed to transform the Information Bureau of Representatives of the Factory Committees into a soviet of workers' deputies. The Menshevik fraction in the Duma also favored a soviet. Skobelev wrote that "on February 22–25 vanguard workers from various neighborhoods had already been to us at the Tauride Palace seeking advice and guidance as to what to do and how to proceed. We specifically proposed they should immediately set up factory committees and prepare for elections to a soviet of workers' deputies in the factories."[72]

Bolsheviks and Mensheviks alike undertook to organize a soviet, but they understood the question of power differently, and thus understood the significance of the soviet differently. Convinced that power must pass to the bourgeoisie after tsarism was overthrown, the Mensheviks considered the soviet an organization reflecting worker spontaneity and a device to pressure the bourgeois authorities and not a source of power. The Bolsheviks looked upon the soviets otherwise. They believed that even while the savage struggle with tsarism continued, a provisional revolutionary government must be formed to implement the revolutionary democratic dictatorship of the proletariat and peasantry, carry the bourgeois-democratic revolution in Russia through to the end, and embark on a socialist revolution. The Bolsheviks contended the soviet should create such a government.

Representatives of workers' organizations, meeting on February 25 on the premises of the Petrograd Union of Workers' Consumer Societies (Nevskii Prospekt, number 144), mentioned earlier, made one of the first attempts to form a soviet of workers' deputies. At the gathering the representatives voted to create a soviet, and recommended sending information about who had been elected to the workers' cooperatives or medical funds. Those present designated the Petrograd Union of Cooperative Workers the city headquarters where information from the various districts should be sent, and proposed to hold the first session of the soviet the following day.[73] This plan was never realized, however, because many participants at the meeting that evening were subsequently arrested.

Meanwhile, the work of organizing a soviet and electing deputies continued in the factories. Even the tsarist authorities learned that a soviet of workers' deputies was forming. A report filed with the Okhranka on February 26 said: "They are planning to form a soviet of workers' deputies. . . . Elections to it will evidently take place at the factories tomorrow morning and already by evening, it may be operative. This is another reason why all factories must be shut down to prevent meetings tomorrow morning."[74] The authorities failed to carry out this proposal and stop the formation of a workers' soviet. However, lack of organization and a single ruling center delayed its formation. The concept of a soviet was in circulation but was slow to be realized.

After four days of struggle, no workers' soviet had yet been founded. Although the revolution had decisively prevailed over the old regime, it as of yet had no organ to represent it. Further delay in the forming of a soviet was impermissible. The Russian Social Democratic Labor party issued an appeal which spoke of the need to struggle to victory over tsarism and organize a soviet of workers' deputies. To judge by its contents, the Bolsheviks put out this call on February 27. It emphasized that the hour had come to emancipate the revolutionary people and to settle accounts with the government, that the army supported the workers, and that the liberation of freedom fighters from prison had strengthened the union of the revolutionary army with the people. "We must complete the task we have begun. Petersburg workers, carry on and expand the general strike, demonstrations, and fraternization with soldiers and Cossacks. Prepare for an armed struggle. We must organize for victory. The movement needs a guiding center. Election of strike committees at factories must begin immediately. Their representatives will constitute the Soviet of Workers' Deputies, which will undertake to organize the movement and form a provisional revolutionary government."[75]

The Vyborg region took the lead in organizing the soviet. A leaflet bearing the signature "The Incipient Soviet of Workers' Deputies" (*Organizuiushchiisia Sovet rabochikh deputatov*), printed on a duplicating machine, has been preserved. Its contents and memoirs of participants show the Vyborg Bolshevik Committee issued it. A Bolshevik worker, S. Ivanov, wrote that "on February 27 the Vyborg District Party Committee appealed to workers and soldiers to organize soviets."[76] E. Studentsova reported the same thing. "At a meeting on the morning of February 27, the Vyborg District Committee of the party formed an initiative group to hold elections for the Incipient Soviet of Workers' Deputies. This group put out an appeal in the name of the Incipient Soviet of Workers' Deputies."[77] It read: "The longed-for hour has come. The people will take power. The revolution has begun. Don't lose a second. Create a provisional revolutionary government today. Organization alone can strengthen our forces. Above all, elect deputies and have them form a network. Let a soviet come into existence, protected by the troops."[78]

A leaflet issued at that time by a group of Interdistrictites and SRs also called for electing deputies to a soviet. It declared that "a provisional revolutionary government" would supersede the tsarist government. "It must include representatives of the proletariat and the army. Comrades! Elect workers' deputies to a Soviet at once. The army already is electing its representatives. Tomorrow a provisional revolutionary government will at last be formed."[79]

Thus all these leaflets urged organizing a soviet of workers' deputies, which would be the equivalent of a provisional revolutionary government or would be obliged to create such a government. Only how was the soviet to be organized? The RSDRP appeal proposed first to elect factory strike committees, whose representatives would compose the soviet of workers' deputies. Everything was happening so fast and the need to form a soviet became so pressing, however, that indirect elections could delay its organization for a long time. The Vyborg Bolsheviks' appeal and the leaflet of the Interdistrictites and SRs offered a quicker and simpler solution. They called upon workers to elect deputies to the soviet directly at workers' meetings.

Where should the elected deputies meet? The Interdistrictite and SR leaflet did not give a clear answer. "Elect deputies and wait for printed instructions," it said. The "Vyborg leaflet" signed by the "Incipient Soviet of Workers' Deputies" designated the site for the soviet more precisely: "Let the Finland Station become the place where the revolutionary command will gather." This seemed a good choice—the Finland Station was on the Vyborg side, the main stronghold of the rising. Before February 27 it might have become the revolutionary center. But on February 27 the movement took another direction—to the Tauride Palace. The time to create a soviet of workers' deputies in the stronghold of the uprising had slipped by and new elements had entered the struggle by February 27, made their mark on events, and influenced the way the soviet was formed.

It was not the Bolsheviks or workers leading the street battles against tsarism who organized the Soviet of Workers' Deputies, but the petit bourgeois leaders who had been on the *periphery* of the workers' movement. They were members of the Menshevik and Trudovik fractions in the Duma; workers in zemstvos, towns, and cooperatives; lawyers; and journalists. They intended to create a soviet to use in the struggle to get rid of tsarism and establish a bourgeois-democratic regime. Members of the Workers' Group in the Central War Industries Committee—Gvozdev, M. Breido [G. E. Breido—D.J.R.], and others, who made for the Duma after their release from Kresty Prison—strove to achieve these same ends. The bourgeois leaders were anxious to carry out their intentions. N. I. Iordanskii reported that Baron Mandel', director of the War Industries Committee, put Gvozdev in an automobile and "drove with him to the factories with the blessing of the leaders of the War Industries Committee, and deluged workers with calls to elect deputies immediately to the workers' Soviet, as in 1905."[80]

Between 2:00 and 3:00 P.M. on February 27 legal activists who had connections with workers' groups met in the Tauride Palace. Chkheidze, Skobelev, Kerensky, B. O. Bogdanov, Gvozdev, Sokolov, I. G. Volkov, N. Iu. Kapelinskii, A. Grinevich, and others attended. Calling themselves the Provisional Executive Committee of the Soviet of Workers' Deputies, they addressed an appeal to the population of the capital and promptly printed it as a separate leaflet that appeared in *Izvestiia zhurnalistov*, the only newspaper that came out that day. Here is the text:

> Citizens! Representatives of workers, soldiers, and the population of Petrograd who are meeting at the State Duma, announce that the first meeting of their representatives will be held tonight at 7:00 P.M. on the Duma premises. All troops who have joined the people should elect their own representatives on the basis of one from each company. Factories should elect their own deputies, one per each thousand workers. Factories with fewer than 1,000 workers should elect one deputy. [Signed] The Provisional Executive Committee of the Soviet of Workers' Deputies.

The Tauride Palace henceforth became the center organizing the Soviet of Workers' Deputies. The Provisional Executive Committee of the Soviet was accommodated in three rooms of the Duma Budget Commission in the left wing of the palace. It was proposed to hold the first meeting of the Soviet in the most spacious of them, room 12, where a large table covered with a cloth stood. Worker deputies arrived and registered nearby. Members of the intelligentsia also came, some of whom had remained aloof from active revolutionary work. G. S. Khrustalev-Nosar', chairman of the Petersburg Soviet of Workers' Deputies in 1905, appeared. He had discredited himself by openly cooperating with the bourgeoisie and betraying the workers' interests, but he now intended "for old time's sake" to preside over the Soviet. The assembly opposed Khrustalev-Nosar's pretensions. The Bolsheviks protested on the grounds that the renegade, who had contributed to the reactionary newspaper *Novoe vremia* (New Times),[p] was a slanderer and anti-Semite who now was trying to take part in a

[p] *Novoe vremia* was a conservative political and literary paper, edited during the war by A. S. Suvorin.

new militant, revolutionary workers' organ and even aspiring to head it. Khrustalev-Nosar's candidacy to lead the Soviet was rejected.[81]

The few hours that had passed since the publication of the Provisional Executive Committee's appeal were insufficient to disseminate the notice of the first meeting of the Soviet of Workers' Deputies in the factory districts. By the scheduled time, 7:00 P.M., February 27, a number of deputies to the Soviet had gathered in the Tauride Palace, but factory deputies got lost in the shuffle. The Bolsheviks recommended postponing the meeting briefly until two or three dozen genuine workers' deputies had gathered. They intended to use the time to notify workers' districts the Soviet was to meet. Because telephones functioned poorly, factories and plants were shut down, and worker revolutionaries were out in the streets, it was impossible to obtain an adequate representation of workers in the Soviet. On this day mostly the legal organizations and not workers sent deputies to the Soviet. A Bolshevik worker, P. Aleksandrov, remembered how the news about organizing the Soviet got transmitted from the Tauride Palace to the workers' cooperative "The Path of Labor" in the Putilov Plant which elected deputies. "They handed us a paper on which was written 'the bearers of this—S. M. Afanas'ev, V. P. Alekseev, P. P. Aleksandrov, and others—have already been elected by the cooperative "The Path of Labor" to attend the Petrograd Soviet of Workers' Deputies.' . . . When we handed over our credentials, they tied a wide red ribbon to our left sleeve, and we entered the comparatively small room where the Soviet was meeting."[82]

At approximately 9:00 P.M., February 27, the first meeting of the Petrograd Soviet of Workers' Deputies began. Reports about it can be found in an article, "How the 'Petrograd Soviet' Was Formed," in *Izvestiia TsK* (News of the Central Executive Committee) on August 27, 1917, as well as in the memoirs of Shliapnikov, Sukhanov, Rafes, Zenzinov, and others.[83] How many deputies attended the Soviet's first meeting? Sukhanov stated that "at the opening of the meeting there were about 250 people. But new groups were constantly entering the hall."[84] When Shliapnikov wrote that there were 40 to 50 deputies at the Soviet's first meeting he meant worker representatives who constituted a minority in the general group. An article, "How the Soviet Was Organized" (*Izvestiia*, August 27), stated that 125 to 150 deputies and representatives of various organizations attended the Soviet's first meeting. Comparing these data, one can assume those present fell into three groups: deputies with voting rights, deputies with consultative privileges, and guests. Including the latter, there were 250 people at the first meeting and the number of deputies reached 125 to 150 people. Fifty actually voted. Apparently there were deputies to the Soviet with the right to vote.

Calling the first meeting of the Soviet of Workers' Deputies to order, Sokolov displayed more energy than any other member of the Provisional Executive Committee. The deputies elected Chkheidze chairman, and Kerensky and Skobelev, deputy chairmen. The election of these activists in the legal profession was not accidental. Only a narrow circle of individuals knew people engaged in the revolutionary underground and often not by their real names, whereas Kerensky, Chkheidze, and Skobelev were well known because of their activities in the State Duma and in legal meetings. Workers who attended the first meeting of the Soviet rushed to the street and areas where the revolutionary struggle continued. Fractional party conferences had not been called before the meeting opened, and the entire affair was conducted "in a nonpartisan manner."

Chkheidze's speech addressed the significance of the Russian Revolution and the need to struggle to complete it. "Long live the revolution! Long live the revolutionary army!" he proclaimed. Kerensky also said a few words, then quickly went to the right wing of the Tauride Palace where a Duma meeting was in progress. Chkheidze soon followed him. Sukhanov described the scene: "Skobelev stayed to serve as chair. In the chaos and general excitement he had no plan of action, nor could he control the noisy and rather disorderly meeting."[85]

The Soviet meeting was disorganized. No prior agenda had been drawn up, questions were raised and decided in great haste. The situation outside remained uncertain and the struggle continued. Skobelev noted that "reports from the localities made it clear the insurgents by no means hold all districts in the city, and those involved in the uprising lack organization and leadership. The meeting did not last long and all members of the Soviet were told to return to their districts immediately to inform workers and soldiers a soviet had been formed and to organize the uprising."[86] Apparently, the Soviet of Workers' Deputies largely limited itself that day to discussing organizational questions, for its leaders believed it premature to have it take up the question of power. Although they negotiated this with Duma members and obviously wanted to keep freedom of action, they could not avoid the narrower question of what was to be their relationship with the Provisional Committee the Duma had just formed. The Bolsheviks opposed cooperation with the Duma Committee. Rafes observed that the Bolsheviks "from the outset demanded a struggle against the Provisional Committee of the State Duma. Whether the Soviet of Workers' Deputies should agree and work with the Duma Committee or oppose it was the common fundament running through the debates."[87]

It is thus not surprising that disputes arose over whether representatives of the Soviet should enter the Provisional Duma Committee.[88] Some deputies took the position that their entry into the Duma Committee would tie the Soviet's hands and allow the bourgeoisie to shift partial responsibility to it. Others believed that to do so would make it easier to oversee the Duma Committee and prevent the bourgeoisie from harming the revolution. This view prevailed. The Soviet favored establishing contact with the Provisional Duma Committee and keeping Chkheidze and Kerensky, who had already entered it, on the committee.

At its first meeting the Soviet of Workers' Deputies elected an Executive Committee composed of Chkheidze, Kerensky, Skobelev, Iu. Steklov, Sukhanov, Kapelinskii, Shliapnikov, Zalutskii, E. Sokolovskii, P. Krasikov

(Pavlovich), and P. Aleksandrovich, and as secretaries of the Soviet, Gvozdev, Sokolov, K. S. Grinevich, and G. G. Pankov.[89] Among all the members of the Soviet Executive Committee, only the Bolsheviks Shliapnikov and Zalutskii boldly and consistently championed the interests of the revolutionary proletariat.[q] The rest of the committee articulated the sentiments of the petite bourgeoisie. The Menshevik, Ermanskii, characterized Sukhanov, Sokolov, Kapelinskii, Grinevich, and Pankov as obscure individuals linked to no organization. He could not understand why they had been elected to the Executive Committee.[90]

Executive Committee members Sokolov, Steklov, and Krasikov (Pavlovich) were considered representatives of the left, even Bolsheviks. In the past, of course, they had been so, but during the war they had withdrawn from party work and no longer supported Bolshevik positions. These individuals entered the Executive Committee as "nonfractional candidates." At first they played a prominent role in the Soviet, especially Steklov, but they supported SR and Menshevik policies and not the Bolshevik point of view.[91] After choosing an Executive Committee, the Soviet of Workers' Deputies decided to supplement it with three representatives each from the Bolsheviks, Mensheviks, and SRs, and one representative from each of these parties' national organizations.

The overwhelming majority of the Executive Committee saw as the Soviet's first task the need to get rid of the autocracy once and for all, establish a bourgeois regime, and defend the interests of the democracy before this regime. From the very first day of its existence, however, the Soviet was compelled to exceed these limits. The tsarist government no longer existed, and a bourgeois regime had not yet been established. The Soviet passed a series of urgent decrees in this transitional period to eliminate the old order and fortify the revolution. At the time, it served as the only real power.

Two pressing problems already confronted the incipient Soviet of Workers' Deputies—the war and the food supply. The uprising against tsarism had swelled and deepened. Workers had taken up arms and soldiers had come over to the people, but neither workers nor soldiers constituted a united armed force. When they joined the revolution the soldiers destroyed the previous military organization and discipline, yet no new organization existed. Lacking arms and officers, most of these soldiers had been separated from their units and blended with civilians. Refusing to return to their barracks where their hated commanders still held sway, groups and individual soldiers roamed the city without food or shelter. Such a situation placed the revolutionary forces in great danger of attack. Even though the revolution had triumphed in Petrograd, no one knew what was going on in other towns or at the front, to say nothing of the Petrograd railroad stations, or other neighborhoods.

This made it necessary to organize the struggle as much as possible, bring

[q] Burdzhalov is stretching the point here, ignoring the extreme positions that some SRs and other non-Bolsheviks took at this time.

separate units together to introduce revolutionary order into the city, and defend the revolution from possible enemy attack. Before the Soviet's first meeting the Provisional Executive Committee had summoned several democratically inclined officers to the Tauride Palace. Together with ordinary soldiers and unit delegates an official of the Military Academy, Lieutenant Colonel S. Maslovskii (Mstislavskii), Naval Lieutenant V. M. Filippovskii (both SRs), and several others formed a Military Commission. The Military Commission first sought to clarify the situation in view of the unfavorable information it received. The revolutionary forces lacked organization and had no artillery, machine guns, command headquarters, or communications. Mstislavskii wrote that, from a military point of view, the revolutionary forces were in an impossible situation. Nevertheless, military standards could not be applied in this instance, for altogether different laws determined how the revolution unfolded. It possessed a moral and political advantage over the tsarist army and steadily grew stronger while the forces of tsarism grew weaker.

Mstislavskii also rehearsed the revolution's advantages. The tsarist authorities had not withdrawn from the dangerous zone across the city line and had not summoned reinforcements to take the offensive against the revolution. Their opponents surrounded the tsarist troops concentrated in the heart of the city. "The revolutionary atmosphere in the city is dividing the government troops more surely than any barricade."[92] But the one advantage the revolution had was insufficient for victory. Lack of united leadership and a general plan compounded the difficulty in the revolutionary camp.

At its first meeting on the evening of February 27, the Soviet of Workers' Deputies decided to organize a revolutionary guard. Representatives from military units that had sided with the revolution attended the meeting. The deputies greeted them warmly. The Soviet empowered the Military Commission already in existence "to continue organizing revolutionary activity." The Soviet appealed to all the troops that had risen up to make contact with the Military Commission immediately and submit to its orders. The first issue of *Izvestiia Petrogradskogo Soveta* (News of the Petrograd Soviet, hereafter *Izvestiia*) reported: "The Military Committee of officials and soldiers in the Tauride Palace is in charge of the revolutionary troops. All units and soldiers are to take their orders from this Committee (Military Commission—E. B.)."

The Military Commission occupied rooms 41 and 42 in the right half of the Tauride Palace where the office of the vice-chairman of the Duma was located. In response to the Soviet's appeal, the revolutionary soldiers turned to the Military Commission. Officers also appeared, but only a few. Unit and platoon commanders of the Petrograd garrison and high-ranking officers were still conspicuously absent. It was primarily young ensigns who came to the Military Commission on leave or on assignment from the front.

Revolutionary workers and soldiers sought help, advice, and instructions from the Military Commission. Concerned with the need to dispose of the hated enemy as soon as possible, they asked the commission to act more energetically and decisively, and to take the initiative. Everyone had questions and made suggestions: Why haven't you occupied the airport? Why don't you have the streets dug up to stop armored cars? Why haven't you taken out the telegraph that the military and police use? Storm the Peter-Paul Fortress, etc., etc.[93]

The Military Commission took measures to destroy tsarism's strongholds in the capital and to organize the defense of the revolution against a possible attack by troops from the front. It formed units of soldiers and workers and dispatched them to the stations and other important points in the city. Their orders and instructions were handwritten. Because neither the Soviet nor the Military Commission had a printing press or official forms, orders and instructions had to be written on whatever was available such as paper found in the desks of the office bearing the letterhead "Vice-Chairman of the State Duma."[94] Although the Military Commission could not control the popular rising, it did help organize the revolutionary armed forces and solved numerous military and technical problems the revolution encountered.

The Soviet of Workers' Deputies set about organizing food supplies. The tsarist authorities had been unable to supply the population with bread and other essential items. Hunger threatened the working people of Petrograd more than other groups and decisive measures were necessary to eliminate it. The Soviet substituted widespread popular action for bureaucratic methods to resolve the food supply crisis, recognizing it essential to involve public organizations and the population itself in the supplying of food. Even before the Soviet meeting, a food supply commission that included N. Groman, M. Novorusskii, and other prominent men was organized. The Soviet approved this commission and adopted a series of decisions regarding the food supply. It resolved "to sequester available flour reserves in state, quartermasters', public, and other warehouses to supply bakeries."[95]

There was an urgent need to feed the revolutionary soldiers. Torn away from their units, the soldiers had no food. Lacking the necessary resources and organization to feed the troops, the Soviet turned to the people for help. On February 27 the Soviet Provisional Executive Committee published in *Izvestiia* an appeal to the inhabitants of the capital: "Comrades! The soldiers who stand with the people have been on the streets, hungry, since morning. The Soviet of Workers', Soldiers' and People's Deputies is doing everything in its power to feed them. But it is difficult to arrange for food at once. The Soviet turns to you, citizens, asking you to share whatever you have with the soldiers." The inhabitants of Petrograd responded to this appeal enthusiastically. Soldier canteens appeared all over the city, in the Tauride Palace itself, in cafeterias, restaurants, academic institutions, offices, and private homes. The population of the capital shared everything it could with the glorious fighters for revolution.

From the outset the Soviet of Workers' Deputies actively organized the press. The workers' press had played a major role in rallying the toiling masses to fight for the victory of the revolution. But the tsarist authorities had shut down workers' newspapers and leaflets and proclamations simply could not replace them. Moreover, a large number of Black Hundred and liberal newspapers sowed confusion and systematically poisoned the population. During the decisive clashes with tsarism these papers became especially dangerous. The workers snatched this ideological weapon from tsarism and the bourgeoisie: the general strike prevented the Black Hundred and bourgeois newspapers from coming out. Petrograd had no periodical press.

The mass of people, excited by the revolution, had to make do with rumors about what was happening. Supporters of the old order spread false reports and caused confusion in the revolutionary ranks. The Petrograd journalists responded by deciding to publish a paper that would inform the population of events. To do so during the general strike, the bourgeois journalists had to ask the Soviet leaders for help. Chkheidze and Kerensky called upon workers to print *Izvestiia zhurnalistov*, which appeared on February 27, when no other paper came out. The Petrograd journalists pledged to print only factual material about ongoing events, but in the selection and transmittal of facts in this journal a definite tendency grew apparent. *Izvestiia zhurnalistov* reflected the attitude of the bourgeois groups and from this point of view "informed" the population what was going on in the capital and the country.

The Soviet leaders saw the need to establish a newspaper that would provide truthful information, interpret the tasks of the working people during the struggle, publicize the decisions of the Soviet, and support its policies. The Soviet of Workers' Deputies thus decided to put out a daily paper, *Izvestiia*. It selected a literary commission including N. Sokolov, A. Peshekhonov, Iu. Steklov, K. Grinevich, and N. Sukhanov "to publish newspapers, leaflets, and appeals." Steklov and V. D. Bonch-Bruevich undertook to get the newspaper out. Bolshevik Bonch-Bruevich went with a detachment of soldiers to occupy one of the largest printing offices in the city belonging to the newspaper *Gazeta kopeika* (The Kopeck Gazette) for the Soviet. Leaflets and proclamations began to appear, and on February 28 the first issue of *Izvestiia* was published. The circulation of the first number of the newspaper together with a supplement that came out that evening amounted to four hundred thousand copies.

On the night of February 27–28 the Soviet Executive Committee met for the first time. It is uncertain whether minutes of this meeting were taken; in any event they have not been found. It is possible to infer what was discussed at the meeting from a short notice in *Izvestiia* and individual memoirs. The first meeting of the Executive Committee discussed the question of arming the workers and forming them into a militia. To ensure the revolution would triumph and continue to develop, it must have an armed force, organize and arm workers' detachments, and bring soldiers who had broken away from their units and were wandering all over the city into organized detachments. The Executive Committee decided to station the armed forces of the people at fixed points, chiefly at factories, under a single leadership. *Izvestiia* published the Executive Committee resolution in its first issue, which designated the following assembly points "for armed workers and troops": Vyborg District, the Society of Consumers and Medical Funds at Parviainen; Petrograd District, the Labor Exchange facing the People's House; Vasilevskii Island, the Labor Exchange at number 46, 13th Line; Rozhdestvenskii District, "Consumers' Cafeteria" on Mytninskaia Street; the Moscow District, the cafeteria of the Dinamo Factory; Nevskii District, the Smolensk Evening School; Narvskii, the Medical Fund in the Putilov Plant. All of these assembly points had been legal centers of workers' organizations before the revolution.

Detachments of the workers' militia were to assemble at the appointed places. Armed workers who had fought police ambushes, sacked police stations, and searched and arrested members of the old regime composed the basic units. The Executive Committee established definite norms for the workers' militia. In the factories and plants of Petrograd one-tenth of all workers were to receive arms.

The question of an armed workers' militia came up again at the Soviet's second meeting on February 28. It resolved to ask officers of socialist persuasion and student groups to join the militia. The meeting also decided "to appeal to the entire population of Petrograd to deliver all of their weapons to the commissariat and ask them to be under arms but not to waste cartridges."[96]

In accordance with this decision the Soviet issued an appeal to the workers.

> The working class badly needs arms now. The success of our struggle closely depends on how well the working class is organized. The Soviet of Workers' Deputies asks all comrade workers who have arms to consign them to commissars it has appointed in the various neighborhoods of the capital. If for some reason this cannot be done, surrender your arms to the Soviet of Workers' Deputies located in the Duma building, the Tauride Palace. Comrade workers! Remember, if the people's cause is to succeed you must arm yourselves, stock up on cartridges, and not waste them. He who fires senselessly into the air is acting foolishly, sowing panic among the inhabitants, and uselessly squandering the ammunition we now need so badly. Comrades, to arms![97]

Because the Soviet could not control all of Petrograd, the question of organizing district soviets came up. Newspapers reported that at its first meeting the Soviet had elected ten provisional commissars to form neighborhood soviets. In all likelihood no detailed discussion of district organizations occurred at that meeting, and the Executive Committee took up this question. The Soviet appointed neighborhood commissars: in Vyborg, Shliapnikov; in Lesnoi, SR Surin; in Petrograd, Popular Socialist Peshekhonov. After the Executive Committee meeting the district commissars conferred, some five or six people in all. Shliapnikov wrote: "We exchanged opinions on how to organize the districts. We as yet had no experience, so therefore the meeting was theoretical in nature and was mostly dedicated to exploring how to implement the decree on organizing an armed force and 'assuring' revolutionary order in the capital."[98]

In most districts, commissars had not played a major role. During the first days of the revolution, district soviets of workers' deputies holding all power were formed. This was particularly true of the Vyborg District, where workers took over the entire management of the region and the local soviet played a decisive role. The commissar of the Executive Committee was the sole link to the Petrograd Soviet. Matters took a different turn on the Petrograd side, where a soviet of workers' deputies formed later. Commissar Peshekhonov chose a group of workers, soldiers, and members of the intelligentsia to organize a district commissariat to maintain law and order. The commissariat linked up with the Provisional Duma Committee, but received no directives from it. "From a conversation with Miliukov," wrote Peshekhonov, "I gained the impression the Duma Committee never discussed the question of local organizations. At any rate it took no decisions nor even floated proposals concerning them."[99]

The Soviet's ongoing work was concentrated in the Executive Committee, housed in room 13, the office of the chairman of the Duma's Budget Commission. Here committee meetings took place and members were available to confer with individual workers and soldiers and with whole delegations arriving at the Soviet in larger numbers. The small Executive Committee staff worked behind a curtain. It was almost constantly in session. Extraordinary communications and special reports often interrupted discussion of regular agenda items. The Executive Committee strove to resolve many major and minor questions.

Regular elections to the Soviet began on February 28. Judging by protocols that have been preserved, workers in the Russian Renault Factory, the Zelenov and Zimin Factory, the Izhorsk Factory, the Voronin, Liutch, and Chesher factories, the State Printing House, and other enterprises elected deputies to the Soviet on that day. Workers in the Putilov Plant, the Putilov Shipyard, the Vulcan Factory, Treugolnik Factory, Lebedev Jute Plant, Semenov Lumberworks, and other factories and plants chose deputies on March 1. In electing their deputies to the Soviet, the workers in several enterprises believed it was a provisional revolutionary government that had been compelled by events to take the administration of the country into its hands. Minutes of a meeting of workers at the Shchetinin Factory read: "A general meeting of workers of the Shchetinin Factory elected Grachev to the provisional revolutionary government, the Soviet of Workers' Deputies, as our signatures attest."[100] However, not all workers saw the Soviet in this light. Since the Soviet met on the premises of the State Duma, some workers confused the two institutions. For example, four thousand workers in the Casings Department in the Petrograd Cartridge Factory on February 28 elected four deputies to what they called the Provisional Workers' Committee of the Duma. Service equipment workers at the First Depot on the Nikolaevskii Railroad authorized a delegate "to represent them in the Duma in order to replace the old regime and create a new one."[101]

When electing deputies to the Soviet, workers in a number of enterprises gave them instructions. Workers in the Nevskii Cotton Mill told their deputies "to support all our interests and needs." A general meeting of workers in the

Northern Textile Mill said to their deputies, "Fight the war to the end if we don't reach agreement with the people of Germany. As for the government—it should be a democratic republic. It is desirable to coordinate the work of the Soviet of Workers' Deputies with that of a committee chosen from the Duma."[102]

It was not just workers in large factories who sent deputies to the Soviet—employees in small enterprises, artisans, and craftsmen did so too. A few groups organized by profession and specialty chose deputies. Woodworkers were invited to a meeting at Chinizelli Circus. "Present events," read an appeal to them, "demand our organized participation. The first step to take is to elect representatives to the Soviet of Workers' Deputies and discuss the most urgent organizational tasks. Come, comrades, fulfill your responsibility to the Great Russian Revolution." A leaflet to leather workers stated: "The old bloodthirsty government has been overturned. The hour has come for the people to rule. The Soviet of Workers' Deputies is in session at the Duma. You, too, comrade tanners, must elect and send representatives there. You must attend a general meeting of tanners on March 2 for this purpose."[103]

Office and professional workers also supported the Soviet. Pharmacists, employees of the city telephone system, the post office, Peter the Great Hospital, and other establishments elected deputies on February 28 and March 1. Some authors consider it unfortunate that representatives of the non-proletarian democratic elements in the city population entered the Soviet.[104] While office and professional workers, craftsmen, artisans, etc., had a petit bourgeois orientation and their representatives sustained the Mensheviks and SRs, it would have been incorrect to have denied them representation on this basis. "It seems to me," Lenin wrote in November 1905, "that the Soviet of Workers' Deputies, as an organization representing all occupations, should *strive* to include deputies from *all* industrial, professional and office workers, domestic servants, farm laborers, etc., from *all* who want and are able to fight in common for a better life for the whole working people, from *all* who have at least an elementary degree of political honesty, from all but the Black Hundreds."[105]

By participating in soviets, the city's toilers showed their faith in the working class to lead the revolution and the people. The task of the proletariat was to use this trust to benefit the revolution and to organize genuine popular sovereignty. The SR-Menshevik leaders in the Petrograd Soviet, however, had other ideas. They aimed to have the workers reach an accommodation with the bourgeoisie and support its power. This can be seen in the first document the Soviet issued, "Address to the People of Petrograd and Russia," published on March [*sic* (February)—D.J.R.] 28 in *Izvestiia*.

The address proclaimed: "Yesterday, February 27, a Soviet of Workers' Deputies was formed in the capital. It comprises elected representatives from factories and plants, military units that rebelled, and democratic and socialist parties and groups." The authors of the appeal, members of the Soviet's Literary

Commission, tried to avoid controversial questions and make the document sound vague and equivocal. Sukhanov wrote: "We decided to keep politics out of the appeal and merely offer an elementary explanation of events, attest that a Soviet of Workers' Deputies had been created as the center of revolutionary democracy, and call for organization and preservation of order. We did not mention the Constituent Assembly, which would embody the democratic order mandated by the revolution, until the end."[106]

The appeal could not avoid politics entirely. It stated that the old order must be finally overthrown and yield to popular rule. "To conclude the struggle successfully in the interests of the democracy, the people must create their own authority. . . . The Soviet of Workers' Deputies, meeting at the State Duma, has undertaken as its main task to organize the people and struggle fully to consolidate political freedom and popular sovereignty in Russia."[107] The appeal left it unclear how the Soviet of Workers' Deputies conceived it would introduce popular sovereignty in Russia. It ended with the words: "All together we shall employ our combined strength to get rid of the old government and to convoke a constituent assembly elected on the basis of general, direct, and equal suffrage." Who would administer the country until a constituent assembly met and who would convoke it? These questions went unanswered.

The Soviet leaders could not conceive of any other authority in the country than that of the bourgeoisie, and they were afraid that if they went too far they would frighten the bourgeoisie away from the revolution. Instead of proclaiming it held power, the Soviet called for a new "organ of authority." Instead of taking control of all the country's affairs, the Soviet proposed "to form local district committees to assume responsibility for all local affairs." This meant the proletariat would have to give way to the bourgeoisie.

What was the bourgeoisie doing?

The Maneuvers of the Bourgeoisie

Not abandoning the possibility that an agreement might be reached with the autocracy, the bourgeoisie counted on achieving a peaceful solution to the political crisis. On the evening of February 26–27 it learned the autocracy had dismissed the Duma. This was a shattering blow to bourgeois hopes. Yet even now the State Duma did not pick up the gauntlet the autocracy had thrown down and openly oppose it. Duma leaders agreed not to protest the dismissal and to leave peacefully. Had the Duma met to hear the tsarist edict? Miliukov's memoirs indicate it had. He wrote that the Duma greeted the tsar's edict with silence, broken only by cries of approval from rightist deputies. Rodzianko, however, declared the Duma did not meet for that purpose: "It was inconceivable to convene the Duma on the 27th, since I thought the army of doubtful quality. To summon the Duma to hear the edict of dismissal would have required us immediately to proclaim the Duma was now a constituent assembly.

I had no authority to convene the Duma after the edict dismissed it . . . I could not jeopardize the Duma. If I had done so, the Duma would have been swept away, and there would not have been any entity in reserve to meet, deliberate, and act as needed at the necessary moment as actually happened."[108] It has been widely claimed the Duma resolved to ignore the edict of dismissal and remain in session. This does not correspond to the facts. Rodzianko wrote: "The Duma obeyed the law, still hoping to find a way out of the complicated situation, and did not pass resolutions to the effect it would not disperse and remain defiantly in session."[109]

After learning they had been dismissed, the Duma deputies became confused and did nothing. A. Tyrkova, a Kadet party activist, in her diary described their behavior on the morning of February 27. "The deputies wandered idly about, and casually discussed the dismissal. 'What do you intend to do? We don't know. What about the street? Who is in charge there? Is there a committee? We don't know.' It was painful to see. 'But, still, gentlemen, you represent the nation, have you no status and authority?' They are hesitating." Another Kadet, S. V. Panina, arrived at the Tauride Palace. She had just witnessed the soldiers' rising and tried to convince the Duma members they had to get control of the movement. "They heard her in silence or said. 'Let them arrest the ministers first.'"[110] Adding that Duma socialists were as much at a loss as other deputies, Duma Deputy S. P. Mansyrev also noticed the Duma members' confusion. "No one felt capable of doing anything at all or had any plan of action."[111]

Nevertheless, rumors that military units had revolted, that soldiers were on their way to the Duma, intent on vengeance, that the tsarist government had lost all authority, and that several ministers had been arrested, began to arouse the deputies and wake them from their lethargy. The Duma members became alarmed. Even clergy who were deputies on the Duma right became agitated. D. O. Zaslavskii, present at the time in the Tauride Palace, remembered how the clergy deputies demanded the Duma go into session right away. "'Where is Rodzianko? Why doesn't he show up?' Good gracious, how they've moved left! They're afraid the people might come to the Duma. 'We've got to do something, start something. . . . Hurry up! . . .' The conservative priests were in a fury. One was not ashamed to cry out, 'if those bastard ministers ran away, we'll have to organize a new ministry.'"[112] But Rodzianko did not want to organize a ministry or convoke the Duma. Rodzianko locked himself in his office, refusing to mingle with the deputies. He avoided deputies and other Duma leaders.

Petit bourgeois leaders tried to shake the Duma out of its torpor. Early on the morning of February 27 the Menshevik N. I. Iordanskii notified Skobelev of the soldiers' uprising and recommended he insist the Duma be convoked promptly. Although Skobelev, like Iordanskii, assumed the bourgeoisie must lead the new movement, he had little hope for the Duma. He said the timid Progressive Bloc would not do serious battle with the tsarist government. Iordanskii objected, contending that the rebel soldiers' arrival at the Tauride Palace would compel it to do so.[113] Appearing at the Tauride Palace, Skobelev and other left deputies called for a speedy convocation of the State Duma to discuss the situation the soldiers' insurrection had created. "We, the extreme left in the Duma," Skobelev later wrote, "insist the Duma majority explain its position and demand it clearly articulate its relationship to events. . . . Miliukov declared he could not formulate his attitude to events since he did not know who was in charge. I replied: 'Like you, we do not know who is in charge. . . . This is a spontaneous mass movement.' "[114]

Along with Skobelev, Kerensky tried to rouse the Duma. " 'Have the Duma meet. It must be on duty,' said Kerensky, proposing to ring the bell to summon the deputies to the hall. No one rang it. 'I shall do it myself.' In a minute the bell pealed throughout the corridors. The deputies hesitated and did not move. After all, the tsar had dismissed the Duma. To convene a session would be flouting the autocrat. 'To the hall, gentlemen,' cried Kerensky, rushing by silent groups. Nobody came."[115]

On the morning of February 27 a Popular Socialist, V. Chernolusskii, passed through the restless city and arrived at the Tauride Palace. He recalled: "After the atmosphere of the city, feverish with revolution, the Tauride Palace conveyed a strange impression. It's true that people had already gathered around it, but it seemed quiet and empty . . . the Duma members were conferring in inside rooms and admitted no one." Chernolusskii reported he saw Rodzianko and other Duma members and told them the revolutionary people and soldiers controlled the entire city, the Romanov dynasty must be dethroned without delay, and the Duma must take power. But Rodzianko and the other Duma leaders refused to take such a step.[116] Duma Vice-Chairman N. V. Nekrasov described the scene: "I remember," he said, "that a prominent public figure approached Rodzianko and stated categorically: 'Declare yourself a provisional government, depose the Romanovs, and expel all the conservatives including the Octobrists.' He had completely forgotten Rodzianko himself was an Octobrist. Rodzianko was taken aback."[117]

Meantime, the revolutionary movement was growing and deepening at lightning speed, threatening not only tsarism, but the Duma as well. Further delay was impossible. From 10:00 to 11:00 A.M. on February 27 a group of deputies burst into Rodzianko's office and insisted the Council of Elders *(sen'orenkonventa)* be convened. But Rodzianko was as unyielding as before. "Please don't disturb me," he said. He was engaged in composing a telegram to the tsar at headquarters. The deputies went without him to the Finance Commission room where Nekrasov chaired a private meeting of the Council of Elders. Kerensky, Skobelev, and others argued that the Duma should not disperse and should take power. Far from all those present agreed with this sentiment.

Skobelev remembered that

> an exchange of views began, but the outside world outstripped our debates. We heard that mutinous soldiers had occupied the Main Artillery Administration on

> Liteinyi Prospekt. Shingarev jumped up and irritably cried: "Only our enemies, the Germans, could do things like that." I replied that a person should choose his words more carefully, since he would be held responsible for them. Rodzianko rushed into the room and cried menacingly, "Who convened the Council of Elders without my permission?" The Bloc leaders explained this was a private not an official Council meeting.[118]

Events overwhelmed Rodzianko. The tsar had not answered the telegram sent the night before. Now with the Duma dissolved, he sent the tsar an even more urgent telegram that the Duma's dismissal had eliminated the last bastion of order, that civil war had begun and was spreading. "The government is utterly powerless to suppress the disorders. The garrison troops are unreliable. The reserve battalions of the guards regiments have mutinied." Rodzianko asked the tsar to form a new authority without delay and to reconvene the legislative bodies, the Duma and the State Council. "The hour has come to decide your fate and the country's. Tomorrow may be too late."[119]

Rodzianko no longer could operate independently. He proposed that the members of the Council of Elders should go over to the office of the chairman of the Duma, where the meeting, now official, continued. The Protocol of Events[120] reveals that Rodzianko discussed the content of the telegrams he had sent to the tsar and informed those in attendance about the situation in Petrograd. Discussing the present situation, the Duma leaders noted the complete inactivity of the tsarist authorities and the frightening anarchy that threatened the country. They spoke of the need to take measures to restore order and tranquility in the capital. Duma deputy I. N. Efremov, a Progressist, subsequently maintained that he had then proposed to ignore the tsarist edict and begin an official Duma meeting at the first opportunity. The protocols, however, indicate no Duma member was willing to do more than call a private meeting. "The Duma leaders," wrote Skobelev, "had absolutely no desire to make a demonstrative gesture by ignoring the government's edict to dissolve the Duma. Their discussions made no reference to a body to lead the rebellious population, but only to the need to present a solid front to the mutinous population."[121]

At 2:30 A.M. on February 27 the Duma members met privately in closed session. No one but they attended and the meeting took place in the adjacent Semicircular Hall instead of the conference chamber. This circumstance obviously underscored the meeting's private character. Yet where they met was not important. Almost 130 years earlier, deputies of the Third Estate in the Estates General of France assembled on a tennis court and declared they were the French National Assembly. This did not occur in Russia in February 1917. The meeting of deputies to the State Duma on February 27 remained a private session and it did not proclaim itself a national assembly. A brief protocol[122] and memoirs by participants in this meeting have been preserved. The confused and contradictory reminiscences reflect the nature of the meeting itself.

The Duma members met under strained circumstances. Crowds of insurgents were on their way to the Tauride Palace. Interrupting the meeting, Duma members went up to the windows to see the new force approaching the very threshold of the ancient Tauride Palace. The demonstrators demanded the deputies declare whom the State Duma supported—the people or the tsarist government. The Duma could find no answer and hesitated. At the height of the meeting Kerensky charged into the Semicircular Hall. He announced delay was no longer possible, the troops were in ferment, and he was on his way to calm the soldiers. "Can I say," he asked, "the Duma is with them?" He hastened off to the troops without any answer from the Duma. When soldiers approached the Tauride Palace several Duma members had to appear before them and receive their delegates.

What did the Duma members discuss at their private meetings on February 27? The central issue was how to establish law and order in the capital. But an overriding question arose: to all intents and purposes the tsarist ministers had been deprived of power. To whom should authority now belong? The majority of Duma members wanted to avoid answering this question or at least to put it off. Opening the meeting, Rodzianko said: "We cannot yet speak with certainty since we still do not know the correlation of forces." Many deputies, anticipating an explanation, confined themselves to a general discussion. Others, however, held it was impossible to delay a solution to the question of power. Nekrasov proposed investing General Manikovskii[r] with dictatorial powers and charging him to establish order with the Duma deputies' support. The proposal to establish a military dictatorship found no favor among the deputies. A recommendation to ask Prince Golitsyn to appoint a general as dictator elicited especially sharp protests. Deputy M. A. Karaulov said all the tsar's ministers "were afraid and had begun to hide. Are we really going to drag out Prince Golitsyn from under the bed?" Karaulov urged Duma members to form a government themselves. Like Nekrasov, N. V. Savich suggested calling upon a general, but proposed it should be A. A. Polivanov, not A. A. Manikovskii.

Menshevik and Trudovik representatives Chkheidze and V. I. Dziubinskii also urged the Duma to form a new government. Dziubinskii favored proclaiming the Duma a constituent assembly. SRs, Mensheviks, Trudoviks, and all the other petit bourgeois groups declared the Duma should establish its credentials to hold power. The Duma members refused to do so, however, and the majority at the meeting adopted a wait-and-see attitude. Miliukov declared it useless to enter into new negotiations with the old government, since it had let power slip from its hands, and pointless for the Duma to declare it was now the government. The Duma was a legislative body and could not assume executive functions. Miliukov did not rule out the possibility of creating a new government, but he believed the time had not yet arrived. He said the extent of the

[r] Evidence suggests that General A. A. Manikovskii had sympathized with the idea of a palace coup that had circulated before the revolution.

"disorders" was unknown and it was still unclear where the loyalty of the majority of soldiers, workers, and the people lay. Shul'gin stressed that the insurgents were making demands the Duma could not accept. "We cannot fully support the part of the population that has rebelled. Imagine, for example, they would want to end the war. We could not agree to that."[123]

In other circumstances the Duma might have had time to indulge in long-winded discourse. But now it was compelled to hurry up. Speeches were limited to five minutes. Soldiers' voices and the clanking of rifles were heard in the hall. The insurgents were inside the Tauride Palace. This is why Rodzianko asked the deputies to pass resolutions more quickly. "Delay is tantamount to death," he said. It was necessary to make a decision as soon as possible. After declining a number of proposals, the private session did no more than resolve to form a provisional committee composed of Duma members. No one understood what this committee was supposed to do, but some new organ had to come into existence. Lasting a bit more than two hours, the private meeting of the Duma members came to an end. It was obviously the shortest meeting in Duma history.

The Council of Elders selected the members of the Provisional Duma Committee. All Duma fractions except the far right were represented: M. Rodzianko, N. Nekrasov, A. Konovalov, I. Dmitriukov, V. Shul'gin, P. Miliukov, V. L'vov, V. Rzhevskii, S. Shidlovskii, and M. Karaulov. Kerensky and Chkheidze joined the ten bourgeois representatives. "In essence," noted V. Shul'gin, "this was the Bureau of the Progressive Bloc with the addition of Kerensky and Chkheidze. . . . Fear of the street had driven Shul'gin and Chkheidze into one collegium."[124]

Rodzianko agreed to head the Provisional Duma Committee only after the Provisional Executive Committee of the Soviet of Workers' Deputies had formed. The Soviet could have swept the Duma away and buried it with tsarism. "When the Bureau of Soviet Deputies came into existence," wrote Skobelev, "Rodzianko was forced to stop temporizing. He sighed deeply and waved his hand as though praying. It looked as though when he agreed to lead the Duma Committee he had rejected the 'sceptered head' that had always charmed him."[125] The new Duma was called the "Provisional Committee of Members of the State Duma for the Restoration of Order and Establishment of Relations with Individuals and Institutions." This long and at first glance obscure title made certain sense. Why Committee of Duma Members and not Duma Committee? Because the tsar had dissolved the Duma and its members did not wish to violate his edict. Why Committee for the Restoration of Order? Because the bourgeoisie had no intention of exceeding the existing system and wanted to restore the old order, not create a new one.

In choosing the Provisional Committee, the Duma deputies were anxious not to deviate from former tsarist "legal" norms. They said the title they had adopted would protect them from prosecution if the revolution should fail. Miliukov later explained: "This clumsy formula had the advantage of satisfying the demands of the moment, without prejudicing the future. By restricting itself to the minimum, it created an entity that absolved the Duma members from any wrongdoing."[126] The Provisional Committee chosen by the Council of Elders was sanctioned at another Duma meeting at 5:00 P.M. on February 27. It was as vague as the earlier one. No one knew how the question of political power would be resolved. Taking a step into the unknown, the assembly wanted all Duma members to accept the resolution. A Trudovik, V. M. Vershinin, proposed that members of the Duma regardless of party should promise "to support and assist the Provisional Committee in all actions it will be obliged to undertake."[127] This proposal was adopted unanimously, although with little enthusiasm. Deputy M. Ichas wrote: "My colleagues and I felt we were electing members to the fisheries or some such Duma commission. No one showed any enthusiasm. I managed to get out: 'Long live the Committee of Salvation!' and several dozen members at the meeting began applauding. The Provisional Committee went off to a session while the remaining three hundred Duma members wandered throughout the gloomy halls of the Tauride Palace."[128]

Now head of the Provisional Committee, Rodzianko hoped that he could persuade Golitsyn to retire and the Duma would help him restore order and tranquility and save the throne for Nicholas II. This is why the committee first started negotiating with the tsar's brother, Mikhail Aleksandrovich. About 6:00 P.M. several members of the Provisional Committee led by Rodzianko and Nekrasov set out for the Mariinskii Palace to meet Grand Prince Mikhail. They had to proceed through streets held by the revolutionary people to the sound of machine-gun and rifle fire, past the burning building of the District Court. After safely traversing the revolutionary zone, the Duma members reached the neighborhood, guarded by troops still loyal to tsarism.

The Duma men told Mikhail Aleksandrovich the situation was dangerous and prompt decisive measures were needed to save the tsar. The Protocol of Events states they explained to the Grand Prince that power must be transferred to the State Duma, since it was the sole body that could form a government authoritative enough to pacify the country.[129] Nekrasov asserts the members of the Provisional Committee proposed Mikhail "accept the regency temporarily until the tsar arrived from headquarters, removed the Council of Ministers, and put a provisional government composed of public figures and headed by a popular general in charge."[130]

Rodzianko maintained that the members of the Provisional Committee suggested Mikhail Aleksandrovich communicate through the Hughes apparatus[s] with the tsar and "tell his brother that he would lose everything if he tomorrow failed to grant the Duma the opportunity to proclaim a responsible ministry and pack Aleksandra Fedorovna off to Livadiia."[131] Rodzianko subsequently wrote that the Duma leaders tried to convince Mikhail Romanov "to become dictator

[s] Invented by D. E. Hughes in 1855, the Hughes apparatus was a type-printing telegraph with a piano-like keyboard.

of Petrograd on his own authority," force government functionaries to retire, and wire the tsar directly, insisting he issue a manifesto "granting" a responsible ministry.[132]

Other memoirs give different accounts of the Duma members' proposals, but all agree on the nature of Mikhail's reply. He stated he had no right to adopt their proposed measures alone and would first have to consult with the Council of Ministers. The Duma members and Mikhail Aleksandrovich conferred with Golitsyn and the tsarist ministers. They tried to convince Golitsyn that "in order to pacify Petrograd and prevent anarchy in the country" his ministry must resign immediately and transfer power to the Duma Committee. Golitsyn and the tsarist ministers still refused. The Protocol of Events indicates that Golitsyn declared he "had requested retirement, but until the tsar approved it he did not consider he had the right to transfer his authority to another person."[133] Mikhail Aleksandrovich would not dream of acting without the consent of the government, although for all practical purposes it no longer existed. Rodzianko woefully regretted: "Grand Prince Mikhail Aleksandrovich's indecisiveness caused a favorable opportunity to slip by."[134]

After the meeting at the Mariinskii Palace, Mikhail Romanov went to the War Ministry to call the tsar through the Hughes apparatus and advise him to take steps to calm the population. He asked General Alekseev to tell Nicholas II he must remove the entire Council of Ministers, put a person at the head of the government who enjoyed the respect of the bulk of the population, and charge him to form a cabinet at his own discretion. He called the chairman of the Zemstvo Union, Prince G. L'vov, such an individual. Because the situation was becoming more serious, Mikhail asked the tsar to empower him to announce this to the population at once, and he advised the ruler to defer his arrival at Tsarskoe Selo. Nicholas II did not negotiate with his brother. Instead, he authorized Alekseev to tell him he did not think he could alter the time of his departure for Tsarskoe Selo and any changes in the composition of the Council of Ministers should be postponed until his arrival. This made Mikhail express apprehension. "I hope the chance has not been lost before His Majesty returns; with the situation as it is now, every hour is precious."[135]

The Duma members returned from the Mariinskii Palace to Tauride late in the evening of February 27. Nekrasov recalled: "From 9:00 to 10:00 P.M. we made our way through the revolutionary city. Zones no longer existed. An unbroken revolutionary wave had engulfed everything. Armored cars often detained us, men asked for passes. Sometimes they were satisfied but sometimes the name Rodzianko provoked hostility . . . everywhere police stations were on fire. The picture was absolutely clear."[136] This was the end of the Duma Committee's attempt "to restore order" with the help of an agreement with the tsarist authorities. The committee had set as a goal "to communicate with individuals and institutions." But there was no one with whom to communicate. Crowds of people had seized the Mariinskii Palace and the ministers in session had gone into hiding.

Could the Duma leaders in such conditions have limited themselves to their original goal? The Duma deputies, lost in the crowd of people cramming the Tauride Palace, had no opportunity to express themselves in this regard, and their committee continued to vacillate. Late in the evening, Colonel B. A. Engel'gardt, a member of the Duma, arrived at the palace. Moving from the group of the center to the Octobrists, he had been active in the Special Defense Commission as a colonel on the General Staff. Exchanging his uniform for civilian clothes to protect himself while going through the streets, Engel'gardt conveyed his impressions to the members of the Duma Committee. He stated that "the military and civil authorities are conspicuous by their absence, that total anarchy threatens, and that the Provisional Committee must take power without delay."[137] V. Shul'gin tried to convince Rodzianko to take this step. He told the Duma president: "Take it because you are a loyal subject. Take it because Russia must have authority . . . if the ministers have decamped you must replace them. . . . This can end only in one of two ways: everything will be all right—His Majesty will appoint a new government—and we shall surrender power to it; or everything will not be all right, we'll refuse to take power and others will."[138]

Rodzianko replied that he was not a rebel and would not break his oath, that he did not want revolution, and that if revolution had broken out, it was because the tsarist ministers had not listened to the Duma. But they had disappeared, leaving the Duma to face the armed people. What should the Duma do? Step aside? Wash its hands of the affair? Leave Russia without a government? Most Duma Committee members felt they must assume power even as a temporary expedient until negotiations with the tsar might begin to preserve the existing order and prevent a transfer of power to the Soviet. Rodzianko refused to do so, even on a temporary basis. Many memoirs describe this moment. Miliukov wrote: "It's time to decide, I said to the chairman of the State Duma. Rodzianko asked for fifteen minutes to reflect and went to his office. It was a difficult quarter of an hour. Much, perhaps even the success of our whole affair, depended upon Rodzianko's decision."[139]

Shidlovskii recalled that while Rodzianko was meditating the telephone rang. His nephew, an officer of the Preobrazhenskii Regiment [Captain Meshcherskii—D.J.R.], reported that the officers of the Preobrazhenskiis had voted to place themselves at the disposal of the Duma leaders. Cries were heard. "There's no reason to vacillate further, a military unit is at our disposal." The news inspired the chairman. Rodzianko left his office and sat down at the table. Engel'gardt related that he leaned back in his chair, pounded his fist on the table and said, "All right, I have decided to take power, but from now on I insist all of you obey me unquestioningly. Aleksandr Fedorovich," he said, turning to Kerensky, "this means you especially." "I shall be glad to cooperate fully with the Provisional Committee of the Duma," Kerensky answered, "but remember, gentlemen, I will have to reckon with what is going on right now in the Budget Commission." Many looked uneasily and with misgivings at the Budget Commission where at that very moment an organization was being born that was destined to play a preeminent role.[140] Describing this scene, Miliukov observed, "Oh mighty Shakespeare! How truly you saw that life's dramatic moments do not lack elements of humor. Mikhail Vladimirovich [Rodzianko] now thought he was dictator of the Russian Revolution. The surprised Kerensky restrained himself and carefully reminded them that there was a comrade chairman in another institution whom he was obliged to obey."[141]

Extreme monarchists subsequently blamed Rodzianko for violating tsarist laws when he took power and "led" the revolution. Clearly sensitive to such accusations, Rodzianko did his best to show how loyal he was. He wrote that on February 27 Golitsyn supposedly had informed him the tsarist government had submitted its resignation. In fact, however, Golitsyn's government did not formally resign on that day. Rodzianko justified himself by contending that a desperate situation had developed and that there was no central authority in the capital. No directives came from the tsar at headquarters, and the city was in the throes of "incipient boundless anarchy."

> The Duma had no alternative but to take power and to try to see whether it could control the anarchy and create a body to which everyone would hearken, one that would be capable of checking burgeoning disaster. Of course the Duma might have refused to lead the revolution, but it should be borne in mind that a power vacuum had developed and if the Duma had withdrawn, total anarchy would have reigned and the country would soon have been ruined. The Duma would have been arrested, all its members would have been killed by the insurgent troops, and power would have at once passed to the Bolsheviks. In the interim the Duma would have to hold things together. Its mandate was incomplete; nevertheless, it had a part to play at this difficult time.[142]

The Provisional Duma Committee decided to assume power at 2:00 A.M., February 28.[143] However, the Duma leaders dated the decree February 27. This made it seem as though the Provisional Committee of the Duma had decided to take power before or simultaneously with the formation of the Soviet of Workers' Deputies.

The committee's first announcement, dated February 27, declared: "The Provisional Committee of the State Duma, faced with difficult conditions of internal chaos caused by the old government, has been compelled to assume responsibility for restoring the government and social order. Conscious of the awesome responsibility of the decision it has taken, the Committee is confident that the people and the army will help in the difficult task of forming a new government, which conforms to the desires of the populace and merits their trust."[144]

Duma leaders had decided to head a popular movement to restore the former state and social order. The Duma Committee's appeals contained no calls for revolutionary actions. They did not indicate what the insurgent people should do, but what they should not do, and what they should avoid. The committee called on the inhabitants of Petrograd and the soldiers of the garrison not to violate state and public institutions, telegraph lines, water towers, electricity stations, and streetcars. The committee declared it was entrusting the defense of factories and plants to the citizenry. It announced that "attacks on the life, person, or property of private citizens" were impermissible.[145]

The evening of February 27–28 the Provisional Duma Committee made known its formation to the army high command. In telegrams to commanders of the fronts and the chief of staff at Supreme Headquarters the committee declared that, with the departure of all the former ministers from the government, power had passed to the committee. The telegram implied it contemplated no changes in domestic or foreign policy. The Provisional Committee assured the commanding officers that the war against the foreign enemy would not be stopped or slackened. "The Provisional Committee in cooperation with military units in the capital and the support of the population will soon establish tranquility at the rear and restore the proper function of government institutions."[146]

That night the Duma Committee dismissed the tsarist ministers and appointed commissars from Duma members to manage various units of the administration until a new government could be formed. Commissars were appointed for the ministries of Internal Affairs, Post, Telegraph and Telephone, War and Navy, Agriculture, Justice, Trade and Industry, Finance, Communications, Education, and for the State Senate and the Petrograd City Governor's office. *Izvestiia zhurnalistov* published this list. They were all Duma deputies—Kadets, Progressists, and left Octobrists, twenty-four in all. The night of February 27–28 the Duma Committee appealed to the railwaymen. It did not ask them to support the revolution or to fight tsarism. The Duma was concerned there should be no interruption of rail service for military purposes. The Provisional Duma Committee wrote: "Trains must move without interruption, with redoubled energy." The committee reminded railway workers and clerks how important transport was for the war effort and supplying the rear.

After declaring it had assumed power, the committee first undertook to form its own dependable force. The revolutionary workers and soldiers had paralyzed the previous military administration. The units that had revolted refused to obey anyone. The Duma Committee set itself the task of restoring the previous military organization, only now subordinate to the committee. Late in the evening of February 27 the Duma Committee co-opted B. Engel'gardt and appointed him commander of the Tauride Palace. But by this time the Military Commission of the Soviet of Workers' Deputies was already at work establishing ties with the military units and organizing them. The Duma Committee decided to make the Military Commission its own organ and have its own people in charge of it. On the night of February 27–28, Rodzianko and Engel'gardt entered room 42, which the commission occupied. N. Sokolov and several staff members of the Soviet also came. S. D. Mstislavskii described the conflict that arose between the leaders of the two bodies, the Duma and the Soviet.

Rodzianko announced: "The Provisional Committee of the State Duma has resolved to assume responsibility for restoring order that has recently been disturbed in the city. You yourselves must understand how necessary restoration of order is for the front as soon as possible. Colonel Engel'gardt, on the General Staff and a member of the State Duma, has been appointed commander of Petrograd."

Mstislavskii related that Rodzianko's pronouncement caused Sokolov to object seriously.

> "Our command has already formed, it's already functioning, our men have been chosen. . . . We don't need any Colonel Engel'gardt here! . . . You have to let those who have been working here ever since the uprising started decide who will command and now especially as it is no longer a question of establishing order but of defeating Khabalov and Protopopov. We want revolutionaries, not 'designates' of His Majesty's Assembly. And it's utterly intolerable that the Petrograd Soviet, the Soviet of revolutionary workers and insurgent soldiers, at present the only real force, should be entirely removed from the command it had created itself to accomplish tasks it itself had set. . . ."
>
> Responding to Sokolov's objections, Rodzianko pounded the table and said: "No, gentlemen, you forced us into this business and so you've got to listen." Sokolov flew into a rage and answered in such language that our officers, who had listened to Rodzianko most respectfully, immediately began to seethe. They clustered around Sokolov. All began shouting at once. Threats were heard. The Soviet side also raised its voice. For a minute it looked like a brawl would break out. We had a hard time to separate those quarreling.[147]

This intense skirmish ended quietly; the Soviet representatives gave way. After the morning of February 28 new leaders controlled the Military Commission, and the members appointed by the Soviet became less influential. Colonel Engel'gardt took charge and named new members, the engineers P. I. Pal'chinskii and Parshin, General Staff officers Tumanov, Iakubovich, Tugan-Baranovksii, Colonel Polovtsev, and others. The staff of the Military Commission changed and so did its appearance.

> Decorously, in the most sophisticated manner, they arranged office desks taken from God knows where in little squares. Several dandyish clerks and two or three coquettish girls as you expect typists to be, with their hair in a bun held together with combs, were already typing away. Strange new people, with shiny shoulder straps and aiguillettes, not seen in the palace during these nights, neat, clean-shaven, and with nicely parted hair, were spreading out official folders on tables . . . aide-de-camps confidently and gaily as if quite at home fluttered about from typewriters to the head tables.[148]

The Military Commission the Soviet had formed was now called the Commission of the Provisional Committee of the State Duma. It tried to assume control of the military and technical aspects of the movement, but lacked the strength and means to do so. The commission operated under the authority of the State Duma and depended on the officer corps. The soldier masses supporting the Soviet of Workers' Deputies obeyed committee directives only when they did not conflict with instructions from the Soviet. Committee members had to reckon with the Soviet. The committee was dependent upon it and to a large degree remained under it.

Although the Duma Committee took up the food supply, it did not create a special body. The Food Supply Commission of the Soviet of Workers' Deputies from the outset had been in contact with it. Duma members A. Shingarev and S. Vostorgin were named to serve on the Soviet's Food Supply Commission, and after that it operated in the name of both the Soviet and the Duma Committee. V. Groman, representative of the Soviet, continued to head it.

On February 28 *Izvestiia* reported that "the Food Supply Commission of the Soviet of Workers' Deputies and the Executive Committee of the Duma announce it has taken charge of all food supply questions." The commission called upon bakers to resume work, recommended they start baking bread, and asked the citizen guard to distribute bread among the population fairly. The Food Supply Commission declared it intended soon "to entrust the distribution of food supplies to local committees, elected by districts by the entire adult population."

The bourgeoisie now strived to concentrate power in its hands. The revolutionary activities of workers and soldiers had put an end to its vacillations and shook it out of its stupor. The bourgeoisie had to side with the revolution and break with the tsarist government so as not to perish with it, but the bourgeoisie wanted to use the revolution for its own interests. The accession of the bourgeoisie hastened the victory of the revolution by further disrupting the cause of the autocracy and further isolating it. When the bourgeoisie joined it, however, the revolution became even more complex and contradictory. While workers and soldiers, the main mass of people, were decisively winning a victory over the tsarist monarchy, the bourgeoisie continued to play a Janus-like role. Although it had renounced the tsarist government, it believed it could save tsarism by making it accept a bourgeois regime.

February 27 witnessed the decisive engagement between the people and the autocracy. When the army joined the people the outcome of the revolution was no longer in doubt. But the victory over tsarism gained that day was not yet complete or final.

What new battles and clashes awaited the revolution?

FOUR

The Second Wave of Revolution

> At the March 2(15) Conference, Chkheidze's closest collaborator, Skobelev, said, according to the newspapers: "Russia is on the eve of a second, real *[wirklich]* revolution." Now that is the truth, from which Skobelev and Chkheidze have forgotten to draw the practical conclusions.
>
> —V. I. Lenin

Dealing the Final Blow to Tsarism

As the morning of February 28 dawned, isolated pockets of support for the autocracy still remained in Petrograd. A detachment of troops, a bicycle battalion, and several other units ensconced in the Admiralty building refused to surrender. Even more significant, some soldiers in the Petrograd garrison had not joined the revolt. Individual units vacillated, occupying a neutral position. Locked in their barracks, they had only a vague notion of what was happening outside. Some remained loyal to their oaths and obeyed their officers' orders. Others, who no longer supported the tsar, expected the workers to help them join the revolution. Reports about the soldiers' moods reached the revolutionary-minded people in various ways. A writer, E. Zozulia, recalled how a mounted soldier wrote something on a dirty scrap of paper: "I saw him throw this note to a group of workers standing on the sidewalk. I saw tears in the eyes of an old man who read it: 'Comrades,' it said in shaky, uneven letters, 'smash the gates of our barracks; they won't let us out into the streets and we all want to join the people.'"[1] The course of the ensuing struggle largely depended upon what the wavering military units would do. The insurgent workers and soldiers had to win over individual military units, draw them into the revolutionary battle, and make the rising in the Petrograd garrison general.

During the first days of the revolution the workers returned to their homes and factories to gain fresh strength in order to resume the struggle the following day. Now the battle with tsarism entered the phase in which they had to inflict sustained blows on the enemy to deal the final blow. The soldiers who had joined the revolution could not return to the barracks under the command of their former officers, as this might undo the entire cause of the armed uprising. A leaflet posted throughout the city read: "Retreat is impossible! Freedom or death! Don't return to your barracks! Don't leave the city! Try to get those not yet involved in the struggle to join the revolution!" Another leaflet made the same appeal to the soldiers: "Soldiers! The people, all of Russia thank you for rising up in the righteous cause of freedom. . . . Soldiers, some of you still hesitate to join your comrades and ours who have revolted. . . . Soldiers, if you are separated from your unit, go to the Duma—there you'll find your comrades and you'll share your happiness and grief with them."[2]

The insurgents now had their own center, the Soviet of Workers' Deputies. An address, evidently composed on February 28, explained that the enemy was still undefeated, that tsarism had mustered a detachment of soldiers to suppress the revolution.

> We must form detachments and units everywhere, organize, support one another in a vigorous comradely manner, and be ready to repulse the enemy anywhere, to secure our victory and hold what we have. You must understand that the people in revolt need to be reinforced by a strong, powerful organization. Onward, Comrades! Everyone to work, everyone take up arms and await with arms in hand the orders of the Soviet of Workers' Deputies to defend all that we have won at such a high price. Better to die for freedom than to be base slaves of the Romanovs. Long live the Great Russian Revolution![3]

A serious threat hung over revolutionary Petrograd. After he learned what was happening there, the tsar decided to take action. Refusing to submit to fate, he decided to subdue the revolution by force and dispatched a punitive expedition of units drawn from the front against insurgent Petrograd. Nicholas II thought General N. I. Ivanov, who had suppressed the 1906 uprising at Kronstadt, should head it. At the beginning of the war he was in command on the southwestern front and he now was at Supreme Headquarters. The tsar appointed General Ivanov commander of the Petrograd Military District and invested him with emergency powers to put down the uprising. A St. George's Cavalry Battalion and front-line units were placed at his disposal. Informing Beliaev of this, Alekseev asked the war minister to form a new staff for Ivanov as soon as possible, composed of officials from the Main Administration of the General Staff, the main staff, and district staff.[4] Khabalov's assistants and Khabalov himself had panicked and had clearly lost faith in the Petrograd high command.

Later Ivanov and other tsarist generals tried to depict this grim mission as a harmless transfer. In April 1917 Ivanov wrote Guchkov that he had maintained that "armed force could not pacify an inflamed populace" and that the intention had been merely to move units from the front to Petrograd for a short time "to relieve the reserve guard battalions in Petrograd needed to protect factories and other enterprises and maintain order in general." The Extraordinary Investigatory Commission of the Provisional Government subsequently upheld this version. A commission member concluded Ivanov had not been invested with any special authority: it had merely been decided to restore order in the capital, and a few units had been sent there to reinforce the garrison. The St. George's Battalion was to protect Ivanov. In fact, however, this was a punitive expedition designed to drown revolutionary Petrograd in blood. Ivanov was declared dictator, all military and civilian authorities of the country, including the Council of Ministers, were to obey him. On February 27 before Ivanov was appointed, Nicholas II told Aleksandra Fedorovna: "After yesterday's news from the city I saw many frightened faces. Fortunately, Alekseev is calm, but he thinks I must name a very decisive individual in order to compel the ministers to work to solve such questions as the food supply, rail transportation, etc. This, of course, is totally justified."[5]

After a conversation with the tsar on the evening of February 27–28, General Ivanov wrote to Alekseev transmitting the tsar's behest: "All ministers are to execute unconditionally all orders from the commander of the Petrograd Military District, Adjutant General Ivanov."[6] Alekseev handed this injunction to Beliaev and instructed him to find a way to convey the tsar's edict to the chairman of the Council of Ministers and other ministers. By that time it had become difficult to deliver tsarist commands to the ministers. Officials in the Petrograd Telegraph office informed Supreme Headquarters that they were surrounded by insurgents, that one could not move freely about the city, and that they could not deliver the tsar's message to Golitsyn and had to telephone it to him.

The Supreme Command ordered the commanders on the northern and western fronts each to make two cavalry and two reserve regiments and one machine-gun detachment immediately available to the new commander of troops of the Petrograd Military District. It was decided to reinforce the infantry and cavalry units with artillery. In a supplementary telegram headquarters ordered both fronts each to send a cavalry and infantry battery to join Ivanov's punitive expedition. Headquarters planned to appoint generals to command these units and to place the Petrograd garrison units still loyal to the tsarist government under Ivanov. General Alekseev explained to General Iu. N. Danilov, chief of the northern front:

> We have to appoint stable generals, since it looks like General Khabalov has lost his head, and furnish General Ivanov reliable, capable, and courageous assistants. The troops should be sent on the fewest possible trains, and you should organize delivery of bread and supplies from the front, since it's difficult to say what is presently happening in Petrograd or whether the local garrison can supply these troops. The situation demands the troops arrive promptly. . . . It's a dangerous time and everything must be done to hasten the arrival of reliable forces. Our future depends on it.[7]

The tsarist generals felt their duty to tsar and country bound them to send units from the front to suppress the revolution, but they did mention the need to conduct the war with the foreign enemy to a victorious end. The commander of the western front, General A. E. Evert, asked his division commanders to communicate to the units assigned to Ivanov his confidence that, imbued with unshakable loyalty to their tsar and devotion to their homeland,

> they will honorably fulfill the responsible assignment given to them during this difficult time for the government, and always remember that order inside Russia, which their sovereign has called upon them to restore, is necessary to ensure victory over our stubborn enemy. . . . When you are exhorting the regiments you have selected to aid the government, I ask you to remind them that they can successfully accomplish their assigned tasks only if they observe the strictest order and are highly disciplined.[8]

In addition to troops from the northern and western fronts, tsarist headquarters also decided to summon units from the more distant southwestern front to quash the revolution. On February 28, Alekseev communicated the tsar's order to the commander of this front. "Assign guards regiments to General Ivanov: the Preobrazhenskii and the Third and Fourth Infantry detachments, and dispatch them as soon as you can, depending upon conditions on the railroads." Alekseev added, "If the situation demands further strengthening of the armed forces in Petrograd, you will have to send a cavalry guards division."[9] Ivanov was also supposed to receive the Vyborg Battalion and two artillery battalions from Kronstadt.

Headquarters hoped reliable forces in Petrograd could struggle with the people, and that with the joint action of units from the front and Petrograd they could put down the revolution. But as each hour went by, fewer and fewer soldiers remained loyal to the government. The revolutionary forces had successfully eliminated the last centers of opposition in the capital.

As on the previous evening, on the morning of February 28 masses of armed workers and soldiers showed up at the bicycle battalion barracks on Sampsonievskii Prospekt. They tried to convince the soldier-bicyclists to join the people, but fearing their officers, they refused as they had before. The cyclists' obstinacy embittered the assembled crowd. Angry voices resounded. "So you're for the tsar. Let's take them by storm! To the barracks! We'll slaughter them all!" When all efforts at persuasion had been exhausted, the besieged resorted to extreme measures: they piled up flammable material and set fire to the wooden barracks of the cyclists; two barracks went up. Armored cars had driven up and opened fire on the other barracks. The bicycle battalion gave in and the soldiers surrendered: "Brothers, forgive us, it's our officers' fault. We would never have gone against the people."

The strongest armed force defending the autocracy was the detachment entrenched at the Admiralty building. It alone posed no threat to the revolutionary forces, for the detachment was vulnerable on all sides and was effectively boxed up in the Admiralty. Nevertheless, if troops arrived from the front it could be used to attack the revolutionary forces. B. Fomin, commander of the

Izmailovskii Reserve Battalion that had joined them, suggested taking advantage of the darkness of night to lead the troops out of the Admiralty to Pulkovo [a nearby suburb—D.J.R.].

> Troops are moving from the front toward Petrograd. In order to join forces with them, to inform them accurately about the situation in Petrograd, and to unify the command, it would be much better for the troop commander not to be surrounded by insurgents and to be outside the zone of the uprising. . . . If we go to Pulkovo, we can supply a detachment with our local resources tomorrow, make contact with the garrison at Tsarskoe Selo, and occupy the rail lines nearest Petrograd, on the Baltic, Warsaw, and Vindavo-Rybinskaia routes."[10]

From a strictly military point of view this plan had its advantages; however, it did not take into account the alignment of political forces and the soldiers' moods. Both the Tsarskoe Selo garrison and the front-line units were ready to join the revolution and no longer defend tsarism, whose day was done. Khabalov rejected the plan, haughtily announcing his place as district commander was Petrograd, not Pulkovo. He would not lead the troops out of the capital and leave the tsarist ministers to their fate. Yet Khabalov was now a commander without troops, and the tsarist ministers were hidden in their apartments in fear of the people's retribution. The military authorities tried to bring the ministers to the Admiralty. They searched and telephoned, but found no one.

About 1:00 A.M. on the morning of February 28, Beliaev instructed the detachment at the Admiralty to proceed to the Winter Palace. Like all the other actions of the hysterical authorities, this order made little sense. A transfer to the Winter Palace would not improve the position of tsarism's defenders. The two divisions of the reserve battalion of the Petrograd Regiment that had been in the palace and the Reserve Cavalry Guards Regiment summoned from the Krechevitskii barracks in Novgorod had reinforced Khabalov's detachment, but these additions could not significantly influence the alignment of forces. After moving to the Winter Palace, the authorities tried to make it a fortress. Frames were put up in many windows and machine guns set up; one stood by a wooden partition, separating the palace rooms from an infirmary where more than five hundred wounded soldiers lay. Still, no matter how much they fortified the Winter Palace, exposed as it was on all sides, it was even more vulnerable than the Admiralty.

Disorder reigned in the detachment of the last defenders of tsarism. Instructions and commands were issued and then changed, commanders came and went, all to no avail. The Reserve Cavalry Regiment left the palace and went back to Novgorod. Toward morning on February 28 the detachment was relocated again: on orders from Grand Prince Mikhail Aleksandrovich the troops were removed from the Winter Palace. They tried to wend their way to the Peter-Paul Fortress and to use it in the struggle against the revolution, but revolutionary units holding Troitskii Bridge blocked the way to the fortress. The defenders of tsarism had to return to the Admiralty. Their situation had become hopeless.

Reports from the military authorities in Petrograd to Supreme Headquarters no longer evoked the soothing assurances of previous days. Earlier, Beliaev and Khabalov had reported on several days at once. Now they wired almost hourly. Earlier, the military authorities of the capital had avoided unpleasantness and kept reassuring the tsar and his entourage in their telegrams. Now they were compelled to tell headquarters how matters stood. At 8:21 A.M. on February 28 Khabalov informed Alekseev: "The number of those still loyal has decreased to 600 infantrymen and about 500 cavalrymen with 15 machine guns, and 12 guns with only 80 cartridges (*sic*—E. B.) The situation is extremely precarious."[11] At 11:22 Beliaev communicated that "the situation remains alarming. Insurgents control the most important buildings all over the city. The troops, tired and exposed to propaganda, are throwing down their arms, crossing over to the insurgents, or turning neutral. At present it's difficult to say exactly how many regiments remain truly reliable. . . . We are desperately anxious for troops to arrive as soon as possible; until reliable forces come insurrection and disorder will continue to grow."[12] At 12:25 Beliaev told headquarters that the Ministry of Communications could no longer do its job. The tsar's command that all ministers must obey the new district commander in chief, Ivanov, had been conveyed to no more than four ministries that were connected to the palace by telephone: "The municipal telephone system is not working and therefore cannot contact the other ministries or the chairman today."[13]

The situation that had developed in Petrograd is reflected in the answers Khabalov gave at 11:30 A.M., February 28, to questions put to him by General Ivanov prior to his arrival in Petrograd from Mogilev to suppress the revolution. The text read:

> 1) Which units are orderly and which are creating disturbances? I have four guards divisions, five squadrons and Cossack units, and two batteries in the main Admiralty building. The rest of the troops have joined the revolutionaries or have agreed with them to remain neutral. Individual soldiers and bands roam the city, firing at passers-by and disarming officers. 2) Which stations are secure? All stations are in the hands of the revolutionaries and tightly guarded by them. 3) Which administrative regions of the city are orderly? The entire city is in the hands of the revolutionaries; the telephone system is not operating, so some parts of the city cannot communicate with another. 4) What authority exists in these parts of the city? I don't know. 5) Are all ministries functioning properly? The revolutionaries have arrested all the ministers. 6) What police units are at your disposal at present? None. 7) What technical and administrative buildings belonging to the military authorities are now at your disposal? None. 8) How much food do you have? I have no food supplies. 9) Have many arms, artillery, and ammunition fallen into the strikers' hands? The revolutionaries have seized all the artillery. 10) What troops and staffs are at your disposal? The head of the district staff is available to me. I have no contact with the other district authorities.[14]

Ivanov's questions and Khabalov's answers graphically demonstrate how little headquarters knew about the situation in Petrograd. Ivanov assumed that troops loyal to the autocracy still guarded railroad stations and held part of the city, that some ministries still functioned, that some police stations, technical and commercial buildings, soldiers and staffs remained at the disposal of the commander of the Petrograd Military District. Khabalov's answers dispelled these illusions: the military authorities in the capital had nothing, they had lost all their positions, all their strongholds. The different way in which both these tsarist generals expressed themselves is also characteristic. Ivanov spoke of insurgents "causing disturbances." Khabalov spoke of revolutionaries holding the entire city and closely guarding the stations. The people had succeeded during several days of uprisings in making the commander of the Petrograd Military District change his tune.

Khabalov's answers expose the hopeless position of autocracy's defenders in Petrograd and that they could no longer put down the workers' and soldiers' revolution. While Khabalov's answers were being transmitted, the Peter-Paul Fortress, one of the last bastions of the autocracy, surrendered. They called this fortress the "Russian Bastille." Several generations of revolutionaries had been imprisoned in it. When the February Revolution broke out the gloomy cells of the Peter-Paul Fortress were almost empty; a year earlier five sailors had been locked up there for participating in the revolutionary movement, but just before the revolution triumphed, on the evening of February 26–27, it held nineteen soldiers who had taken part in the uprising of the reserve battalion of the Pavlovskii Guards Regiment in two prison cells in the Trubetskoi Ravelin. The workers and soldiers had been planning to storm the Peter-Paul Fortress when the garrison indicated it would come over to the people. At approximately noon on February 28 revolutionary detachments of workers and soldiers entered the fortress. They lifted up the soldiers from the Pavlovskii Regiment and carried them out of the Trubetskoi Ravelin to enthusiastic shouts from the crowd.

When the Peter-Paul Fortress fell, the position of the last detachment defending the autocracy entrenched in the Admiralty deteriorated even further. Armed workers and soldiers ready to attack filled the streets next to it and the Aleksandr Garden. The help promised from the front never came. Morale in the Admiralty declined as infantrymen and artillerymen announced they intended to abandon the detachment. This made battle with the insurgents impossible. Realizing that it was useless to keep the tsarist troops in the Admiralty any longer, the command told the soldiers to return to their barracks in an orderly manner. The soldiers decided to leave the Admiralty without weapons, so as not to provoke a clash. They left their rifles in a room in the building and came out without them.

At 1:30 P.M. on February 28 Beliaev reported to headquarters that organized resistance by tsarist troops in the capital had broken off and that the last detachment had capitulated. "About noon on February 28 remaining units still loyal, including four companies, one Cossack unit, two batteries, and two machine-gun divisions were removed from the Admiralty on orders from the naval minister so that the building would not be destroyed. It was decided not to transfer them elsewhere because they were not entirely reliable. The units were distributed among the barracks. To prevent them being disarmed en route, rifles, machine guns, and even gunbolts were handed over to the Naval Ministry."[15]

The workers and soldiers greeted the troops who had come out of the Admiralty with suspicion but not hostility. When they learned that the soldiers were returning to their barracks, which meant the last tsarist camp was being liquidated peacefully and painlessly, an enthusiastic welcome rang out everywhere. The fighters in the Admiralty detachment were not simply quitting the camp of tsarism: workers and soldiers sat on top of the detachable fronts of the artillery guns, the bolts of which remained in the Admiralty, and small red flags had been fastened to the horses' collars. The soldiers of the last tsarist detachment had joined the revolutionary camp. The tsarist authorities vainly sought to console themselves with the thought that the defection of the six or seven hundred men in the Admiralty was a trifle compared with the revolt of an entire garrison. This move marked the victorious culmination of the armed uprising in Petrograd.

Even so, headquarters continued to inform the war minister, who to all intents and purposes no longer held a mandate, what units had been sent to Petrograd, under whose command, and what the further prospects were for forming counterrevolutionary forces.

That day, February 28, the units in the Petrograd garrison that had not yet decided openly to come over to the people hesitated no more, for one could no longer remain neutral. The success of the insurgent workers and soldiers and the course the developing struggle had taken had involved all the soldiers in the revolution. More and more units were coming over.

The night before, their officers had tried to convince the soldiers of the reserve battalion of the Finland Regiment guarding Vasilevskii Island to stand firm for faith and fatherland and not violate their oath. Yet even then the officers' exhortations meant little to the soldiers. Considerable ferment had already heightened emotions in the battalion. Not wishing to be the first openly to revolt, the soldiers in the Finland Regiment waited for the right moment to come out. On the morning of February 28, crowds approached the regiment's barracks. The soldiers refused to fire on them and began to join the insurgents. Seizing the weapons in their barracks, soldiers began going out into the yard, where they removed the guards from the arsenal and the storeroom, and enjoined the guard to leave the building. They released the prisoners held in the stockade, threw open the arsenal doors, and gathered up weapons and cartridges.

A feeling of elation had swept over the workers and soldiers. They all went to the building where the officers had assembled and were holding tight, unwilling to surrender. They began firing. Some of the officers surrendered and gave up their arms, but others donned soldiers' greatcoats and disappeared into the crowd, while another small group ran out behind, climbed a fence and hid in out-of-the-way houses. The Finland soldiers headed to other units.[16]

That same day workers and soldiers approached the Second Baltic Naval Unit. As it was in the city, attempts had been made to employ it in the struggle with the uprising. The detachment of sailors sent to the Kriukov Canal and Blagoveshchenskaia Square district for this purpose, however, turned their weapons on their officers and joined the people. Other sailors locked in their barracks heard voices from the street: "Sailors, join us!" "Down with the autocracy!" "Long live the revolutionary sailors!" The sailors grabbed rifles and cartridges and hastened into the streets, where they fused with the rest of the workers and soldiers and made for Vasilevskii Island. They took part in street clashes and demonstrations, constantly uniting with fresh insurgent groups. Late that night the sailors returned to their unit and took reprisals against their hated commanders.

During these days the cruiser Aurora was docked for repairs at the Franco-Russian Factory. Three workers from this factory remained in the cruiser's guardhouse as of February 27. Turning the ship into a prison made the sailors uneasy. That same evening a guard came for the workers and led them to the upper deck. A loud "Hurrah" resounded, and the sailors rushed to the workers. When the command and the senior ship's officers fired a few rounds at them and mortally wounded a sailor named Osipenko, the rest dispersed. On the morning of February 28 workers gathered on the shore and appealed to the Aurora's complement to unite with the people. Some of the workers boarded the vessel: a fight broke out between officers and sailors, the commander was killed, and the sailors joined the workers. The Aurora became the first battleship to raise the banner of revolt during the February Revolution. The sailors elected a new commander, organized a ship committee, and sent deputies to the Petrograd Soviet.[17]

The behavior of the Cossack units in the capital also suddenly changed. The Cossacks had long been benevolently neutral and had not decided openly to come over to the insurgents. Individual Cossack units dispatched to the city barely resisted when workers and soldiers demanded their arms. A protocol of the command of the reserve detachment of the Combined Cossack Regiment noted that the Cossacks in that unit "were dispersed among the people in small groups of three, four, or five; the civilians began disarming Cossacks and opening fire at the others who were still armed and mounted. The Cossacks were no longer able to insist on their right to bear arms and wished to avoid excesses with the people and unnecessary violence. They were forced to yield."[18] The people took sixty-nine rifles and seventy-five swords from this unit.

The authorities attempted to remove the Fourth Don Cossack Regiment to the Novosaratov settlement near Petrograd in order to prevent Cossacks from joining the insurgent workers and to preserve them as fighting units until troops arrived from the front. They dispatched two Cossack squadrons there on February 28. But the remaining squadrons grew agitated and demanded the return of those sent away. Finally the Cossacks themselves returned those who had been taken away, and the next day the Fourth Don Cossack Regiment went in full strength to the Tauride Palace and announced they would join the revolution.[19]

Just when the soldiers stopped hesitating, the officers began to waver. Most officers remained ready to uphold their oath of loyalty to the autocracy, even though they knew it was impossible to save tsarism without men. They realized the total bankruptcy of the tsarist authorities and the hopelessness of an open struggle with the people. The officers searched for a way out of the situation. The formation of the Provisional Committee of the State Duma, its membership, and the first measures it took inspired the officers to hope there were other ways of saving the ruling order. This new attitude was most prevalent among the officers of the Reserve Battalion of the Preobrazhenskii Regiment. On the night of February 27–28 the officers of this battalion met with the commander, Prince Argutinskii-Dolgorukov, and voted to recognize the authority of the Provisional Duma Committee and help it restore law and order in the capital. Nonetheless, the promise to help was slow in coming. That night the Military Commission directed the battalion command to arrest the tsarist ministers whom they believed were close to their headquarters at the Admiralty. The battalion command avoided this task, arguing that strong infantry and artillery forces guarded the Council of Ministers and that the Preobrazhenskii Regiment could not attack them. But on February 28, when the situation in the capital reached a crisis, the commanders and officer corps of the Preobrazhenskii Battalion finally broke with the tsarist authorities.

On February 28 only a few officers had announced they would side with the people. Most still sat it out in barracks, officers' meetings, and private apartments. After deciding to take power, the bourgeoisie strove to win over garrison commanders. Appealing to officers, the Duma Committee called upon them "to hasten to join the general movement, not to be left out, isolated from their units. . . . If the officer corps wants to take part in the national struggle to emancipate Russia and conduct the war to a glorious end, it must not leave the soldiers without superiors. Delegations from officers' groups would find the information they needed and orders on the walls of the Tauride Palace."[20]

The Provisional Duma Committee and the Military Commission promulgated an order calling upon garrison officers in the capital and others in Petrograd on leave or on assignment who had not received a charge from the Military Commission to come on March 1 and 2 to the building in which the Army and Navy office was located "to receive permanent certification and exact registration and to obtain the Commission's authorization to organize soldiers who have joined the people to guard the capital. Delay in the officers' appearance at their units will undermine their prestige. . . . It is essential to organize the military. Only this will guarantee the strength of our army and final triumph. . . . Don't lose a precious minute of time."[21]

From February 28 on, the supporters of tsarism in Petrograd waited for troops from the front to help them suppress the revolution. That day military units arrived in the capital, but with an altogether different purpose. They had come from Oranienbaum, Strelna, and other Petrograd suburbs to help the workers and soldiers consolidate victory and overthrow tsarism. At the time the First Reserve Machine-Gun Regiment was in Oranienbaum, the second in Strelna. Both contained approximately thirty-six thousand soldiers. Some machine-gun regiments prepared to proceed to the front, but the order was delayed. Oranienbaum also was site of a gunsmith's school and a number of other technical units composed primarily of workers. The proximity to proletarian Petrograd revolutionized the Oranienbaum garrison. The tsarist authorities tried to isolate it from the capital by forbidding transfers to Petrograd and by not permitting soldiers outside the barracks gates.

Despite all of the obstacles, news about the revolution spread among the Oranienbaum soldiers, and they decided to support their Petersburg comrades. The evening of February 27 a call rang out in Oranienbaum: "To arms! Out in the yard!" The technical units, the armory school, and the First Machine-Gun Regiment enthusiastically responded to the call, overcame the resistance of some noncommissioned officers, and went into the street. A soldier, Skorodumov, related: "We had no clear plan because everything happened spontaneously, without organization. The Petersburg events and our hatred of the autocracy guided our actions. Then the insurgent soldiers gathered near the barracks of the machine-gun regiment and decided to go to help the Petersburg regiments and workers."[22]

At first there were only a few arms—several rifles and training machine guns. To obtain weapons, soldiers stormed armory warehouses and grabbed up rifles, machine guns, and cartridges. Officers tried to stop them, calling for discipline, and threatening reprisals. Influenced by the officers, some soldiers hid in the barracks. The majority went boldly into the street, however, and to the station to go to Petrograd. Trying to cut off aid to the revolutionary capital, the officers fired machine guns at the soldiers on the way to the station. A fight broke out. The soldiers routed the officers and commandeered a suburban train, but when a rumor spread that the officers had prepared an ambush and would derail the train the soldiers decided to march to Petrograd on foot.

It was 1:00 A.M. when the soldiers departed. Almost no officers accompanied them. They marched through Martyshkino, Strelna, Sergeev, and Ligovo. In Peterhof the soldiers approached the ensigns' and junkers' schools. The commanders ordered the doors locked and all confined. But doors broke down from the blows of heavy rifle butts and soldiers tore into the building. Some junkers resisted, while others cried out, "Don't shoot!" and came over to the soldiers. Shouts rang out: "Long live freedom!" The soldiers advanced toward Petrograd.

A participant in the events, Bolshevik S. Petrikovskii, observed that the crowd grew to monstrous proportions. "We tried to organize people and control them, but to no avail."[23] Although disorganized, the movement had a clear goal. Units along the road joined the soldiers. They broke into armories, storehouses, seized rifles and machine guns, and snatched up bread and fodder. "It was spectacular," recalled the soldier I. Bulat, "there was no order at all. There were machine-gun units, batteries, cavalry, infantry, and other units. An armed mass of soldiers surged forward, filled with hatred for the war and tsarism. The crowd extended in a huge line."[24]

On the morning of February 28 soldiers from the Petrograd suburbs reached the Narva Gate. Not knowing whose side they were on, the Putilov workers met them with suspicion. Suddenly soldiers shouted: "Workers, we're with you! Down with the tsar!" This prompted enormous enthusiasm among the Putilovites: "The soldiers are with us! Long live the revolution!" everyone cried. The workers brought the soldiers bread, food, cigarettes, and warm clothing. A hidden machine gun opened fire on them. The soldiers shot back, however, wiping out the machine-gun station, and moving to the center of town. The soldiers' arrival from Oranienbaum, Strelna, and other neighboring garrisons played a vital role in the victory of the revolution. Reaching Petrograd the day after the uprising involving the Petersburg soldiers began, the new group actively battled with the gendarmes and police, eliminated enemy machine-gun nests, and guarded bridges and factories. These troops came to revolutionary Petrograd's assistance at the decisive moment, aided the insurgent workers and soldiers, and helped them deal tsarism the coup de grace.

Soldiers in Tsarskoe Selo, where the family of Nicholas II and other members of the royal household were staying, followed the Oranienbaum soldiers. At the time of the Paris Commune, Thiers had converted the royal residence of Versailles into a bastion of counterrevolution and used it to drown the rising of the French people in blood.[a] During the February Revolution reactionary forces failed to make Tsarskoe Selo their stronghold, even though it seemed that tsarism's most loyal units were concentrated there. A commander of one of these units noted that a "rebellious spirit" had even penetrated the Tsarskoe Selo garrison: "There is more than enough flammable material here to light a revolutionary fire." On February 28 commanders of the units at Tsarskoe Selo turned to the tsar's uncle, the elderly Grand Prince Pavel Aleksandrovich, to issue orders if disturbances should break out. Seeking to calm the agitated commanders, Pavel Aleksandrovich declared that Nicholas II would return to Tsarskoe Selo the next day: "I am sure he will grant the responsible ministry so desired, if only it isn't too late. The heir and the empress are at Tsarskoe Selo and it is our responsibility to protect them."[25]

But the soldiers did not want to wait for the tsar to "grant" a responsible ministry. The Reserve Battalion of the First Rifle Regiment, a composite

[a] Adolphe Thiers (1797–1877) French statesman, journalist, and historian who led the right-wing liberals in the Second Republic and Second Empire. Chosen chief executive during the Franco-Prussian War, he ferociously suppressed the Paris Commune of 1871, which was set up in Paris at the end of the war in opposition to Thiers's government at Versailles.

regiment of the tsar's personal forces and other units in the Tsarskoe Selo garrison, responded to the Petersburg soldiers' call to revolt. Ten days before the revolution a guards naval unit had been transferred from the front to Tsarskoe Selo to strengthen the forces protecting the tsar's family. After the revolution broke out, a demolition detachment in the unit received an order to blow up the highway to prevent revolutionary units advancing from the capital to Tsarskoe Selo. The sailors refused to obey and decided to march to revolutionary Petrograd. Officers' threats and exhortations fell on deaf ears. Two thousand uniformed, armed sailors set out for Petrograd. Fired by powerful revolutionary emotions, they marched twenty kilometers almost without stopping. A participant, F. Sorokin, wrote: "At sunrise Petrograd clearly began to take shape before us . . . the Putilov Plant . . . a large crowd of people . . . everywhere you turned was full of people. When our battalion approached the plant, a loud solemn 'Hurrah!' rang out. Men's and women's hats, caps, and white kerchiefs flew up in the air. The workers, several thousand strong, hailed the sailors who had come to join them."[26]

On February 28 almost the entire Petrograd garrison had come over to the revolutionary camp. The Military Commission calculated that the number of soldiers in revolt on the evening of that day totaled 127,000 men.[27] Military units solemnly proceeded to the Tauride Palace. Whereas the night before soldiers had marched to the palace in disorganized crowds, they now marched in an orderly manner, in close formation, often to the music of military bands. Whereas the night before no officers were with them, some officers now had joined the soldiers and were in command. From insurgents, the soldiers had turned into organized demonstrators. Order had replaced disorder. From Liteinyi Prospekt along Kirochnaia, Furshadskaia, Zakharevskaia, and Tavricheskaia streets and Suvorovskii Prospekt thick columns of soldiers marched to the Tauride Palace with red flags and red ribbons on their chests. Huge crowds filled the streets and hailed each new military unit.

The troops approached the entrance of the Tauride Palace or went inside, where they lined up along the walls in the spacious Catherine Hall. Deputies of the State Duma and of the Soviet of Workers' Deputies addressed them. Military commands were clearly heard, greetings rang out, music played, and cries of "Hurrah" rent the air. The Guards Naval Crew commanded by the tsar's cousin, Grand Prince Kirill Vladimirovich, appeared with other units at the Tauride Palace. He was the first member of the royal family to violate his oath to the tsar and to announce to the Duma deputies that he and his men were on their side. News about this received broad dissemination and influenced the officers' future behavior significantly.[28]

Workers from the environs of Petrograd joined the insurgent proletariat that day. N. A. Emel'ianov, an old Bolshevik worker who had fought back in 1905 and had been in prison and exile, told the people of Sestroretsk of what was happening in Petrograd. On February 28 workers in the Sestroretsk Armament Factory quit work and held a mass meeting. A Bolshevik, V. Tvorogov, said power must belong to the workers. Another Bolshevik, V. I. Zof, proposed forming a revolutionary committee to manage the factory and town. Workers elected a committee and sent two deputies (Zof and Emel'ianov) to the Petrograd Soviet. The Sestroretsk workers went to the arsenal, confiscated fifteen thousand rifles and other weapons, armed themselves and supplied their comrades in Petersburg with rifles, revolvers, and cartridges. They formed a patrol and food supply committee, replaced the factory elder with a new one, and arrested the police chief and other representatives of the tsarist government. The Sestroretsk workers established control over the railroads, the railway administration, and occupied important approaches to Petrograd. All this was vital to the revolution.

Hearing of the revolution in Petrograd, workers in the Shlisselburg Gunpowder Factory struck. Five thousand workers assembled at a mass meeting, crossed the Neva, and advanced into the city carrying banners and slogans. After involving workers from the Manufacturing Factory in their movement and holding another, larger meeting, they made for Shlisselburg Fortress, site of a prison for freedom fighters for two hundred years. Decembrists, populists, and revolutionary workers had been held there. Now the people in revolt came to free the last prisoners from Shlisselburg. A workers' delegation negotiated with the prison administration, and on February 28, sixty-four political prisoners were set free. The next day the rest of the prisoners were released.[29] A revolutionary committee now controlled power in Shlisselburg and its environs.

By February 28 the free people held all Petrograd in their hands. With the desperation of the doomed, the autocracy's defenders fought back, using machine guns extensively. Officers and police in civilian clothing fired on peaceful inhabitants, spreading panic. Many machine guns were set up in church belfries.[30]

Protopopov had ordered this. The machine gunners were called "Protopopov's men" and of him it was said:

> A pious man, of all such people
> who can say why he went mad
> and on the very top of steeples
> placed machine guns that he had

But machine guns could not save the autocracy. Tsarism's resistance on the streets of Petrograd now resembled the flickers of a fire that was dying out. On February 28 people poured into the streets of the capital, sweeping away any remaining tsarist strongholds. Police stations continued to be ransacked, as on the night before. People destroyed a station on Zagorodnyi Prospekt. They tossed paper through the broken windows. Two huge fires blazed up; papers and portraits of the tsars were flung into them. A firetruck pulled up, a patrol arrived: "We must put the fires out." "No way," said a man earnestly. "We're burning papers of the pharaohs. And portraits of the tsars too. No way!" The flames kept on blazing.[31]

That day, February 28, the people started destroying symbols of the tsarist autocracy. People climbed on buildings, drugstores, and shops that had supplied the imperial house and tore off the coat of arms bearing the double-headed eagle and monograms of the royal family. Crowds joyfully cast aside these emblems of the hateful old regime. At Anichkov Bridge and Fontanka, people cheered when several double-headed eagles were hurled down.

The battle continued. Liteinyi Prospekt was barricaded at the corner of Sergievskaia Street; two guns installed there were aimed at Nevskii Prospekt. The barricade had been set up in case it was necessary to ward off tsarist troops coming from the railway stations, a reminder that danger to the revolution still existed. But it was not needed and became covered with more and more snow.

The revolution had transformed the entire city. Petrograd had been colored red. Red flags hung from buildings, red bunting brandished from the bayonets of soldiers' and workers' rifles and Cossacks' sabers, red bows appeared on military men and civilians, red scraps adorned coat buttons and cockades. Excited people filled the streets. With joy the crowds greeted trucks and vans with armed people and red flags careening through the city. "Clearly," wrote an eyewitness, "this was the first revolution in history to use automobiles. Like enormous bristling hedgehogs endowed by the will of some supernatural power with the speed of lightning, snorting and squealing, cars large and small, cars with people armed to the teeth flew by one after another, passing or driving around each other when they met."[32]

When the basic forces of the autocracy had capitulated, the enemy resorted to resistance of another form: they scattered throughout the entire city. This resulted in widespread dispersion of the insurgent people. To destroy separate enemy nests now became the main task of the revolution; otherwise, the people could not enjoy a stable and final victory. The masses themselves displayed initiative and independence, which was especially important in achieving this task. A leaflet disseminated throughout the city advised the insurgent workers and soldiers: "The remaining police, Black Hundred, and other scoundrels have lodged themselves on top of buildings and in private apartments. Try to rout them out everywhere at once with your weapons or with a frontal attack. Soldiers, maintain order everywhere. . . . Don't forget to reconnoiter dangerous places, maintain communications, and guard your posts. . . . Don't permit hooligans to offend peaceful citizens, no looting of stores or ransacking apartments—this will harm the cause of freedom."[33] Workers, soldiers, and students on their own burst into attics in houses and bell towers, charged police and gendarme ambushes, seized their machine guns and rifles, and disposed of an enemy that had been firing at people from around a corner.

The activities of the numerous revolutionary detachments hastily formed and poorly coordinated, operating all over the vast city, have left little trace in the sources. Only a partial list can be compiled, based on reports to the Military Commission of the State Duma on February 28 and March 1. These reports indicated from which buildings machine guns fired, stated that government armored cars operated between the People's Home and the Peter-Paul Fortress, and that in the Kolomenskoe District "policemen, armed with machine guns, gathered in attics, fired at groups of people, and sowed panic among the soldiers."[34] They also said that police had laid an ambush behind Moscow Gate. The Military Commission was asked to send armed detachments to defend railway stations, factories, and buildings. Medical orderlies in the field hospital in the Winter Palace pleaded for "a detachment of troops to arrest individuals hiding there, to stop machine-gun fire from roofs, and to guard the palace. The palace now is a no man's land. The guards are gone, but supporters of the tsarist regime are still inside." A patrol from the reserve battalion of the Kegsgolmskii Regiment guarding the Senate building asked for orders, what to do and whom to obey, saying "it would be criminal to leave the Senate building to the whims of fate, because documents of great importance are there."[35] The Military Commission received requests for soldiers to defend the Petrograd Cartridge Warehouse, Okhta Gunpowder Factory, Ammunitions Factory, and other enterprises. The commander of the Main Artillery Administration, General A. A. Manikovskii, petitioned the Military Commission to allow him to enter the administration building where he proposed to appeal to the workers to remain at work and organize the defense of factories. "I am powerless to do anything myself. Please help me," he wrote.

The members of the Military Commission issued numerous instructions about establishing order in various neighborhoods of the city, taking over government buildings, transferring arms, and guarding factories. Usually Engel'gardt, Filippovskii, Pal'chinskii, Maslovskii (Mstislavskii), and Potapov, or sometimes Tumanov, Chikolini, Dimitriev, and other members or associates of that organization signed the orders. It assigned men to meet military units that had arrived at the Baltic Station, to occupy the waterworks on Shpalernaia Street, to deliver twenty thousand cartridges from the Cartridge Works (Patronnyi Factory), to dispatch armored cars to Nikolaevskii Station, etc. The Military Commission directed units to occupy and guard the Central Telephone Exchange, the State Bank, Tsarskoe Selo Station, an electrical station belonging to the Belgian Co., the Savings Bank, the main Telegraph Office, Nikolaevskii Station, the Hermitage, the Aleksandr III Museum, the ammunition warehouse, etc. It instructed Ensign Liubavskii "to take command of the junkers in the Nikolaevskii Engineering School"; Staff Captain Miagkov "to take over the Volynskii Regiment"; Ensign Andrusov, "to take command of your men in the Pavlovskii Regiment"; Ensign S. Ivanov, "to go to the Petrograd side to maintain order in the streets"; Colonel Tsemirov, "to take steps to maintain order in your Third Railroad Workers' Battalion," and the like. An order was signed to "Volunteer[b] Dmitrii Tairov and private Vladimir Maiakovskii to conduct elec-

[b] *vol'noopredeliaiushchiisia*—a person with a secondary education serving in the tsarist army on privileged conditions.

tions for representatives in the military automobile school, and get cars repaired."[36]

Later, summarizing the results of its work, the Military Commission wrote that it had served as the headquarters for the revolution during those days. "The seriousness of the situation, opposition of the defenders of despotism, lack of a plan, unexpected and technical difficulties, and apprehensions whether the revolution would succeed demanded authority and a high command. The Provisional Committee empowered the Military Commission, and it cooperated enthusiastically with the Executive Committee of the Soviet of Workers' and Soldiers' Deputies and brought the revolution to a triumphant conclusion."[37] The Military Commission was not as influential as this document suggests, though, for in the overwhelming majority of cases the masses took the initiative, without waiting for instructions from above. They did not always carry out the Military Commission's directives, sometimes because people had no faith in the commission, and in those cases demanded the Soviet of Workers' Deputies or Duma deputies confirm its directives.

S. Mstislavskii related: "People come, and go, and change. They demand details and orders. I write sheet after sheet, all on the same Duma forms. And it seems just as if I'm casting these pitiful pages covered with meaningless scrawls that change nothing, feeble trifles, into a kind of whirling vortex. Those who receive orders don't carry them out; those who act do so without orders."[38] Instructions from the Military Commission were often late, and frequently the insurgents would seize a building without an order. The soldiers refused to obey many commanders and leaders appointed by the Military Commission. Workers and soldiers guarded important places on their own. Even though the commission had to predate all orders to keep up with what the people had done, it had some value because it provided people with a major organized center.

During those days anarchy and spontaneous excesses threatened Petrograd. Robbers and criminals released from prisons, hooligans, and the like tried to loot shops and apartments and seize liquor warehouses. Tsarist agents often provoked such excesses in order to drown the revolution in a wave of rioting and robbery. The people themselves put a stop to such harmful provocation. Sometimes reports of robberies and other excesses turned out to be exaggerated or even prefabricated, and supporters of the old order frequently circulated them deliberately to confuse the insurgents and discredit the revolution.

Workers played the decisive role in the struggle against violations of revolutionary order, and even representatives of the bourgeois camp were forced to recognize this. A letter to the Petrograd City Duma on March 2 said: "Self-controlled and organized workers protected public institutions, factories, etc., and the entire capital from the half-formed intention of the rabble to take advantage of a favorable opportunity to rob and commit other excesses. Armed force promptly and decisively suppressed any moves of this kind."[39]

The overthrow of tsarism raised the question of power in all its intensity. The future course of the struggle and the results of the revolution itself depended upon resolving this question.

What kind of struggle developed over the question of power on the day after the decisive engagement with tsarism?

The Soviet of Workers' Deputies and the Provisional Committee of the State Duma

By February 28 two political centers had formed in Petrograd: the Soviet of Workers' Deputies and the Provisional Committee of the State Duma. Both had quarters in the Tauride Palace, where the Duma was pressed for space and armed workers and soldiers had occupied halls, corridors, and rooms. An armed camp had grown up nearby: delivery vans and motorcycles were parked there, bags of sand lay about, and military units were in position. The people's revolution charged into palace halls and rooms, brilliant with their white walls and columns and sparkling floors. "The sudden chaos of restoration," noted Mikhail Kol'tsov, "soared through the ancient building, widening it, expanding it, and making it vast. Like a newborn child it embraced the revolution and all of Russia. The Catherine Hall became a barracks, military parade ground, auditorium to hold mass rallies, hospital, bedroom, theater, the cradle of a new country. Alabaster, chipped from the walls, crunched underfoot; machine-gun bandoliers, paper, lists, and rags lay scattered about. Thousands of feet tramped through the rubbish, moving about in a confused, joyful muddle nobody understood."[40] E. Zozulia wrote that during those days the Tauride Palace resembled a third-class provincial railway station when troops were embarking. "It smelled like leather, soldiers' uniforms, and bread. Everywhere along the walls soldiers slept side by side. Thousands of other soldiers, sailors, civilians, students armed with rifles, and officers bustled along corridors and up and down stairs."[41]

Leaders of the defunct tsarist regime also found room in the occupied Tauride Palace. Beginning on the evening of February 27, detachments of workers and soldiers started arresting tsarist officials, ministers, and generals, brought them to the Tauride Palace, and placed them in the Ministerial Pavilion. Recently the lords of Russia, they now proceeded through the crowd, hanging their heads. Many were trembling and glancing to the side because they feared the people. The soldiers guarded them carefully, however, and no violence took place in the palace.

The chairman of the State Council, the hated reactionary I. G. Shcheglovitov, was one of the first to be brought to the palace, escorted by students. Rodzianko came up. "Ivan Grigor'evich," he said to Shcheglovitov, "please come to my office." The students remained clustered around Shcheglovitov, and the crowd grew agitated. Kerensky appeared. "Slowly, emphasizing his sibilants, he declared: 'Shcheglovitov is a prisoner of the people. He will be dealt with according to law.' Turning to the students, he said: 'Take him to the Ministerial Pavilion.' Rodzianko lowered his head, fell silent, and left."[42] To the Ministerial Pavilion they brought the former war minister, Sukhomlinov. The crowd demanded he be handed over. Yet no reprisals against the hated tsarist ministers were permitted. Among others arrested and brought to the palace was Metropolitan Pitirim,[c] notorious for his ties with Rasputin. He stated in writing that his high position in the church hierarchy had always been a burden and now he wished to retire. It was decided to send Pitirim back to the Aleksandr Nevsky Monastery.

The arrested dignitaries were accommodated in the Ministerial Pavilion. Kerensky assumed responsibility for them. He himself wrote on the letterhead of the chairman of the State Duma: "The Provisional Committee charges Duma member Kerensky to administer the Ministerial Pavilion where very important individuals are held."[43] Rodzianko signed this attestation. The Ministerial Pavilion of the Duma at the time presented a curious spectacle. "Those incarcerated in the building," wrote the journalist Khaganskii, "at first looked like the top brass at a festive gathering. The shining shoulder straps and decorations of the generals, and quite a few bald pates. . . . On a large office desk covered with a white cloth lay heaps of books . . . and here too were empty glasses and the remains of the prisoners' supper. The room was silent as a tomb since the prisoners were strictly forbidden to converse among themselves."[44] Conditions for the arrested tsarist officers soon improved. They were allowed to read and talk as long as they left political questions alone. In a few days tsarist ministers and other prominent individuals were transferred to the Peter-Paul Fortress.

Leading members of the old regime were brought to the Tauride Palace, along with minor functionaries—officers, gendarmes, and policemen. Many came voluntarily and, fearing the crowd, asked to be placed under arrest. Dressed in civilian clothing, gendarmes and policemen, trembling for their lives, lined up and waited to be placed under guard by revolutionary soldiers. Their numbers increased until it was difficult to hold them all in the palace. The galleries of the meeting hall, buffets, and other rooms were allocated to this purpose.

The Duma Committee had never intended to conduct large-scale arrest of representatives of the regime and officially disassociated itself from them. Issue number 3 of *Izvestiia zhurnalistov* on February 28, 1917, stated: "The Provisional Committee of the State Duma announces that it has ordered no arrests and henceforward no one will be arrested without the Committee's special instruction."

Insofar as it was impossible to issue a separate directive in each case, the

[c] Pitirim had been bishop of Samara before his 1915 appointment as metropolitan of Petrograd. His move to the capital caused much excitement because he was considered a "Rasputinite" and also because he ousted Metropolitan Vladimir without the sanction of the Holy Synod.

Duma Committee had to publish a blanket order concerning who was subject to arrest. An order on March 1, signed by Duma member Karaulov, averred that those who disturbed the peace, were drunk, arsonists, people firing into the air, etc., those who pretended to be police auxiliaries or gendarmes, as well as individuals conducting searches and arrests without special authorization, would be immediately arrested. Karaulov's order provided for "detaining" tsarist officials and generals. It recommended that the arrested be taken to the commandant's headquarters or the city governor's office, to military prisons, and the like, while senior officials and generals were to be brought to the Tauride Palace.[45] Next day the directive was supplemented: gendarmes were not liable to arrest.

Thus the Duma Committee attempted to limit and control arrests and searches and to protect officials from the armed detachments of workers and soldiers. The committee, however, had no power to enforce these orders. The detachments of armed workers and soldiers did not follow the Duma Committee's directives or wait for its instructions; they carried out arrests and searches motivated by a revolutionary sense of justice. They acted quickly and decisively to destroy the hated tsarist regime and disarm its supporters. Leaders of the Duma Committee complained their instructions concerning arrests and searches were not carried out. Rodzianko wrote: "The supreme authority and power of the State Duma and its chairman, in the capital at any rate, is less than it seems from the provinces. . . . The Provisional Committee has repeatedly declared such arrests are illegal, but they continue to occur with striking regularity."[46]

Such a situation came about because the Soviet had real power. The armed workers and soldiers considered the Soviet their sole leader and obeyed it. The Soviet of Workers' Deputies was linked to the whole capital, factories, and barracks. People went to it for advice, orders, and instructions. The masses instinctively felt an unprecedented, new organization had come into being, destined to play an immense role in their lives.

The second meeting of the Soviet of Workers' Deputies was held on February 28. Like earlier meetings, it took place in room 13. The room was crowded and the number of Soviet members and guests continued to grow. Chairs had to be taken away to make room; people stood pressed against each other. This session was extraordinarily animated. Speeches from representatives of military units repeatedly interrupted the agenda. Delegates from the reserve battalions of the Volynskii, Pavlovskii, Lithuanian, Finnish, and other guards regiments, infantry, and special units received stormy ovations from those present when they assured the Soviet that their units were joining the people in the struggle for freedom. "The hall listened," wrote Sukhanov, "like children hearing a wonderful fairy tale touching the emotions and known by heart, as they held their breath. . . . An enthusiastic ovation met the name of each glorious regiment that launched the revolution. The same enthusiasm greeted the names of the new units that had recently joined the ranks of the popular revolutionary army and that were leading it to victory.[47]

The applause had barely subsided and the Soviet resumed activities when a young soldier in the reserve battalion of the Semenovskii Guards Regiment made an impassioned speech. This was the regiment considered a bastion of tsarism since the First Russian Revolution. He said: "To the last man we are all resolved to join the people against the accursed autocracy and we vow to serve the people's cause to the last drop of our blood." The Semenovskii soldier's speech provoked a new wave of speeches from representatives of the military units that had joined the revolution. The Soviet meeting was transformed into a mighty demonstration of the solidarity between the army and people and gave strength to the idea that workers' and soldiers' deputies might form a single soviet.

On February 28 the Workers' Soviet passed new resolutions on a number of important questions. It decided to register all automobiles and organize its own automobile detachment under the Executive Committee. It resolved to approach the Duma Committee for finances while the Soviet asked the population to make donations for revolutionary needs. The appeal read: "Comrades and citizens! The Soviet of Workers' Deputies is asking everyone who values the victory over the old regime to donate as much money and supplies as they can to help the revolution. . . . Apart from nationwide measures, which will provide it with needed resources on a large scale as the revolution spreads, the Soviet of Workers' Deputies recommends that all citizens make financial contributions to advance the cause of freedom and organize canteens for soldiers and militia everywhere, cafeterias, etc. The Soviet has established finance and food supply commissions to which you should send money and contributions. They are in room 13 of the Tauride Palace."[48] Voluntary contributions from organizations and private individuals constituted the Soviet's main source of support. The Duma Committee and later the Provisional Government did not want to have anything to do with financing the Soviet.

The Soviet decided to augment the Executive Committee with representatives from the parties. The Bolsheviks sent K. I. Shutko, P. A. Zalutskii, and V. M. Molotov; the Mensheviks, B. Baturskii, B. O. Bogdanov, and V. Krokhmal'; the SRs, V. M. Zenzinov; the Bund, M. Rafes and Genrikh Erlikh; the Trudoviks, L. Bramson; the Interdistrictites, I. Iurenev; the Polish Social Democrats, M. Kozlovskii; the Latvian Social Democrats, P. Stuchka. The last three members of the Executive Committee supported the Bolsheviks, but the new party representatives mostly strengthened the rightist, conciliatory wing. The Bolsheviks remained a minority.[49]

A manifesto by the Central Committee of the RSDRP, actually initiated by the Vyborg Bolshevik Committee, had determined the Bolsheviks' position on the revolution. The Vyborg Bolsheviks at first had wanted to join the members of the Central Committee Bureau in writing the manifesto but, unable to find them, they set down to compiling it themselves. Kaiurov related that he and Khakharev wrote the manifesto, that Molotov and Zalutskii edited it, and that it was printed and posted on the streets.[50]

Shliapnikov gave a somewhat different version. According to him, the draft was put together by Khakharev, Lebedev, and Kaiurov and was brought early in the morning of February 28 to the Tauride Palace where the Central Committee Bureau was located. "Along with Comrade Molotov," wrote Shliapnikov, "we discussed the 'Manifesto,' made corrections and improvements, and decided to print it in the name of the Central Committee of the Social Democratic Labor party."[51] The manifesto was published as a supplement to the first issue of *Izvestiia* on the evening of February 28 and in separate leaflets. V. Bonch-Bruevich remembered that the SR-Menshevik leaders in the Soviet were indignant because the Bolshevik manifesto appeared in *Izvestiia*. "I tried to console malevolent critics by informing them that apart from publishing the Manifesto in the Soviet's newspaper, I had printed 100,000 separate copies of it; it already has been posted throughout Petrograd, circulated to factories, mills, and barracks, and sent all over Russia."[52] It is clear that the printing house of the newspaper *Den'* (Day) had also published it.[53]

The manifesto of the Central Committee of the RSDRP set as one of the most important tasks of the working class and revolutionary army "the formation of a provisional revolutionary government to lead the new incipient republican order. The provisional revolutionary government must assume responsibility for devising temporary laws to defend the people's rights and freedoms, confiscate monastery, landlord, absentee, and crown lands, and transfer them to the people, introduce the eight-hour workday, and summon a constituent assembly elected on the basis of universal, direct, equal, and secret sufferage."

The manifesto considered it the Provisional Government's immediate and urgent task: "To contact the proletariat of the warring countries and have them wage a revolutionary struggle in all countries against their oppressors and enslavers, royal governments and capitalist cliques, and at once cease the beastly butchery unleashed upon enslaved peoples." The RSDRP Central Committee manifesto called upon workers and soldiers to elect representatives immediately to a provisional revolutionary government. It appealed to all of Russia to raise the red banner of revolt and create a revolutionary people's government in all towns and villages. "Forward! No turning back! Wage a merciless struggle! Under the red banner of revolution! Long live a democratic republic! Long live the revolutionary working class! Long live the revolutionary people and the insurgent army!"[54]

The manifesto defined where the struggle should go: form an authentic revolutionary government to establish a democratic republic, implement the other demands in the Social Democratic minimum program, and bring the imperialist war to an end at once. Lenin highly approved the manifesto.

> In this document there is not a word about either supporting the Guchkov government or overthrowing it; the workers and the soldiers are called upon to

> organize around the Soviet of Workers' Deputies, to elect representatives to it for the fight against tsarism and for a republic, for an eight-hour day, for the confiscation of the landed estates and grain stocks, and chiefly for an end to the predatory war. Particularly important and particularly urgent in this connection is our Central Committee's absolutely correct idea that to obtain peace relations must be established with the *proletarians of all belligerent countries*."[55]

The manifesto did not say how to choose a provisional revolutionary government or anything about the Soviet,[56] but it stated with absolute clarity that power must pass to the revolutionary people, and the entire document appealed for the formation of a provisional revolutionary government.

The Mensheviks and SRs thought otherwise. Although they attacked the autocracy, they did not urge workers and soldiers to take power and form a provisional revolutionary government. The Mensheviks and SRs had always been convinced that bourgeois power must transform the tsarist monarchy into a bourgeois-democratic state, and that the task of the proletariat was to help the bourgeoisie attain this objective. Since Mensheviks and SRs controlled the Soviet leadership, it reflected their position on this important question.

Possessing real power, the Soviet of Workers' Deputies acted with authority. At the meeting on February 28 the Soviet discussed the railroads. "The Soviet of Workers' Deputies believes the food supply crisis requires restoration of rail service between Petrograd and Moscow. A Special Commission has been charged to examine the question of controlling freight traffic and, in cooperation with the food supply commission, justifying whether a particular line should function." The Soviet considered communications important. It empowered the Executive Committee "to solve the question of supervising the post and telegraph by forming special commissions if necessary." The Soviet opposed the resumption of streetcar service in Petrograd, considering it premature.[57]

The Soviet established a finance commission and on its recommendation decided to remove all state financial resources from the old authorities immediately. "To achieve this, revolutionary patrols must occupy and mount guard over: a) the State Bank; b) the Central and Provincial Treasuries; c) the Mint; d) the Currency Exchange." The Soviet, however, did not undertake this most important task itself, and instead entrusted it to the Provisional Duma Committee. The Duma Committee and the Soviet resolved to create a finance committee, like the existing war and food supply commissions. The Soviet charged this committee to do everything necessary to put the country's finances in order; supervise and control the normal flow of all money and credit at every credit institution, estimate what allocations revolutionary institutions need, and shut off credit when necessary, for which the old authorities were responsible, etc.[58] Despite this resolution, no finance committee was formed. The Soviet of Workers' and Soldiers' Deputies tried to get its resolution through the Duma Committee and secure its cooperation, but the Duma Committee sought to act independently, as though it enjoyed full power.

Because the bourgeoisie did not want the workers' militia guarding the city, it set up its own agencies to maintain public order, modeled on and similar to the old ones. In place of General Balk, the Provisional Duma Committee named a professor at the Military-Medical Academy, V. Iurevich, as city governor of Petrograd, adding the word "public" *(obshchestvennyi)* to his title. On February 28 Iurevich issued an announcement: "I have been appointed Petrograd Public City Governor by the Provisional Committee of the State Duma. . . . All measures are being taken to protect citizens' safety and property. Neighborhood civilian committees are forming to maintain order and to supply citizens with food."[59]

Adding the adjective "public" changed nothing. The new supervisor of public safety, Iurevich, settled down with his aides and assistants surviving from tsarist times in the city governor's spacious building, published *Vedomosti* (Gazette) which few read, and signed the mandatory decrees, to which few paid attention. The city governor was actually as outmoded as the tsarist regime and existed through inertia, lacking real power or concerns. The tsarist city governor had relied on his police. The public city governor had none. The task of maintaining public safety belonged to others.

The City Duma, not the city governor, created the police force. In an emergency session on February 28 deputies of the City Duma resolved "in the interests of safeguarding the life and property of the population" to establish a city militia, entrusted its organization to deputy D. A. Kryzhanovskii, and made credits available from the city budget to do so.[60] After choosing the head of the city militia, the City Duma designated places for the militiamen to assemble and appointed district supervisors mainly from among its own members. The Military-Technical Assistance Committee, which comprised the Russian Technical Society, societies of technologists, electrical and civil engineers, the Metallurgical Society, and other scientific and technical organizations, took part in setting up the militia. It drew up regulations about rendering service and the responsibilities of patrols and asked students to register for it. In an appeal of February 28 the Military-Technical Assistance Committee declared that the tasks of the new organization included: "1) stopping senseless shooting; 2) disarming juveniles and drunks; 3) preventing robberies; and 4) maintaining order in the streets and public places, etc."[61]

The city militia administration was first housed in the City Duma building, and later in the city governor's building. The secretary of the militia, Z. S. Kel'son, related that it began by making white arm bands with the letters "C.M." (City Militia), a number, and the city seal. Although ten thousand arm bands were made, the number of militiamen was considerably less. It was primarily office workers, students, and schoolboys who entered the organization. Kel'son even called it a "militia of infants." The militia staff asked the population to give arms to the City Duma, and this made it possible to arm the militiamen.

The city's inhabitants brought their everyday needs to the militia administration. They came for permission to arrange a funeral, proceed freely through the city, bear arms, and so on. They reported thefts and acts of violence, and asked the militia to guard particular buildings or apartments. They brought in police arrested on the street. The administration fulfilled many of the people's requests, but during the first days of the revolution the militia did not exist as a fighting force. Even though Kel'son claimed that the armed guards functioned as a definite, regulated entity by March 3,[62] this is clearly an exaggeration. During the first days of the revolution several independent organizations defended the city. Kel'son acknowledged that by February 28 an appeal from the Soviet of Workers' Deputies resulted in the formation of fighting cells at factories, which he called "Red Guards," that commissariats of the people's militia existed in the Moscow, Narva and Vyborg regions, "organized independently, having nothing to do with the city militia," and that this worker's militia was not just a body for preserving order, but a fighting force for defending the conquests of the revolution.[63]

While organizing the armed workers' units, the Soviet encouraged formation of the City Duma militia. The order for the city militia read that it was formed "in accordance with a directive of the Provisional Committee of the State Duma and the Soviet of Workers' Deputies." On March 1 *Izvestiia* published an appeal to revolutionary students, signed by student Social Democrats, Socialist Revolutionaries, and Bundists. It invoked the Soviet of Workers' Deputies when asking students to join the civilian paramilitary organization under the auspices of the City Duma. It said:

> The City Duma is organizing a civilian militia. Students are summoned to take part in it: The representative of the revolutionary proletariat, the Executive Committee of the Soviet of Workers' Deputies, has decided to join the central organ of workers' commissariats (a district and its units—E.B.) with the Duma organization. This leads us to summon student comrades to enroll with enthusiasm in the new guard. Remember, comrades, you are participating in the militia at the instance of the Soviet of Workers' Deputies. Remember that the Soviet of Workers' Deputies is your Highest Authority.

And, indeed, workers, soldiers, and students saw the Soviet of Workers' Deputies as "the highest authority," and not the Duma Committee. That is why the City Duma could not create its own armed guard without the Soviet's support.

Resigned to the destruction of a bastion of the autocracy, the police, and to forming new organs to maintain public order with the help of the Soviet, the bourgeoisie tried to leave the rest of the administrative apparatus intact. The revolution had deprived former state institutions of their leaders. The chief tsarist officials either had been arrested by insurgent workers and soldiers or were in hiding, in fear of the people's wrath. Nevertheless, inertia allowed the wheels of the state machine to keep turning; officials went to work, and as before they scratched away with quill pens, attended meetings, circulated papers, pounded typewriters. The commissars appointed to ministries and departments by the State Duma committee were more like observers than representatives of authority. They rarely interfered and routine work went on as before, as if no revolution had taken place. Progressist A. A. Bublikov at the Ministry of Communications was the most active Duma commissar, for it was impossible to ignore this branch of the government administration. Bublikov was compelled personally to give instructions to the railroad administration on questions of train movements, military transport, etc. His directives could not, however, be implemented without the support of railroad and office workers, loyal to the Soviet of Workers' Deputies. They controlled and made absolutely sure the railroads would not be used to the detriment of the revolution.

The most pressing question, on which the fate of the revolution depended, was the question of its armed forces. Unlike the police, the tsarist army had not been destroyed, even though the revolution had badly undermined its base. The bourgeoisie had no wish to reconcile itself to the loss of so important a component of the old state apparatus as the army, and did all it could to revive it in a slightly altered form. Deciding not to disarm workers, it strove to disarm soldiers, restore the authority of their former officers, and revive discipline with the cane. The bourgeoisie wanted the Petrograd garrison to return to its previous military structure in order to stop further development of the revolution and guarantee continuation of the imperialist war. The Provisional Duma Committee defined its task thus:

> The Duma will strive to bring officers and the lower ranks together. There is a pressing need to organize the armed masses. Although they are filled with the best intentions, they are still not organized because events are happening too quickly. Therefore officers are invited to do all they can to assist the State Duma in this difficult work. . . . All must understand the danger that disorganization poses. Citizens, organize!—this is now the fundamental slogan. Our salvation and strength lie in organization. Listen to the Provisional Committee of the State Duma.[64]

The danger the army might disintegrate was actually very great. Upon leaving their barracks, most soldiers broke up into a host of small groups, joined the workers, and dispersed throughout the city. The Military Commission received a note from an unknown author that

> unorganized groups of soldiers are roaming the city; similarly, disorder is manifest both inside and outside the Tauride Palace. Anarchy reigns in the barracks. Many ordinary soldiers with no proper place to spend the night returned to the barracks where they receive no information about what is happening. We suggest that the Commission take the following steps immediately: 1) muster soldiers by regiment in their regular places; 2) appoint temporary commanders and junior officers; 3) set up patrols, occupy roads, stations, and other important public and governmental establishments; 4) stop automobiles aimlessly and unnecessarily roaming the streets; 5) organize the food supply according to regiments and barracks by borrowing bread and other items from places they are available; 7) make sure soldiers are not left in their barracks for a long time without any

> attention, leadership, or information from the insurgent people; 8) transform the Peter-Paul Fortress and the Tauride Palace into resistance bases for all Petrograd; 9) turn the local barracks of individual regiments into district centers; 10) segregate officers who have not joined the people and do not permit them into the barracks; arrest those officers (those heroes at the rear) who might be a bad influence on the soldiers.[65]

The memorandum ended: "In the name of the people and freedom act decisively and forcefully."

The measures outlined in this memorandum did not suit the leaders of the Duma Committee. They wanted to revive the Petrograd garrison along old lines, under the command of the former officer corps. Engel'gardt related that after taking charge of the Military Commission, he decided first to make soldiers return to the barracks and restore previous discipline in the units. The night of February 27–28 he and Bublikov wrote and Rodzianko signed the following order to the units of the Petrograd garrison in the name of the Provisional Committee of the State Duma: "1) all ordinary soldiers and military units must immediately return to their barracks; 2) all officers must return to their units and take all measures to restore order; and 3) unit commanders must report to the State Duma for instructions at 11:00 A.M., February 28."[66]

Duma leaders made the same appeal to soldiers at meetings in the Tauride Palace and in military units. They praised the virtues of order, discipline, and obedience to officers, incessantly gambling on the soldiers' immaturity and their habit of blind obedience. Rodzianko thanked the grenadiers for coming to help restore order. "Support the traditions of a splendid Russian regiment," he said, "listen to your officers. Without superiors a military unit becomes a mob, incapable of establishing order. . . . Your superiors and I ask you to return to your barracks quietly and do whatever your officers tell you."[67] Rodzianko said the same thing to the soldiers in the Reserve Battalion of the Preobrazhenskii Guards Regiment. "Thank you for coming to help the State Duma restore order. . . . I ask you to obey and trust your officers, as we do. Return quietly to your barracks, so that you will be there as soon as you are needed." To junkers attending the Mikhailovskii Artillery School, Rodzianko said that soldiers and officers must reunite and wait for orders from the Provisional Committee of the State Duma. "This is the only way to win."[68]

The speeches Menshevik and SR leaders made to the soldiers differed from those of the Duma representatives. They talked about the struggle against the tsarist regime, the revolution, and democracy. But the SR and Menshevik leaders also told the soldiers to maintain order and unquestioningly obey their officers. "We must," said Kerensky "have complete calm in the city and complete order in our ranks within three days." Kerensky urged soldiers and officers to join together and trust one another. Duma leaders stressed the fact that their activities had the approval of all members of the Duma committee, including socialists. "Tasks of the State Duma's Executive Committee," published February 28 in *Izvestiia zhurnalistov,* declared that "despite deep differences in the political and social ideals held by members of the State Duma who have joined the Provisional Committee, at this present difficult time they are in total agreement."

The bourgeoisie saw that the Soviet of Workers' Deputies was emerging as a new organ of power; it strove to prevent dual power *(dvoevlastie)* and to concentrate all authority in its own hands. Bourgeois leaders appealed to military units to obey no one else but the Provisional Duma Committee and its orders. Speaking to soldiers of the Grenadier Battalion on February 28, Miliukov argued in favor of sole authority: "This authority is the Provisional Committee of the State Duma. You must obey it and no other. Dual power is dangerous for it threatens to fragment and dissipate our forces." The battalion commander spoke next: "Be sure the State Duma will always act honorably. We will be at its service." Miliukov also expounded the danger of dual power to officers of the First Reserve Regiment stationed in Okhta. "At present we have a single authority to whom everyone must listen, the Provisional Committee of the State Duma. There cannot be dual power." Miliukov told the soldiers of this regiment: "You must side with your officers who will march with the State Duma."[69]

Officers told soldiers the same. In an appeal published in *Izvestiia zhurnalistov* a group of officers asked soldiers to return to their units to cooperate with their officers to restore order. "Let's all work together to achieve final victory over the enemy at the front and at home." The officers assured the Duma Committee they would comply with all the committee's instructions. The commander of the Ninth Reserve Cavalry Regiment told a group of soldiers: "I am going to do everything the chairman of the State Duma orders of me." Soldiers as well made such declarations. During the general elation that marked the first days of the revolution, many soldiers had failed to grasp who their friends and enemies really were. The unctuous speeches of Rodzianko, Miliukov, and other leaders of the Duma Committee confused them, and they often answered calls for union, discipline, and order with the familiar words: "We'll be glad to try." But they soon got over it. Struggling to prevent revival of tsarist norms, discipline of the rod, and the unlimited authority enjoyed by former superiors, they did not take Rodzianko's and Miliukov's advice.

Guchkov entered the fray on behalf of the army. Leader of the Octobrists, chairman of the former Duma, now a member of the State Council, and representative of the War Industries Committee, he tried during the first days of the revolution to suppress the popular uprising as the best way to resolve the situation. Guchkov conferred with General M. I. Zankevich and other military leaders, explained the balance of forces, and, convinced the army could not put down revolution, joined the Duma committee. Guchkov had connections with the army command and was considered an expert on military matters. He had been marked for the army ministries. The Duma Committee appointed Guchkov head of the Military Commission. Engel'gardt was still on the commission, but now he became commander of the Tauride Palace and head of the garrison. When Guchkov was dispatched to units of the Petrograd garrison to bring about the "necessary order" the soldiers greeted him with hostility. Firing at Guchkov's car, they killed one of his companions.[d]

The soldiers resisted the Duma Committee's attempts to restore the previous military system and extend its authority over the troops of the Petrograd garrison. In this, as in many other matters as well, the Duma Committee could not function effectively, for it did not enjoy the trust of the armed people. Lacking a firm base, it vacillated, maneuvered, avoided controversial questions, and tried to refrain from conflicts with the Soviet.

That the liberals displayed such lack of authority, timidity, and indecisiveness distressed writer Zinaida Gippius:

> The liberals have no ties with the revolutionary movement and no concrete plan of action. . . . The Duma leaders are powerless. They don't know what they want, they don't even know whether there should be a tsar or not. All they do is carefully avoid all questions and answers. Take a look at the Committee notices Rodzianko signs. They represent nothing but timidity, confusion, and indecisiveness. This is because the liberals still desperately hope that the tsar will designate the Duma Committee as the official government and give it broad authority. . . . The revolution, not they, has overturned this authority. They but mechanically remain on the surface, passively, without anyone's permission. Of course they have no power, they can't take it themselves; somebody has to give it to them and give it to them from above.[70]

Above all else, the Duma lacked authority because it had no real power: The insurgent workers and soldiers recognized and supported the Soviet of Workers' Deputies instead. The Duma Committee declared itself the authority but in fact lacked power. It issued orders only as long as they did not counteract the directives of the only genuine center of power—the Soviet of Workers' Deputies. It is true that at the time and later the Duma Committee was referred to as "the government," and bourgeois-landlord organizations like the Union of Towns and Union of Zemstvos, the War Industries Committee, the Petrograd City Duma, etc., and even the Allied states recognized it as the Provisional Government. On March 1 *Izvestiia zhurnalistov* printed in boldface: "The French and English ambassadors have officially announced to the chairman of the State Duma that the governments of France and England are negotiating with the Provisional Executive Committee of the State Duma, which expresses the will of the people and is the sole Provisional Government of Russia." Neither recognition by bourgeois-landlord organizations, however, nor negotiations with France and England could endow the Duma Committee with the necessary authority.

[d] Guchkov's aide, Prince D. M. Viazemskii, was killed.

The Duma leaders themselves, and above all by means of a telegram a Duma commissar, Bublikov, sent February 28 all over Russia, created a false notion about the power of the Duma and its committee. Using the railway telegraph system, he informed railwaymen about what was happening in Petrograd. The text declared:

> The Committee of the State Duma has today instructed me to take over the Ministry of Communications. I am promulgating the following order from the chairman of the State Duma: "Railwaymen! The old authorities, who have created chaos in all branches of the administration, are now powerless. The State Duma assumes responsibility for creating a new authority. I appeal to you in the name of the fatherland to save our country. It expects you to do more than discharge your responsibilities—it expects heroism. Trains must move uninterruptedly, better than before. Technical weaknesses and lack of equipment must be compensated for by your wholehearted effort, love of country, and consciousness of how important transport is for the war effort and for serving and supplying the rear. [Signed] Duma Chairman Rodzianko." As one of you, I am convinced you can respond to this appeal and justify the hopes our country places in you. All employees are to remain at their posts. [Signed] Duma Member Bublikov.[71]

This telegram, transmitted to every railroad station, was the first intimation the provinces had of events in Petrograd. Yet it distorted what had taken place. Bublikov related that the draft order from the Duma chairman he gave Rodzianko to sign had begun with the following words: "'The old authorities have fallen.' Rodzianko observed: 'How can you say fallen? Has power really fallen?' He substituted these other words: 'The old authorities are now powerless' and signed the order."[72] The telegram implied that a change had taken place because the old authorities had caused havoc in the state administration and had proved powerless (in what?—E.B.). The telegram also implied that the Duma had expelled the previous government and was forming a new one.

Bublikov's closest assistant, Iu. V. Lomonosov, acknowledged:

> From Bublikov's telegram everyone learned that on February 28 the Duma to all intents and purposes already held power. But was that actually true? Of course not! Bublikov had acted like Bismarck with his Ems Dispatch[e]: he corrected reality, he delayed the natural course of the revolution by surrounding the Duma with a totally undeserved halo. First impressions are always the strongest. All of Russia first heard the news of the revolution this way and thought that the Duma had made it. Months had to pass before the Russian people at large realized this was false.[73]

[e] In 1870 Otto von Bismarck edited a telegram he had received from the Prussian king, which summarized a discussion between the king and the French foreign minister that had taken place at Ems. Bismarck edited the telegram for publication, making it appear as if the Prussian king and French foreign minister had exchanged insults. The Ems Dispatch spurred Napoleon III to declare war on Prussia.

In fact the Duma had not made any revolution. It broke with the tsarist government after the fate of tsarism had for all practical purposes been decided, hoping that it could head up the popular movement and move it in the direction it wanted. Nevertheless, it failed to take charge of the movement. Engel'gardt noted that he, Rodzianko, and others had not joined the revolutionary camp because they wanted to pursue such a course. "We accepted the revolution as an accomplished fact and three days later it looked as if we were leading it, but in reality we were lagging behind and, at the same time, making hopeless efforts to hold back its development."[74]

The Provisional Committee of the State Duma was not the "First Provisional Government" as some authors have written.[75] A peculiar situation had arisen: the Duma Committee declared that it had taken power, yet its power was illusory. The Soviet of Workers' Deputies did not claim power, yet in reality power belonged to it. It was the Soviet, and not the Duma Committee that reflected the will of the people and was the only lawful provisional government of Russia. As the revolution progressed, the influence and authority of the Soviet of Workers' Deputies steadily grew. Peshekhonov wrote:

> Overnight the Soviet, which yesterday had appeared an utterly accidental and unauthorized entity, succeeded in communicating with factories and plants and demanded they send deputies, and these deputies had already been elected and had even arrived. Many elements in the population already knew the Soviet existed as their own elected body. Since yesterday evening its proclamations have been circulating, are read on the streets, etc. The masses apparently know nothing about the Duma Committee. They know of the Duma, but it is not hard to consign it to the old order and discard it along with the other tsarist authorities.[76]

Peshekhonov compared the Soviet to a small crystal in a saturated solution which attracted all active elements. Bourgeois authors also wrote of its growing role. "The self-proclaimed Soviet of Workers' Deputies," noted Duma Deputy S. P. Mansyrev (we must do him justice), "worked to its utmost. By the evening of February 27 it had sent messengers to Petrograd factories and military units to have deputies promptly elected. There were already more than 120 individuals chosen mainly from factories and plants. The Soviet began to be transformed from a self-styled into a real institution, based on the will of the workers." Mansyrev wrote that "the Soviet is constantly in session. Delegations coming to it have been given a most enthusiastic reception; there are detailed conversations, instructions are given; present events are explained and delegates look to the future."[77]

Although the Soviet of Workers' Deputies possessed enormous power, it did not take maximum advantage of it. It fulfilled particular governmental functions but did so incompletely, inconsistently, "without attracting attention." Convinced that only bourgeois power could replace tsarism, the Soviet was not master of the situation when a second wave of revolution swelled up after the autocracy had been overthrown. This decided the question whether the revolution would stop halfway or go on to the finish, make a clean break with the past, and place Russia on the road to the future. A second wave of revolution followed the first.

Against whom was this second revolutionary wave directed?

The Struggle against Bourgeois Power

It was easier to overthrow tsarism after the bourgeoisie had broken with it. Although all elements in the population appeared united on the surface, efforts to reconcile the interests of the bourgeoisie with those of the people were doomed to failure. The contradictions between the bourgeoisie and the workers and soldiers intensified. Before the first wave of revolution against tsarism subsided, the working people began a struggle against the Provisional Duma committee and bourgeois power to consolidate the power of the revolutionary people.

The very course of the strife developed and clarified the demand to form a provisional revolutionary government advanced by the Bolsheviks during the first days of the revolution. The Duma committee and the government it had devised could not respond to popular aspirations and become organs of popular authority. Only the Soviet of Workers' Deputies could create an authentic revolutionary government. The majority in the Soviet hesitated to embark upon this path. "But still," noted Shliapnikov, "no other body capable of creating a revolutionary government existed, and therefore we decided to put our conception of a provisional revolutionary government squarely based on revolutionary democracy and organized in the Soviet before the Petersburg Committee and the Soviet Executive Committee. In theory we assumed it was possible to form a provisional government from the socialist parties that held a majority in the Soviet."[78]

A drive to resolve the question of power in this way assumed an especially grand scale in the Vyborg District. This district, the first to rise against tsarism, had become the center from which the second revolutionary wave mounted. Numerous mass rallies of workers and soldiers took place on the Vyborg side on March 1 and 2, mostly in the building belonging to the Sampsonievskii Brotherhood on Bolshoi Sampsonievskii Prospekt in the heart of the region. This modest building bore no resemblance to the luxurious Tauride Palace. During these days it was not filled with people from all walks of life, from distinguished Duma figures to soldiers, but with a uniform mass of working people, possessing a single goal and will.

On March 1 the Vyborg Bolshevik Organization held its first legal meeting in this building of the Sampsonievskii Brotherhood. The large auditorium in the building was overflowing; a huge number of nonparty workers came to the meeting, and a general political rally took place before the start of the party convocation. The working masses gathered there vehemently opposed the bourgeois-landlord State Duma and its committee. Addressing the gathering, Shutko, a member of the Petersburg Bolshevik Committee, argued that to develop and strengthen the revolution the democracy must forge an organ capable of turning the victory of the revolution in Petrograd into a victory of the revolution all over Russia. Shutko concluded that such a body could only be a provisional revolutionary government which the Soviet of Workers' Deputies must organize.

F. Dingel'shtedt remembers that Ivan Chugurin called the meeting to order and that, following Shutko's report, Vladimir Zalezhskii and other comrades spoke. "The meeting, which had responded with alarm to the news of the organization of a Duma government, passed a resolution by majority vote calling for its removal and transferring power to the Soviet, and for the members of this bastion of the tsarist regime to renounce their plenary powers."[79] The resolution adopted at this meeting was published as a leaflet. A report of the Publications Commission of the Vyborg District Committee of the RSDRP said, "A poster containing the resolution approved at the general meeting of the Vyborg District Committee on March 1 has been published. It called for the election of a provisional revolutionary government to which the Provisional Committee of twelve Duma members would be subordinated, and for members of the State Duma to lay down their authority since it remained a bastion of the tsarist regime."[80]

The complete text of the resolution passed at the general meeting of the Vyborg Organization of the RSDRP on March 1 and published as a leaflet runs as follows:

> A general meeting of the Vyborg District of the RSDRP discussed the present political situation and resolved that: 1) To bring the great cause of revolution to victorious completion it is necessary to form a provisional revolutionary government immediately, squarely based on the insurgent workers and soldiers. 2) To this end the insurgent soldiers must reorganize to finish overthrowing those who have been and still are loyal to the tsarist regime. 3) The emergent Soviet of Workers' Deputies, constantly attracting new revolutionary ranks from among the insurgent people and army, must proclaim itself a provisional revolutionary government and seek to directly subordinate the Provisional Committee of twelve Duma members to the Provisional Revolutionary Government. 4) The Duma should be denied the right to represent the people since it has been elected under a law that served the interests of the tsarist regime that has been overthrown.[81]

Did this resolution mean that the Bolsheviks now favored the creation of a republic of soviets? No, that slogan came later. The Bolsheviks did not yet support Soviet power as a distinct form of state order. They considered the Soviet an organ of revolutionary democracy, the only body enjoying the authority to give the country the provisional revolutionary government necessary to liquidate the tsarist regime once and for all, convoke a national constituent assembly, and establish a democratic republic. In February and March 1917 the Bolsheviks did not demand a Soviet republic, but took a step in that direction, which had considerable significance. On the model of 1905 the Bolsheviks regarded the soviets as organs of the revolutionary-democratic dictatorship of the proletariat and peasantry.

Bolsheviks of the Vyborg side appeared before the masses demanding the Soviet be declared a provisional revolutionary government. On March 1 and 2 Bolshevik agitators spoke at numerous political rallies and meetings. These gatherings passed resolutions based on the declaration of the Vyborg Organization of the RSDRP on March 1.

> 1) All power must be concentrated in the Soviet of Workers' and Soldiers' Deputies, the sole revolutionary government, until convocation of a constituent assembly. 2) The army and people must follow only the orders of the Soviet of Workers' and Soldiers' Deputies and consider instructions emanating from members of the (Provisional—E. B.) Executive Committee of the State Duma invalid. 3) All officials and officers who served the old regime must be neutralized and removed from administration. Similarly, all persons and organizations that are not in sympathy with the Soviet of Workers' and Soldiers' Deputies must also be removed from the administration of the country and the city. 4) The Soviet of Workers' and Soldiers' Deputies must strive to convoke a national constituent assembly to deal with the question of a new state structure and end the war. 5) The Soviet of Workers' and Soldiers' Deputies is requested to hail the revolutionary German proletariat that has begun a struggle against its government.[82]

Vanguard workers supported the Bolshevik call to dismiss the Duma Committee and recognize the Soviet as a provisional revolutionary government. Zalezhskii noted that the workers considered it quite natural that the provisional government would be created by the insurgent people, and that similar resolutions to the effect were not isolated instances. F. Dingel'shtedt went so far as to claim "not one political rally or workers meeting would have rejected this resolution of ours if someone had only proposed it."[83] He described a large rally that took place March 1 in the auditorium of the Ural Cinema. Two thousand workers and soldiers assembled. Dingel'shtedt began reading the manifesto of the Central Committee of the RSDRP, and urged those assembled to fight to create a democratic republic, not waiting for a constituent assembly to implement the basic demands of the revolution—the eight-hour workday, confiscation of landowners' estates, and other measures. Pakhomov, a Bolshevik who had just returned from exile, emphasized that the bourgeoisie had organized the Duma Committee to take power, and appealed to workers and soldiers to assume responsibility for their fate.[84]

To be sure, not all meetings carried such resolutions, as some workers had different attitudes. Although those meeting in the Zibel' Factory on February

28 expressed concern about the individuals in the Provisional Duma Committee, they voted "not to rise against other classes of the population." A meeting of workers in the Geisler Factory on March 1 passed a resolution to the effect that "the success of the revolutionary movement can be guaranteed only when all classes who have taken part in and sympathize with it unite." Vanguard workers, however, had no use for such unity among social classes. They sharply criticized the idea of unity with the bourgeoisie and its Duma Committee. Nevertheless, some workers supported the former position.

Mistrust of the bourgeois Duma Committee was reflected in the pages of *Izvestiia,* although the paper generally cooperated with the bourgeoisie. An article, "A People's Economy," published on March 2, stated that commissars of the Duma Committee had temporarily replaced the old ministers

> but no instructions have been issued about changing the whole system of administration of the country's economic life, not just personnel. The Provisional Duma Committee believes peasant agriculture can succeed without providing peasants land. Does the Provisional Committee think our industrial production will progress without an eight-hour workday? . . . We have no idea of what they intend to do in order to solve the vital, controversial questions the revolution has posed. Can we expect the economy will be for the people? All Russia anxiously awaits answers to these questions.

The working masses kept demanding the creation of a genuinely revolutionary government based on the Soviet even after the bourgeois Provisional Government had been formed with the Soviet's sanction. On March 3 a political rally of one thousand workers and soldiers discussed how the Soviet of Workers' and Soldiers' Deputies had recognized the Provisional Government and resolved:

> 1) This Provisional Government does not truly reflect the people's interests; it is inadmissible to give it authority over the rebellious country, even temporarily. It is inadmissible to empower it to convoke a constituent assembly that has to be convened in unrestricted freedom. 2) The Soviet of Workers' and Soldiers' Deputies must immediately remove this Provisional Government of the liberal bourgeoisie and proclaim itself the Provisional Revolutionary Government.[85]

Political rallies articulating such demands regularly met in the auditorium of the Sampsonievskii Brotherhood building. A Bolshevik named Sudakov told of a rally held there the evening of March 4. The auditorium overflowed with workers from the Vyborg region and soldiers of the Moscow Regiment, many of whom came armed with rifles. M. Latsis chaired it. Sudakov expounded the demands of the RSDRP minimum program and declared it necessary to transfer power to the soviets. Next a student engineer from the railways called for support for the Duma and Provisional Government. A loud uproar broke out in the auditorium, and indignant cries forced the speaker to step down. Taking his place, a Bolshevik, Kuz'min, exposed the true meaning of the slogan to support the Provisional Government, and he met with the sympathy of the assembled group. Sudakov correctly noted the importance of meetings in the Sampsonievskii Brotherhood building in mustering support for the Bolshevik position and in opposing the State Duma and the bourgeois government. They were the first calls from the humble masses of Russia to establish Soviet power.[86]

Vanguard workers asked the soldiers to help as they had done during the first days of the revolution when the fate of tsarism hung in the balance, and now again in the struggle to remove the bourgeoisie and form a genuinely revolutionary government. The conjunction of these two forces ensured victory at this new stage of the revolution, as it had during the first stage. The Vyborg District Committee of Bolsheviks appealed to the soldiers on March 1 to elect representatives to the Soviet: "We must organize, and create a new authority, a provisional revolutionary government that will summon a constituent assembly." The appeal went on:

> Only a constituent assembly convened by a provisional revolutionary government can improve the situation, give the people freedom, and end the sanguinary war. We did not raise the revolutionary banner and spill blood on the streets just to change those in power! We are fighting for a democratic republic, we demand that monastery, crown, absentee, and landlord land be confiscated and transferred to the peasants. We demand establishment of the eight-hour workday. Our representatives in the Soviet of Workers' Deputies must uphold these demands. Comrade soldiers! Up to now you have staunchly defended the cause of freedom. Finish the job you've begun, march in step with the workers.[87]

The Interdistrict Committee of the RSDRP and a group of SRs put forward very much the same slogans in a joint appeal to the soldiers on March 1. Its authors urged the soldiers not to trust the bourgeois authorities but join the workers in forming a provisional revolutionary government to carry out the fundamental demands of the people:

> Petrograd has been in the hands of the soldiers and workers for two days. The Duma, which had been dissolved, picked a Provisional Committee and dubbed it a Provisional Government two days ago. So far you have not heard a single word from Rodzianko or Miliukov about whether land will be taken from the landlords and given to the people. The chances are slim! Soldiers! Watch out! The gentlemen landlords don't fool the people! Go and ask the Duma: will there be land, will there be freedom, will there be peace. . . . Put an end to autocratic arbitrariness. Let's finish the job! Summon a constituent assembly to which all the peasants and workers can send deputies: not like the present Duma, where all that matters is who is richer and of higher rank, or else the cause of the people is ruined.

The leaflet urged soldiers to send representatives to the Soviet. "Your representatives and worker deputies must become a provisional revolutionary government of the people. It will give you land and freedom."[88]

The workers and soldiers who had united to rise against tsarism also had interests in common during the next stage of the revolution, although the soldier masses had not yet formulated their major goals as effectively as the vanguard workers had done. The soldiers had been combating specific actions by the bourgeoisie, particularly the restoration of the old ways in the army. In such cases they, like the leading workers, voiced mistrust of the bourgeoisie and demanded the Soviet of Workers' Deputies form a genuinely revolutionary government. Making the general demands of "bread, peace, and freedom more specific," they spoke out in favor of putting the basic points of the Social Democratic minimum program into practice.

The struggle the revolutionary proletariat waged with the bourgeoisie to win over the soldiers determined how the revolution would develop further. The bourgeoisie wanted to destroy the union between workers and soldiers and subordinate the latter to itself. Yet the soldiers stubbornly opposed these attempts. Rodzianko's order, mentioned above (p. 235), that soldiers must return to their barracks and obey their former officers was correctly assumed by the soldiers to be the first act of counterrevolution, aimed at restoring the old ways in the army. Soldiers demanded the order be immediately repealed. Rafes reported that the Executive Committee of the Soviet listened to Chkheidze's and Kerensky's explanation on this account as members of the Duma Committee. They announced that "the Committee has not yet discussed this order, the Committee cannot assume responsibility for it, it is Rodzianko's own personal initiative. . . . During the debate over the order very caustic and passionate speeches were made, including clear calls to arrest Rodzianko and the Provisional Committee of the State Duma and accusations of provocative action and treason, etc."[89] B. Engel'gardt wrote: "The Soviet considered the wish to restore some semblance of discipline and order among the soldiers as an attempt to check or even stifle the young revolution. The charge of counterrevolution was first made."[90]

Engel'gardt reported that workers refused to print Rodzianko's directive, and the members of the Executive Committee of the Soviet declared they had forbidden its distribution. Nevertheless, the command was actually printed and distributed. V. Bazarov related that he was on duty at the print shop when they brought Rodzianko's order in.

> Two laconic directives to soldiers: return to the barracks and obey officers; not a word about the new regime, about the struggle against the enemy, about supporting it [the new regime—D.J.R.]. . . . We were very confused to receive such a document from the revolutionary authority: the intelligent soldiers with us in the print shop showed their shock. They implored us to induce the Provisional

> Committee of the Duma not to publish this act, maintaining quite reasonably that the soldiers would interpret it as a counterrevolutionary gesture, an attempt to lock insurgent regiments up in their barracks and reimpose the old ways with the help of the officers, supporters of the tsarist government.

For a long time all efforts to convince the Duma Committee to repeal the order came to nothing. Only toward morning "did we succeed in bringing the Provisional Committee to its senses and secure instructions to stop circulating the appeal (the order—E.B.). But it was too late. A Duma automobile had managed to obtain some printed copies and distributed them to the soldiers."[91]

The Bolsheviks tried to harness the spontaneous explosion of discontent Rodzianko's order evoked, rally the soldiers around the Soviet, and have it influence the course of events. Bazarov noted "the revolutionary army displayed amazing restraint and self-control. Instead of rushing with the outraged masses to the Tauride Palace, which could have had disastrous consequences, the soldiers quickly organized, elected representatives, one from each company, and sent them to the Duma to insist upon their demands. The Soviet of Workers' Deputies was transformed into a Soviet of Workers' and Soldiers' Deputies. And the first act of this new body was the famous Order No. 1."[92]

Soldier representatives had not attended the first session of the Soviet of Workers' Deputies on February 27, as the Soviet had not yet formed ties with the garrison in the capital. Shliapnikov noted that the idea of a joint soviet of workers' and soldiers' deputies met with no favor from SRs and Mensheviks. They feared involving the army in the political struggle and declared it was inadmissible to "corrupt" their purely proletarian organ with petit bourgeois elements. Their most conservative part expressed apprehension that "revolutionary work and politics can render the army unfit for combat, and thus they were not anxious to attract soldiers into the organization."[93] Mensheviks and SRs did indeed harbor such attitudes, yet they did not overtly oppose soldiers entering the Soviet. In any case, the Provisional Executive Committee, composed of SRs and Mensheviks, in its first address to the Soviet on elections had urged all troops who had come over to the people "to elect representatives immediately, one for each company." It was impossible to retreat from this appeal.

The soldier masses, awakened by the revolution, looked to the Soviet. N. I. Podvoiskii related: "The soldiers, anxious for directives from the Soviet, addressed each member but did not achieve satisfaction. I remember the night of February 27–28. Two members of the Central Committee Bureau, myself, and a few other comrades in the Tauride Palace decided to harness the movement among the soldiers there for instructions. We proposed they return to their battalions, elect representatives, and demand the workers' deputies allow soldiers' deputies into the Soviet." The next day soldier representatives came to the Soviet meeting to express their views on the Duma Committee and officers. Podvoiskii recalled that SR and Menshevik leaders tried to conceal this from the

Soviet, but the soldiers insisted "they be admitted to the meeting to report on counterrevolutionary steps being taken in several regiments. They did not want to admit them. Soldiers broke into the meeting hall, climbed on the tables, and forced the rest to hear them."[94]

The soldiers' deputies in the Soviet expressed indignation at Rodzianko's directive, regarding it as a manifestation of the policies of the bourgeoisie to defend the old order and as a first strike at the revolution. Here is what Soviet deputies and soldiers said at the meeting on February 28: Gribkov scored the reactionary attitude of the Duma leaders; Sukharevskii declared Rodzianko's instruction a counterrevolutionary act and demanded that only orders signed by the Soviet be considered valid; Savinkov spoke of how Rodzianko's actions were directed against the cause for which workers and soldiers had shed their blood. Many considered it necessary to demand an explanation from Rodzianko. Molotov suggested that Rodzianko's directive be declared a counterrevolutionary provocation and that the Soviet should burn it.

Conciliatory voices also rang out. There were proposals to clarify, elaborate, reach an agreement . . . lodge a protest against Rodzianko's order with Duma Committee members Chkheidze and Kerensky, and protest in the name of the Social Democratic and Trudovik fractions in the Duma, not the Soviet. "Don't aggravate relations," declared the Bundist Rafes. Chkheidze urged, "It's not time to skin a live bear; too much is at stake."[95] The Soviet leaders eventually succeeded in soothing passions and in postponing discussion of major issues to the Soviet's next meeting. No report on what had been said at the meeting appeared in the press. *Izvestiia* merely noted that on the question of measures to organize the army the Soviet decided to clarify the relationship between the State Duma Committee and the Soviet of Workers' Deputies and the first question the latter would take up at its next meeting would be working-class tactics in regard to the general political situation.[96]

Rodzianko's order exacerbated relations between the Duma Committee and the Soviet of Workers' Deputies. Engel'gardt related that at a meeting of the Military Commission on March 1, representatives of the Soviet accused the Duma Committee members of pandering to the counterrevolutionary officers and actually encouraging them. Rodzianko wanted "to wind down the revolution." Faced with such charges, Duma Committee and Military Commission leaders had to fall back on their word. Engel'gardt admitted that Duma attempts to overturn the revolution had encountered staunch opposition from the popular masses. After organizing the Provisional Duma Committee, the bourgeoisie had decided to check further development of the revolution and "restore order." "But the democracy looked at things differently and thought Rodzianko's order premature as tsarism was still a force to reckon with. Counterrevolution was possible, and besides, there was much more to be done."[97] Hoping to calm the soldiers, Engel'gardt signed an order: "Today, March 1, a rumor has circulated among the soldiers in the Petrograd garrison that regimental officers have allegedly been collecting arms from the soldiers. These rumors were investigated in two regiments and proved to be false. As Chairman of the Military Commission of the State Duma, I declare that the most resolute measures will be taken to prevent similar actions by officers including the firing squad for the guilty."[98]

Engel'gardt's order received wide circulation. V. Bonch-Bruevich suggested the printing shop of *Izvestiia* publish 100,000 copies. "Print in the form of a large leaflet Engel'gardt's order that officers who take arms from soldiers will be shot."[99] In his memoirs a Bolshevik, E. Orlov, claims that Chkheidze issued a ruling forbidding disarming soldiers and arresting counterrevolutionary officers in the name of the Executive Committee of the Soviet even before Engel'gardt's order. However, no text of such an order by Chkheidze has been found.[100]

The Soviet Executive Committee straddled the fence. It urged soldiers to obey their officers but at the same time to join the workers:

> The Provisional Committee of the State Duma aided by the Military Commission is structuring the army and appointing commanders to its units. Unwilling to interfere in the struggle with the old regime, the Executive Committee of the Soviet of Workers' Deputies recommends that soldiers maintain a stable organization and obey the Military Commission and the leaders it has appointed. It also advises all military units to elect a representative from each regiment to the Soviet of Workers' Deputies immediately to create a single united front of all elements in the working class. Each soldier should show an active interest in events and do all he can to prevent anyone from undertaking actions contrary to the interests of the people. Comrade soldiers, organize and join your brother workers![101]

Urging soldiers to ignore Rodzianko's order, the Bolsheviks resolutely condemned the Duma leaders. In an appeal to the soldiers of March 1, the Vyborg District Bolshevik Committee wrote: "Officers using the name of Rodzianko and of the entire Executive Committee are calling you to return to the barracks, hand over your weapons, and obey your old superiors. Don't listen to them! This means a return to the old order and to former enslavement."[102] The Bolsheviks proposed that the soldiers hold on to their rifles, not trust the reactionary officers, and choose committees to guide the units. A group of Interdistrictites and SRs made the very same appeal to the soldiers. "Don't let that Romanov gang of nobles and officers deceive you. Take power into your hands. Elect platoon, company, and regimental commanders; elect company committees to deal with the food supply and to control all officers. Accept only officers you know are friends of the people. Obey only deputies from the Soviet of Workers' and Soldiers' Deputies."[103]

A return to the old order in the army posed the threat that the tsarist regime that had just toppled would be restored. The cause for which workers and soldiers had spilled their blood in the streets of the capital was in mortal danger. The masses of workers and soldiers took action and rose up to fight for and defend the revolution and strengthen and consolidate its gains. The officers' attempts to take weapons from soldiers failed miserably. In the Eighteenth Naval and other units soldiers shot several commanders when they tried to disarm them.

The Duma Committee caused tremendous excitement on the streets of Petrograd. Workers and soldiers expressed distrust of the bourgeois leaders and saw the Soviet as the sole defender of their interests. A member of the Vyborg District Food Supply Committee made a "Bureau Report" at the Tauride Palace:

> People appeared among us, inciting the crowd and soldiers not to listen to orders signed by Rodzianko like the one to billet troops in barracks by units. The intent of this command was to disarm and slaughter them with machine guns. Rodzianko alone instigated this, not the Soviet deputies. People requested directives be signed by the Soviet of Workers' Deputies, not by Rodzianko. Individuals began insulting (Rodzianko—E.B.) saying he should be arrested . . . they insisted on an end to the war, for they assumed the German comrades were demanding and working toward the same goal.[104]

In a letter to the Provisional Duma Committee a group of officers reported on the spread of such feelings. "On all the streets one can hear speakers to whom soldiers and people are beginning to listen, charging that the Provisional Government and particularly its chairman have betrayed the people, that they wish to hand the people back to the old authorities, and have every intention to prevent the people from introducing a republican system and convening a constituent assembly."[105]

With no faith in the Duma Committee, the soldiers turned to the Soviet of Workers' Deputies. On March 1 their representatives appeared at the Soviet to discuss the situation in the units with the workers, and devise new forms of military organization. Sokolov made a special report to the soldier deputies, in which he discussed the Soviet's organization and functions and the relations it had with the Provisional Committee of the State Duma and its Military Commission. The soldier deputies' entry into the Soviet led Sokolov to augment the Executive Committee with their representatives. Chosen were A. D. Sadovskii (Menshevik-Internationalist, Sixth Engineering Battalion), A. N. Paderin (Bolshevik, Preobrazhenskii Regiment), F. F. Linde (Menshevik-Internationalist, Finland Regiment), A. Borisov (Menshevik, Lithuanian Regiment), I. G. Barkov (Tsarskoe Selo garrison), Klimchinskii (Izmailovskii Regiment), V. I. Badenko (Menshevik-Internationalist, Reserve Infantry Regiment), Vakulenko (Bolshevik, Egerskii Regiment), Iu. A. Kudriavtsev (SR, Automobile Division of the Red Cross), and Sokolov (a sailor).[106] Thus its third meeting (March 1) saw the Soviet of Workers' Deputies reorganized as the Soviet of Workers' and Soldiers' Deputies. The title of its newspaper also changed accordingly. Beginning with issue number 3 it appeared as *Izvestiia Soveta rabochikh i soldatskikh deputatov* (News of the Soviet of Workers' and Soldiers' Deputies).

Sokolov chaired most of the Soviet meeting on March 1, which discussed

Delegates of the Petrograd Soviet. From a photograph in the Museum of the Hungarian Labor Movement, Budapest.

First session of the Soldiers' Section of the Petrograd Soviet. From a photograph in the Museum of the Hungarian Labor Movement, Budapest.

what should be the new foundations of military life. On scraps of paper he wrote down the basic resolutions passed by the assembly. A report on this topic had not been made to the Soviet, because the matter had been initiated by the soldiers themselves not by the Executive Committee. They were the main speakers. Rejecting Rodzianko's command to return to their barracks and give up their arms, the soldiers bitterly assailed the bourgeois Duma Committee for trying to force them under the old yoke. A soldier, (Maksim) Klivanskii, spoke "of the menacing behavior of the Provisional Committee of the Duma toward the revolutionary army." He asserted the Duma leaders were "a party of order that is trying to turn the toiling people into a bunch of sheep. These leaders fear that workers, soldiers, and peasants will no longer obey them, and they want to use the units loyal to them to strangle the revolution. . . . Soldiers must not give up their weapons, and must obey only the Soviet in political matters."[107]

A soldier, Marchenko, related that officers calculated thus—let the soldiers get it out of their system and then we'll take charge again and they'll have it worse than before. But the soldiers would not let the old officers return and elected their own. The representative of the Egerskii Battalion told how soldiers in the unit expelled officers who had not joined the revolution, elected battalion and company commanders, and took control of the arms depot. A soldier of the Lithuanian Regiment noted that insofar as the Military Commission was the preserve of officers, a Military Commission of soldiers should be formed. A soldier, Kudriavtsev, recommended establishing control over the existing Military Commission. The sailor Sokolov appealed to take up arms and not trust the State Duma and Rodzianko.

A. Tarasov-Rodionov's narrative sheds further light on the soldiers' actions at the March 1 Soviet meeting. One soldier representative said indignantly:

> Is this why we made a revolution, so the State Duma can hang officers around our necks once more?! Of course we agree we have to defend ourselves, but you have to let us decide what officers we want on our own. Those who bashed us in the snout, sympathized with tsars and princes, and those who want to open up the front against the Germans—these we don't need. . . . Now we have our Soviet and now we all recognize we have to have company committees in every unit to look after the food supply and to keep an eye on officers. Let these elected committees and no one else control all arms so that officers receive nothing under any circumstances or on anyone's orders. Don't issue them arms, comrades![108]

The soldier Borisov inquired: "Who will defend our freedoms, who will defend our Soviet? I propose that our Executive Committee immediately publish the strongest possible military edict forbidding the entire revolutionary garrison of Petrograd be sent away under any circumstances." Cornet Saks from the Ninth Cavalry Regiment reported that Guchkov and Engel'gardt had dismissed the entire previous complement of the Military Commission and appointed officers from the General Staff. "It is impossible to leave the military staff of the revolution in such a position. It will now be necessary to scrutinize all their orders and instructions very carefully and, when in the slightest doubt, resort to the Executive Committee of the Soviet of Workers' Deputies. To have our military representatives also on it (the Military Commission—E.B.), I would propose to elect an equal number from the soldiers' section of our Soviet to serve."[109]

A Bolshevik soldier, Paderin, from the Preobrazhenskii Regiment, asserted that officers had the right of command only when troops were in formation or on duty. In political matters, soldiers should obey only the Soviet. "Off duty and out of formation soldiers should be absolutely equal in all political and civil rights. All this stupid rising, facing, and saluting off duty and out of formation must be abolished altogether. We have met in our Soviet not to deal with trifles, but to make revolution. We alone, the representatives of the revolutionary workers and soldiers, are the provisional revolutionary power."[110]

The Soviet allowed only the soldier deputies to vote on these questions. They passed a resolution comprising eight or nine points. An excerpt from the minutes of the meeting on March 1, published in number 3 of *Izvestiia*, enumerated the following ones: "Do not give up arms. Elect company and battalion committees to be in charge of all internal order in the regiments. Group the soldier masses around the Soviet of Soldiers' and Workers' Deputies. Obey instructions of the Military Commission only when they do not conflict with resolutions of the Soviet of Workers' Deputies. Assign soldiers as representatives on the staff of the Military Committee (Commission)." Sokolov related the Soviet had also ruled that "the officer corps has no authority over the soldiers beyond purely military relations," and political leadership must belong to the Soviet of Workers' and Soldiers' Deputies.[111]

In raising the issue of new rules for the army before the Soviet, representatives from several garrison units also wanted to have the Duma Committee approve at least some of them. Engel'gardt recalled that late in the evening of March 1, elected soldier deputies from twenty garrison units came and informed him they "cannot trust their officers, who had not taken part in revolutionary activity, and demand an order be published mandating the conducting of elections in companies, squadrons, batteries, and detachments."[112] The soldiers proposed publishing an order to elect officers, to give soldiers control of all economic operations in the units and establish new relations between leaders and the lesser ranks.

Engel'gardt presented the soldiers' demands to the Duma Committee. Committee members and Guchkov categorically opposed adoption. They instructed Engel'gardt to calm the soldiers by promising them that a commission would be formed in the immediate future to undertake a detailed revision of army life, which would pay particular attention to the problems raised by the soldiers. After pacifying them somehow, Engel'gardt returned to the Duma Committee. Soon representatives from the army units summoned him again. A soldier who introduced himself as a member of the Soviet of Workers' Deputies said: "'A delegation from a number of units insists upon new rules of military organization. The Soviet is vitally interested in this question and invites the Provisional Committee of the Duma to work on them together.' 'I told him,' wrote Engel'gardt, 'the Provisional Committee finds publication of such rules impermissible.' 'So much the better,' the soldier said to me, 'we'll write them ourselves.' Turning sharply, he went away, without another word."[113] This was the end of any attempt to involve the Duma Committee in compiling new rules of military organization.

As mentioned above, the Soviet of Workers' and Soldiers' Deputies passed the new principles of military organization on March 1. It remained to turn them into a single document. Sokolov wrote that at the meeting someone proposed to frame the adopted resolutions as an army order, since "we military men are accustomed to obeying orders, not resolutions." The assembly chose a commission to carry out this proposal and empowered it to sign the order in the name of the Soviet of Workers' and Soldiers' Deputies.[114] A. Sadovskii reported that the drawing up of the document was entrusted to soldiers chosen by the members of the Soviet Executive Committee, not to a special commission. "The night of March 1–2," recalled Sadovskii, "soldiers and members of the Executive Committee gathered in a room (I don't remember which one) with Sokolov. Soldiers surrounded him and dictated the order point by point. Sokolov edited them and the result was Army Order No. 1. Kudriavtsev ran to a shop that printed the order during the night, and it was distributed to all units in the morning."[115]

Shliapnikov, Sadovskii, and Sukhanov all give approximately the same account of the order's origin. Sokolov sat at a long table covered with green cloth, surrounded by soldiers, who were members of the Executive Committee or the special commission. They dictated the paragraphs of the order to him. "Often the group broke into argument. Then everyone would get up, walk over to a window facing a garden lightly sprinkled with snow, and then return to the table and resume writing."[116]

The soldier members of the commission or the Executive Committee of the Soviet led by Sokolov did not draft a new document, but merely reduced the resolution already adopted by the Soviet to an order. The Soviet was the collective author of Order No. 1; this historical document was very much a product of the people's creativity.[117]

The protocols of the Executive Committee and the plenum of the Soviet gave no indication that these bodies sanctioned Order No. 1. After final editing it was apparently read aloud to deputies still present and evoked a storm of delight. Shliapnikov remembered how "soldiers and workers listened to the order in breathless silence. You would have had to see the soldiers' faces to understand the revolutionary significance the document carried. A roar of approval, like a gigantic sigh of relief, rolled through the stuffy overflowing rooms of the Soviet."[118] The next day Order No. 1 appeared in *Izvestiia* under the signature of the Soviet of Workers' and Soldiers' Deputies.

Order No. 1 defined the nature of the new army and established who would control the armed forces, as well as whom they would obey. The first paragraph read: "In all companies, battalions, regiments, depots, batteries, squadrons, various individual service units of the military administration and on naval vessels, committees of elected representatives from the lower ranks of the above-mentioned military units should be elected immediately." Units that had not yet chosen deputies to the Soviet were advised to do so promptly, one from each company. The order ruled that "a military unit obeys the Soviet of Workers' and Soldiers' Deputies and its committees in all political action. . . . Orders of the Military Commission are to be obeyed except when they contradict the orders and resolutions of the Soviet of Workers' and Soldiers' Deputies." This established that the orders and resolutions of the Soviet were the supreme authority for military units.

After coming over to the people and acknowledging the Soviet as their political leader, the soldiers could not allow the old command structure, a bastion of tsarism and the bourgeoisie, to continue to control arms. The revolutionary soldiers had to do so. The fifth paragraph read: "All weapons, rifles, machine guns, armored cars, and so on are to be under the device and control of company and battalion committees and are not under any circumstances to be issued to officers, even on demand."

In subordinating the army to the interests of the revolution, the Soviet could not leave its organization unchanged. Order No. 1 defined a new form of army life and established new relations between soldiers and officers. The order stated:

> In formation and on duty soldiers are to observe the strictest military discipline, but outside the service and the ranks, in their political, civilian and private life, soldiers cannot in any way be deprived of the rights enjoyed by all citizens. In particular, standing at attention and compulsory saluting outside of service has been abolished. In the same manner forms of address for officers such as Your Excellency, Your Honor, and the like have been replaced with Mr. General, Mr. Colonel, etc. Rudeness toward soldiers of any military rank and in particular addressing them with 'thou' *(ty)* is forbidden, and soldiers are obliged to report to company committees every infraction of this rule, as well as all misunderstandings between officers and soldiers.

Thus was the denigration of a soldier's self-respect, which had existed since the days of serfdom, eliminated. No longer part of a docile "herd of cattle," but a revolutionary fighter, the soldier won the right to be a full citizen of Russia.

Order No. 1 was a new constitution for the army. Like every constitution, it defined and strengthened what had already been won in the Petrograd garrison and spread the benefits of the revolution throughout the entire army. The Petrograd Soviet of Workers' and Soldiers' Deputies published the order in the interests of the garrison of the Petrograd District. "To all soldiers of the guard, army, artillery, and navy for immediate and precise execution and to Petrograd workers for their information." The insurgents who controlled the telegraph transmitted Order No. 1 at once to all armies and garrisons, and it became a guide to action everywhere. The rising in Petrograd was of critical significance for the victory of the revolution throughout the country, and the orders and instructions of the Petrograd Soviet were vital to all units of the field army and rear garrisons.

Capitalists and landowners met no step taken during the first days of the revolution with so much hostility as Order No. 1. This is understandable, for it robbed them of the army. The bourgeoisie and the high command believed the order caused "the disintegration" of the army. It was considered a call for unauthorized attacks upon officers. In reality, however, it urged soldiers to observe the strictest military discipline and made attacks upon officers difficult. A session of the Soviet on March 11, in which the command of the military district took part, noted that the Soviet had published Order No. 1 at a time when units of the Petrograd garrison had been without superiors and some officers were opposing the revolution. Thus it was Order No. 1 that made it possible to gain control of the movement and prevent excesses.[119] S. D. Mstislavskii's memoirs make the same claim. He wrote that during the revolution the main task was "to direct the raging sea of soldiers to orderly and disciplined shores, for the old tsarist system was useless. The fact that no officer had taken part in the February Revolution complicated the situation. In view of the mass abstention of the officers, restoration of order could only be undertaken by the soldiers themselves with whatever resources lay at their disposal. Because the officers had chosen to abstain, soldiers had to organize without them."[120]

Order No. 1 brought the "raging sea of soldiers to new shores, not old ones. It signified the beginning of the end of the tsarist army as a stronghold of the bourgeoisie and landlords and an instrument to carry out their imperialist designs. Order No. 1 laid the base for a new revolutionary army. This was precisely the reason why the bourgeoisie and the army high command hated it. Yet their hatred lacked substance, for they lacked power. Engel'gardt later told General Kuropatkin that after taking command of the troops in Petrograd, he was "master of the situation for no more than six hours. Then actual power passed to the Soviet of Soldiers' and Workers' Deputies and he was powerless to stop publication of Order No. 1."[121] Guchkov related that he learned about the order when he returned from Pskov. He immediately telegraphed to inform headquarters about this "arbitrary" action of the Soviet of Workers' and Soldiers' Deputies and asked that steps be taken to stop its circulation, but did nothing himself. "At the center," wrote Guchkov, "the government was powerless to influence the Soviet that was independent of it. We could formulate domestic policy only if we tried for agreement between the Provisional Government and the Soviet of Workers' Deputies. . . . Of course, I could have used my authority as a minister to abrogate the order, but it would not have had any practical consequences."[122]

Order No. 1 strengthened the Soviet of Workers' and Soldiers' Deputies.

Sokolov noted that before this order Duma leaders had treated the Soviet condescendingly and even asked when it would leave the Tauride Palace.

> With the publication of Order No. 1 the position of the Soviet of Workers' Deputies changed dramatically for the better. That was the moment the Soviet realized it was a real factor relying on a genuine force, the Petrograd garrison. Even the so-called friends of the revolution on the right recognized the Soviet as a viable force, the Kadets and similar elements, who up to then had "merely tolerated" the Soviet in the Tauride Palace. . . . Before publication of Order No. 1, soldiers came in crowds to the Tauride Palace and had announced their desire to meet someone from the government. Now they went directly to the Executive Committee to make themselves known and sign up.[123]

The soldiers read more into Order No. 1 than was really there, and they went further than had been intended. The order had weakened the officers' authority over the soldiers, and the soldiers tried to eliminate the officers' authority entirely. Although Order No. 1 had called for the election of company and battalion committees, the soldiers had actually popularized the principle of electing officers.[124]

New procedures were underway in the army even before official promulgation of Order No. 1. Many units in the Petrograd garrison began removing old officers and electing new ones on March 1. The Reserve Battalion of the Egerskii Regiment removed commanders who were "unsuitable to be officers of revolutionary guards units." Soldiers in the Petrograd Cavalry Division elected a division commander, a commander of the noncombatant division, squadron commanders, and other commanders and superiors from officers who had joined the revolutionary movement. A general meeting of the Okhtenskii Infantry Command on March 1 resolved: "Not to accept into the command Colonel Sheludchenko, Ensign Kokhanov, and Sergeant Major Ziulin, who lack our trust and who have not joined the movement. Ensign Bunakov has been asked to take charge of the unit and Staff Captain Aleksandrov and Ensign Kubyshkin to serve as the junior officers."[125]

On March 1 the soldiers of the Reserve Battalion of the Moscow Guards Regiment discussed whether they would take back the officers who had abandoned them during the decisive days of the revolution.

> They decided not to take them back. They all went out onto the parade ground. The Provisional Government's order urging officers to join their units was brought out. Officers were delighted, but the soldiers began to shout: 'We don't need them. Arrest them!' Soldiers from other units came up. . . . They demanded the officers surrender themselves and their arms. . . . They elected company commanders from among their comrade soldiers, arrested two officers, and sent them to the Tauride Palace.[126]

In several instances Bolshevik workers participated in the election of officers. Kaiurov related how he met two companies of soldiers in the engineering corps.

The commander made a speech to them congratulating them on the overthrow of the old government and went on to say that it now remained to vanquish the foreign foe. The Provisional Government appealed to soldiers to remain calm, to return to their barracks, and to obey their officers as before.

> Several individuals cried out: "We're happy to try!" The majority looked around in confusion. I asked to be recognized. "Comrades, has workers' blood been spilled in the streets of Petrograd for three days so as to replace one landlord with another?. . . The proletariat will not return to work until it has won its rights . . . we cannot rest until workers and peasants are in power. . . ." The officers were silent. . . . I proposed to arrest them and to choose new officers from among the men. A roar of approval followed. Company commanders were elected on the spot.[127]

Thus began the struggle for the army. Would the relationship between the rank and file and the command change? Would the old army continue serving the tsarist regime, or would this vital part of the state apparatus be reconstructed along new lines? The bourgeoisie strove to prevent fundamental change in the tsarist army and make it serve its interests. The workers and soldiers wanted to destroy the old army and to lay the groundwork to build a revolutionary armed force.

The Duma Committee relied on the old officer corps to implement its policies. As the revolution became national these officers could not come to the defense of tsarism and after grave doubt and vacillation they were forced to break with it and recognize the Provisional Duma Committee. The overwhelming majority of Petrograd garrison officers declared they would unquestioningly carry out all instructions from the Duma Committee and loyally and honorably serve the new order which had replaced the tsarist regime. For two days, March 1 and 2, the garrison officers were registered in accordance with the order of the Duma Committee. A crowd of officers of all ranks filled the rooms, corridors, and the staircase in the vast building of the Army and Navy Assembly. The officers put their commissions on large trays or in baskets for registration. The signature of a staff member of the Duma Military Commission authenticated the documents. The Military Commission gave the officers individual charges, placed them at the head of units, or held them in reserve in the anticipation of future tasks.

Officers in the capital met in the same army and navy building on March 1. The fifteen hundred participants in this meeting passed the following resolution: "Officers in Petrograd, marching shoulder to shoulder with the people, have assembled at the recommendation of the (Provisional—E.B.) Executive Committee of the State Duma. They realized that the people must be organized and concerted work undertaken at the rear as soon as possible to bring the war to a victorious conclusion and unanimously resolve to recognize the authority of the Executive Committee of the State Duma until convocation of a constituent assembly."[128] Another two thousand officers in the capital passed a similar resolution the next day.

The officers' support could not shore up the Provisional Duma Committee, as the soldiers expressed their mistrust of the officer corps and of the State Duma. They doubted the officers had sincerely and permanently joined the people; after all, this had happened after the revolution had already triumphed. Stankevich recalled that the soldiers of the engineering battalion responded rather coldly to his report that the Duma Committee had formed a Provisional Government and, although he spoke with enthusiasm, "a chill could be felt in the auditorium."[129]

The soldiers undermined the authority of the officers and of the entire organization of the old army. They foiled the counterrevolutionary Provisional Committee of the State Duma designed to restore the old system in the army, and above all refused to disarm. The soldiers kept their weapons and thereby shattered the military power of tsarism. This weakened the new bourgeois authorities. The soldiers and workers threatened the very existence of bourgeois power. A journalist named V. Karik wrote in his diary on March 2 that there was agitation against Rodzianko, Miliukov, and other moderate members of the government, and many Bolsheviks were calling upon soldiers not to obey their officers. In a later entry (March 14) he wrote "the workers, spurred on by the Bolsheviks, have taken the bit in their teeth and regardless of circumstances, are demanding implementation of the maximum program—nothing short of that."[130] Karik greatly exaggerated, for no one was demanding the realization of the maximum program, even though a struggle to implement the Social Democratic minimum program and end the imperialist war had definitely begun. At numerous political rallies loud appeals for peace, establishment of a democratic republic, and transferring the land to the peasants rang out.

At one meeting a speaker revealed the true nature of Rodzianko, who had been agitating for war to a victorious conclusion.

> No wonder! He's got something to save. Just take a trip to Ekaterinslav province. There he has thousands and thousands [of acres-D.J.R.] of black earth, and what fine land at that, comrades! Whose land is it, you'll ask? It's Chairman Rodzianko's, they'll tell you, comrades. Then go and ask the same question in Novgorod and Smolensk provinces: who owns these rich estates and endless forests? Duma Chairman Rodzianko, they'll tell you, comrades. And then just go and ask: who owns these immense wineries? Who owns this big factory supplying stocks for rifles at exorbitant prices for the millions in our army? The Duma chairman, they'll tell you, comrades. Well, then, you ask, comrades, why doesn't Duma Chairman Rodzianko fight for total victory?

His words found universal favor with the soldiers. Irate cries rang out: "Down with Rodzianko! Down with the war!"

On March 1 Rodzianko informed Ruzskii that "a frightful revolution has broken out that will be hard to combat." He expressed apprehension he might be incarcerated in the Peter-Paul Fortress, "since the agitation is directed at everything moderate and restrained in its demands."[131] On March 3, in a telephone conversation with Ruzskii, Rodzianko reported that a soldiers', essentially a peasants', revolt had broken out in Petrograd; soldiers, after all, were "peasants taken from their plows, and now they are advancing all their peasant demands." "All the crowds were saying was: 'Land and freedom!,' 'Down with the dynasty!' 'Down with the Romanovs!' 'Down with the officers!' And in many units men have begun striking officers. Workers join in and total anarchy reigns."[132]

What Rodzianko called anarchy was actually a further development in the revolution. When cries of anarchy and disorder came up soldiers pointed out not without reason: "What anarchy? The minute the land question is mentioned it's anarchy. So everything is anarchy then!" From February 28 to March 2 the revolution in Petrograd had developed at breakneck speed. What looked extremely radical in the morning was doubtful by noon, and by evening was already out of date. A clear pattern emerged. "The evening of March 1, when the victory of the revolution was no longer in doubt," wrote Engel'gardt, "a second revolutionary wave crested against the old customs, the old way of life, and the old discipline."[133] During this new phase of the struggle, the workers and soldiers moved to get rid of the bourgeoisie they distrusted as well as to destroy the tsarist regime completely.

The Duma Committee and the staff of the Military Commission followed events in the streets of the capital with growing alarm and glanced uneasily at the left wing of the Tauride Palace, where the Soviet of Workers' Deputies was housed. Rumors circulated that crowds of people were on their way to the Tauride Palace to disperse the State Duma, arrest the Duma Committee, and transfer power to the Soviet. Colonel Polovtsev in the Military Commission wrote that the Soviet of Workers' and Soldiers' Deputies was becoming a more and more "disagreeable" institution, that it was speaking out against the State Duma and had sent observers to watch the Military Commission. "On the morning of March 1 someone said today would be famous and perhaps would be celebrated the way the French celebrate the storming of the Bastille. To this, Palchinskii observed that 'perhaps we are now prisoners in the Bastille.' And, indeed, it was quite unpleasant to hear speakers from the Duma platform urge the crowds to destroy the bourgeoisie, which meant us."[134]

A. Tyrkova also observed that the forces on the left grew stronger. She wrote in her diary that "terrible news" came in from the regiments. While Kadet leaders (generals without an army—emphasized Tyrkova) tried to prove the need to preserve the monarchy and one of them, V. Maklakov, maintained the street had no right to change the fundamental laws of the empire, political rallies and demonstrations took place all over the city; workers and soldiers carried red banners inscribed with "Land and Freedom" and "A Democratic Republic." On March 3, Tyrkova jotted down: "On the whole, less threatening than yesterday. But it's still dangerous."[135]

Supreme Headquarters received reports from the capital during these days confirming that a new revolutionary wave had swollen up between February 28 and March 2. They originated with the military authorities, who were especially alarmed by the mood of the soldiers who would not obey their officers and marched to the Soviet with the workers. On February 28 the Chief Naval Staff reported: "The Duma is trying to get the troops back into their barracks and subordinate them to their officers. Only it needs action by the government that would initiate the calming process." The staff pointed out that delay was extremely dangerous; "a workers' organization may form, raise the socialist banner, and eliminate the Duma."[136] The next day, March 1, the Naval Staff informed headquarters: "It is very difficult to maintain order. A dangerous possibility exists of a schism within the Duma Committee itself, and the far left revolutionary parties may break away from the Soviet of Workers' Deputies and form their own group."[137] Duma member Oznobishin later reported that Rodzianko proposed a secret meeting of several Duma members, which was held in a library in one of the Duma's remote areas. The meeting showed that the State Duma was gradually losing power, which was passing to the Soviet of Workers' Deputies. "We have to do something. Yet no one could say for sure what it was. Then Karaulov said, 'we must arrest the Soviet of Workers' Deputies. If the State Duma will give me a proper mandate, I'll do it myself with my Cossacks.' Such a practical, sensible, sober solution to the problem confused the meeting. A brief exchange of views began, accompanied by timid glances at the door. No one said 'yes' or 'no,' but the number of participants at the meeting quickly began to thin out."[138] The Duma leaders' indecisiveness was entirely understandable. They had no forces to remove much less arrest the Soviet, for even the Cossacks could not be considered reliable. The Duma leaders had no choice but to reach an agreement with the Soviet.

Carrying out the responsibilities of the head of the Main General Staff, General Aver'ianov telegraphed Alekseev on March 2:

> The Provisional Committee is doing everything it can to prevent the troops from going over to the workers' party of the extreme left and make them obey their officers, but the vigorous propaganda of the Soviet of Workers' Deputies is undermining these efforts. Although the Provisional Committee and the Soviet of Workers' Deputies agreed today it was necessary to restore order in the armed forces and establish ties with their leaders, the agreement is unstable and disruption among the troops goes on.[139]

Events occurring from February 28 to March 2 strengthened the Soviet of Workers' and Soldiers' Deputies and made it the leading political force. Colonel Domanevskii, whom the General Staff had sent to lead the punitive expedition for General Ivanov, told the latter only an agreement between Duma moderates and the Duma Committee could stop the burgeoning movement. Domanevskii remarked:

> The insurgents display two clear tendencies: some side with the Provisional Government chosen by the Duma; others support the workers' Soviet. The

former have remained loyal to the monarchist principle and wish only a few reforms, since their goal is to eliminate the disorders as quickly as possible in order to get on with the war. The latter have gone to extremes and want to end the war. Prior to March the Duma government enjoyed high prestige and was genuinely in control of the situation, at least in the capital. But it was clear that every day the position of the Duma government, lacking lawful legitimacy, was becoming more difficult, and that it was more likely power might pass to the extreme left. All this led to the conclusion that at present an armed struggle would only complicate and worsen the situation, that each hour was dear, and that order and normality might most easily be restored by agreement with the Provisional Government.[140]

A new onslaught by the workers and peasants advanced the revolution aimed against the monarchy and also established bourgeois power. The proletarian vanguard insisted the Soviet of Workers' Deputies form a provisional revolutionary government. It is true that many elements in the working class and most soldiers had not yet come out directly in favor of this demand. In distrusting the State Duma and its committee, however, they objectively fought to implement this goal. Creating a provisional revolutionary government by the Soviet would not as yet have meant establishing a dictatorship of the proletariat. Even though the Soviet of Workers' and Soldiers' Deputies then still seemed to be an organ of a revolutionary-democratic revolution, it was destined to bring about a quick and painless transition to a socialist revolution.

Lenin called his first "Letter from Afar," written on March 7, 1917, "The First Stage of the First Revolution." Quoting Skobelev's words, cited in the epigraph to this chapter, Lenin remarked:

> I cannot judge from here, from my accursed afar, how near this second revolution is. Being on the spot, Skobelev can see things better. . . . I am merely emphasizing the confirmation by Skobelev, an "outside witness," i.e., one who does not belong to our party, of the *factual* conclusion I drew in my first letter, namely: that the February–March revolution was merely the *first stage* of the revolution. Russia is passing through a peculiar historical moment of *transition* to the next stage of the revolution, or, to use Skobelev's expression, to a "second revolution."[141]

The second revolutionary wave that burst out between February 28 and March 2 indicated the bourgeois-democratic revolution was becoming a socialist revolution. The bourgeoisie saw the threat and did everything it could to hold back the wave. It wanted to remove the Soviet of Workers' and Soldiers' Deputies and take all power itself in order to stop the further development of the revolution. The power struggle intensified.

How did it proceed and what results did it bring?

FIVE

Dual Power

> The highly remarkable feature of our revolution is that it has brought about a *dual power.*
>
> V. I. Lenin

The Formation of the Provisional Government

The bourgeoisie had been preparing a new Russian government for a long time. It wanted the tsar to grant a "responsible ministry" or at least a "ministry of confidence." Lists of candidates for the new ministers circulated already back in 1915, and were even published. During the first days of the revolution the Duma leaders likewise insisted on a new government. The tsar procrastinated, however, when Rodzianko began negotiating with members of the Romanov dynasty, located at Tsarskoe Selo and in Petrograd, to find a mutually acceptable way out of the situation.

Rodzianko had contacted the tsar's uncle, Grand Prince Pavel Aleksandrovich, commander of the guards. Rodzianko's aide, the lawyer N. I. Ivanov, relayed messages between the Tauride Palace and Pavel Aleksandrovich at Tsarskoe Selo. Since it was known that Nicholas II had left headquarters for Tsarskoe Selo, Pavel Aleksandrovich agreed to be the first to explain to him why it was necessary "to grant" a ministry responsible to the Duma and thereby lay the foundation for a constitutional system. It was proposed to shroud the tsar's concession in the form of a manifesto, which was already being drawn up. Fearing that Aleksandra Fedorovna would somehow convince her husband to act otherwise, the initiators of this venture wanted to speak with the tsar before he saw his wife.

But time lapsed and the tsar did not show up or send any orders. Nicholas II had been unable to break through to the capital where, in the meanwhile, events had become extremely threatening for the monarchy. It was decided to send under the tsarina's and grand princes' signatures a draft manifesto to the tsar at Supreme Headquarters regarding a "responsible ministry." Although Aleksandra Fedorovna rejected the scheme,[1] the three oldest grand princes approved it.

The manifesto document said that the tsar had intended to reorganize the government on a broad popular basis as the war drew to a close, but that recent events made it necessary to introduce reforms sooner. Not supported by legislative institutions, the government had failed to foresee and prevent the unrest occurring in Petrograd. The manifesto called the growing revolution a "disturbance" and expressed the hope that it would be quelled. In the name of the tsar the manifesto proclaimed: "We grant the Russian government a constitutional system and decree the resumption of the State Council and State Duma session, which had been interrupted. We entrust the chairman of the State Duma to form a provisional cabinet at once that enjoys the country's confidence and which, in agreement with us, will convoke a legislative assembly needed to consider the government's urgent proposal for new fundamental laws for the Russian empire."[2]

Pavel Aleksandrovich endorsed the draft manifesto of March 1. He signed it, crossed himself, and exclaimed: "What a coincidence. Today is the anniversary of my brother's death!" Such thoughts must have haunted Pavel, for on March 1, 1881, members of the People's Will[a] had killed his brother Alexander II. I wish you "Good luck!" Pavel Nikolaevich said to Ivanov, who sped off to Mikhail Aleksandrovich and Kirill Vladimirovich in Petrograd, next in line to succeed to the throne.

"I am in complete agreement that this is absolutely necessary," Kirill said, affixing his signature. "I also believe there is no other way out and such a measure is necessary," Mikhail Aleksandrovich declared while signing. On February 28 he informed his wife, M. Brasova: "Our minds aren't given a moment's peace. It is imperative for us to make arrangements with the [provincial] authorities where we rent an estate." The next day Mikhail wrote his wife less elusively. "Events are developing with dreadful speed. . . . I signed a manifesto that His Majesty should have signed. On it are the signatures of Pavel Aleksandrovich and Kirill and now mine, the oldest of the grand princes. This manifesto marks a new beginning for Russia."[3]

A new beginning for Russia was indeed underway, but it had nothing to do with the manifesto. On March 1 the document was presented to the Duma, apparently for its approval and dispatch to the tsar. Unable to deliver it by car, Ivanov walked through the streets that were packed with people and realized that the manifesto would not satisfy the embittered masses. He wrote:

> I carried the manifesto to the Provisional Committee, and with each step I became more and more convinced that the Romanov cause was lost, that Rodzianko would not escape with his cabinet, and that the masses needed a bigger sacrifice. This time Rodzianko did not appear as a solemn triumvir in the

[a] One of the more colorful and historically significant populist groups in nineteenth-century Russia. Its goals were to overthrow the autocracy and establish a democratic republic based on "the people's will." Believing a political struggle was necessary to achieve their goals, they advocated the use of individual terror.

> revolutionary chariot, but as a helpless driver who had lost the reins. He even seemed to have outwardly given up. "I think this is too late," I said about the manifesto. "I am of the same opinion," he answered. "I will give the manifesto to Miliukov and he will confirm its receipt."[4]

The draft manifesto apparently never reached the tsar. Moreover, events were unfolding with such speed and determination that it was impossible to stop them with a promise to grant a new version of the ill-starred manifesto of October 17 [1905—D.J.R.]. The draft manifesto reflected an early stage of the revolution that had even been surpassed by the First Russian Revolution. Ivanov answered Mikhail Aleksandrovich's question about the fate of the manifesto he had signed. "The manifesto is already history. Those considered masters of the situation are not dictating what happens in the Tauride Palace. . . . The role of the Provisional Duma Committee is actually declining. Rodzianko, Kerensky, and others of that ilk are bobbing like buoys in a raging sea and merely legalize everything the crowd decides. No one dares predict what's in store for us tomorrow."[5]

Events pushed the Duma leaders further than they had intended to go. To save the monarchy, they had to sacrifice Nicholas himself. The State Duma Committee back on February 28 had discussed a long-existing plan for Nicholas II's abdication in favor of his son Aleksei, under Mikhail Aleksandrovich's regency. The Duma protocols read: "The rush of events, the mood of the army units, of their commanding officers and of the masses would indicate that Nicholas II's abdication is unavoidable."[6] When the Duma Committee drafted this abdication document on February 28, the committee discussed sending Rodzianko and Shidlovskii to present it to the tsar. At first the Duma leaders decided to postpone the trip, as no one knew where the tsar was. Then the Soviet's opposition to the trip became known, and without its sanction, railwaymen would not provide trains. Thus, Rodzianko's actions were duplicitous—he negotiated with Pavel Aleksandrovich to preserve the throne for Nicholas II, yet at the same time planned to secure the tsar's abdication.

Shidlovskii's memoirs confirm the official version of the discussion of the abdication. According to him, the Provisional Duma Committee decided to demand Nicholas II's abdication and to send Shidlovskii and Rodzianko to the tsar. "Our proposed trip was poorly planned. The possibility of our arrest was not considered, nor that troops loyal to the tsar might resist. On the other hand, we discussed arresting the tsar, but not where to take him or what to do with him. In general the undertaking was amateurish. I began to await our departure. One o'clock came, two, three. We phoned the Nikolaevskii Railway Station repeatedly and asked whether a train was ready, but to no avail. For some reason none were."[7]

As mentioned in the preceding chapter, the situation in Petrograd had become even more alarming and dangerous for the bourgeoisie. The Duma Committee lacked authority. The insurgent people did not trust it and were obeying the Soviet instead. In view of this, Duma leaders continued their efforts to contact the tsar but decided to organize a government before receiving his sanction. On March 1, 1917, the Provisional Duma Committee resolved: "To stave off anarchy and restore public order following the overthrow of the old regime, the Provisional Committee of the State Duma has decided to organize a new government before convocation of a constituent assembly that will determine the future form of government of the Russian state. For this purpose the Provisional Committee has set up a Provisional Council of Ministers composed of the following individuals, whose former civic and political activities ensure them the country's trust."[8]

Membership in "the ministry of trust" was based on the list compiled before the revolution. Prince G. L'vov, named prime minister, was summoned from Moscow without delay. On March 1 he met with the Duma Committee. Miliukov subsequently wrote that this conversation disappointed him greatly. "We did not sense a leader before us. The prince, evasive and cautious, responded to events with vague formulations and generalities." "He is weak-willed and unresourceful," Miliukov said of him afterward. The character alone of the future chairman of the Provisional Government, however, cannot explain L'vov's behavior at this meeting. The bourgeoisie's precarious situation also contributed to L'vov's submissiveness and caution.

In organizing a government, the Provisional Duma Committee counted on the bourgeoisie, whose organizations expressed complete trust in the Duma Committee and approved its efforts to establish a government. In an appeal to the people of Russia, the Central War Industries Committee said that creation of a single provisional authority was now necessary, that "such an authority can emanate only from the State Duma, for it alone can muster authority in the eyes of the entire country, the entire army, and our valorous allies."[9] The bourgeois statesmen heading the War Industries Committee enjoined the population to place power at the State Duma's disposal, and not to tolerate reprisals, disagreements, and uncoordinated actions.

The Duma Committee welcomed the support of the industrial barons united in the Congress of Representatives of Trade and Industry. On March 2 the congress declared "it is placing itself at the complete disposal of the Provisional Duma Committee. It regards the committee's orders and instructions as obligatory, until the creation of a new state administration." The congress called on "Russia's entire merchant-industrial class to forget party and social differences that can now only benefit the enemies of the people, and to unite more cohesively around the Provisional Duma Committee and place all of our resources at its disposal."[10]

Such support did not prevent the Duma from recognizing it was treading water. It lacked real power. The armed worker and soldier masses believed in and followed only the Soviet. That is why, after deciding to form a government, the Duma Committee failed to do so without the Soviet's support. Up until this point the bourgeoisie had favored reaching an agreement with the tsar. Now, after it was no longer advantageous to do so, the bourgeoisie had to reorient itself and find other allies. Up until this point the bourgeoisie had waited for the tsar to form a ministry of trust. Now it had to form such a ministry with the autocracy's enemies.

The Provisional Duma Committee began conferring with the Soviet Executive Committee over the formation of a government. Duma leaders challenged the Soviet either to support the government that the Duma would create, or take power itself. Yet the Soviet leaders were not about to seize power. Maintaining that the revolution was bourgeois in nature, they believed that power must belong to the bourgeoisie, and they therefore looked upon creation of a government by the Duma Committee as altogether natural. SR and Menshevik leaders said that without the bourgeoisie it was impossible to defeat tsarism, govern the country, end economic ruin, etc. The Soviet's support of the Provisional Government created by the Duma Committee signified in essence a voluntary capitulation to the bourgeoisie, a transfer of power to it that had been won by the people. Sukhanov averred that in salvaging the revolution, fortifying its victory over tsarism, and establishing a democratic regime, the victorious people would have to "transfer power to their class enemies, to the privileged bourgeoisie."[11]

The Soviet, without any reservations or strings attached, carried resolutions to do just this. The majority of Soviet leaders held, however, that in yielding power to the bourgeoisie they must demand limits upon the bourgeoisie's authority and political rights and freedoms for the population. The Soviet leaders maintained that, in transferring power to the bourgeoisie, they must neutralize bourgeois power and not give it the opportunity to be used against the people. Moreover, the Soviet leaders feared that workers' excessive demands would frighten the bourgeoisie, whose refusal to take power would be catastrophic. This is why the Soviet Executive Committee did not present socioeconomic demands to the future government, did not bring up such matters as the eight-hour workday or confiscation of landlords' estates, did not question the state's foreign policy, or raise the question of ending the war. The Soviet leaders especially tried to skirt this last concern, even removing it from the agenda, for it was most likely to provoke disagreement with Duma leaders.

The Soviet Executive Committee discussed the question of power on March 1. The protocol of this meeting has been lost and memoir accounts must be consulted to reconstruct what took place. Urgent matters interrupting discussion of the question of power kept the committee from the main business. Although the Executive Committee reached relative agreement while discussing military, technical, and organizational questions, it was rent by discord while debating the question of power. Sharp disagreements between the parties of the revolutionary proletariat and the petit bourgeois groups now surfaced. In accord with the manifesto of the Central Committee Bureau of the RSDRP, the Bolsheviks proposed that the revolutionary democracy seize the country's administration and form a provisional revolutionary government from among members of the Soviet. According to Shliapnikov, eight of the thirty members of the Executive Committee championed this view: A Shliapnikov, P. Zalutskii, V. Molotov, K. Shutko, A. Paderin, A. Sadovskii, P. Aleksandrovich, and I. Iurenev. The Bolshevik proposal stemmed from the entire course of events; the revolution had brought the insurgent people to the point of realizing a provisional revolutionary government. The armed masses of workers and soldiers supported the Soviet, whose Executive Committee had absolute revolutionary authority at its disposal. The Soviet could have removed the bourgeoisie from power easily.

"We proposed to the Executive Committee," wrote Shliapnikov, "to form a provisional revolutionary government from those parties that had joined the Soviet. The implementation of the minimum demands of both socialist parties' [Bolshevik and Menshevik—D.J.R.] programs, as well as ending the war, must be its agenda."[12] This was exactly what the SRs and Mensheviks who made up the majority in the Executive Committee did not want. Wishing to maintain good relations with the Duma Committee, they dissociated themselves from the Bolsheviks' antibourgeois and antiwar policies and spoke out against revolutionary power. The Soviet Executive Committee advocated a transfer of power to the bourgeoisie and formation of a bourgeois government.

But should representatives of the democracy take part in such a government? Some Mensheviks, SRs, and Bundists backed participation in the bourgeois government. They argued that the revolution otherwise would not be brought "to a favorable end," and that the old authorities would not be completely swept away. On the day the Executive Committee met, March 2, an article appeared in *Izvestiia*, "The Democracy's Participation in the Provisional Government," which articulated this point of view. It noted that, in entering the government, representatives of the democracy would prevent the bourgeois parties and Duma Committee from compromising with the old order, and would not give the Provisional Government the opportunity to stop at half reforms, but would encourage it to call a constituent assembly and create a republican order. According to the article, a rupture between the Soviet and Provisional Government would set the bourgeoisie back, and the democracy alone could not create a state apparatus. The democracy "alone in the struggle with the coalition of all bourgeois elements was not yet strong enough to carry out state-organizational work of such colossal magnitude."

The question of the socialists' entry into the Provisional Government was a practical one. The Duma Committee offered the Ministry of Labor to Chkheidze and the Ministry of Justice to Kerensky. Chkheidze refused the office, but Kerensky wavered at first and then accepted the post. The Soviet Executive Committee did not want representatives of the democracy to join the Provisional Government, and favored preserving its strictly bourgeois character. As Sukhanov reported, this decision was carried by a vote of thirteen against seven or eight. Rafes also noted that a significant majority of the Executive Committee opposed participation in the government, but added that the committee postponed final resolution of this matter until the views of the ruling party committees were clarified. The Soviet Executive Committee decided to leave the appointment of ministers completely to the Duma Committee, merely insisting that it be notified of the candidates; where appropriate, it retained the right to reject the most unacceptable of them.[13]

In transferring power to the bourgeois government, the Soviet Executive Committee demanded the Duma Committee and government carry out three political reforms: the declaration of political freedoms, a complete and general political amnesty, and the speedy convocation of a constituent assembly. Proposals were carried to extend all civil rights to soldiers, to abolish the police and replace it with a decentralized people's militia, and to democratize organs of local government through general elections as soon as possible. To defend the revolution, it was proposed to pressure the government not to disarm and remove from Petrograd military units that had taken part in the revolution.

Was the demand made at this Executive Committee meeting to establish a democratic republic? According to Sukhanov, "the immediate declaration of a democratic republic was promoted more urgently than other points during the Executive Committee's deliberations."[14] Sukhanov himself opposed this demand, fearing that it would drive away the bourgeoisie. He maintained that the Soviet Executive Committee had decided not to insist on the declaration of a democratic republic and to limit itself to a call for the convocation of a sovereign constituent assembly. The Soviet Executive Committee's report to the plenum that day, however, suggests otherwise. Judging by this report and several memoirs, the Executive Committee favored a democratic republic but withdrew this demand later, under pressure from Duma leaders.

Once the Duma enlisted the Soviet Executive Committee's support, its representatives began conferring with the Duma Committee. Sukhanov in detail and Miliukov in brief described these deliberations. On the basis of their memoirs it is possible to judge how and to what both sides agreed. The talks took place on the evening of March 1–2. Chkheidze, Sokolov, Steklov, and Sukhanov represented the Soviet Executive Committee. Miliukov took the most active part in the discussions from among the Duma Committee. According to Sukhanov, the future head of government, Prince L'vov, did not utter a single word during the talks. Nor did Kerensky, who sat in gloomy meditation, take part in the negotiations, which were conducted as a private conversation. No one chaired them or took minutes.

Concerned most with "the reign of anarchy" in the capital, the Duma Committee tried to convince the Soviet's representatives "to restore order." Yet there was no need for the Duma members to force an open door. The Soviet's representatives announced that their main "technical" task lay in the struggle against anarchy, which was as important to them as it was to the Duma Committee, and that the Soviet was taking measures to improve relations between soldiers and officers. Further, the Soviet's leaders made it clear that this was not the purpose of the meeting. It was called to create a new government.

> The Soviet of Workers' Deputies' appeals to the privileged elements to form a provisional government . . . and the Soviet, as the organizational and ideological center of the popular movement, as the only organ capable of controlling this movement, as the only organ in the capital having real force at its disposal, wishes to express its attitude toward the government being formed by the political right and to clarify how it sees the government's tasks and, to avoid misunderstandings, to make demands on behalf of the entire democracy to the government, created by the revolution.[15]

Steklov presented the Soviet's position. He cited historical examples and the Western European experience, and expressed the hope that the new government would accept the Soviet's demands and publish them as its own program. "Extreme demands" were not put forth, the questions of land and the eight-hour workday were not raised by anyone, discussion of the question that especially alarmed the Duma leaders, that of war and peace, was avoided. Satisfied that the Soviet Executive Committee did not promote the slogan "Down with the War," which resounded on the streets of Petrograd, Miliukov exclaimed: "Yes, in listening to you I realized how radical our workers' movement has become since 1905."[16]

Although the Duma Committee for the most part found the Soviet Executive Committee deputies' demands acceptable, many of the claims prompted the bourgeois leaders' objections. They argued it was impossible both to hold elections to the constituent assembly during the war and to undertake sweeping democratization of the army. Discussion of the form of the new state order sparked the sharpest debate. Miliukov, proposing to present the throne to Aleksei under Mikhail's regency, favored preserving the monarchy. He declared the Romanovs no longer dangerous: Nicholas was out of the picture, Aleksei was a sick child, and Mikhail was a fool. Chkheidze and Sokolov found Miliukov's plan unacceptable and utopian in view of the universal hatred toward the monarchy. They said that an attempt to save the Romanovs was "totally absurd, senseless, and in general would amount to nothing. . . . But the bourgeois leader was implacable. Seeing the futility of the argument, he addressed the remaining points."[17]

The contracting parties left the question of the form of the state administration unresolved and instead discussed the other points in the government's declaration. The reorganization of the army ignited a major controversy. The Duma leaders rejected a radical democratization of the army and election of officers, but were forced to recognize the extension to soldiers of political rights granted to the citizens of Russia, and to agree with the Soviet's demands not to disarm and remove military units from Petrograd that had taken part in the revolution. They made this and other concessions in order to enlist the Soviet's support, without which their authority meant nothing.

The Duma leaders accepted the Soviet Executive Committee's plan and asked it to take the necessary measures to restore order in the city, to call on soldiers to obey officers, and to declare that the Soviet agrees to the Provisional

Government's formation, trusts it, and supports its program. The Soviet complied. It was then decided to issue two declarations, one by the Provisional Government, the other by the Soviet, and publish them side by side so they could be read together. By morning, March 2, both sides had agreed to most points. They broke up to draw up their separate declarations and then assembled again to confirm them.

A serious hitch owing to Guchkov took place at this concluding phase of the negotiations. He had left for the military units and had not participated in talks with the Soviet's representatives, returning to the Tauride Palace after an agreement on the declaration of a government had already been reached. Guchkov objected to several points in the agreement accepted by the Duma members, in particular to extending political rights to soldiers. He did not want to break off even temporarily agitation for the continuation of the imperialist war.[18] On March 2 a leaflet appeared under Guchkov's signature, as chairman of the Military Commission, which called for war to total victory. This appeal conflicted with the agreement that had been concluded, which had postponed resolution of the question of how to relate to the war. When the Soviet's Executive Committee banned dissemination of this leaflet, Guchkov threw a scandal. Sukhanov recalled: "Both the real strength of our forces and the government's weakness were revealed, and this clearly shook Guchkov. The incident involving this proclamation demoralized him greatly, for it was both unexpected and unbearable. He refused to take part in a government that could not express itself on the cardinal question of its future policies and could not issue a simple proclamation."[19]

Members of the Duma Committee objected to the Soviet's draft declaration, written by Sokolov, on the formation of the Provisional Government. Although it mentioned the need to establish "contact" between soldiers and officers, the document actually called upon the rank and file not to trust the command. Duma Committee members grew alarmed when they read Sokolov's document and declared it impossible to achieve unity if the Soviet held such a position. A serious threat thus jeopardized the agreement just reached.

An outraged Kerensky protested, maintaining that the ill-considered actions of several Executive Committee members undermined the agreement with the Duma and would result in the triumph of anarchy.[20] But Kerensky's apprehensions were exaggerated: the bourgeoisie was not about to jeopardize its relations with the Soviet. It understood that it could control the chaotic elemental revolutionary activity and come to power only with the Soviet's help. The Soviet's and Duma Committee's desire to create a bourgeois government forced them to search for a compromise that would end the negotiations satisfactorily. After rejecting Sokolov's draft, both sides in close cooperation began composing a new one. Steklov wrote the first paragraph of the Soviet's declaration, Sukhanov the second, and Miliukov the third.

At 2:00 P.M. on March 2 the Soviet of Workers' and Soldiers' Deputies discussed the question of power. The Executive Committee was to have reported to the Soviet on the outcome of the negotiations with the Duma Committee. Danger from the left and right threatened the Soviet leaders' efforts to establish bourgeois power on conditions agreed upon with the Duma leaders. The danger from the left alarmed the Executive Committee leaders the most. Sukhanov noted that the Bolsheviks' rejection of transferring power to the bourgeoisie

> could easily have been fortified by taking the struggle to the street—if Bolshevik and Left SR groups had shown sufficient resolve and energy. It would have been extremely hard if not impossible to overcome a movement of this sort by "internal" means, through influence or persuasion. . . . To defend the interests of the "privileged" before the masses, before the Soviet, which possessed real power, was uncommonly difficult. The excitement and alarm of the soldier masses magnified this difficulty tenfold. When the privileged refused to part with the monarchy and dynasty they doomed, if a street movement had started up, the entire "combination" to failure.[21]

The Executive Committee's spokesman, Steklov, exhaustively reported to the Soviet on the negotiations with the Duma. He said the Soviet's representatives had entered into the talks, striving to avoid a conflict with the Duma members and to prevent skinning a live bear. He mentioned that the Soviet's Executive Committee had demanded a number of concessions on behalf of workers and soldiers and wanted to place the new government under popular supervision.

At first, Executive Committee representatives insisted on the immediate promulgation of a democratic republic, but then agreed to postpone doing so until the formation of a constituent assembly, whose convocation was the new government's most urgent task. The Executive Committee proposed the Soviet call upon the population to support the incipient Provisional Government "only insofar as" (*postol'ku, poskol'ku*) it proceeded to undertake the aforementioned tasks.[22] Thus, for the first time, the well-known formula of support for the Provisional Government, "only insofar as," was enunciated, which was the basis of the Soviet majority's conciliatory policies.

Steklov reported that the Executive Committee debated whether the democracy should take part in the Provisional Government. The majority opposed participation, arguing they did not want to be bound by or assume direct responsibility for the future government's domestic and foreign policies. The Executive Committee saw to it that especially odious individuals, well known for their opposition to the revolutionary movement, did not enter the government, and that the most important ministries went to progressive people.

As already mentioned, Kerensky disagreed with the Executive Committee's decision on banning socialists from entering the government. He longed for power and strove at all costs to receive a ministerial portfolio. Failing to elicit a sympathetic response from the Executive Committee, Kerensky turned for support to the Soviet plenum, despite the Executive Committee's decision. Steklov had barely finished his report when Kerensky asked to be recognized.

The auditorium turned to him, applause broke out, and the future minister resorted to his skilled demagogy to persuade the masses. Raising, then lowering his voice, he posed pithy questions, designed to generate applause. "Do you trust me?" Kerensky asked. "We trust you," resounded the reply. "I am speaking, comrades, from the bottom of my heart. I am ready to die if necessary," Kerensky exclaimed and then continued. "Because a new government had already been formed, I had to respond at once whether or not I would accept the offer made to me to become minister of justice, without waiting for your formal sanction. Comrades, representatives of the old authorities were in my hands, and I could not bring myself to release them. . . . I first ordered the immediate freeing of all political prisoners without exceptions, and the dignified return from Siberia of our comrade Duma deputies who had represented the democracy." Kerensky thus took credit for what the people had accomplished—the arrest of government officials and release of political prisoners.

Kerensky's account greatly impressed those present and, as the newspapers wrote, elicited "stormy applause and general enthusiasm." Inspired by success, he continued: "Insofar as I accepted the responsibilities of minister of justice before receiving formal authorization from you to do so, I hereby resign as deputy chairman of the Soviet of Workers' Deputies. I am prepared, however, to resume this office should you deem it necessary."[23] Enthusiastic applause and cries broke out, "Yes, please." Then Kerensky tried to convince those assembled that, as a proponent of a democratic republic, he would represent the democracy within the government. Protests broke out in the auditorium that Kerensky had accepted the ministerial portfolio without the Soviet's sanction, but cries of approval drowned them out. Kerensky's performance at the Soviet ended.

Kerensky quit the Soviet meeting and almost never showed up there again afterward. Interpreting the Soviet majority's applause as a sign of approval, Kerensky settled down in the Provisional Government. The Soviet leaders could not bring themselves to speak out against Kerensky's actions, even though the overwhelming majority opposed coalition government. Yet silence is a sign of approval. In reacting to Kerensky's speech as they had, they in effect upheld his entry into the capitalist government.

At this Soviet meeting, Bolsheviks sharply rebuked the Executive Committee's conciliatory policies. Petrov said that in not creating a government of the people and in leaving the fate of the monarchy unresolved, the Executive Committee had struck a deal with the bourgeoisie. Molotov emphasized that the new government was not revolutionary. Shutko proposed adoption of tactics that would accelerate the revolutionary struggle. Shliapnikov favored formation of a provisional revolutionary government that would implement the Social Democratic minimum program that included a democratic republic, the eight-hour workday, and confiscation of landowners' estates, and also democratize the army. The Bolsheviks criticized the program the government and Duma leaders had worked out, pointing out its silence on such matters as the war, land, eight-hour workday, etc. The official report of the Soviet's March 2 meeting reads: "During the debates the Soviet of Soldiers' and Workers' Deputies exhibited a tendency to reject all collaboration with the Duma Committee and to demand formation of a provisional government."[24]

In contrast with the Bolsheviks, the right wing of the Soviet fought for even closer contact with the Duma Committee than the Executive Committee contemplated. Representatives of this wing appealed to the Soviet not to push things too quickly and get carried away, but to cooperate closely with the bourgeoisie. They advocated creation of a coalition provisional government with the participation of representatives of the democracy. According to Rafes, the Mensheviks' Organizational Committee and the Bund championed this point of view in particular. The Mensheviks, however, lacked the support of the majority of Executive Committee members, and decided not to back this strategy openly. As Rafes put it, "the Bolshevik representatives presented the strongest possible case against supporting the bourgeois government. Members of the Executive Committee had to defend their policy tenaciously. A proposal to participate in the Provisional Government would hardly have met with support at the Soviet plenum if the majority of the Executive Committee opposed it. It would only have played into the Bolsheviks' hands."[25]

The Soviet also dealt with the controversial question of the monarchy's future. The report that the bourgeoisie had not rejected tsarism but wanted to continue it under Aleksei and Mikhail aroused the deputies' irate protests. The Soviet denounced the monarchy. In wishing to reach an agreement with the Duma, however, it did not demand the immediate establishment of a democratic republic in Russia and agreed that the question of Russia's political future should be left to the constituent assembly.

The Soviet deputies pointed out that the new government's program lacked such an elementary demand as the abolition of governmental restrictions on the rights of nationalities and insisted on its inclusion in the program.

The Soviet did not create a provisional revolutionary government. An overwhelming majority approved the Executive Committee's transfer of power to the government formed by the Duma Committee and also the government's program worked out during negotiations with the Duma members. The Soviet merely introduced corrections and additions in the government's program: "1) The Provisional Government agrees to carry out all of the enumerated reforms despite the war; 2) The Manifesto of the Provisional Government must be signed by both Rodzianko and the Provisional Government; 3) The Provisional Government's program will grant all nationalities the right of national and cultural self-determination; 4) The Soviet of Soldiers' and Workers' representatives will form a committee to monitor the Provisional Government."[26]

Although the Soviet's resolution laid the basis for concluding an agreement with the Duma Committee, serious obstacles remained. While the Soviet agreed to postpone the demand for a democratic republic and leave the question of the form of the country's administration to the constituent assembly, the

Duma leaders fought doggedly to preserve the formal political structure, still hoping that replacing the monarch would save the monarchy. A March 1 *Izvestiia* article called reaching an agreement with the old authorities inadmissible. "The question must be posed clearly and boldly: either a new government or a compromise with the old." Appealing for clarity and decisiveness, the newspaper purposefully expressed itself vaguely on this very issue: "We intentionally have not yet dotted all the i's. But we shall do so next time if the ambiguity continues."

It did. A compromise with the former authorities took shape in the form of Nicholas II's abdication, declaration of Aleksei as tsar, and establishment of a regency under Mikhail. *Izvestiia* insisted only a constituent assembly had the right to resolve the question of the country's state order. In an article, "The Regency and the Constituent Assembly," the newspaper wrote that "the Provisional Government does not have the right to determine any permanent form of administration. To protect the people from counterrevolutionary machinations and to help it consummate the revolution before convocation of a constituent assembly is the entire purpose of the Provisional Government." The establishment of a regency would unleash civil war, for the democracy would interpret it "as a counterrevolutionary measure, as a dangerous encroachment on the gains of the revolution."[27]

It was Miliukov who heralded the regency. In a conversation with representatives of the Reuters News Agency and Associated Press on March 2, he stated that "the new government holds that the abdication has officially taken place and that a regency has temporarily been established under Grand Prince Mikhail Aleksandrovich. Such is our decision and we consider it impossible to change it."[28]

In midday on March 2, Miliukov addressed a large mass of soldiers and workers in the Catherine Hall of the Tauride Palace. In this well thought-out speech the bourgeois leader announced the formation of the new government. Miliukov spared no derogatory words or bitter epithets in referring to the old authorities. "History," he said, "knows no other government that has been so stupid, so dishonest, so cowardly, and so treacherous as this one. The deposed government has disgraced itself, has deprived itself of all support and respect." What would the policies of the new authorities be? Mentioning that the Provisional Government's program was under discussion by the Soviet, Miliukov avoided sensitive questions that would alarm the masses and did not say a word about the government's attitude toward the war. He proposed to avoid temporarily all political arguments and disagreements among separate parties and groups and to establish normal relations between soldiers and officers. Miliukov spoke on behalf of unity, which was advantageous to the bourgeoisie.

The crowd asked Miliukov: "Who elected you?" And he arrogantly responded: "No one elected us, for if we had waited for popular elections we could not have seized power from the enemy. The Russian Revolution elected us." Miliukov announced that the people who had entered the government were sacrificing themselves and that as soon as they were told the nation no longer needed them, they would resign, but "we will not give up power now, when it's needed to consolidate the people's victory." Applause interrupted Miliukov's speech, but the more he spoke the louder the cries of indignation and the more biting the questions became. "Who are the new ministers?" rang out from the hall. Miliukov began naming them, giving a short description of each. "We have placed at the head of our ministry a man whose very name signifies organized Russian society," he said. Cries of "privileged society" resounded in reply. "Prince L'vov, head of the Russian Zemstvo, will be our example." "Privileged," the crowd answered once again. Miliukov cautioned those at the meeting: "Now I will mention a name I know will arouse objections." He named Guchkov. In order to sweeten the pill he added: "Right now, while I am in this hall speaking to you, Guchkov is in the streets of the capital consolidating our victory." In fact, however, Guchkov at this time was not consolidating any sort of victory, but had gone with Shul'gin to the tsar to save the monarchy.

His speech ended, Miliukov answered a question that had provoked especially vituperative discussion—the fate of the dynasty. "You ask about the royal family," Miliukov said. "I know in advance that my answer will not please everyone, but I will tell you anyway. The former despot who brought Russia to the brink of ruin will either voluntarily abdicate or will be deposed (applause). Power will be transferred to the regent, Grand Prince Mikhail Aleksandrovich (continuous, indignant cries and exclamations: 'Long live the republic!' 'Down with the dynasty!' Weak applause, drowned out by a new explosion of indignation). The heir to the throne will be Aleksei (shouts: 'that's the old dynasty')."[29] Miliukov was forced to back off in order to calm passions. Declaring himself a supporter of a constitutional monarchy, he announced that the form of the state order was not being decided conclusively now, but would be resolved by the constituent assembly. Yet no stipulations could help anymore. Miliukov had laid all of his cards on the table.

Similar antimonarchy moods prevailed at other political rallies taking place at the time in Petrograd. Sukhanov recalled that "from the porch onto which I had barely managed to go out, I saw a crowd the likes of which I had never seen before in my life. The endless faces and heads looking at me filled the entire courtyard, square, street; the people carried banners, placards, flags. . . . I recounted how the Executive Committee had resolved the question of power, I named the main ministers who had been proposed, and I spelled out the program the Soviet dictated to the L'vov-Miliukov government." But they soon began to interrupt Sukhanov with questions about the monarchy and dynasty. "And I personally," observed Sukhanov, "had not given the matter much thought until now and for the first time saw how important it was to the masses. In reply to the clamor, I told how the disagreement between the privileged ones and the Executive Committee over the monarchy had not yet been resolved. I expressed confidence that the entire nation would favor a democratic republic. . . . An enormous, but at the same time peaceful, demonstration against the dynasty and on behalf of a republic then took place."[30]

The account of officer Tugan-Baranovskii, a member of the Military Commission, confirmed the masses' support for a democratic republic. "On March 2," he said, "a difficult situation arose in the Duma. Placards bearing the inscription 'Down with the Romanovs' appeared. The crisis came to a head. I had to speak with the deputies and answer whether the Romanovs would continue to reign or whether we would have a republic. I had to reply in generalities because exact information was unavailable. The situation became impossible."[31]

Miliukov's report on keeping the monarchy and establishing a regency caused a storm of indignation and protest among workers and soldiers. The insurgent people had fought to topple the tsarist regime, not for a change in tsars. They rejected an absolute, constitutional, or any other form of monarchy. Late in the evening of March 2, a group of infuriated officers announced to the Duma Committee in the Tauride Palace that officers would be unable to return to their units if Miliukov did not repudiate what he had said. Rodzianko asked Miliukov to do this, and he was compelled to declare in print that the proposal to offer the throne to Aleksei under Mikhail's regency was simply his personal opinion. "This, of course, was untrue, for in all previous discussions the question was considered to have been resolved jointly, as Miliukov had set forth. The Provisional Committee, however, frightened by the growing ferment, silently disavowed its former stance."[32]

In view of this situation, only a few monarchists continued to favor preserving the throne for Nicholas. Among them were members of the Romanov dynasty. In a letter sent to Kirill Vladimirovich on March 2, Grand Prince Pavel Aleksandrovich expressed the hope that through concessions, promised in the draft tsarist manifesto, it was still possible to keep the throne for Nicholas II. "You know that through N. I. (Ivanov—E.B.) I am in constant contact with the State Duma. Yesterday evening I recoiled at a new attempt to appoint Misha as regent. This is intolerable and impossible, and is nothing more than Brasova's intrigues.[b] Perhaps it's only gossip, but we have to be on guard, and in every way possible preserve the throne for Nicky. If Nicky will sign a manifesto for us establishing a constitution, this will end the demands of the people and the Provisional Government. Negotiate with Rodzianko and show him this letter." The next day a tearful Pavel Aleksandrovich asked Rodzianko to do everything he could to preserve the throne for Nicholas II. He wrote: "I know that you are devoted to him. . . . I would not alarm you at such a time if I hadn't read Minister of Foreign Affairs Miliukov's speech in *Izvestiia* and his comments about the Grand Prince Mikhail Aleksandrovich as regent. The very thought of removing His Majesty from the scene distresses me."[33]

Rodzianko's dedication to the tsar aside, neither he nor anyone else could

[b] Rumors widely circulated in the capital at this time that Mikhail Aleksandrovich's ambitious wife had been campaigning on behalf of her husband.

keep Nicholas II on the throne. He had to be sacrificed. Rodzianko wrote to Mikhail Aleksandrovich: "It is too late. Only abdication on behalf of the heir under your regency can pacify the country. I beseech you to use your influence so that this will come to pass voluntarily, then things will calm down. I personally am dangling by a thread and can be arrested and hanged at any moment. . . . You cannot turn down the regency. May God help you take my advice—convince His Majesty."[34]

That same day the Duma leaders realized it was impossible to limit itself to this concession. The insurgent people demanded a democratic republic. Supporters of the monarchy feared the Duma Committee would take this step under pressure from the people. On March 2 a group of officers addressed a memorandum to the State Duma Committee. "The Provisional Government does not have the right to follow the instructions of individual groups of people. . . . The Provisional Government must clearly and precisely express its intention to let the people themselves choose a form of government through a constituent assembly, which can be convoked only after establishing complete order in the country, so necessary for proper elections."[35]

The enticement of a constituent assembly saved the bourgeoisie. Menshevik and SR leaders who ran the Soviet did not take advantage of the favorable situation to promulgate a democratic republic. In continuing to cooperate with the bourgeoisie, as they had done during the first days of the revolution, they agreed to postpone discussion of establishing a democratic republic until the constituent assembly was formed.

On March 2 the negotiations resumed between representatives of the Duma Committee and the Soviet Executive Committee regarding the Provisional Government's declaration. The new revolutionary onslaught made the Duma leaders more complaisant. The third point in the government's declaration, on the form of government, received special consideration. Miliukov even now continued to support a monarchy and the Romanov dynasty that had been toppled by the people. The Soviet's representatives argued that Miliukov's stand would exacerbate an already strained situation and that nothing would come of attempts to keep the Romanovs on the throne. Finally, the Duma members assented to delete the point on the monarchy from the declaration. In turn, the Soviet's representatives did not demand a democratic republic and agreed not to include a commitment in the government's declaration "to take any steps that would predetermine the future government's form." The call for the constituent assembly was the platform of agreement between both sides. Neither a democratic republic nor a monarchy! Let the constituent assembly resolve the question of Russia's future state order.

When things were most critical, on the evening of March 2, the Provisional Government released a statement to the population, not waiting for the publication of a joint declaration. It said: "The Provisional Government formed by the State Duma Committee hereby announces that the government's program includes convocation of a constituent assembly on the basis of universal, direct, equal, and secret suffrage, which will determine the country's form of government." This appeal, signed by Prince L'vov, Miliukov, and Kerensky, was immediately given to the Soviet and the Military Commission and was widely disseminated in Petrograd.[36]

Other points in the government's declaration did not cause controversy. The Duma members accepted the Soviet's amendment, and the text of the declaration was edited for the last time and signed by the members of the Provisional Government and Rodzianko. The Soviet's proclamation in regard to the formation and announcement of the Provisional Government was also approved.

Soviet representatives did not interfere in the appointment of ministers, which was left exclusively to the Duma Committee. The Soviet's Executive Committee did not utilize its right to remove "especially objectionable individuals." It saw none. Rafes noted that only Guchkov's candidacy met with protests, but that they were not universal and categorical. The Soviet merely asked whether Guchkov would receive any special powers in the Provisional Government. Miliukov answered in the negative, stating that the entire Provisional Government was responsible for Guchkov's actions. "The question of personality was thus eliminated."[37]

The Provisional Duma Committee appointed the following individuals ministers to "the first public cabinet": chairman of the Council of Ministers and minister of internal affairs, Prince G. E. L'vov; minister of foreign affairs, P. N. Miliukov; minister of war and of the navy, A. I. Guchkov; minister of communications, N. V. Nekrasov; minister of trade and industry, A. I. Konovalov; minister of finance, M. I. Tereshchenko; minister of education, A. A. Manuilov; procurator of the Holy Synod, V. N. L'vov; minister of agriculture, A. I. Shingarev; minister of justice, A. F. Kerensky; state comptroller, I. V. Godnev. The new government was thus unquestioningly made up of capitalists and landowners. Four of the ministers—Miliukov, Manuilov, Nekrasov, and Shingarev—were Kadets. G. L'vov sympathized with them; Guchkov and Godnev were Octobrists; Konovalov was a Progressist; V. L'vov belonged to the center. Tereshchenko considered himself nonaligned, but he, too, was close to the Kadets. Finally, Kerensky—leader of the Trudovik faction in the Duma—declared himself an SR during the revolution.

The Provisional Government's declaration determined which considerations would guide its activities. In the course of negotiations, representatives of the Duma Committee and Soviet had agreed on eight points.

> 1) complete and immediate amnesty for all political and religious prisoners, including those incarcerated for terrorism, mutiny, agrarian crimes, etc.; 2) freedom of speech, union, assembly, and the right to strike, with the extention of political freedoms to the armed forces prescribed by military-technical considerations; 3) the lifting of all class, religious, and national restrictions; 4) immediate preparations for the convocation of a constituent assembly on the basis of universal, equal, direct, and secret suffrage, which will determine the form of government and the country's constitution; 5) replacement of the police by a people's

> militia with elected leaders, subordinate to organs of local administration; 6) elections to organs of local administration also on the basis of four-tailed suffrage; 7) no disarmament and no withdrawal from Petrograd of army units that had taken part in the revolution; 8) the extention to soldiers of all public rights enjoyed by civilians and the preservation of strict military discipline in formation and in carrying out military service.

In accord with the Soviet's proposal, the Provisional Government concluded that "henceforth it did not intend to use the war as an excuse for postponing the aforementioned reforms and undertakings."[38]

Rodzianko informed the high command that the Duma leaders made significant concessions to the Soviet in forming a new government. He told Ruzskii:

> As a result of lengthy negotiations with deputies from the workers I was able to reach some sort of agreement only by evening today. It called for convocation of a constituent assembly so that the people could express their opinion about the form of government. It was only then that Petrograd sighed with relief and the night passed calmly.[39]

Rodzianko reported to Lukomskii at Supreme Headquarters on March 3 in the same vein:

> Yesterday we had to reach an agreement with the leftist parties, establish several basic guidelines, and secure their promise to end all disorders. Downright anarchy has set in, indiscriminate and uncontrollable, and much more intensive than in 1905. . . . To avoid bloodshed, we made up our mind to reach an agreement, the main point of which was recognition of the need to elect a constituent assembly.[40]

Thus the bourgeoisie received state power from the Soviet in exchange for several important concessions. The Provisional Government's declaration stated that it was formed by the Provisional Duma Committee in agreement with the Soviet. Henceforth the Duma Committee had to concede its place to the Provisional Government. It is true that the committee tried to play a role in administering the country even after the government's formation. Viewing the Duma as the source of the Provisional Government's authority, several Duma leaders wanted to preserve for it supervisory or legislative functions. Nonetheless, not even the majority of bourgeois leaders shared such a view of the Duma Committee. On March 9 the Kadet party Central Committee resolved "to recognize as desirable the retention of the Provisional Duma Committee for practical work, mainly of a propagandistic nature, but not to attach any formal juridical significance to it as a source of power."[41]

The Duma Committee was not a source of authority for the new government because it lacked power itself. The Duma Committee's transfer of authority to the Provisional Government had the same nominal character as its own power. The only real source of power was the Soviet, which had conceded authority to the Provisional Government under specific conditions. The Provisional Government could neither have been formed nor could have existed without the Soviet's support. This explains why the Duma leaders helped edit the Soviet Executive Committee's communiqué that outlined its relationship to the new authority and insisted that it be published simultaneously with the government's declaration, and even printed on the same sheet. And this is how it was done. The Soviet Executive Committee's announcement, whether in leaflets or newspapers, appeared alongside the government's declaration.

The Soviet Executive Committee's statement (*Izvestiia*, March 3) said that the broad democratic circles must welcome the reforms decreed by the new government made up "of society's socially moderate strata." "To the extent that the new government moves to implement these obligations and to struggle decisively with the old authorities, the democracy must support it." In this manner the formula "only insofar as," adopted by the Soviet Executive Committee the night before, was confirmed. The announcement spoke of the inadmissibility of "disunity and anarchy" and the need to stop all excesses, robberies, property damage, arbitrary seizures of institutions, etc., at once. The Soviet Executive Committee appealed to soldiers to "work together with officers in a concerted and friendly manner, not stigmatizing the entire officer corps for the foolish behavior of a few individuals, and to show patience and ignore immaterial breaches against the democracy by those officers who have resolutely joined in the final struggle you are leading against the old regime."

After concluding the agreement with the Soviet representatives on the Provisional Government, the bourgeois leaders hastened to inform the population about it so that the order they needed would be restored more quickly. On March 2 the Provisional Duma Committee published a decree: "The difficult period we were living through is over. A Provisional Government has been established. . . . Recognizing its responsibility, it will take all measures to guarantee order, based on freedom, and to save the country from internal and external collapse. The unavoidable short-lived period of confusion is already drawing to an end. Citizens of Russia, first and foremost those swept up by events in the capital, must resume work. Soldiers also must resume a normal life."[42]

Official representatives and unofficial supporters of the bourgeoisie appealed to the entire population for unity. The writer B. Gurevich[c] said at a meeting in the Tauride Palace on March 2: "Miliukov has asked me to stress how pointless it is to harbor doubts. The quickest possible preparation of elections to the Constituent Assembly based on universal, direct, equal, and secret suffrage remains the Provisional Government's prime and unshakable responsibility." The speaker from the liberals announced that "the time for petty disagreements

[c] Burdzhalov may be referring here to B. L. Gurevich, a Menshevik writer better known by his *nom de guerre*, B. Dvinov.

is over," and he applauded the courage and honesty of the Duma Committee and Soviet that have joined together in the name of freedom. "The Time for Brotherly Agreement" was the title of the leaflet containing this speech.[43]

Calls to "forget quarrels," "avoid all arguments and indecision" became the bourgeois liberals' primary appeals. The Kadets had been compelled to seek conciliation with the leftist elements, with the petit bourgeois democracy, and with the masses of armed people. A. Tyrkova wrote in her diary: "Those first days we did not distinguish ourselves from the left. When I heard Skobelev tell the soldiers that freedom and order were indissoluble, I thought we supported the same thing. And the word 'comrade,' altogether foreign to me and heard everywhere, seemed natural. . . . We wanted no quarrels." On March 2 she wrote in her diary: "I met with Skobelev. We (still) warmly shook hands. I thanked him for his earlier speeches."[44]

The second revolutionary wave ebbed with the publication of the Provisional Government's declaration and the Soviet Executive Committee's announcement calling for a constituent assembly. The vanguard elements among the Petrograd proletariat, led by the Bolsheviks, continued to battle for establishing power of the revolutionary people. The majority of workers and soldiers, however, having won major concessions from the bourgeoisie and broad democratic rights, accepted bourgeois power and banked on placing it under the Soviet's control. They followed their petit bourgeois leaders, who called upon them to show their faith in the new government insofar as it implemented the program it agreed to with the Soviet.

Nonetheless, even after the Soviet and Provisional Duma Committee leaders reached an agreement, the situation in Petrograd did not stabilize. The new government lacked a firm base in the army. Summarizing the communiqués received at Supreme Headquarters, Alekseev reached some unpleasant conclusions for the bourgeoisie. On March 3 he informed commanders of the fronts that the turmoil in Petrograd had not yet abated, the situation remained threatening and uncertain, the leftist parties, strengthened by the Soviet of Workers' Deputies, had amassed tremendous influence and rendered powerful pressure on the Duma Committee, "the troops in the Petrograd garrison are completely under the spell of workers' deputies and pose a dangerous threat to everyone, including the moderate elements of the Provisional Government."[45]

Neither Supreme Headquarters nor the Duma Committee nor the Provisional Government, however, could remove the revolutionary soldiers from Petrograd or repress them. They had no choice other than to resign themselves to the presence of these troops, try to reestablish the former status quo in the garrison, and discipline them and subordinate them to the former officers.

While negotiating with the Soviet over the formation of a new government, the Duma Committee simultaneously intended to appoint a new commander to the Petrograd Military District and replace Khabalov, whom the people had arrested. The committee decided that a dauntless hero from the front would best be able to restore order in the garrison. They chose General L. G.

Kornilov, who was known as a tough-willed commander, distinguished in combat. In telegram number 158 to Alekseev, sent on March 2, the Provisional Duma Committee maintained that it was necessary to appoint General Kornilov commander of the Petrograd Military District and dispatch him at once to Petrograd to restore order and save the capital from anarchy.

Petrograd military authorities backed the Duma members' request. General Aver'ianov cabled Alekseev on March 2: "It is absolutely necessary to carry out the measures set forth in telegram number 158 from the chairman of the State Duma, that is, the immediate dispatch of General Kornilov, whose valorous name all members of the Duma Committee agreed on, in order to save Petrograd from anarchy and terror and to bolster the Provisional Committee, which is trying to save the monarchy."[46]

Kornilov commanded a division on the southwestern front. Realizing that Kornilov would have to respond to a difficult political situation in Petrograd, commander of the southwestern front General Brusilov opposed Kornilov's appointment. "Conscience requires me to report," he cabled Alekseev, "that I consider Kornilov inappropriate for such a post. He is known for his bluntness and excessive fervor."[47] Alekseev thought otherwise. Believing that Kornilov would be able to restore law and order quickly, he supported the Duma Committee's proposal. Alekseev asked the tsar to grant permission to appoint Kornilov and to recall General Ivanov to headquarters. The tsar agreed. Thus, upon the initiative of the Duma Committee and with the tsar's sanction, a new "dictator" of Petrograd was appointed.

On March 2 Nicholas II continued signing imperial commands as emperor of all the Russias. Yet Petrograd workers and soldiers had already decided his fate. Following them, Moscow workers rose up against the autocracy. Revolution spread to the provinces and to the front, and everywhere met with the people's complete support.[48] To all intents and purposes, the autocracy had been overthrown.

How was this made official?

The Tsar's Abdication

The tsar was at Supreme Headquarters, protected by his staff, when the revolution broke out. Army commanders strove valiantly to save the tsar and the monarchy. Complying with Nicholas II's order, General Ivanov departed at 2:00 A.M. on February 28 from headquarters with a St. George's Cavalry Battalion, hoping to reach Tsarskoe Selo by 8:00 A.M. on March 1. Units from the front were also to have been sent there to be at his disposal. Ivanov's train arrived late at Tsarskoe Selo. The new district commander was unfamiliar with the situation both there and in Petrograd. Summoning the commander of the Tsarskoe Selo garrison to his car to familiarize himself with local conditions, Ivanov discovered that things were not going well for the monarchy. Unrest had already spread to the units located at Tsarskoe Selo. Learning of the arrival of Ivanov's echelon earmarked for stamping out the revolution, military units began occupying all station exits and surrounding the echelon. The local authorities were confused. They feared clashes with local troops would break out should the St. George's cavalrymen try to disembark, and this would endanger Nicholas II's family and other members of the imperial household living at Tsarskoe Selo.

In view of these considerations, Ivanov decided to retreat to a more favorable site to assemble units from the front assigned to his punitive expedition. Ivanov signed an order stating he had set about fulfilling the responsibilities the tsar had placed on him. The directive was dated "March 1, 1917, Vyritsa Station," but was stamped at Tsarskoe Selo. It read: "An Imperial Order of February 28, 1917, appointed me commander of the Petrograd Military District. I arrived at this district that same day and assumed command of its troops and total administration of the region. I hereby announce this to all troops without exception, to religious authorities, civil authorities, institutions, establishments, and the entire population residing within the district."[49]

But Ivanov had no one to command. Railroad workers had detained units sent for his disposal from the northern front and they had sided with the revolution. General A. Martynov, commander of the Fifteenth Cavalry Division, two regiments of which had moved on Petrograd, wrote: "Not having gone the nineteen versts to Pskov, our train was stopped at Cherskaia Station under the pretext that the track was occupied. They delayed us more than a day. The railwaymen and telegraph operators mysteriously double-checked everything and reported they could not help in any way. I suspected that a railroad strike had broken out, but later found out a special train occupied the track near Pskov and that near Luga two infantry regiments sent from the northern front a day earlier had mutinied, sided with the workers, and set up machine guns."[50] Revolutionary-minded soldiers had also delayed the Sixty-Eighth Borodin Infantry Regiment, included in Ivanov's expedition.

Nor could Ivanov travel freely. *Izvestiia* (March 5, 1917) reported that machinist Petr Deriabin and his assistant Vasilii Trunov conducted General Ivanov's train with the St. George's Battalion and "forced him to give up the proposed march on Petrograd." Representatives of the Provisional Duma Committee also took control of rail service to the capital, maintaining that the arrival of a punitive expedition would exacerbate the situation and make a peaceful resolution of the crisis more difficult.

Lieutenant Grekov, the manager of the Nikolaevskii Station appointed by the Military Commission, honored the Duma Committee's order, instructing all stations and post and telegraph departments to inform him of "all military trains without exception, of their composition, size, and armaments, moving on Petrograd." He demanded similar information on all freight trains carrying munitions.[51] In reply, Quartermaster of the Supreme Command A. S. Lukomskii ordered the military command and railroad administration to guarantee the uninterrupted movement of all trains, to follow orders only "of lawful

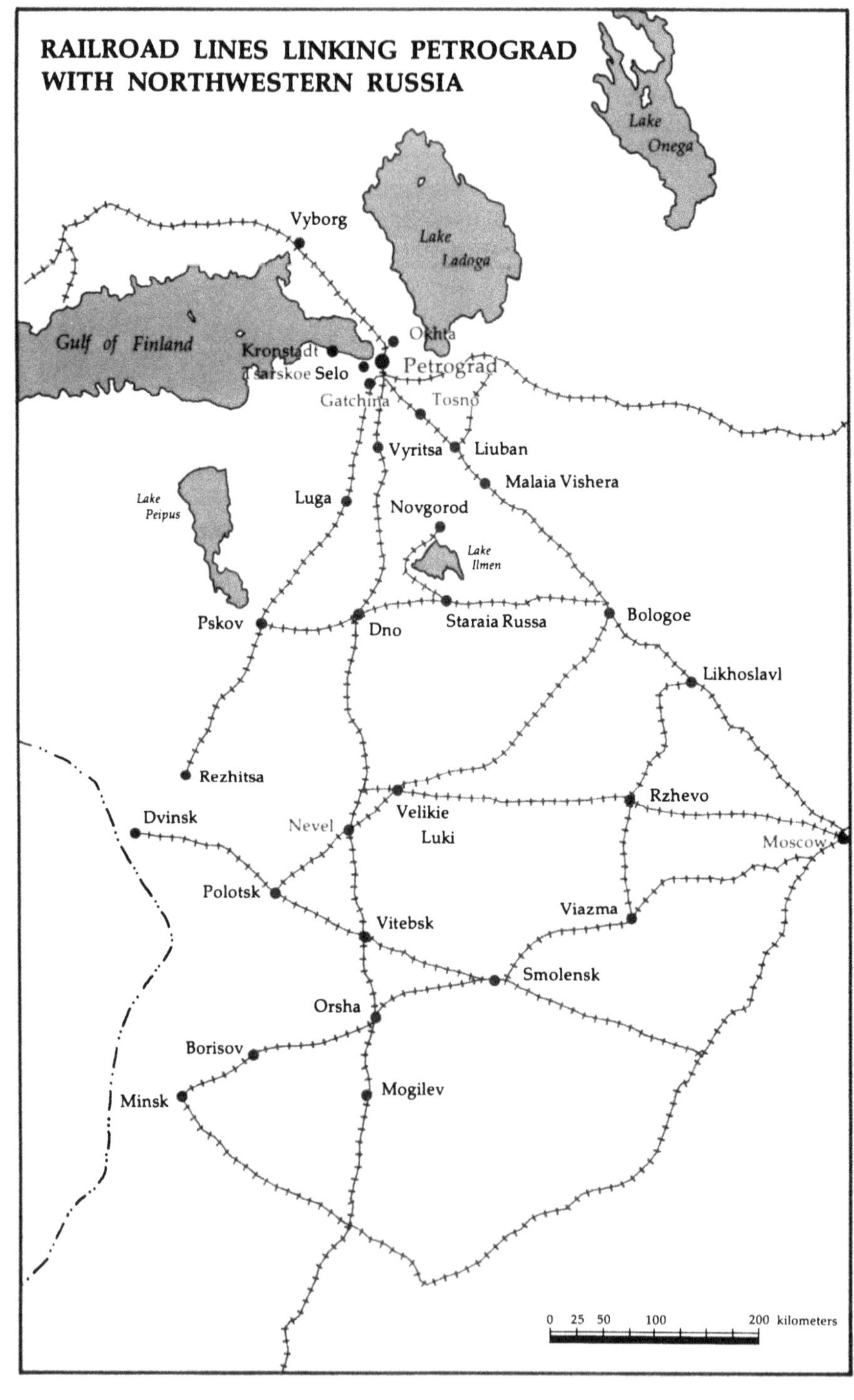

RAILROAD LINES LINKING PETROGRAD WITH NORTHWESTERN RUSSIA
Lake Onega
Lake Ladoga
Vyborg
Gulf of Finland
Kronstadt
Okhta
Petrograd
Tsarskoe Selo
Gatchina
Tosno
Vyritsa
Liuban
Malaia Vishera
Lake Peipus
Luga
Novgorod
Lake Ilmen
Pskov
Dno
Staraia Russa
Bologoe
Likhoslavl
Rezhitsa
Rzhevo
Dvinsk
Nevel
Velikie Luki
Moscow
Polotsk
Viazma
Vitebsk
Smolensk
Orsha
Borisov
Minsk
Mogilev
0 25 50 100 200 kilometers

authorities," and to deal with those who would violate the orders with the strictness of military law.

Apprehensive that units from Ivanov's detachment would somehow break through to the capital despite orders, Commissar Bublikov of the Provisional Duma Committee enjoined the director of traffic on the Vindavskaia line on March 1 "to dispatch immediately two freight trains, one after the other, from Dno Station in the direction of Bologoe and have them occupy a section of double track, possibly east of Dno, and make it physically impossible for trains to move from Bologoe toward Dno. Failure to obey this order or to do so promptly will be considered an act of treason."[52] Supreme Headquarters, lacking a clear idea of the extent and nature of the Petrograd events, believed that the very appearance in the capital of several well-armed disciplined units from the front would deter the rebels and make it possible to end the disorders. Headquarters did not send large formations to Petrograd and did not undertake major actions against revolutionary Petrograd because it did not want to make the front vulnerable and also because it doubted the reliability of front-line units in suppressing civilian disorders. Moreover, the command feared that bloody clashes between separate units would sap the strength of the entire army and lower the prestige of the government even further in the eyes of the Allies.

It gradually became even more obvious that headquarters had sent inadequate forces to suppress the revolution in Petrograd. General Lukomskii wrote that it would have been necessary to organize units of unquestionable reliability from several front divisions to achieve the desired goal, and that this would have demanded ten or twelve days during which revolution would have swept across the entire country. Lukomskii noted that a decision to drown the revolution in Petrograd and Moscow in blood threatened to interrupt operations at the front and force the conclusion of peace with the enemy. "It was necessary to do everything possible to end the revolution peacefully, provided that operations at the front against the enemy are not jeopardized."[53] Headquarters and the high command gave top priority to conducting the war, and they dealt with all other issues with this in mind. Later the high command would subordinate the war against the foreign enemy to the need to snuff out revolution. However, in late February and early March such was not yet the case. An armed attack against Red Petrograd would have triggered civil war. The tsarist generals sought to prevent this and instead to direct all of the country's energies into the war with Germany. Fear of armed skirmishes at the rear restrained their warlike aspirations in regard to the internal enemy and pushed them to search for peaceful solutions to the crisis. The army command pressured the tsar into making some concessions, in particular in agreeing to a "responsible ministry." It also hoped that such a ministry would be able to deal with economic difficulties more successfully and with the domestic revolutionary movement, and would be able to help conduct the war better than the previous government had done. This is why Supreme Headquarters, having dispatched a punitive force against revolutionary Petrograd, at the first opportunity tried to combat revolution in another fashion.

At 1:15 A.M. on March 1 Alekseev cabled in pursuit of Ivanov: "Private sources have it that complete calm was restored to Petrograd on February 28. The troops, all of whom have recognized the Provisional Government, are returning to order. . . . The Provisional Government's appeals to the population speak of how essential the monarchy is for Russia, about the need to elect and appoint a government on new foundations. They eagerly await His Majesty's arrival in order to present the aforementioned demands and request that he accept the people's wish."[54] Alekseev had succumbed to wishful thinking. As of February 28 disorder still reigned in Petrograd, the revolution continued, and the establishment of new principles for forming a government hardly represented the people's desire. The people were fighting to destroy the monarchy. The bourgeoisie alone intended to limit itself to forming a responsible ministry and waited to wring this concession from the tsar. The bourgeoisie and army command believed that this would end the crisis and prevent an armed clash, so undesirable during war. "If this information is correct," continued Alekseev,

> it changes the nature of your actions. Negotiations will lead to conciliation in order to avoid shameful civil strife, so desired by our enemy, and to preserve institutions and factories and start them up again. In a roundabout way I got hold of the appeal to railroad workers from the new minister of communications, Bublikov, which calls for redoubled work from everyone to restore transport. Report all of this to His Majesty with the conviction that things can be brought to a peaceful and positive conclusion that will strengthen Russia.[55]

Duma leaders also sought to resolve the conflict peacefully. The Duma Committee did not detain Colonel Domanevskii, appointed commander of Ivanov's unit, when he appeared in the Tauride Palace and instead negotiated with him to reach an agreement with Ivanov. B. A. Engel'gardt emphasized that the die had been cast and that there was no turning back.

> Ivanov could hold the revolution within the limits that seemed to me at that time obtainable—we could only be allies and collaborators on these grounds. However, Ivanov had to make a concession and recognize the Provisional Committee as the lawful authority. Domanevskii admitted that an agreement with Ivanov was possible . . . but the uncertain mood of Ivanov's troops distressed Domanevskii, who doubted the St. George's cavalrymen's selfless devotion to the throne. In the soldiers' view, preserving order was tantamount to restoring tsarist authority, for which they were not about to fight. In general, he had little faith in the success of Ivanov's mission.[56]

Thus, both sides formulated plans to end the revolution by avoiding armed conflict and by reaching an agreement between tsarism and the monarchist State Duma.

Heady revolutionary events destroyed the possibility for such an agreement. Ivanov could not negotiate without the tsar's sanction and Nicholas was nowhere to be found. Where, in fact, was he? Disturbed by events in the capital, he had left Mogilev for Tsarskoe Selo at 5:00 A.M. on February 28. As always, a special train with the tsar's retinue was sent ahead (both trains were unmarked). Everything began according to plan. Military and police authorities and the railroad administration met the two trains at Smolensk, Viazma, Rzhevo, and other stations to pay their respects, and the trains proceeded on schedule. At first no one knew what was taking place in Petrograd, but the closer they came to the capital, the more alarming the news that reached the tsar and his staff became. A report arrived that the entire Petrograd garrison had sided with the revolution and that the rebels had occupied the railway stations and controlled traffic. It became known that a committee had been formed in Petrograd led by Rodzianko, that a telegram circulated by Bublikov had enjoined the population to subordinate itself to this committee, and that a Lieutenant Grekov had been instructed to direct the unmarked trains not to Tsarskoe Selo, but directly to Petrograd. If some unknown lieutenant were responsible for the emperor's trains, major changes must have taken place in the capital.

In Malaia Vishera the tsar learned that revolutionary troops had occupied the stations at Liuban and Tosno, through which the trains were to pass. Then both trains returned to Bologoe to be rerouted to Tsarskoe Selo in a roundabout way via Staraia Russa, Dno, and Vyritsa. Because it turned out that that route also was unreliable and that the bridge had been destroyed on the Vindavskaia branch-line, this route also had to be rejected. All routes to Tsarskoe Selo and the capital had been cut off.

The revolutionary units' seizure of railway stations disrupted rail communications and severed ties between Supreme Headquarters and the capital. The high command protested orders that had made the Provisional Duma Committee responsible for the railways, believing these measures had undermined discipline without which victory over the foreign enemy was impossible. Alekseev cabled Rodzianko on March 1, 1917, that the interruption of communications between headquarters, Tsarskoe Selo, and the central organs of the war ministry augured terrible misfortune. Alekseev asked the committee to issue an urgent order to permit the unmarked trains to pass, to restore direct ties between headquarters and the central offices of the war ministry, and to abolish controls over headquarters' direct relations with these bodies. "If these controls are not lifted," threatened Alekseev, "I will be forced to break off all ties with the central administration."[57]

The Provisional Duma Committee had no intention of undermining discipline or complicating headquarters' actions or access to the war ministry. Nevertheless, having seized power, it tried to place the committee and headquarters under its control. Fearing that the arrival of Ivanov's detachment would end efforts at pacification and would unleash civil war, the Duma Committee did not wish to allow this unit into the capital. Instead, it intended to negotiate directly with the tsar to obtain concessions with which they could prevent the revolution from spreading. This is why the Duma leaders hampered the movement of tsarist troops, but did not delay the movement of the tsar himself to Petrograd.

The weakness of the tsarist authorities and of the Duma leaders told on the outcome of such efforts. The masses of workers and soldiers who had risen up in struggle were deciding things in their own favor. Rodzianko informed Ruzskii that the soldiers sent from the front to suppress the Petrograd uprising had mutinied, disembarked at Luga, and had "declared that they had sided with the State Duma and had decided to seize all weapons and not allow anybody to pass, not even the imperial trains. I took measures at once to free the track for the tsar's trains, but don't know whether they were successful."[58] They apparently were not.

Forces were at work on both the telegraph and railway lines that neither Alekseev's orders nor Rodzianko's instructions had foreseen. Acting on their own initiative, supporters of the revolution had blocked the route of the imperial trains to the capital. There is a record of a conversation of an unknown railwayman, who requested to report to the commander of the Nikolaevskii Station, Grekov, that the imperial trains had been returned to Bologoe and from there to Dno and that all lines to Bologoe had been taken out of service. A perplexed representative of the Military Commission replied that there had been an order to permit the imperial trains to pass through to Tosno. But his conversation partner pleaded ignorance of this instruction, refused to name his whereabouts, saying that he could no longer remain where he was talking "since supporters of the old administration might find me." He added: "I speak for the motherland and the new government." Both trains were sent back to Bologoe.[59]

Failing to break through to Petrograd, the imperial trains turned back to Pskov, where headquarters of the northern front were located. Why there? Opinions of those closest to the tsar differ on this. D. N. Dubenskii noted that the tsar and his entourage were intending to use the troops of this front, the closest to the capital, to launch a campaign against Petrograd. Lukomskii maintained that the tsar had counted on finding stronger support from General Ruzskii than he found from Alekseev. Refuting this contention, Colonel A. Mordvinov said that the tsar "unconditionally placed less trust" in Ruzskii "than in his own chief of staff, and our arrival in Pskov had been forced on us and had been absolutely unforeseen at the time of our departure. His Majesty, striving to join his family as soon as possible, also sought to be nearer to the capital, so far removed from Mogilev."[60] It appears that Mordvinov's testimony is closer to the truth. Nicholas hardly had intended to form a new punitive expedition against Petrograd composed of troops from the northern front.

Palace commander V. Voeikov reports that Nicholas II told him that he wanted to get to the closest town with a Hughes apparatus. Pskov was such a place. One can suppose that Nicholas sensed the threatening danger and, unaware of what exactly was happening, aimed for the largest nearby town,

Pskov, in order to be protected by troops from the northern front, to establish ties over direct wire with Petrograd, Tsarskoe Selo, and Supreme Headquarters, and to become apprised of the situation so that he could determine a further plan of action against the revolution. Neither Nicholas himself nor Alekseev nor Ruzskii had any reason to suspect that the imperial trains would end up in that town.

When Supreme Headquarters learned that the tsar and his entourage had headed for Pskov, it sent a telegram at 4:00 A.M. on March 1 to the commander of the northern front for delivery to the tsar upon his arrival at the front's headquarters. The cable updated events. At the onset of the revolution the tsar and the army high command had counted on isolating Petrograd and relying on the front, Moscow, and the provinces to put down the uprising. There were no longer grounds for such thinking. Revolutionary Moscow had risen up against tsarism shortly after Petrograd had. On February 28 the commander of the Moscow Military District, General Mrozovskii, reported to Supreme Headquarters that almost all factories had shut down and that workers had taken to the streets with red flags and revolutionary slogans. On March 1 he reported that "total revolution" had gripped Moscow and that the army units were siding with the people. Reports of revolutionary actions in Kronstadt and of the Baltic fleet's recognition of the Duma Committee also reached headquarters.

Alekseev informed the tsar of all of this in a telegram, observing that the disorders could spread to other cities, disrupt rail communications, interrupt the delivery of food supplies and cause hunger, possibly advancing the revolution and ending the war. "Before it's too late," he pleaded,

> it is necessary to take urgent measures to pacify the population and restore normality in the country. Under present conditions, the use of force to suppress the disorders is dangerous and would lead Russia and her army to ruin. So far the State Duma is trying to restore whatever order is possible, but if His Excellency does not respond with appropriate measures that would contribute to the general pacification, power will pass tomorrow to the extremist elements and Russia will live through all the horrors of revolution. I implore His Majesty, for the sake of saving Russia and the dynasty, to place an individual in charge of the government whom Russia believes in and empower him to form a cabinet. This is the only salvation. It is impossible to delay any further. It is necessary to take these steps at once.[61]

Headquarters' actions also conveyed a sense of urgency. Within two hours after this telegram was dispatched, General Klembovskii, assistant to the staff of the high command, telephoned the commander of the northern front. Klembovskii asked that General Alekseev's and the Grand Prince Sergei Mikhailovich's request to take the measures enumerated in the telegram be delivered to the tsar, and that an individual who enjoyed the population's trust be placed at the head of the government. Sergei Mikhailovich considered Rodzianko such a person.[62] Several other military leaders also appealed to the tsar to resolve the situation "peacefully." On the evening of March 1, A. A. Brusilov asked Count V. B. Frederiks to convey to the tsar his request "to accept the fait accompli and peacefully and quickly end the terrible situation." He pointed out that domestic conflict would mean the indisputable loss of the war and catastrophe at home. "Each minute of delay," Brusilov wrote, "will senselessly entail more victims and will complicate finding a favorable outcome to the crisis."[63]

Not minutes but whole hours passed, however, as the revolution spread deeper and the high command had to advise the tsar to agree to even greater concessions. Initially, they had asked Nicholas to appoint an individual in whom "Russia could believe" to head the government. Now they asked him to appoint a ministry responsible to legislative chambers. At twenty past ten on the night of March 1, Alekseev cabled the tsar once again, this time pointing to the urgent need "to issue an imperial act immediately, capable of calming people," and to call to power a ministry responsible to the people's representatives headed by Chairman of the State Duma Rodzianko. Alekseev hoped Duma leaders led by Rodzianko would still be able to end the general turmoil. This same telegram contained the draft manifesto for granting a responsible ministry, compiled by headquarters. Alekseev implored Nicholas II to sign it without further delay.

The document began by mentioning the need to continue the war to a victorious end at all costs. "Striving to unite more closely all forces in the country for the quickest attainment of victory, I deem it essential to summon a ministry responsible before representatives of the people, and to charge its formation to the chairman of the State Duma who enjoys the trust of all of Russia."

After vacillating, the tsar agreed to sign the manifesto about forming a responsible ministry. This resulted in the direct halt of armed actions against revolutionary Petrograd. At 12:20 A.M. on March 2 a telegram was sent to General Ivanov at Tsarskoe Selo which read: "I hope that you arrived safely. I ask you not to take any actions before my arrival and to report to me. Nicholas."[64] That very night Supreme Headquarters instructed the commanders of the northern, western, and southwestern fronts to delay dispatch of troops against Petrograd.

The tsarist generals hoped the formation of a responsible ministry would restore calm and all would come to pass as it had been written: In Petrograd the disturbances would end, the people would be pacified, the threat of civil war and the danger of undermining the front would be dissipated, and Nicholas II would happily continue his reign. Except that it was the bourgeoisie and not the people who demanded a responsible ministry. This slogan was absent from the banners of Petrograd's demonstrators. Workers and soldiers had stained Petrograd streets with their blood not for this pitiful handout from the tsar but to eliminate the tsarist regime. Alekseev and Ruzskii envisioned Rodzianko as the head of the new government, although in fact the Duma Committee did not possess real power. Other forces held sway over Rodzianko and the Duma Committee, as Ruzskii put it, "the extremist elements of the time."

Ruzskii received the manifesto signed by the tsar and communicated it directly to Rodzianko. The tsar's agreement to form a responsible ministry, however, could no longer influence the course of events. Hopes to arrest the further development of the revolution with the help of such measures were dashed. In a conversation with Ruzskii on March 1, Rodzianko said that the tsar and Ruzskii apparently had not realized what was happening in Petrograd.

> One of the most awful of revolutions has broken out that will not be so easy to put down. . . . The interruption in the activities of the legislative bodies fanned the flames and gradually such anarchy set in that the State Duma in general, and I in particular, could only try to take charge of the movement so as to avoid, in view of such social stratification, a level of anarchy that threatens to bring down the government. Unfortunately, I failed miserably. The people's passions had become so enflamed that it was impossible to cool them.[65]

Rodzianko informed Ruzskii that the formation of a responsible ministry would no longer satisfy the people. Hatred of the tsar had become so pervasive that it posed the question of the dynasty's future point-blank. The demand for Nicholas's abdication in favor of his son under a regency of Mikhail Aleksandrovich was being raised. The manifesto establishing a responsible ministry had been delayed, "the opportunity had slipped and there was no turning back." At the start of the conversation Rodzianko boasted that everyone believed in and listened to him. In complete contradiction Rodzianko said at the end of this conversation: "I myself am hanging by a thread, power is slipping from my hands, and anarchy is reaching such levels that I will have to appoint a provisional government this evening. . . . I pray to God that he grants me the strength to contain the present confusion of minds, ideas, feelings, but I fear, no matter what, that things will get even worse."[66]

Rodzianko stated that Nicholas had to be sacrificed and replaced by another tsar to save the monarchy and continue the imperialist war. After becoming familiar with the contents of Rodzianko's conversation with Ruzskii, headquarters proposed that Ruzskii awaken the tsar at once, inform him of this conversation, and insist that he abdicate. But Ruzskii decided to wait until morning. Believing that Nicholas's "voluntary" abdication was the only way out of the situation, the chief of staff decided to defer to the opinion and authority of the front commanders. On the morning of March 2, Supreme Headquarters informed them that "the dynastic question has been posed directly and the war can be continued to a victorious end only by meeting the demands made once again in regard to the tsar's abdication on behalf of his son under a regency of the Grand Prince Mikhail Aleksandrovich." Representatives from headquarters declared it was essential to get all commanders to act in concert in order to save, through major concessions, the army from disintegration and to continue the war against the foreign foe. General Klembovskii added: "Although His Majesty is wavering, the unanimous opinion of the commanders may prompt him to make the one decision capable of saving Russia and the dynasty."[67]

Some of the commanders were reluctant to commit themselves over direct wire. Commander of the western front A. E. Evert limited himself to saying that the question "can be resolved in the army's best interests only if it is resolved at the top." Chief of staff at the Rumanian front V. V. Sakharov said: "No matter how sad, it apparently is necessary to accept this one way out. I am drafting a telegram, but wouldn't it be better to send it after receiving a final decision from you based on the opinions of all the others?" Sakharov wanted to know Nikolai Nikolaevich's opinion beforehand. "It would be extremely desirable, if not absolutely necessary, to know the response from the Caucasus." Commander of the southwestern front A. A. Brusilov was more emphatic. "There is no time to vacillate. Time will not wait. I am in absolute agreement with you."[68]

Afterward, the front commanders submitted written responses to the tsar and headquarters. They favored abdication. Nikolai Nikolaevich begged the tsar to save Russia and the heir: "While blessing him, bequeath him your legacy. There is no other alternative." Brusilov emphasized the "importance of acting quickly to put out the conflagration that flared up and was spreading. Otherwise it will entail incalculably catastrophic consequences. This act will save the dynasty itself for the lawful heir." Evert requested the tsar make a decision, "in the name of saving the motherland and dynasty," in accordance with the chairman of the State Duma's announcement, as the only possible way of ending the revolution. Although Sakharov called Rodzianko's announcement criminal and disgraceful and the Duma itself a gang of rogues who conceived the villainous act, he, too, was compelled to admit that the Duma's recommendation provided the best way out.[69] The commanders' opinions were shaped by their belief that it was impossible to rely on the army to quell "internal disorders" and that it must be spared from political turmoil for the war against the Central Powers. Nicholas II could save his dynasty only by abdicating.

At 10:00 A.M., March 2, Nicholas learned of Ruzskii's conversation with Rodzianko. He understood that the manifesto announcing a responsible ministry would no longer save him. It was necessary to abdicate. He wrote in his diary: "March 2. Ruzskii showed up in the morning and read his lengthy conversation over the Hughes apparatus with Rodzianko. In his words, the situation in Petrograd was such that a ministry composed of Duma members would no longer be able to accomplish anything, since the Social Democratic party in the form of a workers' committee is competing with it. My abdication is necessary."[70]

Once he knew that inquiries had been made to ascertain the opinions of the front commanders, the tsar decided to wait for their responses. By 2:00 P.M. they had been received. Accompanied by the chief of staff of the northern front, G. N. Danilov, and the front's quartermaster, S. S. Savich, Ruzskii went to the tsar, read the responses of the front commanders, reported to him on everything that had occurred during the past few hours, and then offered his personal view. Seeing no way out of the situation, the tsar resolved to abdicate. At 3:00 P.M. he cabled Alekseev and Rodzianko that he was stepping down on behalf of his son, who would remain with him until he came of age, under a regency of Grand Prince Mikhail Aleksandrovich. The telegram, however, was held up.

When he made this decision, Nicholas knew the views of Rodzianko and the commanders, but he had not had the opportunity to consult with his chief advisor, the tsarina. Ties had been broken between Pskov and Tsarskoe Selo. Aleksandra Fedorovna had sent two carriers to the tsar with her letters, but they had not yet reached him. In letters to Nicholas dated March 2, Aleksandra Fedorovna wrote that Rodzianko and his cohorts sought to prevent their meeting "before you sign some piece of paper, constitution, or other such horror." Still hopeful matters would improve, she wrote: "Perhaps you can address troops in Pskov and elsewhere and rally them around you? . . . There are two groups—the Duma and the revolutionaries—two snakes that, I hope, will bite each other's heads off. That would save the situation. I feel that God will intervene."[71]

But the decision to abdicate had already been made. The tsar, however, did not hasten to sign the abdication received from headquarters, because a report arrived that the chairman of the State Duma was on his way to Pskov, and the tsar decided to wait for him. Rodzianko did not show up. He told Ruzskii there were two reasons for this: the troops sent to quash the revolution had mutinied and were not allowing any trains to pass, and without his presence in Petrograd, it was impossible to end the rampant horrors. Nevertheless, Rodzianko failed to mention the major cause of his delay—the Soviet's opposition.

Available sources shed little light on how the Soviet related to the tsar's abdication. Apparently, the Soviet Executive Committee, like the Duma Committee, did not advocate proclamation of the forced deposition of the tsar but wanted to achieve his voluntary resignation. As Rafes remembered, at midday on February 28, N. Sokolov informed the Soviet Executive Committee in strictest confidence that the Provisional Duma Committee was taking measures to obtain Nicholas II's removal. He proposed that the Executive Committee independently obtain this from Nicholas. "We cannot trust the Executive (Provisional—E.B.) Duma Committee 100 percent. This committee could draft an abdication document that would give us a regency and would preserve the monarchy." Rafes reported that "Sokolov has received the necessary authority and appropriate military guard. But several hours later it became clear that he had been too late—representatives of the Duma Committee had already carried out the task."[72] Other sources do not corroborate this report. It was not that Sokolov had been too late: it was not just a few hours, but two entire days that had lapsed between the Soviet Executive Committee's discussion and the Duma representative's departure. In all likelihood, the Soviet Executive Committee did not take any independent steps, but intended to act through the Duma Committee as in other matters.

Apprehensive that the Duma would strike a deal with the tsar, the Executive Committee did not want Rodzianko to reach him. According to the Soviet's protocols, on the evening of February 28 Chkheidze told the Provisional Duma Committee that the Soviet had discussed the chairman of the State Duma's trip to the emperor to demand his abdication, and that it had decided that "the trip can take place only if he, Chkheidze, takes part in it and only if the second part of the abdication act, in regard to bequeathing the throne to the heir Aleksei under a regency of the Grand Prince Mikhail Aleksandrovich, is omitted. A powerful force of revolutionary troops must accompany the train. In the event the Provisional Committee does not agree to these conditions, the Soviet of Workers' and Soldiers' Deputies will not provide a train for the Duma chairman."[73] Skobelev wrote that the Soviet's leaders had taken the initiative in preventing Rodzianko's travel. They had issued the appropriate instructions to railwaymen and had appointed Skobelev commissar of the Petrograd line to establish political control over the railroads.[74]

Despite the obstacles, the Duma representatives nevertheless met with the tsar. Shul'gin relates that late in the evening of March 1, members of the Duma Committee convened. Guchkov was present, but because Kerensky and Chkheidze were not, they spoke freely. Guchkov said that although it appeared that Nicholas II could no longer remain in power, the monarchy must be saved at all costs, because if the masses were to take the initiative they would put an end to the monarchy. According to the protocols, Guchkov, upon his return from visiting the military units, reported it necessary to follow through with plans that had been drawn up on February 28: go to the tsar and obtain his abdication. Then comparative calm would ensue and they would not have to fear "a return to the past"; until the oath is withdrawn, many will try to vindicate the old order and not avoid bloodshed. Rodzianko reported that he had wanted to go to the tsar but that the Soviet had not let him, demanding that Chkheidze accompany him with a battalion of soldiers. Then Guchkov suggested traveling to the tsar clandestinely, and presenting the Soviet with a fait accompli of "giving Russia a new tsar." Guchkov even wanted to undertake this venture at his own risk if the Duma Committee did not sanction his negotiations with the tsar about abdication. Provisional Duma Committee member Shul'gin declared his desire to accompany Guchkov. He wrote: "We exchanged a few more words. I tried to clarify what we had agreed to: the Duma Committee recognized the emperor's resignation as the only way out of the present situation and charged the both of us to report this to His Majesty and, should he agree, empowered us to bring the document to Petrograd. The abdication must be made on behalf of the heir, tsarevich Aleksei Nikolaevich. We must travel together and in complete secrecy."[75]

How did avowed monarchists like Guchkov and Shul'gin reach such a conclusion? "I understood very well why I was going," wrote Shul'gin.

> I felt the abdication was inevitable and it was improper to have Chkheidze confront the sovereign. . . . The resignation must be in the monarchists' hands to

> save the monarchy. . . . I knew that in the event the abdication took place (that is, in the event the monarchists took responsibility for it—E.B.) there would be no revolution. The sovereign would willingly step down, power would pass to a regency, which would appoint a new government. The State Duma, which obeyed the dismissal order and assumed power only because the old ministries had dispersed, would give this authority to a new government. In a juridical sense, there would be no revolution.

It seemed to Shul'gin there was no other way to end the revolution and save the monarchy. "Any other alternative would demand real power. We needed bayonets at the ready that would obey us and it was precisely this kind that were lacking."[76]

Fearing the Soviet's opposition, the Duma leaders kept Guchkov's and Shul'gin's trip to the tsar a secret. Shidlovskii, apparently, had not taken part in the Duma Committee meeting that sanctioned this trip, and therefore knew nothing about it. According to his memoirs, Guchkov, who had been appointed war minister, had disappeared during the first days of the Provisional Government. They searched for him everywhere but to no avail. Shul'gin also disappeared. "A day later it became known that Shul'gin and Guchkov, without the knowledge of the Provisional Duma Committee and Soviet of Workers' Deputies, had contrived to sneak away from the Warsaw Station with an engine and car and take off for Pskov."[77]

In fact, however, Guchkov and Shul'gin had set off to the tsar with the knowledge and at the behest of the Duma Committee and were to negotiate with him on its behalf. They had taken the draft manifesto with them, apparently written by Shul'gin. Judging by the rough draft, this document said that "in this time of such serious trials for Russia, we, lacking the power to save the Empire from the severe misfortune that has befallen it, faced with the foreign enemy, for the good of the country and to satisfy the desire of the entire Russian nation, lay down the task of governing entrusted to us by God."[78] The monarchist leaders of the bourgeois-landlord Duma had sent Guchkov and Shul'gin to the monarch to save the monarchy. "We traveled like the doomed," wrote Shul'gin. "And this had to be. . . . We embarked upon this route because we had come up against opposition everywhere. . . . Here at least was a glimmer of hope. . . . Here was a possible way out. . . . But signals from all around told us to 'give up hope.'" Shul'gin tried to console himself with the thought that the transfer of power from one tsar to another had often "saved Russia" in the past.[79]

Guchkov and Shul'gin arrived in Pskov late on the evening of March 2. Guchkov wanted to meet with Ruzskii first, but the colonel who met Guchkov and Shul'gin at the station informed them the tsar wanted the deputies to come to him at once. Shul'gin recalled that he went to the tsar with the ominous feeling that the most horrible thing conceivable was taking place and that it was impossible to avert it. "Still one more stupid thought" bothered him: "It was awkward for me to appear before the tsar unshaven, in a crumpled collar and jacket."[80]

At 10:00 P.M. on March 2 the discussion on the imperial train began. Guchkov spoke first. Quite upset, he avoided making eye contact with the tsar and detailed unpersuasively what had occurred in Petrograd. Judging by the protocols kept by the head of the field office, K. A. Naryshkin, Guchkov said that he had arrived with Shul'gin to apprise the emperor of the real conditions in Petrograd and to seek advice on measures that could save the situation. Guchkov reported the state of affairs in Petrograd was extremely threatening, the disorders had spread to the outlying regions, there was not a single reliable unit, troops arriving from the fronts promptly sided with the insurgents, and although a Provisional Duma Committee had been formed, it lacked power. Moreover, extremist elements considered the moderate Duma members traitors and were fighting to eliminate the monarchy and establish a socialist republic. "Besides us, a committee of the workers' party is meeting and we are under its influence and censorship. . . . The leftist elements are already beginning to sweep us away. Their slogan is: proclaim a socialist republic. The movement has infected the lower classes and even the soldiers, who are promised land." Guchkov pointed out that the contagion might spread to the front, that in view of the army's present mood it was impossible to preserve the throne for Nicholas. The only way out is to transfer power to others—the abdication of Nicholas II in favor of his son under a regency of Mikhail and the formation of a new government was the only way "to save the monarchical order, to save the dynasty."[81]

Guchkov subsequently recalled that Ruzskii supported him, confirming that "there is not a single unit reliable enough to be sent to suppress the revolution. The tsar looked completely unshaken. The only thing that could be read on his face was that this long speech was unnecessary." And, in fact, the question of abdication had been resolved before the arrival of the Duma Committee's representatives. The protocols of the abdication compiled by Naryshkin state that Nicholas, having heard Guchkov out, commented: "I thought about this during the morning and in the name of general well-being, peace, and Russia's salvation, I was ready to abdicate in favor of my son, but now, reconsidering the situation, I have come to the conclusion that because of his illness I must abdicate at the same time both for my son and for myself, since I cannot part with him."[82]

Nicholas abdicated in favor of his brother Mikhail. The Duma representatives, arriving with a proposal to make Mikhail regent, not tsar, had not anticipated such a decision. They asked that they be given the opportunity to reflect on the "new terms" of the abdication. Then Guchkov announced they did not oppose the tsar's recommendation. Their confederates in the Duma subsequently criticized Guchkov's and Shul'gin's acceptance of Mikhail's candidacy. Attempting to justify his behavior, Shul'gin observed: "How could we have disagreed? . . . We had arrived to tell the tsar the Duma Committee's opinion . . . which coincided with the tsar's. . . . And if it hadn't, what could we have done? . . . We could have returned [to Petrograd] if they let us . . . for we, after all, had not resorted to 'clandestine violence' as was done in the eighteenth and the beginning of the nineteenth centuries. . . ." Shul'gin wrote that whether Aleksei or Mikhail would be tsar was, in the final analysis, a mere detail and that Mikhail's candidacy actually had some advantages. Mikhail could swear allegiance to a constitution to pacify the people, and if need be, he could renounce the throne like his brother, something a minor such as Aleksei could not do. The main thing was that time would be won.[83]

Guchkov gave the tsar the draft abdication manifesto. Nicholas left, returned shortly, and handed a paper to Guchkov. It was the document previously formulated at headquarters, and not the one presented by the Duma delegates. They had wanted Nicholas's successor to grant a constitution. They had argued that the greatest danger came from the leftist elements who were striving to declare a republic, and that if the new tsar were bound by a constitution this would weaken the position of those advocating a republic. As Shul'gin said: "We are preserving the country's symbol. . . . It's hell in the Duma, a real madhouse. We'll have to get embroiled in a decisive fight with the leftist elements and some sort of basis is necessary for this. . . . Should your brother Mikhail Aleksandrovich as the legitimate monarch swear to uphold a new constitution upon his ascension to the throne, this would contribute to a general pacification."[84] In accordance with this request, a phrase was added to the abdication manifesto that the new emperor must take an inviolable oath to govern in concert with the people's representatives.

The tsar's manifesto said that "it has pleased God to lay on Russia a new and painful trial," that the newly arisen popular domestic disturbances imperil the successful prosecution of the war, which must be carried out to a victorious end no matter what happens. The document read: "In agreement with the State Duma, we think it best to abdicate the throne of the Russian State and lay down the supreme power. Not wishing to be separated from our beloved son, we hand down our inheritance to our brother, Grand Prince Mikhail Aleksandrovich, and give him our blessing on ascending the throne of the Russian State. We enjoin our brother to govern in concert and harmony with the people's representatives in legislative institutions on such principles as they shall deem fit to establish, and to bind himself by oath in the name of our beloved country."[85]

The Duma delegates did not wish to create the impression they had extorted the manifesto from the tsar. Although it was approaching midnight, the tsar, at the deputies' request, dated the manifesto 3:00 P.M. The document was typed in two copies, signed by Nicholas II in pencil, and countersigned by the court minister. N. Vishniakov, a bourgeois activist and Moscow City Duma deputy, gave an interesting interpretation of this curious detail. "The pitiful excuse for a tsar could not even see fit to sign his abdication in ink like a real man, but did so in pencil. It was as if he were so indifferent to it all, as others are when they scribble notes in pencil to a friend or make a list of dirty laundry. What despicable people! And it was precisely they who had controlled the fate of a great empire for centuries."[86]

The Duma delegates recommended Nicholas sign one more document. Guchkov said: "Workers and soldiers who took part in the disorders are convinced a return to the old system would result in reprisals against them and therefore a complete change is necessary. The popular imagination needs a crack of the whip that would change everything. I hold that the decision you have reached must be accompanied by the appointment of Prince L'vov as chairman of the Council of Ministers."[87] Nicholas signed the ukase to the State Senate in regard to Prince L'vov's appointment as chairman of the Council of Ministers and the Grand Prince Nikolai Nikolaevich as commander in chief. Insofar as Nicholas had already abdicated, his orders lacked authority. To impart "legality" to them, they were dated 1:00 P.M., March 2, that is, much earlier than they were actually signed.

At the end of their conversation, Guchkov and Shul'gin asked the tsar about his personal plans following his abdication. He answered that he intended to spend several days at Supreme Headquarters, then visit his mother, and return to Tsarskoe Selo. The deputies assured him they would do everything in their power to facilitate his plans.

On the evening of March 2–3, the imperial train pulled out of Pskov Station for Mogilev. It was the train of the last representative of the Romanov monarchy. Nicholas II, branded by universal contempt and hatred, was even abandoned by the most loyal members of his retinue. Concerning the reaction of those closest to the tsar to the abdication, Guchkov wrote: "Literally no one tried to block us, literally no one supported the tsar. . . . Total emptiness surrounded the throne."[88]

The next day, March 3, the former tsar cabled Mikhail Aleksandrovich: "Events of the past days have forced me to decide unconditionally on such an extreme step. Forgive me, if we distressed you and failed to warn you. I remain eternally loyal to my brother. I am returning to headquarters, from where I hope to travel to Tsarskoe Selo in a few days."[89]

The tsar's abdication was not unexpected, but stemmed logically from all of the events that had preceded it. Dem'ian Bednyi[d] wrote in *Izvestiia* on the occasion (March 4, 1917):

> Even without a manifesto we knew
> Tsar Nicholas had been deprived of his just due.
> Still, we must address the people and let them know
> So as to avoid confusion others might sow.
> "Candidates" one and all surely will moan
> When they learn there no longer is any "throne."

Had the victorious revolution resulted in the tsar's abdication or deposition? The latter, of course. The revolution had overthrown Nicholas II, and only

[d] pseudonym of Efim Alekseevich Pridmorov (1883–1945), a Russian poet who joined the Bolshevik party in 1912 and later became one of the founders of the socialist realist school in Soviet poetry.

afterward was this presented as a voluntary resignation. Nicholas II had not stepped down in the first days of the revolution when he still intended to drown the unarmed people in blood with the help of troops from the front. The tsar abdicated when the unreliability of these units became manifest, when the revolution had spread to Moscow and other cities, when the tsar's cause had failed and all options had closed. The insurgent people had dethroned Nicholas themselves, and the "voluntary abdication" merely legalized this act by antedating it. Former subjects of the Russian tsar said he had abdicated himself long ago from the people.

Not for nothing did the bourgeoisie give the tsar's dethronement the form of a voluntary act. As Guchkov put it, "I was afraid that in the event he had refused to renounce the throne, the Soviet of Workers' and Soldiers' Deputies would depose Nicholas II."[90]

The tsar's so-called voluntary abdication freed the army from its oath and made it easier for it to join the revolution. It paralyzed the reactionary officers corps's opposition as well as that of other supporters of the old regime. Monarchists would not be able to defend the throne if it were vacant, if no one agreed to wear the crown knocked from Nicholas II's head. They had to accept the fall of the monarchy, at least temporarily.

The form in which the autocrat's abdication was presented, however, kept the path open for the monarchy's restoration. Calling for the abolition of the monarchy and establishment of a democratic republic, *Izvestiia* rightly noted that the dethronement was shrouded in such a manner that the possibility existed it would be overruled, that the path to restoring the monarchy was not closed. Nicholas's resignation on behalf of his brother and the latter's on behalf of the Provisional Government (see below) preserved the continuity of power and created more favorable conditions for the restoration of the monarchy than the direct deposition of the tsar and proclamation of a republican order.

Supporters of the autocracy depicted the tsar's abdication as a noble gesture, as a sacrifice he made for the well-being of the fatherland. They subsequently maintained that this measure, forced upon them, was illegal, that Nicholas II was not empowered to act for his son and that therefore the Romanov dynasty had not lost its rights to the Russian throne. Aleksandra Fedorovna held that things would return to normal. Believing that all it would take was granting a responsible ministry and constitution, she wrote her husband: "If you are forced to make concessions, you are not obliged to carry them out, since they were wrung from you. . . . It's absolutely criminal that you were compelled to do this simply because you lacked an army. Such a promise will no longer be valid when power is in your hands again. . . . God will save you and restore all of your rights to you."[91] Aleksandra Fedorovna continued to believe this even after Nicholas II had abdicated. On March 3 she wrote the former tsar: "I swear we shall see you once again on your throne which you will ascend with your people and troops for the glory of your reign."[92]

General V. I. Gurko, commander of the Special Army, who not long before the revolution had served as acting chief of staff, wrote the former tsar on March 4 that he hoped the country would return to its "legal sovereign" and that the present heir would be called upon to accept the throne.[93]

The tsar's voluntary abdication in favor of Mikhail did not end further efforts to abolish the monarchy. Workers and soldiers had to take new decisive steps to render Nicholas II and other members of the overthrown dynasty harmless and to prevent a possible restoration of the monarchy.

The deposed tsar had appointed the head of the new Russian government. At 2:17 A.M., March 3, Guchkov and Shul'gin telegraphed Petrograd that the sovereign had agreed to step down on behalf of the Grand Prince Mikhail Aleksandrovich, under the condition that he be bound to uphold a constitution, and that he had entrusted Prince G. E. L'vov to form a new government. L'vov's appointment had clearly come too late. Guchkov and Shul'gin thought that the Provisional Duma Committee would hold off declaring the formation of a new government until their return, but upon their arrival in Petrograd they saw posters on the streets announcing the formation of a Provisional Government headed by that very L'vov, and set up not with the tsar's "blessing," but with that of the Soviet of Workers' and Soldiers' Deputies.

The proclamation of Mikhail Romanov as emperor of Russia did not correspond to the situation that had arisen in the capital or the rest of the country. The broad masses of the people opposed the monarchy in any form. Mikhail's accession to the throne under these conditions could set off a powerful revolutionary explosion that would destroy not only the new tsar but the Duma Committee as well as the Provisional Government, and could pave the way for genuine popular rule. In view of this the overwhelming majority of Duma members realized that if they did not submit today they could lose everything tomorrow. They yielded to the necessity of sacrificing Mikhail and agreeing to the convocation of a constituent assembly, thereby averting a new revolutionary onslaught. In any case, the question of Mikhail's accession was subject to discussion. The manifesto recording Nicholas II's abdication on behalf of his brother had already been transmitted to the fronts and military districts when the Duma Committee released a new command to delay its publication.

At 6:00 A.M. on March 3 Rodzianko informed Alekseev: "Events here have far from abated, the situation has become more threatening and unclear, and I urge you not to release any manifesto until you hear from me how we might put an end to the revolution." Rodzianko told Alekseev that Mikhail's accession to the throne could unleash civil war because his candidacy was unacceptable to everyone.[94] He added that he had failed to reach any agreement on this basis and that a truce was concluded by consenting to convoke a constituent assembly.

Within two hours Rodzianko told Ruzskii approximately the same. "The point is," he said over the Hughes apparatus, "that only with great difficulty have we held the revolutionary movement within more or less acceptable limits, the situation has not normalized, and civil war remains a distinct possibility. People would probably accept the accession of the tsarevich under a regency of the grand prince, but the latter's accession as emperor is totally unacceptable." Rodzianko emphasized that after the agreement with the Soviet to convoke a constituent assembly was reached "the troops slowly but surely returned to order during the night. The proclamation of Mikhail Aleksandrovich as emperor, however, would fuel the fire once again and the merciless destruction would begin of everything capable of being destroyed. We are losing and yielding all of our authority and nothing will be able to pacify the people, not even the return of the monarchy in the proposed form."[95]

It follows from Rodzianko's reports that the Duma leaders intended to restore the dynasty through the constituent assembly and that until its convocation, they hoped to preserve the Provisional Committee, the State Duma, State Senate, and the ministry responsible to them as organs of power. This decision did not please the high command. Promising Rodzianko he would hold back publication of the tsar's manifesto, Alekseev said: "That which you have informed me is far from pleasant. An uncertain situation and a constituent assembly—both are dangerous when applied to the army in the field."[96] Ruzskii regretted that the Duma Committee deputies who had gone to Pskov to negotiate with the tsar had failed to illuminate sufficiently the state of affairs that had arisen in Petrograd. Rodzianko responded it was impossible to blame the deputies. "A totally unexpected soldiers' mutiny had flared up, the likes of which I had never seen before." In fact the situation in Petrograd had become further strained on March 2 and the Provisional Duma Committee had to retreat even further. Guchkov and Shul'gin had left for Pskov to save the monarchy by replacing the tsar, and now members of the Duma Committee were proposing to hold back proclamation of the new emperor.

Upon his return to Petrograd, Shul'gin addressed the soldiers that had gathered at the station, calling upon them to rally around the new tsar, Mikhail, and to obey him. "He shall lead us! Hurrah for the sovereign, Emperor Mikhail II!" It seemed to Shul'gin that the new tsar firmly occupied the Russian throne, that he had traveled to Nicholas II for the sake of the monarchy, and that the monarchy had been saved. Shul'gin was mistaken. Immediately after his speech, he received instructions over the telephone from Miliukov: "Don't release the manifesto. . . . Major changes have taken place." Shul'gin replied that he had already mentioned the new emperor Mikhail to the crowd of soldiers. "You shouldn't have done that," said Miliukov. "The state of affairs has sharply deteriorated since you left Petrograd. . . . They transmitted the text to us. . . . It is altogether unsatisfactory . . . for it is absolutely essential to mention the Constituent Assembly. . . . Don't take any further measures . . . grave misfortunes could follow."[97] Shul'gin promptly went in search of Guchkov to tell him what Miliukov had said.

Guchkov, meanwhile, was addressing a rally of railroad shop workers. Shul'gin recalled that when he entered the large shop where the workers had gathered, the chairman of the meeting was speaking.

> "Take for example the formation of the new government. . . . Who is in it? Do you think, comrades, that representatives of the people have been included? Of the very people who won freedom for themselves? If only that were the case! Here, read this . . . Prince L'vov . . . prince" (the crowd began to grumble). The chairman continued: "Why, then, did we make a revolution! . . . We've all suffered at the hands of these very same princes and counts. . . . We freed ourselves—and for you! Prince L'vov!" (the crowd began to seethe). He continued. "For example, who, comrades, is our new minister of finance? Who would you say? Maybe someone who has personally experienced how the poor live? No, our new finance minister is Mr. Tereshchenko who owns ten sugar plants, and a hundred thousand desiatinas of land. He's worth thirty million!"[98]

Another worker spoke out in the same vein.

> "They've arrived. And look what they've brought with them! Who knows them? Who knows what they've brought back with them? Maybe they've brought what the revolutionary democracy doesn't need. Who asked them anyway? . . . On whose behalf did they go? The people's? The Soviet of Soldiers' and Workers' Deputies'? No! The State Duma's! And who belongs to the Duma? Rich landowners. I would advise you comrades not to let Aleksandr Ivanovich leave here."

The crowd responded to the speaker and shut the shop doors. "It was becoming most unpleasant," Shul'gin observed.

At that point an engineer spoke against taking Guchkov into custody. "We ourselves invited them," he said, "they trusted us and came here. . . . You want to lock the doors? Threaten them?" Cries rang out: "Open the doors!" The doors were opened. Guchkov began to speak. Then Shul'gin. In view of the mood at the rally they wisely did not attempt to support Mikhail's candidacy for the Russian throne. "At this very moment an important meeting is taking place in the State Duma between the Provisional Duma Committee and the Soviet of Workers' Deputies. Everything will be decided at it. Maybe the decisions taken will please everyone. . . . In any event, Aleksandr Ivanovich and I must leave at once." "Well, go then, who's stopping you?" they cried out in reply. "The crowd began to part and we began to make our way to the exit."[99] Thus ended Guchkov's and Shul'gin's attempt to proclaim Mikhail the new emperor.

How did Mikhail feel? After arriving from Gatchina he wandered about Petrograd for a long time, not risking an appearance at the Mariinskii or Winter palaces. He settled down in the private apartment of Princess Putiatina on Millionnaia Street, not far from the Winter Palace. It was there that he found out about Nicholas II's manifesto. News of the tsar's abdication in his favor purportedly dismayed the grand prince greatly. The crown of the Russian empire was bestowed upon Mikhail, and he not only lacked real force at his disposal, but he could not even find refuge for himself from revolution in the capital of his empire. He did not know what to do. He said that he had never wanted the throne anyway, and had not prepared himself for it, that the Provisional Government would function better without him. "How do you like

L'vov," Mikhail asked N. Ivanov. "He's a smart one, isn't he? And Kerensky has character. Perhaps he'll gain control over the masses."[100]

On the morning of March 3 members of the Duma Committee and the Provisional Government assembled in Princess Putiatina's apartment to discuss whether Mikhail Aleksandrovich should ascend the throne. Only Miliukov among those assembled supported Mikhail's candidacy. Miliukov spoke at great length, detailing the situation in the country, arguing that it was necessary for Mikhail to accept the throne. Addressing Mikhail Aleksandrovich, Miliukov said: "If you refuse . . . Your Excellency, everything will be ruined! . . . Russia will lose the symbol that holds it together. . . . If you refuse, anarchy will set in . . . chaos, bloody confusion. . . . If you refuse, things will take a terrible turn . . . toward complete uncertainty." Shul'gin observed that "advice to accept the throne now means to head a loyal regiment and pit yourself against the socialists and cut them down with machine guns."[101]

What was Miliukov counting on by taking such a dangerous position? He later said he favored taking a risk, counting on the help of the Moscow garrison. Miliukov proposed going to Moscow to organize forces to support Mikhail Aleksandrovich. Like Miliukov, Guchkov felt Mikhail should accept the throne. However, taking present conditions into account, he made a conciliatory proposal and advised Mikhail to assume the throne not as tsar but as regent, and in this capacity lead the country until the constituent assembly decided who would rule Russia. What disturbed him most was the possibility that Mikhail's refusal to become tsar would break the continuity of authority and form a serious break between the old and new governments. Others protested Guchkov's suggestion, citing the law codes. There could not be a regent without a tsar. The overwhelming majority present concluded that there was no other alternative than to reject the throne and regency temporarily. Kerensky spoke up in favor of refusing the throne. He said to Mikhail Aleksandrovich: "I am a republican by conviction and am against the monarchy. . . . By assuming the throne you will not save Russia. . . . Russia needs complete unity to face the foreign threat. I implore you in the name of Russia to make this sacrifice. . . . I cannot vouch for your safety, Your Excellency." After consulting privately with Rodzianko and L'vov, Mikhail decided not to accept the throne.

The Duma Committee and the Provisional Government summoned the jurist Baron B. E. Nol'de to Princess Putiatina's, and he, together with Nabokov and Shul'gin, drafted a proclamation. They wrote it in Putiatina's daughter's study, sitting at a school desk, writing in a school notebook. It was established that Mikhail Aleksandrovich refused to accept the throne, and instead deferred the question to the constituent assembly. But who would hold power until it was convened? They decided to proclaim all power belonged to the Provisional Government. The draft document resembled the manifesto and began: "We by the grace of God, Mikhail, emperor and autocrat of all the Russias, etc." Mikhail was not tsar, however, and asked that these words be struck out. He also recommended including in the proclamation a call to pray for God's blessing and a request to all citizens of the empire to recognize the Provisional Government's authority.

An agreement between the Soviet and the Provisional Duma Committee had given rise to the Provisional Government. Now the last Russian emperor Mikhail gave his blessing. The Romanov dynasty had begun with a Mikhail[e] and now ended with one. Mikhail signed the document, embraced L'vov, and wished him well. Turning to Mikhail, Kerensky said: "Believe me, Your Excellency, we will preserve your precious authority until the Constituent Assembly meets, not losing a single bit of it."[102] Nicholas II was dissatisfied with such a turn of events. He wrote in his diary that "it so happens that Misha has abdicated. His Manifesto ends with the call for elections to a constituent assembly through four-tailed suffrage within six months. God only knows who advised him to sign such nonsense."[103]

Subsequently explaining why the Duma monarchists opposed Mikhail Aleksandrovich's accession to the throne, Rodzianko wrote that the workers and the entire revolutionary democracy of Petrograd would not have allowed it.

> It was absolutely clear to us that the grand prince would reign for only a few hours before enormous bloodshed would occur in the capital, launching civil war. It was clear to us that the grand prince would be murdered immediately and all of his supporters with him. He did not have any loyal troops at his disposal and therefore could not rely on any armed force. Mikhail Aleksandrovich asked me point-blank whether I could guarantee his life if he accepted the throne and I was compelled to tell him no. . . . Nor was it possible to slip him out of Petrograd secretly, for not a single automobile or tram would be allowed out of the city.[104]

That very day, March 3, an extra supplement to the fourth issue of *Izvestiia* carried the headline: "Abdication from the throne. Deputy Karaulov appeared at the Duma and announced that the sovereign, Nicholas II, has abdicated in favor of Mikhail Aleksandrovich who in turn has abdicated to the people. Grandiose rallies and ovations are taking place in the Duma. The rapture defies description."

In preparing the abdication documents for publication, arguments arose over what to call them. Were they the manifestos of two emperors? Could Mikhail Aleksandrovich be considered emperor and autocrat of all the Russias? Some argued that he did not have any power and therefore did not reign. Others disagreed, maintaining that he had been emperor from the moment Nicholas II abdicated, that is, almost for a full day, that young and feeble-minded monarchs also had lacked authority, but they had reigned, and that Mikhail's abdication made juridical sense only if it was agreed that he had been emperor. "The disagreement got bogged down in state law," said Bublikov. "Finally, about two

[e] Burdzhalov is referring to Mikhail Fedorovich (1596–1645), first member of the Romanov dynasty. He ascended the throne in 1613, in the wake of the Time of Troubles, and ruled until his death.

o'clock that night an agreement was reached. Nabokov wrote the documents' titles on separate sheets of paper: 1) The abdication of His Sovereign Emperor Nicholas II from the Russian throne on behalf of Grand Prince Mikhail Aleksandrovich; and 2) The Grand Prince Mikhail Aleksandrovich's refusal to accept supreme authority and his recognition that supreme power rests with the Provisional Government, formed on the initiative of the State Duma. We should have entitled these documents 'The result of the first six hours of the Provisional Government's activity.'"[105]

The document Mikhail Romanov signed said that "I have decided to accept the supreme power, only if that be the desire of our great people, expressed at a general election of their representatives to the Constituent Assembly, which should determine the form of government and the new fundamental laws of the Russian empire." Mikhail enjoined the citizens of Russia "to subordinate themselves to the Provisional Government, which has been created by and invested with full power by the State Duma, until the earliest possible convocation of a constituent assembly, elected by universal, direct, equal, and secret ballot, which shall form a government in accord with the will of the people."[106] In this manner the continuity of power was established from Nicholas to Mikhail Romanov and from Mikhail Romanov to the Provisional Government.

Guchkov and Miliukov opposed Mikhail's unwillingness to take power and refused posts in the new ministry. To the bourgeois leaders' alarm, the Provisional Government had barely been formed when it began collapsing. Members of the Central Committee of the Kadet party turned to Miliukov to persuade him to retract his resignation. Miliukov agreed to remain in the government, and he convinced Guchkov to do the same. The latter observed that "Miliukov had little hope that events would turn out favorably, and he was the greater optimist." The crisis hanging over the newly formed Provisional Government had been averted. The government, as announced to the populace, buckled down to work.

On March 4 tsarist officials cheerfully greeted the new ministers who appeared in the ministry. Shingarev warmly thanked officials in the Ministry of Agriculture for their congratulations and wishes. "We're happy to try," they said, assuring the minister they would serve the government loyally and honestly. The new ministers removed the throne from the Synod and issued instructions that the tsar and members of the imperial family were not to be mentioned in prayers. The very Synod that had defended the autocracy and Rasputin's excesses now promulgated a pastoral message to believers, which began: "God's will is done. Russia has embarked upon a new path of statehood." Miliukov requested directors of departments and divisions in the Ministry of Foreign Affairs to remain at their posts and continue work. Other ministers of the Provisional Government turned with similar appeals to officials in their respective ministries. The tsarist officials replied that they recognized the Provisional Government and were glad to have lived to see this day.

The Provisional Government left the state apparatus it inherited from tsarism almost untouched. It limited itself to abolishing the special people's courts, the police, Okhranka, and gendarmerie. All other tsarist institutions were preserved, and their officials continued fulfilling their former functions. In leaving the top officialdom virtually unscathed, the bourgeoisie intended to use it to strengthen its own authority. The Provisional Government thus relied on the prerevolutionary bourgeois public organizations—zemstvos, city dumas, war industries committees, trade and industrial and financial associations. Activists in the Council of Congresses, representatives of industry and trade, of banking, mining, the metallurgical industry, war industries committees, and other commercial establishments voiced their complete faith in the new government and readiness to continue the war with even greater resolve.

Nonetheless, the bourgeois government lacked the people's support. "Who should one obey?" queried a leaflet put out by the Kadets. It answered, "Our Provisional Government, headed by G. E. L'vov, founded by the State Duma in accord with the Soviet of Workers' Deputies is the only Supreme Authority we have. . . . Absolute power belongs solely to it. Only the Provisional Government has the right to issue orders, equally binding for Russian citizens of all classes, estates, nationalities, and religions."[107] The broad masses of people, though, recognized another authority—the Soviet of Workers' and Soldiers' Deputies.

At their very first meeting on March 2, the Provisional Government's ministers already admitted that in view of present conditions the Provisional Government must take the Soviet's opinion into account, but that the Soviet's interference in the government's affairs amounted to dual power which was unacceptable. Therefore the Provisional Government "must familiarize itself with the Soviet's intentions at its private meetings before examining these questions at official meetings of the Council of Ministers."[108] The Provisional Government could advocate familiarizing itself with the Soviet's intentions, but could not eliminate its interference in governmental affairs.

The second revolutionary wave had not achieved its main goal. The bourgeoisie remained in power, a provisional government had been formed, and the basic demands of the minimum programs of the RSDRP were yet to be realized. Nonetheless, the new revolutionary onslaught did not recede without leaving a trace. It overthrew the tsarist monarchy and strengthened the organ of genuine popular authority—the Soviet of Workers' and Soldiers' Deputies, and this was of paramount importance for the revolution's further development.

What exactly did the Soviet do?

The Soviet's Activities

During its first three days of sessions, the Petrograd Soviet evolved into a powerful force. By March 3 the number of deputies had swelled to thirteen hundred. Because tiny room number 13 located in the left wing of the Tauride

Palace could no longer accommodate them, the Soviet moved that day to the palace's White Hall, where the State Duma had met for eleven years. New individuals now occupied the seats so familiar to the Provisional Government's ministers. Showing up in tattered fur and cloth coats and soldiers' greatcoats, the Soviet's deputies and guests packed the auditorium. The reading of the abdication manifesto electrified the audience. A gilded frame still hung over the chairman's desk, but because the tsar's portrait had been removed from it, it gaped vacantly.

Opening the meeting, Chkheidze said: "Let this room where the last State Duma of the Third of June met behold who is assembled here now. . . . Long live our comrades who sat here at one time but who, until today, languished at hard labor." The Soviet's leaders, however, believed the workers' and soldiers' representatives were filling the Duma benches only temporarily. They presumed they were in session to promote a national assembly. "Your very presence," Chkheidze addressed the Soviet's deputies, "portends that within a short while deputies of a national constituent assembly will occupy these seats."[109]

The union between workers and soldiers forged by the revolution was the source of the Soviet's power. Yet efforts to undermine this solidarity continued. That very day, March 3, four hundred soldier representatives, congregated in the Chinizeli Circus, elected a provisional commission and empowered it to create a separate soldiers' organization. Those at the Soviet meeting who supported such a body argued that it would be easier to preserve unity this way. Maksim (Klivanskii), for example, argued that the practical tasks facing workers and soldiers differed. Soldiers have already "discussed forming company committees. Tomorrow we must clarify how to begin training. . . . Although these matters do not interest a single worker, they're extremely important for the revolution. We're speaking of the creation of a revolutionary army. . . . Soldiers must set up their own institution."[110] The majority of deputies, though, opposed election of a separate soldiers' organization. They agreed to keep the Soviet united, but in view of its unwieldy size and of the various issues of specific interest to workers and soldiers, they formed separate workers' and soldiers' sections. The Soviet's plenums were designed to discuss matters of a general political nature and to formulate joint policy.[111]

Relations between soldiers and officers also appeared as a topic on the Soviet's March 3 agenda. Soldiers reported that officers supporting the old order had tried to disarm soldiers, confiscate political literature, etc. "The majority of speakers insisted on the pressing need to take decisive measures to prevent the disarming of soldiers and avert conflicts between the lower ranks and commanders."

The Soviet confirmed the decision made earlier to elect district workers' soviets to organize the population of a given neighborhood, and it favored letting soldiers quartered in the same neighborhoods participate in the soviets with workers. The Petrograd Soviet chose a special organizational commission, and proposed that it "report on the expedient organization of soviets and neighborhood committees."[112] It also discussed establishing an All-Russian Soviet of Workers', Soldiers' and Peasants' Deputies. In the meantime the Petrograd Soviet was to fill this function.

That same day, March 3, the Soviet's Executive Committee set up commissions representing all parties in the Soviet to deal with problems of both local and national importance. The Soviet established commissions for food supplies, agitation, transportation and communications, literature, publications, finance, automobiles, information, managing the concerns of publishing houses, and others.[113] Within a day new commissions that dealt with other towns and legislative activities appeared.

The Soviet published its daily newspaper, *Izvestiia*, edited by Steklov, on whom the Executive Committee bestowed enormous power. On March 7, 1917, it "granted Steklov the right of discretionary (unconditional) power over all matters concerning publications as an Executive Committee commissar. B. Avilov, I. Gol'denberg (Meshkovskii), V. Bazarov, V. D. Bonch-Bruevich, and G. Tsiperovich joined the editorial board.[114] *Izvestiia* enjoyed broad popularity, especially during the first days of the revolution when other papers were not published. It set up shop in the publishing house of the newspaper *Kopeika*, which Bonch-Bruevich had requisitioned for the Soviet. The first issues of the paper were distributed free. Soldiers designated to control the crowds queuing up for *Izvestiia* soon began fulfilling broader functions. According to an editorial board report, "these soldiers on their own initiative began to deal with organizational problems, management, determining the number of copies to be printed, sales, accounts receivable, etc. . . . They eagerly filled each provincial subscription, regardless of whether money accompanied it or not, for they saw it as a way to spread the Soviet's influence."[115]

Workers welcomed *Izvestiia*. M. Koltsov recalled that "on the corner of Liteinyi and Nevskii two excited and ecstatic men ran up to us. 'Take a paper!' With a loud racket, they jumped down and dragged bales of papers from the sidewalk to the car. Tabloid-sized *Izvestiia* was fresh and had a holiday appearance. Chasing after the trucks, people tore the papers from each other's hands, demanded them, and begged for them."[116]

Izvestiia published exposés of those who supported the tsarist regime, particularly the generals, but on the fundamental question of political power it backed the SR-Menshevik Soviet leadership and defended the policy of supporting the bourgeois Provisional Government "only insofar as" it carried out the people's demands.[117]

The revolution's victory expanded the Soviet's role even further, but its activities were not well planned or organized. In a sense, they reflected the spontaneous character of the revolution that had created the Soviet. The Soviet met almost daily for hours on end, and sometimes the meetings turned into political rallies. It, and especially its Executive Committee, wrestled not only with major issues but also with less important ones. There were so many of the latter that the major questions drowned in the "endless flow" of pressing concerns that many deputies scornfully referred to as "vermicelli." They said dealing with them was like "playing leap-frog." Yet it was the "endless flow" of a major revolutionary cause, without which the people's victory would have been impossible. Discussion of agenda items alternated with that of matters not formally presented, coupled with urgent announcements at the meetings of both the Soviet and Executive Committee. This was natural enough, since the revolution raised questions that could not have been foreseen and included on the agenda.

Several Executive Committee members were dissatisfied with this aspect of the Soviet's work. Sukhanov wrote: "The Soviet greatly exacerbated the overcrowding, noise, disorder, and confusion in the palace of the revolution. This finally became unbearable for the exhausted members of the Executive Committee. Besides this . . . it was necessary 'to get away' from the Soviet and the crowds of thousands who were drawn to the palace, if only for a day."[118] It was impossible to conclude the never-ending sessions. As a product of the revolution, the Soviet drew more and more people into its orbit. Its membership grew continuously as new groups of working people sent representatives to it. Numerous delegations from factories and military units arrived at the Soviet's meetings. Rank-and-file participants in the revolution, not authorized by any group, also showed up. They considered it their obligation to observe the work of their highest governing body carefully and to inform it of the thoughts and aspirations of the working masses.

The Soviet's composition and activities reflected the working people's level of consciousness and organization. The worker and soldier masses' poor understanding of their own class interests and the influence of petit bourgeois elements stirred by the revolution shaped the alignment of forces within the Soviet. The majority of its deputies were under the authority of the Mensheviks and SRs; the Bolsheviks turned out to be in the minority. Many authors maintain the Mensheviks' and SRs' strength within the Soviet was attributable to the unfair norms of representation established by the Executive Committee. Each thousand workers sent one deputy to the Soviet. Workers from enterprises with fewer than one thousand workers jointly elected deputies or participated in elections by profession, according to the same norm of one deputy per one thousand workers. In some instances, though, factories with fewer than five hundred workers independently elected deputies.

Lack of coordination naturally meant there could not be complete conformity in the elections held at large, middle-sized, and smaller enterprises. Nevertheless, it is incorrect to maintain that delegates from the largest factories floundered among those from smaller handicraft enterprises, or that "at the time of the Petrograd Soviet's formation, SRs and Mensheviks granted the large factories and plants of Petrograd, whose indigenous proletariat supported the Bolsheviks, as many places in the Soviet as the small enterprises whose workers sprang from a petit bourgeois milieu."[119] In reality, the majority of workers' deputies in the Soviet represented the capital's large and middle-sized enterprises. The six largest factories in Petrograd alone sent about one hundred deputies to the Soviet.[120] Menshevik and SR influence predominated then even at these enterprises.[121] The majority of Soviet deputies from the Putilov, Pipe, Baltic, Metalworks, and several other of the largest factories supported the Mensheviks and SRs for deep-lying reasons, especially owing to changes in the composition of the working class during the war, when workers from the petite bourgeoisie infiltrated the largest industrial enterprises.

Soldiers made up an even broader base of support for the SRs and Mensheviks. Politically inexperienced and incited by the revolution to active struggle for the first time, they backed the SRs and Mensheviks, and believed their assertions for the need to establish national unity and continue the war to defend the revolution from German militarism. Soldiers were well represented in the Soviet and numerically dominated the workers' deputies. Soldiers elected one deputy to the Soviet from each company, the basic unit of military organization during the revolution (in reserve battalions, which composed a major part of the Petrograd garrison, companies contained one thousand to fifteen hundred soldiers). The principle of representation by company was established not only by the Provisional Executive Committee in the Soviet's address of February 27 but also by the appeal issued that day by the Vyborg Bolsheviks and published within a day as Order No. 1.

Not only companies sent one deputy each to the Soviet but also staff commands, military hospitals, storehouses, and other support groups that included an insignificant number of soldiers. As Zalezhskii noted, "among the smaller units no revolutionary work had been conducted until now and political consciousness was quite low. It therefore is natural that these units elected as deputies 'chatterboxes,' such as clerks, educated persons serving on privileged conditions, officer trainees, and others from the petit bourgeois ranks. These deputies were attracted to the SR and Menshevik parties, which were psychologically more kindred to them."[122] Although Bolshevik influence was greater in the largest military units, petit bourgeois influence also predominated in them with rare exception.

As already noted, another circumstance told on the Soviet's membership. The Bolsheviks struggling on the streets of the capital did not participate actively enough in electing deputies, so many people were elected to the Soviet by chance. "The most progressive, active members," wrote Shliapnikov, "were involved in all sorts of revolutionary work and in the heat of passion ignored the elections."[123] As Bolshevik Putilovite F. Lemeshev put it, "in the first days of the revolution all party members were in the streets . . . not enough attention was given to elections to the Soviet of Workers' Deputies."[124] This explains the petit bourgeois wave that swelled in the aftermath of the workers' uprising, carrying SRs and Mensheviks at its crest, and placing them at the leadership of the Soviet. The Soviet's activities reflected SR and Menshevik influence: leaders of the Petrograd Soviet appealed to the proletariat not to drive away the bourgeoisie. Since power had been transferred to the Provisional Government, the Soviet's Executive Committee strove to avoid encroaching upon the government's territory. It advised, asked, sometimes even demanded, but tried not to resolve, order, or instruct. However, it was difficult to hold this line, for the struggle compelled the Soviet to take independent actions. In the revolutionary atmosphere of those days, in which the Soviet was under intense pressure from the masses, the Soviet and its Executive Committee discussed the most diverse problems and often acted as organs of power.[125] They published orders for the garrison, appointed commissars to military units, commandeered printing offices, determined the makeup of the police, prohibited the shipment of Black Hundred literature, carried resolutions to arrest leaders of the old regime, to replace individuals, etc. Without the Soviet's sanction it was impossible to put out newspapers, resume work at factories, reassign military units, and implement an array of other measures.

The Provisional Government was powerless to stop the arrest of leaders of the old regime, for various organizations and groups of workers and soldiers carried them out without authorization. On March 12 the commissar of Petrograd and the Tauride Palace, Duma deputy L. Pushchin, citing the agreement signed by the Provisional Duma Committee, Ministry of Justice, Staff of the Petrograd Military District, and Petrograd Soviet, ordered that directives for the arrest or searching of individuals who had compromised themselves during the revolution and of those who had committed crimes against the people under the old regime could be issued only by "1) the Provisional Committee of the State Duma; 2) the Ministry of Justice; 3) and the Executive Committee of the Soviet of Workers' and Soldiers' Deputies. These orders are to be executed by the chief of staff of the Petrograd Military District. . . . The incarceration of looters and individuals carrying out arbitrary arrests, violence, and disorders will be conducted under instructions from neighborhood police commanders or commanders of military patrols."[126]

Unauthorized searches and arrests, however, continued. Tsarist officials, officers, gendarmes, police, and all sorts of suspicious individuals were locked up. Many of them were directly handed over to the Tauride Palace; they were brought there at all hours, and not only from Petrograd and its environs but also from the more distant towns of Pskov, Nizhnyi Novgorod, Kostroma, and elsewhere. A special commission comprising jurists and members of the State Duma took charge of cases involving the most prominent military and civil officials arrested during the revolution (these cases were then transferred to the procurator of the Petrograd Law Court and the Extraordinary Investigatory Commission of the Provisional Government). Another commission was organized to examine cases involving ordinary officials, namely the city police and Okhranka agents. It hastily interrogated those detained, after which it continued to hold them under arrest or release them: officers were usually placed under the jurisdiction of the Military Commission.

The Provisional Government and the Soviet next examined the matter of resuming publication of newspapers. Because of the general strike in Petrograd not a single newspaper had been published except for *Izvestiia*. Newspaper publishers and editors as well as journalists protested against the strike, saying that the absence of newspapers "would spawn dangerous rumors." In the name of freedom of the press and in order to keep the population informed, they demanded an end to the strike at printing offices and resumption of newspaper publication. Members of the All-Russian Society of Editors of Daily Newspapers hailed the Provisional Duma Committee as "the only authoritative organ" and asked it to take measures "to guarantee the regular appearance of newspapers."[127] But the editors had to discover for themselves that the Duma Committee was not the "only authoritative organ" and that its measures were insufficient to reactivate the silenced press. Not a single paper could be published without the Soviet's permission. It understood that to permit newspapers to resume publication during the strain of revolution would serve to fortify the defenders of the old order and strike a blow at the revolutionary camp. Publishers and editors waxed indignant and protested, but neither they nor the Provisional Government could do anything about it.

The press's fate remained in the Soviet's hands. "No one doubted," wrote Sukhanov, "that the Soviet of Workers' and Soldiers' Deputies should resolve this question (about the resumption of newspaper publication—E. B.), that only it was capable of doing so. No one doubted that this act of defending the revolution was no longer needed. There was no reason to leave it to the discretion of the new government of the right, there was no need to ask its sanction or even inform it. Only the Soviet had real power at its disposal, in particular, the entire army of typographical workers."[128]

Although the most reactionary Black Hundred newspapers had been totally discredited, their editorial offices sacked by the insurgent people, and their employees dispersed, the danger of their revival could not be ruled out. On March 5 the Soviet's Executive Committee passed a decree "to prohibit publication of all Black Hundred publications such as *Zemshchina* (The Populace), *Golos Rusi* (Voice of Rus'), *Kolokol* (The Bell), *Russkoe znamia* (Russian Banner), and others." The extreme reactionary paper *Novoe vremia* went to press without the Executive Committee's permission, so it decided "to shut the paper down until further notice."[129]

The Society of Journalists and Editors challenged the Executive Committee's decision, declaring that it considered "any sort of censorship inadmissible on principle." The Soviet's Executive Committee ignored this protest. The protocol of the March 6 meeting read: "The Executive Committee discussed the press representatives' statement and reconfirmed its previous position on this question, that is, 1) to forbid publication of counterrevolutionary papers and 2) to permit publication of the newspaper *Novoe vremia* and, if technical conditions make it possible, the newspaper *Kopeika*." The committee decided to add representatives of Russian and foreign journalists to the Soviet's publication-printing-office commission.[130] The decision to issue *Novoe vremia* and to open its printing office was made after the owner pledged to the Soviet in writing that he would not publish antirevolutionary literature.

The Soviet's Executive Committee granted permission to publish each paper on an individual basis. Even the newspaper *Pravitel'stvennyi vestnik* (Government Herald) had to turn to the Soviet for permission to publish and circulate. On March 6 the Executive Committee received a memorandum: "Acting in accord with instructions of the Petrograd City Governor to publish the paper *Vestnik Petrogradskogo Obshchestvennogo Gradonachal'stva* (Herald of the Petrograd Public City Governor), your most humble servant requests the Soviet's Executive Committee to permit typesetters, composers, skilled workmen, and others to begin publishing the paper. (Signed) The editor." [131]

At first the Soviet's Executive Committee gave permission to publish newspapers for several days only. On March 10 it decided that "all publications can henceforward appear without prior sanction of the Executive Committee." The bourgeois press once again began to speak out, but it had to reorient itself thoroughly. All of the newspapers now welcomed the revolution, proclaiming that the sun of freedom had risen over Russia and appealing for the union of all the country's vital forces. *Novoe vremia* fired the most reactionary employees from the editorial staff and tried to convince its readers of its loyalty to the new order. *Russkaia volia* (Russian Will), also purged its staff, formerly from the Kadet paper *Rech'* (Speech), and promoted the slogan "Democratic Republic," printing these words each day on its first page in boldface type. Several bourgeois newspapers, resorting to cheap sensationalism to win popularity, described intimate secrets of the House of Romanov, detailed the tsarina's private life, printed stories about Rasputin's escapades, etc. The bourgeois press gradually began attacking the revolutionary forces. Although the Soviet had rescinded its prohibition on the publication of reactionary papers, bourgeois leaders accused the Soviet of violating "freedom of the press."

The fate of the former tsar and other members of the deposed Romanov dynasty was one of the most serious questions facing the Petrograd Soviet. A member of the Union of Republican Officers, Liubarskii, stated that members of this organization and soldiers had discussed measures that should be taken to prevent the monarchy's restoration. They decided to arrest Nicholas II but not the entire royal family as long as it recognized the new regime. They feared Nicholas would leave for Supreme Headquarters or for the south to suppress the revolution. As a result, detachments of workers and soldiers were dispatched to cut off Nicholas's path to either potential stronghold.

On March 3 the Soviet's Executive Committee discussed the fate of Nicholas II and other members of the imperial family. It resolved

> to arrest the Romanov dynasty and to propose to the Provisional Government that it make the arrest together with the Soviet of Workers' and Soldiers' Deputies; to inquire how the Provisional Government would react if the Executive Committee carried out this arrest itself, should the Provisional Government refuse to join it;

> to arrest Mikhail but formally declare him subject only to the surveillance of the revolutionary army; to summon Nikolai Nikolaevich to Petrograd as a preliminary step and to establish strict surveillance over him en route, in view of the danger of arresting him in the Caucasus; to arrest the women of the house of Romanov when necessary, depending on the role each of them played in the affairs of the old regime.[132]

Indecisiveness permeated this Executive Committee ruling. Although the Executive Committee understood the need to take the former tsar and other members of the Romanov dynasty into custody, it did not carry out this important measure independently. Chkheidze and Skobelev informed the Provisional Government of the Executive Committee's decision to arrest Nicholas and waited for a reply from the government. Meanwhile, the deposed tsar contemplated leaving for England for the duration of the war and returning to Russia afterward. Nicholas negotiated this with the Provisional Government through Alekseev. Nicholas Romanov's memorandum said: "I demand the following guarantees from the Provisional Government: 1) unencumbered passage for me and those accompanying me to Tsarskoe Selo; 2) a safe stay in Tsarskoe Selo with those same individuals until my children recover; 3) unencumbered passage to Romanov-on-the-Murman (now the city of Murmansk—E.B.); 4) permission to return to Russia at the end of the war for permanent residence in the Crimea, in Livadiia." Alekseev supported all of Nicholas II's demands except the last. The Provisional Government also agreed to these so-called guarantees. On March 6 L'vov wrote Alekseev that "the Provisional Government is deciding all of these questions affirmatively, and will take all necessary measures to guarantee unimpeded passage to Tsarskoe Selo, a stay there, and passage to Romanov-on-the-Murman."[133]

Judging by this answer, the Provisional Government had decided to send the former tsar to England through the port of Romanov. The government may have intentionally kept this decision from the Soviet because it feared opposition. On March 6, Chkheidze reported to the Soviet's Executive Committee that the government had not yet given a final answer to Nicholas's request to stay at Tsarskoe Selo, received through Alekseev, to which the Provisional Government apparently did not object. After hearing Chkheidze out, the Executive Committee ordered the Military Commission to arrest Nicholas Romanov at once.[134] But measures were not taken this time either. Demands became more and more insistent for the arrest and handing over of Nicholas Romanov to a people's court. The masses were indignant that the former tsar and several members of the House of Romanov were at Supreme Headquarters, in contact with the field army. Suspicions surfaced that the generals, under the aegis of the tsar, were preparing a plot against the revolution.

On March 7 the Soviet Executive Committee received a statement signed by ninety-five individuals.

> We the undersigned members of the Soviet of Workers' and Soldiers' Deputies announce that 1) extreme indignation and alarm exist among workers and soldiers

who have won freedom for Russia because the deposed Nicholas II the Bloody, his wife who is guilty of betraying Russia, his son Aleksei, his mother Mariia Fedorovna, and also all other members of the House of Romanov remain free, traveling throughout Russia, even at the theater of military operations. This is absolutely intolerable and extremely dangerous for the restoration of law and order in the country and army, and for Russia's successful defense against the foreign foe; 2) We order the Executive Committee to demand at once that the Provisional Government take the most urgent measures to isolate all members of the House of Romanov in a single designated place under the reliable guard of the people's revolutionary army.[135]

Fearing the Soviet would arrest Nicholas and his family on its own, the Provisional Government decided to preempt its actions. On March 7 it finally resolved "to recognize that the deposed Nicholas II and his wife are deprived of freedom and should be delivered to Tsarskoe Selo."[136] The Provisional Government sought to soften the blow as much as possible. It placed Aleksandra Fedorovna under house arrest in Tsarskoe Selo. As for Nicholas, Duma members Bublikov, Vershinin, and Gribkov went to Mogilev without the Soviet's knowledge to deliver the dethroned emperor to Tsarskoe Selo. This was reminiscent of the manner in which Guchkov and Shul'gin had traveled to Pskov unbeknown to the Soviet to secure the tsar's abdication. The Provisional Duma Committee's injunction to Vershinin said he was going "to accompany the deposed Nicholas II the entire way from Mogilev to Tsarskoe Selo."[137]

The Duma deputies arrived at Mogilev at 3:00 P.M. on March 7, but decided not to meet Nicholas. Believing it would be easier for the tsar to learn of his arrest from someone closer to him, they asked Alekseev to tell him. Yet no arrest followed. As usual, the imperial train contained the tsar, his retinue, and servants. The Duma deputies, with soldiers at their disposal, boarded a car attached to the imperial train without having seen the tsar. The train started out for Tsarskoe Selo. The deputies issued instructions about which stops to make and the route to take, examined telegrams received along the way, and apprised the authorities in the capital of the train's progress. As the train approached Tsarskoe Selo Station, Nicholas hopped off, jumped into an automobile, and sped off to the Aleksandr Palace. The tsar's papers had not yet been confiscated, so he now had the opportunity to destroy many of them. "I continued to burn letters and papers," Nicholas II wrote in his diary on March 11, 1917.[138]

After permitting the former tsar to take up residence in the Aleksandr Palace, the Provisional Government negotiated with the British government to send Nicholas Romanov and his family to England. In his memoirs, George Buchanan said that on March 8, when the former tsar was still at headquarters, he asked Miliukov whether Nicholas II had been arrested. "I therefore reminded him," wrote Buchanan,

that the Emperor was the King's near relative and intimate friend, adding that I should be glad to receive an assurance that precaution would be taken for his safety. Miliukoff gave me this assurance. He was not, he said, in favor of the

Emperor proceeding to the Crimea, as His Majesty had originally suggested, and would prefer that he should remain at Tsarskoe until his children had sufficiently recovered from the measles for the Imperial family to travel to England. He then asked whether we were making any arrangements for their reception. On my replying in the negative, he said that he was most anxious that the Emperor should leave Russia at once. He would, therefore, be grateful if His Majesty's Government would offer him asylum in England, and if they would accompany this offer with an assurance that the Emperor would not be allowed to leave England during the war.[139]

Within a day Buchanan informed Miliukov that the king and government of England would be pleased to honor the Provisional Government's request and offer Nicholas II and his family asylum in England. "In the event of this offer being accepted, the Russian government would naturally, I added, have to make suitable provision for their maintenance. While assuring me that a liberal allowance would be made them, Miliukoff begged that the fact that the Provisional Government had taken the initiative in the matter should not be published. I subsequently expressed the hope that no time would be lost in arranging for Their Majesties' journey to Port Romanoff."[140]

On March 8 the Soviet's Executive Committee carried another resolution more categorical than the first. The Soviet's protocols read: "On the arrest of Nicholas II and his family. It was decided to arrest the entire family, to confiscate their property, and deprive them of their civil rights immediately. [The Soviet resolved] to send its envoy with the delegation that would conduct the arrest."[141] It was impossible to delay implementation of this decision. On the night of March 8–9 the Soviet's leaders learned of the tsar's proposed flight abroad, which posed a serious threat to the revolution. An *Izvestiia* report on March 10 said: "The Soviet Executive Committee considered it disastrous for the Russian revolution to permit Nicholas II to remain free or to depart abroad where he, disposing of colossal sums stashed away for a rainy day in foreign banks, would be able to hatch conspiracies against the new regime, fund Black Hundred intrigues, send hired assassins, etc."

The Soviet Executive Committee finally took independent steps to render the former tsar harmless, prevent his departure abroad, and arrest him. The Executive Committee ordered units loyal to the Soviet to occupy all stations in the capital. The Soviet sent commissars to Tsarskoe Selo, Tosno, and Zvanka. In the name of the Soviet's Executive Committee a radio message was broadcast to all railroads, communication centers, commissars, local committees, and military units, which said: "Herein be informed that Nicholas II is intending to flee abroad. Tell your agents and committees along the entire track that the Executive Committee of the Petrograd Soviet of Workers' and Soldiers' Deputies orders the arrest of the former tsar. Report immediately to the Executive Committee at the Tauride Palace for further instructions."[142]

At a meeting on March 9 the Soviet Executive Committee resolved "to inform the Provisional Government at once of the Executive Committee's determination to prevent Nicholas Romanov's departure for England and to arrest him. It has been decided to confine Nicholas Romanov in the Trubetskoi Ravelin of the Peter-Paul Fortress, changing its commander for this purpose. It has been decided to give top priority to arresting Nicholas Romanov, even at the risk of severing relations with the Provisional Government."[143] As soon as the Soviet's Executive Committee learned that the former tsar's train had arrived at Tsarskoe Selo, it dispatched there Colonel S. Maslovskii, Second Lieutenant A. Tarasov-Rodionov, and a detachment of soldiers. Why? Skobelev maintained that "we wanted to see for ourselves whether the tsar was guarded closely enough."[144] The detachment's real purpose was actually quite different. The text of the March 9 order to Colonel Maslovskii has been preserved: "Upon receipt of this you are instructed to leave for Tsarskoe Selo as a special commissar of the Executive Committee of the Soviet of Workers' and Soldiers' Deputies and to assume all administrative and military power in Tsarskoe Selo. The Tsarskoe Selo garrison is enjoined to obey Colonel Maslovskii's orders in carrying out the important political task given him. [Signed] Chairman of the Executive Committee of the Soviet Chkheidze. Secretary Kapelinskii."[145] The text of the order to form a detachment of 250 soldiers "at the disposal of Second Lieutenant Tarasov-Rodionov, acting under the authorization of the Executive Committee," is also available.[146]

It is difficult to believe such a large contingent of soldiers was sent to Tsarskoe Selo merely to ascertain "whether the tsar was guarded closely enough." Tarasov-Rodionov told how they went there to prevent the former tsar's departure for England, to arrest and imprison him in the Peter-Paul Fortress, "to seize Nicholas Romanov and escort him to Petrograd dead or alive."[147] Nonetheless, the Soviet's orders were not carried out. Maslovskii arrived at Tsarskoe Selo, negotiated with the garrison commander and with the commander of the Aleksandr Palace and other superiors, demanding they hand over Nicholas Romanov. They refused Maslovskii and declared that, in accordance with the instructions of the commander of the military district, they could not release the former tsar to anyone. The matter ended when Maslovskii was shown Nicholas alive and well and was convinced that the deposed monarch was under reliable guard. "I saw the tsar," Maslovskii reported to Tarasov-Rodionov. "I insisted that they show him to me. And that was enough. . . . Why, they ask, do you want to remove him from here? I spoke with the soldiers . . . and they've sworn not to release Nicholas."[148] Maslovskii telephoned the Executive Committee and received approval for his actions. His mission was considered accomplished.

Both the Provisional Government and the Soviet made concessions. The Soviet no longer demanded the last tsar's imprisonment in the Peter-Paul Fortress and the government rejected (evidently temporarily) plans to send Nicholas Romanov to England, especially since it did not seem possible to carry this out, for workers and soldiers controlled all of the stations and roads. The government promised not to make any decisions in regard to Nicholas II and his family without the Soviet's approval.

Chkheidze reported at a Soviet Executive Committee meeting on March 9:

"Pressured by the Executive Committee, the Provisional Government has rejected the idea of permitting Nicholas Romanov to leave for England without the Executive Committee's special approval. He has been left temporarily at Tsarskoe Selo. The Provisional Government and Minister of Justice Kerensky guarantee he will not go anywhere. The Provisional Government agrees that the Executive Committee should appoint a commissar to Tsarskoe Selo to make sure Nicholas II does not flee."[149] That same day, Maslovskii and Tarasov-Rodionov informed the Executive Committee that "revolutionary troops are responsible for guarding the palace. The order has been issued not to let anyone in or out. All telephones and telegraph equipment have been disconnected. Nicholas Romanov is under close guard. There are about 300 soldiers there from the Third Infantry Regiment. . . . All letters and telegrams are delivered to the sentry room. The representative (of the Soviet—E.B.) was inside and personally saw Nicholas Romanov. The regiment asked me to report that it will be on permanent guard and will not release him. . . . Convinced of the guard's reliability, the representatives (of the Soviet—E.B.) believe it possible to leave Nicholas as is." One Executive Committee member asked the Soviet's representatives: "Why didn't you transfer him to the Peter-Paul Fortress?" When no one else picked up on this suggestion the matter was dropped. After discussing the report the Soviet Executive Committee "dispatched S. D. Maslovskii as commissar of the Executive Committee to supervise the guard and organize the entire affair."

Although the revolutionary workers and soldiers had prevented Nicholas Romanov's flight abroad, it was not ruled out that this might occur later. At a Soviet meeting on March 10 Sokolov admitted the possibility. He therefore proposed to settle the question of Nicholas's property, personal estate, and large financial deposits in English and other foreign banks in the interests of the people. "Before doing this it does not make sense to release him abroad." Thus the door abroad for the former tsar had not been slammed shut. But it was recognized that "the question of Nicholas II's departure and that of other members of the imperial family can be resolved only by an agreement between the Provisional Government and the Soviet of Workers' and Soldiers' Deputies."[150]

The Soviet's opposition prevented the Russian and English bourgeoisie from carrying out their plans for Nicholas. "There was nothing more that we could do," wrote Buchanan.

> We offered the Emperor an asylum, in compliance with the request of the Provisional Government; but as the opposition of the Soviet, which they were vainly hoping to overcome, grew stronger, they did not venture to assume the responsibility for the Emperor's departure, and receded from their original position. . . . It would, moreover, have been useless for us to insist on the Emperor being allowed to come to England, seeing that the workmen had threatened to pull up the rails in front of his train. We could take no steps to protect him on his journey to Port Romanoff. The duty devolved on the Provi-

sional Government. But, as they were not masters in their own house, the whole project eventually fell through.[151]

Even though the Soviet remained in control of the situation after the formation of the Provisional Government, the bourgeoisie strove to concentrate all power in its own hands. Several bourgeois and petit bourgeois leaders recognized the Soviet's role in the past, and wanted to limit its influence in the present. The Kadet V. Kuz'min-Karavaev later wrote: "It (the Soviet—E.B.) was a legacy of the Revolution of 1905. For twelve years the revolution was considered to have been under no leadership other than its. It was formed with the first rifle shot. . . . Let it play a historical role in the past. It played—and then should have been spent as a fighting organization, as an organization for struggle. The Soviet is not meant for creative work, let alone for state building." After handing over power to the bourgeoisie the Soviet could not disband, and the bourgeoisie, no matter how hard it tried, could not do away with it. It was this that created the political instability so characteristic of dual power.

Although Popular Socialist V. Miakotin recognized the Petrograd Soviet's services in overthrowing tsarism, he censured it for trying to act as a government, for addressing direct orders and instructions such as Order No. 1 to the population.[152] Political realities had pushed the Soviet to take such actions. Dual power reflected the true alignment of forces that had taken shape as a result of the overthrow of the autocracy. The Soviet voluntarily had abdicated power on behalf of the bourgeoisie, but the interests of the proletariat and bourgeoisie were so contradictory that, with the support of the armed forces and the trust of the people, the Soviet in reality remained the country's unofficial government.

Thus the February Revolution resolved the main question, that of political power, in a contradictory and inconsistent manner. Other questions touching the vital interests of the toiling people also went unanswered. Only the revolution's further deepening, its transition to a new, socialist stage could guarantee their resolution.

How did the revolution develop further in Petrograd immediately following the overthrow of tsarism?

Petrograd after the Overthrow of the Monarchy

The overthrow of the monarchy gave the revolutionary forces burrowed in the underground the opportunity to carry out legal activity. On February 28, when the battle had not yet abated in the streets and shooting was still breaking out at the barracks of the bicycle battalion, members of the Vyborg Committee of the RSDRP, representatives of the Central Committee Bureau, and party workers newly released from prison gathered in Kaiurov's apartment on Bolshoi Sampsonievskii Prospekt, not far from the barracks. They decided to organize a

Petersburg Bolshevik Committee at once from among former members and to let the Vyborg Committee resume its own responsibilities. One of the first steps of the Vyborg District Committee was creation of an agitational board. At the time Zhenia Egorova, Semen Roshal', and M. Latsis ("Uncle"), and others conducted especially active agitational work in the district.

The transportation breakdown during the revolutionary chaos made it difficult to restore the all-city party committee and establish ties among separate neighborhoods of the expansive city. "We were up to our necks in work," Latsis recalled.

> Everyone was running around; we were as busy as bees. Streetcars weren't running and there were no horses or automobiles. They were available, but not to us. During the first couple of days the authorities could not figure out what was going on and sometimes let us have them. Now the authorities no longer provide the party committee with any because it has shown its true revolutionary character. . . . We're all dead tired and hungry. And then there's the spring slush. In crushed boots we trample from one factory to another. Automobiles rush past . . . the victors are going for a ride.[153]

The Bolsheviks recently released from prison or those returning from the underground and drawn into the revolution were unable to link forces immediately. On March 10, N. Tolmachev wrote from Petrograd to his relatives in Rostov-on-the-Don.

> Dear ones, congratulations on Russia's glorious emancipation. In these days of general amnesty, grant amnesty to me for my criminal silence. Swept up into the revolutionary movement, I thought of nothing and of no one, I forgot everyone and everything. . . . While going to work on the 27th, I became so involved in a demonstration, some 20,000-people strong, that I simply could not come to my senses until the last couple of days. I was everywhere: in the first demonstrations, at the shootings, at the soldiers' uprising, and then, together with soldiers in the Peter-Paul arsenal, I seized revolvers, rifles and drove in an automobile to arrest the police. I was at rallies, at meetings. I, myself, spoke. It was impossible to be on the sidelines. I just now came to my senses. After falling into the whirlpool of events, you become an insignificant bit of debris caught up in the whirling vortex.[154]

V. Shmidt related:

> We old PCs (members of the Petersburg Committee—E.B.) released from prison got lost in the crowd. Somehow we searched each other out; some ran off to the neighborhoods to restore old ties, others to set up legal printing presses or to find lodging. Although we agreed to meet the next day to form a Petersburg committee, we succeeded in doing so only on March 2.[155]

The first meeting of the Petersburg Committee of the RSDRP took place on March 2 at the city Stock Exchange, a place workers knew well and which was headed by the Bolshevik L. Mikhailov (Politikus). By this time ten district party committees already existed in Petrograd as well as a students' Social Democratic organization. Not all of them were represented at this meeting. Present were delegates from the Vyborg, Narva, and Vasilevkii Island regions, the Latvian Social Democrats, the Social Democrats of Poland and Lithuania and from several workers' organizations, old party workers, in all forty people. Those present felt they did not have the right to create a permanent party committee and therefore elected a Provisional Petersburg Committee, which included authorized district representatives and also former committee members. Zalezhskii, Kalinin, Avilov, Shutko, Podvoiskii, Orlov, Antipov, and other comrades joined the Petersburg Committee. Mikhailov was elected chairman, and Shmidt, secretary. Antipov was empowered to form an agitators' board and Shutko a commission responsible for party literature. The committee proposed that Orlov, who was responsible for organizational matters, establish ties at once with the neighborhoods and invite delegates from districts still not represented to join the committee.

The Petersburg Committee of the RSDRP saw its major task in strengthening and broadening the party's ranks and establishing the widest possible contact with the worker and soldier masses. It launched a recruitment drive and resolved to agitate workers and to infiltrate the barracks in order to agitate soldiers. The Petersburg Committee instructed Bolshevik speakers to explain to the masses the need to continue the revolutionary struggle to achieve the total abolition of the monarchical order and the speedy convocation of a constituent assembly. It decided to issue party literature, leaflets, and appeals to workers and soldiers, to publish the program and statutes of the RSDRP as well as posters, and to set up a library.

Shmidt noted that work went well, that ties to the neighborhoods were quickly reestablished. Nonetheless, the first days of the revolution had been lost, and the Mensheviks had taken advantage of this. People constantly crowded into the low, stuffy rooms of the upper floor of the Stock Exchange that accommodated the Petersburg Bolshevik Committee. The Petersburg Committee and its executive commission were almost in continuous session. "Shmidt was the main organizer, carrying out the responsibilities of secretary, and Podvoiskii maintained contact with the neighborhoods and with party visitors from whom there was no respite. He issued directives to agitators and maintained ties with the editorial offices of *Pravda* (all information about us was channeled there through him); Vladimir (Zalezhskii—E.B.) enthusiastically participated in the constant discussion of tactical questions, and also fulfilled representative functions, speaking on behalf of the Petrograd Committee at large rallies and representing the party to nonparty organizations."[156] The Petersburg Committee drew its support from local district and factory organizations. On March 5 *Pravda* observed that "the district organizations of the party are growing not by the day, but by the hour. Organized workers are not satisfied with organizations at the district level and are forming party cells at the subdistrict level and even at individual factories."[157]

The Central Committee Bureau of the RSDRP, the temporary national party center, also carried on important party work. During the first days of the revolution it had settled down in the Tauride Palace, where its members set up a duty schedule and organized its small staff. E. D. Stasova, who had returned to Petrograd from exile shortly before the revolution, had been arrested by the tsarist authorities on the eve of February 25. Freed from police detention by the insurgent people, she now headed the secretariat of the Central Committee Bureau. Stasova wrote: "My responsibilities included receiving comrades, answering their questions on all aspects of party activities, and supplying them with literature. Second, I kept the minutes of the Orgbureau [Organizational Bureau—D.J.R.]. Third, I wrote and circulated all of the Central Committee directives. Fourth, I managed finances."[158]

The members of the Central Committee Bureau who had emerged from the underground (Shliapnikov, Zalutskii, Molotov) could not cope with the enormous volume of work without help. Because it was impossible to wait for a party congress or conference to elect party leaders, the Central Committee Bureau began to co-opt party workers released from prison or exile. On March 7, 1917, it passed a resolution. "In view of the need to enlarge the Central Committee Bureau, as the present membership cannot handle all of the work at the moment and because the former members had just been released from prison, it has been decided to include K. Eremeev, K. Shvedchikov, M. Kalinin, K. Shutko, and M. Khakharev." Zalezhskii, G. Bokii, responsible for maintaining ties with the provinces, A. I. Elizarova, M. I. Ul'ianova, M. Ol'minskii, and others also joined the bureau. At its March 12 meeting it ratified the principle of co-opting new members. "The Central Committee Bureau recruited individuals considered useful, based on their political reliability, but it did not make membership dependent on fulfilling some specific function. The Bureau invited valuable theoreticians into its staff and only then divided up work among them."[159]

After emerging from the underground, the Central Committee Bureau and Petersburg Committee of the RSDRP hastened to renew publication of *Pravda*. K. Eremeev, A. Gertik, N. Poletaev, K. Shvedchikov, S. Zaks-Gladnev, D. Arskii, and other old Pravdists ardently undertook this mission. With a mandate from the Soviet Executive Committee and a small detachment of soldiers, they appeared at the printing office of the newspaper *Sel'skii vestnik* (Village Herald), which belonged to the Ministry of Internal Affairs, to utilize it for printing *Pravda*. The manager read the Executive Committee's order and announced that it said nothing about paper. "But Eremeev interrupted him. 'So you think it's possible to print a newspaper on something other than paper?' This argument had an effect on the manager, not so much because of its logic, as because of the armed patrol of Pavlovites. Cringing, the frightened manager hastened to inform us that the paper reserve totaled 16,000 poods." Shortly thereafter, Fabrikevich (Gnevich), N. Podvoiskii, V. Molotov, and others showed up and began to plan the first issue.[160]

Zaks-Gladnev wrote that the first issue of *Pravda* was composed with difficulty.

> We revolutionaries had forgotten how to write for a newspaper. Besides, the feverish events of the last few days had not yet taken on meaning for us, thoughts had not yet taken concrete shape, formulas had not yet crystallized. . . . Collective creativity played a tremendous role in composing the first issue. I myself wrote two articles. From the first, I remember, they kept one phrase and tacked it on to somebody else's article. My second essay—on our party's program and statutes—made it into the paper, only heavily abridged and edited. A similar fate befell other authors' work. . . . There were almost no technical workers. Many of us stayed around to work as proofreaders, distributors, etc. . . . There was no one to sell the paper in the morning, and there was no one to post the first issue to the provinces.[161]

Appearing on March 5, 1917, the first edition of *Pravda* was distributed free to Petrograd's factories, plants, and barracks and was sent to other cities. The lead editorial spoke the celebrated words: "The working class after years of struggle and thousands of victims, supported by the revolutionary army, has won freedom. *Pravda* was correct. Freedoms for which the workers' paper fought are being realized by the powerful force of the working class. The dawn of a new era has set in and a workers' paper is being revived. . . . Just as the workers' newspaper *Pravda* served as the organ of the revolutionary working class during the difficult days of the autocracy, the workers' newspaper *Pravda* will serve the working class in time of revolution and freedom."

Molotov, Eremeev, Kalinin, and A. I. Elizarova, in the capacity of secretary of the editorial board, joined *Pravda*'s first editorial staff. M. I. Ul'ianova also helped put out the paper. The seasoned party journalist M. Ol'minskii, summoned from Moscow to work on it, soon made his influence on the paper felt. His articles, sometimes two or three at a time, appeared in the first issues of *Pravda*. As before the revolution, workers' contributions financed the paper. The first issue of *Pravda* beseeched: "Comrade workers! Remember that now, just as in the past, the workers' press can exist only on the financial resources of the workers themselves." The newspaper proposed to launch a donation drive for a special operating fund.

The party of the revolutionary proletariat addressed the difficult question of how it should relate to the Soviet. At a March 2 meeting Petersburg Bolshevik Committee members sharply criticized the Soviet. They argued that Mensheviks, who had usurped places in it, did not represent the mood of the majority of conscious workers, that *Izvestiia* did not promote a revolutionary point of view, and that the Soviet's leaders were trailing behind the Duma Committee, which was trying to make a deal with the deposed tsar. The Bolsheviks proposed to carry out agitation more extensively in the districts, to criticize the Soviet's actions, to pressure it from below, and to advance their position more consistently at Soviet meetings.[162]

The Bolsheviks did not criticize the Petrograd Soviet aggressively enough. Gathering after the Soviet had adopted the resolution on rendering conditional support to the Provisional Government, the Central Committee Bureau decided to continue the struggle to create a genuine revolutionary government capable of executing the people's demands. However, it did not enumerate the forms of this struggle and did not rule out the possibility that the masses might influence bourgeois power. On March 3 the bureau carried a resolution on its relationship to the Provisional Government and introduced it to the Petersburg Committee so that the latter could recommend the Petrograd Soviet adopt it. It read:

> Insofar as the Provisional Government represents the interests of the prominent bourgeoisie and large landowners and is trying to reduce the impact of a real democratic revolution by substituting one ruling clique for another, and therefore is incapable of implementing the basic revolutionary demands of the people, the Soviet of Workers' and Soldiers' Deputies believes that: 1) the major task is to struggle for formation of a provisional revolutionary government which is the only one able to carry out these fundamental demands; 2) the Soviet of Workers' and Soldiers' Deputies must reserve complete freedom to determine how to carry out the basic demands of the revolutionary people and, in particular, to select ways of influencing the Provisional Government; 3) establishing control over the Provisional Government in the form of a special Soviet Control Commission is a palliative measure that does not achieve the recognized aim of controlling the implementation of the basic demands of the revolutionary democracy.[163]

Molotov proposed this resolution at the March 3 meeting of the Petersburg Committee of the RSDRP on behalf of the Central Committee Bureau. It evoked lively debate and opinions were divided. A minority supported the Central Committee Bureau's resolution (Shutko, Kalinin, Tolmachev, and others). A majority (including Zalezhskii, Shmidt, Mikhailov, Antipov, Fedorov, and others) voted it down and decided to support a policy more in line with that of the Soviet majority. The resolution carried at this meeting read: "The Petersburg Committee of the RSDRP, taking into account the resolution on the Provisional Government passed by the Soviet, announces that it will not oppose the authority of the Provisional Government insofar as its actions further the interests of the proletariat and of the broadest democratic masses of people, but will struggle mercilessly against efforts by the Provisional Government to restore the monarchy in any form."[164] This resolution ended talk of creating a provisional revolutionary government and gave rise to the illusion that the actions of the bourgeois authorities could "further the interests of the proletariat and of the broadest strata of people."[165]

On March 5 the Petersburg Committee again discussed its relationship to the Provisional Government. A representative of the Vyborg Bolsheviks introduced a resolution that "our present task is to form a provisional revolutionary government, based on the union of local soviets of workers', peasants', and soldiers' deputies from all of Russia." The resolution called for the partial seizure of power in the provinces to facilitate a complete seizure of power in Petrograd. The Petrograd Committee rejected this resolution as it had the one of the Bureau of the Central Committee and confirmed its resolution on the Provisional Government, adopted on March 3. After rejecting the Vyborg Bolsheviks' resolution, the Petersburg Committee did not raise the question of eliminating bourgeois power and did not dissociate itself from the formula of conditional support for the Provisional Government, advanced by the SR-Menshevik majority in the Petrograd Soviet.

The complicated political situation after the overthrow of the monarchy prevented the leaders of the Petrograd Bolshevik Organization from adopting a correct tactical position. They failed to form, or to develop in accord with the new situation, the notion of a revolutionary-democratic dictatorship of the proletariat and peasantry and creation of a provisional revolutionary government, which the Bolshevik party had promoted since 1905. They likewise failed to devise a tactic that would guarantee the most favorable conditions for the transfer to a socialist revolution.

The Mensheviks and SRs did not promote a socialist revolution. They considered socialism a matter of the distant future and limited the struggle of the working people to the confines of the capitalist order. In *Izvestiia* on March 1 the Menshevik Organizational Committee entreated the masses to join forces for the decisive defeat of the old authorities and for formation of a provisional government that would create "conditions for the organization of a new, free Russia." Who was to compose the government and what sort of new Russia would it create? The Menshevik appeal did not answer these and many other questions. The Organizational Committee emphasized that if the proletariat would unite and organize its forces it "would be able to overthrow the old regime and also win for itself the strongest situation possible under the new order." Toward this aim the Menshevik leaders called upon workers to struggle during the revolution. They continued to do so after tsarism had been overthrown.

The central Menshevik organ *Rabochaia gazeta* (Workers' Newspaper), the first issue of which appeared on March 7, held that Russia faced a long period of capitalist development, during which state power must remain in the hands of the bourgeoisie. It explained that the Soviet could not take power because it did not enjoy the support of the bourgeoisie, which played the leading role in the country's economy. Soviet power would be "illusory power, power that would immediately lead to civil war." *Rabochaia gazeta* adjured the democracy not to remove the Provisional Government from power, but to apply to it "maximum pressure to carry out democratic demands," to help it take the bourgeois revolution to its natural conclusion. The newspaper advised the Provisional Government itself to act in the interests of the democracy. And then "it will unquestioningly enjoy the trust of the people and the struggle will be conducted on a single front against the mutual enemy—the legacy of the old order."[166]

The SRs conducted a similar policy. There existed in Petrograd at the time a group of SR Internationalists who occupied leftist positions, which included P. Aleksandrovich, S. Maslovskii, and others. During the revolution this group, together with the Interdistrictites, urged the people not to give power to the bourgeoisie but to form a government of the revolutionary people. Kerensky, Zenzinov, and other SR leaders condemned these appeals. On March 2 a Petrograd Conference of SRs was held, which was attended by only twenty to twenty-five individuals. One SR activist, S. Postnikov, admitted that "the party in the real sense of the word did not yet exist in March 1917. During this month the process of mustering party forces, which up until now had been disorganized, took place."[167] The conference of SRs dissociated themselves from the position of the SR Internationalists, registered its support for cooperating with the Provisional Government, and approved Kerensky's entry into it. According to the resolution that was adopted, the pressing need was to "support the Provisional Government insofar as it carries out the political program it itself declared." The conference called for a struggle "against all efforts that undermine the organizational work of the Provisional Government for the realization of political provisions put forward by it."[168]

Close to the SRs on tactical matters, the Trudoviks occupied the far right flank of the democracy. This faction called upon the population to support the Provisional Government wholeheartedly and to obey its decrees. As a Trudovik appeal to the population of March 4 put it: "At present there is no room, nor can there be, for party quarrels or misunderstandings in the ranks of the insurgent people. Arm-in-arm, all those sympathetic to the cause of the people's emancipation must storm the last strongholds of power, selflessly obeying the Provisional Government organized by the State Duma." The March 5 edition of the daily newspaper *Den'* expressed the position of the populist parties and groups (SRs, Trudoviks, and Popular Socialists): "We will support the Provisional Government, but will not give up our right and obligation to criticize its mistakes. As the workers' and democratic organizations' unity and internal discipline grow, we will seek confirmation that the Provisional Government remains firmly committed to the country's revolutionary transformation on which it has embarked." The newspaper believed that the Provisional Government "was on top of things." It censured the Bolsheviks' *Pravda* and approved of the Petrograd Soviet "for its deep understanding of the moment, its political farsightedness and moderation in dealing with the Provisional Government."

Despite calls for unity, concessions, and agreements, a bitter struggle, which manifested itself in many ways, broke out between classes and parties. The day after the overthrow of tsarism, Petrograd workers discussed whether they ought to continue the general strike that had heralded the beginning of the Russian Revolution. The bourgeoisie strove to return life in the capital to normality as quickly as possible by resuming work at enterprises. This could not be achieved, however, without the Petrograd Soviet's support. On March 3 the Soviet backed the resumption of streetcar transportation and of post and telegraph services. The Soviet explained that "the interruption of the tram system is no longer essential and actually inconveniences the population and makes it difficult to transport essential food items."[169]

The Soviet proposed to the population of Petrograd: 1) not to obstruct regular streetcar traffic, 2) to facilitate as much as possible the difficult work of streetcar employees, 3) to pay their fare accurately, 4) to return wrenches used for operating the cars and commandeered during the uprising to agents-on-duty. The Soviet established guidelines for using trams. "The lower ranks of all arms of service and the city militia riding individually are granted free fare both inside cars and on running boards."[170] District soviets and public organizations appealed to citizens to maintain order while using streetcars, to stay in line at stops, not to overload the cars, etc. Yet snow drifts made it impossible to renew all streetcar movement. The trams were running once again in the capital only on March 7. The cars, adorned with flags and slogans, had taken on a festive appearance.

It was one thing to resume streetcar transportation, but another to end the strike at factories. The latter issue involved a bitter controversy that had great significance for the fate of the revolution. The general political strike had accomplished its task—it had furthered the downfall of the autocracy and the establishment of democratic freedoms. The socioeconomic questions of pressing concern to the working masses, especially that of the eight-hour workday, remained unresolved. In the past, economic strikes had often grown into political ones. This time economic demands had surfaced in the course of a political strike, and many workers championed continuing it until these demands were met.

During the revolution factory owners were unable to resort to such timeworn means of dealing with strikes as lockouts or sending workers eligible for military service to the front. Now resolution of the strike was altogether in the hands of the working class. The Soviet did not exploit this circumstance to the proper extent.

The Soviet's Executive Committee at first agreed to the resumption of work at factories manufacturing war-related items, and to continuing the strike at the others. The Bolsheviks vigorously condemned such a dichotomy. At a meeting of the Petersburg Committee of the RSDRP on March 4, M. Khakharev, K. Orlov, N. Podvoiskii, and others argued that a resumption of work would scatter the revolutionary forces and that reactionary officers would take advantage of the end of the strike "to disarm soldiers and put an end to the revolution." M. Kalinin, on the other hand, deemed it necessary to call workers back to work to prevent possible economic exhaustion. He said that after a prolonged strike "it would be impossible to count on a new revolutionary explosion from them (the workers—E.B.)." V. Zalezhskii said that the main thing was to preserve the working class's revolutionary impulse. "If the strike is long-term or is overused as a political tool, the revolutionary impulse vanishes."[171]

A March 4 decision of the Petersburg Committee criticized the division of workers between those working for defense and those who were not. It maintained that "the time to end the strike must be determined exclusively by considerations that safeguard the maximum preservation and development of revolutionary proletarian energies." The Petersburg Committee did not say whether or not such a moment had set in, but voiced its resolve in the event the strike ended to look vigilantly after "all clandestine and overt steps, both of the deposed autocracy and of the Provisional Government replacing it, so as to keep the masses informed and to quickly resolve questions concerning further actions."[172]

The question of terminating the strike appeared on the Soviet's March 5 agenda. Reporting on the matter, Chkheidze said: "The old regime has been reduced to ashes and now, with the winning of freedom, workers must strengthen what they have won through sound local organization. The criminal old regime has seriously undermined the economy and productivity of the motherland and it is necessary in the name of freedom to return to normality by resuming work. But if the enemy even entertains a restoration, the united proletariat must make demands and protest."[173] Chkheidze admitted that the proletariat could not work under past conditions. "We have returned to work and now must hammer out acceptable working conditions."[174] Although Chkheidze summoned workers to be on guard and to take to the streets at the very first signal, it was another thought that permeated his report: "The time has come for peaceful work."

Five worker and soldier speakers debated Chkheidze's report. The workers backed prolonging the strike while soldiers insisted upon ending it. From the draft protocol it appears that workers demanded the strike be continued until certain of their demands were satisfied, e.g., introduction of the eight-hour workday, review of the makeup of factory administrations, and improvement in work conditions. A member of the Executive Committee of the Moscow Soviet of Workers' Deputies, the Menshevik Pumpianskii, also spoke out at this meeting on behalf of resuming work. He announced that the Moscow workers had decided to return to work, but were waiting to see what their Petrograd brothers did. "Think seriously about the consequences your decision will have. . . . We now have won the right to organize and political rights. We now have new methods of struggle. We now must get down to organizing without losing a precious moment. . . . The strike is paralyzing trade unions. We must resume work to have the opportunity to assert our rights." Therefore Pumpianskii appealed "in the name of the revolution to end immediately the strike directed against the tsarist regime and to mobilize our forces to struggle for a constituent assembly."[175]

An overwhelming majority of members of the Petrograd Soviet (1,170 against 30) voted to end the strike. "In recognizing that the first determined onslaught of the insurgent people against the old order was crowned with success and had sufficiently secured the working class's position in its revolutionary struggle, the Soviet of Workers' and Soldiers' Deputies believes it now possible to begin work in the Petrograd area but to strike once again at the first call. The resumption of work at present seems desirable since strikes seriously threaten to exacerbate economic conditions in the country, already undermined by the old regime."[176] The Soviet petitioned workers "to create and strengthen workers' organizations of all types at once, as strongholds for the continuation of the revolutionary struggle, and to use them to liquidate the old regime and advance the class ideals of the proletariat." The Soviet concomitantly considered it necessary to wind up the strike and work out a program of economic demands workers could present to their employers.

The Soviet's resolution to end the strike alarmed workers because it had not been discussed beforehand at factories, in district soviets, or in the workers' section of the Petrograd Soviet. The decision had been made at the top, at a joint meeting of both sections of the Soviet. Should this decision be obeyed? Workers in some enterprises thought not. A resolution adopted by Petrograd Dinamo Factory workers said: "We will not obey the Soviet of Workers' and Soldiers' Deputies because: 1) a resolution against the resumption of work was not discussed; and 2) the Soviet did not take into account the fact that the revolutionary wave has not yet washed across all of Russia. Putting it otherwise, there can be no talk of bringing the strike to a close until the old authorities have been replaced and victory achieved."[177]

The Organizational Committee of the Soviet of Workers' Deputies of Petrograd's Moscow Region also disagreed with the Petrograd Soviet's decision to start up work. At a meeting on March 6 it called the Soviet's resolution to go back to work "erroneous" and demanded the Soviet reexamine the matter.[178] Representatives of the Vyborg District Bolsheviks attending a meeting of the Petersburg Committee likewise voiced their dissatisfaction with the Soviet's resolution but announced they would obey it to avoid disorganization in the workers' ranks.[179]

The seven-thousand-strong collective of the New Lessner Factory resolved that "the question of ending the strike is premature. Nevertheless, to coordinate and unify revolutionary forces in the country, we will obey the Soviet of Workers' and Soldiers' Deputies' decision and declare that at the first call from workers' and soldiers' representatives we will go out on strike to further the struggle for the [realization of the] basic slogans of the proletariat and peasantry—the eight-hour workday, a democratic republic, and the confiscation of all land for the peasants."[180]

A resolution passed unanimously by workers from six factories (Erlikh, Iakor, Lipin, Vegman, Asler, and Borman) noted that the struggle with tsarism was not yet over, so terminating the strike would be premature. Not wishing to disrupt the ranks of the democracy, however, they agreed to resume work at the first summons in order "to be ready to act as a single united force." The workers proposed that the Soviet notify the entire world of the overthrow of the autocracy in Russia and implore all nations to join together to conclude the war.[181]

The strike did not end at all Petrograd enterprises on the date earmarked for resuming work—March 6. Returning to their benches, workers at many factories presented economic demands to their bosses. Of the eighteen factories in the Vyborg District that had begun work, only two obeyed the Soviet's resolution without reservations; the rest submitted demands to their employers on the introduction of the eight-hour workday and other economic reforms.[182] Judging by local reports made on March 7 in the Workers' Section of the Soviet, the same situation also prevailed at enterprises in other Petrograd neighborhoods.[183]

Summing up the reports, the chairman of the Soviet's Workers' Section, B. O. Bogdanov, a Menshevik, spoke of the unprecedented disorganization and of the need to improve the workers' economic situation in an organized fashion. "In general workers resumed work; in some places, though, only partially. Other workers did not return to work. In the Moscow Region they completely distrust us."[184] Noting that workers in a number of enterprises had not terminated the strike, the Workers' Section of the Soviet on March 7 issued a decree: "1) to recognize the resolutions of the Soviet of Workers' and Soldiers' Deputies as obligatory for the entire working class of Petrograd; 2) to confirm the binding force of the Soviet's resolution on resumption of work at Petrograd's factories and plants; 3) to obligate the Moscow Region to resume work at once."[185]

Even the second resolution by the Soviet to end the strike, however, failed to restore work at all Petrograd factories. Workers at several factories and plants refused to return to their jobs as long as their economic demands were not satisfied. At some enterprises work began, but was stopped shortly thereafter. The administrations' refusal to give in to workers' economic demands or to pay workers during the revolutionary strike triggered a new wave of strikes. In vain the Mensheviks' *Rabochaia gazeta* tried to convince workers that the strike's political goal had been achieved and that its continuation exacerbated the precariousness of the country's economy. Workers at a number of factories continued to strike, advancing their pressing economic demands.

At a meeting of workers' deputies from the Petrograd side, held on March 8, few local representatives reported that workers had gone back to work on the indicated date and under the old conditions. They stated that workers strongly opposed the Soviet's decision to resume work and that those who returned to work did so rather haphazardly. The introduction of the eight-hour workday "in a revolutionary manner" *(iavochnym poriadkom)* accompanied the ending of the strike in the majority of enterprises. Speakers at the meeting on the Petrograd side called the Soviet's decision "premature" because it ignored the mass mood and lack of organization. The meeting proposed that the Soviet "1) reach such decisions henceforth only after a more serious and thorough discussion of them and only after taking into account local moods; 2) reorganize the Soviet and its Executive Committee as soon as possible; 3) develop and implement radical reforms in the economic realm at once."[186]

Petrograd workers returned to their benches not to don the yoke of the former capitalist exploitation; they had spilled their blood on the streets of the capital to achieve a better life. After the overthrow of the autocracy, the battle between labor and capital unfolded with new vigor. The Soviet strove to harness this struggle and keep it within prescribed limits. The Soviet's Executive Committee maintained that the workers must win their demands with the help of factory and local committees, trade unions, and the Soviet. Calling for an end to the strike, the Executive Committee announced that a special commission had been empowered "to work out a list of general economic demands that will be presented to the factory owners and government in the name of the working class." Noting that several industrialists were closing their enterprises and throwing workers out into the street in response to workers' demands, the Executive Committee warned that in the event of similar unlawful actions on the part of the capitalists, "the Soviet will raise before the working class, city government, and Provisional Government the question of the municipalization of such enterprises or their transfer to workers' collectives."[187]

The major working-class demand was the introduction of the eight-hour workday. On March 7, 1917, the Petersburg Bolshevik Committee discussed it. M. Khakharev proposed appealing to the Soviet to introduce the eight-hour workday and insisted it be established by decree. He also considered "it necessary for the neighborhoods to conduct agitation locally—at factories and plants—and through their deputies to direct analogous demands to the Soviet so that pressure will be rendered on the Soviet Executive Committee by the neighborhoods."[188] The decision of the Vyborg District Committee was read at the meeting, which called for the implementation of the eight-hour workday in a revolutionary manner and simultaneously insisted that the Soviet introduce this measure legally. Representatives from Vasilevskii Island, Kolpinskii, and other regions were also adamant about introducing the eight-hour workday. The Petersburg Committee on March 7 resolved that the Soviet's Executive Committee should "decree the eight-hour day at once in all areas of production."[189]

The Soviet's leaders did not take this step, however, for fear of frightening the bourgeoisie away from the revolution. The Mensheviks' *Rabochaia gazeta* argued it was dangerous to move beyond the limits of the political revolution and get down to the fundamental resolution of socioeconomic problems. "Our revolution is a political revolution. We are destroying the bastions of political despotism, but the foundations of capitalism remain in place." *Rabochaia gazeta* maintained that the working class was unable to battle on two fronts—with the tsarist reaction and with capitalists. "We will not respond to the capitalists' challenge. We will begin the economic struggle only when necessary."[190] The Menshevik paper accepted the possibility of establishing the eight-hour workday in separate branches of industry, but opposed its introduction "everywhere by force." "This is tantamount to leaving one revolution unfinished and rushing unprepared into a second."[191]

Some Petrograd workers responded sympathetically to these warnings. The majority, however, fought to have socioeconomic reforms, especially the eight-hour workday, carried out at once. Workers at the Izhora and Franco-Russian factories, Neva Shipyard, and other enterprises did not wait for a government decree or resolution from the Soviet and introduced the eight-hour workday on their own. Workers at several smaller enterprises also behaved in this manner. Two hundred fifty workers of the Woodworks and Mechanical Factory of the House of Khlebnikov & Co. resolved to resume work on March 8, to introduce the eight-hour workday, to fire the manager and foreman, and to choose new ones instead.[192]

Factory and plant owners failed to preserve the status quo at the workplace; the eight-hour workday and other socioeconomic measures were being introduced in a revolutionary manner. The Petrograd Society of Factory and Plant Owners turned to the Soviet for help. On March 9 the Soviet's Executive Committee discussed this society's "desire to negotiate with the Soviet of Workers' and Soldiers' Deputies in connection with the conflicts that were arising with workers." At this meeting the Executive Committee formed a Department of Labor and ordered it to negotiate the formation of conciliatory boards for settling conflicts between workers and proprietors. The Department of Labor and Society of Factory and Plant Owners discussed how they could join forces to direct workers toward peaceful activities. Its delegates, Gvozdev and G. Pankov, announced that the Soviet "understands the gravity of the situation and is concerned with the restoration of work as soon as possible, but can influence the working masses only through appeals. It cannot cite any concrete improvements in the working masses' former disenfranchised status, brought about by the revolution."

The Soviet's representatives told proprietors it was necessary to "reform factory life" on the basis of an agreement between workers and capitalists, and they tried to persuade them the Soviet would not permit the use of force in doing so. Soviet delegates proposed that the Society of Factory and Plant Owners reach an agreement on the most important question—the introduction of the eight-hour workday—and announced this "would immediately soothe the working masses and would give the Soviet the opportunity to use this real improvement to resolve all other questions in a less urgent manner and in the process of normal factory life."[193]

Factory and plant owners realized there was no other way to satisfy workers, and they were forced to make a major concession to the proletariat. An agreement was reached between the Soviet and Petrograd Society of Factory and Plant Owners "on the introduction of the eight-hour workday, factory committees, and conciliatory boards at factories and plants." *Izvestiia* published it under the headline "A Great Working-Class Victory." The agreement established that until publication of a law on the normalization of the workday at all factories, the eight-hour workday would be introduced on all shifts, and the workday would be seven hours on Saturdays. Moreover, the shortening of the workday would not affect wages, and overtime was permitted if approved by the factory committees.

The agreement called for establishment of factory committees at all factories and plants, which were to be chosen by workers through general and equal elections. The committees would represent workers of a given enterprise in their dealings with governmental and public organizations, survey opinions on work conditions, resolve problems arising among workers themselves, and represent workers in settling conflicts with owners and factory administrations. Conciliatory boards were to be set up at all factories to resolve misunderstandings between management and workers. The boards were to be composed of an equal number of elected representatives from workers and the administrations, and in the event that the factory conciliatory boards could not reach agreements, the disputed question was to be submitted to the Central Conciliatory Board made up of an equal number of representatives from the Soviet and Society of Factory and Plant Owners. The firing of foremen or administrators without a hearing before the conciliatory board, especially their forced removal, would no longer be permitted.

The introduction of the eight-hour workday represented an important working-class achievement, the realization of a long-standing dream, of one of the points in the minimum program of the RSDRP. This measure also extended to factories under the military and naval authorities and to enterprises under the city government's jurisdiction. The Executive Committee of the Petrograd Soviet proposed that the government publish a decree implementing the eight-hour workday across Russia in all branches of industry. Although such a decree was never issued, a major victory had nonetheless been gained. A March 12 *Pravda* article, "The First Step," said: "The editorial board of *Pravda* congratulates Petersburg workers and along with them the Soviet of Workers' and Soldiers' Deputies, who have won the eight-hour workday in the revolutionary struggle. . . . We join the demand of the Soviet of Workers' and Soldiers' Deputies for the immediate introduction of the eight-hour workday in all of Russia, in all branches of industry." The newspaper emphasized that the RSDRP had promoted this demand in its program and had fought both for political and economic changes. "The Russian Revolution is a great revolution because it is carrying out not only the political demands of the proletariat and peasantry but also major economic demands: the eight-hour workday, and then the transfer of landlord estates to the emancipated people."

The revolution was to have satisfied the vital interests of both workers and soldiers. This was impossible within the confines of traditional military organization. Moreover, the bourgeoisie sought to preserve this organization after the overthrow of the autocracy and wanted the armed forces to subordinate themselves to it as quickly as possible so that it could become master of the situation and establish its own rule without the Soviet. Troops at the front and rear remained ignorant of what had occurred in the capital, and the State Duma Committee had already planned to administer a new oath to the incipient Provisional Government. In a conversation with Lukomskii on the morning of March 3, Rodzianko reported: "Tomorrow, for General Alekseev's examination, I will transmit to you over direct wire the text of an oath for the troops which you will deign to administer."[194] But the chairman of the State Duma was in too big of a hurry. His recommendation was not acted upon, in part because it was unclear to whom the new oath would be made.

Another attempt by the bourgeoisie to restore the status quo in the army and to demonstrate the troops' unity with the bourgeois government also failed. Petrograd military authorities planned a parade of garrison troops on March 4. The Provisional Government was supposed to salute the troops, but the Petrograd garrison was in ferment. Soldiers were setting up new procedures in the army, and they were not about to take part in parades to honor the Provisional Government—the hated tsarist parades, after all, were still fresh in their memory. On March 3 representatives of the military units convened at district headquarters to discuss the upcoming parade. Serving as commander in chief of the district, General Anokhin argued it was necessary to organize a parade of revolutionary troops so they could present themselves to the new authorities. This suggestion aroused a spate of protests. Some of the soldiers and officers saw it as a machination on the part of the old regime. As one soldier put it: "We made a revolution, we organized ourselves, and our authoritative organ is the Soviet. I don't know whether you've spoken with it, but I know the Soviet opposes all counterrevolutionary parades reminiscent of the old regime."[195]

The Soviet discussed the parade on March 3, but did not reach any conclusive decisions as reported at the district headquarters' meeting. The Soviet refrained from interfering in the actions of the military authorities. It decreed: "Since the instruction of Minister of War Guchkov to organize a parade is an order for the garrison and since the Soviet recognizes the necessity of military discipline, this order will not be discussed by the Soviet of Workers' and Soldiers' Deputies."[196] Despite such "neutrality" on the part of the Soviet, the military authorities failed to implement their order. The soldier masses were stirred against their venture. Recognizing the Soviet as its leader, they did not wish "to present themselves" to the bourgeois government. Because it was impossible to review the troops without the Soviet's backing, the parade never materialized.

Only the Soviet enjoyed indisputable authority among soldiers. They supported the Soviet, believed its appeals, and agreed with its program. Soldier committees made sure that speakers who disagreed with the Soviet's policies did not address political rallies in the barracks. "Members of company or detachment committees are permitted to interrupt speeches if they contradict the Soviet's program."[197] The committee of the Reserve Battalion of the Moscow Regiment on March 9 decreed "that shells and all else necessary for the army be sent to the front with the consent of the Executive Committee of the Soviet of Workers' and Soldiers' Deputies, under its control, and in such a manner as not to harm the revolutionary army."

Order No. 1 had alarmed bourgeois leaders and military authorities, but they were not in the position to revoke it.[198] Duma Committee leaders tried to convince the Soviet's representatives that this order was detrimental to the army and had to be rescinded. Under pressure from military authorities and bourgeois organizations, the Soviet's Executive Committee frequently discussed the order. Following are excerpts from its resolutions on this matter. From March 3: "In view of misunderstandings arising from Order No. 1 in the Petrograd garrison, the Military Commission is entrusted to elucidate this order." From March 4: "After an exchange of opinion at a joint meeting of representatives of the officer corps and the Executive Committee it was decided to regulate relations between officers and soldiers on the bases set forth in Order No. 1. This order is to be elucidated to put an end to misunderstandings arising from it." From March 6: "In view of the fact that Order No. 1 caused a number of misunderstandings and rumors it is resolved to publish Order No. 2 for all garrisons, which explains the meaning of Order No. 1 and confirms its fundamental principles. Order No. 2 will be issued by the Executive Committee and minister of war."[199]

In this manner, then, the Soviet's Executive Committee confirmed the basic provisions of Order No. 1. The committee wanted, together with the minister of war, to explain it, to clear up "misunderstandings and false rumors." But the latter was a firm opponent of Order No. 1. Guchkov had no intention of signing orders jointly with the Soviet; if anything, he tried to avoid cooperating with it. On March 6 the Soviet's Executive Committee discussed "Minister of War Guchkov." It became clear that "the minister of war in every possible way shuns direct relations with the Executive Committee and apparently is not inclined to obey the decisions of the Soviet of Workers' and Soldiers' Deputies." It was decided to send a delegation to the war minister to negotiate publication of Order No. 2. The delegation was instructed to promote a number of new provisions which stemmed from Order No. 1 to Guchkov:

> to insist upon the necessity of electing officers and the creation of an arbitration tribunal made up of two soldiers and two officers and a fifth elected at large. The arbitration tribunal would regulate relations between officers and soldiers. Moreover, the delegation was commissioned to insist upon the abolition of the guards, permission to wear civilian clothing outside of service, the abrogation of saluting and the like in accordance with the principles set forth in Order No. 1. The delegation must report the results of its negotiations to the Executive Committee for a final resolution of the question of Order No. 2.[200]

The Soviet Executive Committee's delegation comprised of Skobelev, Sokolov, Gvozdev, Steklov, Kudriavtsev, and an officer called upon the war minister. Afterward, in reporting on the results of its meeting with him, the delegation said that Guchkov had agreed to issue the order to the front, to present it to the Executive Committee beforehand, and to sign the telegram that would inform the front.[201] It is unclear from this report whether he had agreed to sign the new order earmarked for the Petrograd garrison. In any event, Order No. 2 of March 7, 1917, bore the signature only of the Executive Committee of the Petrograd Soviet.

Order No. 2 explained that soldiers' committees were being formed not in order to choose new officers. "These committees must be elected so that soldiers in the Petrograd garrison are organized and able, through their committee representatives, to take part in the country's political life in general, and to inform the Soviet of Workers' and Soldiers' Deputies of their views on any given measure in particular. The committees must also be in charge of the public needs of each company or unit."[202] Order No. 2 held that the election of officers had been entrusted to a special commission but that election of officers that already had taken place remained in force. It was recognized that until the matter of electing officers was resolved, the committees of individual units had the right to protest the appointment of any officer by directing their complaints to the Soviet's Executive Committee, which in turn would present them to the Military Commission. Order No. 2 confirmed that soldiers must follow the Soviet in their public and private lives, but that they must obey their military superiors when on duty. Citing the Provisional Government's pledge not to disarm the Petrograd garrison, the order proposed that company and battalion committees "see to it that weapons are not taken away from Petrograd soldiers."

The history of these orders did not end here. Soldiers were in turmoil, fearing that Order No. 2 had limited or possibly abrogated Order No. 1. The military authorities insisted on revoking both orders. The Central Committee of the Kadet party again denounced the Soviet's orders, demanding new explanations and clarifications. As a result, a new document, which sometimes is called Order No. 3 and which in reality was an appeal to soldiers at the front, appeared. Deputy Chairman of the Executive Committee Skobelev and Chairman of the Duma's Military Commission Major General Potapov, who had replaced Guchkov, signed this appeal. Order No. 3 recognized the victory over the old regime, pointed out the necessity of regulating relations between soldiers and officers who had accepted the new order, and called upon the latter "to show respect for the citizen-soldier both on duty and off." It reported that Orders No. 1 and 2 concerned only troops in the Petrograd Military District, and that new rules for determining relations between soldiers and officers at the front would be worked out by the war minister in accord with the Soviet's Executive Committee. The document concluded: "This appeal was composed in agreement with War Minister A. Guchkov."[203]

The bourgeois authorities counted on taking the garrison of the capital into their hands with the help of the new commander in chief of the Petrograd Military District, L. G. Kornilov, who arrived in Petrograd on March 5. He was given unlimited powers; in particular, he received the right to remove officers on his own authority, including those at the very highest ranks and replace them. Large sums were placed at his disposal for conducting propaganda in the units. Because of the continuation of the revolutionary struggle, the new commander in chief was no better able than his predecessor to muster total control. He was compelled to take the Military Commission into account, especially the Soviet, and to cope temporarily with limitations on his authority. On March 10 Military Commission member Pal'chinskii informed the Soviet's Executive Committee that "Kornilov wishes to maintain contact with the Executive Committee and Military Commission. He proposed to confirm via orders issued to the district those individuals approved by the Military Commission. Kornilov reported he was relieving all unelected individuals of their responsibilities, if their hostile attitudes toward the revolution warranted it. He also would approve all orders pertaining to troop movement, etc." Pal'chinskii supposed that "General Kornilov had completely mastered the situation and could be retained as commander of the district."[204]

Despite Pal'chinskii's assurances, the Soviet's Executive Committee distrusted Kornilov. At this same Executive Committee meeting someone said that it was necessary "to be wary of Kornilov, for he is a general of the old cloth who wants to end the revolution." One Executive Committee member not named in the protocols advised adopting a neutral position on the matter of strengthening Kornilov's authority. Skobelev recommended informing Kornilov of the doubts certain people had about him.[205] Such declarations, however, went no further. Kornilov remained at his post. In order to subordinate the troops of the Petrograd Military District to his authority, he declared himself a supporter of the revolution and established contact with the Soviet. Yet formal contact could not eliminate real differences.

Neither Guchkov's actions nor those of Kornilov and other ministers and commanders could change the alignment of forces or create staunch military support for the bourgeois authorities in Petrograd. In explaining the reason for this, Guchkov lamented the weakness and inexperience of the garrison's command, its inability to establish firm discipline among soldiers. Moreover, he admitted that the government's promise not to remove troops from Petrograd who had participated in the revolution precluded creation of an armed force loyal to the Provisional Government.[206] This recognition reflected the farsightedness of the workers' and soldiers' demand for strengthening and developing the victory they achieved in February 1917.

The bourgeoisie's appeals for law and order went unheeded, for weapons remained in the hands of workers and soldiers. The presence of the Soviet, drawing on the armed people, opened new perspectives for the further development of the revolution.

Maintaining there were few victims, bourgeois historians and publicists usually call the February Revolution of 1917 in Russia "bloodless." Although this revolution had been bloodless for the bourgeoisie, the working people of Russia had endured heavy losses during their decades-long struggle with the autocracy and, in the last days of its existence, it was their blood that stained the streets of the capital to win freedom.

The workers and soldiers of Petrograd demonstrated heroism and selflessness in their battle against tsarism. They steadfastly fought in the streets of the capital against police and troops loyal to the government. About two thousand people were killed or wounded during the revolution in Petrograd. The social composition of these unfortunate ones is not surprising. Of the 1,224 individu-

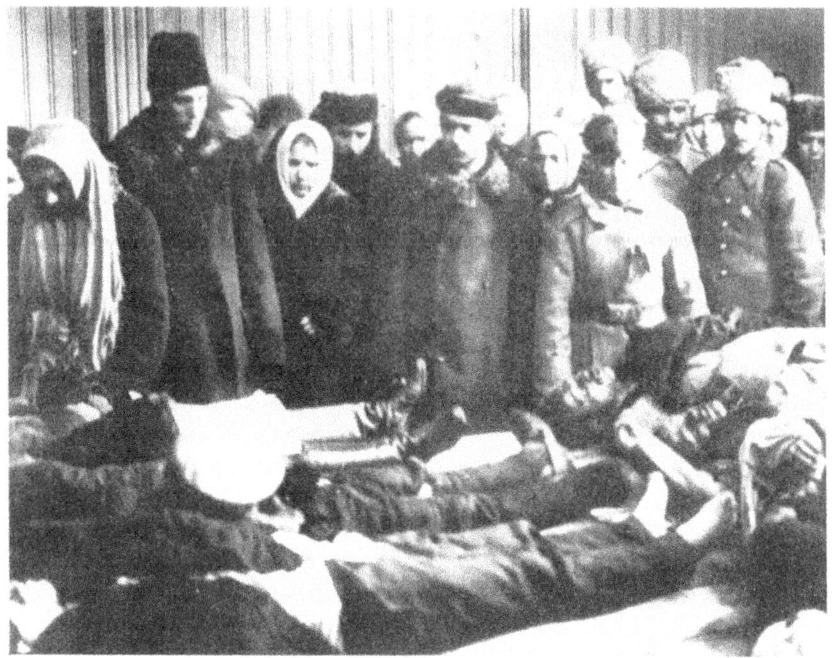

Victims of the February Revolution in the city morgue. Eric Baschet, *Russie 1904–1924: La Révolution est là* (Paris, 1978).

als the Petrograd city authorities listed as killed or wounded, there were 585 soldiers, 315 workers, and 106 office workers. The remainder were students, school-age children, and people of unknown professions.[207] A member of the Petersburg Committee of the RSDRP, a worker named Petr Koriakov, was among those brave souls who met their death. He was only twenty years old when he arrived in Petrograd in 1912 and joined the party. Koriakov then worked in Ekaterinoslav, escaped from arrest, and again showed up in the capital. All day on February 27 he fought in the streets of the city, took part in skirmishes with the police, and was killed in one of them.

The working people of the capital decided to bury the freedom fighters with dignity. The Petrograd Soviet took the initiative to organize a funeral. The protocol of the March 5 meeting said: "A number of delegates made emotional speeches dedicated to the heroes of the uprising against tyranny. It was decided to organize a funeral for the victims of the revolution on March 10. Palace Square was chosen as the place of internment, for it was here that the dead and wounded fell on January 9, 1905, and it symbolized the downfall of the place from which the multifarious evil, the Romanovs, ruled."[208] The Soviet decided to turn the funeral into a commemoration of those who had suffered at the hands of the autocracy. When it became clear that more time was needed to organize the funeral and demonstration, the burial day was postponed to March 23. The place of internment was also changed to the Field of Mars.

The Petrograd Soviet set up a Funeral Commission. Tremendous preparation got underway for the funeral and first free demonstration in the Russian capital. Memories were still alive of the disaster at Khodynka [see note m, chap. 2—D.J.R.], when thousands of people were crushed to death while celebrating Nicholas II's coronation. The victorious workers and soldiers were determined that the overthrow of tsarism and the funeral of its last victims would not be marred by a new Khodynka. The Funeral Commission appealed to all citizens of Petrograd: "On March 23 our city, the first to have raised up the banner of the Great Revolution, commits to the earth and to glorious and eternal memory the bodies of the freedom fighters. May this day of national commemoration of the freedom fighters be free of any accidental deaths whatsoever, as someone could fall in the large mass of people who will participate in the solemn procession. We invoke the civic pride of each of you and ask your utmost assistance in maintaining order during the procession and in preventing senseless excesses unworthy of us."[209]

On March 23, 1917, the working people of Petrograd buried the fallen freedom fighters. An enormous procession passed through the streets of Petrograd. A million people took part in it. It was the first free demonstration organized by the people themselves in the capital of Russia. "In this gala procession of hundreds of thousands of people," wrote Maksim Gorky, "it was felt, and for the first time, that the Russian people, yes, the Russian people had made a revolution. It rose from the dead to join the great cause of the world—the building of new and ever-so-free forms of life."[210]

Complete order reigned at the funeral of those who fought for the revolution. Red coffins covered with flowers were carried from the hospitals. Behind them marched the working people of Petrograd, the sounds of "La Marseillaise" and of a funeral march rang out, red banners fluttered with the inscriptions "We sing to the glory of the foolhardy brave," "Your death lit the great torch of freedom," "We vow to be worthy of those who perished for the cause of freedom." The people proceeded to the Field of Mars, where the coffins with the bodies of the fallen heroes were lowered into communal graves. The guns of the Peter-Paul Fortress sounded a salute. The last columns marched at twilight with torches, paying their last respects to the victims of the autocracy. Appeals to further struggle resounded. The slogan "Long live the democratic republic" was inscribed on many banners.

Before us are lists of those buried in the Field of Mars, compiled by the Funeral Commission: four graves each containing 46 bodies, for a total of 184. Among them are individuals who could not be identified. But the names and occupations of the overwhelming majority of them have been accurately ascertained—they are workers, soldiers, sailors. Even bourgeois leaders were compelled during the revolution to recognize the role workers played in the struggle for freedom. At a congress of the Kadet party that took place at the time Miliukov gave "an impassioned speech in praise of the leftist revolutionary people and revolutionary army." "We must," he said, "humbly bow down to those whose red coffins we saw at the bottom of a deep grave in the Field of

Mars. . . ."[211] At this same congress another Kadet leader, M. Vinaver, announced: "We can speak of the heroic deeds of the Petrograd garrison only with a feeling of noble remembrance." The newspaper *Birzhevye vedomosti* (Stock Exchange Gazette) on March 23 noted: "The workers and soldiers who crossed to the side of righteousness and freedom were the first to face Protopopov's machine guns unarmed. They began the revolution. This is their great service."

On the day of the funeral the Bolsheviks' *Pravda* discussed the meaning of the victorious revolution. "Today the attention of all those without rights and the downtrodden throughout the entire world is directed at Russia, at this city where heroic workers and a disenfranchised peasantry cast off the yoke of the tsarist autocracy. . . . Along with songs of sorrow for the fallen freedom fighters rise up in the spring sky millions of voices of an exultant chorus singing of the triumph of the revolution." *Pravda* wrote of the victory of the ideas of scientific socialism, which had enabled Russian socialists to define the inevitability and proximity of the revolution and to lead the proletariat along the correct path. "It was not the call for civil peace put forth during the predatory war of aggression among capitalist states, but the call for civil war that led Russia to the great revolution."

The modest monument raised by the emancipated people on the Field of Mars bears the inscription: "At the bid of tyrants, nations tormented each other. You rose up, working-class Petrograd, and were the first to begin the war of the oppressed against all oppressors." The Russian Revolution was but the beginning of this just war. The entire course of the country's socioeconomic development had prepared it. The masses of people had awaited it, and several generations of revolutionaries had selflessly fought for its victory. Tsarism had sought to suppress the revolution with the help of partial reforms and bloody repressions. The last Russian tsar remained in the people's memory as Nicholas the Bloody. But neither repression nor reform could snuff out revolution. Deep objective processes had undermined the autocracy and made the revolution inevitable. New fighters replaced those who had fallen, and the struggle continued with renewed force.

The Petrograd proletariat played the main role in the victory of the February Revolution. The workers of Petrograd initiated and inspired the uprising against tsarism. They were the first to enter the struggle and, carrying along the soldier masses, they were able to win freedom. "The revolution," wrote V. I. Lenin, "was decided by the Petrograd workers. . . . Petrograd aroused Russia. Petrograd freed her. Great was the cause of the Petrograd workers."[212]

The Petrograd proletariat scored a victory in the capital and undermined the foundations of the tsarist authorities from one end of the country to the other. Moscow, the provinces, and the front rose up in the revolutionary struggle after Petrograd. The revolution was victorious throughout Russia. The workers and peasants of Russia overthrew tsarism and under Bolshevik leadership directed the revolution toward its socialist stage.

Notes

Translator's Introduction

1. Western reviewers warmly praised the book when it appeared. Paul Avrich called it "one of the finest historical works to be published in the Soviet Union since the death of Stalin." William G. Rosenberg hailed it as "an extremely good book: thoughtful, objective, comprehensive, and thoroughly documented." Nancy W. Heer pronounced "there had been nothing in Soviet historiography on the early months of 1917 approaching this level of scholarship and integrity of argument since the 1920s." For reasons that will become obvious later in this essay, no Soviet historical journal reviewed the study, but historians O. N. Znamenskii and V. I. Startsev, in their review published in the journal of the Soviet Writers' Union, *Novyi mir* (New World), maintained that the book's merits have won a place for it "among the most significant achievements in the field of history in our day." Tsuyoshi Hasegawa, author of the most exhaustively researched Western-language examination of the February Revolution, considered Burdzhalov's "the best monograph to date on the February Revolution in any language. . . ." And, more recently, the Study Group of the Russian Revolution, an international association of historians, concluded that Burdzhalov's *Vtoraia russkaia revoliutsiia* "still remains the finest account." See Paul Avrich's review in *The American Historical Review*, no. 1 (1971), pp. 171–72; Rosenberg's review in *Kritika*, vol. 4 (1968), pp. 1–12; Nancy W. Heer's study, *Politics and History in the Soviet Union* (Cambridge, Mass., 1971), p. 196; O. N. Znamenskii's and V. I. Startsev's review, "Istoriia Fevral'skoi revoliutsii," in *Novyi mir*, no. 3 (1968), pp. 270–73. Hasegawa's assessment is found in Tsuyoshi Hasegawa, *The February Revolution: Petrograd 1917* (Seattle, 1981), p. xii, and that of the Study Group of the Russian Revolution in *Sbornik: Papers of the Ninth International Conference of the Study Group of the Russian Revolution*, no. 9 (Leeds, 1983), p. 8. Eastern European scholars also spoke highly of Burdzhalov's accomplishments. See Jozef Lewandowski, *Z pola walki*, no. 1 (Warsaw, 1968), pp. 231–35, and M. Reiman, "Problemy historicke interpretace," *Revue dějin socialismus*, no. 1 (Prague, 1968), pp. 134–40.

2. E. N. Burdzhalov, *Istoriia SSSR (vtoraia chetvert' XIX veka)* (Moscow, 1946); *Istoriia SSSR. Otmena krepostnogo prava i revoliutsionno-demokraticheskoe dvizhenie v Rossii 50-60-kh godov XIX v. Razvitie kapitalizma posle krest'ianskoi reformy* (Moscow, 1946); *SSSR v period bor'by za sotsialisticheskuiu industrializatsiiu strany (1926–1929 gg.)* (Moscow, 1950); *Podgotovka i provedenie Velikoi Oktiabr'skoi sotsialisticheskoi revoliutsii* (Moscow, 1951); *Sovetskii Soiuz v bor'be za zavershenie stroitel'stva sotsialisticheskogo obshchestva i postepennyi perekhod k kommunizmu (1939–1941 gg.)* (Moscow, 1951); *Sovetskii Soiuz v provedenie Stalinskoi konstitutsii (1935–1937 gg.)* (Moscow, 1951); and *Velikaia otechestvennaia voina Sovetskogo Soiuza (1941–1945 gg.)* (Moscow, 1953).

3. See the lead article in *Voprosy istorii*, "O zadachakh sovetskikh istorikov v bor'be s proiavleniiami burzhuaznoi ideologii," no. 2 (1949), pp. 3–13, which formulated the meaning of cosmopolitanism.

4. Aleksandr Nekrich, *Otreshis' ot strakha: Vospominaniia istorika* (London, 1979), p. 53. Nekrich's memoir offers a fascinating account of the trials of the historical profession during Stalin's last years. See in particular, pp. 37–118. Other analyses of this period can be found in Konstantin F. Shteppa, *Russian Historians and the Soviet State* (New Brunswick, 1962), pp. 209–360, and P. K. Urban, *Smena tendentsii v sovetskoi isto-*

riografii, Institut zur Erforschung der UdSSR, series 1, no. 44 (Munich, 1959), pp. 11–19.

5. Thomas B. Larson, "What Happened to Stalin," *Problems of Communism,* no. 2 (1967), p. 83. Burdzhalov, incidentally, published a 70-page booklet at the end of 1953, which mentioned Stalin only once and in far from adulating tones. The booklet had a press run of 200,000 copies and was published in November. See E. N. Burdzhalov, *V chem sostoit znachenie Velikoi Oktiabr'skoi sotsialisticheskoi revoliutsii* (Moscow, 1953).

6. A. M. Pankratova, "K itogam X mezhdunarodnogo kongressa istorikov," *Voprosy istorii,* no. 5 (1956), p. 16.

7. See "Konferentsiia chitatelei zhurnala 'Voprosy istorii,'" *Voprosy istorii,* no. 2 (1956), pp. 199–213.

8. "XX s"ezd KPSS i zadachi issledovaniia istorii partii," *Voprosy istorii,* no. 3 (1956), pp. 3–12.

9. For an overview of this period, see Alexander Dallin, "Recent Soviet Historiography," in *Russia under Khrushchev: An Anthology from "Problems of Communism"* (New York, 1962), pp. 470–88, and Urban, *Smena tendentsii,* pp. 19–33.

10. E. N. Burdzhalov, "O taktike bol'shevikov v marte-aprele 1917 goda," *Voprosy istorii,* no. 4 (1956), pp. 38–56, and "Eshche o taktike bol'shevikov v marte-aprele 1917 goda," *Voprosy istorii,* no. 8 (1956), pp. 104–14.

11. Heer, *Politics and History,* p. 187.

12. Moreover, a memoir written by F. I. Drabkina on the All-Russian Bolshevik conference in March 1917, also appearing in the same issue of *Voprosy istorii,* added punch to Burdzhalov's essays by describing the differences of opinion in the party's ranks and Stalin's moderate, "non-Leninist" stance on several key issues. See "Vserossiiskoe soveshchanie bol'shevikov v marte 1917 goda," *Voprosy istorii,* no. 9 (1956), pp. 3–16.

13. The most exhaustive account of the events of 1956–57 can be found in Heer's *Politics and History,* pp. 69–95. See also Larry F. Holmes, "Soviet Historical Studies of 1917 Bolshevik Activity in Petrograd," Ph.D. dissertation, University of Kansas, 1968, especially pp. 292–304; M. Fainsod, "Soviet Russian Historians, or: The Lessons of Burdzhalov," *Encounter,* no. 102 (1962), pp. 82–89; Leonard Schapiro, "Continuity and Change in the New History of the CPSU," in John Keep and Liliana Brisby, eds., *Contemporary History in the Soviet Mirror* (New York, 1964), pp. 69–82; Dallin, "Recent Soviet Historiography," pp. 470–88; Vera Piroschkov, "Sowjetische Geschichtswissenschaft im inneren Widerstreit (1956–1959), *Saeculum,* nos. 1–2 (1960), pp. 180–98; Nekrich, *Otreshis' ot strakha,* pp. 143–47; and Shteppa, *Russian Historians,* pp. 374–78. The decree of March 9, 1957, and the statement of *Voprosy istorii*'s editorial board can be found in Marin Pundeff, comp. and trans., *History in the USSR: Selected Readings* (San Francisco, 1967), pp. 232–45.

14. M. E. Naidenov, "Sovetskaia istoricheskaia nauka nakanune XXII s"ezda KPSS," *Voprosy istorii,* no. 10 (1961), p. 5.

15. For a discussion of the spate of Soviet publications during this period, see Martin Dewhirst, "L'Historiographie Soviétique récente de l'histoire de la Révolution," *Cahiers du monde Russe et Soviétique,* no. 4 (1964), pp. 549–66.

16. As late as 1959, there were only fifteen full professors and nine doctors of historical science among the 5,250 teachers of party history in the country's institutes of higher education. Many of the teachers lacked academic degrees and conducted no research. See A. A. Zemskov and I. G. Mitrofanov, "O nekotorykh voprosakh izucheniia istorii KPSS v vysshei shkole," *Voprosy istorii,* no. 10 (1959), pp. 150–51.

17. See Schapiro's "Continuity and Change."

18. George M. Enteen, "Soviet Historians Review Their Own Past: The Rehabilitation of M. N. Pokrovsky," *Soviet Studies,* no. 3 (1969), pp. 306–20.

19. Naidenov, "Sovetskaia istoricheskaia nauka," p. 6.

20. Kurt Marko, "History and the Historians," *Survey,* no. 56 (1965), pp. 71–82.

21. *Vsesoiuznoe soveshchanie o merakh uluchsheniia podgotovki nauchno-pedagogicheskikh kadrov po istoricheskim naukam* (Moscow, 1964). Ponomarev's opening and concluding remarks are available in English translation in *Soviet Studies in History*, no. 1 (1963).

22. E. N. Burdzhalov, "Nachalo vtoroi russkoi revoliutsii," in *Materialy i issledovaniia po istorii SSSR* (Moscow, 1964), pp. 131–59.

23. Discussions of Soviet historiography during this period can be found in Hans Rogger, "Politics, Ideology and History in the USSR: The Search for Coexistence," *Soviet Studies*, no. 3 (1965), pp. 253–75; Arthur P. Mendel, "Current Soviet Theory of History: New Trends or Old?" *American Historical Review*, no. 1 (1966), pp. 50–73.

24. See Nekrich, *Otreshis' ot strakha*, pp. 217–40.

25. The article is "Zhurnal i istoricheskaia nauka," *Voprosy istorii*, no. 1 (1966), pp. 3–14. See pp. 6–7.

26. Nekrich, *Otreshis' ot strakha*, pp. 257–69. The verbatim discussion of Nekrich's book as well as a discussion on a proposed text of the third volume of the History of the CPSU, a closed meeting at the Institute of History between Old Bolsheviks and party historians, have been published in *Survey*. See "The Personality Cult," no. 63 (1967), pp. 159–80.

27. Kurt Marko, "Ghosts behind the Ghost—Stalin under Revision," *Survey*, no. 60 (1966), p. 112.

28. Rosenberg review, *Kritika*, p. 5.

29. Znamenskii and Startsev, "Istoriia Fevral'skoi revoliutsii," p. 272.

30. Tsuyoshi Hasegawa, "The Bolsheviks and the Formation of the Petrograd Soviet in the February Revolution," *Soviet Studies*, no. 1 (1977), pp. 86–107.

31. In Burdzhalov's own words: "Research on the second Russian Revolution virtually stopped. No monograph on . . . [it] was published. Dissertations, general course books, and textbooks made no serious contribution to the scholarly study of the February Revolution and were mostly of a primitive, oversimplified kind." E. N. Burdzhalov, "Istochniki i literatura po istorii vtoroi russkoi revoliutsii," in *Sverzhenie samoderzhaviia: Sbornik statei*, ed. I. I. Mints et al. (Moscow, 1970), p. 272.

32. See, for example, E. D. Chermenskii, "Fevral'skaia burzhuazno-demokraticheskaia revoliutsiia 1917 goda," *Voprosy istorii*, no. 2 (1957), pp. 3–18; Id., *Fevral'skaia burzhuazno-demokraticheskaia revoliutsiia 1917 goda v Rossii* (Moscow, 1959); P. V. Volobuev, *Ekonomicheskaia politika vremennogo pravitel'stva* (Moscow, 1962); Id., *Proletariat i burzhuaziia Rossii v 1917 g.* (Moscow, 1964); I. P. Leiberov, "Petrogradskii proletariat v bor'be za pobedu Fevral'skoi revoliutsii," *Istoriia SSSR*, no. 1 (1957), pp. 41–73; Id., "Stachechnaia bor'ba Petrogradskogo proletariata v pervoi mirovoi voine," *Istoriia rabochego klassa Leningrada*, vyp. 2 (1963), pp. 156–86; Id., "O revoliutsionnykh vystupleniiakh petrogradskogo proletariata v gody pervoi mirovoi voiny i Fevral'skoi revoliutsii," *Voprosy istorii*, no. 2 (1964), pp. 63–77.

33. For example, V. S. Diakin, *Russkaia burzhuaziia i tsarizm v gody pervoi mirovoi voiny, 1914–1917* (Leningrad, 1967).

34. For example, *Oktiabr'skoe vooruzhennoe vosstanie: Semnadtsatyi god v Petrograde. Kniga pervaia* (Leningrad, 1967) and I. I. Mints, *Istoriia Velikogo Oktiabria* (Moscow, 1967), vol. 1, *Sverzhenie samoderzhaviia*.

35. I. I. Mints et al., eds. *Sverzhenie samoderzhaviia: Sbornik statei* (Moscow, 1970) and *Rossiiskii proletariat: Oblik, bor'ba, gegemoniia* (Moscow, 1970). Resolutions condemning these volumes criticized their "careless propositions and formulations" and the editors of *Sverzhenie samoderzhaviia* (but not Burdzhalov specifically) for exaggerating the role of spontaneity. For analyses of some of the more significant trends in Soviet historiography at this time, see *Soviet Studies in History*, no. 3 (1983–84); George M. Enteen, "A Recent Trend on the Historical Front," *Survey*, no. 4 (1974), pp. 122–31; David Longley, "Some Historiographical Problems of Bolshevik Party History (The

Kronstadt Bolsheviks in March 1917)," *Jahrbücher für Geschichte Osteuropas*, no. 4 (1975), pp. 494–514. A conference held in March 1973, devoted to the development of historical sciences in the USSR, criticized these volumes and others. See "Vazhnye zadachi istoricheskoi nauki," *Voprosy istorii KPSS*, no. 5 (1973), pp. 7–23.

36. John L. H. Keep, "The Current Scene in Soviet Historiography," *Survey*, no. 1 (1973), p. 3.

37. Burdzhalov, "Istochniki i literatura," pp. 251–82.

38. E. N. Burdzhalov, *Vtoraia russkaia revoliutsiia: Moskva, front, periferiia* (Moscow, 1971).

39. Chermenskii, for example, has continued studying the crisis at the top while Leiberov has chronicled the labor movement during the war and February Revolution. E. D. Chermenskii, *IV Gosudarstvennaia duma i sverzhenie tsarizma v Rossii* (Moscow, 1976). I. P. Leiberov, *Na shturm samoderzhaviia: Petrogradskii proletariat v gody pervoi mirovoi voiny i Fevral'skoi revoliutsii (iiul' 1914–mart 1917 g.)* (Moscow, 1979). It is indicative of recent trends that Leiberov praises Burdzhalov's analysis of the Bolsheviks' dealings with the other revolutionary parties during February and even his controversial discussion of the role of spontaneity vs. consciousness, but criticizes Burdzhalov for underestimating the coordinating and ruling role of the unified Bolshevik center in Petrograd and the presence of a worked-out plan for the preparation and implementation of a general strike. See pp. 8–9.

40. Take, for example, the book by M. E. Solov'ev, *Bol'sheviki i Fevral'skoi revoliutsii 1917 goda* (Moscow, 1980). Although the author criticizes Burdzhalov, grossly overstates the role of the Bolsheviks, and attacks Sukhanov and other "falsifiers," he nonetheless has had to strike a more balanced chord on Stalin who, the author admits, tended to favor union with the Mensheviks on such issues as the war, relations with the Provisional Government, and the Soviet (p. 167).

41. This is apparent even when the author exaggerates the Bolsheviks' role and the importance of Bolshevik leadership as in the study by I. M. Pushkareva, *Fevral'skaia burzhuazno-demokraticheskaia revoliutsiia 1917 goda v Rossii* (Moscow, 1982). More successful in this regard is V. I. Startsev, *27 fevralia 1917* (Moscow, 1984).

42. Michael T. Florinsky, *The End of the Russian Empire* (New Haven, 1931); Bernard Pares, *The Fall of the Russian Monarchy* (New York, 1939); W. H. Chamberlin, *The Russian Revolution, 1917–1921*. 2 vols. (New York, 1935).

43. George Katkov, *Russia 1917: The February Revolution* (New York, 1967). S. P. Mel'gunov, *Martovskie dni 1917 goda* (Paris, 1961); see also his *Na putiakh k dvortsovomu perevorotu* (Paris, 1931), and *Legenda o separatnom mire* (Paris, 1957).

44. See, for instance, Allan K. Wildman, *The End of the Russian Imperial Army: The Old Army and the Soldiers' Revolt (March–April, 1917)* (Princeton, 1980); and David Longley, "The Divisions in the Bolshevik Party in March 1917," *Soviet Studies*, no. 1 (1972), pp. 61–76, and "Some Historiographical Problems of Bolshevik Party History (The Kronstadt Bolsheviks in March 1917)," *Jahrbücher für Geschichte Osteuropas*, no. 4 (1975), pp. 494–514.

Preface

1. *Rech'*, March 9, 1917.

2. David Lloyd George, *Voennye memuary* (Moscow, 1935), vol. 3, pp. 373–74. [I have provided the appropriate quotation from the English-language original. See David Lloyd George, *War Memoirs of David Lloyd George* (Boston, 1934), vol. 3, *1916–1917*, p. 483—D.J.R.]

3. Quoted from G. Z. Ioffe, "Anglo-amerikanskaia burzhuaznaia istoriografiia o Fevral'skoi revoliutsii v Rossii," *Istoricheskie zapiski*, 78 (1965), p. 10.

4. R. P. Browder and A. F. Kerensky, eds., *The Russian Provisional Government, 1917: Documents* (Stanford, 1961), vol. 1, p. 21.

5. E. D. Chermenskii, *Fevral'skaia burzhuazno-demokraticheskaia revoliutsiia 1917 goda v Rossii* (Moscow, 1959); I. P. Leiberov, "Petrogradskii proletariat v bor'be za pobedu Fevral'skoi burzhuazno-demokraticheskoi revoliutsii v Rossii," *Istoriia SSSR*, no. 1 (1957), pp. 41–73; Id., "O revoliutsionnykh vystupleniiakh Petrogradskogo proletariata v gody pervoi mirovoi voiny i Fevral'skoi revoliutsii," *Voprosy istorii*, no. 2 (1964), pp. 63–77.

6. The authors of the recently published second volume of *The History of the Communist Party of the Soviet Union* (Moscow, 1966) are the only ones to devote a special chapter to the February Revolution, and to illuminate its history more completely and accurately than previous historical works on the party.

1. The Revolutionary Crisis

1. See V. I. Lenin, *Collected Works* (Moscow, 1964), vol. 25, p. 364. [All references to Lenin's collected works will provide citations from the official English-language fourth edition published in the Soviet Union. Volume numbers and page numbers will differ from the Russian-language fifth edition of *Polnoe sobranie sochinenii* (Moscow, 1960–65) cited by Burdzhalov—D.J.R.]

2. Ibid., vol. 25, p. 364.

3. *Gosudarstvennaia duma, chetvertyi sozyv: Stenograficheskii otchet zasedanii 26 iiulia 1914 g.*, p. 25.

4. Ibid., p. 19.

5. It's not surprising that the declaration appeared in the stenographic report and the press in a drastically shortened form. Rodzianko deleted all places in the declaration that mentioned the inadmissibility of cooperating with the tsar. The full declaration can be found in A. E. Badaev, *Bol'shevistskaia fraktsiia IV Gosudarstvennoi Dumy i revoliutsionnoe dvizhenie v Peterburge: Vospominaniia* (Moscow and Leningrad, 1930), pp. 346–48.

6. G. V. Plekhanov, *O voine* (Petrograd, 1917), p. 15.

7. O. A. Ermanskii, *Iz perezhitogo* (Moscow and Leningrad, 1927), p. 119.

8. V. A. Bystrianskii, ed., *Listovki Peterburgskikh bol'shevikov, 1902–1917 gg.* (Moscow, 1939), vol. 2, pp. 116–17. Bolshevik leaflets issued during the war are signed by the "Petersburg Committee of the RSDRP." At the beginning of the war the tsarist government renamed the capital "Petrograd." The Petersburg Committee of the RSDRP, however, kept its former name, believing that a change in name would be a concession to chauvinism.

9. Thus wrote in particular the former British consul in Moscow, one of the organizers of the anti-Soviet intervention [during the civil war], Sir Bruce Lockhart: "But for the War and the antiquated inefficiency of the Russian military organisation, the Tsar would still be on his throne." [R. H. Bruce Lockhart, *Memoirs of a British Agent* (London and New York, 1932), p. 66. Burdzhalov cites the Russian-language edition, *Memuary britanskogo agenta* (London and New York, 1932), p. 59—D.J.R.]

10. Lenin, *Collected Works*, vol. 21, p. 176.

11. A. N. Iakhontov, "Tiazhelye dni: Sekretnye zasedaniia Soveta Ministrov—16 iiulia-2 sentiabria, 1915 goda," *Arkhiv russkoi revoliutsii*, 18 (Berlin, 1926), p. 37.

12. *Rossiia v mirovoi voine 1914–1918 gg. (v tsifrakh)* (Moscow, 1925), p. 5.

13. P. I. Liashchenko, *Istoriia narodnogo khoziaistva SSSR* (Moscow, 1950), vol. 2, p. 635.

14. A. G. Rashin, *Formirovanie rabochego klassa Rossii* (Moscow, 1958), p. 233.

15. P. V. Volobuev, *Proletariat i burzhuaziia Rossii v 1917 godu* (Moscow, 1964), p. 16.

16. *Ivanovo-Voznesenskie bol'sheviki v period podgotovki i provedeniia Velikoi Oktiabr'skoi revoliutsii* (Ivanovo, 1947), p. 36.

17. *Bol'sheviki v gody imperialisticheskoi voiny, 1914-fevral' 1917: Sbornik dokumentov mestnykh bol'shevistskikh organizatsii* (Moscow, 1939), p. 65.

18. Bolshevik activities in this regard are examined in the article by I. P. Leiberov, "O vozniknovenii revoliutsionnoi situatsii v Rossii v gody pervoi mirovoi voiny (iiul'-sentiabr' 1915 g.)," *Istoriia SSSR*, no. 6. (1964), pp. 33–59.

19. A. F. Bessonova et al., comps., "Antivoennaia rabota bol'shevikov v gody pervoi mirovoi voiny," *Istoricheskii arkhiv*, no. 5 (1961), p. 87.

20. Ibid., p. 88.

21. *Bol'sheviki v gody imperialisticheskoi voiny*, pp. 67–68.

22. "Iz perepiski russkogo biuro TsK s zagranitsei v gody voiny (1915–1916 gg.) s predisloviem A. I. Elizarovoi," *Proletarskaia revoliutsiia*, no. 7–8 (102–103) (1930), p. 185.

23. Lenin, *Collected Works*, vol. 21, p. 402.

24. Ibid., p. 401.

25. *Bol'sheviki v gody imperialisticheskoi voiny*, pp. 62, 74.

26. Bystrianskii, *Listovki Peterburgskikh bol'shevikov*, vol. 2, p. 200.

27. *Petrogradskii proletariat i bol'shevistskaia organizatsiia v gody imperialisticheskoi voiny* (Leningrad, 1939), p. 146.

28. Bystrianskii, *Listovki Peterburgskikh bol'shevikov*, vol. 2, p. 197.

29. Ibid., p. 209.

30. G. Shokanov, "K desiatiletiiu stachki na Brianskom zavode," *Proletarskaia revoliutsiia*, no. 9 (56) (1926), p. 218.

31. Bystrianskii, *Listovki Peterburgskikh bol'shevikov*, vol. 2, p. 219.

32. TsGAOR SSSR, f. perliustratsii (opening and inspection of correspondence) d. 1062, l. 12.

33. Ibid., l. 65; d. 1067, l. 38.

34. B. B. Grave, ed., *Burzhuaziia nakanune Fevral'skoi revoliutsii* (Moscow, 1927), p. 134.

35. M. Vol'fovich and E. Medvedev, eds., *Tsarskaia armiia v period mirovoi voiny i Fevral'skoi revoliutsii: Materialy k izucheniiu istorii imperialisticheskoi voiny* (Kazan, 1932), pp. 39–40.

36. *Bol'sheviki v gody imperialisticheskoi voiny*, p. 129.

37. N. E. Kakurin, ed., *Razlozhenie armii v 1917 godu* (Moscow and Leningrad, 1925), p. 7.

38. TsGAOR SSSR, f. DPOO, 1917, d. 293, ch. 82, lit. B, l. 1.

39 I. R. Gelis, comp. "Revoliutsionnaia propaganda v armii v 1916–1917 gg.," *Krasnyi arkhiv*, no. 4 (17) (1926), p. 39.

40. Ibid., p. 45.

41. Grave, *Burzhuaziia nakanune Fevral'skoi revoliutsii*, p. 133.

42. Vol'fovich and Medvedev, *Tsarskaia armiia*, p. 26.

43. O. Chaadaeva, *Armiia nakanune Fevral'skoi revoliutsii* (Moscow and Leningrad, 1935), pp. 68–69.

44. P. N. Miliukov, *Istoriia vtoroi russkoi revoliutsii* (Sofia, 1921), vol. 1, p. 85. [Volume I of Miliukov's history is available in English translation. See *The Russian Revolution* (Gulf Breeze, Fl., 1978), vol. 1, *The Revolution Divided: Spring, 1917*, trans. Tatyana and Richard Stites and ed. Richard Stites—D.J.R.]

45. TsGAOR SSSR, f. 627, op. 1, d. 115, l. 3.

46. Ibid., f. 579, op. 1, d. 1108, l. 1.

47. *Kanun revoliutsii* (Petrograd, 1918), p. 76.

48. TsGAOR SSSR, f. 601, op. 1, d. 997, l. 2.

49. *Rech'*, August 26, 1915.

50. V. V. Shul'gin, *Dni* (Belgrade, 1925), p. 134.

51. Grave, *Burzhuaziia nakanune Fevral'skoi revoliutsii*, p. 50.

52. *Russkie vedomosti,* September 27, 1915.
53. *Perepiska Nikolaia i Aleksandry Romanovykh* (Moscow and Petrograd, 1923), vol. 3, p. 244.
54. Iakhontov, "Tiazhelye dni," p. 39.
55. V. P. Semennikov, *Politika Romanovykh nakanune revoliutsii: Ot Antanty-k Germanii* (Moscow and Leningrad, 1926), p. 85.
56. *Gosudarstvennaia duma, chetvertyi sozyv: Stenograficheskii otchet,* session IV, p. 1225.
57. Ibid., p. 1323.
58. Grave, *Burzhuaziia nakanune Fevral'skoi revoliutsii,* p. 74.
59. M. Paleologue, *Tsarskaia Rossiia vo vremia mirovoi voiny* (Moscow, 1923), p. 207.
60. V. P. Semennikov, *Monarkhiia pered krusheniem* (Moscow and Leningrad, 1927), p. 12.
61. Ibid., p. 282.
62. Lenin, *Collected Works,* vol. 21, p. 379.
63. Bystrianskii, *Listovki Peterburgskikh bol'shevikov,* vol. 2, p. 224.
64. *Petrogradskii proletariat i bol'shevistskaia organizatsiia,* p. 173.
65. *Kanun revoliutsii,* p. 80.
66. TsGAOR SSSR, f. DPOO, 1917 g., d. 45, l. 50.
67. *Petrogradskii proletariat i bol'shevistskaia organizatsiia,* pp. 181–82.
68. *Bol'sheviki v gody imperialisticheskoi voiny,* p. 203.
69. *Arkhiv Oktiabr'skoi revoliutsii Leningradskoi oblasti,* f. 4000, op. 7, ll. 13–15.
70. P. N. Miliukov, *Vospominaniia, 1859–1917* (New York, 1955), vol. 2, p. 277. [An abridged English-language edition of Miliukov's memoirs is available. See Paul Miliukov, *Political Memoirs, 1905–1917,* ed. Arthur P. Mendel and trans. Carl Golberg (Ann Arbor, 1967)—D.J.R.]
71. Ibid., p. 278.
72. *Gosudarstvennaia duma, chetvertyi sozyv: Stenograficheskii otchet,* session V, p. 81.
73. TsGAOR SSSR, f. perliustratsiia, d. 1063, ll. 6, 9; d. 1066, l. 118; d. 1070, l. 64.
74. Ibid., d. 1063, l. 58; d. 1064, l. 60.
75. Ibid., d. 1062, l. 9.
76. Grave, *Burzhuaziia pered Fevral'skoi revoliutsii,* p. 156.
77. TsGAOR SSSR, f. 5913, op. 1, d. 16, l. 31.
78. *Russkie vedomosti,* November 27, 1916.
79. Former Deputy Minister of Internal Affairs V. I. Gurko afterward admitted that Rasputin's appearance "only speeded up the process of the breakup of the state system, but in and of itself did not cause it." (V. Gurko, *Tsar' i tsaritsa* [Paris, 1927], p. 123.)
80. *Gosudarstvennaia duma, chetvertyi sozyv: Stenograficheskii otchet,* session V, p. 287.
81. A. A. Sergeev, ed. "Dnevnik Nikolaia Romanova," *Krasnyi arkhiv,* no. 20 (1) (1927), p. 125.
82. TsGAOR SSSR, f. perliustratsiia, d. 1068, l. 98.
83. Ibid., d. 1067, l. 51.
84. Ibid., d. DPOO, d. 20, ch. 7, l. 1.
85. Ibid., f. perliustratsiia, d. 1070, l. 11.
86. *Padenie tsarskogo rezhima: Stenograficheskie otchety doprosov i pokazanii dannykh v 1917 g. v Chrezvychainoi Sledstvennoi Komissii Vremennogo Pravitel'stva* (Moscow and Leningrad, 1926), vol. 5, p. 209.
87. A. A. Blok, *Poslednie dni imperatorskoi vlasti. Prilozhenie.* (Petrograd, 1921), p. 139. Another well-known member of the Black Hundreds, a deputy of the State Duma, N. Markov II, proposed to change the electoral law that had established

elections by social estates before holding new elections. "A Duma elected by estates," he wrote, "will not be liberal." I. Tobolin, ed., "Programma soiuza russkogo naroda pered Fevral'skoi revoliutsii," *Krasnyi arkhiv*, no. 20 (1) (1927), p. 242.

88. *Perepiska Nikolaia i Aleksandry Romanovykh*, vol. 5, pp. 172, 185, 189.

89. Lenin, *Collected Works*, vol. 23, p. 129.

90. In an interesting work dedicated to this question *(Politika Romanovykh nakanune revoliutsii)* V. P. Semennikov correctly notes that the Rasputin-Romanov authorities consciously, although quite discreetly, strove for a separate peace with Germany, but did not take the decisive step toward achieving it for three reasons: 1) they were afraid to break with Anglo-French capital; 2) they feared that the liberal-imperialist Russian bourgeoisie would oppose conclusion of a separate peace; 3) they could not agree on which conditions of peace would satisfy tsarism (p. 186). Semennikov recognized that the decisive step toward a separate peace had not been taken, but nonetheless maintained that tsarism did turn from the Entente to Germany. In P. N. Sobolev, ed., *Istoriia Velikoi Oktiabr'skoi sotsialisticheskoi revoliutsii* (Moscow, 1962), it is argued that "the tsarist government decided to conclude a separate peace with Germany" (p. 12). The authors, however, do not provide any proof.

91. V. Storozhev, "Diplomatiia i revoliutsiia," *Vestnik Narodnogo komissariata po inostrannym delam*, nos. 4–5 (1920), pp. 70, 74. On the eve of the revolution the German government made one more attempt to issue feelers for a separate peace with Russia. This was done through the Bulgarian diplomat Rizov, who tried to establish ties with the Russian ambassadors in Sweden and Norway (*Sovremennye zapiski*, 1928, no. 35). [I was unable to find this reference in *Sovremennye zapiski*—D.J.R.]

92. Storozhev, "Diplomatiia i revoliutsiia," p. 74.

93. Sir George W. Buchanan, *My Mission to Russia and Other Diplomatic Memoirs* (Boston, 1923), vol. 2, p. 49. [Burdzhalov cites a Russian-language edition, *Moia missiia v Rossii* (Berlin, 1929), vol. 2, p. 38—D.J.R.]

94. Paleologue, *Tsarskaia Rossiia*, p. 261. Buchanan's daughter Meriel, who lived with him in Russia, spoke out in his defense. In the book *Krushenie velikoi imperii* (vol. 2 [Paris, 1932], pp. 31–32) she writes: "the British Embassy was perhaps the only house where a Palace Revolution was *not* discussed . . . it is certainly not true that he (Buchanan) wavered for one moment in his loyalty to the Emperor. . . ." [English edition cited here, see *The Dissolution of an Empire* (London, 1932), pp. 154–55—D.J.R.]. *Istoriia Grazhdanskoi voiny v SSSR* (vol. 1 [Moscow, 1935], pp. 57–58) claims that Buchanan's memoirs implicate him in a conspiracy against Nicholas II, but from them it is impossible to draw such a conclusion.

95. Buchanan, *My Mission to Russia*, vol. 2, p. 100.

96. Ibid., pp. 55–56.

97. [This quote and the one below come from the English-language original—D.J.R.] Lloyd-George, *War Memoirs*, vol. 3, p. 452. Lloyd-George maintains that he induced the British government to establish more direct contact with Russia.

98. Ibid., p. 468.

99. Buchanan, *My Mission to Russia*, vol. 2, p. 55.

100. Semennikov, *Monarkhiia pered krusheniem*, p. 85.

101. Paleologue, *Tsarskaia Rossiia*, p. 274.

102. M. V. Rodzianko, *Krushenie imperii* (Leningrad, 1927), p. 207.

103. Paleologue, *Tsarskaia Rossiia*, p. 302.

104. See A. I. Guchkov's memoirs in *Poslednie novosti*, September 9 and 13, 1936. Guchkov gave almost similar testimony on this question to the Extraordinary Investigatory Commission of the Provisional Government.

105. Recalling his discussion with General Krymov, Rodzianko maintains that he unequivocally spoke out against a coup and even forbade people to speak of it in his

home. (Rodzianko, *Krushenie imperii*, pp. 205–206.) The question of a palace coup, however, was discussed in Rodzianko's home, despite the "ban" of the proprietor.

106. *Den'*, September 2, 1917.

107. *Materialy Komissii oprosov Obshchestva izucheniia revoliutsii 1917 g*. A small portion of these materials can be found in the personal archival fund of professor M. A. Polievktov, which is kept by his widow, professor R. N. Nikoladze. She graciously provided the opportunity for the author to use them.

108. P. N. Miliukov, *Rossiia na perelome: Bolshevistskii period russkoi revoliutsii* (Paris, 1927), vol. 1, pp. 27–28. Miliukov later declared that he didn't know a thing about preparations for a palace coup and that "none of these preparations had the slightest influence on the real course of events." ("Pervyi den'," *Poslednie novosti*, March 4, 1924.)

109. TsGAOR SSSR, f. DPOO, 1917, d. 27, ll. 17–18.

110. TsGAOR SSSR, f. 5962, op. 1, d. 4, l. 13.

111. V. A. Maklakov, "Nekotorye dopolneniia k vospominaniiam Purishkevicha i kn. Iusupova ob ubiistve Rasputina," *Sovremennye zapiski*, no. 34 (1928), p. 80.

112. M. N. Pokrovskii, ed., "Ekonomicheskoe polozhenie Rossii pered revoliutsiei," *Krasnyi arkhiv*, no. 3 (10) (1925), p. 69.

113. TsGAOR SSSR, f. perliustratsiia, d. 1066, ll. 4, 115.

114. A. M. Anfimov, "Tsarskaia okhranka o politicheskom polozhenii v strane v kontse 1916 g.," *Istoricheskii arkhiv*, no. 1 (1960), pp. 204–205. Despite the severe description of the mood of the population, an official of the Ministry of Internal Affairs found that the report did not illuminate reality accurately enough. He instructed: "The report was compiled too cautiously, for it seems that the true extent of the crisis was not reflected in it. Instruct the head of the Moscow Department of the Okhranka to be more honest and truthful on these questions."

115. Grave, *Burzhuaziia nakanune Fevral'skoi revoliutsii*, p. 136.

116. TsGAOR SSSR, f. DPOO, d. 20, lit. B, l. 1.

117. Ibid., f. perliustratsiia, d. 1066, l. 19, d. 1070, l. 33.

118. Ibid., f. DPOO, 1917, d. 341, ch. 91, l. 2.

119. Ibid., d. 20, ch. 13, l. 3.

120. Ibid., f. 5913, op. 1, d. 16, l. 31.

121. *Perepiska Nikolaia i Aleksandry Romanovykh*, vol. 5, p. 190.

122. TsGAOR SSSR, f. 6065, op. 1, d. 1, l. 31.

123. Ibid., f. DPOO, 1917, d. 75, ch. 57, l. 3.

124. TsGIA SSSR, f. 1276, op. 12, d. 1816, l. 12.

125. TsGAOR SSSR, f. The Extraordinary Investigatory Commission of the Provisional Government, (ChSK) op. 1, d. 448, l. 72.

126. Ibid., f. POO, 1917, d. 630, l. 70.

127. TsGAOR SSSR, f. POO, d. 507, l. 50.

128. "Dokumenty Biuro TsK RSDRP v Rossii (iiul' 1914 g.-fevral' 1917 g.) (Iz materialov mnogotomnoi istorii KPSS. Okonchanie)," *Voprosy istorii KPSS*, no. 9 (1965), p. 81.

129. TsGAOR SSSR, f. DPOO, 1917, d. 9, ch. 46, lit. B, l. 11.

130. Ibid., l. 10.

131. Ibid., f. POO, d. 644, l. 295.

132. A. Shliapnikov, ed., "Fevral'skaia revoliutsiia v dokumentakh: Listki, vozzvaniia, korrespondentsiia," *Proletarskaia revoliutsiia*, no. 1 (13) (1923), p. 261.

133. TsGAOR SSSR, f. DPOO, 1917, d. 347, ch. 28, l. 2 ob. (obverse).

134. Shliapnikov, "Fevral'skaia revoliutsiia v dokumentakh," p. 266. A letter of the Executive Committee of the Petersburg Committee of the RSDRP read: "In general, on the basis of these incomplete data, one can fix the number of strikers at 160,000–170,000

participants; others put the figure at 200,000 and higher" (ibid., p. 265). The difference between the data of the Central Committee of the Petersburg Committee and the Bureau of the Central Committee is significant. In a footnote to the publication of these documents in the journal *Proletarskaia revoliutsiia*, Shliapnikov confirms the figure given in the "Information Sheet." He writes: "According to data verified at the time by our Bureau of the Central Committee, the number of strikers reached up to 300,000 workers (ibid., p. 266).

135. Ibid., p. 264.
136. *Petrogradskii proletariat i bol'shevistskaia organizatsiia*, p. 191.
137. Shliapnikov, "Fevral'skaia revoliutsiia v dokumentakh," p. 266.
138. *Nakanune velikoi revoliutsii* (Moscow, 1922), p. 39.
139. *Bol'sheviki v gody imperialisticheskoi voiny*, p. 161.
140. TsGAOR SSSR, f. DPOO, 1917, d. 158, l. 6.
141. Shliapnikov, "Fevral'skaia revoliutsiia v dokumentakh," p. 267.
142. *Bol'sheviki v gody imperialisticheskoi voiny*, pp. 163–66.

2. The Beginning of the Insurrection

1. "Dokumenty Biuro TsK RSDRP v Rossii," p. 81.
2. TsGAOR SSSR, f. DPOO, 1917, d. 5, ch. 57, lit. B, ll. 3–4.
3. Bessonova, "Antivoennaia rabota bol'shevikov," p. 97.
4. TsGAOR SSSR, f. DPOO, 1917, d. 341, ch. 88, lit. B, ll. 10, 14.
5. TsGIA SSSR, f. 1278, op. 10, d. 10, l. 41. According to data from the Extraordinary Investigatory Commission, the Petrograd garrison on February 1, 1917, consisted of 180,000 soldiers (TsGAOR SSSR, f. ChSK, d. 471, p. 19). Based on data from the Quartermasters' Administration, B. Kochakov gives other figures: 271,000 soldiers in Petrograd and 195,000 soldiers in the nearest suburbs (B. Kochakov, ed., *Ocherki istorii Leningrada*, [Moscow and Leningrad, 1956], vol. 3, p. 64). Kochakov includes troops from the service units (from storehouses and workshops and others) and those recuperating in field hospitals.
6. A. G. Shliapnikov, *Semnadtsatyi god* (Moscow, 1923), vol. 1, pp. 69–70.
7. N. K. Krupskaia, *Vospominaniia o Lenine* (Moscow, 1957), p. 271. In quoting this passage, many Western bourgeois historians maintain that Lenin did not foresee the imminent victory of the revolution. In fact, however, Lenin believed that a revolutionary crisis had ripened in Russia already by the fall of 1915. The entire report on the twelfth anniversary of the Revolution of 1905 is permeated with confidence that the new revolution would take place in the immediate future. Lenin told the Swiss comrades that Europe was fraught with revolution, though, of course, he was unable to pinpoint the exact date it would take place.
8. Lenin, *Collected Works*, vol. 23, p. 270.
9. Ibid., vol. 35, p. 288.
10. TsPA IML, f. 17, op. 7, d. 27024, ll. 1–2.
11. *Kanun revoliutsii*, pp. 99–100.
12. Shliapnikov, *Semnadtsatyi god*, vol. 1, pp. 32–33.
13. *Kanun revoliutsii*, p. 7.
14. Shliapnikov, *Semnadtsatyi god*, vol. 1, Appendix, p. 281.
15. Grave, *Burzhuaziia nakanune Fevral'skoi revoliutsii*, p. 183.
16. *Bol'sheviki v gody imperialisticheskoi voiny*, p. 172.
17. TsGAOR SSSR, f. POO, 1917, d. 630, l. 135.
18. Bystrianskii, *Listovki Peterburgskikh bol'shevikov*, vol. 2, p. 245.
19. Shliapnikov, *Semnadtsatyi god*, vol. 1, p. 43.
20. Ibid., Appendix, p. 290.

21. TsGVIA, f. 10/l, d. 614. Lists of the condition of personnel, armaments, and the battle complement.

22. The tsarist authorities later denied they had armed the police ahead of time with machine guns to battle against the revolutionary movement. The Extraordinary Investigatory Commission of the Provisional Government carried out an investigation, verified the number of machine guns seized during the street battles in Petrograd, and concluded that all of them belonged to the military units. It's doubtful, however, that the police were armed with machine guns obtained from the military during the revolution itself and that they could have used them without preliminary preparation. Evidently, a plan prepared by the tsarist authorities beforehand had envisaged the police using machine guns against the people.

23. Rodzianko, *Krushenie imperii*, p. 216.

24. Iu. I. Korablev, ed., *Rabochee dvizhenie v Petrograde v 1912–1917 gg.: Dokumenty i materialy* (Leningrad, 1958), p. 535.

25. *Rech'*, February 10, 1917.

26. Ibid.

27. Miliukov, *Vospominaniia*, vol. 2, p. 286.

28. Shliapnikov, *Semnadtsatyi god*, vol. 1, p. 309.

29. TsGAOR SSSR, f. DPOO, 1917, d. 525, l. 91.

30. Ibid., d. 307, lit. A, l. 40.

31. Ibid., d. 59, ch. 28, ll. 1–2.

32. Ibid., d. 20, ch. 50, l. 3.

33. Ibid., f. ChSK, d. 782, ll. 19–20.

34. Ibid., l. 22 ob. Miliukov subsequently wrote regarding the matter of a responsible ministry: "To the very end the majority in the Duma fought against the notion of achieving these purposes by revolutionary means. But seeing that the way of forceful overthrow would be chosen anyway, quite apart from what the Duma did, it began planning for the peaceful channeling of the revolution which it preferred to see come from above rather than below." (Miliukov, *Istoriia vtoroi russkoi revoliutsii*, vol. 1, p. 22.) [The translation provided here is from Tatyana and Richard Stites, *The Russian Revolution* (Gulf Breeze, Fl., 1978), vol. 1, *The Revolution Divided: Spring, 1917*, pp. 22–23.—D.J.R.]

35. TsGAOR SSSR, f. DPOO, d. 27, ch. 46, lit. B, l. 4 ob.

36. Ibid., l. 5.

37. Rodzianko, *Krushenie imperii*, p. 218.

38. *Gosudarstvennaia duma, chetvertyi sozyv: Stenograficheskii otchet*, Session V, pp. 1343–44.

39. TsGAOR SSSR, f. perliustratsiia, d. 1071, l. 45.

40. Bystrianskii, *Listovki Peterburgskikh bol'shevikov*, vol. 2, p. 248.

41. Lenin, *Collected Works*, vol. 27, p. 481.

42. Shliapnikov, *Semnadtsatyi god*, vol. 1, p. 73.

43. Korablev, *Rabochee dvizhenie v Petrograde v 1912–1917 gg.*, pp. 544–45.

44. V. G. Naumkin, "Na Izhorskom zavode nakanune Fevral'skoi revoliutsii," *Krasnaia letopis'*, no. 1 (40) (1931), p. 175.

45. *Putilovets v trekh revoliutsiiakh: Sbornik materialov po istorii Putilovskogo zavoda* (Moscow and Leningrad, 1933), pp. 310–12. M. Mitel'man, B. Glebov and A. Ul'ianskii in *Istoriia Putilovskogo zavoda, 1789–1917* (Moscow and Leningrad, 1939) describe these events in a detailed and colorful manner but err in noting that "all of the workshops of the factory struck on February 21" (p. 576). This mistake is repeated in a number of other works. As a matter of fact, however, the strike that day involved workers from several workshops only.

46. *Leningradskii gosudarstvennyi istoricheskii arkhiv*, f. 569, op. 10, d. 530, l. 64.

47. *Arkhiv Oktiabr'skoi revoliutsii Leningradskoi oblasti*, f. 4000, op. 5, d. 1063, l. 12.

48. V. M. Zenzinov, "Fevral'skie dni," *Novyi zhurnal*, vol. 34 (1953), p. 189.

49. In the essay "Fevral'skaia revoliutsiia 1917 goda v Rossii—reshaiushchaia predposylka Velikoi Oktiabr'skoi sotsialisticheskoi revoliutsii," (*Uchenye zapiski kafedr istorii SSSR i novoi istorii Moskovskogo gosudarstvennogo pedagogicheskogo instituta imeni V. I. Lenina*, vyp. 1, vol. 112, Moscow, 1958), M. E. Solov'ev points out: "From that day (Feb. 18—E.B.) the February Revolution in essence began to grow, which led to the fall of tsarism" p. 13). The introductory essay to the collection *Rabochee dvizhenie v Petrograde v 1912–1917 gg.* says: "The strike that began in February at the Putilov Plant under Bolshevik leadership was transformed into a citywide strike and the latter into an armed uprising that ended with the victory of the revolutionary people over the rotten and criminal tsarist autocracy (p. 24)." Evidently, for this reason the collection does not include materials on the workers' movement after February 18. However, a strike at the gun-carriage press workshop of the Putilov Plant that took place that day, like the other strikes of the Putilov workers in January–February 1917, was not the beginning of the Second Russian Revolution. I. Gaza in the preface to the collection cited above, *Putilovets v trekh revoliutsiiakh*, correctly defines their place: "the January–February strikes of the Putilov workers were the prelude to the February Revolution" (p. XII).

50. TsGIA SSSR, f. 1282, op. 1, d. 741, l. 114.

51. *Leningradskii gosudarstvennyi istoricheskii arkhiv*, f. 569, op. 24, d. 3, ll. 69–70.

52. TsPA IML, f. 124, op. 1, d. 2122, ll. 28–29.

53. Shliapnikov, "Fevral'skaia revoliutsiia v dokumentakh," p. 283.

54. *Arkhiv Oktiabr'skoi revoliutsii Leningradskoi oblasti*, f. 4000, op. 5, d. 74, l. 27; op. 6, d. 45.

55. V. Kaiurov, "Shest' dnei Fevral'skoi revoliutsii," *Proletarskaia revoliutsiia*, no. 1 (13) (1923), p. 158.

56. Shliapnikov, *Semnadtsatyi god*, vol. 1, Appendix, p. 314. I. P. Leiberov in the article "O revoliutsionnykh vystupleniiakh" correctly emphasizes the leading role of the metalworkers in the revolution but incorrectly contrasts them with the rest of the workers. "It was not the spontaneous economic actions of hungry working men and women," he writes, "that determined the basic and serious nature of the revolutionary struggle in the course of the citywide strike, but the massive political strike activities of the metalworkers" (p. 75). What emerges from his argument is that only the metalworkers carried out a political struggle, while the other working men and working women, suffering from hunger, voiced only economic demands. In fact, the economic and political struggle became interwoven for all workers.

57. *Leningradskaia pravda*, March 12, 1926.

58. I. Gordienko, *Iz boevogo proshlogo* (Moscow, 1957), pp. 56–57.

59. Kaiurov, "Shest' dnei Fevral'skoi revoliutsii," p. 158.

60. *Leningradskaia pravda*, March 12, 1927; I. Mil'chik, *Rabochii fevral'* (Moscow and Leningrad, 1931), pp. 61–62.

61. I. Markov, "Kak proizoshla revoliutsiia: Zapis' rabochego," *Volia Rossii*, no. 3 (1927), p. 87.

62. A. Taimi, *Stranitsy perezhitogo* (Petrozavodsk, 1955), p. 171.

63. TsGAOR SSSR, f. DPOO, 1917, d. 341, ch. 57, l. 9v.

64. *Gosudarstvennyi muzei Velikoi Oktiabr'skoi sotsialisticheskoi revoliutsii* (Leningrad), f. 6, Vospominaniia N. Ignatova.

65. TsGIA SSSR, f. 1282, op. 1, d. 741, l. 118.

66. Ibid., ll. 134, 143, and elsewhere.

67. Mitel'man, Glebov, Ul'ianskii, *Istoriia Putilovskogo zavoda*, p. 579.

68. TsGAOR SSSR, f. 628, op. 1, d. 19, ll. 75–79.

69. *Gosudarstvennyi muzei Velikoi Oktiabr'skoi sotsialisticheskoi revoliutsii* (Leningrad), f. 6, Vospominaniia M. Baikova.

70. Personal archive of M. Polievktov. *Materialy Komissii oprosov. Beseda s Chikolini.*

71. *Voina i dorogovizna v Rossii*, published by the TsK RSDRP, 1915.

72. TsGAOR SSSR, f. DPOO, 1917, d. 341, ch. 57, l. 9b.

73. Ibid., POO, op. 5, d. 699, l. 2.

74. Leiberov, "O revoliutsionnykh vystupleniiakh," p. 65.

75. TsGAOR SSSR, f. ChSK, d. 19, l. 49.

76. A. Kuznetsov, "Shtormovye etapy," *Leningrad*, no. 10 (1931), p. 21.

77. *Arkhiv Oktiabr'skoi revoliutsii Leningradskoi oblasti*, f. 4000, op. 6, d. 91, ll. 13–14.

78. *Vozrozhdenie*, September 8, 1928.

79. *Gosudarstvennaia duma, chetvertyi sozyv: Stenograficheskii otchet*, Session V, p. 1657.

80. Ibid., p. 1649.

81. Ibid., p. 1650.

82. *Delo naroda*, March 15, 1917.

83. Ermanskii, *Iz perezhitogo*, p. 140.

84. N. N. Sukhanov, *Zapiski o revoliutsii* (Petrograd, 1919), vol. 1, p. 16.

85. TsGAOR SSSR, f. 6065, op. 1, d. 1, l. 34.

86. Ibid., f. ChSK, op. 1, d. 446, l. 49.

87. *Rech'*, February 24, 1917.

88. TsGAOR SSSR, f. POO, 1917, d. 630, l. 186.

89. Lenin, *Collected Works*, vol. 26, p. 31.

90. Ibid., vol. 29, p. 396.

91. According to a report by Shliapnikov, the Petrograd Bolshevik Organization numbered approximately 3,000 members at the beginning of the revolution (*Petrogradskaia pravda*, March 12, 1920).

92. A. G. Shliapnikov, "Fevral'skie dni v Peterburge," *Proletarskaia revoliutsiia*, no. 1 (13) (1923), p. 82.

93. *Petrogradskaia pravda*, March 14, 1923.

94. However, in several works the start of the Second Russian Revolution is not linked to this date. For example, in *Istoriia Velikoi Oktiabr'skoi sotsialisticheskoi revoliutsii* nothing is said about the disturbances prompted by lack of bread, or about International Women's Day. This work maintains that workers from the majority of large factories struck already on February 22 (p. 13), which is not the case.

95. *Pravda*, March 5, 1917.

96. L. S. Gaponenko et al., eds., *Revoliutsionnoe dvizhenie v Rossii posle sverzheniia samoderzhaviia: Dokumenty i materialy* (Moscow, 1957), p. 9.

97. B. G., "Fevral'skaia revoliutsiia i okhrannoe otdelenie," *Byloe*, no. 1 (29) (January 1918), p. 167.

98. Gordienko, *Iz boevogo proshlogo*, p. 57.

99. Kaiurov, "Shest' dnei," p. 159.

100. Shliapnikov, *Semnadtsatyi god*, vol. 1, p. 92.

101. A. Tarasov-Rodionov, *Fevral'* (Moscow, 1931), pp. 84–85.

102. Kaiurov, "Shest' dnei," p. 161.

103. "Fevral'skaia revoliutsiia i okhrannoe otdelenie," p. 166.

104. According to the data of the Petrograd secret police, 158,583 workers were on strike on February 24, and 201,248 on February 25; according to the data of the city authorities, the number of strikers was 197,000 and 240,000 respectively, (TsGAOR SSSR, f. ChSK, d. 471, l. 27). On the basis of data from the secret police, the factory

inspectorate, reports of police supervisors, factory administrations, and other sources, Leiberov adduces a more exact figure for those striking: 214,111 on February 24, and over 300,000 on February 25 (Leiberov, "O revoliutsionnykh vystupleniiakh," p. 75).

105. K. Kondrat'ev, "Vospominaniia o podpol'noi rabote Peterburgskoi organizatsii RSDRP(b) v period 1914–1917 gg.," *Krasnaia letopis'*, no. 7 (1923), p. 64.

106. TsGAOR SSSR, f. DPOO, 1917, d. 5, ch. 57, l. 31.

107. R. Kovnator, "Nakanune fevralia: Otryvki iz vospominanii, 1905–1917," in *Revoliutsionnoe iunoshestvo* (Leningrad, 1924), p. 189.

108. I. Gavrilov, "Na Vyborgskoi storone v 1914–1917 gg.," *Krasnaia letopis'*, no. 2 (23) (1927), p. 51.

109. *Pravda*, March 12, 1919.

110. *Arkhiv Oktiabr'skoi revoliutsii Leningradskoi oblasti*, f. 4000, op. 5, d. 1319, ll. 3–4.

111. Taimi, *Stranitsy perezhitogo*, pp. 171–72.

112. "Fevral'skaia revoliutsiia i okhrannoe otdelenie," p. 169.

113. TsGAOR SSSR, f. 5881, op. 1, d. 528.

114. "Fevral'skaia revoliutsiia i okhrannoe otdelenie," p. 174.

115. TsGAOR SSSR, f. ChSK, d. 471, l. 35.

116. A. Kugel', "Poslednii maskarad," *Ogonek*, April 24, 1927.

117. *Leningradskii gosudarstvennyi istoricheskii arkhiv*, f. 569, op. 10, d. 443, ll. 54, 59, 61, 64.

118. TsGAOR SSSR, f. ChSK, d. 471, ll. 13–14.

119. V. Shepelev, "Fevral'skie dni," *Ogonek*, no. 7 (1927).

120. In the article "Petrogradskii proletariat vo vseobshchei politicheskoi stachke 25 fevralia 1917 g.," in *Oktiabr' i grazhdanskaia voina v SSSR: Sbornik statei k 70-letiiu akademika I. I. Mintsa* (Moscow, 1966), Leiberov, on the basis of police data, maintains that not less than seventeen embittered skirmishes with mounted and regular police and gendarmes took place on February 25, of which workers used weapons in eleven cases (revolvers in seven instances, bombs in three, and grenades in one). In the remaining six they used rocks, bottles, pieces of metal and ice, shovels, and billets of wood. Leiberov concludes: "These facts cogently testify to the move on the part of the proletarian masses of Petrograd from peaceful defense to the offense, to an armed struggle" (pp. 42–43). However, such a conclusion is hardly substantiated. There were considerably more clashes with the police than one can establish from police reports preserved by chance. Nevertheless, one should not maintain on the basis of eleven instances "in which weapons were used" that the movement had turned into an armed battle on February 25.

121. *Petrogradskaia pravda*, March 14, 1923.

122. Shliapnikov, *Semnadtsatyi god*, vol. 1, p. 90.

123. P. Zalutskii, "V poslednie dni podpol'nogo Peterburgskogo komiteta bol'shevikov v nachale 1917 g.," *Krasnaia letopis'*, no. 2 (35) (1930), p. 37.

124. TsGAOR SSSR, f. DPOO, 1917 g., d. 5, ch. 97, ll. 30–32. In the draft of the document the mentioned activities were erroneously dated a day earlier.

125. Bystrianskii, *Listovki Peterburgskikh bol'shevikov*, vol. 2, pp. 249–50.

126. Shliapnikov, *Semnadtsatyi god*, vol. 1, p. 109.

127. Bystrianskii, *Listovki Peterburgskikh bol'shevikov*, vol. 2, pp. 250–51.

128. TsPA IML, f. 17, op. 1, d. 151, l. 1.

129. I. Iurenev, "'Mezhraionka' (1911–1917 gg.)," *Proletarskaia revoliutsiia*, no. 2 (25) (1924), p. 141.

130. Zenzinov, "Fevral'skie dni," p. 190.

131. Ermanskii, *Iz perezhitogo*, pp. 141–42.

132. Sukhanov, *Zapiski o revoliutsii*, vol. 1, pp. 35–36.

133. Ibid., p. 39.

134. Personal archive of M. Polievktov. *Materialy Komissii oprosov. Beseda s M. Tereshchenko*.
135. A. P. Aleksandrov, *Za Narvskoi zastavoi: Vospominaniia starogo rabochego* (Leningrad, 1963), p. 126.
136. Shliapnikov, *Semnadtsatyi god*, vol. 1, Appendix, pp. 332–33.
137. *Gosudarstvennaia duma, chetvertyi sozyv: Stenograficheskii otchet*, Session V, pp. 1730–31.
138. Ibid., p. 1714.
139. Ibid., p. 1723.
140. Ibid., p. 1728.
141. I. V. Gessen, *V dvukh vekakh* (Berlin, 1937), p. 355.
142. Personal archive of M. Polievktov. *Materialy Komissii oprosov. Beseda s M. V. Rodzianko*.
143. *Padenie tsarskogo rezhima*, vol. 7, p. 158.
144. "Fevral'skaia revoliutsiia i okhrannoe otdelenie," pp. 174–75.
145. *Perepiska Nikolaia i Aleksandry Romanovykh*, vol. 5, p. 209.
146. Sergeev, "Dnevnik Nikolaia Romanova," pp. 135–36.
147. *Perepiska Nikolaia i Aleksandry Romanovykh*, vol. 5, p. 214.
148. Ibid., pp. 218–19.
149. "Fevral'skaia revoliutsiia 1917 goda: Dokumenty stavki verkhovnogo glavnokomanduiushchego i shtaba glavnokomanduiushchego armiiami severnogo fronta," *Krasnyi arkhiv*, no. 21 (2) (1927), p. 4.
150. Ibid., pp. 4–5.
151. *Perepiska Nikolaia i Aleksandry Romanovykh*, vol. 5, p. 224.
152. *Padenie tsarskogo rezhima*, vol. 1, p. 190.
153. Ibid., p. 191.
154. TsGAOR SSSR, f. pechatnykh izdanii, inv. no. 584.
155. "Fevral'skaia revoliutsiia 1917 goda: Dokumenty stavki," p. 5.

3. The Decisive Clash

1. I was unable to uncover lists of those arrested or more detailed information about them. According to Department of Police data, the number of people immured in Petrograd prisons and police stations on February 26–27 increased by 114. (TsGAOR SSSR, f. DPOO, 1917, d. 371, ch. 57, ll. 24, 29).
2. *Arkhiv Oktiabr'skoi revoliutsii Leningradskoi oblasti*, f. 4000, op. 5, d. 995, l. 14.
3. Ibid., d. 1053, ll. 17–18.
4. Ermanskii, *Iz perezhitogo*, p. 145.
5. Kaiurov, "Shest' dnei Fevral'skoi revoliutsii," p. 165.
6. TsGAOR SSSR, f. ChSK, d. 471, l. 42.
7. Markov, "Kak proizoshla revoliutsiia," p. 58.
8. TsGIA SSSR, f. 1278, op. 5, d. 1353.
9. *Padenie tsarskogo rezhima*, vol. 2, p. 226.
10. "Fevral'skaia revoliutsiia 1917 goda: Dokumenty Stavki," *Krasnyi arkhiv*, no. 21 (2), pp. 5–6.
11. *Poslednie novosti*, March 12, 1921.
12. TsGAOR SSSR, f. DPOO, 1917, d. 341, ch. 57, l. 46.
13. Ibid.
14. Ibid., f. pechatnykh izdanii, inv. no. 2342.
15. Iu. Volin, "Rozhdestvo svobody," *Revoliutsiia v Petrograde* (Petrograd, 1917), pp. 39–40, 43. [I was unable to verify this source—D.J.R.]
16. Zenzinov, "Fevral'skie dni," p. 210.

17. *Shestoi s"ezd RSDRP (bol'shevikov): Protokoly* (Moscow, 1958), p. 49.
18. "Fevral'skaia revoliutsiia i okhrannoe otdelenie," p. 171.
19. Ibid.
20. Shliapnikov, *Semnadtsatyi god*, vol. 1, p. 127.
21. "Fevral'skaia revoliutsiia i okhrannoe otdelenie," p. 174.
22. TsGAOR SSSR, f. 5856, op. 1, d. 362.
23. Kaiurov, "Shest' dnei Fevral'skoi revoliutsii," p. 166.
24. Shliapnikov, *Semnadtsatyi god*, vol. 1, pp. 132–33.
25. *Narvskaia zastava: Sbornik vospominanii* (Moscow, 1959), p. 25.
26. Several contradictory descriptions exist of the mutiny of the Volynskii Regiment. S. Mstislavskii has identified seven such versions. Several of them clearly exaggerate the role of the noncommissioned officer T. Kirpichnikov, who the Provisional Government made into a hero of the February Revolution because of his assiduous service to the bourgeoisie, and decorated with the St. George's Cross and promoted to the rank of ensign. One also comes across in the literature claims that Kirpichnikov was a Putilov worker, but this does not correspond to reality. In describing the uprising of the reserve battalion of the Volynskii Regiment, I have mainly utilized the version of the soldiers themselves. See *Revoliutsiia 1917 goda: Ocherk, napisannyi soldatami uchebnoi komandy Volynskogo polka* (Petrograd, 1917).
27. O. Sipol', "Iz vospominanii," *Petrogradskaia pravda*, March 12, 1920.
28. M. Slonimskii, *Kniga vospominanii* (Moscow and Leningrad, 1966), pp. 13–14.
29. N. I. Iordanskii, "Voennoe vosstanie 27 fevralia: 1917 g. v Petrograde," *Molodaia gvardiia*, no. 2 (1928), p. 168.
30. L. Dobronravov, "Revoliutsiia (Zapiski)," *Sovremennyi mir*, no. 2–3 (1917), pp. 282, 284.
31. Kaiurov, "Shest' dnei Fevral'skoi revoliutsii," p. 167.
32. Shliapnikov, *Semnadtsatyi god*, vol. 1, pp. 134–35.
33. Mil'chik, *Rabochii fevral'*, p. 87.
34. TsPA IML, f. 131, op. 1, d. 75, ll. 5–6.
35. TsGAOR SSSR, f. DPOO, 1917, d. 341, ch. 57, l. 29.
36. M. I. Kalinin, *Za eti gody: Stat'i, besedy, rechi* (Moscow and Leningrad, 1929), vol. 3, p. 432.
37. F. Lemeshev, "Na Putilovskom zavode v gody voiny," *Krasnaia letopis'*, no. 2 (23) (1927), p. 38.
38. V. Shmidt, "V 'Krestakh'," *Pravda*, March 12, 1927.
39. S. Budantsev, "Povest' o stradaniiakh uma," *Krasnaia nov'*, no. 3 (1931), p. 85.
40. *Bol'shevizatsiia Petrogradskogo garnizona v 1917 g.: Sbornik dokumentov* (Leningrad, 1932), p. vi. (The figures are adduced by the compilers of the document collection on the basis of materials of the Military Commission of the Provisional Committee of the State Duma.)
41. "Fevral'skaia revoliutsiia 1917 goda: Dokumenty Stavki," *Krasnyi arkhiv*, no. 2 (21), p. 8.
42. *General Kutepov: Sbornik statei* (Paris, 1934), p. 161.
43. TsGAOR SSSR, f. 6375, op. 1, d. 2, ll. 11–12.
44. V. Shklovskii, "Zhili-byli," *Znamia*, no. 8 (1961), p. 195.
45. *General Kutepov*, p. 169.
46. *Padenie tsarskogo rezhima*, vol. 2, p. 266.
47. Ibid., p. 239.
48. TsGAOR SSSR, f. ChSK, d. 480, l. 231.
49. *Novoe vremia*, August 1, 1923.
50. TsGAOR SSSR, f. 6515, op. 1, d. 1, l. 34.
51. Ibid., f. ChSK, d. 480, l. 11.
52. *Padenie tsarskogo rezhima*, vol. 2, p. 267.

53. M. Rodzianko, *Gosudarstvennaia duma i Fevral'skaia 1917 g. revoliutsiia* (Rostov-on-the-Don, 1919), p. 41.

54. "Fevral'skaia revoliutsiia 1917 goda: Dokumenty Stavki," *Krasnyi arkhiv,* no. 2 (21), p. 8.

55. Ibid., p. 9.

56. Ibid., pp. 15–16.

57. Ibid., pp. 14–15.

58. Lenin, *Collected Works,* vol. 23, p. 350.

59. *Istoriia Kommunisticheskoi partii Sovetskogo Soiuza* (Moscow, 1966), vol. 2, p. 677. The authors of this volume cite a characteristic statement by Shliapnikov. "All of our thoughts were riveted on the grandiosely unfolding street battle. . . . Questions relating to how to conduct the battle relegated to the back burner the tasks of leading the movement and of creating a ruling center for the battle that, in case of victory, would be recognized by all." (Shliapnikov, *Semnadtsatyi god,* vol. 1, p. 97).

60. S. Skalov, "27 fevralia 1917 g. v Peterburge: Vospominaniia uchastnika vosstaniia," *Krasnaia nov',* no. 3 (1931), p. 118.

61. Personal archive of M. Polievktov. *Materialy Komissii oprosov. Beseda s A. F. Kerenskim.*

62. V. N. Zalezhskii, *Iz vospominanii podpol'shchika* (Kharkov, 1931), p. 159.

63. Shliapnikov, *Semnadtsatyi god,* vol. 1, p. 104.

64. M. G. Rafes, "Moi vospominaniia," *Byloe,* no. 19 (1922), p. 186.

65. Ibid., p. 187.

66. S. D. Mstislavskii, "Fevral'skaia revoliutsiia," *Krasnaia panorama,* March 11, 1927.

67. Lenin, *Collected Works,* vol. 27, p. 87.

68. *Izvestiia,* March 12, 1924.

69. *Literaturnaia gazeta,* November 6, 1965.

70. Gordienko, *Iz boevogo proshlogo,* p. 58.

71. Sukhanov, *Zapiski o revoliutsii,* vol. 1, pp. 27–28.

72. M. I. Skobelev, "Gibel' tsarizma: Vospominaniia M. I. Skobeleva," *Ogonek,* no. 11 (1927).

73. V. Kaiurov, "Kak obrazovalsia Petrogradskii Sovet," *Izvestiia tsentral'nogo ispolnitel'nogo komiteta i Petrogradskogo Soveta rabochikh i soldatskikh deputatov,* August 27, 1917.

74. "Fevral' skaia revoliutsiia i okhrannoe otdelenie," pp. 174–75.

75. *Revoliutsionnoe dvizhenie v Rossii posle sverzheniia samoderzhaviia,* p. 5. The compilers of the collection who published this document write that it was issued by the Central Committee Bureau of the RSDRP (p. 752), however they do not document this claim. The leaflet was not signed by any specific committee of the RSDRP, but judging by its contents, it may be considered to have been Bolshevik inspired.

76. *Gosudarstvennyi muzei Velikoi Oktiabr'skoi sotsialisticheskoi revoliutsii* (Leningrad), f. 6, Vospominaniia S. Ivanova, p. 12.

77. *Vyborgskaia storona: Sbornik statei i vospominanii* (Leningrad, 1957), p. 29.

78. *Petrogradskii proletariat i bol'shevistskaia organizatsiia,* p. 217.

79. *Gosudarstvennaia publichnaia biblioteka imeni M. E. Saltykova-Shchedrina,* f. listovok, inv. no. 1a.

80. Iordanskii, "Voennoe vosstanie 27 fevralia," p. 169.

81. M. Rafes maintains that Khrustalev-Nosar' and Gvozdev initially were elected members of the mandate commission, but then were removed from it. (Rafes, "Moi vospominaniia," p. 189).

82. Aleksandrov, *Za Narvskoi zastavoi,* pp. 128–29.

83. Information provided in these sources is contradictory, and protocols of the meeting have not been preserved or else were not kept.

84. Sukhanov, *Zapiski o revoliutsii*, vol. 1, p. 96.
85. Ibid., p. 97.
86. Skobelev, "Gibel' tsarizma."
87. Rafes, "Moi vospominaniia," p. 190.
88. The formation of this committee is discussed below.
89. Kaiurov, "Kak obrazovalsia Petrogradskii Sovet."
90. Ermanskii, *Iz perezhitogo*, p. 158.
91. Later, all three returned to the Bolshevik party and took active part in it.
92. S. D. Mstislavskii, *Piat' dnei: Nachalo i konets Fevral'skoi revoliutsii* (Berlin, Petrograd, and Moscow, 1922), pp. 20–21.
93. Ibid., p. 16.
94. Orders and instructions with such titles promoted the spreading of the false impression that the State Duma played the leading role in the revolution.
95. *Izvestiia Petrogradskogo Soveta rabochikh i soldatskikh deputatov*, February 28, 1917. Addendum.
96. Ibid., March 1, 1917.
97. Ibid.
98. Shliapnikov, *Semnadtsatyi god*, vol. 1, p. 154.
99. A. V. Peshekhonov, "Pervye nedeli: Iz vospominanii o revoliutsii," In *Fevral'skaia revoliutsiia* (Moscow and Leningrad, 1925), p. 438.
100. *Arkhiv Oktiabr'skoi revoliutsii Leningradskoi oblasti*, f. 7384, op. 1, d. 7, l. 32.
101. Ibid., d. 8, l. 13.
102. Ibid., op. 5, d. 7, ll. 32, 82.
103. TsGAOR SSSR, f. listovok.
104. For example, G. I. Zlokazov notes that "the conciliatory-minded leadership of the Petrograd Soviet literally 'gave the green light' to the most ill-sorted elements in order to strengthen its position." (G. I. Zlokazov, "Sozdanie Petrogradskogo Soveta: Fevral' 1917 g.," *Istoriia SSSR*, no. 5 [1964], p. 110.)
105. Lenin, *Collected Works*, vol. 10, p. 20.
106. Sukhanov, *Zapiski o revoliutsii*, vol. 1, pp. 105–107.
107. *Izvestiia Petrogradskogo Soveta rabochikh i soldatskikh deputatov*, February 28, 1917.
108. Personal archive of M. Polievktov. *Materialy Komissii oprosov. Beseda s M. V. Rodzianko*. [Shortly after the February Revolution, A. E. Presniakov established a commission to investigate the revolution. It was composed of students who interviewed the major participants. Some of the materials the students assembled ended up in the hands of Professor M. A. Polievktov and later of his wife, R. N. Nikoladze. Burdzhalov is the only historian I know who cites these sources—D.J.R.]
109. Rodzianko, *Gosudarstvennaia duma i Fevral'skaia 1917 g. revoliutsiia*, p. 40.
110. TsGAOR SSSR, f. 629, op. 1, d. 19, l. 10.
111. S. P. Mansyrev, "Moi vospominaniia," in *Fevral'skaia revoliutsiia* (Moscow, 1926), p. 264.
112. D. Zaslavskii, "V Gosudarstvennoi dume," *Krasnaia panorama*, March 11, 1917.
113. Iordanskii, "Voennoe vosstanie 27 fevralia," pp. 165–66.
114. *Vecherniaia Moskva*, March 11, 1927.
115. Zaslavskii, "V Gosudarstvennoi dume," p. 7.
116. *Izvestiia tsentral'nogo ispolnitel'nogo komiteta*, March 12, 1927.
117. Personal archive of M. Polievktov. *Materialy Komissii oprosov. Beseda s N. N. Nekrasovym*.
118. Skobelev, "Gibel' tsarizma."
119. "Fevral'skaia revoliutsiia 1917 goda: Dokumenty Stavki," *Krasnyi arkhiv*, no. 2 (21), pp. 6–7.

120. According to Duma deputy Vershinin, "The Protocol of Events" was compiled during the first days of the revolution by the director of the Duma office Ia. Glinka. The protocol covers the period from February 27 through March 2, 1917, that is, from the formation of the Provisional Committee of the State Duma to the abdication of the tsar. It was meant to have been published, but apparently was not. The draft is found in the archives among Vershinin's papers. (TsGAOR SSSR, f. 5990, op. 1, d. 2) (hereafter cited as *Protokol sobytii*).
121. Skobelev, "Gibel' tsarizma."
122. The protocol was published in the newspaper *Volia Rossii*, March 15, 1921.
123. Ibid.
124. Shul'gin, *Dni*, p. 162.
125. Skobelev, "Gibel' tsarizma."
126. Miliukov, *Vospominaniia*, vol. 2, p. 293.
127. *Protokol sobytii*, p. 9.
128. *Poslednie novosti*, March 12, 1927.
129. *Protokol sobytii*, p. 10.
130. Personal archive of M. Polievktov. *Materialy Komissii oprosov. Beseda s N. N. Nekrasovym*.
131. Ibid. *Beseda s M. V. Rodzianko*.
132. Rodzianko, *Gosudarstvennaia duma i Fevral'skaia 1917 g. revoliutsiia*, p. 40.
133. *Protokol sobytii*, p. 10.
134. Rodzianko, *Gosudarstvennaia duma i Fevral'skaia 1917 g. revoliutsiia*, p. 40.
135. "Fevral'skaia revoliutsiia 1917 goda: Dokumenty Stavki," p. 12.
136. Personal archive of M. Polievktov. *Materialy Komissii oprosov. Beseda s N. N. Nekrasovym*.
137. *Gosudarstvennaia biblioteka SSSR imeni V. I. Lenina*, Rukopisnyi fond, f. 306, d. 2. (B. Engel'gardt, *Potonuvshii mir [Vospominaniia]*.) Excerpts from B. Engel'gardt's memoirs were published in the newspaper *Obshchee delo*, March 16, 17, 18, 1921.
138. Shul'gin, *Dni*, p. 179.
139. *Poslednie novosti*, March 12, 1927.
140. *Obshchee delo*, March 16, 1921.
141. *Poslednie novosti*, March 12, 1927.
142. Rodzianko, *Gosudarstvennaia duma i Fevral'skaia 1917 g. revoliutsiia*, p. 41.
143. *Protokol sobytii*, p. 12.
144. TsGAOR SSSR, f. pechatnykh izdanii, inv. no. 1391.
145. Ibid., inv. no. 1394.
146. *Protokol sobytii*, p. 14.
147. Mstislavskii, *Piat' dnei*, pp. 17–18.
148. Ibid., p. 26.

4. The Second Wave of Revolution

1. E. D. Zozulia, "Chto zapomnilos'," *Ogonek*, no. 12 (1925).
2. *Tsentral'nyi gosudarstvennyi muzei revoliutsii SSSR*, f. listovok, inv. no. 3693/224. These leaflets were unsigned.
3. Ibid., no. 68/3.
4. "Fevral'skaia revoliutsiia 1917 goda: Dokumenty Stavki," *Krasnyi arkhiv*, no. 2 (21), p. 11.
5. *Perepiska Nikolaia i Aleksandry Romanovykh*, vol. 5, p. 224.
6. "Fevral'skaia revoliutsiia 1917 goda: Dokumenty Stavki," *Krasnyi arkhiv*, no. 2 (21), p. 19.
7. Ibid., p. 10.
8. Ibid., p. 27.

9. Ibid., p. 24.
10. TsGAOR SSSR, f. 6515, op. 1, d. 1, l. 37.
11. "Fevral'skaia revoliutsiia 1917 goda: Dokumenty Stavki," *Krasnyi arkhiv*, no. 2 (21), p. 19.
12. Ibid., p. 20.
13. Ibid., p. 25.
14. Ibid., p. 20–21.
15. Ibid., p. 27.
16. *Pravda*, March 10, 1917.
17. *Baltiiskie moriaki v podgotovke i provedenii Velikoi Oktiabr'skoi sotsialisticheskoi revoliutsii: Sbornik dokumentov* (Moscow, 1957), p. 16.
18. TsGVIA, f. 10/l, d. 614, l. 557.
19. I. Ul'ianov, *Kazachestvo v pervye dni revoliutsii: K 3-ei godovshchine Velikoi rossiiskoi revoliutsii* (Moscow, 1920), pp. 18–19.
20. TsGAOR SSSR, f. 3348, op. 1, d. 169, l. 12.
21. Ibid., f. pechatnykh izdanii, inv. no. 2117.
22. *Pravda*, March 7, 1917.
23. Personal archive of S. Petrikovskii. *Vospominaniia o Fevral'skoi revoliutsii*, p. 4.
24. TsPA-IML, f. 124, op. 1, d. 273, l. 5.
25. TsGIA SSSR, f. 2856, op. 1, d. 84, l. 15.
26. F. Sorokin, *Gvardeiskii ekipazh v fevral'skie dni 1917 g.* (Moscow, 1932), pp. 47–48.
27. *Bol'shevizatsiia Petrogradskogo garnizona v 1917 g.*, p. iv.
28. This did not prevent Kirill Vladimirovich from later aspiring to the Russian throne. Rodzianko claims to have shuddered when he learned a member of the imperial family had appeared at the Tauride Palace with a red bow in his lapel and to have expressed his surprise that Kirill had violated his oath, asking him to leave the palace and lead away the Guards Naval crew. The former Duma president made this up afterward, however, and in fact at the time actually thanked the grand prince for siding with the revolution and recognizing the Provisional Committee. Otherwise, how could Rodzianko justify the fact that he had violated his own oath to the tsar? (*Izvestiia Komiteta petrogradskikh zhurnalistov*, March 1, 1917).
29. N. Saratov, "Fevral' na Shlissel'burgskom porokhovom zavode: Dni revoliutsii 1917 g.," *Proletarskaia revoliutsiia*, no. 1 (13) (1923).
30. The reports of the Provisional Government's Extraordinary Investigatory Commission list churches, belfries, and buildings in which people with machine guns and machine-gun cartridges were found between February 27 and March 2. One of the lists names fifty-four such places, the other, seventy-nine. Eleven machine guns were set up in St. Isaac's Cathedral alone. Others were found in the Mariinskii Theater, Anichkov Palace, Putilov Plant, Troitskii Cathedral, and elsewhere.
31. L. Dobronravov, "Revoliutsiia: Zapiski," *Sovremennyi mir*, no. 4 (1928). [The author's name is probably D. Dobronravov—D.J.R.]
32. V. F. Bulgakov, "Revoliutsiia na avtomobiliakh: Petrograd v fevrale 1917 g.," *Na chuzhoi storone*, no. 6 (1924), p. 10.
33. *Gosudarstvennyi muzei Velikoi Oktiabr'skoi sotsialisticheskoi revoliutsii* (Leningrad), f. listovok, inv. no. 816.
34. F. D., ed., "Fevral'skaia revoliutsiia v Petrograde (28 fevralia–1 marta 1917 g.)," *Krasnyi arkhiv*, no. 41–42 (1930), p. 73.
35. Ibid., p. 62. [Original citation is incorrect—D.J.R.]
36. TsGAOR SSSR, f. 3348, op. 1, d. 168, ll. 10–14, 20, 31, 32.
37. TsGIA SSSR, f. 1278, op. 10, d. 19, l. 3.
38. Mstislavskii, *Piat' dnei*, p. 20.
39. *Leningradskii gosudarstvennyi istoricheskii arkhiv*, f. 680, op. 1, ll. 8, 10.

40. M. Kol'tsov, *Fevral'skii mart* (Moscow, 1927), p. 6.
41. E. D. Zozulia, *Piat' dnei; rasskaz. 27 fevralia 1917 g.: Stikhotvorenie* (Petrograd, 1917), p. 68.
42. *Vecherniaia Moskva*, March 14, 1917.
43. TsGAOR SSSR, f. 3348, op. 1, d. 185, l. 15.
44. G. P. (G. Peretts), *V tsitadeli russkoi revoliutsii: Zapiski komendanta Tavricheskogo dvortsa 27 fevralia-23 marta 1917 g.* (Petrograd, 1917), p. 62.
45. *Izvestiia Komiteta petrogradskikh zhurnalistov*, no. 4 (1917).
46. Rodzianko, *Gosudarstvennaia duma i Fevral'skaia 1917 g. revoliutsiia*, p. 50.
47. Sukhanov, *Zapiski o revoliutsii*, vol. 1, pp. 98–99.
48. *Izvestiia Petrogradskogo Soveta rabochikh i soldatskikh deputatov*, March 1, 1917.
49. It is impossible to identify all of the party representatives who joined the Soviet's Executive Committee. The names mentioned above were taken from lists published in *Petrogradskii Sovet rabochikh i soldatskikh deputatov: Protokoly Ispolnitel'nogo Komiteta* (Moscow and Leningrad, 1925), pp. 361–62. Many party representatives who entered the Executive Committee were later replaced.
50. Kaiurov, "Shest' dnei Fevral'skoi revoliutsii."
51. Shliapnikov, *Semnadtsatyi god*, vol. 1, p. 185.
52. V. D. Bonch-Bruevich, *Na boevykh postakh Fevral'skoi i Oktiabr'skoi revoliutsii* (Moscow, 1931), pp. 10–11.
53. Printer M. Ageev confirms this. He writes in "Ot aresta do osvobozhdeniia," *Pechatnik*, no. 7–8 (1928), p. 11: "That very same evening the printing house of the newspaper *Den'*, which we had seized, composed and printed the 'Manifesto of the Russian Social Democratic Labor party (Bolshevik).'" In a research note published in *Voprosy istorii KPSS* ("O pervom izdanii Manifesta TsK RSDRP(b) 'K vsem grazhdanam Rossii,'" no. 6 [1964], pp. 64–65), Kh. M. Astrakhan points out that the typeface of the leaflet found in the Museum of the October Revolution in Leningrad is identical to that of the newspaper *Den'*, whereas the typeface of other copies of the leaflet with the manifesto are identical to that of the newspaper *Izvestiia*. It appears that the manifesto was printed by the printing houses of both *Izvestiia* and *Den'*. Moreover, it's possible that the manifesto was also hectographed. It is more difficult to pinpoint the leaflet's publication date. *Pravda*, which reprinted the manifesto on March 5, erroneously stated that "the Manifesto was put out on February 26." Despite the fact that the manifesto's contents refute this date ("The Strongholds of Tsarism Have Fallen") and that Shliapnikov back in 1923 exposed the error, several authors as late as 1956 insisted that it was correct. (E. Bugaev, "Kogda utrachivaetsia nauchnyi podkhod," *Partiinaia zhizn'*, no. 14 (1956), pp. 69–70). In fact, the leaflet with the manifesto could not have appeared earlier than the evening of February 27.
54. *Izvestiia Petrogradskogo Soveta rabochikh i soldatskikh deputatov*, February 28, 1917. Addendum.
55. Lenin, *Collected Works*, vol. 23, p. 320.
56. Lenin wrote that the manifesto appealed to the masses to organize around the Soviet. But there were no original texts of the manifesto abroad. Lenin read a not altogether correct excerpt of it published in *Frankfurter Zeitung* (See *Polnoe sobranie sochinenii*, vol. 49, pp. 412, 553.)
57. *Izvestiia Petrogradskogo Soveta rabochikh i soldatskikh deputatov*, March 1, 1917.
58. In 1905 the Petrograd Soviet had limited itself to an appeal to the populace to withdraw all deposits from banks and to withhold taxes. But now the question of liquidating the entire tsarist financial system had been raised.
59. *Izvestiia Komiteta petrogradskikh zhurnalistov*, no. 2, February 28, 1917.
60. *Leningradskii gosudarstvennyi istoricheskii arkhiv*, f. 513, op. 19, d. 852, ll. 2–3.

61. TsGIA SSSR, f. 691, op. 1, d. 21.

62. Z. Kel'son, "Militsiia Fevral'skoi revoliutsii: Vospominaniia," *Byloe*, no. 1 (29) (1925), p. 168.

63. Ibid., p. 171. A recently published work by V. I. Startsev mentions that during the first days of the revolution in Petrograd, eighty-five district and subdistrict commissariats existed and that the enormous territory encompassing the industrial regions of the capital were protected by a workers' militia. See *Ocherki po istorii Petrogradskoi krasnoi gvardii i rabochei militsii* (Moscow and Leningrad, 1965), pp. 52–53.

64. *Izvestiia Komiteta petrogradskikh zhurnalistov*, no. 2, February 28, 1917.

65. TsGAOR SSSR, f. 3348, op. 1, d. 170, ll. 6–7.

66. TsGIA SSSR, f. 1175, op. 2, d. 4, l. 1.

67. *Izvestiia Komiteta petrogradskikh zhurnalistov*, no. 2, February 28, 1917.

68. Ibid.

69. Ibid.

70. "O dniakh Peterburgskikh (iz dnevnika Z. Gippius)," *Vozrozhdenie*, September 14, 1928.

71. *Izvestiia Petrogradskogo Soveta rabochikh i soldatskikh deputatov*, March 1, 1917.

72. A. A. Bublikov, *Russkaia revoliutsiia: Vpechatleniia i mysli ochevidtsa i uchastnika* (New York, 1918), p. 23.

73. Iu. V. Lomonosov, *Vospominaniia o martovskoi revoliutsii 1917 goda* (Stockholm and Berlin, 1921), p. 27.

74. *Gosudarstvennaia biblioteka SSSR imeni V. I. Lenina*, Rukopisnyi fond, f. 306, d. 3, l. 726.

75. This is what D. V. Oznobishin maintains in the article "Vremennyi komitet gosudarstvennoi dumy i vremennoe pravitel'stvo," *Istoricheskie zapiski*, vol. 75 (1965), p. 275. Citing Lenin, Oznobishin overlooks the fact that it was from abroad that Lenin called the Duma Committee the First Provisional Government. When he returned to Russia, however, Lenin discovered that power originally had been in the hands of the Soviet which voluntarily had conceded it to the bourgeois government. In a speech at the all-city party conference on April 14, 1917, he said: "Only here on the spot did we learn that the Soviet had surrendered power to the Provisional Government." (Lenin, *Collected Works*, vol. 24, p. 142).

76. Peshekhonov, "Pervye nedeli," p. 438.

77. Mansyrev, "Moi vospominaniia," p. 271.

78. Shliapnikov, *Semnadtsatyi god*, vol. 1, pp. 186–87.

79. F. Dingel'shtedt, "Vesna proletarskoi revoliutsii: Iz vpechatlenii agitatora v marte 1917 g.," *Krasnaia letopis'*, no. 1 (12) (1925), p. 193.

80. *Pravda*, March 8, 1917.

81. *Revoliutsionnoe dvizhenie v Rossii posle sverzheniia samoderzhaviia*, p. 6. Shliapnikov published a slightly different text of the resolution given to him by K. Shutko, which was adopted at this meeting. Instead of the ambivalent statement that the insurgent soldiers must reorganize "to finish overthrowing those who have been and still are loyal to the tsarist regime," the text conveyed by Shutko contains a more precise wording: "it is necessary to create a single revolutionary organ which, involving still more and more insurgent workers and soldiers, will reorganize the army and replace officers who remain loyal to the tsarist regime with revolutionary workers and peasants." See Shliapnikov, *Semnadtsatyi god*, vol. 1, pp. 226–27.

82. Shliapnikov, *Semnadtsatyi god*, vol. 1, p. 236.

83. Dingel'shtedt, "Vesna proletarskoi revoliutsii," p. 194.

84. Ibid., p. 193.

85. *Pravda*, March 9, 1917.

86. *Arkhiv Oktiabr'skoi revoliutsii Leningradskoi oblasti,* f. 4000, op. 5, d. 1053, ll. 19–20.
87. *Vyborgskaia storona,* p. 77.
88. TsGAOR SSSR, f. pechatnykh izdanii, inv. no. 3470.
89. Rafes, "Moi vospominaniia," p. 193.
90. *Obshchee delo,* March 16, 1921.
91. V. Bazarov, "Pervye shagi russkoi revoliutsii," *Letopis',* no. 2–4 (1917), p. 381.
92. Ibid., pp. 381–82.
93. Shliapnikov, *Semnadtsatyi god,* vol. 1, p. 193.
94. *Shestoi s"ezd RSDRP (bol'shevikov),* p. 59.
95. *Arkhiv Oktiabr'skoi revoliutsii Leningradskoi oblasti,* f. 1000, op. 73, d. 1, l. 15.
96. *Izvestiia Petrogradskogo Soveta rabochikh i soldatskikh deputatov,* March 1, 1917.
97. Personal archive of M. Polievktov. *Materialy Komissii oprosov. Beseda s B. A. Engel'gardtom.*
98. *Izvestiia Komiteta petrogradskikh zhurnalistov,* March 2, 1917.
99. TsPA-IML, f. 17, op. 1, d. 15, l. 1.
100. K. Orlov maintained that Chkheidze, under pressure from a group of Bolsheviks, ordered that not a single rifle be taken from workers or soldiers, and that arms seized from military units be returned and counterrevolutionary officers arrested. See K. Orlov, *Zapiski rabochego revoliutsionera* (Moscow, 1929), p. 42. Orlov's book contains the following editorial comment: "This fact adduced by Orlov has not been published before. The editorial board has verified it with such participants as Shmidt, Khakharev, and Zaitsev."
101. TsGAOR SSSR, f. pechatnykh izdanii, inv. no. 4313.
102. *Vyborgskaia storona,* p. 77.
103. TsGAOR SSSR, f. pechatnykh izdanii, inv. no. 3470.
104. TsGAOR SSSR, f. 3348, op. 1, d. 185, ll. 15–16.
105. *Protokol sobytii,* p. 45.
106. Party affiliation of these individuals is adduced on the basis of A. Sadovskii's records. Sadovskii himself joined the Bolshevik party in July 1917. (See TsPA-IML, f. 124, op. 1, d. 1699, ch. 2, ll. 243, 268). Afterward, soldier deputies formed a separate section, ruled by a new executive commission. A meeting of soldiers' deputies on March 6 confirmed appointment of almost eighty-five members to the commission. An SR, Utgov, was elected chairman of the Soldiers' Section of the Soviet.
107. *Izvestiia Petrogradskogo Soveta rabochikh i soldatskikh deputatov,* March 2, 1917; *Arkhiv Oktiabr'skoi revoliutsii Leningradskoi oblasti,* f. 1000, op. 73, d. 2, l. 5.
108. Tarasov-Rodionov, *Fevral',* p. 205.
109. Ibid., p. 206.
110. Ibid., p. 207.
111. N. D. Sokolov, "Kak rodilsia Prikaz No. 1," *Ogonek,* no. 11 (1927).
112. *Obshchee delo,* March 18, 1921.
113. Ibid.
114. Sokolov, "Kak rodilsia Prikaz No. 1."
115. TsPA-IML, f. 124, op. 1, d. 1699, ch. 2, l. 269.
116. Shliapnikov, *Semnadtsatyi god,* vol. 1, pp. 211–12.
117. In light of this it is incorrect to consider N. Sokolov, who was only involved in publishing the order, as the author of Order No. 1, or worse yet, to name Iu. Steklov the author as is done in the foreward to Iu. Steklov, *Vospominaniia i publitsistika* (Moscow, 1965), p. 4.
118. Shliapnikov, *Semnadtsatyi god,* vol. 1, p. 212.
119. TsGAOR SSSR, f. 5827, op. 1, d. 6, ll. 4–6.

120. Mstislavskii, *Piat' dnei,* p. 86.

121. M. N. Pokrovskii, comp., "Iz dnevnika A. N. Kuropatkina," *Krasnyi arkhiv,* no. 20 (1) (1927), p. 72.

122. *Poslednie novosti,* September 20, 1936.

123. Sokolov, "Kak rodilsia Prikaz No. 1."

124. Volume One of *Istoriia grazhdanskoi voiny v SSSR* (Moscow, 1935) maintains that the Petrograd Soviet's Order No. 1 had called for election of officers "but that in the process of publishing the order in the newspaper this point was deleted under Sokolov's insistence (p. 79). No evidence, however, is adduced to support this contention. In the Petrograd Soviet's resolution, determined to be the basis of Order No. 1, there is no call for election of officers. V. Miller's note, "Iz istorii Prikaza No. 1 Petrogradskogo Soveta," *Voenno-istoricheskii zhurnal,* no. 5 (1966), pp. 109–13, points out the groundlessness of the contention cited above and links the call for the election of officers with the leaflet put out by the Interdistrictites and SRs (see page 248 of my work).

125. TsGIA SSSR, f. 1278, op. 10, d. 34, l. 60.

126. *Pravda,* March 11, 1917.

127. Kaiurov, "Shest' dnei Fevral'skoi revoliutsii," p. 170.

128. *Gosudarstvennyi muzei Velikoi Oktiabr'skoi sotsialisticheskoi revoliutsii* (Leningrad), f. listovok, no. 10851.

129. V. B. Stankevich, *Vospominaniia, 1914–1919* (Moscow, 1928), p. 35.

130. M. R. Popov, "L. A. Volkenshtein," *Golos minuvshego,* no. 4–6 (1918), p. 73.

131. "Fevral'skaia revoliutsiia 1917 goda: Dokumenty Stavki," *Krasnyi arkhiv,* no. 2 (21), p. 56.

132. Ibid., no. 3. (22), p. 28.

133. *Obshchee delo,* March 17, 1921.

134. P. A. Polovtsev, *Dni zatmeniia* (Paris, n.d.), pp. 20–21.

135. TsGAOR SSSR, f. 629, op. 1, d. 20, ll. 10–11.

136. "Fevral'skaia revoliutsiia 1917 goda: Dokumenty Stavki," no. 2 (21), p. 29.

137. Ibid., pp. 42–43.

138. A. Oznobishin, *Vospominaniia* (Paris, 1927), p. 263.

139. "Fevral'skaia revoliutsiia 1917 goda: Dokumenty Stavki," no. 3 (22), p. 6.

140. TsGAOR SSSR, f. ChSK, d. 466, l. 129. Domanevskii is wrong. The Duma Committee was not in charge of the situation even before March 1.

141. Lenin, *Collected Works,* vol. 23, pp. 322–23.

5. Dual Power

1. The tsarina subsequently wrote Nicholas: "Pavel, who received the most awful dressing down from me because he had done nothing with the guards, is now nobly and foolishly trying to save us all: he composed an idiotic manifesto calling for a constitution after the war and the like." (*Perepiska Nikolaia i Aleksandry Romanovykh,* vol. 5, p. 227).

2. "Kulisy istorii. Novye dokumenty k istorii fevral'skogo perevorota (Manifest b. Velikikh kniazei; Proekt otrecheniia, napisannyi V. Shul'ginym; Pervyi sostav Vremennogo pravitel'stva)," *Ogonek,* no. 1 (1923).

3. TsGAOR SSSR, f. 622, op. 1, d. 22, ll. 85, 87. Mikhail Romanov ironically inscribed on one of the envelopes: "To Comrade Natalia Sergeevna Brasova from Comrade M.A.R."

4. Ibid., f. 6439, op. 1, d. 1, l. 11.

5. Ibid., d. 3, l. 1.

6. *Protokol sobytii,* p. 20.

7. S. I. Shidlovskii, "Vospominaniia," in *Fevral'skaia revoliutsiia* (Moscow and Leningrad, 1925), p. 294.

8. TsGAOR SSSR, f. 6, op. 2, d. 120, l. 1.
9. *Izvestiia Komiteta petrogradskikh zhurnalistov*, no. 6, March 2, 1917.
10. Ibid., no. 8, March 3, 1917.
11. Sukhanov, *Zapiski o revoliutsii*, vol. 1, p. 168.
12. Shliapnikov, *Semnadtsatyi god*, vol. 1, p. 220.
13. Sukhanov, *Zapiski o revoliutsii*, vol. 1, p. 191; Rafes, "Moi vospominaniia," p. 196.
14. Sukhanov, *Zapiski o revoliutsii*, vol. 1, p. 194.
15. Ibid., p. 205.
16. Ibid., p. 212. Rafes illuminates this matter somewhat differently. He writes that in reporting on the negotiations at a meeting of the Soviet's Executive Committee, Steklov announced that members of the Duma Committee had raised the matter of continuing the war, but this provoked a rebuff from Rafes, Sukhanov, and Sokolov. They maintained that "the working class and the Soviet of Workers' Deputies had carried out a revolution not to fight a war but to democratize the country, and therefore only matters concerning the domestic life of the state must be included in the Provisional Government's program if it wishes the support of the Soviet of Workers' Deputies." Rafes, "Moi vospominaniia," p. 195.
17. Sukhanov, *Zapiski o revoliutsii*, vol. 1, pp. 208–209.
18. Miliukov, *Vospominaniia*, vol. 2, p. 308.
19. Sukhanov, *Zapiski o revoliutsii*, vol. 1, p. 221.
20. Ibid., p. 222.
21. Ibid., p. 231.
22. *Izvestiia Petrogradskogo Soveta rabochikh i soldatskikh deputatov*, March 3, 1917.
23. Ibid.
24. Ibid.
25. M. G. Rafes, *Dva goda revoliutsii na Ukraine: Evoliutsiia i raskol "Bunda"* (Moscow, 1920), p. 31. In memoirs published in the journal *Byloe* (no. 19, 1922), Rafes writes that the Bolsheviks demanded "the overthrow of the Duma Committee and formation of a new Provisional Government" (p. 197). The conflict thus revolved around overthrowing or supporting bourgeois power.
26. *Izvestiia Petrogradskogo Soveta rabochikh i soldatskikh deputatov*, March 2, 1917.
27. Ibid., March 3, 1917.
28. *Russkie vedomosti*, March 3, 1917.
29. *Izvestiia Petrogradskogo Soveta rabochikh i soldatskikh deputatov*, March 3, 1917.
30. Sukhanov, *Zapiski o revoliutsii*, vol. 1, pp. 245–46.
31. Personal archive of M. Polievktov. *Materialy Komissii oprosov. Beseda s Tugan-Baranovskim*.
32. Miliukov, *Istoriia vtoroi russkoi revoliutsii*, vol. 1, p. 52.
33. TsGAOR SSSR, f. 640, op. 2, d. 43, ll. 1–3.
34. B. V. Nikitin, *Rokovye gody* (Paris, 1937), pp. 201–202.
35. *Protokol sobytii*, p. 45.
36. Ibid., p. 46.
37. Rafes, *Dva goda revoliutsii na Ukraine*, p. 196.
38. *Revoliutsionnoe dvizhenie v Rossii posle sverzheniia samoderzhaviia*, pp. 419–20.
39. "Fevral'skaia revoliutsiia 1917 goda: Dokumenty Stavki," *Krasnyi arkhiv*, no. 3 (22), p. 28.
40. Ibid., p. 40.
41. *Gosudarstvennaia publichnaia biblioteka imeni M. E. Saltykova-Shchedrina*,

Otdel rukopisei, f. 482, d. 186, l. 3. D. Oznobishin writes in *Istoricheskie zapiski*, vol. 75, p. 286: "The functions of a supreme authority remained with the Provisional Duma Committee after formation of the Provisional Government. Rodzianko tried in every way possible to emphasize the supreme legislative character of the Duma's authority." Rodzianko's strivings, however, should not be confused with what actually happened. The Duma Committee did not possess power either before or after formation of the Provisional Government.

42. *Izvestiia Komiteta petrogradskikh zhurnalistov*, no. 7, March 3, 1917.

43. TsGAOR SSSR, f. pechatnykh izdanii, inv. no. 4450.

44. Ibid., f. 629, d. 20, ll. 5–6, 9.

45. "Fevral'skaia revoliutsiia 1917 goda: Dokumenty Stavki," *Krasnyi arkhiv*, no. 3 (22), p. 23.

46. Ibid., pp. 6–7.

47. Ibid., p. 8.

48. As mentioned in the Preface, the events in Moscow, the provinces, and at the front are illuminated in volume 2 of this work.

49. TsGAOR SSSR, f. pechatnykh izdanii, inv. no. 2520.

50. Ibid., f. 6536, op. 1, d. 1, l. 4.

51. "Fevral'skaia revoliutsiia 1917 goda: Dokumenty Stavki," *Krasnyi arkhiv*, no. 2 (21), p. 33.

52. Ibid., p. 36.

53. A. S. Lukomskii, "Iz vospominanii," *Arkhiv russkoi revoliutsii*, vol. 2 (1921), p. 22.

54. "Fevral'skaia revoliutsiia 1917 goda: Dokumenty Stavki," *Krasnyi arkhiv*, no. 2 (21), p. 31.

55. Ibid.

56. *Gosudarstvennaia biblioteka SSSR imeni V. I. Lenina*, Rukopisnyi otdel, f. 306, d. 3, l. 743.

57. "Fevral'skaia revoliutsiia 1917 goda: Dokumenty Stavki," *Krasnyi arkhiv*, no. 2 (21), p. 45.

58. Ibid., p. 55.

59. TsGAOR SSSR, f. 3348, op. 1, d. 172, l. 9.

60. A. Mordvinov, "Poslednie dni imperatora," in *Otrechenie Nikolaia II: Vospominaniia ochevidtsev i dokumenty*, ed. P. E. Shchegolev (Leningrad, 1927), p. 94.

61. "Fevral'skaia revoliutsiia 1917 goda: Dokumenty Stavki," *Krasnyi arkhiv*, no. 2 (21), pp. 39–40.

62. Ibid., p. 42.

63. Ibid., p. 47.

64. Ibid., p. 53.

65. Ibid., p. 56.

66. Ibid., pp. 58–59.

67. Ibid., p. 68.

68. Ibid., pp. 68–70.

69. Ibid., p. 72–74.

70. Sergeev, "Dnevnik Nikolaia Romanova," *Krasnyi arkhiv*, no. 1 (20) (1927), p. 136.

71. *Perepiska Nikolaia i Aleksandry Romanovykh*, vol. 5, pp. 226–28.

72. Rafes, *Dva goda revoliutsii na Ukraine*, p. 194.

73. *Protokol sobytii*, p. 21.

74. Skobelev, "Gibel' tsarizma."

75. Shul'gin, *Dni*, pp. 240–41.

76. Ibid., pp. 241–42.

77. S. I. Shidlovskii, *Vospominaniia* (Berlin, 1923), vol. 1, p. 85.

78. "Kulisy istorii," *Ogonek*.
79. Shul'gin, *Dni*, p. 265.
80. Ibid., p. 266.
81. "Protokol otrecheniia Nikolaia II (Po zapisi generala K. A. Naryshkina)," in *Otrechenie Nikolaia II*, ed. P. E. Shchegolev, pp. 185–86 [Error in original—D.J.R.].
82. Ibid., p. 186 [Original incorrectly cites p. 218—D.J.R.].
83. Shul'gin, *Dni*, pp. 270–71.
84. "Protokol otrecheniia Nikolaia II," p. 186 [Original incorrectly cites p. 218—D.J.R.].
85. "Manifest otrecheniia Nikolaia II," in *Otrechenie Nikolaia II*, ed. P. E. Shchegolev, p. 189 [Original incorrectly gives p. 221—D.J.R.].
86. TsGAOR SSSR, f. 875, op. 1, d. 20, l. 272.
87. "Protokol otrecheniia Nikolaia II," pp. 186–87.
88. TsGAOR SSSR, f. 5856, op. 1, d. 600, l. 9.
89. Nikitin, *Rokovye gody*, p. 202.
90. *Poslednie novosti*, September 13, 1926.
91. *Perepiska Nikolaia i Aleksandry Romanovykh*, vol. 5, pp. 226, 229.
92. Ibid., p. 232.
93. *Izvestiia tsentral'nogo ispolnitel'nogo komiteta i Petrogradskogo Soveta rabochikh i soldatskikh deputatov*, September 21, 1917.
94. "Fevral'skaia revoliutsiia 1917 goda: Dokumenty Stavki," *Krasnyi arkhiv*, no. 3 (22), pp. 25–26.
95. Ibid., pp. 27–28.
96. Ibid., p. 27.
97. Shul'gin, *Dni*, pp. 286–87.
98. Ibid., p. 289.
99. Ibid., pp. 291–92. Sources usually claim that railroad workers arrested Guchkov because he proclaimed Mikhail emperor. Judging by Shul'gin's account, however, the matter never came to an actual arrest.
100. TsGAOR SSSR, f. 6439, d. 3, l. 5.
101. Shul'gin, *Dni*, p. 299.
102. B. E. Nol'de, *Dalekoe i blizkoe: Istoricheskie ocherki* (Paris, 1930), p. 145.
103. Sergeev, "Dnevnik Nikolaia Romanova," p. 137.
104. Rodzianko, *Gosudarstvennaia duma i Fevral'skaia 1917 g. revoliutsiia*, p. 45.
105. Bublikov, *Russkaia revoliutsiia*, p. 70.
106. *Rech'*, March 4, 1917.
107. TsGAOR SSSR, f. pechatnykh izdanii, inv. no. 1710.
108. Ibid., f. 601, op. 1, d. 2103, l. 1. Here I cite the unofficial protocol of the Provisional Government's first meeting. V. Nabokov, who was managing governmental affairs, said that he was not satisfied with this protocol but that he was unable to correct it since he was not present at the government's first meeting. The minutes of this meeting were not included in the published protocols.
109. *Izvestiia Petrogradskogo Soveta rabochikh i soldatskikh deputatov*, March 5, 1917.
110. *Arkhiv Oktiabr'skoi revoliutsii Leningradskoi oblasti*, f. 1000, op. 73, d. 5, l. 17.
111. Ibid., f. 1000, op. 73, d. 5, l. 18.
112. *Izvestiia Petrogradskogo Soveta rabochikh i soldatskikh deputatov*, March 5, 1917.
113. *Petrogradskii Sovet rabochikh i soldatskikh deputatov*, p. 10.
114. Ibid., p. 23.
115. TsGAOR SSSR, f. 1244, op. 1, d. 42, l. 2.
116. *Izvestiia tsentral'nogo ispolnitel'nogo komiteta*, March 12, 1927.
117. Iu. Steklov thought it curious that the SRs and Mensheviks, composing a

majority in the Soviet and in its Executive Committee, were not represented on the editorial board of *Izvestiia* and that the newspaper was "edited if not in a definite Bolshevik spirit then at least in a clearly revolutionary one, which was at variance with the general mood of the Soviet majority (*Zhurnalist*, no. 3 [1927], p. 4). In fact, Steklov, Gol'denberg, Bazarov, and Avilov had been Bolsheviks formerly. During the war and February Revolution they were closer to the Mensheviks and the tone of *Izvestiia* was not at odds with "the general mood of the Soviet majority." Later Gol'denberg and Steklov again joined the Bolshevik party.

118. Sukhanov, *Zapiski o revoliutsii*, vol. 2, p. 48.

119. *Istoriia grazhdanskoi voiny v SSSR* (Moscow, 1955), vol. 1, pp. 74–75; S. Murashov, *Kak pobedila Velikaia Oktiabr'skaia sotsialisticheskaia revoliutsiia* (Moscow, 1957), p. 10.

120. S. A. Artem'ev, "Sostav Petrogradskogo Soveta v marte 1917 g.," *Istoriia SSSR*, no. 5 (1964), p. 123.

121. Artem'ev in the article cited above and M. Potekhin in the essay "K voprosu o vozniknovenii i sostave Petrogradskogo Soveta v 1917 g.," *Istoriia SSSR*, no. 5 (1965), pp. 233–35, correctly note this. For example, the gigantic Obukhov Factory did not send a single Bolshevik deputy to the Soviet. M. Rozanov wrote: "The small Bolshevik organization at the factory turned out to be inadequately prepared for the elections. . . . Political trustfulness, political inexperience, and intoxication with the victory over tsarism prevented the Obukhov workers from making sense of the complex situation." See *Bastiony revoliutsii* (Leningrad, 1957), pp. 139–40.

122. V. N. Zalezhskii, "Pervyi legal'nyi Peka," *Proletarskaia revoliutsiia*, no. 1 (13) (1923), p. 142.

123. Shliapnikov, *Semnadtsatyi god*, vol. 1, pp. 203–204.

124. F. A. Lemeshev, "Narvskii raionnyi komitet bol'shevikov ot Fevralia k Oktiabriu 1917 goda: Ocherk," *Krasnaia letopis'*, no. 5–6 (1932).

125. From March 3 the protocols of the Soviet's Executive Committee were published in *Izvestiia*. Unfortunately, these protocols were summarized and therefore do not give a clear notion of what occurred at the Executive Committee's meetings.

126. TsGAOR SSSR, f. 1235, op. 53, d. 40, ll. 26–27.

127. *Izvestiia Komiteta petrogradskikh zhurnalistov*, no. 5, March 2, 1917.

128. Sukhanov, *Zapiski o revoliutsii*, vol. 1, p. 111.

129. *Petrogradskii Sovet rabochikh i soldatskikh deputatov*, p. 14.

130. Ibid., p. 18.

131. *Arkhiv Oktiabr'skoi revoliutsii Leningradskoi oblasti*, f. 4000, op. 1, d. 9, l. 6.

132. *Petrogradskii Sovet rabochikh i soldatskikh deputatov*, p. 9.

133. "Fevral'skaia revoliutsiia 1917 goda: Dokumenty Stavki," *Krasnyi arkhiv*, no. 3 (22), pp. 54–55.

134. *Petrogradskii Sovet rabochikh i soldatskikh deputatov*, p. 17.

135. "Trebovanie naroda o zakliuchenii Nikolaia Romanova v krepost'," *Krasnyi arkhiv*, no. 81 (2) (1937), pp. 122–23.

136. TsGAOR SSSR, f. 6, op. 2, d. 3, l. 15.

137. Ibid., f. 1278, op. 10, d. 6, l. 22.

138. Sergeev, "Dnevnik Nikolaia Romanova," p. 138.

139. Buchanan, *My Mission to Russia*, II, p. 104.

140. Ibid., p. 105.

141. *Petrogradskii Sovet rabochikh i soldatskikh deputatov*, p. 28.

142. *Tsentral'nyi gosudarstvennyi muzei revoliutsii SSSR*, f. listovok, inv. no. 23316/21.

143. *Petrogradskii Sovet rabochikh i soldatskikh deputatov*, p. 29.

144. Personal archive of M. Polievktov. *Materialy Komissii oprosov. Beseda s M. I. Skobelevym.*

145. *Tsentral'nyi gosudarstvennyi muzei revoliutsii SSSR*, f. listovok, inv. no. 12/200.
146. Ibid., inv. no. 12/429.
147. Tarasov-Rodionov, *Fevral'*, p. 315.
148. Ibid., p. 322.
149. *Petrogradskii Sovet rabochikh i soldatskikh deputatov*, p. 30.
150. *Izvestiia Petrogradskogo Soveta rabochikh i soldatskikh deputatov*, March 10, 1917.
151. Buchanan, *My Mission to Russia*, II, pp. 105–6.
152. V. Miakotin, *Velikii perevorot i zadachi momenta* (Petrograd, 1917), p. 7.
153. *Krasnaia gazeta*, March 12, 1922.
154. *Arkhiv Oktiabr'skoi revoliutsii Leningradskoi oblasti*, f. 4000, op. 7, d. 2094, ll. 20–21.
155. *Pravda*, March 12, 1927.
156. Dingel'shtedt, "Vesna proletarskoi revoliutsii," p. 201.
157. *Pravda*, March 5, 1917.
158. E. D. Stasova, *Stranitsy zhizni i bor'by* (Moscow, 1957), pp. 84–85.
159. "Protokoly i rezoliutsii Biuro TsK RSDRP(b) (mart 1917 g.)," *Voprosy istorii KPSS*, no. 3 (1962), p. 143.
160. S. Zaks-Gladnev, "Vozobnovlenie 'Pravdy'," *Zhurnalist*, no. 2 (1927), pp. 17–18.
161. Ibid.
162. *Pervyi legal'nyi Peterburgskii komitet bol'shevikov v 1917 godu* (Moscow and Leningrad, 1927), p. 4.
163. Ibid., pp. 10–11. This resolution has been published in the document collection *KPSS v bor'be za pobedu sotsialisticheskoi revoliutsii v period dvoevlastiia* (Moscow, 1957) with the annotation: "not earlier than March 9, 1917" (p. 30). In a scholarly note "O pervoi rezoliutsii Biuro TsK RSDRP(b) v marte 1917 goda," *Voprosy istorii KPSS*, no. 3 (1966), pp. 105–11, V. Lavrin rightfully concludes that this dating is incorrect. The resolution quoted by us in the text must be dated March 3, 1917.
164. Ibid., p. 11.
165. V. Zalezhskii subsequently noted that the Petrograd Bolshevik Committee took the formula adopted by the Soviet on supporting the Provisional Government "only insofar as" and slightly changed it. This rendered it harmless, without causing conflict with the Soviet. See *Iz vospominanii podpol'shchika*, p. 166. In reality the difference between the contents of the Petrograd Committee's formula and that of the Soviet was slight: "supporting" was replaced with "not acting against."
166. *Rabochaia gazeta*, March 7, 1917.
167. TsGAOR SSSR, f. 6065, op. 1, d. 1, l. 46.
168. *Izvestiia Petrogradskogo Soveta rabochikh i soldatskikh deputatov*, March 4, 1917.
169. Ibid.
170. *Biblioteka Instituta marksizma-leninizma pri TsK KPSS*, f. listovok, inv. no. 27939.
171. *Pervyi legal'nyi Peterburgskii komitet bol'shevikov v 1917 godu*, p. 13.
172. Ibid., p. 14.
173. *Arkhiv Oktiabr'skoi revoliutsii Leningradskoi oblasti*, f. 1000, op. 73, d. 7, l. 1.
174. *Izvestiia Petrogradskogo Soveta rabochikh i soldatskikh deputatov*, March 6, 1917.
175. *Arkhiv Oktiabr'skoi revoliutsii Leningradskoi oblasti*, f. 1000, op. 73, d. 7, l. 6.
176. *Izvestiia Petrogradskogo Soveta rabochikh i soldatskikh deputatov*, March 6, 1917.
177. *Revoliutsionnoe dvizhenie v Rossii posle sverzheniia samoderzhaviia*, pp. 465–66.
178. *Arkhiv Oktiabr'skoi revoliutsii Leningradskoi oblasti*, f. 7384, op. 9, d. 293, l. 5.

179. *Pervyi legal'nyi Peterburgskii komitet bol'shevikov v 1917 godu*, p. 27.
180. *Pravda*, March 9, 1917.
181. *Rabochee dvizhenie v 1917 godu* (Moscow and Leningrad, 1926), p. 32.
182. *Pervyi legal'nyi Peterburgskii komitet bol'shevikov v 1917 godu*, p. 27.
183. *Izvestiia Petrogradskogo Soveta rabochikh i soldatskikh deputatov*, March 10, 1917.
184. F. Matveev, *Iz zapisnoi knizhki deputata 176 pekhotnogo polka* (Leningrad, 1932), p. 25.
185. *Izvestiia Petrogradskogo Soveta rabochikh i soldatskikh deputatov*, March 10, 1917.
186. *Revoliutsionnoe dvizhenie v Rossii posle sverzheniia samoderzhaviia*, p. 231.
187. *Izvestiia Petrogradskogo Soveta rabochikh i soldatskikh deputatov*, March 9, 1917.
188. *Pervyi legal'nyi Peterburgskii komitet bol'shevikov v 1917 godu*, p. 26.
189. Ibid., pp. 27–28.
190. *Rabochaia gazeta*, March 7, 1917.
191. Ibid., March 10, 1917.
192. TsGIA SSSR, f. 27, op. 1, d. 194, l. 4.
193. Volobuev, *Proletariat i burzhuaziia Rossii v 1917 godu*, p. 107.
194. "Fevral'skaia revoliutsiia 1917 goda: Dokumenty Stavki," *Krasnyi arkhiv*, no. 3 (22), p. 40.
195. TsGAOR SSSR, f. 1248, op. 1, d. 25, l. 8.
196. *Izvestiia Petrogradskogo Soveta rabochikh i soldatskikh deputatov*, March 5, 1917.
197. TsGVIA, f. 11, d. 3883, l. 1.
198. The Kadets insisted on abrogating Order No. 1. It appears that Kerensky and Chkheidze promised them they would refuse to acknowledge it as well. On March 4 the Central Committee of the Kadet party resolved to publish and distribute Kerensky's and Chkheidze's announcement refuting Order No. 1. (A. S. Izgoev, *Sotsialisty vo vtoroi russkoi revoliutsii* [Petrograd, 1917], p. 12). However, the Soviet's Executive Committee disagreed with Kerensky and Chkheidze and their announcement was not published.
199. *Petrogradskii Sovet rabochikh i soldatskikh deputatov*, pp. 10, 11, 16.
200. Ibid., p. 17.
201. Ibid., pp. 20–21.
202. *Den'*, March 7, 1917.
203. *Rabochaia gazeta*, March 9, 1917. Guchkov, who began his ministerial activities by disapproving Order No. 1, was compelled to confess this to troops in the Petrograd Military District.
204. *Petrogradskii Sovet rabochikh i soldatskikh deputatov*, pp. 34–35.
205. Ibid., p. 36.
206. *Poslednie novosti*, September 20, 1936.
207. *Birzhevye vedomosti*, March 13, 1917. The Petrograd Soviet gave financial compensation to the wounded and to the families of those killed during the revolution. Among the 218 victims who received help were 90 workers, 91 soldiers, 10 sailors, and 27 individuals from various professions. (TsGAOR SSSR, f. 6978, op. 1, d. 922, l. 13.)
208. *Izvestiia Petrogradskogo Soveta rabochikh i soldatskikh deputatov*, March 6, 1917.
209. *Gosudarstvennyi muzei Velikoi Oktiabr'skoi sotsialisticheskoi revoliutsii* (Leningrad), f. listovok, inv. no. 832.
210. Bazarov, "Pervye shagi russkoi revoliutsii," p. 308.
211. *Rech'*, March 28, 1917.
212. Lenin, *Polnoe sobranie sochinenii*, t. 31, p. 458. [A translation does not appear in the English-language edition of Lenin's works—D.J.R.]

Bibliography

Archives

Arkhiv Oktiabr'skoi revoliutsii Leningradskoi oblasti (Leningrad Oblast Archive of the October Revolution)
f. 1000.
f. 4000.
f. 7384.

Biblioteka instituta marksizma-leninizma pri TsK KPSS (Library of the Institute of Marxism-Leninism, Moscow)
f. listovok.

Gosudarstvennaia biblioteka SSSR imeni V. I. Lenina, Rukopisnyi fond (V. I. Lenin State Library, Manuscript Division, Moscow)
f. 306 (B. A. Engel'gardt, "Potonuvshii mir: Vospominaniia.")

Gosudarstvennaia publichnaia biblioteka imeni M. F. Saltykova-Shchedrina (M. E. Saltykov-Shchedrin State Public Library, Leningrad)
f. listovok.
f. 482 (Manuscript Division).

Gosudarstvennyi muzei Velikoi Oktiabr'skoi sotsialisticheskoi revoliutsii (State Museum of the Great October Socialist Revolution, Leningrad)
f. 6.
f. listovok.

Leningradskii gosudarstvennyi istoricheskii arkhiv (Leningrad State Historical Archive)
f. 513.
f. 569.
f. 680.

Personal archive of S. Petrikovskii, *Vospominaniia o Fevral'skoi revoliutsii*.

Personal archive of M. Polievktov, *Materialy Komissii oprosov. Beseda s Chikolini*.
Beseda s M. I. Tereshchenko.
Beseda s M. V. Rodzianko.
Beseda s A. F. Kerenskim.
Beseda s N. N. Nekrasovym.
Beseda s B. A. Engel'gardtom.
Beseda s Tugan-Baranovskim.
Beseda s M. I. Skobelevym.

TsGAOR SSSR (Central State Archive of the October Revolution, Moscow)
f. DPOO (The Department of the Police).
f. POO (The Department of the Petrograd Okhranka).
f. Chsk (The Extraordinary Investigatory Commission of the Provisional Government).
f. perliustratsiia (Opening and inspection of correspondence).
f. pechatnykh izdanii.
f. listovok.

f. 6 (Chancellery of the Provisional Government).
f. 579.
f. 601, 622, 627, 628, 629, 640.
f. 875.
f. 1235, 1244, 1248, 1278.
f. 3348.
f. 5827, 5856, 5881.
f. 5913, 5962, 5990.
f. 6065.
f. 6375.
f. 6439.
f. 6515, 6536.
f. 6978.

TsGIA SSSR (Central State Historical Archive of the USSR, Leningrad)
f. 27, op. 1.
f. 691, op. 1.
f. 1175, op. 2.
f. 1276 (The Council of Ministers), op. 12 (The State Duma).
f. 1278 (Chancellery of the Ministry of Internal Affairs), op. 1.
f. 1282, op. 1.
f. 2856, op. 1.

Tsentral'nyi gosudarstvennyi muzei revoliutsii SSSR (Central State Museum of the Revolution of the USSR, Moscow)
f. listovok.

TsGVIA SSSR (Central State Military History Archive of the USSR, Moscow)
f. 10.
f. 11.

TsPA-IML (Central Party Archive of the Institute of Marxism-Leninism of the Central Committee of the Communist Party of the Soviet Union, Moscow)
f. 17.
f. 124.
f. 131.

Documents

Anfimov, A. M. "Tsarskaia okhranka o politicheskom polozhenii v strane v kontse 1916 g." *Istoricheskii arkhiv*, no. 1 (1960): 203–208.

Baltiiskie moriaki v podgotovke i provedenii Velikoi Oktiabr'skoi sotsialisticheskoi revoliutsii: Sbornik dokumentov. Moscow, 1957.

Bessonova, A. F., et al., comps. "Antivoennaia rabota bol'shevikov v gody pervoi mirovoi voiny." *Istoricheskii arkhiv*, no. 5 (1961): 74–107.

Bol'sheviki v gody imperialisticheskoi voiny, 1914-fevral' 1917: Sbornik dokumentov mestnykh bol'shevistskikh organizatsii. Moscow, 1939.

Bol'shevizatsiia Petrogradskogo garnizona v 1917 g.: Sbornik dokumentov. Leningrad, 1932.

Browder, R. P., and A. F. Kerensky, eds. *The Russian Provisional Government: Documents*. 3 vols. Stanford, 1961.

Bystrianskii, V. A., ed. *Listovki Peterburgskikh bol'shevikov, 1902–1917 gg*. 2 vols. Moscow, 1939.

"Dokumenty Biuro TsK RSDRP v Rossii (iiul' 1914 g.-fevral' 1917 g.) (Iz materialov mnogotomnoi istorii KPSS. Okonchanie)." *Voprosy istorii KPSS*, no. 9 (1965): 79–86.

F. D., ed. "Fevral'skaia revoliutsiia v Petrograde (28 fevralia-1 marta 1917 g.)." *Krasnyi arkhiv*, no. 41–42 (1930): 62–102.
"Fevral'skaia revoliutsiia 1917 goda: Dokumenty stavki verkhovnogo glavnokomanduiushchego i shtaba glavnokomanduiushchego armiiami severnogo fronta." *Krasnyi arkhiv*, no. 2 (21) (1927): 1–78; no. 3 (22) (1927): 3–70.
Gaponenko, L. S., et al., eds. *Revoliutsionnoe dvizhenie v Rossii posle sverzheniia samoderzhaviia: Dokumenty i materialy*. Moscow, 1957.
Gelis, I. R., comp. "Revoliutsionnaia propaganda v armii v 1916–1917 gg." *Krasnyi arkhiv*, no. 4 (17) (1926): 36–50.
Gosudarstvennaia duma, chetvertyi sozyv: Stenograficheskii otchet, 1914–1917.
Iakhontov, A. N. "Tiazhelye dni: Sekretnye zasedanii Soveta Ministrov—16 iiulia-2 sentiabria 1915 goda." *Arkhiv russkoi revoliutsii*, vol. 18 (1926): 5–136.
Ivanovo-Voznesenskie bol'sheviki v period podgotovki i provedeniia Velikoi Oktiabr'skoi revoliutsii. Ivanovo, 1947.
"Iz perepiski russkogo biuro TsK s zagranitsei v gody voiny (1915–1916 gg.) s predisloviem A. I. Elizarovoi." *Proletarskaia revoliutsiia*, no. 7–8 (102–103) (1930): 177–95.
Kakurin, N. E., ed. *Razlozhenie armii v 1917 godu*. Moscow and Leningrad, 1925.
Korablev, Iu. I., ed. *Rabochee dvizhenie v Petrograde v 1912–1917 gg.: Dokumenty i materialy*. Leningrad, 1958.
Materialy Komissii oprosov Obshchestva izucheniia revoliutsii 1917 g.
Padenie tsarskogo rezhima: Stenograficheskie otchety doprosov i pokazanii dannykh v 1917 g. v Chrezvychainoi Sledstvennoi Komissii Vremennogo Pravitel'stva. 7 vols. Moscow and Leningrad, 1924–1927.
Perepiska Nikolaia i Aleksandry Romanovykh. 5 vols. Moscow and Petrograd, 1923–1927.
Petrogradskii Sovet rabochikh i soldatskikh deputatov: Protokoly Ispolnitel'nogo Komiteta. Moscow and Leningrad, 1925.
Pokrovskii, M. N., ed. "Ekonomicheskoe polozhenie Rossii pered revoliutsiei." *Krasnyi arkhiv*, no. 10 (3) (1925): 67–94.
———., comp. "Iz dnevnika A. N. Kuropatkina." *Krasnyi arkhiv*, no. 20 (1) (1927): 56–77.
"Protokoly i rezoliutsii Biuro TsK RSDRP(b) (mart 1917 g.)." *Voprosy istorii KPSS*, no. 3 (1962): 134–57.
Putilovets v trekh revoliutsiiakh: Sbornik materialov po istorii Putilovskogo zavoda. Moscow and Leningrad, 1933.
Rossiia v mirovoi voine 1914–1918 gg. (v tsifrakh). Moscow, 1925.
Sergeev, A. A., ed. "Dnevnik Nikolaia Romanova." *Krasnyi arkhiv*, no. 20 (1) (1927): 123–52; no. 21 (1927): 79–96; no. 22 (3) (1927): 72–91.
Shestoi s"ezd RSDRP (bol'shevikov): Protokoly. Moscow, 1958.
Shliapnikov, A. G., ed. "Fevral'skaia revoliutsiia v dokumentakh: Listki, vozzvaniia, korrespondentsiia." *Proletarskaia revoliutsiia*, no. 1 (13) (1923): 259–351.
Tobolin, I., ed. "Programma soiuza russkogo naroda pered Fevral'skoi revoliutsiei." *Krasnyi arkhiv*, no. 20 (1) (1927): 242–44.
Vol'fovich, M., and E. Medvedev, eds. *Tsarskaia armiia v period mirovoi voiny i Fevral'skoi revoliutsii: Materialy k izucheniiu istorii imperialisticheskoi voiny*. Kazan, 1932.

Revolutionary Leaders' Writings

Lenin, V. I. *Polnoe sobranie sochinenii*. Izd. 5. 55 vols. Moscow, 1960–1965. [English language edition cited as *Collected Works*. Izd. 4. 45 vols. Moscow, 1960–1970.]
Plekhanov, G. V. *O voine*. Petrograd, 1917.
Voina i dorogovizna v Rossii. Published by the TsK RSDRP, 1915.

Memoirs

Ageev, M. "Ot aresta do osvobozhdeniia." *Pechatnik*, no. 7–8 (1927): 11.

Aleksandrov, A. P. *Za Narvskoi zastavoi: Vospominaniia starogo rabochego*. Leningrad, 1963.

B. G. "Fevral'skaia revoliutsiia i okhrannoe otdelenie." *Byloe*, no. 1 (29) (January 1918): 158–76.

Badaev, A. E. *Bol'shevistskaia fraktsiia IV Gosudarstvennoi Dumy i revoliutsionnoe dvizhenie v Peterburge: Vospominaniia*. Moscow and Leningrad, 1930.

Bazarov, V. (Pseud. for V. A. Rudnev). "Pervye shagi russkoi revoliutsii." *Letopis'*, nos. 2–4 (1917): 376–86.

Blok, A. A. *Poslednie dni imperatorskoi vlasti. Prilozhenie*. Petrograd, 1921.

Bonch-Bruevich, V. D. *Na boevykh postakh Fevral'skoi i Oktiabr'skoi revoliutsii*. Moscow, 1931.

Bublikov, A. A. *Russkaia revoliutsiia: Vpechatleniia i mysli ochevidtsa i uchastnika*. New York, 1918.

Buchanan, Sir George. *Moia missiia v Rossii*. vol. 2. Berlin, 1929. [*My Mission to Russia and Other Diplomatic Memories*. 2 vols. Boston, 1923.]

Buchanan, Meriel. *Krushenie velikoi imperii*. 2 vols. Paris, 1932–1933. [*The Dissolution of an Empire*. London, 1932.]

Budantsev, S. "Povest' o stradaniiakh uma," *Krasnaia nov'*, no. 3 (1931): 77–96.

Bulgakov, V. F. "Revoliutsiia na avtomobiliakh: Petrograd v fevrale 1917 g." *Na chuzhoi storone*, no. 6 (1924): 5–52.

Dingel'shtedt, F. "Vesna proletarskoi revoliutsii: Iz vpechatlenii agitatora v marte 1917 g." *Krasnaia letopis'*, no. 1 (12) (1925): 190–215.

Dobronravov, D. "Revoliutsiia." *Sovremennyi mir*, no. 4 (1928). [I was unable to verify this citation and believe it may well be the same source as the following entry by L. Dobronravov.—D.J.R.]

Dobronravov, L. "Revoliutsiia (Zapiski)." *Sovremennyi mir*, nos. 2–3 (1917): 273–313.

Ermanskii, O. A. *Iz perezhitogo*. Moscow and Leningrad, 1927.

Gavrilov, I. "Na Vyborgskoi storone v 1914–1917 gg." *Krasnaia letopis'*, no. 2 (23) (1927): 39–61.

Gessen, I. V. *V dvukh vekakh*. Berlin, 1937.

Gordienko, I. *Iz boevogo proshlogo*. Moscow, 1957.

Guchkov, A. I. "Vospominaniia." *Poslednie novosti*, September 9, 13, 1936.

Gurko, V. *Tsar i tsaritsa*. Paris, 1927.

Iordanskii, N. I. "Voennoe vosstanie 27 fevralia: 1917 g. v Petrograde." *Molodaia gvardiia*, no. 2 (1928): 162–72.

Iurenev, I. "'Mezhraionka' (1911–1917 gg.)." *Proletarskaia revoliutsiia*, no. 2 (25) (1924): 114–43.

Izgoev, A. S. *Sotsialisty vo vtoroi russkoi revoliutsii*. Petrograd, 1917.

Kaiurov, V. "Kak obrazovalsia Petrogradskii Sovet." *Izvestiia tsentral'nogo ispolnitel'nogo komiteta i Petrogradskogo Soveta rabochikh i soldatskikh deputatov*, August 27, 1917.

———. "Shest' dnei Fevral'skoi revoliutsii." *Proletarskaia revoliutsiia*, no. 1 (13) (1923): 157–70.

Kalinin, M. I. *Za eti gody: Stat'i, besedy, rechi*. 3 vols. Moscow and Leningrad, 1929.

Kel'son, Z. "Militsiia Fevral'skoi revoliutsii: Vospominaniia." *Byloe*, no. 1 (29) (1925): 161–79.

Kol'tsov, M. *Fevral'skii mart*. Moscow, 1927.

Kondrat'ev, K. "Vospominaniia o podpol'noi rabote Peterburgskoi organizatsii RSDRP(b) v period 1914–1917 gg." *Krasnaia letopis'*, no. 5 (1922): 227–43; no. 7 (1923): 30–70.

Kovnator, Rakhil (Roza). "Nakanune fevralia: Otryvki iz vospominanii, 1905–1917." In *Revoliutsionnoe iunoshestvo: Iz proshlogo sotsial-demokraticheskoi uchashchiesia i rabochei molodezhi, 1905–1915*, pp. 178–92. Leningrad, 1924.
Krupskaia, N. K. *Vospominaniia o Lenine*. Moscow, 1957.
Kugel', A. "Poslednii maskarad." *Ogonek*, April 24, 1927.
Kuznetsov, A. "Shtormovye etapy." *Leningrad*, no. 10 (1931): 5–34.
Lavrin, V. A. "O pervoi rezoliutsii Biuro TsK RSDRP(b) v marte 1917 goda." *Voprosy istorii KPSS*, no. 3 (1966): 105–11.
Lemeshev, F. A. "Narvskii raionnyi komitet bol'shevikov ot Fevralia k Oktiabriu 1917 goda: Ocherk." *Krasnaia letopis'*, nos. 5–6 (1932): 116–34.
Lloyd George, David. *Voennye memuary*. Vol. 3. Moscow, 1935. [*War Memoirs of David Lloyd George*. Vol. 3. Boston, 1934.]
Lockhart, Sir R. H. Bruce. *Memuary britanskogo agenta*. [*Memoirs of a British Agent; Being an Account of the Author's Early Life in Many Lands and of His Official Mission to Moscow in 1918*. London and New York, 1932.]
Lomonosov, Iu. V. *Vospominaniia o martovskoi revoliutsii 1917 goda*. Stockholm and Berlin, 1921.
Lukomskii, A. S. "Iz vospominanii." *Arkhiv russkoi revoliutsii*, vol. 2 (1921): 14–44.
Maklakov, V. A. Letter to Ia. E. Povoltskii in V. M. Purishkevich's *Ubiistvo Rasputina* (1923).
———. "Nekotorye dopolneniia k vospominaniiam Purishkevicha i kn. Iusupova ob ubiistve Rasputina." *Sovremennye zapiski*, no. 34 (1928): 260–81.
Mansyrev, S. P. "Moi vospominaniia." In *Fevral'skaia revoliutsiia*, pp. 256–81. Moscow, 1926.
Markov, I. "Kak proizoshla revoliutsiia: Zapis' rabochego." *Volia Rossii*, no. 3 (1927): 67–107; nos. 5–6 (1927): 54–86; no. 7 (1927): 55–65.
Matveev, F. *Iz zapisnoi knizhki deputata 176 pekhotnogo polka*. Leningrad, 1932.
Miakotin, V. *Velikii perevorot i zadachi momenta*. Petrograd, 1917.
Mil'chik, I. *Rabochii fevral'*. Moscow and Leningrad, 1931.
Miliukov, P. N. *Istoriia vtoroi russkoi revoliutsii*. 3 vols. Sofia, 1921–1924.
———. "Pervyi den'." *Poslednie novosti*, March 4, 1924.
———. *Rossiia na perelome: Bol'shevistskii period russkoi revoliutsii*. 2 vols. Paris, 1927.
———. *Vospominaniia, 1859–1917*. 2 vols. New York, 1955.
Mstislavskii, S. D. "Fevral'skaia revoliutsiia." *Krasnaia panorama*, March 11, 1927.
———. *Piat dnei: Nachalo i konets Fevral'skoi revoliutsii*. Berlin, Petrograd and Moscow, 1922.
Narvskaia zastava: Sbornik vospominanii. Moscow, 1959.
Nikitin, B. V. *Rokovye gody*. Paris, 1937.
Nol'de, B. E. *Dalekoe i blizkoe: Istoricheskie ocherki*. Paris, 1930.
"O dniakh Peterburgskikh (Iz dnevnika Z. Gippius)." *Vozrozhdenie*, September 14, 1928.
Orlov, K. *Zapiski rabochego revoliutsionera*. Moscow, 1929.
Oznobishin, A. *Vospominaniia*. Paris, 1927.
Paleologue, Georges M. *Tsarskaia Rossiia vo vremia mirovoi voiny*. Moscow, 1923.
Perets, G. P. *V tsitadeli russkoi revoliutsii: Zapiski komendanta Tavricheskogo dvortsa 27 fevralia-23 marta 1917 g*. Petrograd, 1917.
Peshekhonov, A. V. "Pervye nedeli: Iz vospominanii o revoliutsii." In *Fevral'skaia revoliutsiia*, pp. 430–65. Moscow and Leningrad, 1925.
Polovtsev, P. A. *Dni zatmeniia*. Paris, n.d.
Popov, M. R. "L. A. Volkenshtein." *Golos minuvshego*, nos. 4–6 (1918): 71–80.
Purishkevich, V. M. *Ubiistvo Rasputina: Iz dnevnika*. Moscow, 1923.
Rafes, M. G. *Dva goda revoliutsii na Ukraine: Evoliutsiia i raskol "Bunda."* Moscow, 1920.

———. "Moi vospominaniia." *Byloe*, no. 19 (1922): 177–97.
Revoliutsiia 1917 goda: Ocherk, napisannyi soldatami uchebnoi komandy Volynskogo polka. Petrograd, 1917.
Rodzianko, M. V. *Gosudarstvennaia duma i Fevral'skaia 1917 g. revoliutsiia*. Rostov-on-the-Don, 1919.
———. *Krushenie imperii*. Leningrad, 1927.
———. "Krushenie imperii." *Arkhiv russkoi revoliutsii*, vol. 17 (1926): 5–169.
Rozanov, M. *Bastiony revoliutsii*. Leningrad, 1957.
Saratov, N. "Fevral' na Shlissel'burgskom porokhovom zavode: Dni revoliutsii 1917 g." *Proletarskaia revoliutsiia*, no. 1 (13) (1923): 239–42.
Shegolev, P. E., ed. *Otrechenie Nikolaia II: Vospominaniia ochevidtsev i dokumenty*. Leningrad, 1927.
Shepelev, V. "Fevral'skie dni." *Ogonek*, no. 7 (1927).
Shidlovskii, S. I. *Vospominaniia*. 2 vols. Berlin, 1923.
———. "Vospominaniia." In *Fevral'skaia revoliutsiia*, pp. 282–315. Moscow and Leningrad, 1925.
Shklovskii, V. "Zhili-byli." *Znamia*, no. 8 (1961): 159–99.
Shliapnikov, A. G. "Fevral'skie dni v Peterburge." *Proletarskaia revoliutsiia*, no. 1 (13) (1923): 71–134.
———. *Semnadtsatyi god*. 4 vols. Moscow and Petrograd, 1923–1931.
Shmidt, V. "V 'Krestakh.'" *Pravda*, March 12, 1927.
Shokhanov, G. "K desiatiletiiu stachki na Brianskom zavode." *Proletarskaia revoliutsiia*, no. 9 (56) (1926): 199–222.
Shul'gin, V. V. *Dni*. Belgrade, 1925.
Sipol', O. "Iz vospominanii." *Petrogradskaia pravda*, March 12, 1920.
Skalov, S. "27 fevralia 1917 g. v Peterburge: Vospominaniia uchastnika vosstaniia." *Krasnaia nov'*, no. 3 (1931): 115–21.
Skobelev, M. I. "Gibel' tsarizma: Vospominaniia M. I. Skobeleva." *Ogonek*, no. 11 (1927).
Slonimskii, M. *Kniga vospominanii*. Moscow and Leningrad, 1966.
Sokolov, N. D. "Kak rodilsia Prikaz No. 1." *Ogonek*, no. 11 (1927).
Stankevich, V. B. *Vospominaniia, 1914–1919*. Moscow, 1928.
Stasova, E. D. *Stranitsy zhizni i bor'by*. Moscow, 1957.
Steklov, Iu. *Vospominaniia i publitsistika*. Moscow, 1965.
Sukhanov, N. N. *Zapiski o revoliutsii*. Vol. 1, Petrograd, 1919; vol. 2, Petrograd, Berlin, and Moscow, 1922.
Taimi, A. *Stranitsy perezhitogo*. Petrozavodsk, 1955.
Tarasov-Rodionov, A. *Fevral'*. Moscow, 1931.
Volin, Iu. "Rozhdestvo svobody," *Revoliutsiia v Petrograde*. Petrograd, 1917. [I was unable to verify this source.]
Vyborgskaia storona: Sbornik statei i vospominanii. Leningrad, 1957.
Zaks-Gladnev, S. "Vozobnovlenie '*Pravdy*'." *Zhurnalist*, no. 2 (1927): 16–20.
Zalezhskii, V. N. *Iz vospominanii podpol'shchika*. Kharkov, 1931.
Zalutskii, P. "V poslednie dni podpol'nogo Peterburgskogo komiteta bol'shevikov v nachale 1917 g." *Krasnaia letopis'*, no. 2 (35) (1930): 34–37.
Zaslavskii, D. "V Gosudarstvennoi dume." *Krasnaia panorama*, March 11, 1917.
Zenzinov, V. M. "Fevral'skie dni." *Novyi zhurnal*, vol. 34 (1953): 188–211; vol. 35 (1953): 208–40.
Zlokazov, G. I. "Sozdanie Petrogradskogo Soveta: Fevral' 1917 g." *Istoriia SSSR*, no. 5 (1964): 103–11.
Zozulia, E. D. "Chto zapomnilos!" *Ogonek*, no. 12 (1925).
Zozulia, E. D., and A. d'Aktil'. *Piat dnei; rasskaz. 27 fevralia 1917 g.: Stikhotvorenie*. Petrograd, 1917.

Newspapers

Birzhevye vedomosti. Petrograd, 1917. Nonparty liberal paper.
Delo naroda. Petrograd, 1917. Socialist Revolutionary newspaper.
Den'. Petrograd, 1917. Right Menshevik paper.
Izvestiia. Official organ of the Soviet government.
Izvestiia Komiteta petrogradskikh zhurnalistov. Petrograd, 1917. Later renamed *Izvestiia revoliutsionnoi nedeli*.
Izvestiia Petrogradskogo Soveta rabochikh i soldatskikh deputatov. Daily organ of the Petrograd Soviet and later of the Central Executive Committee. After August 1 known as *Izvestiia tsentral'nogo ispolnitel'nogo komiteta i Petrogradskogo Soveta rabochikh i soldatskikh deputatov*.
Krasnaia gazeta. Established January 25, 1918. Published by the Petrograd Soviet of Workers' and Peasants' Deputies. Absorbed by *Leningradskaia pravda* as of March 1, 1939.
Leningradskaia pravda. Organ of the Leningrad Communist Party Organization.
Literaturnaia gazeta. Contemporary Soviet literary weekly.
Massovaia gazeta, 1917.
Novoe vremia. Émigré paper published in Belgrade, 1921–1929.
Obshchee delo. Paris, 1919–1921. Émigré weekly edited by V. Burtsev.
Petrogradskaia pravda. Precursor of *Leningradskaia pravda*.
Poslednie novosti. Émigré newspaper published in Paris by P. N. Miliukov.
Pravda. Central organ of the Bolshevik (Communist) party.
Rabochaia gazeta. Petrograd, 1917. Central Menshevik party newspaper.
Rech'. Kadet party newspaper published in Petrograd.
Russkie vedomosti. Moscow, 1917. Liberal daily.
Vecherniaia Moskva. (Various titles.) Published by the Moscow City Committee of the Communist Party of the Soviet Union and by the Moscow Soviet.
Volia Rossii. Prague, SR émigré newspaper.
Zhurnalist. Moscow, 1922–1933. Issued by the Central Committee of Soiuz rabochikh poligraficheskoi promyshlennosti. Superseded in October 1933 by *Bol'shevistskaia pechat'*.

Secondary Works

Artem'ev, S. A. "Sostav Petrogradskogo Soveta v marte 1917 g." *Istoriia SSSR*, no. 5 (1964): 112–28.
Astrakhan, Kh. M. "O pervom izdanii Manifesta TsK RSDRP(b) 'Ko vsem grazhdanam Rossii.'" *Voprosy istorii KPSS*, no. 6 (1964): 64–65.
Bugaev, E. "Kogda utrachivaetsia nauchnyi podkhod." *Partiinaia zhizn'*, no. 14 (1956): 62–72.
Chaadaeva, O. *Armiia nakanune Fevral'skoi revoliutsii*. Moscow and Leningrad, 1935.
Chermenskii, E. D. *Fevral'skaia burzhuazno-demokraticheskaia revoliutsiia 1917 goda v Rossii*. Moscow, 1959.
General Kutepov: Sbornik statei. Paris, 1934.
Grave, B. B., ed. *Burzhuaziia nakanune Fevral'skoi revoliutsii*. Moscow, 1927.
Ioffe, G. Z. "Anglo-amerikanskaia burzhuaznaia istoriografiia o Fevral'skoi revoliutsii v Rosii." *Istoricheskie zapiski*, 78 (1965): 3–30.
Istoriia grazhdanskoi voiny v SSSR. Ed. Maksim Gor'kii et al. Vol. 1. Moscow, 1935.
Istoriia Kommunisticheskoi partii Sovetskogo Soiuza. Vol. 2. Moscow, 1966.
Kanun revoliutsii. Petrograd, 1918.

Kochakov, B., ed. *Ocherki istorii Leningrada*. Vol. 3. Moscow and Leningrad, 1956.
KPSS v bor'be za pobedu sotsialisticheskoi revoliutsii v period dvoevlastiia. Moscow, 1957.
Leiberov, I. P. "O revoliutsionnykh vystupleniiakh Petrogradskogo proletariata v gody pervoi mirovoi voiny i Fevral'skoi revoliutsii." *Voprosy istorii*, no. 2 (1964): 63–77.
———. "O vozniknovenii revoliutsionnoi situatsii v Rossii v gody pervoi mirovoi voiny (iiul'-sentiabr' 1915 g.)." *Istoriia SSSR*, no. 6 (1964): 33–59.
———. "Petrogradskii proletariat v bor'be za pobedu Fevral'skoi burzhuazno-demokraticheskoi revoliutsii v Rossii." *Istoriia SSSR*, no. 1 (1957): 41–73.
———. "Petrogradskii proletariat vo vseobshchei politicheskoi stachke 25 fevralia 1917 g." In *Oktiabr' i grazhdanskaia voina v SSSR: Sbornik statei k 70-letiiu akademika I. I. Mintsa*, pp. 31–46. Moscow, 1966.
Liashchenko, P. I. *Istoriia narodnogo khoziaistva SSSR*. 2 vols. Moscow, 1950.
Miller, V. "Iz istorii Prikaza No. 1 Petrogradskogo Soveta." *Voenno-istoricheskii zhurnal*, no. 5 (1966): 109–13.
Mitel'man, M., B. Glebov, and A. Ul'ianskii. *Istoriia Putilovskogo zavoda, 1789–1917*. Moscow and Leningrad, 1939.
Murashov, S. *Kak pobedila Velikaia Oktiabr'skaia sotsialisticheskaia revoliutsiia*. Moscow, 1957.
Nakanune velikoi revoliutsii. Moscow, 1922.
Naumkin, V. G. "Na Izhorskom zavode nakanune Fevral'skoi revoliutsii." *Krasnaia letopis'*, no. 1 (40) (1931): 168–76.
Oznobishin, D. V. "Vremennyi komitet gosudarstvennoi dumy i vremennoe pravitel'stvo." *Istoricheskie zapiski*, 75 (1965): 273–94.
Pervyi legal'nyi Peterburgskii komitet bol'shevikov v 1917 godu. Moscow and Leningrad, 1927.
Petrogradskii proletariat i bol'shevistskaia organizatsiia v gody imperialisticheskoi voiny. Leningrad, 1939.
Potekhin, M. "K voprosu o vozniknovenii i sostave Petrogradskogo Soveta v 1917 g." *Istoriia SSSR*, no. 5 (1965): 233–35.
Rabochee dvizhenie v 1917 godu. Moscow and Leningrad, 1926.
Rashin, A. G. *Formirovanie rabochego klassa Rossii*. Moscow, 1958.
Semennikov, V. P. *Monarkhiia pered krusheniem*. Moscow and Leningrad, 1927.
———. *Politika Romanovykh nakanune revoliutsii: Ot Antanty-k Germanii*. Moscow and Leningrad, 1926.
Sobolev, P. N., ed. *Istoriia Velikoi Oktiabr'skoi sotsialisticheskoi revoliutsii*. Moscow, 1962.
Solov'ev, M. E. "Fevral'skaia revoliutsiia 1917 goda v Rossii—reshaiushchaia predposylka Velikoi Oktiabr'skoi sotsialisticheskoi revoliutsii." In *Uchenye zapiski kafedr istorii SSSR i novoi istorii Moskovskogo gosudarstvennogo pedagogicheskogo instituta imeni V. I. Lenina*, vyp. 1, vol. 112, pp. 3–47. Moscow, 1958.
Sorokin, F. *Gvardeiskii ekipazh v fevral'skie dni 1917 g*. Moscow, 1932.
Startsev, V. I. *Ocherki po istorii Petrogradskoi krasnoi gvardii i rabochei militsii*. Moscow and Leningrad, 1965.
Storozhev, V. N. "Diplomatiia i revoliutsiia: Obzor predoktiabr'skoi diplomaticheskoi kaniteli." *Vestnik Narodnogo komissariata po inostrannym delam*, nos. 4–5 (1920): 60–104.
"Trebovanie naroda o zakliuchenii Nikolaia Romanova v krepost'." *Krasnyi arkhiv*, no. 81 (2) (1937): 121–27.
Ul'ianov, I. *Kazachestvo v pervye dni revoliutsii: K 3-ei godovshchine Velikoi rossiiskoi revoliutsii*. Moscow, 1920.

Volobuev, P. V. *Proletariat i burzhuaziia Rossii v 1917 godu*. Moscow, 1964.
Vorobtsova, Iu. I. "Zagranichnoe predstavitel'stvo TsK RSDRP(b) v 1917." *Voprosy istorii KPSS*, no. 6 (1966): 30–39.
Zalezhskii, V. N. "Pervyi legal'nyi Peka." *Proletarskaia revoliutsiia*, no. 1 (13) (1923): 135–56.

Index

www.ingramcontent.com/pod-product-compliance
Ingram Content Group UK Ltd.
Pitfield, Milton Keynes, MK11 3LW, UK
UKHW030641040425
457092UK00006B/128